KT-469-543

ORGANIZATIONAL PSYCHOLOGY AND DEVELOPMENT

A Reader for Students and Practitioners

Edited by

Cary L. Cooper

and

Ivan T. Robertson

University of Manchester
Institute of Science & Technology, UK

FRANCIS CLOSE HALL LEARNING CENTRE
UNIVERSITY OF GLOUCESTERSHIRE
Swindon Road
Cheltenham GL50 4AZ
Tel: 01242 532913

JOHN WILEY & SONS, LTD

Chichester · New York · Weinheim · Brisbane · Singapore · Toronto

Copyright © 2001 by John Wiley & Sons, Ltd,
      Baffins Lane, Chichester,
      West Sussex PO19 1UD, England

      National   01243 779777
      International (+44) 1243 779777
      e-mail (for orders and customer service enquiries): cs-books@wiley.co.uk
      Visit our Home Page on http://www.wiley.co.uk
                  or http://www.wiley.com

All Rights Reserved. No part of this publication may be reproduced, stored in a retrieval
system, or transmitted, in any form or by any means, electronic, mechanical,
photocopying, recording, scanning or otherwise, except under the terms of the Copyright,
Designs and Patents Act 1988 or under the terms of a licence issued by the Copyright
Licensing Agency Ltd, 90 Tottenham Court Road, London W1P 9HE, UK, without the
permission in writing of the Publisher.

Other Wiley Editorial Offices

John Wiley & Sons, Inc., 605 Third Avenue,
New York, NY 10158-0012, USA

Wiley-VCH Verlag GmbH, Pappelallee 3,
D-69469 Weinheim, Germany

John Wiley & Sons Australia Ltd, 33 Park Road, Milton,
Queensland 4064, Australia

John Wiley & Sons (Asia) Pte Ltd, 2 Clementi Loop #02-01,
Jin Xing Distripark, Singapore 129809

John Wiley & Sons (Canada) Ltd, 22 Worcester Road,
Rexdale, Ontario M9W 1L1, Canada

Library of Congress Cataloguing-in-Publication Data

Organizational psychology and development : a reader for students and practitioners /
edited by Cary L. Cooper and Ivan T. Robertson.
      p. cm. — (Key issues in industrial & organizational psychology)
      Includes bibliographical references and index.
      ISBN 0-471-49556-5
      1. Psychology, Industrial. 2. Organizational behavior. 3. Work—Psychological aspects.
    I. Cooper, Cary L. II. Robertson, Ivan. 1946– III. Series.

    HF5548.8 .O6953 2001
    658.3'001'9—dc21

                                                      2001017584

British Library Cataloguing-in-Publication Data
A catalogue record for this book is available from the British Library

ISBN 0-471-49556-5

Typeset in 10/12pt Plantin by Dorwyn Ltd, Rowlands Castle, Hants
Printed and bound in Great Britain by Antony Rowe Ltd, Chippenham, Wilts
This book is printed on acid-free paper responsibly manufactured from sustainable forestry,
in which at least two trees are planted for each one used for paper production.

CONTENTS

ABOUT THE SERIES

Each book in this exciting series draws together the most authoritative and important recent developments on a topic of central importance to industrial and organizational psychology. Selected from volumes of the International Review of Industrial and Organizational Psychology, these collections provide students and practitioners with the ideal tool for:

- Essays, dissertations and new projects
- Quickly updating an area of knowledge for the busy professional
- Source material for lecture courses and seminars
- Beginning research students
- Keeping the consultancy library relevant

Key Issues in Industrial and Organizational Psychology
Edited by Cary L. Cooper and Ivan T. Robertson

Current books published in this series are—

Organizational Psychology and Development
A Reader for Students and Practitioners
Edited by Cary L. Cooper and Ivan Robertson

Personnel Psychology and Human Resource Management
A Reader for Students and Practitioners
Edited by Ivan Robertson and Cary L. Cooper

Well-Being in Organizations
A Reader for Students and Practitioners
Edited by Cary L. Cooper and Ivan Robertson

ABOUT THE EDITORS

Cary L. Cooper
Ivan T. Robertson

Manchester School of Management, University of Manchester Institute of Science and Technology, PO Box 88, Manchester M60 1QD, UK.

Cary L. Cooper received his BS and MBA degrees from the University of California, Los Angeles, his PhD from the University of Leeds, UK, and holds honorary doctorates from Heriot-Watt University and Wolverhampton University. He is currently BUPA Professor of Organizational Psychology and Deputy Vice Chancellor of UMIST. Professor Cooper was Founding and current President of the *British Academy of Management* and is a Fellow of the British Psychological Society, Royal Society of Arts, Royal Society of Medicine and Royal Society of Health. He is also Founding Editor of the *Journal of Organizational Behavior* and co-editor of *Stress Medicine*, serves on the editorial board of a number of other scholarly journals, and is the author of over 90 books and 400 journal articles.

Ivan Robertson is Professor of Work and Organizational Psychology in the Manchester School of Management, UMIST, and Pro-Vice-Chancellor of UMIST. He is a Fellow of the British Academy of Management, and the British Psychological Society, and is a Chartered Psychologist. Professor Robertson's career includes several years experience working as an applied psychologist on a wide range of projects for a variety of different organizations. With Professor Cooper he founded Robertson Cooper Ltd (www.robertsoncooper.com), a business psychology firm which offers consultancy advice and products to clients. Professor Robertson's research and teaching interests focus on individual differences and organizational factors related to human performance. His other publications include 25 books and over 150 scientific articles and conference papers.

CONTRIBUTORS

John Arnold — *Loughborough University Business School, Ashby Road, Loughborough LE11 3TU, UK*

Carole Borrill — *Institute of Work Psychology, The University of Sheffield, Sheffield S10 2TN, UK*

David P. Campbell — *Center for Creative Leadership, 850 Leader Way, Colorado Springs, CO 80906, USA*

David Chan — *Department of Social Work & Psychology, National University of Singapore, 10 Kent Ridge Crescent, Singapore, 0511*

Cary L. Cooper — *Manchester School of Management, UMIST, PO Box 88, Manchester M60 1QD, UK*

Russell Cropanzano — *Department of Psychology, Colorado State University, Fort Collins, Colorado 80523–1876, USA*

Catherine S. Daus — *Department of Psychology, Southern Illinois University, Room 0118, Building III, Edwardsville, Illinois 62026, USA*

Carsten K. W. De Dreu — *Department of Psychology, University of Amsterdam, Roetersstraat 15, 1018 W B Amsterdam, The Netherlands*

Jerald Greenberg — *Faculty of Management and Human Resources, Ohio State University, Columbus, Ohio 43210–1399, USA*

Sophia Harinck — *Department of Psychology, University of Amsterdam, Roetersstraat 15, 1018 W B Amsterdam, The Netherlands*

Gerard Hodgkinson — *Leeds University Business School, The University of Leeds, Leeds LS2 9JT, UK*

Udo Konradt — *Christian-Albrechts-Universität zu Kiel, Institut für Psychology, Universität zu Kiel, Olshausenstr. 40, D-24098 Kiel, Germany*

Mike Mälecke — *Christian-Albrechts-Universität zu Kiel, Institut für Psychology, Universität zu Kiel, Olshausenstr. 40, D-24098 Kiel, Germany*

Dennis W. Organ — *Kelly School of Business, Indiana University, Bloomington, IN 47405, USA*

Julia Beth Paine — *Kelly School of Business, Indiana University, Bloomington, IN 47405, USA*

David S. Sanders — *Department of Psychology, Southern Illinois University, Room 0118, Building III, Edwardsville, Illinois 62026, USA*

Renate Schmook — *Christian-Albrechts-Universität zu Kiel, Institut für Psychology, Universität zu Kiel, Olshausenstr. 40, D-24098 Kiel, Germany*

Phyllis Tharenou — *Department of Business Management, Monash University, Caulfield East 3145, Melbourne, Australia*

Kerrie Unsworth — *Institute of Work Psychology, The University of Sheffield, Sheffield S10 2TN, UK*

Annelies E. M. Van Vianen — *Department of Psychology, University of Amsterdam, Roetersstraat 15, 1018 W B Amsterdam, The Netherlands*

Michael West — *Institute of Work Psychology, The University of Sheffield, Sheffield S10 2TN, UK*

INTRODUCTION

Historically, the two related fields of industrial and organizational psychology addressed distinctive but related issues. When members of both sub-fields recognized that the somewhat different emphases (individual-level issues versus organization-level issues) were better combined rather than competing, I/O psychology emerged as a stronger and more comprehensive discipline. The chapters in this volume tackle issues that look at the role of people in organizational contexts and demonstrate very vividly that effective research must sometimes combine the individual and organization perspectives to obtain a full picture.

This volume explores research in a range of topics to do with organizational psychology and development. The chapters are written by leading scholars with international reputations in their fields, from Australia, The Netherlands, Germany, Singapore, the UK and the USA. The book is divided into three broad sections reflecting the different levels of analysis possible in I/O psychology: Individuals in Organizations; Groups and Teams; and Organizational Issues. These distinctions in levels of analysis are helpful and provide a framework which can be used to tackle the various different conceptual and practical problems that arise when attempting to obtain a clear view of issues such as alternative ways of working, career progression and the roles of individuals in teams and groups.

The chapters in the first section focus on individual issues which are not directly related to effective task performance. The major contributions of I/O psychologists to enhancing task performance (e.g. personnel selection and training) are dealt with in another volume in this collection (Personnel Psychology and Human Resource Management. The chapters in the first section of this volume explore the processes of adaptation at work, organizational citizenship, career development and advancement. Although they do not impact on performance directly, these topics are of considerable importance in understanding how people get to grips with organizational life, how they contribute and how their careers develop.

The second section moves to the level of collections of people in teams and groups. Clearly there are different issues involved when considering the effectiveness of people working together, compared with individual performance. Of course, in reality many roles in organizations involve a mixture of individual tasks and tasks where working with others is important to successful performance. Whenever there is an interface between two or more people the possibility of effective combination of effort arises – but so does the possibility of conflict. Both topics are dealt with by the two chapters in this section.

The final section looks at issues that are viewed from the perspective of the overall organization. The distribution of rewards and the procedures for their distribution is a topic that has emerged in more recent years as something of significance for I/O psychologists. It is clearly a topic where the individual and organizational levels of analysis are inextricably connected. The final two chapters in this volume also tackle topics where the interactions between individual behaviour and organization-level policies and practices are crucial.

All of the topics are thoroughly reviewed, drawing on material from the leading volumes of the International Review of Industrial and Organizational Psychology. We hope that this compendium of quality reviews will help to improve research and practice in I/O psychology. In the end, we must attempt to move in the direction of understanding the simple truth of John Ruskin's comments about work in 1852: 'In order that people may be happy in their work, these three things are needed: they must be fit for it; they must not do too much of it; and they must have a sense of success in it.'

Part I

INDIVIDUALS IN ORGANIZATIONS

Chapter 1

CONCEPTUAL AND EMPIRICAL GAPS IN RESEARCH ON INDIVIDUAL ADAPTATION AT WORK

David Chan
National University of Singapore

As we enter into the third millennium, many changes are occurring or have occurred at the workplace. Schmitt and Chan (1998) noted that changes such as advances in communications technology, the increasing use of teams to accomplish work, globalization of corporations, and the increased service orientation of organizations will almost certainly have implications for the ways in which job candidates are selected, what knowledge, skills, abilities, and other characteristics (KSAOs) are most related to performance in organizations, and the manner in which performance itself is defined. Indeed, I predict that changes such as those just described are likely to drive much of the research in industrial and organizational (I/O) psychology for the next few decades.

Despite the variety of changes that are occurring at the workplace, they do share something in common, namely the increased demands they will make on workers to adapt to constant change in the work they do. Hence, it is not surprising that the idea of *individual adaptation* in one form or another underlies many studies carried out in the last decade of I/O psychology. The purpose of this paper is to integrate the relevant but diverse studies in research on individual adaptation at work. I will highlight several conceptual and empirical gaps in the literature and offer some concrete suggestions on ways to bridge these gaps.

LITERATURE ON INDIVIDUAL ADAPTATION

Individual adaptation refers to the process by which an individual achieves some degree of fit between his or her behaviors and the new work demands created by the novel and often ill-defined problems resulting from changing

Conceptual and Empirical Gaps in Research on Individual Adaptation at Work by David Chan taken from IRIOP 2000 v15, Edited by Cary L. Cooper and Ivan T. Robertson: © 2000 John Wiley & Sons, Ltd

and uncertain work situations (Chan, in press-a). Chan identified four elements that seem to characterize what researchers describe when they examine the need to be adaptive: (a) changes and uncertainty in the work situation create novel and ill-defined problems; (b) problems make new work demands on individuals; (c) established and routine behaviors that were successful in the previous work situations become irrelevant, suboptimal, or less useful in the new situations; and (d) adaptive behaviors that are in some way qualitatively different from established routines are successful in the new situation. Note that the essence in the description of individual adaptation is generic in the sense that neither the cause of adaptive behaviors (e.g., individual difference constructs or training) nor the nature of the change or demand created due to the change is specified. If we adopt this description of adaptation, then it is not difficult to see that diverse and sometimes apparently disparate areas of research are in fact investigating a similar process or phenomenon at work. What distinguishes the different research literatures are the assumptions or arguments (implicit or explicit) concerning the cause of adaptive behaviors and the types of substantive contexts of the research (e.g., individual versus team contexts). As argued later in this paper, the nature of the change or demand in the new situation is often not explicated in the different research literatures.

To organize the review, four distinct but related research literatures will be discussed. The four are literatures on (a) individual differences, (b) training, (c) teams, and (d) newcomer socialization. I will briefly review the current state of research in each of these areas. On the basis of the review, several issues constituting conceptual and empirical gaps in the research on individual adaptation at work will be explicated.

Individual Differences Research

In the literature on individual differences, the research on individual adaptation is concerned with *who* are the individuals best suited for functioning in changing and uncertain environments. Adaptation is construed in terms of an individual's level of *adaptability*. That is, successful adaptation is largely a function of the individual's critical KSAOs which are viewed as stable individual difference attributes or traits (e.g., Judge, Thoresen & Pucik, 1996; Mumford, Baughman, Threfall, Uhlman & Costanza, 1993; Paulhus & Martin, 1988). From the individual differences perspective, some people are more adaptable than others, and the ranking of individuals on adaptability is relatively stable across time. The traditional selection paradigm that uses one or more measures of adaptability to predict some job-relevant criterion (e.g., job performance) is the archetype of individual differences research approach to the study of adaptation.

The literature on adaptability as an individual differences construct often treated the construct as unitary, but researchers' diverse operationalizations of adaptability strongly suggest that they have different aspects of adaptation in mind. The diverse measures of 'adaptability' include *cognitive measures* such as tests of fluid intelligence (Snow & Lohman, 1984) and practical intelligence (Wagner, 1986; Sternberg, 1994), *personality measures* such as scales assessing flexibility (Gough, 1987) and change orientation (Jackson, 1967), *structured interviews* focusing on either past experiences (Motowidlo, Carter, Dunnette et al., 1992) or hypothetical situations (Latham, Saari, Pursell & Campion, 1980), *assessment center* exercises such as interview simulations and leaderless group discussions (Chan, 1996), and *biodata* items written specifically to tap adaptability (Schmitt, Jennings & Toney, 1996). The diversity of operationalizations reflects the different aspects of adaptability emphasized by researchers. Schmitt and Chan (1998) suggested that the diversity is due to the different adaptive situations examined across studies, an important point which I will return to later. Suffice now to say that an adequate theory of adaptability is probably one that construes adaptability as a multidimensional construct and identifies the major types of situations or demands requiring adaptation.

Training Research

Training researchers who studied individual adaptation are concerned with how trainees can acquire or learn the important skills required for functioning in changing and uncertain situations. Instead of construing successful adaptation as a function of individual differences in adaptability, the training literature emphasizes and focuses on how training interventions can enable individuals to learn to be adaptive. For example, Kozlowski, Gully, McHugh, Salas and Cannon-Bowers (1996) examined how sequenced mastery training goals can increase trainees' levels of adaptation.

Research on training adaptive expertise has focused on trainees' acquisition of appropriate knowledge structures and metacognitive or self-regulation skills. These cognitive representational and processual constructs pose important measurement and construct validation challenges and some promising advances have been made in the recent training literature (e.g., Ford & Kraiger, 1995; Goldsmith & Kraiger, 1997; Kraiger, Ford & Salas, 1993; Smith, Ford & Kozlowski, 1997). Many of these advances draw on earlier research on development of expertise (Anderson, 1983, 1993; Chi, Feltovich & Glaser, 1981; Holyoak, 1991) and measurement of structural knowledge (e.g., Schvaneveldt, Durso & Dearholt, 1985, 1989). Detailed discussions on training adaptive expertise are available in Chan (in press-a), Ford and Kraiger (1997), and Smith, Ford and Kozlowski (1997).

Teams Research

With the increased use of teams in organizations to accomplish complex tasks and improve productivity, teams have become a hot topic in both research and practice in I/O psychology. The study of individual adaptation in teams research has to be understood in the context of the nature of the teams examined. As noted by Schmitt and Chan (1998), because information exchange and decision-making are primary reasons for the use of teams at the workplace, much of the recent research on teams has focused on the sharing and coordination of information among team members and on the team decision-making process. The exchange between multiple expert sources of information in attempts to effectively arrive at good decisions defines the boundary conditions for much of the recent research on teams, that is, team decision-making under conditions of distributed expertise. The types of teams studied are often those where members with different specialized skills operate together in a dynamic context of high stress and unpredictable events (e.g., military combat units, surgery teams, flight crews). Sophisticated team decision-making models such as the one proposed by Hollenbeck, Ilgen, Phillips and Hedlund (1994) have been developed and empirically tested. Given this framework of teams research, individual adaptation is important to the extent each team member is expected to effectively cope with new information provided by other members and demands created by the constantly changing and uncertain team task environment if he or she is to contribute to successful team decision-making and team performance.

Conceptually, the importance of individual adaptation in the context of naturalistic team decision-making is evident in the fact that most problem situations encountered by teams in organizations are ill-structured and they often involve incompatible or shifting goals (Kozlowski, 1998). But empirically there is little research that has directly examined individual adaptation in teams and established or demonstrated clear links between individual adaptation and team performance or other team functioning. One possible reason is that the understanding of naturalistic decision-making teams requires a conceptual and empirical research base quite different from traditional types of work teams found in business organizations such as quality circles, production teams, and planning committees. Social psychology and group dynamics, which focus on concepts such as group norms and morale as opposed to the notion of distributed expertise, constitute the conceptual and empirical base for many of the traditional team models. It is only recently that researchers examining naturalistic decision-making teams (e.g., Kozlowski et al., 1996) found the literature on adaptive expertise (Holyoak, 1991) to provide a useful conceptual and empirical research base for the study of adaptation in such teams.

The program of research by Kozlowski and his colleagues (Kozlowski, 1998; Kozlowski et al., 1996; Kozlowski, Gully, Nason, & Smith, in press) represents one of the few attempts in teams research to relate individual adaptation to team functioning. Drawing on Holyoak's (1991) characterization of adaptive expertise as a deep comprehension of the problem domain made possible by the individual's possession and application of organized and flexible knowledge structures, Kozlowski and his colleagues argued that adaptive experts in the team are those who are able to recognize changes in task priorities and modify their strategies and actions accordingly. Although the conceptual framework adopted by these authors by no means denies the role of stable individual differences, their focus on the individual team member follows the research on training adaptive expertise described in the preceding section. That is, the foundation for individual adaptation or adaptability is provided by the training or learning of metacognitive and self-regulation skills. The process of building of individual adaptive expertise through training is alluded to in the preceding section and described in detail in Smith, Ford and Kozlowski (1997).

The notion of individual adaptation underlies most of recent team studies that attempt to model team performance (e.g., Cannon-Bowers, Tannenbaum, Salas & Volpe, 1995; Kozlowski et al., 1996). However, the assessment of adaptation and performance both at the individual and team levels raises complex conceptual and measurement issues that are only beginning to be addressed (Chan, 1998a; Tesluk, Mathieu & Zaccaro, 1997). The study of teams provides an excellent context for research on individual adaptation because it often forces the researcher to address the complex but critical issues involving the construct validity and processual nature of adaptation. I will discuss these issues after reviewing the fourth area of research on individual adaptation.

Newcomer Socialization Research

During the first few months in an organization, newcomers are continually trying to make sense of the uncertainties and adapt to the new and changing work environment (Louis, 1980). Thus, the newcomer's experience during organizational entry is often described in recent socialization literature as an individual adaptation process (Ashford & Black, 1996; Bauer & Green, 1994; Morrison, 1993a, b). This adaptation process is seen as critical to the development of attitudes and behaviors that enable the newcomer to function effectively during the transition period and adjust to the new work environment (Vandenberg & Self, 1993).

Early socialization research conceptualized and assessed adaptation outcomes in terms of traditional variables such as job performance, turnover, satisfaction, and organizational commitment (e.g., Feldman, 1981). As recent research construes the newcomer as proactive rather than reactive or passive, the focus of attention is turned to such variables as task mastery, role clarity, and social integration, which are more proximal adaptation outcomes of newcomer proactivities than the traditional outcomes. A detailed review of the literature on newcomer adaptation is provided in Bauer, Morrison and Callister (1998) and hence will not be repeated here.

The central interest in the newcomer individual adaptation process is the intra-individual change that occurs over time during organizational entry.

However, the assessment of intra-individual change has largely been inadequate in previous studies. For example, important individual adaptation questions such as the presence of individual differences in the rate of change in an adaptation outcome and the associations between initial levels of adaptation and rates of change have been neglected. Chan and Schmitt (in press) explicated the weaknesses of traditional approaches to intra-individual change and showed how a latent growth modeling approach can address these weaknesses and directly answers important individual adaptation questions. A more comprehensive version of the modeling approach is provided in Chan (1998b). As argued later, Chan's method provides a powerful and flexible framework for bridging many of the conceptual and empirical gaps in the assessment of intra-individual change and, more generally, the research on individual adaptation.

BRIDGING GAPS IN RESEARCH ON INDIVIDUAL ADAPTATION

The above brief review indicates that diverse research literatures have adopted somewhat different research paradigms and often apparently disparate assumptions in the approach to individual adaptation. This section will argue that each of the four areas of research, however, has not paid sufficient attention to several critical issues. There are both conceptual and empirical gaps that need to be bridged if we are to gain a better understanding of the phenomenon of individual adaptation. These gaps relate to issues of (a) dimensionality, (b) malleability, (c) predictor–criterion relationships, (d) levels of analysis, and (e) change over time.

Dimensionality

As noted in the above discussion on individual differences research, there is no agreement on what specific KSAOs constitute adaptability. With one researcher assessing adaptability using a personality measure and another assessing adaptability using a cognitive ability measure, findings on adaptability relationships across the two studies may not be directly comparable. When results of these studies are combined in a meta-analysis, the meta-analytic findings may not be meaningful and may even be misleading. Advances in the individual differences approach to adaptation are likely to be preceded by the explicit recognition, in terms of both conceptualization and measurement of the multidimensionality of the adaptability construct (Chan, in press-a). There is probably no single unitary individual difference construct (i.e., trait) of adaptability that is applicable to the diverse adaptive situations of interest.

To address the issue of dimensionality, both conceptual and empirical gaps need to be bridged. Conceptually, we have to begin by proceeding in a theory-driven manner to identify the relevant domains of individual difference constructs such as cognitive ability (e.g., fluid intelligence), cognitive style (e.g., field dependency), personality (e.g., openness to experience), and motivational styles (e.g. learning goal orientation) that could form the foundation for adaptability. These adaptability domains, within each of which specific attributes are defined, would constitute the core components of adaptability. As I will argue later, explicating this multidimensionality is important for meaningful theorizing and estimation of predictor–criterion relationships and it provides an important step towards the development of an adequate theory of adaptability.

Bridging the conceptual gap in the dimensionality issue provides the necessary basis for bridging the empirical gaps. A clear conceptual definition of the specific adaptability construct in question would allow precise and valid measures to be developed and potential differences across various adaptability constructs could be empirically assessed. When researchers are explicit in their conceptualization and measurement of their adaptability constructs, meaningful meta-analyses could be performed and primary studies could be coded according to construct to test for moderator effects.

Malleability

The issue of malleability or trainability of an individual's level of adaptability has not received adequate attention in either the individual differences or training research. By construing adaptability in terms of trait-like attributes, individual differences researchers almost always assume that an individual level of adaptability is a given and is stable across time so that it is not susceptible to change (increase or decrease). Training researchers, on the other hand, tend to emphasize the efficacy of interventions or conditions to develop or increase adaptive expertise and have somewhat ignored or downplayed the role of individual differences. Within-group variance is more often treated as error variance than residual variance that may be of substantive interest. In short, while the individual differences researcher has not given sufficient attention to the search for contextual or situational moderators (i.e., training interventions), the training researcher should pay more attention to potential individual differences in trainability. The extent of malleability is likely to differ across different aspects of adaptation or adaptability components. For example, it may be the case that training individuals to adapt to changes in organizational policies is easier than training individuals to adapt to changes in emergency crisis situations. Likewise, it may be the case that adaptability levels are more malleable when they involve learning goal orientations than when they involve cognitive ability or personality traits. This underscores the importance of addressing the fundamental question of dimensionality discussed above.

To address the issue of malleability, an integrative person–situation approach that views the individual differences perspective and training or learning perspective as complementary is necessary (Chan, in press-a). This approach requires the traditional individual differences researcher and training researcher to reconceptualize the notion of residual variance. Instead of treating residual variance as entirely made of random measurement error, it should be treated as unexplained variance due to model mis-specification resulting from omission of important variables from 'the other perspective'. Hence, researchers should consider including both individual differences and training or situational variables when conceptualizing and measuring individual adaptation. Aptitude X Treatment study designs would have to be the rule rather than the exception so that we could assess how effects of individual differences may be dependent on context (i.e., training interventions or other situational variables) and vice versa. Finally, we should specify what demands related to adaptation exist, and measure outcomes focused on whether or not individuals meet these demands. In other words, the issue of malleability cannot be adequately addressed without a clear delineation of the aspects of adaptive situations and outcomes involved. This is essentially a criterion problem. The issue is discussed in more detail in the next section.

Predictor–Criterion Relationships

Conceptual and empirical gaps also exist in the theorizing and estimation of predictor–criterion relationships in research on individual adaptation. The predictors studied are usually some individual difference constructs such as personality traits or other person variables such as job knowledge and work experience. The criteria are adaptive outcomes and are typically some measures of the individual's adaptive performance on some given task. The problem is that many studies appear to uncritically assume a simple linear positive bivariate association between predictor and criterion when they select predictors of adaptive performance and estimate the predictor–criterion relationship. Studies examining more complex predictor–criterion relationships involving curvilinear and interaction terms are virtually non-existent.

A primary reason for the failure to consider such complex relationships is the lack of a construct orientation in either the predictor or criterion space. In Chan (in press-a), I provided a detailed account of how complex predictor–criterion relationships could be revealed when the nature of work experience as a predictor construct is explicated. Using conceptual frameworks (Quinones, Ford & Teachout, 1995; Tesluk & Jacobs, 1998) that emphasize the multidimensional, multilevel, and dynamic nature of the work experience construct; I have argued that experience can either promote or inhibit adaptation. For example, having more experience (amount) of working on different task types which share the same underlying deep structure is likely to increase the probability of successfully abstracting the underlying principles in the structure. That is, for some task domains, work experience of different types at the task level may have a positive effect on the development of adaptive expertise. On the other hand, work experience may inhibit adaptation through the mechanism of routinization. Experience in terms of extensive repeated task practice may lead to compilation of declarative knowledge into procedural productions (condition-action rules). When task performance is proceduralized, the individual quickly or automatically applies well-practiced strategies or solutions to familiar and well-learned problem situations. However, in novel situations requiring new strategies or responses, similar but causally irrelevant (in terms of problem solution) features would match the condition in the individual's production, causing this *routine* (as opposed to adaptive) expert to automatically execute the action. The action executed would be inappropriate to meet the new demands in the novel situation. This would be an instance of a negative association between experience and adaptive performance. Alternatively, there could be a curvilinear (inverted-U shaped) relationship between amount of experience and adaptive performance such that performance increases with initial practice but, with more extensive practice, proceduralization occurs and performance decreases (see function for same task type in Figure 1.1).

The complexity of predictor–criterion relationships also calls for more complex ways of estimating the effects of interest. Consider again the two modes of experience (conceptualized at the task level)—amount and type. Figure 1.1 hypothesizes that (for some given task domain), based on some theory similar

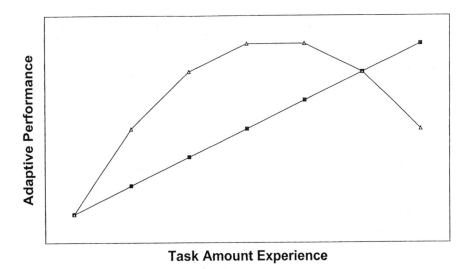

Figure 1.1 A hypothetical polynomial interaction effect between task amount experience and task type on adaptive performance

to the arguments presented in the preceding paragraph, there is a complex interaction effect between task amount experience and task type on adaptive performance. The test of such a hypothesis would require performing a hierarchical regression analysis assessing the unique contribution of a polynomial interaction term. If one is exploring possible interaction effects without a theory of the predictor–criterion relationships, then one is likely to stop at the step where the simple amount X type interaction term is entered into the regression equation. Note that the presence of a polynomial interaction effect, depending on its nature, may or may not imply the presence of a simple interaction effect.

Clearly, the first step in bridging gaps in the theorizing and estimation of predictor–criterion constructs is developing comprehensive and useful conceptual models and valid measures in both the predictor and criterion space. On the predictor side, the literature in differential psychology provides relatively comprehensive models or taxonomies of individual differences variables that can be developed into models of adaptability constructs and relevant valid measures of many of these constructs are likely to be found in the personnel selection literature. In contrast, there is apparently little literature from which we can readily draw to develop conceptual models and valid measures on the criterion side. Campbell's (1990) theory of job performance which decomposes the multidimensional construct of performance into eight components may provide a useful starting point for developing a model of adaptive performance.

Modeling and assessing the criterion space in adaptation research has to go beyond the construct of job performance to develop theory-based and empirically validated taxonomies of adaptation demands and performance outcomes. Pulakos (1996) is probably the first to attempt the development of such a criterion taxonomy. She systematically abstracted the adaptability requirements of a wide variety of jobs and considered potential individual differences correlates of these requirements. She analyzed critical incidents related by job incumbents in a wide variety of military and civilian jobs and classified the types of situations that required adaptation. Her final list of adaptive behaviors ranged from 'handling crisis situations and work stress' to 'learning work tasks and technologies' and 'interpersonal and intercultural sensitivity and adaptability'. Taxonomic efforts as such (both in the predictor and criterion space) require substantial research resources but they are critical to advances in research in individual adaptation. Significant advances will be made if researchers could use these validated taxonomies to derive taxonomic or predictor–criterion linkages and elaborate them into specific models of individual adaptation, which can be further empirically tested (Chan, in press-a).

Levels of Analysis

Organizational phenomena have the properties of dynamic systems, with critical antecedents, processes, and outcomes conceptualized and measured at multiple levels of organizational analysis such as the individual, group, and organization (Chan, 1998a). A number of authors have underscored the importance of adopting a multilevel approach to organizational phenomena and several theoretical frameworks for multilevel research have been proposed (e.g., Chan, 1998a; House, Rousseau & Thomas-Hunt, 1995; Klein, Dansereau & Hall, 1994; Rousseau, 1985). Discussion on important mathematical issues related to the analysis of multilevel data (e.g., Bliese, 1998; Bliese & Halverson, 1998; Ostroff, 1993) and analytical models for structuring multilevel data (e.g., Bryk & Raudenbush, 1987; McArdle & Epstein, 1987; Meredith & Tisak, 1990; Willett & Sayer, 1994) are also available. However, despite the existence of these theoretical frameworks and methodological advances, the fundamental conceptual and measurement issues related to levels are often neglected in substantive research in I/O psychology. Several conceptual and empirical gaps in the research in individual adaptation are results of insufficient attention paid to the multilevel issues raised by these authors. These gaps are most salient in the team and newcomer socialization literatures on adaptation.

A central issue in teams research is gaining a clear understanding of the nature of individual contributions to team effectiveness (Kozlowski et al., in press). Recall that in teams research individual adaptation is important to the extent each team member is expected to effectively cope with new information provided by other members and new demands created by the team task environment. On the surface, it appears that the issue is straightforward. To make a team high in adaptive performance, don't we simply staff the team with individuals who are high in adaptability? The problem is that interaction and coordination among team members are central in team functioning so that team performance is often not a straightforward result of the additive aggregate of individual team members. As noted by Kozlowski et al. (in press), teams research that focuses on identifying the KSAOs that individual team members should possess can only provide a limited gain in our understanding of team effectiveness. Kozlowski et al. presented an elaborate model of the development of adaptive teams. According to this model, the basis for the development of a team's adaptive expertise is the process of team compilation in which team members comprehend patterns of role exchange and relations of these patterns to task contingencies. Because team adaptive performance is the result of dynamic and complex interactions of these network patterns, adaptability at the team level is not simply an additive aggregate of adaptability at the individual level.

But whether the additive aggregate model or some other composition models should be employed is dependent on how the construct of team adaptability is conceptualized. In Chan (1998a), I argued that a fundamental problem in multilevel research is that the issue of construct validation has not been adequately addressed. Specifically, multilevel researchers often do not make explicit their *composition* model(s) when composing 'new' constructs from their lower-level counterparts. A composition model specifies the functional relationships between constructs at the two different levels of analysis. These relationships enable the explicit transformation from the lower-level construct (individual adaptability) to the higher-level construct (team adaptability) which in turn provides conceptual precision in the target construct (team adaptability) hence aiding the derivation of test implications for hypothesis testing. Using the typology of composition models provided in Chan (1998a), the teams' researcher can explicate the conceptual definition of the team-level construct of adaptability, as assumed in his or her study, and the appropriate model for composing the target construct from the lower-level construct of individual adaptability.

Consider the example where individual adaptation is construed essentially as individual self-regulation. The teams researcher proposes that a self-regulation functionally similar to individual self-regulation also exists at the team level (e.g., Kozlowski et al., 1996). At the individual level, self-regulation refers to the activities carried out by the individual to monitor and evaluate his or her own performance with respect to progress toward a goal. The critical parameters of self-regulation include understanding of the coordination of one's actions, error detection, balancing multiple tasks or workloads to stay on track towards goal achievement, and a knowledge of one's task environment (Kanfer & Ackerman, 1989). On the basis of these critical parameters, the teams researcher could employ the *process composition* model described in Chan (1998a) to compose the process of self-regulation from the individual level to the team level. Kozlowski et al. (1996) did just that when they described team self-regulation as team members gaining 'an understanding of how to coordinate member actions, engage in error detection, and monitor each other's performance, so the team can balance workloads and stay on track toward stated objectives' (p. 276). The authors provided the conceptual definition of team self-regulation (team adaptability) by explicating the team-level analogues for the critical parameters of self-regulation (adaptability) at the individual level (individual adaptability).

In practice, composing adaptation from the individual level to the team level is often not easy because the adaptation process of interest is often multifaceted or multidimensional with embedded subprocesses. Unlike the other models (e.g., additive composition, direct consensus composition) in Chan's (1998a) typology, process composition has no concrete empirical algorithm to compose the lower-level process(es) to the higher-level process(es). A challenge for researchers examining adaptive teams is to develop an adequate process composition model and derive explicit hypotheses to be tested as part of the validation of the model. The researcher may have to start by composing the less complex subprocesses of adaptation and systematically integrate these component processes into the complex and multidimensional process of team adaptation. Note also that because multiple constructs may be specified and interrelated in the description of a process, it may be the case that an adequate process composition model of team adaptation has to be preceded by specifying one or more composition forms in Chan's (1998a) typology for composing the relevant higher-level constructs. For example, the process composition may be preceded by an additive composition in which some team adaptability construct (e.g., team ability) is composed from the individual level adaptability construct (cognitive ability).

When we pay attention to issues of levels of analysis and composition models, we will be able to clarify the relationships between individual and team adaptability, both in the individual differences and training literatures. Chan (1998a) provided an example of how construct development of the notion of team adaptability can proceed from the individual differences and learning (training) approaches. In the individual differences approach, we can adopt a static approach of adaptability and begin with the individual-level construct of adaptability defined in terms of a stable individual difference attribute. We then specify an additive (or direct consensus, see Chan, 1998a) composition for composing the individual-level construct to the team level. Hypotheses concerning the new construct could then be formulated. For example, we could hypothesize that this static notion of team adaptability is positively associated with team morale. In the learning or training approach, we begin with the individual-level construct of adaptability defined in terms of a process in which the individual suppressed proceduralized actions and developed new productions when confronted with novel task demands. We then specify a process composition for composing the individual-level construct to the team level. Hypotheses concerning the new construct now could be formulated. For example, we could hypothesize that team mastery orientation is positively associated with this dynamic or process notion of team adaptability.

There are also conceptual and empirical gaps in the newcomer socialization literature on individual adaptation that may be construed as results of insufficient attention paid to levels of analysis. As described earlier, the assessment of intra-individual change over time in extant studies on newcomer adaptation has largely been inadequate. Intra-individual change is assessed using repeated measurements from the same individuals over time and it occurs at a level lower than the individual level of analysis. To put it another way, time is nested within individuals. Traditional approaches to newcomer adaptation research emphasized within-time inter-individual variability (i.e., at the individual level of analysis) and failed to consider across-time intra-individual variability (i.e., at the intra-individual level of analysis). Even when longitudinal studies are performed, the focus has almost always been on change at the aggregate level (typically in terms of mean differences) and thus does not provide an adequate conceptualization and analysis of intra-individual changes over time and inter-individual differences in these changes. Only when a distinction is made between individual and intra-individual levels of analysis are we able to directly address such questions as individual differences in the form of the intra-individual trajectory and the rate of intra-individual change, associations between individual differences at initial status and in rate of change, and associations between rate of change and external correlates. Chan and Schmitt (in press) argued for the importance of these questions to our understanding of the newcomer individual adaptation process. Using data collected from newcomers over four repeated measurements spaced equally at one-month intervals, the authors demonstrated how these and other adaptation questions can be directly addressed using a latent growth modeling approach that explicitly distinguishes between individual and intra-individual levels of analysis.

Change over Time

Individual adaptation does not occur in a time vacuum. Thus, questions concerning different aspects of change over time are directly relevant. In Chan (1998b), I explicated nine fundamental questions on change over time and proposed an integrative analytical model to help conceptualize and assess the different facets of change over time corresponding to these questions. (The reader is referred to Chan, 1998b for the description of the analytical model including details on how aspects of the model are used to address the nine questions on change over time.) I will summarize these questions and relate them to research in individual adaptation. Addressing these questions would bridge many conceptual and empirical gaps relating to change over time as well as to the above discussions on dimensionality, malleability, predictor–criterion relationships, and levels of analysis.

Question 1 asks if the change is to be considered as *systematic differences* or *random fluctuations*. An adequate change assessment in the study of individual adaptation should account for measurement error and allow observed variance to be partitioned into true construct variance, nonrandom (systematic) error variance, and random error variance. When change over time is assessed, the notions of time-specific and time-related errors have to be incorporated in the change assessment. This is because measurement errors may not be homoscedastic and independent within individuals over time. Very often, we do not have a priori reasons to expect the precision with which an adaptation attribute can be measured to remain identical (i.e., homeoscedastic) or change (i.e., heteroscedastic) over time. Even if we do, we need ways of testing the particular assumption. When consecutive measurements are closely spaced in time, errors may also be correlated, especially for identical measures. A failure to adequately model the error covariance structure could lead to biased estimates of the magnitude of true change and even mis-specification of the true change patterns. The model proposed by Chan (1998b) has the capability and flexibility to (a) model a variety of a priori specified error covariance structures and (b) assess the effects of mis-specification of the error to covariance structure on the estimates of true change.

Question 2 asks if the change is to be considered *reversible* or *irreversible*. Change can be unidirectional with no possibility of returning to or restoring previous states or levels, or it can be reversible. The trajectory representing the change over time may be monotonically increasing or decreasing (e.g., linear) so that change is construed as irreversible, or the trajectory may be one of several nonmonotonic functional forms (e.g., an 'inverted U') so that change over time is construed as reversible. Using the procedures described in Chan (1998b), the researcher can capture the form of the change trajectory representing the individual adaptation process by specifying a priori one or more functional forms and assessing the goodness-of-fit of each form and the incremental fit of one form over the other (e.g., the incremental fit of a quadratic over a linear trajectory).

Question 3 asks if the change is to be considered *unitary* or *multipath*. Change can be represented as proceeding in one single pathway or through multiple different pathways. Multiple paths occur when a detour from a single change trajectory is possible as individuals proceed from one point to another. Consider the example of changes in levels on an adaptation outcome as newcomers proceed from Time 1 to Time 4 (through Times 2 and 3). Even if all newcomers share the same level at Time 1 and at Time 4, some newcomers may follow a linear trajectory while others follow a quadratic trajectory. The multiple-group growth modeling procedures described in Chan (1998b) allow the researcher to identify subgroups of individuals that followed different change trajectories.

Question 4 asks if the change is to be considered as (a) a *continuous, gradual, quantitative* phenomenon; (b) *large magnitude shifts* on a *quantitative* variable; or (c) a progression through a series of *qualitatively distinctive* stages. When representing change with a linear trajectory, the change may be construed as (a) or (b) to the extent that the slope of the linear trajectory is gradual or steep. However, the trajectory, linear or otherwise, will be an inappropriate representation when the true nature of change over time is best characterized as (c) in which there is a qualitative shift in the conceptualization of the phenomenon between time points. When such qualitative changes occur, representing and interpreting change over time in terms of the parameters (e.g., slope) of a change trajectory is misleading and not meaningful because we would be comparing apples at one time point with oranges at another. Chan (1998b) argued that the researcher should assess if (c)-type changes occur prior to modeling (a)-type and (b)-type changes. In their study on newcomer adaptation, Chan and Schmitt (in press) demonstrated the absence of (c)-type changes prior to modeling the change trajectories of several adaptation variables. The notion of (c)-type change is described in more detail in Question 5.

Question 5 asks if the change is to be considered as differences in (a) magnitude in an absolute sense, (b) calibration of measurement, or (c) conceptualization. These three types of changes correspond to Golembiewski, Billingsley and Yeager's (1976) *alpha, beta,* and *gamma* change respectively. The issue described in Question 4 is a special instance of this more general and fundamental question concerning the type of change. Alpha change refers to changes in absolute levels given a constant conceptual domain and a constant measuring instrument. In research in individual adaptation, assessment of change over time is often directly based on absolute differences in responses on some measures, that is, true change is assumed to be alpha change. However, the reliance on absolute differences as a direct indicator of change over time assumes measurement invariance (equivalence) of responses across repeated measurements. We can meaningfully speak of alpha change only when there is measurement invariance of responses across time. Measurement invariance across time exists when the numerical values across time waves are on the same measurement scale (Drasgow, 1984, 1987).

Measurement invariance could be construed as absence of beta and gamma changes. Beta change refers to changes in absolute level complicated by changes in the measuring instrument given a constant conceptual domain. Beta change occurs when there is a recalibration of the measurement scale. That is, in beta change, the observed change results from an alteration in the respondent's subjective metric or evaluative scale rather from an actual change in the construct of interest. A difficulty in the training research approach to individual adaptation is that the training intervention may have caused beta change as much as alpha change so that direct comparisons between pre- and post-training may not necessarily be a good indication of changes in adaptation levels on the construct of interest. Sometimes beta change (as opposed to alpha change) may be the idea underlying adaptation in the sense that the recalibration of measurement is critical to adaptive performance. To my knowledge, no research has construed adaptation as such or attempted to separate alpha from possible beta change when examining changes in adaptation due to training. Chan's (in press-b) application of mean and covariance structures analysis to detect differences in item 'evocativeness' of a construct (i.e., uniform differential item functioning) may be used to assess beta change by treating pre- and post-training adaptation measures as different items assessing the same construct.

Gamma change refers to change in the conceptual domain. The change described in Question 4(c) is a gamma change. Gamma change can take a variety of forms. For example, in the language of factor analysis, the number of factors (a factor representing a construct) assessed by a given set of measures may change from one time point to another. Alternatively, the number of factors may remain constant across time, but a differentiation process occurs so that the factor intercorrelations decrease over time, or an integration process may occur so that the factor intercorrelations increase over time. When individuals adapt, their conceptual structures may be undergoing factorial differentiation as they acquire a more differentiated view of the knowledge domain. Or, their conceptual structures may be undergoing factorial integration as previously unrelated dimensions in the knowledge domain get integrated into global undifferentiated dimension. Given the emphasis on the qualitative change in conceptualization of the the task problem domain that purportedly occurs when individuals develop adaptive expertise, it is somewhat surprising that previous research has not explicitly discussed and assessed the various forms of gamma change as measures of individual adaptation. The literature on gamma change is directly relevant for bridging the conceptual and empirical gaps in research that construe adaptation as changes in conceptualization. More discussions on gamma change including measurement issues are available in Chan (1998b), Millsap and Hartog (1988), Schaubroeck and Green (1989), Schmitt (1982), and Vandenberg and Self (1993).

Question 6 asks if the change is to be considered as a shared characteristic of a *group of individuals* over time or to be referred to what occurs *within an individual* over time, or *both*. This issue has been discussed above in the section on levels of analysis. Suffice to say that researchers should be sensitive to the different aspects of change over time that may be occurring at different levels of analysis. Even if the researcher hypothesizes that change occurs at one but not the other level, it is important to collect data at both levels and employ analytical models that estimate effects at both levels so that the assumption of no change at the non-target level can be tested.

Question 7 asks if *individual differences in intra-individual change* in the focal variable are predictable from external variables. For example, in newcomer adaptation research, we may want to know if individual differences in the rate of change in an adaptation outcome are predictable from individual differences in cognitive ability or some individual difference adaptability construct.

Question 8 asks if there are *cross-domain relationships* in change over time. For example, are individual differences in rate of change in adaptive performance during training related to individual differences in rate of change in adaptive performance on the job? For the same set of predictor variables, is the pattern of predictive relationships (e.g., predictor-rate of change associations) invariant across different domains (i.e., training versus job)? Chan (1998b) described how a variety of these cross-domain relationships can be examined by relating predictors and change trajectories from different domains in a single multivariate model.

Question 9, the final question, asks if there is *invariance across groups* with respect to the specific facet of change over time under investigation. These groups could be experimental and control groups in research on training adaptive expertise or they could be natural occurring groups such as gender groups or groups which differ on some adaptability construct. The question of interest is whether a specific change pattern found in one group is equal to (invariant) or differs from (noninvariant), in either magnitude or form, the change pattern in a different group. For example, the trajectory representing changes in adaptive performance on a novel job task may differ in functional form between newcomers and veterans. Or, in training adaptive expertise, the experimental group may undergo a type of gamma change represented by factorial integration of performance measurement so that performance components (factors) become increasingly interrelated over time, whereas the control group may exhibit factorial invariance so that intercorrelations among performance components remain constant over time. Chan (1998b) demonstrated how specific facets of change in patterns in multiple groups can be modeled and compared to determine if invariance exists across groups.

The adequacy of the answers to the relevant questions enumerated above forms the basis for bridging the conceptual and empirical gaps in research on individual adaptation. As discussed, these questions on change over time are inextricably linked to the issues of dimensionality, malleability, predictor–criterion relationships, and levels of analysis.

CONCLUDING REMARKS

There is an increased proliferation of new concepts and assessment technologies in the research on individual adaptation, whether it is in the literature on individual differences, training, team, or newcomer socialization. For example, concepts such as team mental models and team compilation and new assessment technologies or measurement techniques such as the Pathfinder algorithm for eliciting knowledge structures and various cognitive task analysis methods are increasingly employed in recent research. However, as discussed in this paper, several important conceptual and empirical gaps exist. Unless these gaps are satisfactorily addressed, we may end up with a multitude of labels, all of which purportedly refer to scientific constructs or valid measurements concerning individual adaptation but in reality have no incremental explanatory value.

ACKNOWLEDGEMENTS

The author would like to thank Neal Schmitt, Elaine Pulakos, and Paul Tesluk for the fruitful discussions on some of the ideas contained in this paper. Correspondence concerning this paper should be directed to David Chan, Department of Social Work and Psychology, National University of Singapore, 10 Kent Ridge Crescent, Singapore 119260, Republic of Singapore. Electronic mail can be sent to *swkcct@nus.edu.sg*.

REFERENCES

Anderson, J. R. (1983). *The Architecture of Cognition*. Cambridge, MA: Harvard University Press.
Anderson, J. R. (1993). Problem-solving and learning. *American Psychologist*, **48**, 35–44.

Ashford, S. J. & Black, J. S. (1996). Proactivity during organizational entry: The role of desire for control. *Journal of Applied Psychology*, **81**, 199–214.

Bauer, T. N. & Green, S. G. (1994). Effect of newcomer involvement in work-related activities: a longitudinal study of socialization. *Journal of Applied Psychology*, **79**, 219–223.

Bauer, T. N., Morrison, E. W. & Callister, R. B. (1998). Organizational socialization: A review and directions for future research. In G. R. Ferris (Ed.), *Research in Personnel and Human Resource Management*, Vol. 16 (pp. 149–214). Greenwich, CT: JAI Press.

Bliese, P. D. (1998). Group size, ICC values, and group-level correlations: A simulation. *Organizational Research Methods*, **1**, 355–373.

Bliese, P. D. & Halverson, R. R. (1998). Group size and measures of group-level properties: An examination of eta-squared and ICC values. *Journal of Management*, **24**, 157–172.

Bryk, A. S. & Raudenbush, S. W. (1987). Application of hierarchical linear models to assessing change. *Psychological Bulletin*, **101**, 147–158.

Campbell, J. P. (1990). Modeling the performance prediction problem in industrial and organizational psychology. In M. D. Dunnette and L. M. Hough (Eds), *Handbook of Industrial and Organizational Psychology*, Vol. 1, (pp. 687–732). Palo Alto, CA: Consulting Psychologists Press.

Cannon-Bowers, J. A., Tannenbaum, S. I., Salas, E. & Volpe, C. E. (1995). Defining competencies and establishing team training requirements. In R. A. Guzzo & E. Salas (Eds), *Team Effectiveness and Decision Making in Organizations* (pp. 333–380). San Francisco: Jossey-Bass.

Chan, D. (1996). Criterion and construct validation of an assessment center. *Journal of Occupational and Organizational Psychology*, **69**, 167–181.

Chan, D. (1998a). Functional relations among constructs in the same content domain from different levels of analysis. *Journal of Applied Psychology*, **83**, 234–246.

Chan, D. (1998b). The conceptualization and analysis of change over time: An integrative approach incorporating longitudinal means and covariance structures analysis (LMACS) and multiple indicator latent growth modeling (MLGM). *Organizational Research Methods*, **1**, 421–483.

Chan, D. (in press-a). Understanding adaptation to changes in the work environment: Integrating individual difference and learning perspectives. *Research in Personnel and Human Resources Management*.

Chan, D. (in press-b). Detection of differential item functioning on the Kirton Adaptation-Innovation Inventory using multiple-group mean and covariance structures analysis. *Multivariate Behavioral Research*.

Chan, D. & Schmitt, N. (in press). Interindividual differences in intraindividual changes in proactivity during organizational entry: A latent growth modeling approach to understanding newcomer adaptation. *Journal of Applied Psychology*.

Chi, M. T. H., Feltovich, P. J. & Glaser, R. (1981). Categorization and representation of physics problems by experts and novices. *Cognitive Science*, **5**, 121–152.

Drasgow, F. (1984). Scrutinizing psychological tests: Measurement equivalence and equiavalent relations with external variables are central issues. *Psychological Bulletin*, **95**, 134–135.

Drasgow, F. (1987). Study of measurement bias of two standardized psychological tests. *Journal of Applied Psychology*, **72**, 19–29.

Feldman, D. C. (1981). The multiple socialization of organization members. *Academy of Management Review*, **6**, 309–318.

Ford, J. K. & Kraiger, K. (1995). The application of cognitive constructs and principles to the instructional systems model of training: Implications for needs assessment, design, and transfer. In C. L. Cooper and I. T. Robertson (Eds), *Inter-*

national Review of Industrial and Organizational Psychology, Vol. 10 (pp. 1–48). Chichester: Wiley.

Goldsmith, T. E. & Kraiger, K. (1997). Structural knowledge assessment and training evaluation. In J. K. Ford and Associates (Eds), *Improving Training Effectiveness in Work Organizations* (pp. 73–96). Hillsdale, NJ: Erlbaum.

Golembiewski, R. T., Billingsley, K. & Yeager, S. (1976). Measuring change and persistence in human affairs: Types of change generated by OD designs. *Journal of Applied Behavioral Science*, **12**, 133–157.

Gough, H. G. (1987). *Manual for the California Psychological Inventory*. Palo Alto, CA: Consulting Psychologists Press.

Hollenbeck, J. R., Ilgen, D. R., Phillips, J. M. & Hedlund, J. (1994). Decision risk in dynamic two-stage contexts: Beyond the status quo. *Journal of Applied Psychology*, **79**, 592–598.

Holyoak, K. J. (1991). Symbolic connectionism: Toward third-generation theories of expertise. In K. A. Ericsson and J. Smith (Eds), *Toward a General Theory of Expertise* (pp. 301–336). Cambridge: Cambridge University Press.

House, R., Rousseau, D. M. & Thomas-Hunt, M. (1995). The meso paradigm: A framework for the integration of micro and macro organizational behavior. *Research in Organizational Behavior*, **17**, 71–114.

Jackson, D. N. (1967). *Personality Research Form Manual*. Goshen, NY: Research Psychologists Press.

Judge, T. K. A., Thoresen, C. J. & Pucik, V. (1996). Managerial coping with organizational change: A dispositional perspective. Paper presented at the Academy of Management Meetings, Cincinnati, Ohio.

Kanfer, R. & Ackerman, P. L. (1989). Motivation and cognitive abilities: An integrative-aptitude-treatment interaction approach to skill acquisition. *Journal of Applied Psychology*, **74**, 657–690.

Klein, K. J., Dansereau, R. G. & Hall, R. J. (1994). Levels issues in theory development, data collection, and analysis. *Academy of Management Review*, **19**, 195–229.

Kozlowski, S. W. J. (1998). Training and developing adaptive teams: Theory, principles, and research. In J. A. Cannon-Bowers & E. Salas (Eds), *Decision Making Under Stress: Implications for Training and Simulation* (pp. 115–153). Washington, DC: APA Books.

Kozlowski, S. W. J., Gully, S. M., McHugh, P. P., Salas, W. E. & Cannon-Bowers, J. A. (1996). A dynamic theory of leadership and team effectiveness: Developmental and task contingent leader roles. *Research in Personnel and Human Resources Management*, **14**, 253–305.

Kozlowski, S. W. J., Gully, S. M., Nason, E. R. & Smith, E. M. (in press). Developing adaptive teams: A theory of compilation and performance across levels and time. In D. R. Ilgen & E. D. Pulakos (Eds), *The Changing Nature of Work and Perfomance: Implications for Staffing, Personnel Actions, and Development*. San Francisco: Jossey-Bass.

Kraiger, K., Ford, J. K. & Salas, E. (1993). Application of cognitive, skill-based, and affective theories of learning outcomes to new methods of training evaluation. *Journal of Appled Psychology*, **78**, 311–328.

Latham, G. P., Saari, L. M., Pursell, M. A. & Campion, M. A. (1980). The situational interview. *Journal of Applied Psychology*, **69**, 569–573.

Louis, M. R. (1980). Surprise and sense-making: What newcomers experience in entering unfamiliar organizational settings. *Administrative Science Quarterly*, **25**, 226–251.

McArdle, J. J. & Epstein, D. (1987). Latent growth curves within developmental structural equation models. *Child Development*, **58**, 110–133.

Meredith, W. & Tisak, J. (1990). Latent curve analysis. *Psychometrika*, **55**, 107–122.

Millsap, R. E. & Hartog, S. B. (1988). Alpha, beta, and gamma change in evaluation research: A structural equation approach. *Journal of Applied Psychology*, 73, 574–584.

Morrison, E. W. (1993a). Longitudinal study of the effects of information seeking on newcomer socialization. *Journal of Applied Psychology*, 78, 173–183.

Morrison, E. W. (1993b). Newcomer information seeking: Exploring types, modes, sources, and outcomes. *Academy of Management Journal*, 36, 557–589.

Motowidlo, S. J., Carter, G. W., Dunnette, M. D., Tippins, N., Werner, S., Burnett, J. R. & Vaughn, M. J. (1992). Studies of the structured behavioral interview. *Journal of Applied Psychology*, 77, 571–587.

Mumford, M. D., Baughman, W. A., Threfall, K. V., Uhlman, C. E. & Costanza, D. P. (1993). Personality, adaptability, and performance: Performance on well-defined and ill-defined problem-solving tasks. *Human Performance*, 6, 241–285.

Ostroff, C. (1993). Comparing correlations based on individual level and aggregated data. *Journal of Applied Psychology*, 78, 569–582.

Paulhus, D. L. & Martin, C. L. (1988). Functional flexibility: A new conception of interpersonal flexibility. *Journal of Personality and Social Psychology*, 55, 88–101.

Pulakos, E. D. (1996). Proposal for the test of a model of adaptability. (Submitted to Department of Defense Small Business Innovation Research Program.) Washington, DC: Personnel Decisions Research Institutes.

Quinones, M. A., Ford, J. K. & Teachout, M. S. (1995). The relationship between work experience and job performance: A conceptual and meta-analytic review. *Personnel Psychology*, 48, 887–910.

Rousseau, D. M. (1985). Issues of level in organizational research: Multilevel and cross-level perspectives. In L. L. Cummings & B. Staw (Eds), *Research in Organizational Behavior*. Greenwich, CT: JAI Press.

Schaubroeck, J. & Green, S. G. (1989). Confirmatory factor analytic procedures for assessing change during organizational entry. *Journal of Applied Psychology*, 74, 892–900.

Schmitt, N. (1982). The use of analysis of covariance structures to assess beta and gamma change. *Multivariate Behavioral Research*, 17, 343–358.

Schmitt, N. & Chan, D. (1998). *Personnel Selection: A Theoretical Approach*. Thousand Oaks, CA: Sage.

Schmitt, N., Jennings, D. & Toney, R. (1996). Can we develop measures of hypothetical construct? Paper presented at the 1st Biannual Biodata Conference, Athens, GA.

Schvaneveldt, R. W., Durso, F. T. & Dearholt, D. W. (1985). *Pathfinder: Scaling with network structures* (Memoradum in Computer and Cognitive Science, MCCS-85-89, Computing Research Laboratory). Las Cruces: New Mexico State University.

Schvaneveldt, R. W., Durso, F. T. & Dearholt, D. W. (1989). Network structures in proximity data. In G. G. Bower (Ed.), *The Psychology of Learning and Motivation*, Vol. 24, (pp. 249–284). New York: Academic Press.

Smith, E. M., Ford, J. K. & Kozlowski, S. W. J. (1997). Building adaptive expertise: Implications for training design strategies. In M. A. Quinones & A. Ehrenstein (Eds), *Training for a Rapidly Changing Workplace*. American Psychological Association. Washington, DC.

Snow, R. E. & Lohman, D. L. (1984). Toward a theory of cognitive aptitude for learning from instruction. *Journal of Educational Psychology*, 76, 347–376.

Sternberg, R. J. (1994). The PRSVL model of person–context interaction in the study of human potential. In M. G. Rumsey, C. B. Walker & J. H. Harris (Eds), *Personnel Selection and Classification*. Hillsdale, NJ: Erlbaum.

Tesluk, P. & Jacogs, R. R. (1998) Toward an integrated model of work experience. *Personnel Psychology*, 51, 321–355.

Tesluk, P., Mathieu, J. E. & Zaccaro, S. J. (1997). Task and aggregation issues in the analysis and assessment of team performance. In M. T. Brannick, E. Salas & C.

Prince (Eds), *Team Performance Assessment and Measurement: Theory, Methods, and Applications*. Hillsdale, NJ: Erlbaum.

Vandenberg, R. J. & Self, R. M. (1993). Assessing newcomers' changing commitments to the organization during the first 6 months of work. *Journal of Applied Psychology*, **78**, 557–568.

Wagner, R. K. (1986). The search for intraterrestrial intelligence. In R. J. Sternberg & R. K. Wagner (Eds), *Practical Intelligence: Nature and Origins of Competence in the Everyday World*. Cambridge: Cambridge University Press.

Willett, J. B. & Sayer, A. B. (1994). Using covariance analysis to detect correlates and predictors of individual change over time *Psychological Bulletin*, **116**, 363–380.

Chapter 2

THE PSYCHOLOGY OF CAREERS IN ORGANIZATIONS

John Arnold
Loughborough University Business School

In one sense an exhaustive review of the literature on the psychology of careers is overdue—the last one in this series was provided by Michael Driver in 1988. But on the other hand there is no shortage of more recent reviews of career-related topics. In 1991, the *Journal of Vocational Behavior* commissioned a veritable blitz of reviews to mark its 20th anniversary (Borgen, 1991; Chartrand & Camp, 1991; Hackett, Lent and Greenhaus, 1991; London & Greller, 1991; Meier, 1991). Since then, its traditional annual reviews of the whole field of vocational behavior have been replaced by annual reviews of subareas of the field, each subarea appearing once every three years, usually right at the end of the year (Swanson, 1992; Blau, Linnehan, Brooks and Hoover, 1993; Fouad, 1994; Watkins and Subich, 1995). The *Career Development Quarterly* also publishes annual reviews, these mostly concerning the theory and practice of counseling (e.g. Salomone, 1993; Subich, 1994). Meanwhile, in the *Journal of Management*, Ornstein and Isabella (1993) produced a review of aspects of careers more exclusively orientated towards organizational issues. Feldman (1989) did a similar job four years earlier. Also, as we shall see shortly, some topics I would consider to be specific aspects of careers have been reviewed elsewhere, including in this present volume.

I want to use the existence of the generous supply of thorough reviews (albeit from a North American perspective) as an opportunity to take a different approach. Rather than seeking to mention briefly all research and theory produced in recent years in a kind of prose catalogue, I will present some observations and arguments about certain aspects of the psychology of careers in organizations. My primary purposes are to examine what careers are about in a changing world, to identify some topics which reflect current and future concerns, and to report and critically examine literature in those areas.

Ornstein and Isabella (1993, p. 244) commented that a review of the whole field of careers would be 'impossible and somewhat unnecessary' due to the

The Psychology of Careers in Organizations by John Arnold taken from IRIOP 1997 v12, Edited by Cary L. Cooper and Ivan T. Robertson: © 1997 John Wiley & Sons, Ltd

large number of disciplinary approaches brought to bear upon it, and the variety of target audiences for different segments of it. Driver (1988) noted that other writers have characterized the study of careers as fragmented and unsatisfactory in important respects (see also Hall, 1991). Part of the reason for this may be that even amongst behaviorally-orientated writers there seems little consensus about what careers are, or rather what they are construed as being. An examination of some definitional differences will help us to clarify the many strands of career and begin to identify a framework for a structured examination.

WHAT IS A CAREER?

Some authors perhaps wisely do not attempt to define what a career is. Others have grasped the nettle. Below are some not very systematically chosen definitions of career, including some older ones because they have influenced or reflect subsequent work:

1. A sequence of positions occupied by a person during the course of a lifetime (Super & Hall, 1978).
2. A series of related job experiences that fit into some meaningful pattern. If you have a series of odd jobs all your working life, that is hardly a career (DuBrin, 1983).
3. A succession or an accumulation of role-related experiences over time (London & Mone, 1988).
4. A sequence of jobs occupied and performed throughout a person's working lifetime (Gray, Gault, Meyers and Walther, 1990).
5. Occupations that are characterized by interrelated training and work experiences, in which a person moves upward through a series of positions that require greater mastery and responsibility, and that provide increasing financial return (Perlmutter & Hall, 1992).
6. The sequence of negotiations and renegotiations of the psychological contract which the individual conducts with organizations during his or her work life (adapted from Herriot, 1992, referring to organizational careers).
7. The pattern of work-related experiences that span the course of a person's life (Greenhaus & Callanan, 1994).
8. Accumulations of information and knowledge embodied in skills, expertise, and relationship networks acquired through an evolving sequence of work experiences over time. In this context, work experiences constitute the primary mechanism by which careers occur though they are not in themselves a career (Bird, 1994).

Most academics familiar with careers literature agree that a career is NOT confined to upward and/or predictable movement within one kind of work.

Yet this is the image conveyed in definition 2 (in a self-help 'how to be successful' guide), and definition 5 (a lifespan development text). Worse, it is not uncommon to see advertisements along the lines of 'Enrol at Salaryhike College if you want a career, not just a job'. The local newspaper in my current home town entitles its situations vacant section 'Jobs and Careers'. Readers can no doubt think of similar examples of this apparent dual labor market. Therefore, a continuing and pressing concern is that career *is* often thought of as something like definitions 2 and 5 by many people, including some who write about careers. Wider use of less restrictive implicit or explicit definitions of career would surely help social scientists to apply theories and concepts more effectively, enable popular writers to purvey more effective advice, and assist mere mortals to manage their careers better.

One fairly evident common feature of all these definitions is that they refer to *more than one* role, experience, or event. Words like series, sequence, succession, pattern and accumulation are used. This is a key point. The study of career involves study over time rather than taking snapshots of supposedly stable situations. Note also that although the above definitions agree on the 'more than one' aspect, what there is more than one of is in doubt. We are offered positions, related job experiences, role-related experiences, jobs occupied and performed, upward sequence of positions, negotiations, work-related experiences and skills, expertise and relationship networks. In other words, the studies of careers have variously focused on sequences of roles, experiences in those roles, behaviors in the roles, and personal attributes derived from the roles. No wonder it is a diverse field.

For present purposes, we can be said to be considering career if we are thinking about (i) potential or actual sequences of employment-related positions, roles, activities or experiences encountered by, or available to, one or more persons; (ii) their plans, decisions and attitudes concerning such sequences; (iii) their adjustment and development in new or changed employment-related positions, etc.; (iv) their preparation for future ones; and (v) their sense-making about past employment-related positions etc in relation to their present ones. We are also in the realm of careers when we consider (vi) attempts made by focal individuals themselves or others to influence (normally facilitate or shape) any of the first five phenomena; and finally (vii) the interplay between personal and macro- or micro-situational variables and any of the preceding six phenomena.

THE CONTEXT OF CAREERS

It is now well known that the context of employment in the Western world has changed and is still changing. Pressures brought about by globalization of economies and technological advance have led to some quite dramatic transformations in work organizations.

More than one *guru* has skilfully and eloquently described the new landscape. Bridges (1995) has argued that jobs and traditional employment are gone forever. Handy (1989, 1994) described various organizational forms that are emerging. They have in common a core of full-time employees who consider themselves members of the organization, and a periphery of casualized workers, some highly skilled carrying out specialized and limited-term projects and others semi- or unskilled working in contracted-out functions such as cleaning and catering. Some interesting questions revolve around managing the performance and commitment of these latter two groups (Pearce, 1993; Beard and Edwards, 1995). Along similar but more pessimistic lines, UK journalist Will Hutton (Hutton, 1995) has predicted the advent of a 30/30/40 society: 30% either unemployed or economically inactive, 30% in insecure and intermittent employment with few benefits, and 40% relatively privileged usually with marketable skills in relatively stable employment or self-employment. Particularly in countries which embraced the concept (and cost) of a welfare state after World War II, such scenarios have profound implications for social fabric and order, and for personal financial planning which in many countries has long been based on a norm of stable employment.

Perhaps mainly with Hutton's 40% in mind, some writers have referred to new kinds of career. This too has a rather longer history than might be first thought. Hall (1976) referred to the Protean career, where the individual is his or her own agent. More recently, people are urged to regard themselves as self-employed even if they have an employer (Bridges, 1995); to carry a portfolio of skills and experiences and make strategic moves which equip them for future employability (Kanter, 1989; Handy, 1989). Arthur (1994) has coined the term 'boundaryless career' to sum up the trend towards employment experiences which take individuals across employer boundaries. These boundaries are in any case blurred due to the proliferation of mergers and acquisitions (Cartwright & Cooper, 1992), wholly-owned subsidiaries, and autonomous business units. The boundaryless career may well also take a person across different types of work, and it is validated and supported by networks such as professional groups.

Some further trends in employment, and in demography, add detail to this picture. The average age of the population in most Western countries is increasing due to increased longevity and historical patterns of birth rates. In the UK, out of a total labor force of about 30 million, an increase of 2.4 million in the number of 35 to 54 year olds and a drop of 1.6 million under 35s is expected between 1993 and 2006 (*Social Trends*, 1993). Increased participation by women in the labor market is occurring in many countries (Offermann and Gowing, 1990; Wheeler, 1990; Davidson, 1996), and an increasing proportion of the total jobs available are part-time (the two trends are not unconnected, since at present a greater proportion of women than men work part-time). Although somewhat vulnerable to the economic cycle, the proportion of people in self-employment has increased significantly in the UK and to a lesser extent in other European Union countries (Meager, Kaiser & Dietrich, 1992). The number and proportion of people working in small and medium enterprises (SMEs) has increased in many countries—a salutary reminder that analyses of organizational careers must not assume a large organization (in any case, as many have wryly observed, the sure-fire way to run a small business these days is to start with a large one).

So, with the earlier analysis of the nature of careers in mind, what issues arise from the trends described above that should interest psychologists? In no particular order, they seem to me to be those listed below. Having identified the issues, in each case I will then briefly examine recent literature in that area.

1. Job changes happen with increasing frequency (Inkson, 1995), and perhaps involve more radical change for individuals and less predictability than was once the case. Individuals and organizations are under pressure to perform quickly and creatively. Louis (1982) argued that career transitions had been neglected hitherto—has this been rectified in recent years? Psychological investigations of work-role transitions (Nicholson, 1989), relocation, newcomer information-seeking and socialization are all relevant here. So is the literature on commitment, but that is reviewed in Meyer's chapter in this volume. Hence it is not covered here. Also, teleworking, and the transition to it, have been covered recently in this series by Chapman, Sheehy, Heywood, Dooley and Collins (1995). Transitions involving unemployment received some attention from Winefield (1995), also in this series.

2. In some organizations individuals are explicitly told that it is up to them to manage their own careers—the organization as a corporate body will take no part and provide no support. In others, some responsibility is being taken for equipping individuals to manage their own career within a general framework that offers some signposts but fewer than was once the case. There is a strong case to be made that demographic changes and increasing competition mean that organizations need to utilize *all* their people better (Herriot & Pemberton, 1995b). What is the current contribution of the psychologically oriented literature concerning career interventions and their impact upon individuals and organizations?

3. Individuals are having to make and remake career decisions more frequently. They may experience periods of education and training scattered through their life, not just in their childhood and adolescence. The proportion of older people in the population of many countries is increasing. What can the psychological literatures on career, decision-making, aging and lifespan development contribute to an understanding of career?

These three issues seem to me to fall naturally out of the current context. That is not to say there are no others. In particular, I am aware of the need to include in each of the above three areas relevant literature on gender, ethnicity and internationalization in careers. Two other important issues arising from the current context but omitted here due to space constraints and coverage elsewhere are:

4. For many people working in organizations, the old understanding of their employment relationship has been disconfirmed by experiences over the last few years. What implications does this have for their interpretation of present experience relative to past and future? Recent literature on the psychological contract (e.g. Shore & Tetrick, 1994; Herriot, Pemberton, 1995a) and related issues has addressed this.

5. Delayering and downsizing have made promotions harder to obtain, and some organizations have shifted to project- or competency-bases (Lawler, 1994) where relatively constant job descriptions do not exist. For both reasons, externally verifiable career success is more difficult to obtain and to define. Indeed any sort of career map is hard to find. Within a managerial context, issues concerning career success are reviewed by Tharenou (this volume).

CHANGE AND TRANSITION

Incidence and Types of Change

One symptom of what Stephens (1994) has appropriately described as 'increasingly discontinuous and unstable work lives' is increased frequency of voluntary and involuntary work-role transitions. These include changes between jobs, substantial shifts in the requirements or opportunities inherent in an existing job or other employment situation, transitions into and out of employment, relocation of employment, and also changes in attitude to features of one's objective career. Regarding managers, Nicholson and West (1988) reported increasing frequency of job change in the UK. More recent work by Inkson (1995) and Cawsey and Inkson (1992) has reaffirmed this trend in the UK and New Zealand respectively, and noted that it has been relatively impervious to the economic cycle. Also, much of the increase in job changes for managers is accounted for by involuntary and/or sideways or downward status moves. Around half of managers' job changes involve a change of employer. Thus it is appropriate that no less than 12 of Hall's (1991) 'Twenty Questions: research needed to advance the field of careers' specifically refer to work-role transitions.

Potentially useful general typologies and models of work-role transitions were developed some time ago (e.g. Louis, 1980a, b; Nicholson, 1984, 1989) but have been used relatively little in subsequent research, though there are signs that this may be changing. Ashforth and Saks (1995) tested some predictions derived from Nicholson (1984) concerning whether business school graduates in the early months of employment would seek to change their roles (innovate) or be changed by them (personal change). Contrary to prediction, the amount of personal change was unrelated to the discretion and novelty of the new work role. However, as predicted, discretion was positively related to self-reported role innovation. Commenting upon the moderate level of support for their predictions, the authors noted that Nicholson's theory may be limited in that adjustment to new work roles is portrayed as a relatively asocial process. In line with this proposition, Major, Kozlowski, Chao and Gardner (1995) have recently reported that interactions with colleagues and supervisors in the early weeks of a new job can reduce the negative impact of unmet expectations.

In a review of some of the literature in this area, Stephens (1994) has integrated some concepts from the Nicholson (1984) model with others from lifelong approaches to career development. Stephens argued that the Nicholson model is more comprehensive than the perhaps better known Theory of Work Adjustment (Dawis & Lofquist, 1984). Certainly, to me, the Theory of Work Adjustment has a strangely dated appearance. Its prediction that satisfactoriness (of an employee's performance) and satisfaction (the extent to which the job meets the employees' needs) jointly determine job tenure seems to portray stability as the norm, disrupted only by unsatisfactory circumstances. This seems rather implausible these days. Returning to Stephens (1994), he also noted a dearth of research on the effects of work-role transitions on non-transitioners. This is a theme that has been mentioned in socialization literature and recently in job rotation literature but as yet rarely pursued.

Bruce and Scott (1994) adapted Louis' (1980a) typology of transitions to fit the context of the US Navy, where the structured career development system enabled them to test propositions in relatively controlled fashion. The five types of transition were entry events, promotion events, lateral moves, resignation, and retirement. The authors commented as follows upon their results (p. 26): 'In general, the career events studied were moderately high in magnitude and desirability, low in strain and role ambiguity, and seen as causing moderate adjustment difficulty. These events were seen as resulting in gains in both individuals' personal lives and their careers, and there was moderate eagerness toward all events.' Nicholson and West (1988) also noted that many work-role transitions are experienced quite positively, and questioned whether stress-based models were appropriate. Longitudinal work with degree-qualified samples by Newton and Keenan (1990) and Arnold (1994) supports the notion that job-changing produces either neutral or positive outcomes for psychological well-being, though this does not rule out the possibility that stress models may be useful in investigating the *process* of adjustment. The amount of stress experienced by a transitioner may depend partly upon the resources they bring to the transition. Heppner, Multon and Johnston (1994) reported the development and validation of the 40-item Career Transitions Inventory. Five subscales emerged. They did not precisely coincide with the theoretical constructs originally identified by the authors. The subscales are readiness, confidence, perceived support, control, and decision-independence. The Career Transitions Inventory may well prove to be a useful instrument in research and practice.

Relocation

Relocation occurs when one or more employees of an organization move geographically whilst retaining the same employer. They may or may not be performing the same job in their new location as their old, and the move may or may not be of their own instigation. J. M. Brett, Stroh and Reilly (1992) reviewed the then-existing literature in volume 7 of this series. Their own work (Brett, Stroh & Reilly, 1993) with mobile managers in leading US corporations contradicted much earlier research by finding that sex, race and number of children at home were *not* related to willingness to relocate. Neither were work attitudes such as job satisfaction and company loyalty—as the authors point out, this is not surprising since the object of those attitudes is the job or company, not the relocation. The main factor predicting willingness to relocate was age. Older employees were less willing. These findings may be partly due to the sample, which consisted of managers who had relocated in the previous two years. Although not about relocation, a recent article by J.F. Brett, Cron and Slocum (1995) suggests a variable that has been neglected in relocation research. This is economic dependency on work. For some people, relocation is the only way of keeping a job, particularly in group moves.

Munton, Forster, Altman and Greenbury (1993) reported data from over 200 relocating employees and their families at relocation, and then three months and six months later. Respondents' worries focused mostly on extra-employment concerns such as property transactions and guilt at forcing children to move. Fisher and Shaw (1994) reported a study of 150 relocating military employees who provided data before and then three months after their move. Adjustment and attitudes toward the move were more strongly related to anticipated, and then actual, features of the new location than were demographic and pre-move location attributes. Past experience of moves was strongly negatively correlated with adjustment difficulty. However, this last point has not been the case in all research. Martin (1995) found some evidence, albeit in a small sample, that adjustment to relocation was most difficult for those with little experience of it and those with a great deal of experience. In the former case lack of know-how and disruption of community ties may have been the cause. In the latter group it may have been more a case of being worn down by yet another round of tedious and taxing tasks. Lawson and Angle (1994) found a more straightforward effect of prior experience of moving helping adjustment in their survey of 200 families involved in a company move. Overall, family and other extra-employment factors were better predictors of adjustment than were employment-related ones.

The concept of adjustment has come under rather closer scrutiny in the literature on international relocation. Brewster (1994) argues that it is most often construed by researchers as psychological comfort, but in the discussion of data researchers 'find themselves discussing the steps that the expatriate takes to bring his or her behavior into line with that of the host country' (p. 50). Brewster found that Swedish managers in the UK tended to adopt styles more characteristic of the UK than Sweden, and suggested that expatriates' behaviors may change more completely and quickly than is often realized. Janssens (1995) has pointed out that integration into a new environment should not necessarily be seen as a desirable outcome of work-role transitions. Sometimes (and particularly in international assignments) the employing organization's top managers may want the relocatee to retain a 'head office' perspective rather than 'go native'. She found that contact of international relocatees with members and the culture of the host country increased steadily as they spent longer there. This increase was still evident after 5 years and longer. Contrary to Brewster, then, some aspects of adjustment may be long drawn out.

There are of course individual differences in how international relocation is handled. Black and Gregersen (1992) distinguished two dimensions: maintenance of own cultural identity and contact with the host culture. This enabled a 2×2 classification: free agent (low, low); go native (low, high); heart at home (high, low); and dual citizen (high, high). Recent empirical work has reinforced earlier assertions that adjustment of family members is crucial to the work and general adjustment of the international relocatee him or herself. Nicholson and Imaizumi (1993, p. 130) have described this as '. . . a significant flow of adjustment from the domestic to the employment sphere.' W. Arthur and Bennett (1995) found that family situation was perceived as more important in determining success of international location than were job knowledge and motivation, relational skills, flexibility/adaptability and even extra-cultural openness. Furthermore, this finding from a sample of 338 international assignees in 45 multinational companies applied across different types of work and types of company. In an interesting analysis from a psychoanalytical perspective Schneider and Asakawa (1995) examined the role in international adjustment of dependency, separation and individualization, autonomy and control, and intimacy. They contrasted aspects of child-rearing in an attempt to identify differential adult adjustment patterns.

Experiencing Work-role Transitions

Much research on work-role transitions has used samples of young people entering full-time employment for the first time. This is sometimes for good theoretical reasons, but often for convenience. Earlier work (see Arnold, 1990, for a review) tended to find that navigating the transition was not as difficult as previous theorizing had suggested it might be. That work tended to concentrate on adjustment to unfulfilling work for school-leavers, but utilization of skills and commitment in graduate samples. More recent work by

Arnold and Nicholson (1991) and Fournier and Payne (1994) with graduates has examined the nature and extent of self-concept change in the early months and years of employment. There is significant qualitative change, though not necessarily towards potential role models in the organization.

There is perhaps good reason why the education to employment transition of young people has been going out of fashion. Trends towards higher unemployment, education interspersed throughout life, and work experience during education have made this transition less clearcut and uniform than it once was. Nevertheless, a special issue of the *Journal of Vocational Behavior* was recently devoted to the transition for non-college-educated youth. In the lead article, Feij, Whitely, Peiró and Taris (1995) reported a large-scale longitudinal study with cross-validation of young people in eight countries over the first 18 months of school to work transition. The sample was chosen on the basis of being employed in certain occupations. They formulated, tested and modified a model of the development of job content innovation and career enhancing strategies on the part of the young people. They proposed that supervisor relations, work centrality, work values and correspondence between individual and work were implicated in this. Findings supported the importance of relations with the supervisor in influencing the outcome variables.

A series of invited articles critiqued the Feij et al. paper. Hesketh (1995) examined the potential contribution of the Theory of Work Adjustment (Dawis & Lofquist, 1984) to the framing of the study and interpreting its findings. Blustein (1995) argued that it would have been strengthened by inclusion of theoretical constructs from career development and lifespan development theory, as well as more attention to the cultural contexts of the countries concerned. The most critical commentary was by Eldredge (1995), who highlighted Feij et al.'s inappropriate use of some existing literature and their failure to use concepts and measures of socialization and innovation.

One area Eldredge (1995) concentrated upon was the impact of socialization on the role orientation of newcomers. A recent reanalysis by Baker (1995) of data reported by Allen and Meyer (1990) has suggested that socialization tactics adopted by organizations with newcomers have their effect partly through the degree of role certainty as proposed by Allen and Meyer, but also partly through the degree of interaction with incumbents. Baker reiterated Jones' (1986) earlier conclusion that it is difficult to socialize newcomers in such a way that both commitment and innovation are fostered.

At the other end of employed life, there has been a little recent attention to retirement. This too is an increasingly ambiguous transition with respect to its timing, voluntariness, and suddenness. A model of psychological aspects of retirement has recently been presented in this series (McGoldrick, 1996), so coverage here is very brief. Feldman (1994) has called for more research linking decision to retire with subsequent adjustment. He drew on image theory (Beach & Mitchell, 1978) to identify sustaining a stable self-image, resolving approach-avoidance conflicts, and maintaining or regaining control over one's future as three themes that should be central to retirement research. No less than 14 hypotheses for future research were specified. Hanisch (1994) has reported research which made some links between reasons for retiring (work, personal, or health reasons) and subsequent attitudes and behaviors. Talaga and Beehr (1995) uncovered several factors (e.g. presence of dependents in the household) which had differential impacts on the retirement decisions of men relative to women.

Socialization and Information-seeking

The notion that individuals have inflated expectations of their new environment when starting work or making subsequent job changes has a long history (e.g. Vroom, 1966). It has subsequently been developed into unmet expectations—i.e. failure of the reality to live up to anticipation. Although recent research in this area is scant compared with the 1970s and 1980s, Wanous, Poland, Premack and Davis (1992) reported a meta-analysis of 31 studies which showed quite strong relationships between met expectations and job satisfaction, organizational commitment, and intention to leave, and a smaller but still significant one with actual job survival. Study design (experimental vs non-experimental) did not moderate these relationships. Wanous et al. acknowledged some conceptual and methodological limitations of met expectations.

One practical application of the met expectations literature has been realistic job previews—that is, attempts to portray the job to applicants 'warts and all' rather than in an entirely positive light. Again, published research in this area seems to have passed its peak, at least for the time being. However, Meglino, Denisi and Ravlin (1993) reported an investigation of a large sample of correctional officers. Surprisingly, a realistic job preview had significant effects on applicants who already had experience of the role, often in the opposite direction from those who did not have such experience. Findings were also different during the probationary period than subsequently. However, most of the effects were relatively small.

Researchers have devoted quite a lot of attention to learning and socialization in new jobs. Many studies in this area demonstrate a particularly painstaking and thorough approach on the part of their authors. For example, R.F. Morrison and Brantner (1992) investigated correlates of self-reported learning of departmental head jobs in a military setting. Reassuringly, increasing time in the job was positively correlated with learning, though a significant effect in regression analysis for time squared indicated a leveling off of learning towards the end of the 18-month assignments. Learning the job was also associated with low job challenge (presumably the benefits of simplicity more than offset any motivational problems caused by low challenge), and by high perceived importance to the real work of the organization. Self-efficacy (see also Saks, 1995) and role clarity were also positively correlated with learning. One interesting inhibitor of learning was prior experience of the role but in a different context and a subordinate position. The cross-sectional nature of this research inevitably leaves open the question of causality. Some of the correlates listed above could quite plausibly be outcomes of learning.

Chao, O'Leary-Kelly, Wolf, Klein and Gardner (1994) reported a large, impressive and informative study of organizational socialization. Construing organizational socialization as learning on the part of an individual who is adjusting to a new or changed role within an organization, they set out to examine content rather than process. They identified six areas of socialization: performance proficiency, people, politics, language, organizational goals and values, and history. A measure was developed, the factor structure of which reflected the theoretical concepts very well. The questions for four of the factors reflect learning 'about' or 'how to'. Those concerning people reflect social acceptance by others, whilst goals and values predominantly concerns personal acceptance or internalization of those goals and values. Longitudinal data showed that self-reported socialization had a positive impact on the career-related outcomes of career involvement, identity resolution and adaptability. People socialization however showed no relationships with outcomes, and history socialization showed negative ones!

Several studies have built upon earlier work (e.g. Ashford, 1986) concerning the information and feedback-seeking strategies of newcomers. This work is very much in the social-cognitive tradition. The newcomer is viewed as seeking to make sense of their new environment by acquiring and processing various forms of information in a social context. Miller and Jablin (1991) produced an exhaustive conceptual overview of types, sources and tactics of information-seeking as well as its potential costs and outcomes and individual differences. They specified a number of propositions for subsequent research. Some of these have subsequently been addressed (Ostroff & Koslowski, 1992; E.W. Morrison, 1993). Among Ostroff and Koslowski's findings were that newcomers focus primarily on acquiring information about task and role (as opposed to group and organization) and that acquisition of knowledge from supervisors and task knowledge was associated with positive changes in satisfaction, commitment and adjustment. Using somewhat different classifications of types and sources of information, E.W. Morrison (1993) also found cross-time relationships between certain aspects of information and adjustment outcomes.

Overall, the research on work-role transitions could benefit from a more consistent approach to what adjustment is. The term is used a lot, sometimes to mean integration or well-being, and sometimes to signal the individual's approach to their role. The same, only more so, applies to socialization. In spite of quite a rich and long-running literature in this area (see for example Brim, 1968), it is still conceptualized in many different ways. In keeping with the current dominance of social cognition in psychology, current work tends to construe it as learning various aspects of how to be an organizational member. Even so, distinctions are not always made between learning what to do, learning how to do it, and learning when to do it, let alone wanting to do it, believing it is the right thing to do, and viewing oneself as the kind of person who does it. In other words, socialization may cover cognitive learning, behavioral compliance, identification and internalization even though the first has had the vast majority of attention in recent research. The last of these in particular involves change in the self-concept, or at least the constellation of social selves (Schein, 1971). The methods used in most psychological research in this area also miss some of the richness of socialization and adjustment. Many writers have argued, for example, that socialization of women in male-dominated work environments presents women with a number of difficulties and dilemmas that may be qualitatively different from those experienced by men (Alvesson & Billing, 1992) and more acute the more the preponderance of males (Ely, 1994). These include how to respond to uncongenial value systems, whether or not to participate in organizational politics and adopt assertive behavior, with implications for self-concept and integrity. Marshall (1995) has reviewed much of this and other work, and has examined the dilemmas of advocating change whilst also speaking within academic conventions.

Commitment

There is an extraordinarily large literature on organizational commitment, much of it quite recent, and relatively little challenging (as opposed to refining) the concept (for an exception, see Coopey & Hartley, 1991). The organizational commitment literature is reviewed in this volume by one of its leading contributors (Meyer, Chapter 5).

Commitment is not confined to organizations, however. For many years it has been recognized that for some people at work, commitments may be to other referents. Meyer, Allen and Smith (1993) have provided some tentative evidence that the three aspects of organizational commitment (normative, continuance and affective) are also observable in commitment to occupations. The related construct of career commitment has also been developed and measured in recent years. Building on the earlier work of Blau (e.g. 1985), Carson and Bedeian (1994) have recently developed the 12-item Career Commitment Measure (CCM), which incorporates the three dimensions of career identity, career planning and career resilience. The authors argued on the basis of their data that their measure exhibits good construct and content validity, whilst also avoiding some of the problems of Blau's (1985) measure. Carson and Bedeian went to some lengths to explain to people completing the CCM that career includes concepts like line of work, profession, occupation and vocation, but even so the measure clearly refers to quite a narrow concept of career. Another line of research in this area has concerned the compatibility or otherwise of commitment to organization and to occupation. Wallace (1993) reported a meta-analysis of 15 published studies which showed a positive correlation between the two types of commitment. This suggests that the two can go hand in hand. Whilst this is no doubt true in some workplaces, Herriot (1992) amongst others has presented an analysis which shows very clearly that it cannot be taken for granted.

CAREER INTERVENTIONS IN ORGANIZATIONS

Overview

As already noted, the state of flux in most organizations, and contraction in many, is widely held to have led to the abandonment of attempts to manage careers in organizations. This has been replaced by an emphasis on the need for employees to engage in self-development. This concept may be helpful. It has a history in the applied psychology and management literature, and at least some people seem to engage purposefully in it (McEnrue, 1989). However, it now seems to be accompanied by the message that the organization will not even give any clues about what skills and experiences it wants its people to have. So people are expected not only to look after their own development, but also to do so in the absence of any information (Hirsh, Jackson & Jackson, 1995).

Nevertheless, there is a strong case to be made that now more than ever it is advantageous for an organization to play a part in the management of careers. If career paths are necessarily ambiguous (Callanan & Greenhaus, 1992; Arnold & Mackenzie Davey, 1994) and if an organization's competitive advantage lies in its use of human resources (Lawler, 1994), then the organization's task is to provide a context where employees can learn to manage their own careers in conditions of change and uncertainty. This means providing a supportive context without actually doing the managing. It probably also means a shift from using the narrower definitions of career emphasizing advancement within one line of work to much broader definitions (Adams, 1991). Tensions often exist between employee and organizational interests, and it is often argued that successful interventions must reflect both (Gutteridge, Leibowitz & Shore, 1993). In workplaces with many outsourced contract workers, issues arise as to who should be eligible to participate in interventions (Pearce, 1993). Clarity is required about the purpose of any given intervention. Is it for assessment, identifying career options, action planning, skill development, vacancy filling, or some prioritized combination of these? (Hirsh, Jackson & Jackson, 1995). It is doubtful whether the Human Resource Management strategy of making line managers responsible for facilitating the career development of subordinates (Storey, 1992) will be effective. This doubt stems from many observations, not least gaps in perception, understanding and interest between line manager and subordinate (Arnold & Mackenzie Davey, 1992; Herriot, Pemberton & Pinder, 1994).

Career interventions in organizations can take a variety of forms (Russell, 1991). These include internal vacancy notification, career workbooks, career workshops, individual counseling (including outplacement), skills inventories, personal development plans, career pathing, educational opportunities, mentoring, development centers, succession planning, and developmental work experiences. In recognition of the less organizationally-based nature of careers, there are some initiatives to set up career centers for use by individuals but to some extent sponsored by employing organizations (Waterman, Waterman & Collard, 1994).

In spite of quite thorough analyses of how organizational career interventions might be evaluated (e.g. London & Stumpf, 1982, ch. 5), there is little good-quality research assessing the impact of these interventions, nor the necessary conditions for them to work well. As Herr and Cramer (1992, pp. 482–483) put it: 'In some ways the current state of the literature pertaining to career planning in organizations is reminiscent of the writing and research related to the condition of school counseling in the late 1950s and early 1960s—role studies, suggestions, reports of tentative programs, recommendations for practice, rudimentary attempts to link theory with practice, and very little empirical or evaluative research.' Of course it is understandable that evaluation is thin on the ground. It takes time to conduct, especially in a field like careers where any benefits will be medium rather than short term. Some organizations will not wish to go public about what they do and whether it works. The legitimate demands of journal editors for rigor are hard to meet in field settings, particularly over substantial time periods with (almost by definition) a potentially mobile population. Nevertheless, the correlation between use of certain HRM practices and organizational performance at least in some industries (Terpstra & Rozell, 1993; J.B. Arthur, 1994) does give some prospect of career interventions having a demonstrable impact on the bottom line.

Mentoring

Mentoring is the intervention most often investigated in applied psychological research. To some extent this is justified by its apparent increasing popularity, although thorough information about the uptake of interventions is thin on the ground (Iles and Mabey, 1993). In turn, this popularity may be a function of the relatively small visible demands made by mentoring on a training budget and its resonance with preoccupations of baby-boomers reaching middle age. Mentoring can take a number of forms, but probably the most common one fits with the general definition provided by Kram (1985, p. 2): '. . . a relationship between a younger adult and an older, more experienced adult that helps the individual learn to navigate in the world of work.' The person in receipt of mentoring is often referred to as the protégé. A distinction is often made between informal mentoring (Levinson, Darrow, Klein, Levinson & McKee, 1978), where a relationship between mentor and protégé springs up spontaneously, and formal mentoring, where relationships are arranged and overseen by an employing or professional organization.

There is evidence that having had a mentoring relationship as opposed to not having had one is associated with indices of career success and/or socialization (e.g. Whitely, Dougherty & Dreher, 1991; Scandura, 1992; Ostroff & Kozlowski, 1993; Aryee & Chay, 1994), though see Chao, Walz and Gardner (1992) for more equivocal results. An interesting recent study (Pollock, 1995) has found that protégé benefits from mentoring seem to increase after the initial stages of the relationship, though this finding may be jeopardized by the method of asking respondents for retrospective accounts of their mentoring relationships, and leaving unspecified the time period associated with early, middle and late stages of the relationship. There are also data consistent with the idea that protégé individual differences such as socio-economic status (Whitely, Dougherty & Dreher, 1991) and personality (Turban & Dougherty, 1994) mediate and/or moderate the beneficial effects of mentoring for the protégé. Particular concern has been voiced about gender issues in mentoring. There is some feeling that women protégés may be at a disadvantage relative to male ones in obtaining a mentoring relationship and then profiting from it, especially if the mentor is male (e.g. Ragins & Cotton, 1991).

A number of writers seem willing on the basis of the above studies or their own experience and intuition to accept that mentoring normally produces benefits for mentor, protégé and employing organization, particularly the protégé (Clutterbuck, 1993). Attention therefore turns to how mentoring can be implemented effectively and pitfalls avoided. To be sure, those are vital issues, and the practicalities and politics of such interventions are often neglected by I/O psychologists (Johns, 1993). However, it really is necessary to point out a few important truths about the research cited above. Most of it did not distinguish between formal and informal mentoring. In the latter case, it may be that people who were clearly going to be successful were attractive to potential mentors, and that's why they received mentoring. Some experimental evidence in support of this conjecture has been provided by Olian, Carroll and Giannantonio (1993). With the exception of Chao, Walz and Gardner (1992) there were no comparable control groups of people who did not receive mentoring. The range of potentially confounding variables controlled for is rarely comprehensive, and certainly less comprehensive than in some of the related career success literature cited in Tharenou (this volume). Sometimes mentoring is defined as having someone the respondent calls their mentor, and sometimes as being in receipt of functions or benefits associated with mentoring, whatever the source. The research is very predominantly cross-sectional and/ or retrospective. Interestingly, where an assessment is made of what immediate benefits of mentoring are experienced by the protégé, they have been fairly modest (Noe, 1988; Chao, Waltz and Gardner, 1992).

Succession

There has been quite an extensive literature over the years on succession, particularly succession of Chief Executive Officers (CEOs). Unlike most other research on work-role transitions (see above) CEO succession literature focuses very little upon the experiences and adjustments of the incoming CEO. Instead, it concentrates on characteristics of the CEO and impact of his or her arrival upon organizational performance and employees. This is understandable given the supposed influence of CEOs, but it might be informative if more studies addressed how new CEOs are (for example) socialized. Even more to the point, research on other, 'ordinary' work-role transitions could place more emphasis upon the impact of the new arrival on those around them.

The literature on executive succession has recently been reviewed very thoroughly by Kesner and Sebora (1994), who noted that CEO succession happens relatively infrequently, with average CEO tenure of 14 years. They traced succession literature through from the 1950s and 1960s to the 1990s, identifying themes, ambiguities and progress along the way. Kesner and Sebora noted that one recurring theme was successor origin—particularly whether the incoming executive was an organizational insider or outsider. Research in this area has not drawn a clear conclusion about when each type of succession occurs, or whether one produces consistently better results than the other. The search is now on for moderator variables which may account for the variable findings. Cannella and Lubatkin (1993) for example found that in poor performing organizations, appointment of an outside CEO was likely only if there was no heir apparent and if the old CEO had little influence on the selection decision. Mabey and Iles (1993) have also made the point that succession is often a highly political process. Kesner and Dalton (1994) found that outsider CEOs induced more turnover in other upper management positions than outsider CEOs, but contrary to hypothesis, this latter turnover was unrelated to organizational performance. It should be noted, finally, that the outsider vs insider distinction is very broad. There is scope for greater use of more refined typologies of executive career path, such as that recently proposed by White, Smith and Barnett (1994).

Development Centers

There is increasing interest in using assessment center technology to identify developmental needs of existing employees, with a view to possible future job placement, training or promotion rather than immediate selection for a specific post. There is some evidence that candidates see assessment centers as relatively fair means of selecting people for jobs (Robertson, Iles, Gratton & Sharpley, 1991), so on the face of it one might expect those who experience a development center to act upon the feedback they obtain.

Jones and Whitmore (1995) conducted a 10-year follow-up of employees in an insurance company and found that acceptance of the feedback on the part of the assessees was quite high, and that (on the basis of self-report) 48% of developmental recommendations were implemented. This percentage was positively correlated with subsequent promotion, but close analysis showed that this was due to just two of the seven areas of developmental activity investigated. Engelbrecht and Fischer (1995) have also reported a study of insurance company employees. They compared experimental and control groups in an investigation of whether attendance at a development center was positively associated with work performance (supervisor ratings) relative to non-attendees three months later. It was, on nine of the eleven scales measured. However, there was no pre-test, and supervisors were aware of who had attended development centers so conclusions must be tentative.

Development Through the Job

Various factors have provoked a recent career-oriented focus on how people can be developed for future work via present work. The most significant are probably the well-documented problems of transfer of learning in training courses to everyday work (see for example Baldwin & Padgett, 1993) and the increased pressure in organizations for development to interfere with immediate performance as little as possible.

Campion, Cheraskin and Stevens (1994) have reported an investigation of managerial job rotation amongst 255 employees in a large pharmaceutical company. They construed rotation as non-promotional job moves where the employee usually does not remain permanently in the new job but nor does he or she return to the old one. In their study, rotations occurred every one to five years. They found that self-reported knowledge and skill outcomes factored out into three areas: technical, administrative and business. What they termed career management outcomes of rotation included career affect, organizational integration, stimulating work and personal development, though only the last of these could be said directly to reflect on individuals' felt ability to manage their career. Potential costs of job rotation included workload and productivity and learning curve. On the whole, respondents gave numerically higher ratings to the benefits of rotation than to the costs, though they suggested an additional cost of lost motivation or commitment amongst those not rotating. Rate of job rotation was positively correlated with promotion and salary increases, being in early career, being highly educated, and perceived increase in skills. These findings are interesting, though there may well have been an element of self-fulfilling prophecy about some of them. Also, in some contexts job rotation is used to try to maintain the performance and motivation of plateaued staff (see for example Tremblay, Roger & Toulouse, 1995) so it may be of some concern that early career (presumably pre-plateau) employees were more interested in rotation than later career ones. The association between rotation and promotion may also not be replicated elsewhere. Campion and colleagues pointed out that further research could address generalizability issues and a finer analysis of which skills are most effectively developed through rotation as opposed to other means.

In another important line of work, McCauley and colleagues (e.g. Mc-Cauley, Ruderman, Ohlott & Morrow, 1994) have developed and validated the Development Challenge Profile, which is a self-report instrument for assessing the developmental opportunities inherent in managerially oriented jobs. They identified 15 developmental features of jobs, two of which concerned job transitions, nine task-related characteristics and four obstacles. Particularly in the last category, there were some features such as difficult boss that one presumably would not normally seek to build into a job. This leads to the question of what can truly be called developmental as opposed to just plain difficult, and the authors conceded that they underestimated the degree of stress associated with some of the developmental challenges. Ohlott, Ruderman and McCauley (1994) found that although there were no widespread differences between male and female managers in terms of the developmental challenges they experienced, women tended to experience more of the obstacles.

The contribution of on-the-job experiences to career is a fruitful area for further development, and one suspects that much more in this line will be done in the next few years.

Career Counseling

Most counseling occurs outside the person's work organization, but it is sometimes offered to employees as a stand-alone service or as part of a package such as outplacement or a career development workshop. A review of theory and research on career counseling theory, techniques and practice is outside the scope of this chapter, and is in any case provided elsewhere (e.g. Egan, 1990; Nathan & Hill, 1992; Sharf, 1992; see also Hermansson, 1993, for an interesting example of the application of some of Egan's ideas to counseling in organizations). Here I will confine comment to a few points about the evaluation of career counseling.

Most counselors do not seek to give advice. To use an old distinction, they help people to make decisions wisely, not wise (as judged by the counselor) decisions (Katz, 1969). This becomes ever more true as the pace of change increases and it is difficult to discern with confidence what a wise decision is. The need for ready access to counseling by adults throughout their career is increasingly evident (Watts, 1994) as non-normative events buffet us frequently (Vondracek & Schulenberg, 1992). Some of the earlier research evaluating careers counseling and guidance used stability in a job or occupation as a dependent variable, but this seems inappropriate as a goal of counseling now, and perhaps then too (Killeen, White & Watts, 1992). Given the number of other things happening in a person's life, it is difficult if not impossible to isolate the impact of a counseling intervention, which may in any case be additional to earlier interventions with the same person. The interconnections and continuities between different parts of a person's life at any one time also mean that any career counseling intervention must encompass, and may have an impact upon, leisure, personal relationships and so on (Krumboltz, 1993).

However, to the extent that it can be done, evaluation of career counseling work needs to be in terms of the client's cognitive processes (Kidd & Killeen, 1992) as well as outcomes such as job satisfaction. The latter are becoming more ephermeral and in any case are unlikely to be achieved without cognitive processes. These include reflecting on the past and present, monitoring and evaluating self, and exploration, as well as meta-cognitive skills such as knowing when to use these processes. This is touched on again in the next section.

CAREER MANAGEMENT AND LIFESPAN DEVELOPMENT OF INDIVIDUALS

The Nature of Vocational Personality

John Holland's theory (e.g. Holland, 1985) remains the dominant one in the field of vocational personality measurement. Holland has proposed the existence of six 'pure types' of vocational personality, each of which any given individual or work environment can resemble to greater or lesser degrees. The types can be thought of as arranged at the vertices of a hexagon, with their positioning defining the relative similarity of the types. Holland's fundamental proposition concerning effective vocational choices is that a person whose personality is congruent with (i.e. similar to) their environment will, other things being equal, experience more satisfaction in it and perform better than a person not in congruent environment. Surprisingly perhaps, a recent meta-analytic review revealed little support for this prediction (Tranberg, Slane & Ekeberg, 1993).

If we assume that *some* kind of match between person and environment facilitates satisfaction and/or performance, the negative results reported by Tranberg, Slane and Ekeberg may indicate that Holland has not hit upon the optimal way of describing people and environments. One conclusion might be that something like Schein's (1993) career anchors might do a better job. There is no direct evidence for that, but Nordvik (1991) has shown that scores on career anchor measures are relatively independent of scores on Holland vocational personality measures. This leaves open the possibility that career anchors may tap aspects of personality more meaningful to congruence than Holland's. Tokar and Swanson (1995) have found that scores on Holland types correlate in interpretable ways with parts of the five-factor model of personality (McCrae & Costa, 1987), particularly Openness and Extroversion. This is encouraging for Holland's typology in that it should indeed link with other conceptualizations of personality, but discouraging in that large areas of the 'Big Five' do not seem well reflected in the Holland typology.

There have been recent debates concerning the structure of vocational personality. Gati (1991) argued for a hierarchical structure of vocational interests rather than a hexagonal or circular one. A stimulating series of articles in the *Journal of Vocational Behavior* (1992) debated Holland's hexagonal structure. Prediger and Vansickle (1992) advocated a two-dimensional model in which the axes (data-ideas and things-people) could be superimposed onto the hexagon, but with more utility and sensitivity than could be achieved by Holland type scores. Holland and Gottfredson (1992) presented a counter-argument which focused on how some patterns of scores would not be adequately reflected by the Prediger and Vansickle reformulation. Dawis (1992) offered some perceptive further comments, including the observation that the choice of six clusters is arbitrary, and other formulations specify different numbers. Rounds and Tracey (1993) analyzed data from a large number of US studies in an attempt to identify which non-hierarchical structure, if any, best fitted the data. They concluded (p. 886) that '. . . a very simple circular-ordering structure can be validly used in thinking about RIASEC interests.' This means that the Prediger and Vansickle axes are not obviously any better or worse than any other pair of orthogonal axes, and that choosing different numbers and positions on the circle could lead to description of 'pure types' different from those of Holland, but equally valid. Rounds and Tracey also noted the presence of a general factor in response to vocational interest inventories: that is, a tendency to express (or not) interest in activities of all kinds. The interpretation of this factor was identified as an important issue for future research.

Decision Processes and Individual Differences

Holland's theory concerns the content of decisions more than the process of making decisions. Quite a lot of developmentally oriented theorizing some years ago attempted to map out how individuals clarify their sense of self and integrate this with vocational and other life choices (Super & Hall, 1990). Using concepts derived from this line of thinking, Blustein, Pauling, DeMania and Faye (1994) found that the extent to which students reported engaging in exploratory behavior was correlated with progress in vocational decision-making, whereas indices of congruence (see above) were not.

Recently a little attention has been paid to the detail of how individuals go about making and implementing decisions. The literature here concerns either on the one hand 'career' or 'vocation' (normally defined as an area of work) or on the other hand, job. Integration with work on decision-making from other areas of psychology is not particularly high, though for an exception see Gati,

Fassa, and Houminer (1995). Use of concepts from social cognitive psychology is however more prevalent. Moss and Frieze (1993) found that students' preferences amongst job offers could be explained both by the extent to which offers matched students' desired job attributes and by the extent to which students' stereotypes of people working in the jobs offered matched their self-concept. The first of these explained more of the variance in preferences than the second. Gianakos (1995) extended an existing line of research applying sex-role self-concept to career variables. She found that androgynous individuals (i.e. those who described themselves in both stereotypically masculine and feminine terms) felt more able to tackle career decision-making tasks than others, and significantly more so than undifferentiated individuals (i.e. those who scored low on both traditionally feminine and masculine aspects of self-concept). However, in studies of this kind it is important to establish that a person's sex *per se* does not account for the variance in the dependent variable.

A recent monograph by Lent, Brown and Hackett (1994) has applied social cognitive theory to interests, choices and performance in employment and academic settings. The authors argued that existing work tended to view persons in overly static terms, with behavior being seen as a product of a person–situation interaction rather than an aspect of it. They continued: 'By contrast, social cognitive theory emphasizes the situation and domain-specific nature of behavior, relatively dynamic aspects of the self-system, and the means by which individuals exercise personal agency' (p. 82). With an emphasis on self-efficacy, outcome expectancies and personal goals, Lent, Brown and Hackett then built models of interests, choices and performance and specified many hypotheses, some of which they were able to test. This work may well succeed in doing what the authors hoped—to advance on the static trait-oriented views of decision-making and add specificity to the more learning-oriented but rather general development approaches.

The Lent, Brown and Hackett approach may be particularly well suited to a world where people need to make choices with a weather eye toward their future marketability in terms of skills and experiences as well as the congruence between present self and work requirements. Furthermore, individuals have fewer external markers of their progress (see above) and less opportunity to pursue a pre-defined sequence of jobs. All this places a greater emphasis on self-awareness and assessment, learning from experience and coping with uncertainty and setbacks. Some other recent work is also relevant here. Waterman, Waterman and Collard (1994) have referred to career-resilient workers, where career resilience is defined in terms of self-knowledge, long-term goals independent of an employing organization, knowledge of the market, flexibility, and willingness to move on when they no longer fit the organization. Although it was developed in the specific context of Silicon Valley in California, USA, and reflects economic rather than psychological imperatives, the concept of career resilience probably has wider applicability.

London (1993) has explored the concept of career motivation. He suggested that it has three components: career insight, career identity and career resilience. The last of these was defined (rather differently from Waterman, Waterman & Collard) as the ability to adapt to changing circumstances. Career insight is the realism and clarity of the person's career goals, and career identity is the extent to which a person defines him or herself in terms of work. The three constructs and their measurement are clearly important to the study of careers, but combining them and assigning the label motivation to the composite seems less than helpful despite London's attempt to equate them to the energizing, direction and persistence components of motivation. Carson, Carson and Bedeian (1995) have developed a self-report measure of career entrenchment, which is in some respects the opposite of career resilience. It has three components: career investments, emotional costs of changing careers, and limitedness of career alternatives.

Regarding self-assessment of attributes and/or performance, the earlier literature (e.g. Mabe & West, 1982) tended to concentrate on the degree of accuracy of self-assessment (or at least agreement with others' assessments), often with the assumption that accuracy would facilitate effective decision-making. More recent work has taken two rather different directions. First, it seems that agreement of self-ratings with those made by colleagues at work may reflect the possession of some social or self-insight skills which also contribute to a person's objective career success (Bass & Yammarino, 1991; Furnham & Stringfield, 1994). Second, self-efficacy theory suggests, with a little evidence to back the claim, that moderately over-optimistic self-estimates should enhance subsequent performance (Lent, Brown & Hackett, 1994).

Life-span Development and Aging

The influence of development approaches was hinted at in the previous section. Led by the late Donald Super and others, developmental analyses of careers have emphasized the unfolding nature of cognition, emotion and behavior concerning careers. At first, these approaches tended to be confined purely to employment, and quite closely tied to normative age-related phenomena. But the developmental approaches themselves developed. They have increasingly considered roles other than employment and in some cases close links with age have been loosened (Super, 1990; see also Chi-Ching, 1995, for an empirical example).

As Super (1990, p. 194) put it: '. . . what I have contributed is not an integrated, comprehensive and testable theory, but rather . . . a loosely unified set of theories dealing with specific aspects of career development taken from developmental, differential, social and phenomenological psychology and held together by self-concept or personal-construct psychology.' Developmental ideas, even more than most, require longitudinal examination. Thus it is perhaps not surprising that the use of developmental ideas in careers research and practice is common, but tests of theoretical propositions are rare. In the former category, Dix and Savickas (1995) have recently reported an interesting piece of work attempting to elicit from 50 successful male workers how they had tackled the six developmental tasks of the establishment stage of career. The authors pointed out that this helps to make explicit some of the tacit knowledge associated with successful career development. Through use of interviews, critical incident techniques, and content categorizing by expert judges, Dix and Savickas identified between three and eight coping behaviors for each of the six tasks. A similar exercise with female workers is planned, which is important given that this study focused on males, and that developmental approaches are often heavily criticized for working from male, middle-class perspectives.

One contribution often seen as particularly vulnerable on this last point is that of Levinson et al. (1978), (see also Levinson, 1986). On the basis of interviews with 40 men, they proposed a closely age-related developmental pattern which alternated between stable and transitional periods. The former is where a person pursues stable goals within a life structure, and the latter is where they question and perhaps change their goals and/or life structure. Smart and Peterson (1994) have tested these ideas in a cross-sectional analysis of 498 Australian professional women. There were 12 dependent variables, including for example professional commitment, intent to remain and need for achievement. They concluded that the pattern postulated by Levinson et al. was evident for only one of the dependent variables (pay satisfaction). However, it is not obvious to me why one would expect trends in the dependent variables consistent with Levinson et al. As Levinson et al. pointed out, stable periods are not necessarily experienced as stable or calm. A person may have stable goals, and these may include (for example) leaving their employer. During a transitional period they may be considering a different lifestyle, but still intend to build this around (for example) their current profession. Levinson's ideas can only really be tested using detailed case material, with all the practical and analytical problems that involves.

Recently Helms and Piper (1994) have lamented the small amount and simplistic nature of research on racial aspects of vocational behavior and development. Typically racial groups have been defined in nominal terms—that is, people are assigned to a category regardless of how they view themselves. But, '. . . unless one believes that vocational behavior is bio-genetically determined and racial classification is a valid indicator of persons' biogenetic endowments, then there is no valid reason for explaining or anticipating consistent between-group differences on the basis of race *per se* on any of the commonly investigated vocational behavior.' In the same issue of the *Journal of Vocational Behavior*, Evans and Herr (1994) reported results which supported that assertion. Helms and Piper argued that use of racial identity theory (e.g. Helms, 1990) could further our understanding of the vocational development blacks and whites alike. The theory traces stages in the development of racial identity, and may have some parallels with other developmental approaches in careers and in adult cognitive development more generally (see e.g. Commons, Sinnott, Richards & Armon, 1989). Helms and Piper further suggested that racial identity should be seen as a dependent variable (i.e. an outcome of events and experiences) as well as an independent variable.

There is increasing recognition that the demographic trends described earlier require more attention to the psychology of aging and its integration with employment-related contexts (see Davies, Matthews & Wong, 1991 for a review). Sterns and Miklos (1995) have provided a helpful recent review of some key areas here. They disaggregated the concept of aging into five different and not necessarily consistent aspects (chronological/legal, functional, psychosocial, organizational and lifespan) and reviewed research related to each. Consistent with Neugarten's (1977) notion of 'fanning out' of members of a cohort as they progress through adulthood, Sterns and Miklos noted that 'Late careers are often more difficult to study than early careers because there is less consistency in the development tasks' (p. 259). In an article in the same edition of the *Journal of Vocational Behavior*, Hall and Mirvis (1995) have put forward some interesting propositions about the nature of career at midlife and beyond. They argued that the changing nature of the workplace holds both threats and opportunities for older workers. For example, older workers may be better able than younger ones to engage in 'relational' work such as helping and supporting others. This work is especially important when an organization is under pressure, but often goes unnoticed (or worse, it is seen as non-productive) and unrewarded. Hall and Mirvis also drew upon systems theory to suggest that an organization needs to contain at least as much complexity as is present in its environment. One form of complexity is diversity, and one form of diversity is age. 'Careers too are becoming more complex: We would argue that what we are seeing now, instead of one set of career stages spanning a lifespan (as the Super model posits), is a series of many shorter learning cycles over the span of a person's work life. . . . As a result, people's careers will become increasingly a succession of 'mini-stages' (or short-cycle learning stages) of exploration – trial – mastery – exit, as they move in and out of various product areas, technologies, functions, organizations, and other work environments. . . . Thus, the half-life of a career stage would be driven by the half-life of the competency field of that career work' (p. 277). Hall and Mirvis added that if older workers can be removed from various job and health insecurities, they are likely to be able to engage in the continuous learning (as opposed to isolated retraining) demanded by the labour market.

A number of studies have shown that stereotypes of older workers, whilst not wholly negative, are not particularly flattering. A comprehensive recent study in this area has been reported by Warr and Pennington (1994). In a study with 1140 personnel managers, they found that non-managerial jobs perceived as mainly for older workers were also perceived to make fewer cognitive demands, be slower paced and less demanding of energy than those for younger workers. Sterns and Miklos (1995) cited a study by Russell and Curtis (1992) which found that 63% of companies offered pre-retirement programs, but only 23% had programs to reduce obsolescence or plateauing. This is consistent with barriers to the effective development of older workers identified by Hall and Mirvis (1995), which included the perceptions that investment in the development of older workers is too costly, and that older workers are too inflexible and difficult to train.

These perceptions exist alongside research showing that there is little relationship between age and job performance (McEvoy & Cascio, 1989), except within early adulthood. Other work shows that, despite age-related decrements in some aspects of information-processing, the task performance of older people is often at least as good as that by younger people especially where tasks are of a relatively familiar kind and the use of learning strategies is encouraged (e.g. Salthouse, 1990). On the other hand the pace of change in the workplace more often requires learning *un*familiar tasks. Alwin (1994) has noted the existence of different patterns of stability in psychological constructs during adulthood. He suggested that the evidence on intelligence and personality traits indicated a pattern of persistently high stability from early adulthood to old age. Data on self-concepts and attitudes suggested a rather different pattern of low stability in early adulthood followed by stability in midlife and either further stability or more change thereafter. These findings might suggest another problem for older people—they really are less open to change than younger people. On the other hand, as Alwin and others have pointed out, it is wellnigh impossible to disentangle different influences on lifespan development. The pattern of findings may principally reflect typically low pressure in the past for people to change after early adulthood. Nowadays and in the future we may find that necessity is the mother of instability.

Future theory and practice in careers would do well to pay more attention to work on lifespan development, of which Alwin (1994) is just one example, though an impressively far-sighted one. Warr and Conner (1992) presented another impressive contribution in their attempt to link research on intelligence, cognitive style and expertise with job competence, whilst Warr (1993) analyzed key differences between cognitive tasks and linked them to expected patterns of performance of people of different ages. Extension of this kind of work to the cognitive demands made by the self-management of careers offers an exciting and profitable way forward in helping all people, especially older ones, tackle the demands of contemporary life (Kegan, 1994). Another avenue here is the recent work on wisdom by Baltes and colleagues (e.g. Staudinger, Smith & Baltes, 1992). Although this might be criticized for taking a rather narrow and culture-specific view of what wisdom is (Assmann, 1994) it offers a measure of ways of thinking which may be very well suited to career management as we approach the millennium.

CONCLUSIONS

The psychological literature on careers is appropriately diverse in content, though less so in method. Recent years have seen important advances in research in some areas, particularly (in my opinion) the psychological contract and work-role transitions and socialization. In some areas empirical research is relatively plentiful but over-arching theory rather thin. In others, especially developmental approaches to careers, the reverse is true.

A number of impressive contributions exhibiting at least two of methodological excellence, theory development, and practical application have been published in recent years. Most of these are either substantial longitudinal empirical studies or ground-breaking theoretical contributions which more often than not draw heavily upon work in other areas of psychology, particularly social cognition. Indeed, this last point is a real source of optimism— there are signs of increasing integration of career psychology with the rest of the discipline.

Of course, not all in the garden is rosy. A number of papers, including some mentioned in this review, have made at best a modest contribution to our understanding of careers (though in most cases I would have been proud enough to have produced them!). For the purposes of this review (including areas I have excluded from this chapter because of space limitations), I was most consistently impressed by the content of *Academy of Management Journal* and *Personnel Psychology*. Contributions in these journals seemed to me most often to combine rigor with a sensitive attempt to tackle issues of real importance in organizational life. *Journal of Applied Psychology* and *Journal of Vocational Behavior* carried many excellent articles but at times seemed in danger of over-emphasizing 'technical correctness' at the expense of contribution to understanding of issues of practical importance. The *Journal of Organizational Behavior* and *Human Relations* were also very valuable sources of good material, and the latter in particular published papers with diverse methods and varied theoretical orientations. But these two more than the other four journals mentioned also seemed to carry some of the modest contributions alluded to earlier. Often, but not always, cross-sectional and entirely self-report data were the limiting factor.

With large datasets and/or a longitudinal study design it is of course often appropriate for multiple papers to be published. Nevertheless, I felt there were some instances where researchers produced multiple articles from the same data even though a single bigger and more integrative contribution might have developed the field better. There is also a tendency (evident also in this article I suspect) for authors to over-emphasize research conducted in their own country or continent even though they are writing on issues of international importance for international audiences.

The career literature is beginning to reorientate to take account of the changing world of employment. There is much still to be done in developing analyses of how individuals can and should manage their careers, achieve success against their own standards, and make appropriate decisions, but in many of the areas reviewed a start has been made. The Hall and Mirvis (1995) paper is a particularly good example of this.

One of several profitable lines of enquiry will be how people explain to themselves and others their past, present and future in a world with relatively few fixed points or signposts. This endeavor requires attention to discourse and narrative (e.g. Gergen, 1988) which would represent a useful addition to, and change from, the vast majority of existing careers research. It may depart from the positivist assumption that there is one 'truth' (albeit a complex one) waiting to be found. Interestingly, this assumption reflects quite a low level of development in models of cognitive development! But even if it is not really so novel, there is likely to be much value in placing somewhat more emphasis on people's accounts of their behavior and thinking (e.g. Dix & Savickas, 1995), and also more emphasis on direct observation of behavior and assessment of thinking strategies.

REFERENCES

Adams, J. (1991) Issues in the management of careers. In R. F. Morrison and J. Adams (eds), *Contemporary Career Development Issues*. Hillsdale, NJ: Erlbaum.

Allen, N. J. & Meyer, J. P. (1990) Organizational socialization tactics: A longitudinal analysis of links to newcomers' commitment and role orientation. *Academy of Management Journal*, **33**, 847–858.

Alvesson, M. & Billing, Y. D. (1992) Gender and organization: Towards a differentiated understanding. *Organization Studies*, **13**, 73–102.

Alwin, D. F. (1994) Aging, personality and social change: The stability of individual differences over the adult life span. In D. L. Featherman, R. M. Lerner & M. Perlmutter (eds), *Life-Span Development and Behavior*, Vol. 12. Hillsdale, NJ: Erlbaum.

Arnold, J. (1990) From education to labor markets. In S. Fisher and C.L. Cooper (eds), *On The Move: The Psychological Effects of Change and Transition*. Chichester: Wiley.

Arnold, J. (1994) Opportunity for skill use, job changing, and unemployment as predictors of psychological well-being amongst graduates in early career. *Journal of Occupational and Organizational Psychology*, **67**, 355–370.

Arnold, J. & Mackenzie Davey, K. (1992) Self-ratings and supervisor ratings of graduate employees' competences during early career. *Journal of Occupational and Organizational Psychology*, **65**, 235–250.

Arnold, J. & Mackenzie Davey, K. (1994) Graduate experiences of organizational career management. *International Journal of Career Management*, **6**, 14–18.

Arnold, J. & Nicholson, N. (1991) Construing of self and others at work in the early years of corporate careers. *Journal of Organizational Behavior*, **12**, 621–639.

Arthur, J. B. (1994) Effects of human resource systems on manufacturing performance and turnover. *Academy of Management Journal*, **37**, 670–687.

Arthur, M.B. (1994) The boundaryless career: A new perspective for organizational enquiry. *Journal of Organizational Behavior*, **15**, 295–306.

Arthur, W. & Bennett, W. (1995) The international assignee: The relative importance of factors perceived to contribute to success. *Personnel Psychology*, **48**, 99–114.

Aryee, S. & Chay, Y. W. (1994) An examination of the impact of career-oriented mentoring on work commitment attitudes and career satisfaction among professional and managerial employees. *British Journal of Management*, 5, 241–249.

Ashford, S. J. (1986) Feedback-seeking in individual adaptation: A resource perspective. *Academy of Management Journal*, 29, 465–487.

Ashforth, B. E. & Saks, A. M. (1995) Work-role transitions: A longitudinal examination of the Nicholson model. *Journal of Occupational and Organizational Psychology*, 68, 157–175.

Assmann, A. (1994) Wholesome knowledge: Concepts of wisdom in a historical and cross-cultural perspective. In D. L. Feathermen, R. M. Lerner & M. Perlmutter (eds), *Life-Span Development and Behavior*, Vol. 12. Hillsdale, NJ: Erlbaum.

Baker, W. K. (1995) Allen and Meyer's (1990) longitudinal study: A reanalysis and reinterpretation using structural equation modeling. *Human Relations*, 48, 169–186.

Baldwin, T.T. and Padgett, M. (1993) Management development. In C. L. Cooper and I. T. Robertson (eds), *International Review of Industrial and Organizational Psychology*, Vol. 8. Chichester: Wiley.

Bass, B. M. & Yammarino, F. J. (1991) Congruence of self and others' leadership ratings of naval officers for understanding successful performance. *Applied Psychology: An International Review*, 40, 437–454.

Beach, L.R. & Mitchell, T.R. (1978) A contingency theory for the selection of decision strategies. *Academy of Management Review*, 3, 439–449.

Beard, K. M. & Edwards, J. R. (1995) Employees at risk: Contingent work and the psychological experience of contingent workers. In C. L. Cooper and D. M. Rousseau (eds), *Trends in Organizational Behavior*, Vol. 2. Chichester: Wiley.

Bird, A. (1994) Careers as repositories of knowledge: A new perspective on boundaryless careers. *Journal of Organizational Behavior*, 15, 325–344.

Black, J. S. & Gregersen, H. B. (1992) Serving two masters: Managing the dual allegiance of expatriate employees. *Sloan Management Review*, Summer, 61–71.

Blau, G. (1985) The measurement and prediction of career commitment. *Journal of Occupational Psychology*, 58, 277–288.

Blau, G., Linnehan, F., Brooks, A. & Hoover, D. K. (1993) Vocational behavior 1990–1992: Personnel practices, organizational behavior, workplace justice, and industrial/organizational measurement issues. *Journal of Vocational Behavior*, 43, 133–197.

Blustein, D. L. (1995) Toward a contextual perspective of the school-to-work transition: A reaction to Feij et al. *Journal of Vocational Behavior*, 47, 257–265.

Blustein, D. L., Pauling, M. L., DeMania, M. E. & Faye, M. (1994) Relation between exploratory and choice factors and decisional progress. *Journal of Vocational Behavior*, 44, 75–90.

Borgen, F. H. (1991). Megatrends and milestones in vocational behavior: A 20-year counseling psychology retrospective. *Journal of Vocational Behavior*, 39, 263–290.

Brett, J. F., Cron, W. L. & Slocum, J. W. (1995) Economic dependency on work: A moderator of the relationship between organizational commitment and performance. *Academy of Management Journal*, 38, 261–271.

Brett, J. M. (1992) Job transfer. In C. L. Cooper and I. T. Robertson (eds), *International Review of Industrial and Organizational Psychology*. Vol. 7. Chichester: Wiley.

Brett, J. M., Stroh, L. K. & Reilly, A. H. (1992) Job transfer. In C. L. Cooper and I. T. Robertson (eds), *International Review of Industrial and Organizational Psychology*, Vol. 7. Chichester: Wiley.

Brett, J. M., Stroh, L. K. & Reilly, A. H. (1993) Pulling up roots in the 1990s: Who's willing to relocate? *Journal of Organizational Behavior*, 14, 49–60.

Brewster, C. (1994) The paradox of adjustment: UK and Swedish expatriates in Sweden and the UK. *Human Resource Management Journal*, 4, 49–62.

Bridges, W. (1995) *Jobshift: How to Prosper in a Workplace Without Jobs.* London: Nicholas Brealey.

Brim, O. G. (1968) Adult socialization. In J. A. Clausen (ed.), *Socialization and Society.* Boston: Little, Brown.

Bruce, R. A. & Scott, S. G. (1994) Varieties and commonalities of career transitions: Louis' typology revisited. *Journal of Vocational Behavior,* **45,** 17–40.

Callanan, G. A. & Greenhaus, J. H. (1992) The career indecision of managers and professionals: An examination of multiple subtypes. *Journal of Vocational Behavior,* **41,** 212–231.

Campion, M. A., Cheraskin, L. & Stevens, M. J. (1994) Career-related antecedents and outcomes of job rotation. *Academy of Management Journal,* **37,** 1518–1542.

Cannella, A. A. & Lubatkin, M. (1993) Succession as a sociopolitical process: Internal impediments to outsider selection. *Academy of Management Journal,* **36,** 763–793.

Carson, K. D. & Bedeian, A. G. (1994) Career commitment: Construction of a measure and examination of its psychometric properties. *Journal of Vocational Behavior,* **44,** 237–262.

Carson, K. D., Carson, P. P. & Bedeian, A. G. (1995) Development and construct validation of a career entrenchment measure. *Journal of Occupational and Organizational Psychology,* **68,** 301–320.

Cartwright, S. & Cooper, C. L. (1992) *Mergers and Acquisitions: The Human Factor.* Oxford: Butterworth & Heinemann.

Cawsey, T. & Inkson, K. (1992) Patterns of managerial job change: A New Zealand study. *New Zealand Journal of Business,* **14,** 14–25.

Chao, G. T., O'Leary-Kelly, A. M., Wolf, S., Klein, H. J. & Gardner, P. D. (1994) Organizational socialization: Its content and consequences. *Journal of Applied Psychology,* **79,** 730–743.

Chao, G. T., Walz, P. M. & Gardner, P. D. (1992) Formal and informal mentorships: A comparison on mentoring functions and contrast with nonmentored counterparts. *Personnel Psychology,* **45,** 619–636.

Chapman, A. J., Sheehy, N. P., Heywood, S., Dooley, B. & Collins, S. C. (1995) The organizational implications of teleworking. In C. L. Cooper and I. T. Robertson (eds), *International Review of Industrial and Organizational Psychology,* Vol. 10. Chichester: Wiley.

Chartrand, J. M. & Camp, C. C. (1991) Advances in the measurement of career development constructs: A twenty-year review. *Journal of Vocational Behavior,* **39,** 1–39.

Chi-Ching, Y. (1995) The effects of career salience and life-cycle variables on perceptions of work–family interfaces. *Human Relations,* **48,** 265–284.

Clutterbuck, D. (1993) *Everyone Needs a Mentor,* 2nd edn. London: Institute of Personnel Management.

Collin, A. & Watts, A. G. (1996) The death and transfiguration of career—and careers guidance? *British Journal of Guidance and Counselling,* in press.

Commons, M. L., Sinnott, J. D., Richards, F. F. & Armon, C. (eds) (1989) *Adult Development: Comparisons and Applications of Developmental Models.* New York: Praeger.

Coopey, J. & Hartley, J. (1991) Reconsidering the case for organizational commitment. *Human Resource Management Journal,* **1,** 18–32.

Davidson, M. J. (1996) Women and Employment. In P. B. Warr (ed.), *Psychology at Work.* Harmondsworth: Penguin.

Davies, D. R., Matthews, G. & Wong, C. S. K. (1991) Ageing and work. In C. L. Cooper and I. T. Robertson (eds), *International Review of Industrial and Organizational Psychology,* Vol. 6. Chichester: Wiley.

Dawis, R. V. (1992) The structure(s) of occupations: Beyond RIASEC. *Journal of Vocational Behavior,* **40,** 171–178.

Dawis, R. V. & Lofquist, L. H. (1984) *A Psychological Theory of Work Adjustment.* Minneapolis, MN: University of Minnesota Press.

Dix, J. E. & Savickas, M. L. (1995) Establishing a career: Developmental tasks and coping responses. *Journal of Vocational Behavior*, **46**, 93–107.

Driver, M. J. (1988) Careers: A review of personal and organizational research. In C. L. Cooper and I. T. Robertson (eds), *International Review of Industrial and Organizational Psychology*, Vol. 3. Chichester: Wiley.

DuBrin, A. J. (1983) *Human Relations for Career and Personal Success.* Reston, VA: Reston Publishing Co.

Egan, G. (1990) *The Skilled Helper* 4th edn. Pacific Grove: Brooks/Cole.

Eldredge, B. D. (1995) Some things not considered: Evaluation of a model of career enhancing strategic and content innovation with respect to organizational socialization. *Journal of Vocational Behavior*, **47**, 266–273.

Ely, R. J. (1994) The effects of organizational demographics and social identity on relationships among professional women. *Administrative Science Quarterly*, **39**, 203–238.

Engelbrecht, A. S. & Fischer, A. H. (1995) The managerial performance implications of a developmental assessment center process. *Human Relations*, **48**, 387–404.

Evans, K. M. & Herr, E. L. (1994) The influence of racial identity and the perception of discrimination on the career aspirations of African American men and women. *Journal of Vocational Behavior*, **44**, 173–184.

Feij, J. A., Whitely, W. T., Peiró, J. M. & Taris, T. W. (1995) The development of career-enhancing strategies and content innovation: A longitudinal study of new workers. *Journal of Vocational Behavior*, **47**, 231–256.

Feldman, D. C. (1989) Careers in organizations: Recent trends and future directions. *Journal of Management*, **15**, 135–156.

Feldman, D. C. (1994) The decision to retire early: A review and reconceptualization. *Academy of Management Review*, **19**, 285–311.

Fisher, C. D. & Shaw, J. B. (1994) Relocation attitudes and adjustment: A longitudinal study. *Journal of Organizational Behavior*, **15**, 209–224.

Fouad, N. A. (1994) Annual review 1991–1993: Vocational choice, decision-making, assessment, and intervention. *Journal of Vocational Behavior*, **45**, 125–176.

Fournier, V. & Payne, R. (1994) Change in self-construction during the transition from university to employment: A personal construct psychology approach. *Journal of Occupational and Organizational Psychology*, **67**, 297–314.

Furnham, A. & Stringfield, P. (1994) Congruence of self and subordinate ratings of managerial practices as a correlate of supervisor evaluation. *Journal of Occupational and Organizational Psychology*, **67**, 57–67.

Gati, I. (1991) The structure of vocational interests. *Psychological Bulletin*, **109**, 309–324.

Gati, I., Fassa, N. & Houminer, D. (1995) Applying decision theory to career counseling practice: The sequential elimination approach. *Career Development Quarterly*, **43**, 211–220.

Gergen, M. (1988) Narrative structures in social explanation. In C. Antaki (ed.), *Analyzing Everyday Explanation: A Casebook of Methods.* London: Sage.

Gianakos, I. (1995) The relation of sex-role identity to career decision-making self-efficacy. *Journal of Vocational Behavior*, **46**, 131–143.

Gray, D. A., Gault, F. M., Meyers, H. H. & Walther, J. E. (1990) Career planning. In J. C. Quick et al. (eds) *Career Stress in Changing Times.* New York: Haworth Press.

Greenhaus, J. H. & Callanan, G.A. (1994) *Career Management*, 2nd edn. London: Dryden Press.

Gutteridge, T. G., Leibowitz, Z. B. & Shore, J. E. (1993) *Organizational Career Development.* Reading, MA: Addison-Wesley.

Hackett, G., Lent, R.W. & Greenhaus, J. H. (1991) Advances in vocational theory and research: A twenty-year retrospective. *Journal of Vocational Behavior*, **38**, 3–38.

Hall, D. T. (1976) *Careers in Organizations*. Glenview, IL: Scott Foresman.

Hall, D. T. (1991) Twenty questions: Research needed to advance the field of careers. In R. F. Morrison and J. Adams (eds) *Contemporary Career Development Issues*. Hillsdale, NJ: Erlbaum.

Hall, D. T. & Mirvis, P. H. (1995) The new career contract: Developing the whole person at midlife and beyond. *Journal of Vocational Behavior*, **45**, 328–346.

Handy, C. (1989) *The Age of Unreason*. London: Business Books.

Handy. C. (1994) *The Empty Raincoat*. London: Hutchinson.

Hanisch, K. A. (1994) Reasons people retire and their relations to attitudinal and behavioral correlates in retirement. *Journal of Vocational Behavior*, **45**, 1–16.

Helms, J. E. (1990) *Black and White Racial Identity*. New York: Greenwood Press.

Helms, J. E. & Piper, R. E. (1994) Implications of racial identity theory for vocational psychology. *Journal of Vocational Behavior*, **44**, 124–138.

Heppner, M. J., Multon, K. D. & Johnston, J. A. (1994) Assessing psychological resources during career change: Development of the Career Transitions Inventory. *Journal of Vocational Behavior*, **44**, 55–74.

Hermansson, G. L. (1993) Counsellors and organizational change: Egan's systems model as a tool in organizational consulting. *British Journal of Guidance and Counselling*, **21**, 133–144.

Herr, E. L. & Cramer, S. H. (1992) *Career Guidance and Counseling through the Life Span*, 4th edn. New York: Harper Collins.

Herriot, P. (1992) *The Career Management Challenge*. London: Sage.

Herriot, P. & Pemberton, C. (1995a) *New Deals*. Chichester: Wiley.

Herriot, P. & Pemberton, C. (1995b) *Competitive Advantage Through Diversity*. London: Sage.

Herriot, P., Pemberton, C. & Pinder, R. (1994) Misperceptions by managers and their bosses of each other's preferences regarding the managers' careers: A case of the blind leading the blind? *Human Resource Management Journal*, **4**, 39–51.

Hesketh, B. (1995) Personality and adjustment styles: A Theory of Work Adjustment approach to career enhancing strategies. *Journal of Vocational Behavior*, **47**, 274–282.

Hirsh, W., Jackson, C. & Jackson, C. (1995) *Careers in Organizations: Issues for the Future*. Brighton: Institute for Employment Studies.

Holland, J. L. (1985) *Making Vocational Choices*, 2nd edn. Englewood Cliffs, NJ: Prentice-Hall.

Holland, J. L. & Gottfredson, G. D. (1992) Studies of the hexagonal model: An evaluation (or, the perils of stalking the perfect hexagon). *Journal of Vocational Behavior*, **40**, 158–170.

Hutton, W. (1995) *The State We're In*. London: Cape.

Iles, P. & Mabey, C. (1993) Managerial career development programmes: Effectiveness, availability and acceptability. *British Journal of Management*, **4**, 103–118.

Inkson, K. (1995) Effects of changing economic conditions on managerial job changes and careers. *British Journal of Management*, **6**, 183–194.

Janssens, M. (1995) Intercultural interaction: A burden on international managers? *Journal of Organizational Behavior*, **16**, 155–167.

Johns, G. (1993) Constraints on the adoption of psychology-based personnel practices: Lessons from organizational innovation. *Personnel Psychology*, **46**, 569–592.

Jones, G. R. (1986) Socialization tactics, self-efficacy, and newcomers' adjustments to organizations. *Academy of Management Journal*, **29**, 262–279.

Jones, R. G. & Whitmore, M. D. (1995) Evaluating developmental assessment centers as interventions. *Personnel Psychology*, **48**, 377–388.

Kanter, R. M. (1989) *When Giants Learn to Dance*. New York: Simon & Schuster.

Katz, M. R. (1969) Can computers make guidance decisions for students? *College Board Review*, No. 72, Summer.

Kegan, R. (1994) *In Over our Heads: The Mental Demands of Modern Life.* Cambridge, MA: Harvard University Press.

Kesner, I. F. & Dalton, D. R. (1994) Top management turnover and CEO succession: An investigation of the effects of turnover on performance. *Journal of Management Studies*, **31**, 701–713.

Kesner, I. F. & Sebora, T. C. (1994) Executive succession: Past, present and future. *Journal of Management*, **20**, 327–372.

Kidd, J. & Killeen, J. (1992) Are the effects of careers guidance worth having? *Journal of Occupational and Organizational Psychology*, **65**, 219–234.

Killeen, J., White, M. & Watts, A. G. (1992) *The Economic Value of Careers Guidance.* London: Policy Studies Institute.

Kram, K. E. (1985) *Mentoring at Work.* Lanham, MD: University Press of America.

Krumboltz, J. D. (1993) Integrating career and personal counseling. *Career Development Quarterly*, **42**, 143–148.

Kuhl, J. (1992) A theory of self-regulation: Action versus state orientation, self-discrimination, and some applications. *Applied Psychology: An International Review*, **41**, 97–129.

Lawler, E. (1994) From job-based to competency-based organizations. *Journal of Organizational Behavior*, **15**, 3–16.

Lawson, M. B. & Angle, H. (1994) When organizational relocation means family relocation: An emerging issue for strategic human resource management. *Human Resource Management*, **33**, 33–54.

Lent, R. W., Brown, S. D. & Hackett, G. (1994) Toward a unifying social cognitive theory of career and academic interest, choice and performance. *Journal of Vocational Behavior*, **45**, 79–122.

Levinson, D. J. (1986) A conception of adult development. *American Psychologist*, **41**, 3–13.

Levinson, D. J., Darrow, C. N., Klein, E. B., Levinson, M. H. & McKee, B. (1978) *Seasons of a Man's Life.* New York: Knopf.

London, M. (1993) Relationships between career motivation, empowerment and support for career development. *Journal of Occupational and Organizational Psychology*, **66**, 55–69.

London, M. & Greller, M. M. (1991) Demographic trends and vocational behavior: A twenty year retrospective and agenda for the 1990s. *Journal of Vocational Behavior*, **38**, 125–164.

London, M. & Mone, E. (1988) *Career Growth and Human Resources Strategies.* New York: Quorum Books.

London, M. & Stumpf, S. A. (1982) *Managing Careers.* Reading, MA: Addison-Wesley.

Louis, M. R. (1980a) Surprise and sense-making: What newcomers experience in entering unfamiliar organizational settings. *Administrative Science Quarterly*, **25**, 226–251.

Louis, M. R. (1980b) Career transitions: Varieties and commonalities. *Academy of Management Review*, **5**, 329–340.

Louis, M. R. (1982) Career transitions: A missing link in career development. *Organizational Dynamics*, **10**, 68–77.

Mabe, P. A. & West, S. G. (1982) Validity of self-evaluation of ability: A review and meta-analysis. *Journal of Applied Psychology*, **67**, 280–296.

Mabey, C. & Iles, P. (1993) The strategic integration of assessment and development practices: Succession planning and new manager development. *Human Resource Management Journal*, **3**, 16–34.

Major, D. A., Kozlowski, S. W. J., Chao, G. T. & Gardner, P. D. (1995) A longitudinal investigation of newcomer expectations, early socialization outcomes, and the moderating effects of role development factors. *Journal of Applied Psychology*, **80**, 418–431.

Marshall, J. (1995) Gender and management: A critical review of research. *British Journal of Management*, **6** (Special Issue), S53–S62.

Martin, R. (1995) The effects of prior job moves on job relocation stress. *Journal of Occupational and Organizational Psychology*, **68**, 49–56.

McCauley, C.D., Ruderman, M. N., Ohlott, P. J. & Morrow, J. E. (1994) Assessing the developmental components of managerial jobs. *Journal of Applied Psychology*, **79**, 544–560.

McCrae, R. R. & Costa, P. T. (1987) Validation of the five-factor model of personality across instruments and observers. *Journal of Personality and Social Psychology*, **56**, 586–595.

McEnrue, M. P. (1989) Self-development as a career management strategy. *Journal of Vocational Behavior*, **34**, 57–68.

McEvoy, G. M. & Cascio, W. F. (1989) Cumulative evidence of the relationship between employee age and job performance. *Journal of Applied Psychology*, **74**, 11–17.

McGoldrick, A. E. (1996) A psychological model of retirement decision and impact. In C. L. Cooper and I. T. Robertson (eds), *International Review of Industrial and Organizational Psychology*, Vol. 11. Chichester: Wiley.

Meager, N., Kaiser, M. & Dietrich, H. (1992) *Self-Employment in the UK and Germany*. London: Anglo-German Foundation for the Study of Industrial Society.

Meglino, B. M., Denisi, A. S. & Ravlin, E. C. (1993) Effects of previous job exposure and subsequent job status on the functioning of a realistic job preview. *Personnel Psychology*, **46** 803–822.

Meier, S. T. (1991) Vocational behavior, 1988–1990: Vocational choice, decision-making, career development interventions, and assessment. *Journal of Vocational Behavior*, **39**, 131–181.

Meyer, J. P., Allen, N. J. & Smith, C. A. (1993) Commitment to organizations and occupations: Extension and test of a three-component conceptualization. *Journal of Applied Psychology*, **78**, 538–551.

Miller, V. D. & Jablin, F. M. (1991) Information seeking during organizational entry: Influences, tactics, and a model of the process. *Academy of Management Review*, **16**, 92–120.

Morrison, E. W. (1993) Newcomer information-seeking: Exploring types, modes, sources and outcomes. *Academy of Management Journal*, **36**, 557–589.

Morrison, R. F. & Brantner, T. M. (1992) What enhances or inhibits learning in a new job? A basic career issue. *Journal of Applied Psychology*, **77**, 926–940.

Moss, M. K. & Frieze, H. (1993) Job preferences in the anticipatory socialization phase: A comparison of two matching models. *Journal of Vocational Behavior*, **42**, 282–297.

Munton, A. G., Forster, N., Altman, Y. & Greenbury, L. (1993) *Job Relocation: Managing People on the Move*. Chichester: Wiley.

Nathan, R. & Hill, L. (1992) *Career Counselling*. London: Sage.

Neugarten, B. L. (1977) Personality and aging. In J. E. Birren and K. W. Schaie (eds), *Handbook of the Psychology of Aging*. New York: Van Nostrand Reinhold.

Newton, T. J. & Keenan, A. (1990) Consequences of changing employers amongst young engineers. *Journal of Occupational Psychology*, **63**, 113–127.

Nicholson, N. (1984) A theory of work-role transitions. *Administrative Science Quarterly*, **29**, 172–191.

Nicholson, N. & West, M. A. (1989) Transitions, work histories and careers. In M. B. Arthur, D. T. Hall and B. S. Lawrence (eds) *Handbook of Career Theory*. Cambridge: Cambridge University Press.

Nicholson, N. (1990) The transition cycle: Causes, outcomes, processes and forms. In S. Fisher and C. L. Cooper (eds), *On The Move: The Psychological Effects of Change and Transition.* Chichester: Wiley.

Nicholson, N. & Imaizumi, A. (1993) The adjustment of Japanese expatriates to living and working in Britain. *British Journal of Management,* 4, 119–134.

Nicholson, N. & West, M. A. (1988) *Managerial Job Change: Men and Women in Transition.* Cambridge: Cambridge University Press.

Noe, R. A. (1988) An investigation of the determinants of successful assigned mentoring relationships. *Personnel Psychology,* 41, 457–479.

Nordvik, H. (1991) Work activity and career goals in Holland's and Schein's theories of vocational personalities and career anchors. *Journal of Vocational Behavior,* 38, 165–178.

Offermann, L. R. & Gowing, M. K. (1990) Organizations of the future. *American Psychologist,* 45, 95–108.

Ohlott, P. J., Ruderman, M. N. & McCauley, C. D. (1994) Gender differences in managers' developmental job experiences. *Academy of Management Journal,* 37, 46–67.

Olian, J. D., Carroll, S. J. & Giannantonio, C. M. (1993) Mentor reactions to protégés: An experiment with managers. *Journal of Vocational Behavior,* 43, 266–278.

Ornstein, S. & Isabella, L. A. (1993) Making sense of careers: A review 1989–1992. *Journal of Management,* 19, 243–267.

Ostroff, C. & Kozlowski, S. W. J. (1992) Organizational socialization as a learning process: The role of information acquisition. *Personnel Psychology,* 45, 849–874.

Ostroff, C. & Kozlowski, S. W. J. (1993) The role of mentoring in the information gathering processes of newcomers during early organizational socialization. *Journal of Vocational Behavior,* 43, 170–183.

Pearce, J. L. (1993) Toward an organizational behavior of contract laborers: Their psychological involvement and effects on employee coworkers. *Academy of Management Journal,* 36, 1082–1096.

Perlmutter, M. & Hall, E. (1992) *Adult Development and Aging.* 2nd edn. Chichester: Wiley.

Pollock, R. (1995) A test of conceptual models depicting the developmental course of informal mentor-protégé relationships in the workplace. *Journal of Vocational Behavior,* 46, 144–162.

Prediger, D. J. & Vansickle, T. R. (1992) Locating occupations on Holland's hexagon: Beyond RIASEC. *Journal of Vocational Behavior,* 40, 111–128.

Quick, J. C., Hess, R. E., Hermalin, J. & Quick, J. D. (eds) (1990) *Career Stress in Changing Times.* New York: Haworth Press.

Ragins, B. R. & Cotton, J. L. (1991) Easier said than done: Gender differences in perceived barriers to gaining a mentor. *Academy of Management Journal,* 34, 939–951.

Robertson, I. T., Iles, P. A., Gratton, L. & Sharpley, D. (1991) The impact of personnel selection and assessment methods on candidates. *Human Relations,* 44, 963–982.

Rounds, J. & Tracey, T. J. (1993) Prediger's dimensional representation of Holland's RIASEC circumplex. *Journal of Applied Psychology,* 78, 875–890.

Russell, J. E. A. (1991) Career development interventions in organizations. *Journal of Vocational Behavior,* 38, 237–287.

Russell, J. E. A. & Curtis, L. B. (1992) *Career development programs in the Fortune 500.* Paper presented at meeting of the Society for Industrial Organizational Psychology.

Saks, A. M. (1995) Longitudinal field investigation of the moderating and mediating effects of self-efficacy on the relationship between training and newcomer adjustment. *Journal of Applied Psychology,* 80, 211–225.

Salomone, P. R. (1993) Annual review: Practice and research in career counseling and development, 1993. *Career Development Quarterly,* 42, 99–128.

Salthouse, T. A. (1990) Cognitive competence and expertise in aging. In J. E. Birren and K. W. Schaie (eds), *Handbook of the Psychology of Aging*, 3rd edn. London: Academic Press.

Scandura, T. A. (1992) Mentorship and career mobility: An empirical investigation. *Journal of Organizational Behavior*, **13**, 169–174.

Scandura, T. A. & Ragins, B. R. (1993) The effects of sex and gender role orientation on mentorship in male-dominated occupations. *Journal of Vocational Behavior*, **43**, 251–265.

Schein, E. H. (1971) The individual, the organization, and the career: A conceptual scheme. *Journal of Applied Behavioral Science*, 7, 401–426.

Schein, E. H. (1993) *Career Anchors: Discovering your Real Values*. Revised edn. London: Pfeiffer and Co.

Schneider, S. C. & Asakawa, K. (1995) American and Japanese expatriate adjustment: A psychoanalytic perspective. *Human Relations*, **48**, 1109–1127.

Sharf, R. F. (1992) *Applying Career Development Theory to Counseling*. Pacific Grove: Brooks/Cole.

Shore, L. & Tetrick, L. E. (1994) The psychological contract as an explanatory framework in the employment relationship. In C. L. Cooper and D. M. Rousseau (eds), *Trends in Organizational Behavior*, Vol. 1. Chichester: Wiley.

Smart, R. & Peterson, C. (1994) Stability versus transition in women's career development: A test of Levinson's theory. *Journal of Vocational Behavior*, **45**, 241–260.

Social Trends, (1993) No. 23. London: Central Statistical Office.

Staudinger, U. M., Smith, J. & Baltes, P. B. (1992) Wisdom-related knowledge in a life review task: Age differences and the role of professional specialization. *Psychology and Aging*, 7, 271–281.

Stephens, G. K. (1994) Crossing internal career boundaries: The state of research on subjective career transitions. *Journal of Management*, **20**, 479–501.

Sterns, H. L. & Miklos, S. M. (1995) The aging worker in a changing environment: Organizational and individual issues. *Journal of Vocational Behavior*, **47**, 248–268.

Storey, J. (1992) *Developments in the Management of Human Resources*. Oxford: Blackwell.

Subich, L. M. (1994) Annual review: Practice and research in career counseling and development: 1993. *Career Development Quarterly*, **43**, 114–151.

Super, D. E. (1990) Career and life development. In D. Brown and L. Brooks (eds), *Career Choice and Development*, 2nd edn. San Francisco: Jossey-Bass.

Super, D. E. & Hall, D. T. (1978) Career development: exploration and planning. *Annual Review of Psychology*, **29**, 257–293.

Super, D. E. & Hall, D. T. (1990) Career development: Exploration and planning. *Annual Review of Psychology*, **29**, 333–372.

Swanson, J. L. (1992) Vocational behavior 1989–1991: Life-span career development and reciprocal interaction of work and nonwork. *Journal of Vocational Behavior*, **41**, 101–161.

Talaga, J. A. & Beehr, T. A. (1995) Are there gender differences in predicting retirement decisions? *Journal of Applied Psychology*, **80**, 16–28.

Terpstra, D. E. & Rozell, E. J. (1993) The relationship of staffing practices to organizational level measures of performance. *Personnel Psychology*, **46**, 27–48.

Tokar, D. M. & Swanson, J. L. (1995) Evaluation of the correspondence between Holland's vocational personality typology and the five-factor model of personality. *Journal of Vocational Behavior*, **46**, 89–108.

Tranberg, M., Slane, S. & Ekeberg, S. E. (1993) The relation between interest congruence and satisfaction: A meta-analysis. *Journal of Vocational Behavior*, **42**, 253–264.

Tremblay, M., Roger, A. & Toulouse, J-M. (1995) Career plateau and work attitudes: An empirical study of managers. *Human Relations*, **48**, 221–237.

Turban, D. B. & Dougherty, T. W. (1994) Role of protégé personality in receipt of mentoring and career success. *Academy of Management Journal*, **37**, 688–702.

Vondracek, F. & Schulenberg, J. (1992) Counseling for normative and nonnormative influences on career development. *Career Development Quarterly*, **40**, 291–301.

Vroom, V. H. (1966) A study of pre- and post-decision processes. *Organizational Behavior and Human Performance*, **1**, 212–225.

Wallace, J. E. (1993) Professional and organizational commitment: Compatible or incompatible? *Journal of Vocational Behavior*, **42**, 333–349.

Wanous, J. P., Poland, T. D., Premack, S. L. & Davis, K. S. (1992) The effects of met expectations on newcomer attitudes and behaviors: A review and meta-analysis. *Journal of Applied Psychology*, **77**, 288–297.

Warr, P. B. (1993) Age and employment. In M. Dunnette, L. Hough and H. Triandis (eds), *Handbook of Industrial and Organizational Psychology*, Vol. 4. Palo Alto: Consulting Psychologists Press.

Warr, P. B. & Conner, M. (1992) Job competence and cognition. *Research in Organizational Behavior*, **14**, 91–127.

Warr, P. B. & Pennington, J. (1994) Occupational age-grading: Jobs for older and younger non-managerial employees. *Journal of Vocational Behavior*, **45**, 328–346.

Waterman, R., Waterman, J. & Collard, B. (1994) Toward a career resilient workforce. *Harvard Business Review*, July/August.

Watkins, C. E. & Subich, L. M. (1995) Annual review, 1992–1994: Career development, reciprocal work/non-work interaction, and women's workforce participation. *Journal of Vocational Behavior*, **47**, 109–163.

Watts, A. G. (1994) *Lifelong Career Development: Towards a National Strategy for Careers Education and Guidance*. Cambridge, UK: Careers Research and Advisory Centre.

Wheeler, K. G. (1990) Career experiences: Current and future themes. In J C. Quick et al. (eds), *Career Stress in Changing Times*. London: Haworth Press.

White, M. C., Smith, M. & Barnett, T. (1994) A typology of executive career specialization. *Human Relations*, **47**, 473–486.

Whitely, W., Dougherty, T. W. & Dreher, G. F. (1991) Relationship of career mentoring and socioeconomic origin to managers' and professionals' early career progress. *Academy of Management Journal*, **34**, 331–351.

Whitely, W., Dougherty, T.W. & Dreher, G. F. (1992) Correlates of career-oriented mentoring for early career managers and professionals. *Journal of Organizational Behavior*, **13**, 141–154.

Chapter 3

MANAGERIAL CAREER ADVANCEMENT

Phyllis Tharenou
Monash University

It has become increasingly important to understand how advancement into managerial positions occurs. There is the need to advance as managers those who are most effective. The performance of organization leaders has been shown to contribute to organization failure (Levinson, 1994) and profitability (Day & Lord, 1988), with the proportion of effective managers thought to be less than 50% and executives about 33% (Forbes & Piercy, 1991; Hogan, 1994; Hogan, Curphy, & Hogan, 1994). There is the critical need to understand why women and minorities continue to be underrepresented in management (Northcraft & Gutek, 1993). There are different but not understood ways to advance to high positions in contemporary organizations than two decades ago (Kotter, 1995), when there was reliance on career paths based on job ladders, seniority, and tenure. Managerial positions are fewer in flatter, decentralized, downsized organizations, of necessity changing how advancement occurs (Offerman & Gowing, 1993). There are also changed human resources management practices for selection and promotion of managers. Selection practices for management positions are more structured and less subjective than a decade earlier (Shackleton & Newell, 1991), equal employment opportunity/affirmative action has been introduced, and applicant pools for managerial positions are increasingly diverse—more feminized, older, and of more ethnic groups and races (Khojasteh, 1994).

How people advance in the contemporary management hierarchy is not understood (Kotter, 1995). Are qualities of the individual (ambition, intelligence) more important than organizational factors (promotion ladders, line jobs, functional areas), or do they interact? Are merit, performance-based factors—human capital, managerial skills, job performance, job-relevant traits—more important than non-merit, non-performance-based factors—informal networks, discrimination, politics, job-irrelevant traits? Are 'informal' social factors—networks, mentors, politics, group similarity—more explanatory than 'formal' opportunity structures—internal labor markets,

---

Managerial Career Advancement by Phyllis Tharenou taken from IRIOP 1997 v12, Edited by Cary L. Cooper and Ivan T. Robertson: © 1997 John Wiley & Sons, Ltd

seniority, tenure? Knowledge of managerial advancement is from diverse, distinct, highly specific approaches, as yet resulting in questions remaining unanswered. Reviews of the literature have been confined to understanding causes of promotion (Forbes & Wertheim, 1995; Markham, Harlan, & Hackett, 1987; Stumpf & London, 1981) or women's advancement into management (Powell & Mainiero, 1992; Ragins & Sundstrom, 1989). This review examines the causes of career advancement of supervisors, managers, executives, and chief executive officers (CEOs) broadly in terms of managerial promotions, level and pay, as well as of subordinate entry to management positions. It is based on the contemporary empirical research published since 1990.

Managerial career advancement has usually been defined in terms of promotions within managerial ranks and the level of management position ultimately reached (e.g. Miner, Chen, & Yu, 1991), and as level of pay (Rosenbaum, 1984). Managerial promotions signify upward movement in the managerial hierarchy, and managers' levels and pay signify managerial achievement and success (Gattiker & Larwood, 1990; Miner, Chen, & Yu, 1991). Managerial promotions (number or rate) appear to precede increases in level and pay (Brett, Stroh, & Reilly, 1992a; Bretz & Judge, 1994; Gibbs, 1995), and managerial level is used to predict pay (e.g. Boxman, De Graaf, & Flap, 1991; Bretz & Judge, 1994; Lobel & St. Clair, 1992; Reskin & Ross, 1992; Schneer & Reitman, 1995), suggesting promotion increases level which increases pay. The term pay will be used to refer to salary, salary progression or total compensation because results do not differ by pay type and types are highly related (e.g. Judge, Cable, Boudreau, & Bretz, 1995).

The studies to be reviewed have examined organizational and individual causes of managerial career advancement, consistent with past reviews (e.g. Markham, Harlan, & Hackett, 1987; Ragins & Sundstrom, 1989; Stumpf & London, 1981). The studies published since 1990 cover several major categories of variables, as shown in Figure 3.1. In the organizational context, opportunity structures, social structures, the interpersonal context, and promotion processes have been examined, and in regard to individual factors, traits, human capital, managerial skills, and family.

THE ORGANIZATIONAL ENVIRONMENT

Opportunity Structures

Large organizations with long promotion ladders and high growth should provide opportunities for individuals to advance into management. On organization entry, individuals are faced with opportunity structures (Markham, Harlan, & Hackett, 1987). They enter jobs that vary in the extent to which promotion ladders are attached, entering on the bottom rung of the ladder in a

ORGANIZATIONAL   **INDIVIDUAL**

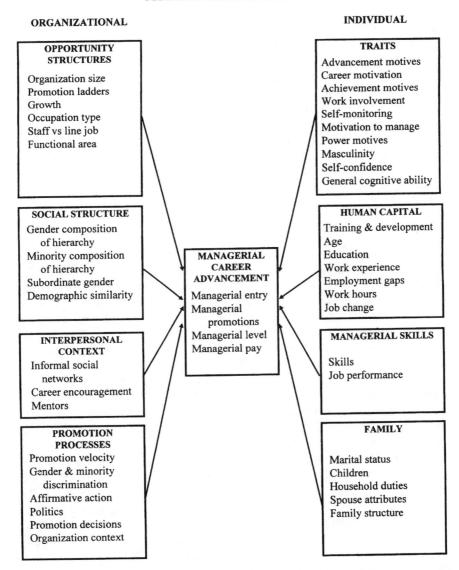

Figure 3.1 The major categories of variables examined in regard to managerial career advancement from the studies to be reviewed

closed internal labor market, or at higher rungs in a more open internal labor market. Promotion is achieved by moves between levels in the ladder, and so ladders need to be long with many levels and to lead to higher level jobs for promotion to occur, and vacancies need to arise. Occupations and job types and functions are also components of internal labor markets that vary in their capacity to allow individuals to move into, or advance in management. Primary jobs and 'organization' jobs (the firm labor market) provide more promotion opportunities than secondary jobs and 'occupation' jobs (Markham, Harlan, & Hackett, 1987). The studies to be reviewed are multivariate, primarily cross-sectional designs, assessing opportunity structures measured either by self-report, little validated measures at individual level, or by more objective means using company and industry records at organization level. Most studies of opportunity structures do not assess their indirect effects on advancement through intervening structures or other factors, and insufficient studies have compared the importance of opportunity structures to individual factors or to other organizational factors.

Organization size

Organization size has been found not related (Cox & Harquail, 1991; Dreher & Ash, 1990; Judge et al., 1995) or weakly related (Nkomo & Cox, 1990; Whiteley & Coetsier, 1993) to managers' promotion. Indirect effects may occur through internal labor markets. Larger organizations than smaller had internal promotion systems for executives (Friedman, 1991), and were more likely to have a fast track and use informal nominations for promotion to middle manager levels (Ferris, Buckley, & Allen, 1992). The influence on actual advancement was not assessed. Organization size was negatively related to managers' managerial levels (Cox & Harquail, 1991; Herriot, Gibson, Pemberton, & Pinder, 1993; Schneer & Reitman, 1994a, 1995), perhaps because larger organizations are more competitive or have fewer managerial positions. Organization size may have greatest effect in late career. Organization size did not increase managerial levels until mid-career when employees were 28 to 44 years old, reaching full impact for those greater than 44 years (Melamed, 1996a), and managers in larger organizations increased their level and pay when older than 44 than in middle years (Herriot et al., 1993). Organization size had inconsistent links to managers' and executives' pay: nonsignificant (Dreher & Ash, 1990; Reskin & Ross, 1992; Whitely & Coetsier, 1993), negative (Herriot et al., 1993; Ingham & Thompson, 1995; Judge et al., 1995), and positive (Meyerson, 1994; Pfeffer & Ross, 1990; Schneer & Reitman, 1995). Organization size was not related to managers' advancement comprising promotion, level and pay (Judge & Bretz, 1994). Organization size was related positively to selection of older business unit managers with more corporation tenure (Guthrie & Olian, 1991) and of insider CEOs than outsiders (Datta & Guthrie, 1994), suggesting larger organizations than smaller may advance insiders to executive positions, perhaps because of larger candidate pools. Organization size has been inconsistently related to women's or minorities' managerial advancement. Using large numbers of companies, organization size was not related to the proportion of women or minorities in management (Konrad & Linnehan, 1995; Konrad & Pfeffer, 1991; Leck &

Saunders, 1992a, b; Leck, Saunders, & St. Onge, 1991; Pfeffer, Davis-Blake, & Julius, 1995), although it has been related, particularly representatively, to hiring for management positions of male and female visible minorities (non-Caucasian, nonwhite) and the disabled (Konrad & Linnehan, 1995; Leck & Saunders, 1992a, b; Leck, Saunders, & St. Onge, 1991). For university executives and managers, organization size was negatively related to hiring of women (Konrad & Pfeffer, 1991) and to pay for positions continuously held by women and positions held by men but formerly held by women, compared to continuing male positions (Pfeffer & Ross, 1990). In summary, not consistent with internal labor markets for advancement, organization size is inconsistently related, either unrelated or weakly related, to managerial career advancement including of women and minorities.

Promotion ladders

Long promotion ladders were related to male and female managers' promotion (Tharenou & Conroy, 1994), but the number of management levels was not related to black managers' managerial promotions (Nkomo & Cox, 1990). Frequency of management vacancies was positively related (Blum, Fields, & Goodman, 1994; Nkomo & Cox, 1990) and unrelated to managers' promotions or managerial levels (Cox & Harquail, 1991). Promotion ladders were negatively related to managers' and executives' managerial levels (Herriot, Gibbons, Pemberton, & Jackson, 1994; Tharenou & Conroy, 1994), perhaps because shorter ladders are reported closer to the top. In a sample ranging in level (43% subordinates), an open versus closed internal labor market was not related to managerial level, but low cohort competition increased women's and not men's managerial levels (Melamed, 1995a). Management vacancies and low management salaries, reflecting institutional pressures, and promotion and development from within and the high proportions of professional and skilled organization positions, reflecting internal labor markets, were related to the percentage of women in management in 279 medium to large private firms (Blum, Fields, & Goodman, 1994). Industrial relations managers' perceptions of organization career reward systems and the fit of their preferences with the system were related, albeit weakly, to pay and job level (Bretz & Judge, 1994), suggesting advancement arises partly from person–environment fit. In summary, not supporting internal labor markets for advancement, promotion ladders are inconsistently related to managerial advancement.

Growth

Organizational growth in two 3-year periods did not assist promotion of two entry cohorts of managers in a US international company, having either small positive effects or negative effects (Hurley & Sonnenfeld, 1994). Periods of high growth had inconsistent links with promotion rates at all managerial levels, and did not assist women and minorities. The promotion rates of men and whites remained much higher (Hurley & Sonnenfeld, 1994). The growth era enhanced the promotions of whichever functional area (operations versus staff) had initially lower promotion rates, suggesting growth equalizes. Women were more likely than men to manage academic and nonacademic departments in two universities when they had smaller budgets and the department was nongrowing, whereas men got the job when the department had a larger budget or was growing (Stover, 1994). In summary, growth may not help managerial career advancement.

Occupation type

Occupations are classified by skill level based on their range and complexity of job duties and formal education, on-the-job training, and experience to do the job. Managerial and administrative occupations are classified highest in skill level and unskilled occupations lowest, with nonmanagerial/administrative occupations (e.g. clerical) having managerial positions. High skill level occupations (primary jobs) offer job security, skill development, and career paths as distinct from low level occupations (secondary jobs; Markham, Harlan, & Hackett, 1987). Using standard government occupational classifications, occupational level was related positively to women's and men's managerial levels for employees ranging in level (Melamed, 1995a), and holding a managerial versus nonmanagerial occupation to managers' higher pay (Reskin & Ross, 1992). The greater percentage of women in an occupation, the less likelihood employees held a supervisory position in a US national sample (Huffman, 1995) and the lower the pay of Australian managers (Martin, 1994). Job titles that qualified public servants to apply to take examinations for managerial positions were disproportionately held by males, with eligibility requirements reducing managerial promotions of women and minorities (Steinberg, Haignere, & Chertos, 1990). In summary, supporting the importance of primary versus secondary job labor markets, occupation level and male gender-linkage are positively related to managerial advancement.

Line versus staff job

Line rather than staff positions should provide more knowledge about the firm and opportunities for visible performance and credibility in critical functions, increasing opportunities for managerial advancement. Line rather than staff positions were related (Nkomo & Cox, 1990; Whitely & Coetsier, 1993) and not related (Cox & Harquail, 1991; Scandura, 1992) to managers' promotions, and not related to managers' levels (Bretz & Judge, 1994; Cox & Harquail, 1991). Women who reached vice-president level reported moving out of staff to line positions in mid-career (Mainiero, 1994a). Entering by line versus staff jobs was related inconsistently to managers' career advancement, and became less important with tenure in the firm (Hurley & Sonnenfeld, 1994). Line rather than staff jobs were positively related to managers' pay (Scandura, 1994) or had no links (Cox & Harquail, 1991; Whitely & Coetsier, 1993), and not related to industrial relations managers' advancement (promotions, level, pay; Judge & Bretz, 1994). In summary, line versus staff jobs are related inconsistently, often unrelated, to managerial career advancement.

Functional area

The type or breadth of functional areas managers occupy may influence opportunities for advancement through increased knowledge, visible performance, credibility, and familiarity (Forbes & Piercy, 1991). For managers, central areas of finance, marketing, and operations were not related to advancement (Cannings, 1991; Cannings & Montmarquette, 1991b; Dreher & Ash, 1990; Schneer & Reitman, 1990; Stroh, Brett, & Reilly, 1992; Whitely, Dougherty, & Dreher, 1991), although they are rarely compared to less central functions of human resources and community relations. Managers in finance had higher pay (Schneer & Reitman, 1994b, 1995). The number of functional areas, and thus breadth of experience, was not related to managers' promotion, level or pay (Cox & Harquail, 1991; Ellis & Heneman, 1990), except for younger compared to middle and older managers' managerial levels (Herriot et al., 1993). International experience was related to executives' promotion but not pay (Judge et al., 1995), and international jobs, living outside the US, and adding one year of international experience gave male managers extra salary payoffs per year but female managers pay reductions (Egan & Bendick, 1994). In studies using archival data and interviews, and without comparison groups, men and women who rose to executive levels had (i) successful performance in critical functional areas and experience on high visibility projects and task forces, especially in the first five years; (ii) experience in corporate headquarters, and breadth of experience through several functional areas, cross-functional areas, assistant to executive positions, and international assignments, especially in late early career, the second five years; (iii) broadening general management experience, especially in mid-career (10 to 20 years); and (iv) major organizational assignments and projects on specific organizational needs in late career (Forbes & Piercy, 1991; Mainiero, 1994a; Piercy & Forbes, 1991). In summary, apart from executive advancement, type and number of functional areas are usually not related to managerial career advancement.

Social Structure

Organizational social structures may influence opportunities for managerial career advancement. Processes of similarity and categorization operate for decision-makers, including when selecting for management jobs. Decision-makers compare themselves to others as similar or different and are attracted to those similar, and perceive and relate to others by social categories when detailed information and contact is lacking (Baron & Pfeffer, 1994). Kanter coined the term 'homosocial reproduction' when insiders replicate themselves when filling jobs (Kanter, 1977), and homophily operates when selectors prefer to choose similar others and job seekers prefer to work with similar individuals (Ibarra, 1993). Homophily is the degree of demographic and identity similarity of interacting individuals (Ibarra, 1993). Male managerial hierarchies are therefore more likely to result in selection and promotion of white men for managerial jobs. In the studies to be reviewed, there are insufficient direct tests of explanations (e.g. effects of similarity) posed for the effects, and few tests of interactions between social structures and individual attributes for managerial career advancement.

Gender composition of hierarchy

Most studies of the impact of gender composition of managerial hierarchies are cross-sectional, self-report survey designs with multivariate analyses and controls. For managers and executives, the extent to which the managerial hierarchy was male was related to women not being promoted but not men, but to neither's managerial levels (Tharenou & Conroy, 1994). Female CEOs were discriminated from matched samples of male CEOs and female top managers from amongst organizational (training, selection), interpersonal (male hierarchy, career encouragement), and individual (personality, non-work, early background) factors by two factors, one of which was the extent the managerial hierarchy was male (Tharenou, 1995). This suggests male hierarchies stop women breaking the glass ceiling, and more female hierarchies help them. In a structural equation analysis, male hierarchies did not affect male or female managers' and executives' career encouragement, and reduced men's and not women's training and development and thus in turn managerial advancement (Tharenou, Latimer, & Conroy, 1994). For middle managers of a finance company, the number of women already in top positions was related to women's motivation to be promoted, but not men's (Cannings & Montmarquette, 1991a).

Studies of university managers are consistent with processes of homosocial reproduction and homophily in selection and promotion practices based on the gender composition of managerial hierarchies. From analysis of objective longitudinal data of a national US sample of 821 colleges and universities, the proportion of female administrators predicted the proportion of female administrators five years later (Pfeffer, Davis-Blake, & Julius, 1995). If the president of the college was a woman or a minority, the greater were the proportion of female administrators and increase in their proportion over five years (Pfeffer, Davis-Blake, & Julius, 1995). A new hire for managerial and executive positions was more likely to be a woman if there was a greater percentage of women in the particular position across institutions and/or in all administrative positions in a university, and if the previous occupant was a woman (Konrad & Pfeffer, 1991). It was hard to get women into positions from which they were formerly excluded, but once first hired for those positions, they were more likely to be hired (Konrad & Pfeffer, 1991). For two university departments, women were more likely than men to manage departments previously managed by a woman (Stover, 1994). In summary, consistent with homophily and homosocial reproduction processes, male managerial hierarchies reduce women's managerial advancement, and increases in women in managerial jobs subsequently increase women's representation in management.

Minority composition of hierarchy

For university executives and managers, the percentage of minorities in management five years earlier and the CEO being a minority were related to the percentage of minorities in management (Pfeffer, Davis-Blake, & Julius, 1995). The greater percentage of minorities in that particular position, or all administrative positions in universities and the previous occupant being a minority were related to minorities being new hires (Konrad & Pfeffer, 1991). The organizations' percentage of black employees was not related to managerial promotions of black managers from self-reports of MBA graduates in several organizations (Nkomo & Cox, 1990). The overall trends are consistent with homophily and homosocial reproduction explanations. In summary, minorities in the managerial hierarchy increase minority representation in management.

Subordinate gender

Higher proportions of female than male subordinates were positively related to the number of women managers (Reskin & Ross, 1992) and university administrators (Stover, 1994), and the percentage of women in nonmanagement positions was related to the percentage of women in management in medium to large private firms (Blum, Fields, & Goodman, 1994). Men were more likely to manage men than women (Reskin & Ross, 1992). In summary, women are more likely to be managers when the subordinates are women rather than men.

Demographic similarity

Social similarity, by providing a familiar frame of reference, is thought to influence choice of job applicants when the decision is more uncertain (Salancik & Pfeffer, 1978), as would be found for high level management jobs. Hence, demographically similar candidates may be promoted to management jobs (Mittman, 1992). For male but not female business school graduates in the first 3 months of their jobs, when the work group had high proportions of women, men were more likely to be promoted at 14 months, but women were not when the workgroup was male (Kirchmeyer, 1995). Cultural (ethnicity, religion) and generational (age, education, lifestyle) similarity were not related to promotion. From analyses of objective public data, individuals' demographic dissimilarity to the team in age, tenure, education, military service and career experiences was not related to promotion from nonelite to elite status in 93 top management teams over a four-year period (Jackson, Brett, Sessa, Cooper, Julin, & Peyronnin, 1991). From archival data, future CEOs were found similar to the organization's executives in middle- or upper-class socioeconomic origins, education level from elite universities, being sons of business executives or professionals, and being from industrialized or metropolitan areas, all indicating familiarity and trust (Forbes & Piercy, 1991). In summary, not supporting a broad social similarity view, demographic similarity is inconsistently related to managerial promotion.

Interpersonal Context

Individuals may be provided in their work environment with emotional/expressive and career/instrumental support for advancement from multiple others or specific individuals. Instrumental behavior provides job-related resources including information and career support, whereas expressive behavior provides emotional support (Ibarra, 1993). Studies have examined multiple contacts using informal social networks. Informal network relationships influencing advancement are formed based on group similarity (i.e. homophily), with same-group ties thought to pull people into and up managerial hierarchies (Ibarra, 1993). Studies have examined individual support using mentors. Mentors provide intensive career and expressive support for advancement (Kram, 1983), using direct interventions, for example, through sponsoring protégés and providing legitimacy (Burt, 1992). Studies of social structure have rarely directly tested the inferred explanations for their effects.

Informal social networks

Employees are said to have a location in the social structure of an organization, giving each employee a network of contacts who are themselves connected to others (Burt, 1992). Social capital is the network of the player's relationships with other players who may be friends, colleagues or other contacts (Burt, 1992). They provide opportunities, because they have information, and enable the player to have more control in negotiations because there are multiple options or choices between them (Burt, 1993). Returns arise because employees are positioned to identify and develop more rewarding opportunities from the information and control benefits of these ties. Structural hole theory (Burt,

1992) proposes that, among similar managers, those who advance most have personal contacts in diverse groups within and beyond the firm. Structural holes are gaps between nonredundant relationships that allow network benefits partly because they are additive rather than overlapping. Networks should be large and have weak ties to provide information and control. The studies of informal networks have analyzed primarily objective data.

Social capital in terms of number of external ties was positively related to pay for executive team members in Swedish public firms through networks based on strong not weak ties (Meyerson, 1994). Social capital added to human capital (education, experience) to explain executives' pay (Meyerson, 1994). Dutch male and female senior managers primarily found their current jobs through informal channels with larger than smaller ranges, with weak ties the most frequent way, especially for those highest educated (Boxman, De Graaf, & Flap, 1991). Using structural equation analysis, social capital in terms of external work contacts and memberships increased managers' pay, net of human capital as education and experience and of position level as number of subordinates (Boxman, De Graaf, & Flap, 1991). Human capital increased social capital. The effects of human capital on pay were greatest for managers with little social capital, and smallest for those with a lot. For male managers in a high technology firm, early and greatest promotions went to managers with more social capital, through having unconstrained, nonredundant networks (Burt, 1992). Except when entry-rank, promotions came more slowly to managers with networks constrained by being too small, too strongly connected, and connected to a single central contact, especially promotions to highest ranks. In summary, supporting social network theorists, informal social networks within or outside the organization increase managerial advancement (pay), with larger networks better than smaller, although not necessarily those with weaker than stronger ties.

For female senior managers in a high technology firm, networks dominated by strong ties to strategic sponsors and few interconnected, redundant contacts led to greatest promotion, especially to highest ranks, opposite to the weak network ties that assisted men (Burt, 1992). Women managers are thought to be not fully trusted and to need greater sponsorship to achieve legitimacy, through an objective source of information, and need to borrow the social capital to get the information and control benefits of structural holes (Burt, 1992). Male managers are thought to have more favorable social networks and personal contacts than female, providing more information, support, and access to jobs, resulting in men gaining higher status jobs than women (Ragins & Sundstrom, 1989). Using confirmatory analysis, male middle managers in a finance company used informal networks for career advice, especially with organizational superiors, more than females did, resulting in more promotion offers (Canning & Montmarquette, 1991b). Women used formal meritocratic procedures in terms of performance, formal promotion bids and education more than men, and gained fewer promotions (Canning &

Montmarquette, 1991b). For managers in internationally related occupations, men gained an additional $5200 per year from using personal networks for job search, whereas women gained $3000 per year (Egan & Bendick, 1994). In summary, informal social networks may provide men with greater managerial career advancement than women.

Career encouragement

Career encouragement by superiors and colleagues in the organization was related to male and female managers' and executives' organizational promotion, but not to their managerial levels (Tharenou & Conroy, 1994). Using structural equation analysis, managers' and executives' career encouragement increased women's training and development more than men's, and training and development in turn led to managerial advancement (Tharenou, Latimer, & Conroy, 1994). Women who reached vice-president level reported widespread top level support in early career (Mainiero, 1994a). One of the two factors distinguishing matched female CEOs, male CEOs, and female top managers was career encouragement (Tharenou, 1995). The women CEOs reported the support was from female colleagues and superiors more than male, who would have been the majority available (Tharenou, 1995). Career encouragement from similar others may thus help women break the glass ceiling. Women are likely to need more interpersonal support than men to reach top jobs because they have substantial barriers, and interpersonal support facilitates persistence in the face of barriers. In summary, career encouragement increases managerial career advancement, perhaps more for women than men.

Mentors

Career mentoring, embracing sponsorship, challenging work, protection, coaching and visibility for the protégé (Kram, 1983), should be more directly related to career advancement than psychosocial mentoring, comprising role modeling, friendship, acceptance, and counseling. For example, sponsoring involves mentors using their influence to gain protéges desirable positions and advancement. Mentor processes are different to those used by nonmentors (supervisors) of managers, who provided fewer mentor functions and for whom a mentoring relationship with stages could not be detected (Pollock, 1995). Sponsored promotion in early career is thought to assist career progress in tournaments in which winning and losing occurs at each career round (Rosenbaum, 1984). Mentoring is thought to assist winning in early rounds, although there are no comparisons with later career stages to assess its early importance.

In cross-sectional, chiefly self-report questionnaire studies controlling for human capital and job and organization variables, mentor presence and mentor career support were related positively to managers' pay and promotions in early career (Whitely & Coetsier, 1993; Whitely, Dougherty, & Dreher, 1991;

Yuen, 1995), as was overall mentor support (Dreher & Ash, 1990). Business graduates who had a mentor in the first 3 months of the job were more likely to be promoted at 14 months, with no effects for general supervisor support and work group fit (Kirchmeyer, 1995). General supervisor support was not related to black or white managers' promotability or plateauing by being in the same position seven or more years (Greenhaus, Parasuraman, & Wormley, 1990). For 183 managerial dyads in a manufacturing firm, supervisor- and subordinate-rated career mentoring were related to middle managers' pay and promotion rate from company records (Scandura & Schriesheim, 1994). Using structural equation analysis, initiation of mentoring resulted in mentoring, which then led to managers' and professionals' self-reported advancement, comprising pay and promotions (Turban & Dougherty, 1994). In early career, career mentoring has been more important to managers' promotions, though not to pay, than individual and other organization variables (Kirchmeyer, 1995; Whitely & Coetsier, 1993; Whitely, Dougherty, & Dreher, 1991), although there are no comparisons with later career stages.

The effects of psychosocial mentoring alone have not been assessed, and moderator effects of the mentoring-managerial advancement relationship appear likely, as found for protégé socio-economic status and promotion (Whitely, Dougherty, & Dreher, 1991). There are insufficient studies to say if mentoring similarly influences managerial advancement by gender or race. Mentor support was related similarly to the pay and promotion of male and female business graduates (Dreher & Ash, 1990), but a mentor was related to men's managerial level and not women's for accountants of whom over half supervised more than five employees (Johnson & Scandura, 1994). Presence of a mentor was related to black managers' managerial promotions (Nkomo & Cox, 1990) and promotability ratings and lack of plateauing (Greenhaus, Parasuraman, & Wormley, 1990). In summary, supporting the process of career mentoring, mentor presence and career support, rather than general supervisor support, increase managers' promotion, especially in early career, and pay.

Promotion Processes

Selection for managerial positions requires matching the candidate's competencies with the nature and demands of the job and organization. At lower management levels, the focus is on the performance demands of the job and the expectations of the organization, whereas at executive levels it is on the match with the organization's business strategy, culture and history and the fit with other senior executives (Forbes & Piercy, 1991).

Promotion velocity

Studies have assessed the effects of favorable starting circumstances and continuity of promotion on managerial career advancement. Career tournament theory proposes that, on organization entry, individuals join a tournament in which players must win rounds at each career round to advance to the next (Rosenbaum, 1990). Employees face a series of progressively more selective competitions. Those who do not win early are eliminated or restricted in play to consolation rounds, whereas winners proceed to the next round but need to keep winning to be still in the tournament (Rosenbaum, 1984, 1990). Those who advance early, by being younger than their peers on their status level, are offered more opportunities for advancement. Winners receive ability signals (job status, career velocity) that affect their prospects for the next higher competition. Promotion leads to more promotion as new jobs create more opportunities for development and networking and signal ability, creating 'career velocity' (Rosenbaum, 1990). Tournaments discourage late-emerging ability and impose low ceilings.

Starting at higher hierarchical levels was related to more managerial promotions and higher levels for managers (Cox & Harquail, 1991). For male and female managers, fast starters, trainees who spent less than average time in their first management job, compared to slow starters, attained higher management levels, and starting in a high power versus lower power department predicted greater promotion and pay over 10 years (Sheridan, Slocum, Buda, & Thompson, 1990). In early career, assignment to career-maker departments and high visibility projects was reported for women reaching vice-president level (Mainiero, 1994a), and promotion to the first management position by the first five years occurred for managers promoted to general manager or functional vice-president by age 39 for those who later became CEOs (Forbes & Piercy, 1991). Analysing longitudinal company data, managers who had been promoted upward still had high chances of being promoted to higher levels (Hurley & Sonnenfeld, 1994) and high advancement desires (Howard, 1991), whereas those who had not been promoted as much reported less chance of still being promoted and had low advancement desires, supporting career tournament theory. Starting opportunities may be less favorable to women's managerial advancement than men's. Female middle managers entered banking at initially lower job levels than male managers (Martin & Morgan, 1995; Morgan, Schor, & Martin, 1993). For university nonacademic staff ranging from subordinates to senior managers who had been promoted, structural equation analysis of objective data showed that the managerial level and status of the prior position influenced the hierarchical level of the new position and, independently, being a woman reduced the level and status of the prior position as well as the new position (Johnsrud & Heck, 1994). Unlike men's, female middle managers' promotion offers led to a decline in promotion bids, perhaps because of an invisible ceiling for women (Cannings & Montmarquette, 1991b). In summary, supporting career tournaments in early career, favorable starting opportunities lead to managerial advancement, but women's initially lower level placements than men's reduces their managerial advancement.

Gender discrimination

Female managers' promotions did not translate to as high managerial levels as males' (Cox & Harquail, 1991; Lewis, 1992). Compared to men, women gained more promotions to reach middle management (Martin & Morgan, 1995; Morgan, Schor, & Martin, 1993), and were promoted less into the professional grades through which public servants needed to pass to apply for supervisory jobs (Naff, 1994). In summary, promotion results in female managers gaining lower managerial levels than male managers.

Statistical discrimination studies assess if there are incremental effects of gender on advancement by first controlling for individuals' productivity and job and organizational variables, using hierarchical regression analysis (see Ragin & Bradshaw, 1991, for a critique). When the incremental variance is significant, statistical discrimination is said to operate. This is said to be based on employers expecting women, on average, to be less productive or to leave the firm sooner than men, and thus assigning individual women to lower level positions than men (Blau & Ferber, 1987; Strober, 1990). The generalizations from statistical reasoning processes about the attributes of average group members constitute gender stereotypes (see Schaller, Boyd, Yohannes, & O'Brien, 1995). Stereotypes save energy by simplifying information processing and response generation in evaluative processes, and are invoked more when evaluative processes are difficult and perceivers' resources depleted (Macrae, Milne, & Bodenhausen, 1994). This is consistent with the sizeable, complex information requirements and uncertain decision-making confronted in selection processes for higher level jobs with large applicant pools. Studies do not directly test the inferred explanations for statistical discrimination, nor test if stereotypes are involved.

The statistical discrimination studies are primarily cross-sectional self-report designs, and cover all career stages. For executives and managers comparable in age, productivity (i.e. work experience, education, performance), career paths and mobility (i.e. starting level, relocation, company changes, employment gaps), job type, organization, and industry, men compared to women were rated higher on promotion potential (Landau, 1995) and gained more managerial promotions (Cox & Harquail, 1991), and more pay (Cannings, 1991; Hanson Frieze, Olson, & Cain Good, 1990; Schneer & Reitman, 1994b, $p <0.10$; Stroh, Brett, & Reilly, 1992; Truman & Baroudi, 1994). Similarly, for employees ranging from subordinates to executives, men gained higher managerial levels than comparable women (Haberfeld, 1992; Melamed, 1995b; Wright, Baxter, & Birkelund, 1995). In an analysis of objective longitudinal data for university managers and executives, statistical discrimination was shown. Pay dropped when the incumbent changed from male to female and increased when the incumbent changed from female to male, worse in private than public universities (Pfeffer & Ross, 1990). Overall, the explanation by gender is weak, but can translate into substantial reductions in pay (e.g. Haberfeld, 1992). Some studies show no statistical discrimination: on managers' promotion (Dreher & Ash, 1990; Stroh, Brett, & Reilly, 1992) or managers' levels (Schneer & Reitman, 1994a; Truman & Baroudi, 1994). In an analysis of objective data, gender was first controlled, and effects assessed of five-year-earlier individual variables (human capital, family), change in individual variables in the five years, and organization (functional area) variables (Shenhav, 1992). Female white scientists and engineers in the private but not public sectors were more likely to be promoted into entry-level management positions than comparable white men, with no differences by race (Shenhav, 1992). In summary, overall, supporting statistical discrimination by gender, higher standards are used for women's managerial career advancement than men's.

Perceived discrimination predicted male and female MBAs' starting pay but not current pay in early to mid-career, although being female still also lowered starting and current pay (Hanson Frieze, Olson, & Cain Good, 1990). Each year since MBA graduation increased the probability that early career women perceived discrimination. In a longitudinal study tracking male and female cohorts of MBA graduates, mid-career was less helpful to women's managerial career advancement than early career, compared to men's (Schneer & Reitman, 1994b, 1995). The full-time women managers earned less and reached top management levels less often than the comparable males (Schneer & Reitman, 1995). The income gender difference first appeared 7–12 years post-MBA and grew larger in the last six years. Women continued to feel more subject to sex discrimination in relation to promotion or position in mid-career as early career than men, although men reported discrimination unlike in early career. Female Singaporean business graduates in mid- but not early career perceived that prejudice against women was negatively related to managerial level in relation to age and pay (Chi-Ching, 1992).

Minority discrimination

Statistical discrimination against minorities has been tested by the incremental variance added by minority status/race after controlling effects of productivity and other relevant variables. Stastical discrimination was shown on rated promotion potential for black compared to white and Asian compared to nonAsian managers and professionals although not Hispanics (Landau, 1995), on supervisor-rated promotability and career advancement opportunities and on career plateauing for black compared to white managers (some professionals; Igbaria & Wormley, 1995), on managers' and executives' pay for minority compared to nonminority status (Pfeffer & Ross, 1990), and on being supervisors or not for Asian American compared to white public servants varying in grade level (Kim & Lewis, 1994). Blacks and other nonwhite managers, especially when male, reported more discrimination for promotion and/or hiring than white managers in early to mid-career (Hanson Frieze,

Olson, & Cain Good, 1990). In a study in which gender was entered first in regression analyses, followed by five-year earlier individual variables, their change in five years, and organizational variables, black male or female scientists and engineers were more likely to be promoted to entry-level managerial positions over comparable whites and more in the public than private sectors (Shenhav, 1992). In summary, overall, supporting statistical discrimination by race, there are higher standards for blacks' managerial career advancement than whites', especially for promotion potential.

Affirmative action

Affirmative action/equal employment opportunity (AA/EEO) implementation was not related to black managers' promotion in a self-report study (Nkomo & Cox, 1990). From analyzing objective survey data for 231 universities, presence of a female or minority AA officer predicted the proportion of female or minority administrators five years later, respectively, with the higher the relative salary of the officer within the university, and thus presumably their status and ability to mobilize resources to get things done, the greater the effect (Pfeffer, Davis-Blake, & Julius, 1995). Studies have surveyed human resource managers to gather data on AA practices and proportions of women and minorities in management. Using structural equation analysis of 116 companies, equity-based (i.e. merit) and equality-based (i.e. target groups) human resource practices were related to the percentage of managers who were women or minorities, as was management support for EEO to minority proportion (Konrad & Linnehan, 1992). For 138 companies, formalized human resource management strategies to promote EEO and AA were in the main not related to women's and people of color's percentage in management and highest ranks (Konrad & Linnehan, 1995). This included identity-blind merit-based structures in which human resource practices do not identify protected groups, and management attitude, or being subject to lawsuits. Identity-conscious human resource management structures explicitly identifying their purpose for protected groups were weakly related to women's highest ranks and people of color in greatest percentages in management, and not being subject to compliance reviews to greater percentages of women in management (Konrad & Linnehan, 1995). The extent of formalization, comprehensiveness and management support of 294 Canadian employment equity programs (EEP) was correlated, weakly, with representative hiring from the external labor pool for management positions of female nonminorities and visible minorities (Leck, Saunders, & St. Onge, 1991), and of women and of male and female visible minorities but not of disabled persons and aboriginal peoples (Leck & Saunders, 1992a). EEP effectiveness explained additional variance in representative hiring for management positions of nonminority but not visible minority women (Leck & Saunders, 1992b; Leck, Saunders, & St. Onge, 1991) and of male and female visible minorities and women, but not disabled persons (Leck & Saunders, 1992a). In summary, affirmative action increases, although weakly, the advancement in management of women and perhaps minorities but not the disabled.

Politics

A political model of promotion is said to characterize the process as a negotiated reality, where the outcome is explained more by connections and interpersonal influence strategies, and less by objective qualifications, performance, and competence (Ferris, Buckley, & Allen, 1992), especially if situations are ambiguous and accountable such as managerial advancement decisions (Ferris & Judge, 1991). Political influence by candidates is defined as behavior designed to maximise short- or long-term interests, comprising primarily self-promotion and ingratiation (Ferris & Judge, 1991).

For middle manager positions, in chiefly interview studies of how promotion occurs in their organizations, politics were reported by candidates and decision-makers as influencing promotion through superiors' choice of managers for developmental opportunities such as training and task forces (Cianni & Romberger, 1995), by organizational connections (Deshpande, Schoderbek, & Joseph, 1994), and by identification of possible candidates, similarity of values and interests, bosses' level of personal comfort with candidates, candidate impression management and ingratiation, and promotion being a negotiated process (Ferris, Buckley, & Allen, 1992; Ruderman & Ohlott, 1994; Ruderman, Ohlott, & Kram, 1995). In a multivariate survey study, managers' use of supervisor-focused tactics based on ingratiation was related to higher overall career advancement, whereas job-focused tactics based on self-promotion were negatively related (Judge & Bretz, 1994). Women's progression from political naïviety to development may help reaching vice-president levels (Mainiero, 1994b). In surveys and interviews in 82 manufacturing and service organizations, organizational strategy was the major influence on promotion to middle manager, influencing who were the selectors, how the choice was made, the criteria utilized, and who was chosen (Ferris, Buckley, & Allen, 1992), resulting in a political process. Outsider CEOs were more likely to be chosen than insiders when organizational performance was poor but, suggesting political influence, especially when there were fewer insiders on the board of directors and less employee ownership, combined with the previous CEO being dismissed or younger than retirement age, or there being no heir apparent (Boeker & Goodstein, 1993; Cannella & Lubatkin, 1993; Cannella, Lubatkin, & Kapouch, 1991; Puffer & Weintrop, 1995). Political influence by candidates and selectors appears as important to managerial promotions as candidate performance, ability and human capital, and organization strategy, structure and needs (Deshpande, Schoderbeh, & Joseph, 1994; Ferris, Buckley, & Allen, 1992; Judge & Bretz, 1994; Ruderman & Ohlott, 1994; Ruderman, Ohlott, & Kram, 1995). In summary, partly supporting a political model of advancement, use of politics by candidates and decision-makers influences managerial career advancement, at least for middle manager to executive positions.

Promotion decisions

Interviews of successful candidates and their decision-makers have examined individual and organization factors perceived to influence managerial promotions. Promotion to middle and senior manager appears to be based on a combination of individual and organizational factors, meritorious and non-meritorious. The individual factors reported linked to promotion included ability, performance, work ethic, preparation, and results (Ferris, Buckley, & Allen, 1992; Ruderman & Ohlott, 1994). The organization factors were strategy, opportunity structure, messages sent by promotions, and long-range staffing goals. The social networks and political influence factors were to do with bosses' identification of, comfort with, and similarity to candidates, candidate impression management and ingratiation, and negotiation through mutual accommodation and adapting jobs for candidates (Ferris, Buckley, & Allen, 1992; Ruderman & Ohlott, 1994). Gender differences in 36 promotions were examined in one of the three companies of Ruderman and Ohlott (1994). Similar reasons were given for men's and women's promotion based on merit (Ruderman, Ohlott, & Kram, 1995). The key differences were bosses' reporting high personal comfort as important when they promoted men, but personal strength and familiarity with job responsibilities when they promoted women. Women, unlike men, reported having to push for the job after a trial. Bosses cited diversity when women were chosen on merit, whereas availability was cited for talented men. Women appeared to have to demonstrate personal strength and prove themselves extensively before they were promoted, in order to reduce perceived risk (Ruderman, Ohlott, & Kram, 1995).

Organization context

Resource dependency theory proposes that top staffing appointments (and removals) are affected by the organization's context (Pfeffer & Salancik, 1978). Top managers and executives are proposed to be selected who can cope with problems and critical internal and external contingencies of their environments. Managers and executives with more years of relevant organization experience who were older, and thus more likely to be insiders, were chosen as general managers of business units when low cost strategic goals were sought (Guthrie & Olian, 1991), and those with fewer years of organization experience, higher education, and in marketing and professional functions rather than engineering and operations, and thus more likely outsiders, when change was occurring through industry instability (Olian & Guthrie, 1991) or deregulation (Guthrie, Grimm, & Smith, 1991). Future CEOs were generalists who had had responsibility for an entire division or business within the same firm or industry when company or industry knowledge was needed and not change (Forbes & Piercy, 1991). Outsider CEOs were chosen, with specialties in one functional area, usually finance or law, gained from company changes, when change and specialized expertise were needed. From analyses of objective, often longitudinal data, insiders advanced to be CEO when insider knowledge was needed, whereas outsiders were more likely than insiders when times were unstable, change and diverse experience were needed, or organization performance was poor (Boeker & Goodstein, 1993; Cannella & Lubatkin, 1993; Cannella, Lubatkin, & Kapouch, 1991; Datta & Guthrie, 1994; Puffer & Weintrop, 1995). In summary, supporting resource dependency theory, organization context influences the attributes of those selected for top management.

INDIVIDUAL FACTORS

Traits

Traits are stable predispositions to certain kinds of actions that, when combined with other factors, are proposed to predict organizationally relevant behaviors, including managerial success (House, Howard, & Walker, 1991; Locke, 1991). Traits may predict advancement because individuals' motives, such as ambition, drive them to gratify their goals through managerial advancement, and because the tasks of the managerial role allow individuals to implement their self-concepts in occupational choice (Super, 1957) through fit. Traits such as cognitive ability, masculinity, and leadership motivation fit the tasks of the managerial role; intelligence, dominance, and masculinity were the traits perceived of leaders (Lord, De Vader, & Alliger, 1986). Traits may also indirectly influence advancement by interacting with the work situation (Fagenson, 1990a). Most studies have used standardized reliable, validated measures of personality and work-related motivation, and company records of managerial advancement, often being longitudinal predictions over many years, rendering confidence in the results. Studies are generally not conducted in which traits interact with the work situation, in which the relative importance of traits is compared to organizational or other individual factors, in which reverse effects are tested, in which comparisons occur of group differences (e.g. gender) in predicting advancement by traits, or in which traits chosen are based on job-relevance or vocational choice theory. Some traits can be classified within the 'Big Five' (Barrick & Mount, 1991). Conscientiousness, as will to achieve, measured as advancement motives, ambition and achievement motives, and openness to experience, measured as general cognitive ability, have clear support, with little evidence for extroversion, agreeableness, and emotional stability.

Advancement motives/ambition

Advancement motivation and need on entry to American Telephone & Telegraph company (AT&T) most predicted, of seven assessment centre dimensions, male managers' promotion into higher levels of management (Howard & Bray, 1990). Advancement motivation increased from entry up to 8 years, and at entry and at 8 years (strongly) predicted, and at 20 years less strongly predicted, 20-year managerial level. Ambition at entry at AT&T most predicted, of six composite measures from 37 personality and motivation tests, managerial level 20 years later (Howard & Bray, 1990). A single-item ambition measure was positively related to promotion and pay of executives and was as important as most human capital and organizational factors (Judge et al., 1995). In summary, advancement motives and ambition predict managerial career advancement.

Career motivation

Ratings of managers' overall career potential by trainers and by peers (trainees) in international management development programs predicted position levels 6 and 3.5 years later, respectively (Hofstede, 1994). Assessment center-rated career motivation in terms of desire for career advancement and development, but not ratings of knowledge or skill dimensions as communication and planning, predicted advancement to division level management 10 years later in an insurance company (Jones & Whitmore, 1995). Supervisor-rated and personality measures of managerial potential were related to managers' position level and pay in a single firm, similarly by gender and race when examined for pay (Thompson, 1994). In summary, career motivation is related to managerial career advancement.

Achievement motives

Achievement motivation as inner work standards, achievement motivation, and need for achievement, from personality tests and assessment center exercises, at 8 and 20 years rather than on entry predicted promotion to higher managerial levels after 20 years at AT&T (Howard & Bray, 1990). It was late-appearing in prediction becoming important by late, early career. Using the same sample, achievement motivation at entry predicted female but not male managers' level for those who stayed in AT&T to become middle managers 12 years later (Jacobs & McClelland, 1994). In summary, from one data set, achievement motivation may predict managerial level.

Work involvement

Managers' work involvement has been measured as either a personality trait, or as preferences. Work involvement, as work orientation, primacy of work, and occupational life theme from personality tests and assessment center exercises, predicted managers' promotion into higher levels of management at AT&T (Howard & Bray, 1990). Work involvement at 8 and especially 20 years, not entry, most strongly predicted 20-year managerial level, thus being late-appearing in prediction at late early career. Being family-involved on entry, measured from interviews, negatively predicted 20-year managerial level, with financial-acquisitive, service and occupational involvements positively predictive (Howard & Bray, 1990). Work centrality is chiefly measured as a single item according points to work out of several areas of life. It was not related to managers' promotions (Nkomo & Cox, 1990; Judge et al., 1995), with a positive exception (Whitely, Dougherty, & Dreher, 1991), nor to managers' and executives' levels (Judge et al., 1995; Schneer & Reitman, 1995; Yuen, 1995). Work centrality and significance were related to executives' and managers' pay (Judge et al., 1995; Lobel & St. Clair, 1992; Schneer & Reitman, 1995), although there were nonsignificant links (Whitely, Dougherty, & Dreher, 1991; Yuen, 1995). Preference for high income, but not for meaningful work, was positively related to male and female managers' pay (Jacobs, 1992). For mostly managers (some professionals), family-oriented women with preschoolers received higher merit increases than family-oriented men with preschoolers, and career-oriented women with preschoolers received lower merit increases than career-oriented women with preschoolers (Lobel & St. Clair, 1992), suggesting allocation based on conformity to gender role stereotypes. In summary, work involvement as personality may be related to managerial level, and work centrality in life is positively related to managers' pay but not promotion or level.

Self-monitoring

High self-monitors are said to regulate or control themselves according to situational and interpersonal cues, adjusting their self-presentations, whereas low self-monitors behave according to how they feel, being less attuned to role expectations and about making a positive impression on others (Snyder & Gangestad, 1982). Male and female managers in early career who were high self-monitors achieved more cross-company promotions five years later and obtained more internal promotions when they stayed in the same company than low self-monitors (Kilduff & Day, 1994). In a structural equation test, management graduates who were high self-monitors initiated more mentoring, which led to gaining more mentoring which, in turn, led to higher career advancement of promotion and pay (Turban & Dougherty, 1994). In summary, the few studies suggest that self-monitoring is related positively to managerial promotions and perhaps pay.

Motivation to manage

According to role motivation theory, motivation to change, the extent to which certain individuals enjoy and perform well in managerial positions in hierarchical organizations, should result in managerial success (Miner, 1993). Motivation to manage was assessed in 36 studies, 25 of managers of which seven were predictive over three to five years. Motivation to manage was moderately related to managers' success as advancement potential, hierarchic level and pay, and to business school students' managerial career choice, similarly for the 1960s to the 1990s (Miner, 1993; Miner, Ebrahimi, & Wachtel, 1995). The effects were found for hierarchic systems but not professional, task and group domains (Miner, 1993). Desire to compete and to exercise power were the most highly predictive subscales. A meta-analysis of 26 studies found that motivation to manage was related, albeit weakly, to managers' position level and pay, and to students' intention to pursue a career in management (Carson & Gilliard, 1993). In summary, supporting hierarchic role motivation theory, motivation to manage predicts career intentions to enter management and managerial career advancement.

Power motives

Three studies used the data of the AT&T sample (Howard & Bray, 1990). The leadership motive pattern on entry distinguished upper management men and women at higher levels (combining those in AT&T and those who left) from those at lower levels 12 years later (Jacobs & McClelland, 1994). The leadership motive pattern is a high need for power with low affiliation needs, tempered with high self-control. Need for power was positively related to men's and women's attained management level. Helpless power at entry was higher for those who remained in lower management levels than for those who attained upper levels 12 years later (Jacobs & McClelland, 1994). High responsible power, combining power motivation and responsibility, predicted managerial level after 16 years in AT&T for men in nontechnical jobs (Winter, 1991). Need for power of university women in senior year did not predict holding a supervisor job or not at age 35, 14 years later. It predicted career advancement comprising improved salary, status, or control positively and more for women in power-relevant jobs than women in nonpower-relevant jobs (self-employed, small business owners, technical managers; Jenkins, 1994). The positive relationship was for relational power jobs (psychologists, noncollege teachers) and not for directive power jobs (college faculty, journalists, nontechnical business executives) such as management. In summary, need for power is related to managerial career advancement depending on job type.

Masculinity/instrumentality

According to gender schema theory (Bem, 1981), gender role traits influence the way individuals organize and process information. The 'masculine' gender role is an instrumental, task orientation focusing on getting the job done or problem solved (Bem, 1981). Individuals high in masculinity process information in masculine terms, and should perceive themselves as suited to the managerial role. The managerial role is perceived as requiring masculine traits of leadership, dominance, forcefulness, tough-mindedness, lack of emotion, independence, and aggressiveness, as observed primarily in business students (e.g. Schein & Mueller, 1992; Schein, Mueller, Lituchy, & Liu, 1996). Masculine individuals emerged as leaders compared to feminine, in groups of undergraduate business students working throughout the semester on class presentations and assignments (Kent & Moss, 1994). In cross-sectional studies, higher level managers reported greater masculinity than lower level managers, male or female (Chusmir & Koberg, 1991; Chusmir, Koberg, & Stecher, 1992; Fagenson, 1990b), although reverse effects could occur. The lack of gender different effects does not support the gender role model (see Gutek, 1993) suggesting women have difficulty in using the sex-role behaviors needed for managing others, especially masculinity. In summary, masculinity is positively related to men's and women's managerial levels.

Self-confidence

Managers' self-confidence was related positively to hierarchical level for men or women (Chusmir, Koberg, & Stecher, 1992) but was not related to hierarchical level when masculinity was included for the same sample (Chusmir & Koberg, 1991). Self-confidence in relation to one's job was not related to managers' and executives' promotion and managerial level, whether male or female (Tharenou & Conroy, 1994). Self-confidence did not lead directly to managerial career advancement comprising level and pay in a structural equation test, but did so indirectly through increasing career encouragement and training and development, similarly for men and women (Tharenou, Latimer, & Conroy, 1994). Reverse effects did not occur on self-confidence. In analyses of the one data set, self-confidence had inconsistent gender differences in the prediction of managerial level, weakly related to male but not female managers' level (Koberg, Chusmir, & Carlin, 1992) or giving no gender differences (Chusmir, Kobert, & Stecher, 1992). Self-confidence was negatively related to female but positively to male public service managers' levels (Melamed, 1996b). On entry to AT&T and at 8 and 20 years, self-esteem, high feelings of self-worth, very weakly predicted 20-year managerial level (Howard & Bray, 1990). In summary, self-confidence is inconsistently related to managers' levels.

General cognitive ability

General cognitive ability, how much and how quickly a person learns, has been measured by validated, reliable verbal and numerical reasoning tests and at times other ability tests. Cognitive ability in early career predicted male and female oil company managers' job grades 5 to 10 years later controlling for skills (Shore, 1992), at entry predicted managerial level 20 years later for AT&T managers (Howard & Bray, 1990), and in the first two years of service predicted job level attained from the third to the twelfth year for oil company managers, as did management judgment (Sparks, 1990). Using the sample of oil company managers, early cognitive ability more strongly predicted job level 14–15 years later for those less successful in early career than more successful, measured as age-graded job level attained in the first four or five years (Dreher & Bretz, 1991), the authors speculating that acquiring knowledge, skills and information depends on cognitive ability when individuals are competing without the advantages of early career signals of high potential, and thus sponsorship. By contrast, general cognitive ability did not predict male middle managers' monetary bonuses one, two, three or four years later, nor did pre-employment cognitive ability (Tziner, Meir, Dahan, & Birati, 1994), or predict the promotions and pay of MBAs 3.5 to 4.5 years after graduation except in interaction with conscientiousness (O'Reilly & Chatman, 1994). A standard deviation increase in conscientiousness at higher cognitive ability levels was worth U.S. $18 780 more in salary and 0.56 more in promotions than at lower levels, similarly by race and ethnicity (O'Reilly & Chatman, 1994). Verbal and nonverbal reasoning were related to supervisors' and managers' level and pay (Thompson, 1994). In summary, general cognitive ability alone or combined with circumstances or other traits predicts long-term managerial career advancement from entry.

Other traits of the 'Big Five'

Extroversion was related to male but not female managers' managerial level (Melamed, in press). Conscientiousness comprising achievement, endurance and order did not directly predict promotion and pay of MBAs 3.5 to 4.5 years after graduation, but did when they were higher not lower in cognitive ability (O'Reilly & Chatman, 1994). Positiveness (i.e. optimism), measured at entry, predicted managerial level 20 years later at AT&T (Howard & Bray, 1990). Using structural equation analysis of the AT&T data, optimism, measured by optimism and general adjustment, and leadership role attractiveness, measured by attraction to the leader role and aversion to the follower role, predicted managerial level taking into account measurement error, stability of variables, and verbal and quantitative ability and education (House, Howard, & Walker, 1991). Entry optimism predicted 8-year managerial level, and 8-year leadership attraction predicted 20-year managerial level. In the only reverse effect, 8-year managerial level increased leadership role attraction at 20 years (House, Howard, & Walker, 1991). Personality traits, including extroversion and cognitive ability, did not start increasing managerial level until employees were 28 to 44 years, and had greatest effects when greater than 44 years (Melamed, 1996a).

Human Capital

Human capital theory proposes that investments in education, on-the-job training and work experience result in increased productivity, which leads to increased pay and job status, causing upward mobility in free market contests (Becker, 1975). Individuals choose to improve their human capital, which results in payoffs later in their careers (Becker, 1993). Gender differences in individuals' chosen investments and types of jobs then explain differences in pay and status. In signaling theory (Spence, 1973, 1974), employers make selection decisions guessing the applicant's productive capabilities from imperfect information. They therefore use signals, the applicants' investments in education, job experience and training, to estimate the probability the applicant will be productive based on conditional probabilities established through past experience. These signals of productivity have rates of return in pay and advancement. Studies providing empirical links for human capital inputs are multivariate, chiefly cross-sectional, self-report survey designs often assessing the importance of another factor (e.g. mentoring) for managerial advancement, and initially controlling human capital. Apart from training and development—usually of interest in its own right—the links found for human capital are for relative importance often when used as controls, prior to other predictor sets, in regression analyses.

Training and development

In human capital theory, on-the-job training increases employee pay and other rewards as work experience increases, because productivity increases, and employers are said to make specific investments such as executive training of their employees (Becker, 1993). Training and development are also proposed to lead to promotion to top management by developing knowledge, skills, credibility, and credentials and thus expertise and power (Ragins & Sundstrom, 1989). Development, learning activities for personal and professional growth and the long term as opposed to training for immediate job performance, is used to prepare managers for future jobs and to lead to promotion (e.g. Campion, Cheraskin, & Stevens, 1994). Using a case study approach, when an organization was faced with many middle managers and supervisors retiring, the strategy to replace them was to prepare individuals for advancement by training (Sandwith, 1993).

Participation in training and development courses over one's career was positively related to manufacturing managers' promotion and pay (Scandura, 1992) and to manager's and executives' managerial levels but not promotion (Tharenou & Conroy, 1994). For research and development professionals, whereas technical training was either not or negatively related, participation in managerial development increased the likelihood of gaining lower level supervisory positions four years later, all objective company measures (Roberts &

Biddle, 1994), and of assessment as promotable to technical management by supervisors, especially when higher on self-reported managerial interests and abilities (Cordero, DiTomaso, & Farris, 1994). Managerial interests also increased promotability indirectly through managerial development opportunities (Cordero, DiTomaso, & Farris, 1994). From company records, job rotation was positively related to managers' and professionals' pay growth and promotion rate (Campion, Cheraskin, & Stevens, 1994), job rotation opportunities in the first year were related to managers' salary progression four years later (Orpen, 1994), and entering by the company's 14-month on-the-job trainee program compared to direct hiring or internal promotion predicted greater managerial promotion and salary progression over 10 years for male and female public utility company managers, but nontrainees reached higher management levels (Sheridan et al., 1990). In a later analysis of the same sample, the training program increased promotion only on the first job and not subsequent jobs (Sheridan, Slocum, & Buda, in press). Implemented assessment center developmental recommendations were not related to attaining division level management 10 years later in an insurance company, nor was participation versus nonparticipation for nominated nonparticipants (Jones & Whitmore, 1995). In summary, consistent with human capital theory, participation in training and development increases managerial advancement, especially if management development.

Ragins and Sundstrom (1989) argued that access to training is used as part of a pattern of tracking that grooms men for promotion into management more than women. Studies have been of comparable men and women. For female but not male managers and executives, being prevented from attending training was related to lack of organizational promotion (Tharenou & Conroy, 1994). Using structural equation analysis, participation in training and development substantially increased managerial advancement for managers and executives, and not the reverse, more for men than women (Tharenou, Latimer, & Conroy, 1994). For managers in internationally related occupations, being designated in a fast-track development program earned men $10 900 per year but women $200 per year (Egan & Bendick, 1994). In summary, participation in training and development increases men's managerial career advancement more than comparable women's.

Age

In career tournament theory, age timetables are proposed in promotion (Rosenbaum, 1984, 1990). Advancement is said to decline with age because employees who do not win early in the tournament are eliminated or restricted later in play to consolation rounds, with sharp declines after a critical age. Some studies are consistent with age—advancement timetables. Age was negatively related to managers' promotion rate (Scandura, 1992) and supervisor-rated promotability (Igbaria & Wormley, 1995). Older managers plateaued more than younger, by having more years in their current position (Igbaria & Wormley, 1995; Tremblay & Roger, 1993). For younger but not older managers, position tenure and education were related positively to promotability (Cox & Nkomo, 1992), and number of jobs, functions and organizations to managerial level and pay (Herriot et al., 1993). High fliers (i.e. younger than their job grade norm) had the highest advancement expectations, and plateaued managers (i.e. older than their grade norm) the lowest for managers in an multinational corporation (Nicholson, 1993). Managerial level increases with age to a certain point and then the rate slows, the curvilinear link supporting career tournaments. Managers' age was related to supervisor-rated promotability when below but not over 45 years (Cox & Nkomo, 1992), and to job grade up to middle manager level with higher levels decreasingly related (Nicholson, 1993). Age positively and age squared negatively were related to the managerial level of employees ranging in level (Haberfeld, 1992). Pay may increase continuously with age. Age and age squared were related to CEOs' pay (Ingham & Thompson, 1995). In summary, there is some support for career tournament age timetables for promotion and managerial level.

Other studies do not test curvilinear links. Age has been used as a proxy for work experience to test human capital theory (Strober, 1990). Age was not related to male and female managers' and executives' promotion (Cox & Harquail, 1991; O'Reilly & Chatman, 1994; Tharenou & Conroy, 1994), with one positive exception (Judge et al., 1995). Age was not related to managers' and executives' managerial levels (Cox & Harquail, 1991; Tharenou & Conroy, 1994), with one positive exception (Herriot et al., 1993). Age may indirectly increase managerial career advancement. Using structural equation analysis, age increased male managers' and executives' years work experience more than females' which, in turn, increased participation in training and development, subsequently increasing managerial career advancement (Tharenou, Latimer, & Conroy, 1994). The impact of men's age was totally captured through work experience, unlike women's, for whom age directly increased managerial advancement. Age was positively related to male and female managers' and executives' pay (Cannings, 1991; Herriot et al., 1993, 1994; Ingham & Thompson, 1995; Judge et al., 1995; Scandura, 1992), although there are nonsignificant links (O'Reilly & Chatman, 1994; Schneer & Reitman, 1993) and negative links with merit increases (Lobel & St. Clair, 1992). In summary, overall, not supporting human capital theory, age is comparatively unimportant to managerial promotions and managerial levels but, in support of human capital theory, has a distinct positive link with managers' pay.

Education

Human capital and signaling theories predict that education increases managerial level and pay, the former theory through increasing knowledge and skills and thus productivity (Becker, 1993) and the latter through providing information when knowledge about potential productivity is imperfect (Spence, 1974; Strober, 1990). Education is likely not to be used as a signal for managerial promotion, because promotion is usually internal to the organization, where more certain information exists on candidates' performance than by external entry.

Education level was not related to male or female managers' and executives' promotion (Cannings & Montmarquette, 1991b; Judge et al., 1995; Powell & Butterfield, 1994; Scandura, 1992; Stroh, Brett, & Reilly, 1992; Tharenou & Conroy, 1994), nor to supervisor-rated promotability of black or white managers (Igbaria & Wormley, 1995), with one positive exception for promotability ratings of black and white managers (Greenhaus & Parasuraman, 1993). Education level was positively related to female and male managers' levels (Gattiker & Larwood, 1990; Melamed, 1996b; Tharenou & Conroy, 1994) and entry to management, although education change was not (Shenhav, 1992). Two studies applying structural equation analysis showed indirect as well as direct effects of education level. Education level directly increased the hierarchical level of jobs to which university administrative employees ranging in level had been promoted, but also indirectly, by increasing the status and level of the prior position held (Johnsrud & Heck, 1994). Education level increased managers' and executives' managerial advancement, similarly for men and women, but indirectly did so by increasing men's participation in training but not women's (Tharenou, Latimer, & Conroy, 1994). Education level was positively related to managers' pay (Gattiker & Larwood, 1990; Jacobs, 1992; Martin, 1994; Reskin & Ross, 1992; Scandura, 1992; Stroh, Brett, & Reilly, 1992; Whitely & Coetsier, 1993), although there were also no links (Cannings, 1991; Dreher & Ash, 1990; Lobel & St. Clair, 1992). In summary, supporting human capital and signaling theories, education level is not related to managers' promotion but is related to managerial level and pay.

Type of degree and educational institution are also relevant. Bachelors' degrees as opposed to noncollege education were positively related to managers' levels (Herriot et al., 1994) and pay (Egan & Bendick, 1994; Herriot et al., 1994; Judge et al., 1995; Martin, 1994), although not promotion (Judge et al., 1995) nor Singaporean business graduates' level or pay (Yuen, 1995). Bachelor degrees and professional majors in business or engineering predicted the first and subsequent promotions over a 10-year period of entry level public utility managers, with lack of them having negative effects for low performers, and resulted in faster promotion than for those with comparable performance who had different educational backgrounds (Sheridan, Slocum, & Buda, in press). Law degrees were more highly related to executives' pay than other degrees, but not to promotion (Judge et al., 1995). Masters' degrees, usually MBAs, were positively related to managers' pay (Bretz & Judge, 1994; Dreher & Ash, 1990; Egan & Bendick, 1994; Judge et al., 1995; Whitely & Coetsier,

1993; Whitely, Dougherty, & Dreher, 1991) but not managers' promotions (Dreher & Ash, 1990; Whitely & Coetsier, 1993; Whitely, Dougherty, & Dreher, 1991) nor pay, level and overall advancement (Bretz & Judge, 1994; Judge & Bretz, 1994; Judge et al., 1995). Masters' degrees had negative links with private sector scientists' and engineers' entry to management (Shenhav, 1992). PhDs had negative links to entry to and level in management (Bretz & Judge, 1994; Judge & Bretz, 1994; Shenhav, 1992) with a positive exception for managers' pay (Bretz & Judge, 1994). Ivy League schools and quality degrees versus others were positively related to managers' and executives' pay but not promotion (Judge et al., 1995). Grade point average was not related to managers' and executives' advancement (Bretz & Judge, 1994; Judge & Bretz, 1994; Judge et al., 1995). Men in internationally related occupations received greater additional pay per year than women from bachelor and graduate degrees, law or business degrees, and degrees from prestigious schools (Egan & Bendick, 1994). This is consistent with signaling theory. Employers offer returns on education using probability distributions that interact with unalterable observable indices such as gender, resulting in the rate of return to men's external signaling of education applying only to other men and not to women, for whom payoffs are different (Spence, 1973). In summary, gaining a bachelors' degree is positively related to managers' level and pay but not promotion, masters' degrees are related positively only to managers' pay, and PhDs decrease managerial advancement. Women may gain less managerial advancement indirectly or directly from educational attainment than men.

Work experience/tenure

Years of company tenure were positively related to managers' and executives' promotions (Cox & Harquail, 1991; Naff, 1994; Nkomo & Cox, 1990; Stroh, Brett, & Reilly, 1992), with one nonsignificant exception (Scandura, 1992). Although company tenure was positively related, average job tenure (i.e. job change) was negatively related to managers' promotion and level (Cox & Harquail, 1991), suggesting loyalty is rewarded. Similarly, stable company tenure from the second five years of employment, combined with less inter-firm and more intra-firm job change was found for men who rose to CEO status (Forbes & Piercy, 1991; Piercy & Forbes, 1991). Company tenure and company tenure squared were positively related to managers' promotions (Stroh, Brett, & Reilly, 1992), suggesting promotion continues to increase with tenure. Years of company tenure were positively related to managerial entry (Shenhav, 1992) and managers' levels (Herriot et al., 1993; Yuen, 1995) for men's and women's levels (Melamed, 1996b) with one exception (Gattiker & Larwood, 1990). It took fewer years of company experience for male middle managers in a bank to reach that level than female (Martin & Morgan, 1995; Morgan, Schor, & Martin, 1993). Company tenure was positively related to managers' pay (Cannings, 1991; Gattiker & Larwood,

1990; Herriot et al., 1993; Lobel & St. Clair, 1992; Reskin & Ross, 1992; Scandura, 1992; Stroh, Brett, & Reilly, 1992; Whitely, Dougherty, & Dreher, 1991; Yuen, 1995), with one negative exception (Judge et al., 1995). Company tenure but not company tenure squared were related to managers' pay (Stroh, Brett, & Reilly, 1992), suggesting a linear link. Using structural equation analysis, work experience of occupational and organizational years indirectly increased male managers' and executives' managerial advancement comprising level and pay more than females' through increasing men's participation in training and development more (Tharenou, Latimer, & Conroy, 1994). In summary, supporting human capital theory and also notions of rewards for loyalty, company tenure is positively related to managers' promotion, levels and pay.

Years of position tenure were negatively related to black and white managers' promotability ratings (Greenhaus & Parasuraman, 1993), and positively related to university executives' and managers' pay (Pfeffer & Ross, 1990). Suggesting a curvilinear link, position tenure in the current level was related to middle managers' promotion, being lowest in the first year, peaking in the second, and declining thereafter (Gibbs, 1995), and position tenure positively and position tenure squared negatively were related to managers' overall advancement (Judge & Bretz, 1994). Candidate employment in the hiring department, being at the highest grade and years at that grade, was positively related to panel evaluations and referrals for the senior executive service (Powell & Butterfield, 1994). Only employment in the hiring department was positively related to the selecting official's actual selection decision of those referred; years at the highest grade were negatively related. Position tenure squared was not related to building society CEOs' pay (Ingham & Thompson, 1994), implying a linear link. In summary, promotion may rise, peak and fall with position tenure, and position tenure may be positively related to managers' pay.

Total years of work experience were positively related to managers' promotion (Cox & Harquail, 1991; Dreher & Ash, 1990; Stroh, Brett, & Reilly, 1992; Whitely & Coetsier, 1993; Whitely, Dougherty, & Dreher, 1991), and negatively related to panel evaluations and referral decisions for the senior executive service, but not to the selecting official's actual selection decision of those referred (Powell & Butterfield, 1994). Total years of work experience had a curvilinear relationship with panel evaluations; highest evaluations were received by applicants with 10 years experience and lower evaluations as experience increased beyond 10 years. Total years of work experience were not related to managers' levels (Schneer & Reitman, 1994a, 1995) but combined with organizational and occupational years were related to managers' and executives' promotion and managerial level (Tharenou & Conroy, 1994). Total years of work experience were positively related to managers' pay (Dreher & Ash, 1990; Martin, 1994; Stroh, Brett, & Reilly, 1992; Whitely & Coetsier, 1993; Whitely, Dougherty, & Dreher, 1991) with no links in some early career studies (Cox & Harquail, 1991; Schneer & Reitman, 1995) and a negative link in mid-career (Schneer & Reitman, 1994a, 1995). Pay appears to rise, peak and then decrease in rate of rise with years of employment. Total years of work experience were positively related and total years squared negatively related to male or female managers' pay (Cannings, 1991; Jacobs, 1992; Martin, 1994), with one exception suggesting a linear link (Stroh, Brett, & Reilly, 1992). In summary, supporting human capital theory, total years of work experience are positively related to managerial promotions but, supporting a career tournament view, may have a curvilinear link with managers' pay.

Employment gaps

Employment gaps have often been measured as gaps/no gaps (continuous employment), reducing variance. Employment gaps were negatively related to managers' promotions (Dreher & Ash, 1990) when low not high in socio-economic status (Whitely, Dougherty, & Dreher, 1991), but not related to managers' levels (Bretz & Judge, 1994; Schneer & Reitman, 1995; Yuen, 1995) or overall advancement (Judge & Bretz, 1994). Employment gaps were not related (Bretz & Judge, 1994; Schneer & Reitman, 1994a; Stroh, Brett, & Reilly, 1992; Whitely & Coetsier, 1993), positively related (Whitely, Dougherty, & Dreher, 1991), and negatively related (Yuen, 1995) to managers' pay. Employment gaps were related to lower pay for male but not female MBA graduates in early career (Schneer & Reitman, 1990), suggesting adverse effects for men who do not follow a traditional career path. For the same sample six years later, the impact of the early career employment gap on mid-career pay was not sustained when controlling for earlier pay, and mid-career gaps reduced mid-career pay, similarly for men and women (Schneer & Reitman, 1994b). In another MBA sample, early career employment gaps decreased early career pay and accumulated gaps at mid-career decreased mid-career pay, controlling for earlier pay (Schneer & Reitman, 1995). In summary, employment gaps may be negatively related to promotion, are not related to managerial level, and are either not or negatively related to managers' pay.

Work hours

Hours worked per week were not (Judge et al., 1995; Whitely, Dougherty, & Dreher, 1991) or positively (Whitely & Coetsier, 1993) related to managers' promotions. Hours worked per week were related to managers' job levels (Bretz & Judge, 1994) and pay (Bretz & Judge, 1994; Jacobs, 1992; Judge et al., 1995; Schneer & Reitman, 1993, 1995; Whitely & Coetsier, 1993; Whitely, Dougherty, & Dreher, 1991). Hours worked per week were not related to managers' pay (Reskin & Ross, 1992) including in mid-career for either early career or mid-career hours, when controlling for earlier pay

(Schneer & Reitman, 1994a). Hours worked per week were related to managers' overall advancement (Judge & Bretz, 1994). Evenings worked per month and desired work hours were related to executives' pay and promotion (Judge et al., 1995). Reverse effects were not tested for work hours. An additional eight hours work per week gained male middle managers in internationally related occupations an estimated extra $7300 per year but female managers an extra $4300, controlling relevant variables (Egan & Bendick, 1994). In summary, weekly hours are positively related to managers' pay.

Job change

Managers appear to change jobs frequently, every two years in a British study (Nicholson, 1990), and increased changing jobs and company relocations from 1978 to 1989 (Stroh, Brett, & Reilly, 1994). Managers on an executive search firm's files gave advancement as the reason for job search (Krausz & Reshef, 1992). Number of company/employer changes was not related to managers' promotion (Whitely & Coetsier, 1993), and organization and geographic moves were negatively related to managers' and executives' promotion (Tharenou & Conroy, 1994). Changing companies more frequently was associated, weakly, with managers' lower levels (Brett, Stroh, & Reilly, 1992a; Ellis & Heneman, 1990) or not related to managers' levels (Melamed, in press). Number of employing organizations was related positively to managers' levels and pay for those young but not middle-aged and older (Herriot et al., 1993). Number of company changes was not related to managers' pay (Cox & Harquail, 1991; Ellis & Heneman, 1990; Stroh, Brett, & Reilly, 1992; Whitely & Coetsier, 1993), and was negatively related for men and women (Brett, Stroh, & Reilly, 1992a). For managers from middle managers to CEOs, not changing companies increased advancement (Brett, Stroh, & Reilly, 1992a; Ellis & Heneman, 1994; Forbes & Piercy, 1991; Piercy & Forbes, 1991). In early and not mid-career, female Singaporean business graduates reported limited organization change was related to lower pay and age-adjusted managerial levels (Chi-Ching, 1992). Number of position changes was positively related to managers' levels (Melamed, 1996b) and to younger but not middle and older managers' levels and pay (Herriot et al., 1993). In summary, changing employers and positions is inconsistently related to managers' levels, and changing employers is not related to managers' pay.

Relocation moves for current and previous employers predicted high managerial level and pay for Fortune 500 transferees, most middle managers (Brett, Stroh, & Reilly, 1992a; Stroh, Brett, & Reilly, 1992). Relocation for the company was the most important predictor of several factors of female managers' managerial level, more than males' (Brett, Stroh, & Reilly, 1992a), and managers at high levels, mostly men, had not moved for their spouse's career (Stroh, Brett, & Reilly, 1992). The most highly paid managers relocated rather than not, and were promoted in their companies rather than changing companies. Relocation increased managerial levels for public sector middle managers (Lewis, 1992) and senior executive service officers (Naff, 1994). By contrast, relocations were not related to the pay or level of the male 45–50-year-old managers on an executive search firm's files (Ellis & Heneman, 1990). Moving for advancement was related to men's but not women's managerial levels (Tharenou & Conroy, 1994). In summary, job change by relocation may be positively related to managers' levels and pay.

Investment in human capital in early career is important to early and later managerial career advancement. Workforce experience, education, and employment gaps were more important than other individual variables for managers' advancement in early career (Cox & Harquail, 1991; Schneer & Reitman, 1990, 1995; Whitely & Coetsier, 1993; Whitely, Dougherty, & Dreher, 1991) although there is little comparison with organizational variables. Human capital (education, position tenure, job and organization changes) gained managers more advancement in early than in late career (Cox & Nkomo, 1992; Herriot et al., 1993). At an early career stage, career choices of short organization tenure and more job changes combined with choosing occupations with high levels and prestige explained managerial level, but other individual variables and organization opportunity structures did not for British employees ranging in level, 43% subordinates (Melamed, 1996a). Managerial level was more explained by human capital inputs, organizational structure, and career choices in late (>44 years) career than early (18 to 28 years old), conflicting with greater links of human capital with the advancement of younger than older managers (Cox & Nkomo, 1992; Herriot et al., 1993). Education level, but also traits, parenthood (negatively), and industry type and company size did not increase managerial level until mid-career when employees were 28 to 44 years old, reaching their full impact when greater than 44 years in late career (Melamed, 1996a).

Managerial Skills

Skills are important for leaders' effectiveness because they provide specific capacities for action from traits (Locke, 1991), and should increase performance and subsequently advancement. Managerial skills have been classified as people and administrative/task skills (Locke, 1991). Management performance has been classified into interpersonal dealings and communication, leadership and supervision (both people domains), technical activities and the mechanics of management (the task domain), and personal behavior and skills (Borman & Brush, 1993). Studies have not been based on theories of managerial skills or performance, and do not consider indirect links of skills to advancement through performance, nor the relative importance of managerial skills and performance compared to other factors.

Skills

Cross-sectional usually self-report studies have assessed managers' work-related skills, often with validated, reliable measures, as background experiences, skills demonstrated in assessment centers, and on-the-job leadership skills. Background experiences (self-rated leadership, general responsibility, personal financial management) were related positively to supervisors' and managers' levels and pay in a single firm (Thompson, 1994). Interpersonal skills and administrative skills assessed by an assessment center at entry predicted managerial level 20 years later at AT&T (Howard & Bray, 1990). For those who ultimately remained at lower management, managerial skills assessed in assessment centers decreased by the eighth year and further by the twentieth year compared to the increase for those who rose to higher levels in AT&T (Howard, 1991). Interpersonal skills and performance skills from an assessment center in early career each predicted oil company managers' job grade 5 to 10 years later, similarly for men and women, controlling for cognitive ability, the 'other' skill, and the overall assessment center rating (Shore, 1992). Female managers' higher performance skills than males' did not translate into higher advancement. Male middle managers' managerial performance, communication and interpersonal interaction abilities assessed in an assessment center did not predict monetary bonuses over the next four years (Tziner et al., 1994).

Subordinate- and self-reported problem-solving, planning/organizing, networking, clarifying, and motivating behaviors were correlated with mid- and upper-level managers' age-graded managerial level, similarly for self- and subordinate-reports (Kim & Yukl, 1995), although several behaviors were not consistently related or related at all. Bosses' assessments of 20 of 25 skills predicted managers' organization promotion (demoted/termination, no/lateral movement, promoted) 2 to 2.5 years later (McCauley & Lombardo, 1990). Most predictive were: perseveres, hires talented staff, builds team, learns quickly, easy with job transition, is flexible, resourceful, and is decisive. In early career, supervisory skills, technical skills, skills in critical functional areas and, additionally in mid- and late career, broadening and general management skills, appeared to facilitate men reaching CEO using archival data (Forbes & Piercy, 1991) and women reaching vice-president levels using self-report interviews (Mainiero, 1994a). In studies without comparison groups, retrospective interviews of senior executives or ratings by supervisors and peers, perhaps subject to self-serving distortions, indicated that poor managerial skills, including adaptability, strategic, interpersonal and participative skills derailed executives and managers in late career (McCauley & Ruderman, 1991; Van Velsor & Leslie, 1995). Derailed managers resign, are fired, retire early, do not rise further with high potential, or rise and fail.

The managerial skills found related to managerial advancement can be classified into people skills, both interpersonal and communication (interpersonal, clarifying, conflict management, team-building, networking) and leadership and supervision (leadership, motivating, supervisory, supporting), administrative skills/mechanics of management and technical skills (planning, decision-making, problem-solving, meeting objectives, administration, delegating, hiring, technical skills, performance), and personal behavior and skills (adaptability, responsibility, learning, flexibility, perseverance, resourceful). In summary, consistent with Borman and Brush's (1993) managerial performance dimensions, interpersonal, leadership, task, and personal skills are related to entry into and managerial advancement at all career stages, including later advancement.

Job performance

Studies of job performance have used chiefly company records of supervisor performance appraisal ratings, which are subject to errors and validity problems, reducing confidence in what the construct is being measured. Managers' job performance has been said to comprise task and contextual performance, the latter being the 'extras' employers look for in outstanding performance, such as citizenship and prosocial behavior (Landy, Shankster, & Kohler, 1994). Managers' job performance is usually judged by superiors, for whom high contextual performance is thought to lead to early promotion recommendations (Landy, Shankster, & Kohler, 1994). Studies are multivariate with substantial statistical controls.

Using across-organization samples, job performance was not related to managerial promotions, levels, or pay (Cannings, 1991; Cox & Harquail, 1991; Nkomo & Cox, 1990), or to panel evaluations and referral decisions for the senior executive service, but was positively related to the selecting official's actual selection of those referred (Powell & Butterfield, 1994). Successful early performance in critical functional areas was found for men reaching CEO status from archival data (Forbes & Piercy, 1991; Piercy & Forbes, 1991) and reported by women reaching vice-president level (Mainiero, 1994a). Using samples from single firms, job performance was related to promotability ratings of municipality supervisors by their managers, more for those below 45 years than above (Cox & Nkomo, 1992), to middle managers' promotion for performance measured currently and last year but not two years earlier (Gibbs, 1995), to male managers' promotions (Korenman & Neumark, 1991), and to entry to first level supervisor positions four years later for technical professionals (Roberts & Biddle, 1994). For US private sector white male scientists and engineers, managers came from higher paid technical workers, a proxy for performance, and successful managers were also more successful technicians in terms of pay (Biddle & Roberts, 1994). In summary, particularly within single firms, managers' job performance is positively related to managerial entry and advancement, especially for technical jobs.

Five studies analysed the same data set in multivariate analyses with substantial controls. For pairs of lower- to middle-level managers and their supervisors in three companies in communications, banks and electronics, job performance was related to supervisor-rated promotability for younger (23–49 or 23–54 years) but not older (50–63 or 55–63 years) managers (Siegel, 1993), consistent with the direction in Cox and Nkomo (1992). Younger managers appear preferred for promotion despite similar performance by older managers, with performance gaining managers more advancement in early than in late career. Using the communications company managers, job performance was positively related to promotability and to not being non-plateaued (Igbaria & Greenhaus, 1992). For black and white, chiefly managerial (rest professional) information systems employees of one of the companies, job performance was related to supervisor-rated promotability and future career advancement opportunities and to career plateauing (Igbaria & Wormley, 1995). Supervisor-rated internal performance attributions of ability and effort were not related to the advancement measures. Using the full sample from the three companies, black lower and middle level managers were rated lower on job performance by their supervisors than comparable whites, resulting in lower promotability assessments (Greenhaus, Parasuraman, & Wormley, 1990). Being black thus resulted in lower performance ratings which resulted in lower promotability ratings. In another analysis, blacks were rated as less promotable than whites primarily because they were rated as performing less effectively, but also because their job performance was less likely to be attributed to their ability than comparable performance of whites (Greenhaus & Parasuraman, 1993). Supervisors' ability attributions for the performance of their subordinate managers were associated with their promotability ratings; the strongest impact was when performance was moderately rather than highly successful, perhaps because performance is open to different explanations. In summary, supervisor performance attributions are not consistently related to managers' promotability ratings, but being black results in lower performance ratings and lower internal attributions for job performance than being white, resulting in lower promotability ratings.

Family

Psychological and labor market theories propose that a family has a negative impact on women's managerial career advancement, and a positive one on men's. Male managers are usually married fathers, whereas female managers are likely to be single or married and, if married, childless (Brett, Stroh, & Reilly, 1992a; Gutek, Searle, & Klepa, 1991; Lobel & St. Clair, 1992; Schneer & Reitman, 1995; Parasuraman & Greenhaus, 1993). From a psychological view, women's multiple roles of family and work impose time limitations and cause role overload and work–family role conflict, limiting factors leading to managerial advancement such as years of work experience, work hours, training, and relocation (Ragins & Sundstrom, 1989; Tharenou, 1990). By contrast, men's role in the workplace is consistent with the family 'provider' role (Bielby & Bielby, 1989), separating them from the home role and possible time constraints and role overload or conflict, resulting in a positive career impact. From a labor market view, men need to perform better in the labor market to support a family, and employers need to advance men to cater for family needs, unlike women. According to human capital theory, household duties reduce married women's time in the labor force, discourage their investment in human capital, and cause them to seek low-energy-intensive jobs (Becker, 1985), resulting in lower pay and status. According to distributive justice theory (Pfeffer & Ross, 1982), employers allocate rewards based on individual employee needs. Fathers need to provide for the family's financial needs, but women should be supported by spouses. According to wife-as-resource view (Kanter, 1977; Pfeffer & Ross, 1982), wives provide men with additional resources to invest in their careers through the extra roles they take on, especially if not employed outside the home, advantaging married over single men.

Studies assessing the impact of family are usually cross-sectional, self-report multivariate designs with extensive controls. Most do not consider the effects of family on intervening processes such as managers' tenure, work hours, or training that then affect managerial advancement, or directly test the theoretical explanations proposed for effects of family.

Marital status

Marital status was not related to male or female managers' and executives' promotion (Dreher & Ash, 1990; Judge et al., 1995; Korenman & Neumark, 1991; Tharenou & Conroy, 1994; Whitely, Dougherty, & Dreher, 1991). Marital status or marrying or changing to single did not predict the entry of scientists and engineers into managerial positions five years later (Shenhav, 1992), nor was marital status related to managers' levels (Melamed, 1996b). By contrast, single managers had lower managerial levels than married (Bretz & Judge, 1994), and marital status increased managers' levels which then increased pay, although there was a small wage premium on pay caused by marital status alone (Korenman & Neumark, 1991). Single managers had less overall managerial advancement than married (Judge & Bretz, 1994) and earned less (Bretz & Judge, 1994; Judge et al., 1995; Korenman & Neumark, 1991; Landau & Arthur, 1992), although there are also no links between marital status and pay (Dreher & Ash, 1990; Whitely, Dougherty, & Dreher, 1991). Being married was negatively related to female managers' pay and positively to males' (Jacobs, 1992). Single or never-married female managers and professionals earned less than married women, especially dual-career (Brett, Stroh, & Reilly, 1992b; Landau & Arthur, 1992; Schneer & Reitman, 1993). Single men earned less than divorced male managers and professionals who earned less than married men (Korenman & Neumark, 1991; Landau & Arthur, 1992). The lesser pay of single managers than married is consistent with distributive justice theory (less financial need), human capital theory (lack of stability), or social expectations theory (Pfeffer & Ross, 1982), not conforming to social stereotypes, although the explanations are not assessed. In summary, not consistent with a multiple role view, both female and male single managers may be lower in managerial level and are paid less than married managers.

Children

Number of children was not related to female or male managers' and executives' organization promotion (Tharenou & Conroy, 1994). For male and female scientists and engineers, number of children was not related to entry into management, and having children was negatively related to entry for the private not public sector (Shenhav, 1992). Children were related very weakly to managers' levels (Bretz & Judge, 1994), but not to female or male managers' levels (Melamed, 1996b). Number of children was not related to female or male managers' pay (Bretz & Judge, 1994; Cannings, 1991; Jacobs, 1992; Korabik & Rosin, 1995; Lobel & St. Clair, 1992), nor were pregnancy leave (Landau & Arthur, 1992) or preschool children (Lobel & St. Clair, 1992). Children under age six were negatively related to female but not male manager's pay (Jacobs, 1992). For a chiefly managerial sample (rest were professionals), men with children at home earned more than men with no children at home, whereas there was no relationship between having children and pay for women (Landau & Arthur, 1992). For a sample of Australian managers without post-secondary education and not necessarily full-time, women earned less than men increasingly more from having no children to one or two children to three or more children (Martin, 1994). Time devoted to dependant care was not related to executives' (93% men) pay or promotion (Judge et al., 1995), child-minding was not related to male or female managers' and executives' promotion or managerial level (Tharenou & Conroy, 1994), and dependant responsibilities were not related to managers overall advancement (two-third's men; Judge & Bretz, 1994). In summary, not consistent with a multiple role view, number or care of children is not related to managerial promotions, level, or pay for women (or men).

Marital status and children

Female CEOs could be discriminated from matched male CEOs but not from matched female top managers by being childless and not having a spouse (Tharenou, 1995), suggesting that lack of a family is not the reason women break the glass ceiling. A family, combining martial status and children, was not related to managers' and executives' managerial level or organization promotion (Tharenou & Conroy, 1994). For five of six countries (except Canada), the self-selection hypothesis whereby women voluntarily make themselves less available for promotion into management because of family responsibilities, was not supported for employees ranging from subordinates to top managers (Wright, Baxter, & Birkelund, 1995). There were no differences in workplace authority in terms of managerial level or authority between unmarried women, childless women with husbands providing household help, and mothers with little husband help (Wright, Baxter, & Birkelund, 1995). Parasuraman and Greenhaus (1993) proposed that families interrupt women's work experience, which reduces training amongst other things, and, in turn, affects career advancement. In support, structural equation analysis revealed that a family (spouse and children) reduced women's work experience but increased men's (Tharenou, Latimer, & Conroy, 1994). In turn, work experience led to training and development and subsequently managerial career advancement. In summary, marriage and children do not decrease women's managerial advancement but, consistent with a multiple role view, may reduce processes leading to it.

Household duties

Household responsibilities were not related to managers' (most men) overall advancement (Judge & Bretz, 1994). For married middle-level managers, household labor was more negatively related to men's levels and pay than women's, especially for those with graduate degrees (Konrad & Cannings, 1994). The career-family men (above the median on participation in household labor) of the sample had lower hierarchical levels than career-primary men (below the median), with career-family women in between (Konrad & Cannings, 1994). Employers may have sanctioned men for participating in household labor because it violates gender roles. Career-family women managers were paid less than career-primary men managers, who were similar in pay to career-family men (Konrad & Cannings, 1994). Extent of full responsibility for household duties were negatively related to women's but not men's pay (Cannings, 1991). In summary, inconsistent with multiple role effects for women alone, household duties may disadvantage men's or women's managerial advancement.

Spouse attributes

Male and female managers reported that spouse assistance had enhanced their careers (Grossbard-Shechtman, Izraeli, & Neuman, 1994). Spouse support was related to male and female managers' and executives' managerial level but not promotion (Tharenou & Conroy, 1994). Managers (87% male) with spouses working full-time rather than part-time had not plateaued more (Tremblay & Roger, 1993), and employed spouses were not related to male (chiefly) executives' promotion, but were to their lower pay (Judge et al., 1995). Managers' assessment that they had not constrained their careers for spouses gained male managers an extra $21 900 per year and women $1700 (Egan & Bendick, 1994). Work–family conflict was related to male and to female managers' and executives' managerial level but not promotion (Tharenou & Conroy, 1994). Because the study is cross-sectional, high managerial level could have caused role conflict. In summary, the few studies suggest that spouse support may help managers' levels, and spouse employment may affect male managers' pay.

Family structure

Family structures are derived from the interaction between marital status, parental status, and spousal employment status, providing family types: single childless, single-career families including traditional families with married fathers whose spouses are not employed outside the home, and dual-career families including post-traditional families of employed fathers or mothers whose spouses are also employed outside the home. Most studies assess only links with pay.

For managers, traditional men, fathers with not-employed spouses, earned more than other men, including childless counterparts and dual-career married fathers and childless men, and single childless men (Landau & Arthur, 1992; Schneer & Reitman, 1993), with greater salary progression and promotion in a longitudinal study than dual-career fathers (Brett, Stroh, & Reilly, 1992b). Effects were weak (Landau & Arthur, 1992). Post-traditional fathers do not necessarily earn less than other men, apart from traditional fathers. Dual-career fathers had similar pay compared to men combined from all other family structures for MBA graduates in mid-career (Schneer & Reitman, 1995) and to dual-earner childless men in early career (Schneer & Reitman, 1993). Dual-career fathers were promoted less than dual-career childless men and traditional single-earner fathers for managers who were all transferees (Brett, Stroh, & Reilly, 1992b), but had similar managerial levels to men combined into all other family structures (Schneer & Reitman, 1995). Post-traditional women, mothers with employed spouses, earned as much as other married women and mothers but more than single or never married women (Brett, Stroh, & Reilly, 1992b; Landau & Arthur, 1992; Schneer & Reitman, 1993, 1995), had similar promotion to dual-career childless women (Brett, Stroh, & Reilly, 1992b), and had similar managerial levels to women combined from all other family structures (Schneer & Reitman, 1995). Female managers whose spouses did not have a career earned more than dual-career counterparts (Landau & Arthur, 1992). In summary, for managers, traditional fathers earn more than other men, chiefly supporting distributive justice and wife as resource views; with that proviso, post-traditional fathers do not necessarily earn less; and post-traditional mothers earn as much as other women but more than single women, not supporting multiple role views.

INTEGRATORY STUDIES

Multivariate Studies

Organization or individual?

A few comprehensive, chiefly self-report studies were able to estimate the relative importance of organizational and individual factors simultaneously, most using hierarchical regression analysis. Most studies measured more individual than organizational variables, and only one (Bretz & Judge, 1994) considered interactions between the two in their effects on managerial career advancement. For 1270 Australian managers and executives (Tharenou & Conroy, 1994), managerial level and promotion were related to self-reported organization opportunity (organization size, promotion ladders, public sector) and social structures (male hierarchies, career encouragement) and training and development opportunities, but not to individuals' personalities (self-confidence, attributions, willingness to move), early socialization, and family responsibilities. Human capital (work experience, education) added to the explanation by the organization variables. In a stepwise regression analysis of 16 predictors for 136 British public service managers, human capital inputs (education, tenure), organizational opportunity structures (line position, promotion opportunities for the grade above), and personality (low self-control) explained managerial level, with other personality measures, mental ability, family (marital status, children), job changes, and objectively measured industry opportunities unimportant (Melamed, 1996b). Four studies measured more individual than organization variables, and so found they were more important. Using multivariate multiple regression, pay and promotion of 1388 US executives on a search firm's database were more related to human capital (education, tenure), demographic (male, marital status), and motivational (ambition, work hours) variables than to objectively measured organizational and industry opportunity variables (Judge et al., 1995). For 873 US industrial relations managers, human capital (education, work hours) most explained pay and job level, with explanation added by the perceived organization reward environment and the fit of the person's preferences to this reward environment, but little by demographic variables (gender, race, family), industry, or personal reward preferences alone (Bretz & Judge, 1994). For the same sample, political skills of the supervisor- and job-focused tactics and human capital inputs explained overall career advancement more than demographic, motivational and industry variables (Judge & Bretz, 1994). For 200 US managers from several firms, work experience was more important to managerial level than were career choice, success criteria and family influence on work (Gattiker & Larwood, 1990).

The multivariate studies show family variables have no or little relative importance, and human capital inputs have the most consistent relative importance. Organizations' internal labor markets as organization size, promotion ladders, line jobs and the reward environment have inconsistent links, but appear more related than family roles, early socialization, and personality. Personality is inconsistently related to managerial career advancement when compared to organizational and individual factors, but may be relatively important when conceptually linked (e.g. ambition). In summary, individual factors, especially human capital of education and work experience, and organization factors, mainly promotion opportunities, are related to managerial advancement.

Integratory models

Most studies testing integratory models have applied structural equation modeling to cross-sectional chiefly self-report questionnaire data. For 1359 senior Dutch private sector managers and executives, human capital increased position level and social networks, and all in turn increased pay (Boxman, De Graaf, & Flap, 1991). The internal locus of control, emotional stability and self-monitoring of 147 US managers and professionals led to initiating mentoring, resulting in mentoring gained that, in turn, increased overall career advancement (Turban & Dougherty, 1994). For 513 women and 501 men Australian public and private sector managers and executives, self-confidence increased the career encouragement and training and development received, and career encouragement increased women's participation in training and development more than men's (Tharenou, Latimer, & Conroy, 1994). Education increased men's, not women's participation in training and development and, for both, increased managerial advancement. A family increased men's work experience and reduced women's, and work experience led to greater participation in training and development by men than women. Training and development had the major impact on managerial advancement (Tharenou, Latimer, & Conroy, 1994). For 646 middle managers of a Canadian finance company, informal social networks increased men's offers of promotions more than women's, and human capital of performance and company tenure increased women's promotion more than men's, with men being offered more promotions (Cannings & Montmarquette, 1991b). In a study testing mediator effects by regression analysis for 457 British employees from subordinates to general manager level (Melamed, 1996a), human capital, but not organization structure, was related to career choices that influenced managerial level. Human capital of education and work experience, but also mental ability and being single were related to career choices of more prestigious and professional jobs and short tenure and frequent change of jobs, that in turn increased managerial levels.

In summary, tests of integratory models suggest that, apart from direct effects, individuals' human capital (work experience, education) and personality (e.g. self-confidence, self-monitoring) influence the use of organization social networks, career support, and training and development opportunities, and individuals' career choices that, in turn, lead to managerial career advancement. Marriage may affect career choices and reduce work experience, thus decreasing managerial career advancement.

CONCLUSION

Organization opportunity structures of internal labor markets, as provided by large organization size, long promotion ladders and growth, appear not important to advancing in management. The traditional path to advancement of employees stepping onto career ladders on entry and then subsequent promotion up the ladder may therefore not hold. The type of position and functional area is also not related to managerial advancement, although broadening experiences in critical functional areas, including general management at mid-career and late career, may assist advancement to executive levels. High level occupations with high percentages of males increase managerial level, providing opportunities for development of skills and the career paths needed to advance. Overall, being in the 'right' place at the 'right' time appears relatively unimportant to advancement, except being in the right occupation counts.

Social structures are important to managerial career advancement. Women are more likely to gain initial management jobs and advance in the hierarchy including to executive positions when the managerial hierarchy is less proportionately male and subordinates are women rather than men. Minorities are likely to advance under corresponding circumstances. Decision-makers appear attracted to those similar to them in identity and group affiliation, and comfortable with those with whom they are familiar, resulting in their reproducing themselves socially in selection and promotion. This causes white men to gain more managerial advancement than other groups. Who individuals are like counts.

Informal social networks and career support facilitate entering and advancing in management, at least in mid- and late career, and including to the top. Informal networks of personal contacts inside or external to the organization provide career information, control of options and support. Bigger networks are better. Networks assist men's managerial advancement more than women's, even though social networks with large range and strong sponsors are needed for women's managerial career advancement. Career encouragement from peers and supervisors increases managerial advancement, perhaps more for women than men, and interpersonal support appears especially important for women to overcome barriers including breaking the glass ceiling. Having a mentor who provides career support, as distinct from general supervisor support, results in increased managerial promotions, especially in early career, and managerial pay for men and women managers. Who individuals know and who knows them counts.

Promotion processes have important effects on entry into and advancement in the managerial hierarchy. Starting in favorable circumstances including higher levels and on faster tracks predicts later managerial advancement. Career tournaments operate from entry with winners and losers at each career stage, and winners may keep winning. They may do so because promotion provides developmental and network opportunities, opening up further promotion. Favorable starting processes are found more for men than women. Female managers also gain lower managerial levels and pay from promotion and incur higher promotion and advancement standards than comparable, similarly situated men, including in early and mid-career. This is discrimination, presumably based on stereotypes held about women as a group, perhaps in regard to productivity or labor force attachment or just lack of comfort of the male managerial majority through dissimilarity. Blacks appear discriminated against for managerial career advancement based on race. To counteract discrimination, affirmative action programs clearly delineating target groups increase entry into managerial jobs, increasing women's and minorities' representation in management. Politics influences who advances in management, especially from mid-career, including to the top. Use of political skills by candidates including managing impressions and ingratiation increases their managerial advancement, as does supervisor political influence through recommendations, candidate identification, comfort levels, and negotiations. How political individuals are counts. Promotion to middle and upper management and executive levels is determined by individuals' abilities and accomplishments and organization needs, including context, but also by social networks and politics. The organization's context and needs are important to characteristics of those chosen to be executives.

Individuals' traits predict managerial career advancement in the short and long term, and are important to initial managerial advancement and to reaching the top. Certain traits may allow taking advantage of organization opportunities, by seeking or accepting training and development and career support and making career choices that increase managerial advancement. There appear to be four major facets of individuals who advance in management. First, they are ambitious, advancement- and career-motivated, and self-monitoring, especially in early career, and have high achievement needs and work involvement, important as careers progress to mid- and late career to sustain advancement. These ambition and achievement motives drive individuals to seek and accept managerial advancement. Second, those likely to advance into management are motivated to manage, including prior to employment. Third, they are intelligent, especially relevant to early career progress in learning complex jobs. Fourth, they are instrumental, suited to the task demands of managerial jobs. The latter three traits allow individuals to implement their self-concepts in occupational choice; the traits fit with and are relevant to the managerial role. Drive and person fit count.

Human capital investments increase managerial career advancement. Managers who invest in their education level and quality, company tenure, full-time years of work experience, weekly work hours, geographical job transfers, and management training and development are likely to gain initial managerial positions and advance, including to the top. This is the traditional way of getting ahead, working hard and increasing skills and knowledge and thus productivity, for which rewards are given, and establishing credentials, credibility and visibility in the organization to provide signals on which advancement decisions are made. Human capital investments are as, or more important to, managerial career advancement as other significant factors. Human capital directly influences advancement into management and also indirectly through increasing factors that lead to advancement: social networks, training and development, and career choices. Investing in human capital, especially company tenure and education, pays back at the time in managerial advancement, and in mid- and late career. What individuals know and can do counts throughout their careers.

Managerial skills at each career stage increase managerial career advancement at that stage and later. Important are interpersonal, leadership, administrative, and personal skills. Ineffective people and strategic skills may derail managers in late career. Managers rated as high performers by their supervisors are more likely to gain entry into management and to advance as managers within organizations, reflecting task performance but perhaps also citizenship. High performance in critical functional areas is important to gain top level advancement. Age and racial bias may reduce promotability ratings, affected by attributions for performance. Overall, what individuals can do and how well counts.

Family roles appear relatively unimportant to advancement in management compared to other factors. Being a single male or female disadvantages, and being a traditional father advantages, managers' pay, perhaps because employers allocate pay based on individual need and/or perceived stability and conformity. Multiple roles of home and work do not appear to cause women's lesser managerial advancement than men's, and dual-career mothers advance as much as other women except singles, although women's multiple roles may impede processes that lead to advancement such as work experience and training.

In summary, the empirical literature since 1990 suggests that individual qualities and work environment factors combine to facilitate individuals entering and advancing in management in hierarchical organizations. Individuals choose certain occupations and, when they are high level occupations with high proportions of white men, they provide opportunities for advancement. Employees who are ambitious, want to manage, are instrumental, and intelligent seek advancement continuously. They invest in education, work experience, and training and development to do so, increasing their productivity and developing credentials, credibility and visibility. Because of these attributes, they are viewed as suitable for entry to, and advancement in management and seek and are provided with developmental experiences, social networks, career encouragement and mentor support, providing the information, resources, control, and support needed to advance. Interpersonal support comes from the male managerial hierarchies of organizations, more to men than women. Individuals who gain early promotion increase in the hierarchical level of their jobs, resulting in continued challenging work and development experiences, gaining credibility, visibility and familiarity, and thus more opportunities for promotion. The managerial momentum and career velocity need to be maintained. To be promoted, managers need to have high managerial skills especially in critical areas and general management, perceived so by their bosses, have favorable political circumstances and use political skills, and be similar in attributes to the majority of the managerial hierarchy. Decision-makers select and advance those who are similar to them and in the same social categories, and use stereotypes to help them process information about possible candidates. The selection and promotion process is thus imperfect, resulting in higher promotion standards for groups dissimilar to the majority. Advancement at highest levels in the hierarchy is influenced by similarity and fitting in, by politics, and with fulfilling organization needs, requiring a fit with organization context.

REFERENCES

Baron, J. N. & Pfeffer, J. (1994) The social psychology of organizations and inequality. *Social Psychology Quarterly*, 57, 190–209.

Barrick, M. R. & Mount, M. K. (1991) The big five personality dimensions and job performance: A meta-analysis. *Personnel Psychology*, 44, 1-26.

Becker, G. S. (1975) *Human Capital.* Chicago: University of Chicago Press.

Becker, G. S. (1985) Human capital, effort, and the sexual division of labor. *Journal of Labor Economics*, 3, 533–558.

Becker, G. S. (1993) *Human Capital.* Chicago: University of Chicago Press.

Bem, S. L. (1981) Gender schema theory. *Psychological Review*, 88, 354–364.

Biddle, J. & Roberts, K. (1994) Private sector scientists and engineers and the transition to management. *Journal of Human Resources*, 29, 82–107.

Bielby, J. M. & Bielby, D. D. (1989) Family ties. *American Sociological Review*, 54, 776–789.

Blau, F. D. & Ferber, M. A. (1987) Occupations and earnings of women workers. In K. S. Koziara, M. H. Moskow, & L. D. Tanner (eds), *Working Women: Past, Present, Future.* Washington, DC: Bureau of National Affairs.

Blum, T. C., Fields, D. L., & Goodman, J. S. (1994) Organization-level determinants of women in management, *Academy of Management Journal*, 37, 241–268.

Boeker, W. & Goodstein, J. (1993) Performance and successor choice. *Academy of Management Journal*, 36, 172–186.

Borman, W. C. & Brush, D. H. (1993) More progress toward a taxonomy of managerial performance requirements. *Human Performance*, 6, 1–21.

Boxman, E. A. W., De Graaf, P. M., & Flap, H. D. (1991) The impact of social and human capital on the income attainment of Dutch managers. *Social Networks*, **13**, 51–73.

Brett, J. M., Stroh, L. K., & Reilly, A. H. (1992a) Job transfer. In C. L. Cooper and I. T. Robertson (eds), *International Review of Industrial and Organizational Psychology* (pp. 323–362). New York: Wiley.

Brett, J. M., Stroh, L. K., & Reilly, A. H. (1992b) What is it like being a dual career manager in the 1990s? In S. Zedeck (ed.), *Work, Families and Organizations* (pp. 138–167). San Francisco: Jossey-Bass.

Bretz, R. D. & Judge, T. A. (1994) Person–organization fit and the theory of work adjustment. *Journal of Vocational Behavior*, **44**, 32–54.

Burt, R. S. (1992) *Structural Holes: The Social Structure of Competition.* Cambridge, MA: Harvard University Press.

Burt, R. S. (1993) The social structure of competition. In R. Swedgerb (ed.), *Explanations in Economic Sociology* (pp. 65–103). New York: Russell Sage Foundation.

Campion, M. A., Cheraskin, L., & Stevens, M. J. (1994) Career-related antecedents and outcomes of job rotation. *Academy of Management Journal*, **37**, 1518–1542.

Cannella, A. & Lubatkin, M. (1993) Succession as a socio-political process. *Academy of Management Journal*, **36**, 763–793.

Cannella, A., Lubatkin, M., & Kapouch, M. (1991) Antecedents of executive selection. *Academy of Management Proceedings*, **51**, 11–15.

Cannings, K. (1991) An interdisciplinary approach to analyzing the managerial gender gap. *Human Relations*, **44**, 679–695.

Cannings, K. & Montmarquette, C. (1991a) The attitudes of subordinates to the gender of superiors in a managerial hierarchy. *Journal of Economic Psychology*, **12**, 707–724.

Cannings, K. & Montmarquette, C. (1991b) Managerial momentum. *Industrial and Labor Relations Review*, **44**, 212–228.

Carson, K. P. & Gilliard, D. J. (1993) Construct validity of the Miner Sentence Completion Scale. *Journal of Occupational and Organizational Psychology*, **66**, 171–175.

Chi-Ching, E. Y. (1992) Perceptions of external barriers and the career success of female managers in Singapore. *Journal of Social Psychology*, **132**, 661–674.

Chusmir, L. H. & Koberg, C. S. (1991) Relationship between self-confidence and sex-role identity among managerial women and men. *Journal of Social Psychology*, **131**, 781–790.

Chusmir, L. H., Koberg, C. S., & Stecher, H. D. (1992) Self-confidence of managers in work and social situations. *Sex Roles*, **26**, 495–512.

Chusmir, L. H. & Parker, B. (1991) Gender and situational differences in managers' values. *Journal of Business Research*, **23**, 325–335.

Cianni, M. & Romberger, B. (1995) Perceived racial, ethnic, and gender differences in access to developmental experiences. *Group & Organization Management*, **20**, 440–459.

Cordero, R., Di Tomaso, N., & Farris, G. F. (1994) Identifying and developing promotability in R&D laboratories. *Journal of Engineering and Technology Management*, **11**, 55–72.

Cox, T. H. & Harquail, C. V. (1991) Career paths and career success in the early career stages of male and female MBAs. *Journal of Vocational Behavior*, **39**, 54–75.

Cox, T. H. & Nkomo, S. M. (1991) A race and gender-group analysis of the early career experience of MBAs. *Work and Occupations*, **18**, 431–446.

Cox, T. H. & Nkomo, S. M. (1992) Candidate age as a factor in promotability ratings. *Public Personnel Management*, **21**, 197–210.

Datta, D. K. & Guthrie, J. P. (1994) Executive succession. *Strategic Management Journal*, **15**, 569–577.

Day, D. V. & Lord, R. G. (1988) Executive leadership and organizational performance. *Journal of Management*, **14**, 453–464.

Deshpande, S. P., Schoderbek, P. P., & Joseph, J. (1994) Promotion decisions by managers. *Human Relations*, **47**, 223–232.

Dreher, G. F. & Ash, R. A. (1990) A comparative study of mentoring among men and women in managerial positions. *Journal of Applied Psychology*, **75**, 539–546.

Dreher, G. F. & Bretz, R. D. (1991) Cognitive ability and career attainment. *Journal of Applied Psychology*, **76**, 392–397.

Egan, M. L. & Bendick, M. (1994) International business careers in the United States. *International Journal of Human Resource Management*, **5**, 33–50.

Ellis, R. & Heneman, H. G. (1990) Career pattern determinants of career success for mature managers. *Journal of Business and Psychology*, **5**, 3–20.

Fagenson, E. A. (1990a) At the heart of women in management research. *Journal of Business Ethics*, **9**, 1–8.

Fagenson, E. A. (1990b) Perceived masculine and feminine attributes as a function of sex and level in the organizational hierarchy. *Journal of Applied Psychology*, **75**, 204–211.

Ferris, G. R., Buckley, M. R., & Allen, G. M. (1992) Promotion systems in organizations. *Human Resource Planning*, **15**, 47–68.

Ferris, G. R. & Judge, T. A. (1991) Personnel/human resources management: A political perspective. *Journal of Management*, **17**, 447–488.

Forbes, J. B. & Piercy, J. E. (1991) *Corporate Mobility and Paths to the Top*. New York: Quorum Books.

Forbes, J. B. & Wertheim, S. E. (1995) Promotion, succession, and career systems. In R. Ferris, S. D. Rosen, & D. T. Barnum (eds), *Handbook of Human Resource Management* (pp. 494–510). Cambridge, MA: Blackwell Business.

Friedman, S. D. (1991) Why hire from within? *Academy of Management Best Paper Proceedings*, **51**, 272–276.

Gattiker, U. E. & Larwood, L. (1990) Predictors for career achievement in the corporate hierarchy. *Human Relations*, **43**, 703–726.

Gibbs, M. (1995) Incentive compensation in a corporate hierarchy. *Journal of Accounting and Economics*, **19**, 247–277.

Greenhaus, J. H. & Parasuraman, S. (1993) Job performance attributions and career advancement prospects. *Organizational Behavior and Human Decision Processes*, **55**, 273–297.

Greenhaus, J. H., Parasuraman, S., & Wormley, W. M. (1990) Effects of race on organizational experiences, job performance evaluations, and career outcomes. *Academy of Management Journal*, **33**, 64–86.

Grossbard-Shechtman, S. A., Izraeli, D. N., & Neuman, S. (1994) When do spouses support a career? *Journal of Socio-Economics*, **23**, 149–167.

Gutek, B. A. (1993) Changing the status of women in management. *Applied Psychology: An International Review*, **42**, 301–311.

Gutek, B. A., Searle, S., & Klepa, L. (1991) Rational versus gender-role expectations for work–family conflict. *Journal of Applied Psychology*, **76**, 560–568.

Guthrie, J. P., Grimm, C., & Smith, K. G. (1991) Environmental change and management staffing. *Journal of Management*, **17**, 735–748.

Guthrie, J. P. & Olian, J. D. (1991) Does context affect staffing decisions? *Personnel Psychology*, **44**, 261–291.

Haberfeld, Y. (1992) Employment discrimination: An organizational model. *Academy of Management Journal*, **35**, 161–180.

Hanson, Frieze, I., Olson, J. E., & Cain Good, D. (1990) Perceived and actual discrimination in the salaries of male and female managers. *Journal of Applied Social Psychology*, **20**, 46–67.

Herriot, P., Gibbons, P., Pemberton, C., & Jackson, P. R. (1994) An empirical model of managerial careers in organizations. *British Journal of Management*, **5**, 113–121.

Herriot, P., Gibson, G., Pemberton, C., & Pinder, R. (1993) Dashed hopes. *Journal of Occupational and Organizational Psychology*, **66**, 115–123.

Hofstede, G. (1994) Predicting managers' career success in an international setting. *Management International Review*, **34**, 63–70.

Hogan, R. (1994) Trouble at the top: Causes and consequence of managerial incompetence. *Consulting Psychology Journal*, **46**(1), 9–15.

Hogan, R., Curphy, G. J., & Hogan, J. (1994) What do we know about leadership? *American Psychologist*, **49**, 493–504.

House, R. J., Howard, A., & Walker, G. (1991) The prediction of managerial success. *Academy of Management Best Paper Proceedings*, **51**, 215–219.

Howard, A. (1991) Managerial roles that span careers. In J. W. Jones, B. D. Steffy, & D. W. Bray (eds), *Applying Psychology in Business* (pp. 452–462). Lexington, MA: Lexington Books.

Howard, A. & Bray, D. W. (1990) Predictions of managerial success over long periods of time. In K. E. Clark & M.B. Clark (eds), *Measures of Leadership* (pp. 113–130). West Orange, NJ: Leadership Library of America.

Huffman, M. L. (1995) Organizations, internal labor market policies, and gender inequality in workplace supervisory authority. *Sociological Perspectives*, **38**, 381–397.

Hurley, A. E. & Sonnenfeld, J. A. (1994) Organizational growth and employee advancement. In M. London (ed.), *Employees, Careers and Job Creation* (pp. 31–48). San Francisco, CA: Jossey-Bass.

Ibarra, H. (1993) Personal networks of women and minorities in management: A conceptual framework. *Academy of Management Review*, **18**, 57–87.

Ibarra, H. (1995) Race, opportunity, and diversity of social circles in managerial ranks. *Academy of Management Journal*, **38**, 673–703.

Igbaria, M. & Greenhaus, J. H. (1992) The career advancement prospects of managers and professionals. *Decision Sciences*, **23**, 478–499.

Igbaria, M. & Wormley, W. M. (1995) Race differences in job performance and career success. *Communication of the ACM*, **38** (3), 83–92.

Ingham, H. & Thompson, S. (1995) Mutuality, performance and executive compensation. *Oxford Bulletin of Economics and Statistics*, **57**, 295–308.

Jackson, S. E., Brett, J. F., Sessa, V. I., Cooper, D. M., Julin, J. A., & Peyronnin, K. (1991) Some differences make a difference. *Journal of Applied Psychology*, **76**, 675–689.

Jacobs, J. A. (1992) Women's entry into management. *Administrative Science Quarterly*, **37**, 282–301.

Jacobs, R. L. & McClelland, D. C. (1994) Moving up the corporate ladder. *Consulting Psychology Journal*, **46**, 32–41.

Jenkins, S. R. (1994) Need for power and women's careers over 14 years. *Journal of Personality and Social Psychology*, **66**, 155–165.

Johnson, N. B. & Scandura, T. A (1994) The effects of mentoring and sex-role style on male–female earnings. *Industrial Relations*, **33**, 263–274.

Johnsrud, L. K. & Heck, R. H. (1994) Administrative promotion within a university. *Journal of Higher Education*, **65**, 23–43.

Jones, R. G. & Whitmore, M. D. (1995) Evaluating developmental assessment centers as interventions. *Personnel Psychology*, **48**, 377-388.

Judge, T. A. & Bretz, R. D. (1994) Political influence processes and career success. *Journal of Management*, **20**, 43–65.

Judge, T. A., Cable, D. M., Boudreau, J. W., & Bretz, R. D. (1995) An empirical investigation of the predictors of executive career success. *Personnel Psychology*, **48**, 485–519.

Kanter, R. M. (1977) *Men and Women of the Corporation.* New York: Basic Books.

Kent, R. L. & Moss, S. E. (1994) Effects of sex and gender role on leader emergence. *Academy of Management Journal,* 37, 1335–1346.

Khojasteh, M. (1994) Workforce 2000 demographic characteristics and their impacts. *International Journal of Public Administration,* 17, 465–505.

Kilduff, M. D. & Day, D. V. (1994) Do chameleons get ahead? *Academy of Management Journal,* 37, 1047–1060.

Kim, H. & Yukl, G. (1995) Relationships of managerial effectiveness and advancement to self-reported and subordinate-reported leadership behaviors from the multiple-linkage model. *Leadership Quarterly,* 6, 361–377.

Kim, P. S. & Lewis, G. B. (1994) Asian Americans in the public service: Success, diversity and discrimination. *Public Administration Review,* 54, 285–290.

Kirchmeyer, C. (1995) Demographic similarity to the work group. *Journal of Organizational Behavior,* 16, 67–83.

Koberg, C. S., Chusmir, L. H., & Carlin, W. B. (1992) Gender and hierarchical level coalignment with managers' self-confidence. *Psychology, A Journal of Human Behavior,* 29, 14–17.

Konrad, A. M. & Cannings, K. (1994) Of mummy tracks and glass ceilings. *Relations Industrielles,* 49, 303–333.

Konrad, A. M. & Linnehan, F. (1992) The implementation and effectiveness of equal opportunity employment. *Academy of Management Best Paper Proceedings,* 52, 380–384.

Konrad, A. M. & Linnehan, F. (1995) Formalized HRM structures. *Academy of Management Journal,* 38, 787–820.

Konrad, A. M. & Pfeffer, J. (1991) Understanding the hiring of women and minorities in educational institutions. *Sociology of Education,* 64, 141–157.

Korabik, K. & Rosin, H. M. (1995) The impact of children on women managers' career behavior and organizational commitment. *Human Resource Management,* 34, 513–528.

Korenman, S. & Neumark, D. (1991) Does marriage really make men more productive? *Journal of Human Resources,* 26, 283–307.

Kotter, J. P. (1995) *The New Rules: How to Succeed in Today's Corporate World.* New York: Free Press.

Kram, K. E. (1983) Phases of the mentor relationship. *Academy of Management Journal,* 26, 608–625.

Krausz, M. & Reshef, M. (1992) Managerial job change. *Journal of Business and Psychology,* 6, 349–359.

Landau, J. (1995) The relationship of race and gender to managers' ratings of promotion potential. *Journal of Organizational Behavior,* 16, 391–400.

Landau, J. & Arthur, M. B. (1992) The relationship of marital status, spouse's career status, and gender to salary level. *Sex Roles,* 27, 665–681.

Landy, F. J., Shankster, L. J., & Kohler, S. S. (1994) Personnel selection and placement. *Annual Review of Psychology,* 45, 261–296.

Leck, J. D. & Saunders, D. M. (1992a) Canada's employment equity act. *Population Research and Policy Review,* 11, 21–49.

Leck, J. D. & Saunders, D. M. (1992b) Hiring women. *Canadian Public Policy – Analyse de Politiques,* 18, 203–220.

Leck, J. D., Saunders, D. M., & St. Onge, S. (1991) Achieving a diversified workforce with employment equity programs: Effects on hiring women. *Academy of Management Best Paper Proceedings,* 51, 385–389.

Levinson, H. (1994) Why the behemoths fall. *American Psychologist,* 49, 428–436.

Lewis, G. B. (1992) Men and women towards the top. *Public Personnel Management,* 21, 473–491.

Lobel, S. A. & St. Clair, L. (1992) Effects of family responsibilities, gender, and career identity salience on performance outcomes. *Academy of Management Journal*, **35**, 1057–1069.

Locke, E. A. (1991) *The Essence of Leadership*. New York: Lexington Books.

Lord, R. G., De Vader, C. L., & Alliger, G. M. (1986) A meta-analysis of the relationship between personality traits and leadership perceptions. *Journal of Applied Psychology*, **71**, 402–410.

Macrae, C. N., Milne, A. B., & Bodenhausen, G. V. (1994) Stereotypes as energy-saving devices: A peek inside the cognitive toolbox. *Journal of Personality and Social Psychology*, **64**, 37–47.

Mainiero, L. A. (1994a) Getting anointed for advancement: The case of executive women. *Academy of Management Executive*, **8**, 53–67.

Mainiero, L. A. (1994b) The political seasoning of powerful women executives. *Organizational Dynamics*, **22** (4), 5–20.

Markham, W. T., Harlan, S. L., & Hackett, E. J. (1987) Promotion opportunity in organization. *Research in Personnel and Human Resources Management* (pp. 223–287). New York: JAI Press.

Martin, L. R. & Morgan, S. (1995) Middle managers in banking. *Quarterly Journal of Business and Economics*, **34**, 55–68.

Martin, W. (1994) Understanding class segmentation in the labour market. *Work, Employment & Society*, **8**, 355–385.

McCauley, C. D. & Lombardo, M. M. (1990) Benchmarks. In K. E. Clark & M. B. Clark (eds), *Measures of Leadership* (pp. 535–545). West Orange, NJ: Leadership Library of America.

McCauley, C. D. & Ruderman, M. N. (1991) Understanding executive derailment. In J. W. Jones, B. D. Steffy, & D. W. Bray (eds), *Applying Psychology in Business* (pp. 483–488). Lexington, MA: Lexington Books.

Melamed, T. (1995a) Career success: The moderating effect of gender. *Journal of Vocational Behavior*, **47**, 35–60.

Melamed, T. (1995b) Barriers to women's career success. *Applied Psychology: An International Review*, **44**, 295–314.

Melamed, T. (1996a) Validation of a stage model of career success. *Applied Psychology: An International Review*, **45**, 35–66.

Melamed, T. (1996b) Career success: An assessment of a gender-specific model. *Journal of Occupational and Organizational Psychology*, **69**, 217–242.

Meyerson, E. M. (1994) Human capital, social capital and compensation. *Acta Sociologica*, **37**, 383–399.

Miner, J. B. (1993) *Role Motivation Theories*. Routledge: London.

Miner, J. B., Chen, C. C., & Yu, K. C. (1991) Theory testing under adverse conditions. *Journal of Applied Psychology*, **76**, 343–349.

Miner, J. B., Ebrahimi, B., & Wachtel, J. M. (1995) How deficiencies in motivation to manage contribute to the United States' competitiveness problem (and what can be done about it). *Human Resource Management*, **34**, 1–25.

Mittman, B. S. (1992) Theoretical and methodological issues in the study of organizational demography and demographic change. *Research in the Sociology of Occupations*, **10**, 3–53.

Morgan, S., Schor, S. M., & Martin, L. R. (1993) Gender differences in career paths in banking. *Career Development Quarterly*, **41**, 375–382.

Murrell, A. J., Olson, J. E., & Frieze, I. H. (1995) Sexual harassment and gender discrimination. *Journal of Social Issues*, **51**, 139–149.

Naff, K. C. (1994) Through the glass ceiling. *Public Administration Review*, **54**, 507–514.

Nicholson, N. (1990) The transition cycle. In S. Fisher & C. L. Cooper (eds), *The Psychology of Change and Transition* (pp. 83–108). New York: Wiley.

Nicholson, N. (1993) Purgatory or place of safety? *Human Relations*, **46**, 1369–1389.
Nkomo, S. M. & Cox, T. (1990) Factors affecting the upward mobility of black managers in private sector organizations. *Review of Black Political Economy*, **19**, 39–58.
Northcraft, G. & Gutek, B. (1993) Discrimination against women in management. In E. A. Fagenson (ed.), *Women in Management: Trends, Issues and Challenges in Managerial Diversity* (pp. 131–161). Newbury Park, CA: Sage Publications.
Offerman, L. R. & Gowing, M. K. (1993) Personnel selection in the future. N. Schmitt & W. C. Borman (eds), *Personnel Selection in Organizations* (pp. 385–417). San Francisco: Jossey-Bass.
O'Reilly, C. A. & Chatman, J. A. (1994) Working smarter and harder. *Administrative Science Quarterly*, **39**, 603–627.
Orpen, C. (1994) The effect of initial job challenge on subsequent performance among middle managers: A longitudinal study. *Psychology, A Journal of Human Behavior*, **31**, 51–52.
Parasuraman, S. & Greenhaus, J. H. (1993) Personal portrait. In E. A. Fagenson (ed.), *Women in Management* (pp. 186–211). Newbury Park, CA: Sage.
Pfeffer, J., Davis-Blake, A., & Julius, D. J. (1995) The effect of affirmative action officer salary changes on managerial diversity. *Industrial Relations*, **34**, 73–94.
Pfeffer, J. & Ross, J. (1982) The effects of marriage and a working wife on occupational and wage attainment. *Administrative Science Quarterly*, **27**, 66–80.
Pfeffer, J. & Ross, J. (1990) Gender-based wage differences: The effects of organization context. *Work and Occupations*, **17**, 55–78.
Pfeffer, J. & Salancik, G. R. (1978) *The External Control of Organizations: A Resource Dependence Perspective*. New York: Harper & Row.
Piercy, J. E. & Forbes, J. B. (1991) The phases of the chief executive's career. *Business Horizons*, **34**, 20–22.
Pollock, R. (1995) A test of conceptual models depicting the developmental course of informal mentor–protégé relationships in the workplace. *Journal of Vocational Behavior*, **46**, 144–162.
Powell, G. N. & Butterfield, D. A. (1994) Investigating the 'glass ceiling' phenomenon. *Academy of Management Journal*, **37**, 68–86.
Powell, G. N. & Mainiero, L. A. (1992) Cross-currents in the river of time. *Journal of Management*, **18**, 215–237.
Puffer, S. M. & Weintrop, J. B. (1995) CEO and board leadership. *Leadership Quarterly*, **6**, 49–68.
Ragin, C. C. & Bradshaw, Y. W. (1991) Statistical analysis of employment discrimination. *Research in Social Stratification and Mobility*, **10**, 199–228.
Ragins, B. R. & Sundstrom, E. (1989) Gender and power in organizations. *Psychological Bulletin*, **105**, 51–88.
Reskin, B. F. & Ross, C. E. (1992) Jobs, authority, and earnings among managers. *Work and Occupations*, **19**, 342–365.
Roberts, K. & Biddle, J. (1994) The transition into management by scientists and engineers. *Human Resource Management*, **33**, 561–579.
Rosenbaum, J. E. (1984) *Career Mobility in a Corporate Hierarchy*. New York: Academic Press.
Rosenbaum, J. E. (1990) Structural models of organizational careers. In R. L. Breiger (ed.), *Social Mobility and Social Structure* (pp. 272–397). Cambridge: Cambridge University Press.
Ruderman, M. N. & Ohlott, P. J. (1994) *The Realities of Management Promotion*. Greensboro, NC: Center for Creative Leadership.
Ruderman, M. N., Ohlott, P. J., & Kram, K. E. (1995) Promotion decisions as a diversity practice. *Journal of Management Development*, **14** (2), 6–23.

Salancik, G. R. & Pfeffer, J. (1978) Uncertainty, secrecy, and the choice of similar others. *Social Psychology*, **41**, 246–255.

Sandwith, P. (1993) A hierarchy of management training requirements: The competency domain model. *Public Personnel Management*, 22, 43–62.

Scandura, T. A (1992) Mentorship and career mobility: An empirical investigation. *Journal of Organizational Behavior*, **13**, 169–174.

Scandura, T. A. & Schriesheim, C. A. (1994) Leader–member exchange and supervisor career mentoring as complementary constructs in leadership research. *Academy of Management Journal*, **37**, 1588–1602.

Schaller, M., Boyd, C., Yohannes, J., & O'Brien, M. (1995) The prejudiced personality revisited. *Journal of Personality and Social Psychology*, **68**, 544–555.

Schein, V. E. & Mueller, R. (1992) Sex role stereotyping and requisite management characteristics. *Journal of Organizational Behavior*, **13**, 439–447.

Schein, V. E., Mueller, R., Lituchy, T., & Liu, J. (1996) Think manager–think male. *Journal of Organizational Behavior*, **17**, 33–41.

Schneer, J. A. & Reitman, F. (1990) Effects of unemployment gaps on the careers of MBAs. *Academy of Management Journal*, **33**, 391–406.

Schneer, J. A. & Reitman, F. (1993) Effects of alternate family structures on managerial career paths. *Academy of Management Journal*, **36**, 830–843.

Schneer, J. A. & Reitman, F. (1994a) Effects of early and mid-career employment gaps on career outcomes. *Academy of Management Best Paper Proceedings*, **54**, 63–67.

Schneer, J. A. & Reitman, F. (1994b) The importance of gender in mid-career. *Journal of Organizational Behavior*, **15**, 199–207.

Schneer, J. A. & Reitman, F. (1995) The impact of gender as managerial careers unfold. *Journal of Vocational Behavior*, **47**, 290–315.

Shackleton, V. & Newell, S. (1991) Managerial selection. *Journal of Occupational Psychology*, **64**, 23–36.

Shenhav, Y. (1992) Entrance of blacks and women into managerial positions in scientific and engineering occupations. *Academy of Management Journal*, **35**, 889–901.

Sheridan, J. E., Slocum, J. W., Buda, R., & Thompson, R. C. (1990) Effects of corporate sponsorship and departmental power on career tournaments. *Academy of Management Journal*, **33**, 578–602.

Sheridan, J. E., Slocum, J. W., & Buda, R. (in press) Factors influencing the probability of employee promotions. *Journal of Business and Psychology*, **11**.

Shore, T. H. (1992) Subtle gender bias in the assessment of managerial potential. *Sex Roles*, **29**, 499–515.

Siegel, S. R. (1993) Relationship between current performance and likelihood of promotion for old versus young workers. *Human Resource Development Quarterly*, **4**, 39–50.

Snyder, M. & Gangestad, S. (1982) Choosing social situations. *Journal of Personality and Social Psychology*, **43**, 123–135.

Sparks, C. P. (1990) Testing for management potential. In K. E. Clark & M. B. Clark (eds), *Measures of Leadership* (pp. 103–111). West Orange, NJ: Leadership Library of America.

Spence, A. M. (1973) Job market signaling. *Quarterly Journal of Economics*, **87**, 355–375.

Spence, A. M. (1974) *Market Signaling: The Information Transfer of Hiring and Related Processes*. Cambridge, MA: Harvard University Press.

Steinberg, R. J., Haignere, L., & Chertos, C. H. (1990) Managerial promotion in the public sector. *Work and Occupations*, **17**, 284–301.

Stover, D. (1994) The horizontal distribution of female managers within organizations. *Work and Occupations*, **21**, 385–402.

Strober, M. H. (1990) Human capital theory: Implications for HR managers. *Industrial Relations*, **29**, 214–359.

Stroh, L. K., Brett, J. M., & Reilly, A. H. (1992) All the right stuff. *Journal of Applied Psychology*, 77, 251–260.

Stroh, L. K., Brett, J. M., & Reilly, A. H. (1994) A decade of change. *Human Resource Management*, 33, 531–548.

Stumpf, S. A. & London, M. (1981) Management promotions. *Academy of Management Review*, 6, 539–549.

Super, D. E. (1957) *The Psychology of Careers*. New York: Harper.

Tharenou, P. (1990) Psychological approaches for investigating women's career advancement. *Australian Journal of Management*, 15, 363–378.

Tharenou, P. (1995) Correlates of women's chief executive status. *Journal of Career Development*, 21, 201–212.

Tharenou, P. & Conroy, D. K. (1994) Men and women managers' advancement. *Applied Psychology: An International Review*, 43, 5–31.

Tharenou, P., Latimer, S., & Conroy, D. K. (1994) How do you make it to the top? *Academy of Management Journal*, 37, 899–931.

Thompson, J. W. (1994) An international validation of London House's STEP battery. *Journal of Business and Psychology*, 9, 81–99.

Tremblay, M. & Roger, A. (1993) Individual, familial, and organizational determinants of career plateau. *Group and Organization Management*, 18, 411–435.

Truman, G. E. & Baroudi, J. J. (1994) Gender differences in the information systems managerial ranks. *MIS Quarterly*, 18, 129–142.

Turban, D. B. & Dougherty, T. W. (1994) Role of protégé personality in receipt of mentoring and career success. *Academy of Management Journal*, 37, 688–702.

Tziner, A., Meir, E., Dahan, M., & Birati, A. (1994) An investigation into the predictive validity and economic utility of the Assessment center for the high management level. *Canadian Journal of Behavioral Science*, 26, 228–245.

Van Velsor, E. & Leslie, J. B. (1995) Why executives derail. *Academy of Management Executive*, 9 (4), 62–73.

Whitely, W. T. & Coetsier, P. (1993) The relationship of career mentoring to early career outcomes. *Organization Studies*, 14, 419–441.

Whitely, W. T., Dougherty, T. W., & Dreher, G. F. (1991) Relationship of career mentoring and socioeconomic origin to managers' and professionals' early career progress. *Academy of Management Journal*, 34, 331–351.

Winter, D. G. (1991) A motivational model of leadership. *Leadership Quarterly*, 2 (2), 67–80.

Wright, E. O., Baxter, J., & Birkelund, G. E. (1995) The gender of workplace authority. *American Sociological Review*, 60, 407–435.

Yuen, E. C. (1995) Does having a mentor make a difference? *International Journal of Employment Studies*, 3, 1–15.

Chapter 4

A NEW KIND OF PERFORMANCE FOR INDUSTRIAL AND ORGANIZATIONAL PSYCHOLOGY: RECENT CONTRIBUTIONS TO THE STUDY OF ORGANIZATIONAL CITIZENSHIP BEHAVIOR

Dennis W. Organ and Julie Beth Paine
Kelley School of Business

INTRODUCTION

From its earliest days as a distinct area within the behavioral and social sciences, industrial/organizational psychology has recognized 'performance' as perhaps its 'ultimate' dependent variable, if not its *raison d'etre*. Interest in other matters, such as workplace attitudes and work group dynamics, implicitly derived from the eventual connections to knowledge about how to make organizations more effective.

Of course, I/O psychology emerged in the early years of this century, a time we now characterize as the 'Machine Age.' In this era, 'performance' for the rank and file of workers consisted of well-defined sequences of motor responses, dictated and paced by the needs of machines. Also, the securest fund of empirical knowledge in psychology at that time had to do with sensory perception, the topography of motor responses, and the measurement of mental and motor abilities. Thus, it occasions no surprise that industrial psychologists of that period justified their calling either by designing physical work environments or by selection and placement systems that maximized worker output.

In the middle years of the century, industrial psychology broadened its research by drawing from newly developing sectors of the larger discipline, such as social psychology. Hence, the concepts and methods fashioned for

A New Kind of Performance for Industrial and Organizational Psychology: Recent Contributions To The Study of Organizational Citizenship Behavior by Dennis W. Organ and Julie Beth Paine taken from IRIOP 1999 v14, Edited by Cary L. Cooper and Ivan T. Robertson: © 1999 John Wiley & Sons, Ltd

studying human motivation, social attitudes, personality, group dynamics, and leadership were put to use in analyzing workplace phenomena, on the premise that such applications could also add to our knowledge about how to improve 'performance.'

But little such knowledge resulted. There appeared to be little if any connection between workplace attitudes and productivity; no particular mode of leadership or supervision predicted group output; work group cohesion was as likely to be associated with work restriction as it was with greater productivity; and measures of personality traits offered little basis for predicting worker performance aside from measures of ability. Moreover, the strenuous effort that I/O psychologists put into crafting ever more refined measures and ever more complicated theories could not add materially to the variance explained in 'performance.' This is certainly not to say that these efforts were wasted. Knowledge of a sort did accrue from studies of worker satisfaction, measures of leader behavior, an understanding of the motives that people bring to work, the recognition of group forces on workplace behavior, and an array of organizational features that bear upon the quality of life at work. What seemed to be sorely missing was a means of connecting all of this to 'performance.'

In recent years, we have begun to think that perhaps the reason for the dearth of explanatory power of the 'softer' side of I/O psychology in the study of performance has not been because it is too soft, but that our dependent variable, 'performance,' has been too 'hard.' Until recently we have taken our cue from our early forebears and thought of performance as measurable output—with some form of supervisory ratings of 'job performance' as the occasional proxy for output, when measurement of individual output loomed as too formidable a task. In effect, our thinking about performance was frozen in a Machine Age mentality that equated organizational effectiveness with the algebraic sum of the task productivity of individual workers. The problem with this cast of mind is that it leaves the 'organizational' out of organizational psychology. Organized collective effort is efficacious precisely because it is organized; that is the whole is greater than the sum of its parts. To understand how people contribute to organizations, we have to understand not just how they can do their tasks more efficiently, but also what they contribute to the overall character of organization, the value-added 'surplus' by which the whole exceeds the sum of its parts.

And, indeed, that is precisely the tack increasingly taken by I/O psychology in recent years. We have witnessed a growing appreciation for the multi-dimensionality of individual contributions to organizations. Productivity in individually assigned tasks captures only a portion of what participants render to their workplace organizations. That portion, as we shall see, is mainly determined by the skills, ability, experience, and training of the person work-ing on the task—once due account is taken of the effects of technology and work design as they define the task itself. Beyond this are contributions of a different sort that do appear to be related to the 'softer' side of I/O psychology, such as social attitudes and personality. Suddenly it is not 'merely humanistic' to reckon with how we might effect and sustain high levels of job satisfaction, nor is it necessarily 'unscientific' to use impressionistic information from interviews in making hiring decisions. I/O psychologists can now address these questions not only in the assurance of their intellectual respectability, but gratified that they fully qualify as pertaining to the goal of making organizations more effective.

A number of more or less independent works of research and writing (with similarly independent sets of labels) have contributed to the development of our understanding of this larger definition of 'performance.' However, two lines of scholarly inquiry stand out as having provided the cumulative contributions that have defined, shaped, and articulated this domain of I/O psychology: The study of 'organizational citizenship behavior' (OCB) and the research on 'contextual performance.'

These programs of research arose from very different origins and motives. Work on OCB began as an effort to salvage something of value from the much-maligned 'human relations' belief that job satisfaction importantly affected a person's job productivity. Since empirical study undercut the premise that satisfaction was appreciably related to individual output, it was necessary to redefine 'performance' to include something other than output. In a sense, the goal was to 'find something that correlates with job satisfaction.' While an oversimplification, it is fair to state that this work was most often associated with those who identify themselves more with 'organizational' than 'industrial' psychology. Important contributions came from people with connections to schools of business at Indiana University, New York University, Northwestern University, Tulane University, the University of California at Berkeley, and Texas A&M University.

On the other hand, the study of contextual performance was undertaken in order to improve upon what were regarded as disappointingly low validity coefficients of existing measures used as predictors of performance. This work was conducted mainly by psychologists with connections to graduate programs of industrial and organizational psychology, and their interest resided particularly in the use of personality measures for predicting individual work performance. Such predictors had not fared well in accounting for measures of task output. Gradually, disaffection began to focus on the 'criterion'—perhaps the problem was a deficient, unimaginative conceptualization of the dependent variable. Effort was then directed to remapping the domain of what we mean by 'performance', with an eye toward the inclusion of organizationally-relevant contributions that go beyond productivity on a task. The result was the finding that some aspects of personality explained dimensions of performance not accounted for by differences in mental ability. Important studies in this stream of work were carried out by individuals with ties to the University of Minnesota, the

University of Florida, and the University of South Florida, as well as those psychologists involved in the ambitious 'Project A' (Campbell, 1990) for US Army personnel selection and classification.

This chapter will focus primarily on recent developments in the study of OCB. However, this endeavor will necessarily involve some discussion of contextual performance, because the two lines of inquiry—while emanating from quite different origins—have of late begun to merge.

First, we will note that a concern for OCB (or, contextual performance) can be traced back for over a half century to important conceptual work on organizations, and in one guise or another has resurfaced periodically in various treatises on management and collective effort. Following this historical note, we summarize the work done during 1976–1992 that is specifically associated with what is referred to as OCB. The core of the chapter then concentrates on what has been going on in roughly the last five years of study directed to this topic. We conclude with an overview of the broad contours of the published work in this area and some suggestions for those who endeavor to contribute to it.

HISTORICAL ROOTS OF OCB

Chester Barnard's *The Functions of the Executive* has been reprinted at least 20 times since its first appearance in 1939, and with good reason. No one in the first half of this century offered a more penetrating and comprehensive analysis of collective effort, and no conceptual scheme of organization has proved more robust to secular trends in the style, content, or purpose of organized action. Barnard's analysis is not bound by particular technologies, ideologies, nor—so far as we can tell—by culture.

Early on, Barnard notes that 'successful cooperation in or by formal organizations is the abnormal, not the normal condition. What are observed from day to day are the successful survivors among innumerable failures' (Barnard, 1939/1964:5). We suppose that if Barnard were writing today, he might have expressed this observation in terms evocative of sociological thermodynamics, that the normal condition of human effort is toward entropy. The point is that the odds are against the sustaining of collective effort. *Homo sapiens* might be a social animal, but not naturally nor necessarily united in formal collective effort. Thus, some forces must be exerted toward the sheer maintenance of organization itself, over and beyond whatever the organization is intended to accomplish.

For Barnard, the essential condition of organizations is a '*willingness* of persons to contribute efforts to the cooperative system' (p. 83, italics in orig.). This willingness, he adds further, involves a subordination of self; thereby a personal act becomes a contribution to an impersonal system, and the effect is 'cohesion of effort.' Willingness to cooperate is something different from effectiveness, ability, or value of personal contributions. It varies over time and across individuals, but 'the preponderance of persons' at any given time are likely to be characterized by a fragile sense of this willingness.

So we see that Barnard clearly appreciated the importance of individual contributions other than those of performing a particular task. Also critical are the actions expressive of 'willingness to cooperate'. Furthermore, he anticipated the key thrust of work on OCB by suggesting that 'willingness to cooperate, positive or negative, is the expression of the net satisfactions or dissatisfactions experienced or anticipated by each individual in comparison with those experienced or anticipated through alternative opportunities' (p.85). Finally, he foreshadowed the work on contextual performance in his belief that stable differences exist among individuals in their tendencies toward willingness to cooperate.

The famed Hawthorne studies of Western Electric were taking place even as Barnard wrote. Barnard was not directly involved in these studies, but he had connections to Elton Mayo, and others at Harvard, who influenced the course of those studies. *Management and the Worker* (Roethlisberger & Dickson, 1939/1967), the interpretive chronicle of the decade of Hawthorne studies, cites Barnard, so it appears that the latter's ideas had some influence on the lessons derived from Hawthorne. Indeed, Barnard set the precedent for Roethlisberger and Dickson's distinction between the 'formal' and 'informal organization.' What is curious, though instructive, is that Barnard saw the formal organization as evolving from the informal—that is the formal organization at some point becoming an 'institutionalization' of informal collective effort—but the Hawthorne writers keyed on the reverse sequence. Roethlisberger and Dickson took the formal structure as a given and informal organization as emergent from it. The informal organization, guided by the 'logic of sentiment' as opposed to the logic of fact, could take a direction in opposition to the formal system. Nonetheless, the informal organization stood as a 'necessary condition for collaboration.' In a sense, there always is a lag between formal structure and informal organization. The former arises from the latter, but the need for collaboration never can be wholly guaranteed by formal structure. Some account must then be taken of why and how participants go beyond the dictates of the formal structure in order to sustain coherent collective action.

Katz and Kahn (1966), working within an open-system model of organization in their social psychological analysis, drew attention to the qualitatively different classes of behaviors essential to organizational effectiveness. Organizations require patterns of dependable and predictable behavior by their participants, behavior that is roughly synonymous with the roles prescribed for them by the formal structure. But also essential are spontaneous behaviors that meet the demands of unforeseen contingencies:

Within every work group in a factory, within any division in a government bureau, or within any department of a university are countless acts of cooperation without which the system would break down. We take these everyday acts for granted, and few of them are included in the formal role prescriptions for any job. One man will point out to another that his machine is getting jammed, or will pass along some tool that his companion needs, or will borrow some bit of material he is short on. Men will come to the aid of a fellow who is behind on his quota. . . . We recognize the need for cooperative relationships by raising specific questions about a man's capacity for them when he is considered for a job. How well does he relate to his fellows; is he a good team man; will he fit in? (Katz & Kahn, 1966:339)

Katz and Kahn stressed that the same drives or incentives do not necessarily motivate these different classes of behavior. The rewards that accrue to participants because of above-average task proficiency do not logically elicit spontaneous, informal contributions.

By way of concluding this brief historical sketch, let us note a recurring theme of so many celebrated statements about the nature of groups and organizations—the distinction between those activities that accomplish the primary function of the group or the organization and those activities that sustain the inclination to think and act as part of a collective effort. Bales' path-breaking studies of small groups (Bales & Slater, 1955) recognized the role of a task leader but a separate role for the 'maintenance specialist' who helped keep the group together. Fleishman's empirical analyses of supervisory behavior identified not only those leader behaviors (initiation of structure) that addressed task activities, but an independent set of behaviors—consideration—that nurture the affective involvement of participants in the collective enterprise (Fleishman, Harris, & Burtt, 1955).

What we did not have before the early 1980s was a means of translating these organizational imperatives for willingness to cooperate, collaboration, or maintenance into the industrial/organizational psychologist's conception of individual performance. The work done in the late 1970s and 1980s under such rubrics as OCB, prosocial behavior, extra-role behavior, and contextual performance provided the framework for meeting those needs.

OCB, 1977–1992

The origins of the research on OCB date from an essay by Organ (1977), in which he offered some defense for the conventional wisdom that 'satisfaction causes performance.' This notion, said by many to derive from a discredited 'Human Relations' conception of worker psychology, had little support from empirical studies dating back to the 1930s. The more accepted view among academic I/O psychologists was that satisfaction follows from rewards, which might or might not depend on level of performance (Lawler & Porter, 1967). Organ, more or less assuming the role of Devil's Advocate, suggested that perhaps the acceptance by managers and other nonacademic groups of the 'satisfaction causes performance' view was due to their broader definition of 'performance.' Conceivably the practitioner thinks of performance as more than quantity of output or virtuoso technical accomplishments. To those charged with the responsibility of running an organization, 'performance' might also include all of those actions that make the organization easier to run. Thus, people who come to work regularly and on time; accept and follow the rules of workplace governance; show respect for others as well as for organizational assets; and subordinate short-run personal indulgences for the greater good of the group, are 'good performers'—even if their 'productivity' (in measurable output of goods and services) is only 'average' or 'fair.' And, Organ argued, people would be inclined to exhibit these manifold gestures of accommodation and cooperation as a means of reciprocation to the organization for satisfying work experiences and outcomes. Productivity will be constrained by the limits of aptitude, technology, work design, and resources, but participants can adjust their cooperation and compliance more flexibly to match the support given them by management. In this sense, then, 'satisfaction' might indeed 'cause performance,' and therefore the conventional wisdom is indeed wise.

Organ's essay was one of several that had pondered the question of how satisfaction and performance are related. It suggested nothing particularly distinctive as a framework for theory or guide to research, and there is nothing in the essay to indicate that Organ himself had any intention to pursue his notions in any systematic inquiry. However, two doctoral students took him seriously. T.S. Bateman, using Organ's essay as a starting point, developed a measure of what he called 'nonquantitative' performance and conducted a longitudinal, cross-lagged correlational study of this performance and satisfaction in a group of nonacademic professional university employees. The results (published in Bateman & Organ, 1983) were encouraging and quite consistent with the idea that prior satisfaction predicted subsequent 'nonquantitative performance.'

Another student, C.A. Smith, inspired by her close and sympathetic reading of *Management and the Worker*, undertook to elaborate upon Bateman's measure and investigate further the nature and correlates of this 'organizational citizenship behavior.' First, she interviewed several first-line supervisors at different places of work and asked them to think of what they expected and appreciated in a 'good worker' but could neither force them to do nor promise specific rewards for doing. From this material she drafted a tentative measure and tested it with a group of full-time-employed students taking graduate business courses. The data yielded two clearly distinct factors. One factor was defined by helping or cooperating with a specific person (coworker or supervisor) and was dubbed 'altruism.' The other factor was comprised of items describing more general and impersonal conduct in support of the organization and was called 'generalized compliance.' These factors held up in a large field study in two banks, and in that study both were significantly correlated with job satisfaction, with the altruism factor showing the stronger connection (a frequent finding in OCB studies). The data also implicated something like a 'conscientiousness' personality factor as an independent predictor of generalized compliance (see Smith, Organ, & Near, 1983).

Organ used these findings, along with related but independent works such as those by Puffer (1987) and Scholl, Cooper, and McKenna (1987) as an empirical basis for sketching a conceptual model of OCB (Organ, 1988). He used the occasion to suggest other types of OCB, such as sportsmanship, courtesy, and civic virtue (constructive political involvement in the workplace: Graham, 1986). He also drew from the substantial body of empirical literature in experimental social psychology documenting the effect of good mood on prosocial behavior. Organ believed that the correlational studies of OCB and job satisfaction could be interpreted in two different ways: Perhaps people consciously and deliberately use OCB to reciprocate their employers for positive work experiences; alternatively, job satisfaction—as a stable good mood state—leads people to behave spontaneously in a constructive and cooperative fashion. Finally, Organ speculated on the dispositional basis of OCB, noting work by Schneider and Dachler (1978), Staw and Ross (1985), and Staw, Bell and Clausen (1986) in support of dispositional origins of job satisfaction.

From the date of Organ's monograph up through the early 1990s, the published work on OCB developed along three main lines of inquiry:

1.   Podsakoff and MacKenzie, along with various associates, developed measures of types of OCB other than those of altruism and generalized compliance (e.g., Podsakoff, MacKenzie, Moorman, & Fetter, 1990). Four-factor and five-factor schemes have met with varying degrees of success in terms of fitting the intended items of the measures. Regardless of the number of factors yielded by the data, the factors themselves consistently intercorrelate at levels from 0.35 to 0.70 or higher. The most consistent and interpretable breakdown is the split between the 'personal' and 'impersonal' forms of OCB.
2.   Several researchers attempted to tease out that element or aspect of job satisfaction that relates most strongly to OCB. Is it the cognitive or affective element of satisfaction that is most important? If, as some studies (e.g., Organ & Konovsky, 1989) suggest, the cognitive influence predominates, is this cognitive influence translatable into the notion of 'fairness'? And if fairness is the key, is it the distributive, procedural, or interactional dimension of fairness that matters most? (cf. Konovsky & Folger, 1991; Moorman, 1991; Niehoff & Moorman, 1993).
3.   Overlapping the two lines of inquiry noted above was the more general approach of identifying attitudinal and dispositional predictors of OCB and comparing their relative strengths of association with the criterion. In some

instances this approach took the form of testing causal models implicating dispositional factors (e.g., Agreeableness, Conscientiousness, Positive Affectivity) as underlying determinants of both job satisfaction and OCB and thus explaining why the latter two variables are correlated.

Recent Developments, Extensions, and Reinterpretations of OCB

Attitudinal and dispositional predictors: examination of the cumulative empirical record

By the end of 1994 a substantial body of empirical literature concerning OCB had accumulated, and by far the largest portion of this record concerned attitudinal and dispositional correlates of various measures of OCB. Organ and Ryan (1995) conducted a meta-analysis of 55 such studies.

Organ and Ryan concluded that the attitudinal predictors most frequently studied—job satisfaction, perceived fairness, affective commitment, and leader supportiveness—were roughly equal in terms of the estimated population correlations with both of the major dimensions of OCB (altruism and compliance). There simply was no basis for thinking that any one attitude was the 'ultimate' predictor of OCB or that any one of them accounted for the correlation of the others with OCB. The correlations, corrected for attenuation, hover roughly around the 0.30 level, depending on whether one includes studies using self-report ratings of OCB. Organ (1997) has more recently concluded, as a result of structural equations analysis of the estimated population correlations, that a general 'morale' factor underlies the pattern of correlations between job attitudes and OCB. Thus, any self-report measure of participants' assessments or perceptions of their work environments will predict independent ratings of OCB to the extent that such measures tap a diffuse, pervasive state of 'good morale.'

Organ and Ryan found much less support for the connection between personality factors and OCB. The one notable instance of association is that between conscientiousness and the impersonal form of OCB (compliance). Personality measures with strong overtones suggestive of characteristic mood states could not account for the reliable correlations between job attitudes and OCB; the data suggested that it is more likely that affectively toned dispositions predict OCB only to the extent that they predict job attitude measures.

One definite *caveat* is in order here in assessing the strength of dispositional predictors of OCB. For purposes of analysis, Organ and Ryan grouped a variety of measures that they had deemed reflective of the trait of conscientiousness. It is likely that these measures varied considerably in their true (but unknown) validity as indices of conscientiousness, and proper corrections for attenuation due to variable validities might have resulted in a stronger association with OCB. Furthermore, the work of Borman and Motowidlo (1993), Motowidlo and Van Scotter (1994), and Van Scotter and Motowidlo (1996) suggests that conscientiousness, when consistently and specifically defined in terms of personal characteristics such as work orientation and dependability, has stronger links to OCB than one would have guessed from Organ and Ryan's meta-analysis.

Experimental research on OCB

The dominant research paradigm in OCB, as with so much of I/O psychology, has taken the form of the correlational field study. Of course, this fact constrains the confidence we can place in any interpretations of the data. Correlations between so-called predictors and presumed criteria can occur as a function of unmeasured variables that might or might not figure in the stated theoretical framework guiding the research. Also, even when predictors and criteria measures come from different sources (and thus are not vulnerable to the problem of common method variance), one cannot dismiss the possibility that the measures are both distorted by common causes. For example, supervisors (or, for that matter, coworkers) who simply like certain participants might rate them higher in OCB; and those participants report more positive attitudes and perceptions of the workplace by virtue of being liked by those raters. Even 'longitudinal' correlational studies of OCB (which are rare) are hardly free of such problems. Thus, experimental procedures that vary presumed influences on OCB and assess the concomitant changes in OCB would provide valuable checks on the tenability of conclusions based on correlational studies.

Laboratory experiments pose a formidable challenge to researching OCB because they force the researcher to define OCB narrowly. OCB as a construct covers a potentially broad category of behaviors. Moreover, current theoretical approaches regard OCB as a function of attitudes and personality, which predict aggregated indices of thematically related behaviors over the course of time better than they predict any specific behavior at a given moment. Thus, it comes as no surprise that laboratory experiments are conspicuous by their absence in the OCB literature.

A major exception is a study conducted by Wright, George, Farnsworth, and McMahan (1993), in which the researchers varied goal difficulty and goal-contingent rewards with respect to an explicit measure of task productivity. The researchers found that difficult and specific goals, while associated with higher task productivity, reduced the incidence of OCB in the form of helping a late-arriving subject (who was actually a confederate of the experimenters). The lowered OCB was particularly significant among those subjects (students) who reported the higher levels of commitment to the goal. These findings, of course, posed little relevance for questions about attitudinal and personality factors usually studied as correlates of OCB. However, the results demonstrated that some methods for motivating high levels of task productivity can have detrimental effects on OCB. Those who attain high task productivity may do so, in part, because they focus their effort on measurable performance that is contractually rewarded, diverting their energies away from contributions that would not be measured or rewarded. One cannot help wondering what the longer run effect would have been on those who did help the confederate and did not qualify for pay which was contingent on meeting the goal for task productivity. A plausible scenario is that they would have judged the reward scheme unfair and curtailed their efforts to help others, regardless of whether such curtailment would have improved their task performance.

Another laboratory experiment (Hui, Organ, & Crooker, 1994) manipulated time pressure as a task stressor to see how that would affect the willingness of student subjects to contribute subsequently to a supposedly unrelated opinion/suggestion survey conducted by the school administration. The trend of the results suggested that higher time pressure diminished the quality of the subjects' participation in the survey, more so than the proportion of students willing to participate, but overall the findings were weak.

A major contribution to the empirical record of OCB came in the form of a quasi-field experiment conducted by Skarlicki and Latham (1996). They conducted a training program in principles of organization justice for officers in a Canadian union local. The training consisted of four 3-hour sessions conducted over a three-week period, and used lectures, case studies, group discussion, and role-playing. Pre-intervention measures of members' perceptions of union fairness and peer ratings of union citizenship behaviors were administered to the experimental group and to a control group, which was another local affiliate of the same national union. Three months after concluding the training of union officers, experimental and control groups again responded to measures of perceived fairness and OCB. Rank and file members of the intervention group, but not the other local, registered a significant increase in perceived fairness in the manner in which the local was governed an administered. The inference is that the union officers who received the training had in fact applied the training material in their dealings with the membership. Also, peer ratings of member OCB increased significantly in the intervention group but not in the comparison group; this increase occurred in both forms of OCB, one defined by citizenship behaviors directed toward the union as an organization and another comprised of citizenship behaviors vis-à-vis other union members. Interestingly, causal modeling of the data indicated that increased perceived fairness virtually entirely accounted for the increase in the more abstract or organizational expression of OCB, but not in the more personal or collegial form of union citizenship. In other words, while the training apparently changed the union officers' conduct in ways that led to increased perceptions of union fairness, and simultaneously members increased their citizenship behavior in peer interaction, the change in perceived fairness did not by itself account for the rise in OCB. The suggestion is that something other than fairness in officers' behavior had changed. This would not be surprising, as field interventions—however effective in practice—can almost never be 'construct pure' (Cook & Campbell, 1979). Possibly the intervention provided the occasion for other informal (even subtle) changes that improved not simply fairness, but 'morale' in a more general sense.

Skarlicki and Latham (1997) replicated this study with a different union. The original study featured a public sector union comprised of white-collar professional and technical employees; the replication occurred in a private sector union whose members were clerical workers and owned shares in the company. Measures, training program content, and pedagogy matched those of the earlier study. Results were virtually identical, including the finding that increased fairness perceptions mediated the effect of the training on the 'compliance' dimension of OCB, but not on the 'altruism' form of union citizenship behaviors.

Consequences of OCB

The bulk of empirical research on OCB, especially before 1992, concerned itself with antecedents of individual OCB. As noted above, most of this research assessed the relative predictive power of measures of various individual attitudes, perceptions, and traits.

More recently, an increased interest has become manifest in the consequences of OCB. One form of this interest has to do with the consequences for the individual who is regarded as regularly exhibiting more or less OCB—for example, how does OCB affect treatment by superiors? The other consequence of interest is how OCB by the group as a whole affects group performance—performance defined in terms of the group's effectiveness in achieving its goals.

Consequences of OCB: individuals

Performance appraisal. Most supervisors would like to believe that their assessments of employee performance are relatively unbiased and reflect actual employee productivity on defined objectives. However, recent research has shown that in fact there is more to the performance appraisal than either supervisors or employees realize. One of the factors influencing ratings and other outcomes of performance appraisal is the extent to which an employee demonstrates OCB.

The weight given to OCB by supervisors will vary, as will the value of OCB for a given job. However, what is clear is that managers define employee performance beyond simply 'in-role' behavior. There are many possible reasons why managers are influenced by OCB when evaluating performance, including: 'norms of reciprocity' or feelings of obligation toward helpful employees; a search for distinctive or memorable information about an employee (something unique that he or she has done); rating errors such as halo or recency effects because of recent gestures of extra effort; illusory correlations between extra-role performance and outcomes; and schema-triggered affect or the association of an individual with certain categories or stereotypes perpetuated by OCB-type behavior.

In a study by Werner (1994), OCB directed toward individuals (OCB-I) and OCB directed toward the organization (OCB-O) were compared with in-role dimensions of performance to see whether OCB was creating a halo effect in supervisory ratings of employee performance. Results indicated a significant correlation between the level of OCB-I and a halo effect in ratings. In other words, the halo effect was greater for employees when supervisors had highly positive OCB information regarding the employee's behavior. Werner argued that if OCB is in fact desirable for improved overall organizational effectiveness, and if such information explains relevant rating variance, then the value of OCB should be made explicit to employees in the rating process.

Not only does OCB have the potential to cause rating errors, but it also may account for more of the overall evaluation outcome than supervisors realize. Podsakoff, MacKenzie and Hui (1993) and MacKenzie, Podsakoff and Fetter (1993) found that OCB consistently accounted for a larger portion of variance in evaluations of salesperson performance than did objective measures of productivity. While OCB *and* objective productivity accounted for over half of the variance in the evaluations of the sales persons' performance, OCB explained a larger proportion of the variance by itself than did objective measures.

A critical issue associated with the conscious or unconscious effect that OCB has on supervisors in employee performance appraisals is whether employees realize the role that OCB has in evaluations. Employees who take their in-role responsibilities literally and believe they are performing at a high level may feel unfairly treated if they find that they are being judged on criteria not specified beforehand. In making fairness judgments, employees will consider the extent to which evaluation criteria are specified in advance. Feelings of injustice could undermine employee motivation, decrease job satisfaction, or increase the likelihood of withdrawal from the organization.

Moving up the hierarchy. Organ (1988) originally suggested that, 'the higher the rank of an organizational member, the more diffuse are the expected, role-related obligations of that member.' This implies that individuals will demonstrate a wide variety of OCB more often upon reaching higher levels in the organization. OCB may also affect one's chances of getting to those higher levels in the first place. Research by Park and Sims (1989) studied whether OCB affected promotion decisions. They found that subjects who demonstrated OCB were most likely to be considered for promotions. OCB clearly was linked to initial considerations for managerial positions in that without OCB, individuals were not even likely to be considered for promotion.

In concert with the assumption that managerial responsibilities are more diffuse, Borman and Motowidlo (1993) discussed the fact that evaluations of higher level managers may rely more heavily on OCB because of the greater contextual nature of their jobs. They argued that, 'differences between task and contextual components are not as straightforward as in other jobs', and that as much as 30% of managerial performance is contextual. This contextual component would entail OCB-like behavior such as helping others, demonstrating enthusiastic leadership, publicly supporting the organization, and acting as a role model for others.

Recently, MacKenzie, Podsakoff and Paine (1997) considered whether OCB and objective productivity measures had differential effects on evaluations of performance at various hierarchical levels. Findings supported the hypothesis that managers' evaluations of performance are determined at least as much by OCB as they are by objective measures of performance. In addition, results indicated that a larger proportion of evaluations is due to OCB as individuals ascend the organizational hierarchy. In particular, OCB contributed to 43% of managerial evaluations, and was 15 times more important than quantitative performance for managers while only 4 times as important as quantitative performance for employees.

Possible explanations for this occurrence include difficulty in separating managerial from subordinate contributions, difficulty quantifying individual managerial performance at higher levels, greater expectations for members of management, less frequent interaction between managers and *their* managers (thus, a search for distinctive behavioral examples when evaluating performance), and the higher visibility of managerial positions—necessitating a kind of 'role-modeling' toward lower level employees. Findings suggest that OCB is a key component in the selection of managers, and highlight the need to make more explicit the importance of demonstrating OCB at higher levels of management.

Consequences of OCB: organizational/unit levels

One of the original tenets of the concept of OCB was that in the aggregate it improves overall organizational effectiveness and performance. In recent years, research has in fact been able to support this assumption. A study by Karambayya (1991) showed a correlation between OCB and subjective ratings of unit performance. It also reflected the importance of the interdependence between work units in creating an aggregate increase in overall performance.

More recently, Podsakoff, Ahearne, and MacKenzie (1997) tested whether OCB actually improves the effectiveness of organizations. Their study of 40 machine crews in a paper mill revealed that Helping Behavior and Sportsmanship had significant effects on performance quantity, and Helping Behavior also had a significant impact on performance quality. With general support for the relationship between OCB and work group performance, they were able to identify that one-fourth of the variance in quantity and one-fifth of the variance in quality were accounted for by OCB.

In earlier research, Podsakoff and MacKenzie (1992) studied the impact of average unit OCB combined with sales productivity, on overall unit performance in 116 managerial units of a large insurance company. They found that OCB significantly enhanced unit level performance. In particular, the dimensions of Sportsmanship and Civic Virtue most directly enhanced performance, while Helping Behavior had the smallest impact on performance. In contrast to the 1997 article, it was argued that Helping Behavior demonstrated by one employee may or may not actually help the recipient—that in fact it may detract from the ability to get work done by taking time away from the 'doing' of one's job. However, this may vary somewhat due to the nature of the industry being studied, as well as the type of compensation being provided (individual versus group rewards). Overall, the aggregate effect of greater OCB was an increase in unit level performance.

In a study by Walz (1995), 34 General Managers of 'Limited Menu Restaurants' (fast food restaurants with no official wait-staff) were surveyed regarding employee citizenship behavior. Significant differences were found in the levels of OCB demonstrated by employees in high-performance LMRs (with 'performance' measured by several objective criteria) versus the levels of OCB in low-performing LMRs. Building on Walz's research, Walz and Niehoff (1996) found that Helping Behavior was positively related to overall operating efficiency, customer satisfaction, revenue per full-time employee, and quality of performance, and was negatively related to waste. In addition, Sportsmanship and Civic Virtue were negatively related to customer complaints, which was reflected in overall organizational effectiveness ratings on customer surveys.

In contrast to the 1992 Podsakoff and MacKenzie findings, the Walz and Niehoff data showed that Helping Behavior had the greatest overall impact on organization effectiveness, and that OCB did improve the organization's overall efficiency. The aggregate effects of OCB on measures of organizational effectiveness were significantly different for high and low performing organizations. In concluding this study, the authors recommended studying OCB at the aggregate or group level as opposed to the individual level, since a fundamental premise of OCB is that it contributes to *overall* organizational performance.

Going international: cross-cultural perspectives on OCB

OCB as a construct was conceived within the context of North American cultural expressions of organizational behavior, and almost all of the studies up to 1992 studied OCB with settings, subjects, and measures adapted to that culture. Hofstede (1980) and others have amply documented that the prevailing work culture in North America is apt to score much higher in individualism than we would find in Asia, Latin America, and most of Europe, where a more collective ethos reigns. One might well expect that differences in individualism-collectivism would temper the conception of OCB and the forms in which people in the culture recognize its occurrence. We might likewise find that antecedents of OCB are different in more collective cultures, for example, that individual job satisfaction does not figure as importantly as some other perceptions of the work environment. Indeed, we might find that in a collective culture OCB has no real meaning apart from any other conception of member contributions of a holistic sort.

Measurement and construct issues/cultural mediators of OCB

In one of the first non-North American studies looking at leader fairness, Farh, Podsakoff, and Organ (1990) argued that task scope accounts for more variance in the Altruism/Compliance dimensions of OCB than satisfaction. In researching this hypothesis, they surveyed 195 workers from the Taiwanese ministry of communications to see if Taiwanese supervisors dimensionalize OCB the same way that supervisors do in the US. For the dimensions of altruism and General Compliance, the coefficients of congruence were 0.96 and 0.97, respectively.

Overall, the data did not support the hypothesis that satisfaction is a direct cause or antecedent of Altruism or General Compliance, but leader fairness and task characteristics were characterized as causal variables. However, satisfaction was correlated with both leader fairness and task characteristics.

Other researchers have begun to consider the possible cross-cultural nature of OCB. One such study by Konovsky, Elliott, and Pugh (1997) compared the factor structure of OCB in a Mexican sample with that of a similar US sample. Predictors of OCB in Mexico included conscientiousness, achievement striving, and distributive justice. These reflect a similar structure to that found in the US. However, support for the social exchange model of OCB found in the US was not found in the Mexican sample. The authors were interested in whether management practices were transferable between NAFTA countries, and whether these practices would have the same effect on productivity in both countries. In particular, they tested whether the same variables would predict OCB.

The tendency for OCB to be more likely in collectivistic cultures was discussed. This was hypothesized because collectivistic cultures tend to favor interdependence, loyalty, and helping, all of which are reminiscent of OCB-like behavior. However, the actual interpretation of what constitutes citizenship behavior may vary from culture to culture. In the Mexican sample, there was some support for the hypothesis that perceived fairness would explain variance in OCB beyond satisfaction alone. The authors also found that trait conscientiousness predicted OCB (manifested as altruism, courtesy, and civic virtue) in the Mexican sample. Finally, the social exchange model of OCB (which is supported in the US) was found to fit better than an economic exchange model, but did not fit the data as well as in the US.

The implications of these findings is that OCB does have meaning and relevance in different cultures, but in some cases the types of behaviors which define OCB may differ. In addition, the terminology used to identify or classify OCB may have different meaning as well.

Moorman and Blakely (1995) considered Individualism and Collectivism as individual difference predictors of OCB in a within-culture study. Results provided further support for the notion that people with collectivistic tendencies are more likely to demonstrate OCB. Not only do individualistic and collectivistic differences exist across cultures, but they exist within cultures as well, and can impact the level of OCB demonstrated by groups that appear relatively homogeneous.

In some cases, demonstrating OCB (or not demonstrating OCB) may have a similar result in the eyes of an organization's management (increased productivity), but the actual behavior may 'look' very different behavior depending on the culture and workforce. Munene (1995) looked at a behavioral phenomenon in Nigeria called 'Not-on-Seat,' which means reporting to work on time, then leaving the workplace or immediate area, and returning several hours later. This behavior is considered an aspect of an employee's 'service attitude' which in Nigerian business is considered a form of OCB. OCB was defined for purposes of this study as, 'Cooperative acts which are given freely and spontaneously.'

Munene argues that there is a tendency for African organization members to lack professional conscience yet have a strong concern for social obligations. Bureaucrats may be more concerned with what is best for their extended family than for the organization as a whole. Munene also suggests that one cannot rely on job satisfaction as a condition for OCB in Africa because the actual job conditions are often so poor that it would not be a meaningful measurement. Therefore, Munene proposes that for most African workers, job satisfaction would not be related to OCB. Instead, he argues that 'job involvement' or meeting one's needs and having a psychological identification with one's job, as well as having affective commitment based on a need for social approval or group identification, would be more viable precursors to OCB.

In Munene's study, supervisors rated employees on a 9-item conscientiousness scale, while employees rated their job involvement, affective commitment, and job satisfaction. Results showed that job involvement was the variable with the strongest influence on OCB, followed by affective commitment, trust, meeting perceived needs, and then job satisfaction. Thus, the challenge of developing a common definition of OCB which can be applied universally, becomes clearer.

Organ and Lingl (1995) also studied OCB in a cross-cultural setting and found no significant differences in citizenship behavior between work cultures in the United States and Britain. The study, which used survey data from production facilities in both countries, revealed a two-factor structure of OCB, with the traits agreeableness and conscientiousness accounting for variance in satisfaction for both groups, and conscientiousness accounting for variance in Altruism and Generalized Compliance.

Finally, Farh, Earley, and Lin (1997) considered the relationship between OCB and organizational justice in Chinese society. The Western term 'OCB' and its dimensional correlates were analyzed for applicability in Chinese society. Three of the original five dimensions applied, while two additional dimensions were substituted. The five dimensions of OCB in Chinese society were altruism, conscientiousness, identification with the company (similar to Civic Virtue), interpersonal harmony, and protecting company resources.

Using the five Chinese dimensions of OCB, Farh, Earley and Lin found that organizational justice was most strongly related to OCB in a 'traditional', low-modernity culture, and was stronger for men than for women. This 'traditional' society was described as hierarchical, respectful of authority, non-egalitarian, and collectivistic. Both distributive and procedural justice enhanced OCB by nurturing a covenantal contract between the employee and the organization. Overall, organizational justice had a significant impact on two of the five dimensions identified as OCB in China. Farh, Earley, and Lin also suggest that the nature of social ties within a society will influence the display of extra-role behaviors or OCB, and stress the importance of culture-specific construct development.

OCB-I versus OCB-O

An important but subtle phenomenon noted in some of the cross-cultural work on OCB is the strong distinction between OCB directed toward other individuals (OCB-I) and OCB directed toward the organization (OCB-O). In the study mentioned previously by Farh, Earley, and Lin (1997), the tendency toward strong collectivism with regard to one's family meant that organizations had to be very cautious about employees using resources for family gains. Demonstrating OCB-I for one's 'in-group' was taken almost to an extreme.

In an exploratory study by Paine and Organ (1997), a small sample of individuals from 26 different countries provided further support for the importance of defining cross-cultural OCB in terms of OCB-I and OCB-O. Not only did the results of the study reflect a more cynical attitude toward OCB in some countries (e.g., in Japan it is expected but in the UK it is considered 'brown-nosing'), but interviews with subjects reflected strong feelings regarding the delineation between demonstrating OCB for coworkers or friends versus for one's organization. For example, in Australia, the concept of loyalty to one's 'mates' is of the utmost importance and is even expected. However, OCB toward the organization is seen as going considerably beyond the norm.

Construct refinement

Organ defined OCB as 'individual behavior that is discretionary, not directly or explicitly recognized by the formal reward system, and that in the aggregate promotes the effective functioning of the organization' (Organ, 1988:4). Implicitly, this definition marks OCB as 'extra-role' or 'beyond the job description.' Some benefits might accrue to those who contribute much in the form of OCB, but the concept excluded any specific contributions for which the organization provided official recognition and contractual rewards or benefits.

Williams and Anderson (1991) have demonstrated that, whether one uses self-ratings, ratings by peers, or ratings by supervisors, there is clear evidence that the raters discriminate between OCB and 'in-role' performance, just as they distinguish between the impersonal and personal (compliance versus altruism) dimensions of OCB itself. Nonetheless, a recurring controversy among I/O psychologists interested in OCB has involved the objection that much—potentially all—of what is *measured* as OCB is in fact part of the 'job.' Even if certain designated aspects of OCB do not find expression in a formal job description, there often will be expectations by peers, bosses, or the individual that those aspects of performance be rendered. Especially problematic for some is the 'compliance' or impersonal brand of OCB. Since measures include items pertaining to attendance, punctuality, following the rules, and using company time for company-relevant activities only, one could easily argue that the measures spill over into the formal job domain. After all, everyone is expected to be at work and on time, follow the rules, and not use company time for personal business. Some might counter with the argument that there is some *level* of adherence to these norms beyond which higher levels of conduct are discretionary and not formally rewarded. But the distinction certainly becomes blurred.

As illustration of the problem, Morrison (1994) found that a majority of respondents interpreted 18 of the 20 items comprising the intended measure of OCB as 'in-role.' Indeed, the thrust of her findings was that, the broader the subjects themselves defined their 'job,' the higher they were rated in OCB. Perhaps it is no more 'discretionary' to perform OCB than it is in fact ultimately discretionary whether to perform any part of the job.

We have already noted findings that those who are rated higher in OCB tend also to receive higher ratings of overall performance. It would be astonishing if more positive appraisals of performance did not translate into better treatment in some forms of benefits. Such treatment might not occur as a contractual guarantee, but then one has to wonder these days just how much of any claim on organizational rewards rests on formal contracts. Thus, it becomes increasingly difficult to identify contributions that are not part of the 'job' or 'role' (as defined by somebody) and do not meet with tangible rewards about as often and reliably as any form of 'in-role performance.'

To further complicate this issue, other constructs purport to capture 'extra-role behavior' (ERB), and while they might well overlap with some categories of OCB, they certainly do not coincide with OCB. Whistle-blowing (WB: Near & Miceli, 1987) and Principled Organization Dissent (POD: Graham, 1986), for example, would seldom figure as 'part of the job,' as most people would understand it. Also, both WB and POD, to the extent that they uncover and correct various illegal and unethical practices, arguably do contribute to long-run organizational effectiveness, although the short-run effects might include much pain and embarrassment for organizational officials. Yet such 'challenging' or adversarial gestures bear little resemblance to OCB in the forms of altruism, compliance, courtesy, and sportsmanship. One strongly suspects that the predictors of WB and POD would be just as different from OCB as would be the short-run effects of the actions themselves.

Van Dyne, Cummings, and Parks (1995) made a valiant effort to bring some conceptual order to the jumble of ERB constructs. They conclude that a strong case exists for preserving the in-role/extra-role dimension for member behavior. Even though what is extra-role at a given moment might evolve into an in-role practice, and even though different observers (including the actor) might differ in opinion as to whether a specific form of contribution resides in-role or extra-role, the distinction has utility for some theoretical purposes. They would, however, regard OCB as pertaining more to those contributions that have an affiliative or promotive flavor, with POD and WB viewed as extra-role behavior that is challenging or adversarial. Substantively, the main effect this would have on OCB is that it calls for a redefining and perhaps renaming of Civic Virtue. Organ (1988), borrowing from Graham (1986), understood Civic Virtue to encompass those contributions arising from responsible political involvement in the governance and conduct of the collective enterprise. In fact, the measurement of Civic Virtue has operationalized it into a set of mundane tasks (e.g., attending meetings, reading and answering mail, offering opinions, keeping up with what's going on at work) that are more akin to the category of Compliance (indeed, some factor analyses of OCB scale items have Civic Virtue items loading on Compliance).

Curiously, Van Dyne, Cummings and Parks while offering some major help in the tidying up of the ERB domain, made no reference to the work of Borman and Motowidlo (1993), who avoid the in-role/extra-role criterion altogether. Rather, they propose thinking in terms of two basically different kinds of 'performance.' *Task performance* represents 'the effectiveness with which job incumbents perform activities that contribute to the organization's technical core either directly by implementing a part of its technological process, or indirectly by providing it with needed materials or services' (Borman & Motowidlo, 1997:99). Whether it involves welding, writing, driving a delivery truck, classroom teaching, brain surgery, or monitoring a radar screen, task performance is part and parcel of workflow that transforms inputs of energy, information, and materials into outputs in the form of goods and services to some external constituency. By design, different tasks involve different activities and usually require different types of aptitude and training; good task performance by a brain surgeon requires specialized knowledge and a steady hand, while good task performance by a copywriter calls for verbal fluency and imagination. *Contextual performance*, on the other hand, 'has the effect of maintaining the broader organizational, social, and psychological environment in which the technical core must function' (Motowidlo, Borman, & Schmit, 1997:75). Essentially, contextual performance sustains or enhances the collective character of the organization, because it reinforces the linkages between and among individual participants. Unlike task performance, contextual performance—since it deals with psychological linkages between people—is much alike from one job to another or one organization to another. It includes informal helping and cooperation, forbearance, active acceptance and enactment of the 'rules of the game,' and gestures that promote good will between groups. In other words, it sounds much like the enumerated categories of OCB.

The advantage of thinking in terms of task versus contextual performance is that we need not split fine hairs over whether a contribution is or is not part of the job, or whether it is in-role or extra-role. And we do not have to fret over whether rewards accrue to the person making the contribution, and if so, when the rewards come or what form they take.

Empirical work by Motowidlo and Van Scotter (1994) gives some support to the utility of the task/contextual distinction. They found that 'overall performance' ratings of Army personnel were positively and significantly correlated with independent ratings of the task productivity and contextual performance of those personnel. Moreover, while aptitude, job knowledge, and experience were the best predictors of task performance, personality measures of dependability, achievement striving, and work orientation were the key correlates of contextual performance.

A subsequent research report (Van Scotter & Motowidlo, 1996) distinguished two types of contextual performance: 'Interpersonal facilitation' (IF) and 'job dedication' (JD). The measurement items for these two subscales are highly suggestive of the 'altruism' and 'compliance' forms of OCB. Moreover, the data indicate a clearer distinction between IF and task performance than between JD and task performance. This finding echoes the criticisms of compliance as a category of 'extra-role' contributions or 'going beyond the job description.'

Organ (1997) has offered the opinion that conceptual clarity might result from redefining OCB along the lines of contextual performance. However, he would couple this with the observation that much of what we call contextual performance would often represent more discretionary forms of contribution and that rewards for it would generally be more uncertain and indirect than would be true for task performance.

We still must reckon, though, with a considerable degree of conceptual fuzziness when we define OCB or contextual performance as those contributions that maintain the organizational context and psychological climate in which tasks are performed. The problem now is that 'context' and 'climate' are themselves abstract, and we would have a daunting challenge in trying to offer a comprehensive list of their denotative referents. In principle, though, one might be able to demonstrate a high degree of interrater agreement on the extent to which specific behaviors fall into this domain.

Another question concerning OCB that has arisen is: What is its opposite? Are we talking about an area of contribution that varies only in degree of positivity? Or does it have a negative pole anchored by actions that actively and deliberately harm the context and climate of work? More to the point, are the predictors of negative and destructive actions simply the opposite of those that predict OCB, or do very different antecedents come into play?

Skarlicki and Folger (1997) used a measure of 'organizational retaliation behavior' (ORB) operationally defined by peer observations of individuals who had intentionally damaged equipment, pilfered tools or supplies, bad-mouthed the company, purposefully withheld information needed by others, wasted time, or misused time at work. The researchers found strong negative correlations between peer ratings of such behaviors and the rated individuals' reported perceptions of fairness. Procedural and interactional justice were slightly stronger predictors than distributive fairness, and in fact there were significant interactions among the criteria of fairness. Interestingly, their correlations were (in absolute value) quite a bit stronger than the corresponding positive correlations generally found between OCB and justice. In other words, unequivocal perceptions of unfairness might have a stronger functional relationship to ORB than do perceptions of attained fairness with OCB. The texture of the findings would also seem to argue for one continuum from high levels of ORB to high levels of OCB, with the midpoint represented by someone who refrains from destructive acts but offers nothing toward maintaining or enhancing the context of work.

A further distinction might be made between actively harming the work context, or ORB, and deliberately exerting less effort on task performance than is expected. What we have here is something called 'Propensity to Withhold Effort' (PWE: Kidwell & Bennett, 1993; One certainly hopes that this acronym does not invite confusion with 'Protestant Work Ethic'). Kidwell and Bennett propose, and we agree, that this idea is theoretically independent of either OCB or ORB. Their discussion dwelt mainly upon the reductions in effort that occur when several people jointly perform a task and only group, not individual, output can be observed. This phenomenon sometimes goes by the terms 'free-riding' or 'social loafing'. Kidwell and Bennett do hypothesize that PWE is affected not only by group size and task visibility, but also by participants' perceptions of workplace equity. One might also think of PWE as, in a sense, the negative side of compliance, conscientiousness, or Motowidlo and Van Scotter's (1996) 'job dedication.'

How these issues are resolved theoretically will probably require some careful analysis of the relative distribution and importance of both the positive and negative instances of OCB/contextual performance. If the volume and significance of the two are similar—that is if high levels of positive OCB are both infrequent and quite important, but so are high levels of its opposite, and if the best predictors of each are the same but of different sign, then it would seem logical to bring all of these phenomena into the same framework and effect some degree of parsimony. If one is quite rare relative to the other, and the rare occasion is best predicted by something utterly unrelated to the other, then trying to force them into the same framework would probably add to construct confusion.

Linking OCB to other substantive research areas

Existing frameworks of OCB and contextual performance might properly be regarded as 'molar' or 'midrange' theories. Within the range of phenomena explicitly encompassed by OCB, one sees obvious candidates for research topics. For examples one might assess the effect of job morale on OCB, individual differences in tendencies to contribute by way of OCB, effects of reward systems and management practices on OCB, and the effect of OCB on organizational outcomes.

But ideally a molar or midrange theory should do more than explain variance in the components constituting the theory. In addition, such a theory should have some utility within the larger fabric of interrelated theories of organizations. It should not be a 'stand alone' theory that never gets outside itself. It should invite speculation and inquiry about the perspective it sheds on phenomena otherwise addressed by other molar theories.

The last five years show some signs that I/O psychologists are looking at links between OCB and other topics. An illustrative, yet certainly not exhaustive sense of the kinds of links attracting interest can be seen in the literature on psychological contracts, ingratiation, and leader–member exchange.

Psychological contracts

A psychological contract between an employee and an organization refers to the expectations about reciprocal obligations that comprise the employee–organization exchange relationship. It is a set of beliefs about what each party is obligated to give in exchange for contributions from the other (Wolfe-Morrison & Robinson, 1997). This concept primarily is a matter of perception on the part of each participant, and these perceptions may or may not always reflect reality. These contracts tend to be largely relational in nature, often relying heavily on citizenship-type behaviors. They are characterized by being open-ended in nature, long-term, and containing various socio-emotional elements such as loyalty and support.

As Wolfe-Morrison and Robinson (1997) point out, recent trends such as downsizing, restructuring and an increase in foreign competition are greatly affecting employees' psychological contracts. There is greater tendency toward violation of these contracts by organizations, which has been found to have a negative impact on employee behavior. In effect, violation may cause employees to reduce contributions to the organization, or to exit the organization.

This phenomenon relates directly to OCB, as demonstrated by Robinson and Wolfe-Morrison (1995) who predict that employee beliefs about the extent to which their organization has fulfilled its obligations to them will affect their citizenship behavior within the organization (specifically, OCB-O). They demonstrate this through research which shows that OCB is the behavior most likely to suffer when employees experience contract violation. In particular, the aspect of OCB most affected by an employee's perception of contract fulfillment (or violation) is Civic Virtue. This relationship is based on the fact that Civic Virtue is the form of OCB most clearly directed toward the organization.

Robinson and Wolfe-Morrison (1995) surveyed MBA graduates several times over a period of over two years to determine the explicitness of promises made to the employees (time 1), how well expectations were being met (time 2), and the level of trust they had in their employer (time 3). A self-report measure of Civic Virtue was also taken at time 3. Perceived violations of both relational and transactional obligations noted at times 1 and 2 were negatively correlated with Civic Virtue at time 3. In addition, perceived violation was negatively related to trust, which mediated the relationship between relational violation and Civic Virtue.

Results suggest that when employees believe their employer has not fulfilled the terms of the employment contract, employees will be less likely to demonstrate OCB-O in the form of Civic Virtue. Support for their hypothesis led the researchers to argue that due to the inherent value of OCB as a contributor to overall productivity and organizational effectiveness, organizations should understand and attempt to manage employee perceptions and expectations (i.e., via Realistic Job Previews) in order to encourage higher levels of OCB. Employees are also encouraged to take an active role in engaging organization agents in frank discussions designed to clarify expectations. This dialogue is considered critical, since maintaining OCB is vital to the effective functioning of the overall organization.

Ingratiation versus citizenship behavior

The motives to which supervisors attribute employee behavior may affect such things as perceptions of performance, ongoing treatment, and ratings on employee evaluations. Some would argue that if an employee demonstrates behavior that ultimately benefits the organization, then the intent or motive is not relevant. Yet on an individual level, the attributions made by a supervisor regarding an employee's motivation for 'going the extra mile' may actually affect several things.

Feldman (1981) discusses supervisory attributions as they relate to performance appraisals by showing that behavior which departs from basic supervisory expectations receives more conscious attention than expected behavior. Supervisors may seek to explain the unique behavior by categorizing it in some way. The issue becomes one of assigning positive or negative attributions to behaviors that may *look like* citizenship behavior. However, these attributions and categorizations are often riddled with biases, thus making it difficult to know what the true motives of any individual really are. The attributions also have implications for interpretations of future behavior.

Eastman (1994) argues that ingratiation and citizenship behavior may appear similar but that supervisors will respond to them differently when it comes to performance evaluation and reward decisions, depending on the attributions they make. Since employee motives are not always readily apparent, supervisors may determine that behavior is either a form of OCB *or* ingratiation. Eastman's research simulated managerial decision-making regarding pay and performance evaluation under conditions of high or low behavioral *consistency* (generality of behavior across time/place); *distinctiveness* (generality of behavior across multiple targets or individual recipients); and *consensus* (generality of behavior across several employees).

His belief was that conspicuous behavior directed only toward one's supervisor, or opportunistic behavior (only around performance appraisal time) would be seen as ingratiation. He argued that rewards would be greater for those employees considered to be demonstrating OCB versus those classified as ingratiating. Eastman found that consensus accounted for significant variance in attributions regarding employee behavior and that attributions made by supervisors did mediate supervisory decisions about pay and rewards. He also pointed out the danger of a truly good citizen being incorrectly labeled as an ingratiator and finding him or herself in an 'out-group.' If this were to happen, the employee would most likely respond by reducing his or her level of OCB, which would, in turn, be detrimental to the organization's overall effectiveness.

In a related article, Ferris, Judge, Rowland, and Fitzgibbons (1994) studied subordinate influence and performance evaluation. They discussed the difficulty in distinguishing OCB from political influence tactics such as self-promotion or ingratiation. They stressed that certain tactics are considered more or less situationally appropriate, and the perceived appropriateness can influence supervisor affect. This was shown to affect performance evaluations. Employee behavior may be interpreted as job-focused (intended to make an individual seem more competent), or supervisor-focused (intended to increase one's likability). While supervisor-focused behavior is potentially a form of OCB-I, they argue that the true distinction between OCB and self-serving behavior is the intention, not the outcome. There are certainly behaviors which would be considered ingratiating or self-serving that could also benefit the organization.

OCB and leader–member exchange

Virtually from the outset, Organ (1988) treated OCB within the spirit, if not the actual framework, of social exchange. The point of departure was Blau's (1964) distinction between economic and social exchange. Blau defined economic exchange as those transactions involving explicit quid pro quo, occurring at specified times, and based on contractual enforcement rather than trust. Social exchange, by contrast, leaves timing and manner of reciprocation unspecified and depends upon trust in one's exchange partner. Organ (1988) treated OCB as a contribution to the organization that arises from a relationship of trust with the organization. This trust, in turn, is based on the belief that the organization is a just system, one that is fair in both contractual and noncontractual treatment of participants.

In retrospect, it seems puzzling why more of the early treatment of OCB did not borrow from the work of Graen and others on leader–member exchange (LMX: Dansereau, Graen, & Haga, 1975; Graen & Uhl-Bien, 1995). The parallels are all too obvious. In the theory and research on LMX, the assumption is that the leader (e.g., supervisor) has qualitatively different relationships with different subordinates. Relationships between the leader and the 'outs' or 'hired hands' occur mostly in the form of contractual or economic exchange. The leader provides for those people no more and no less than what the organizational role of manager or supervisor requires. For other subordinates, the 'ins' or 'cadres'—who have both the ability and the inclination to contribute more than contractual obligations—the leader enacts more of a social-exchange relationship. The leader, in a sense, 'negotiates' a different role for the subordinate. More is expected, but more is also offered, in the forms of greater input into decision-making and more psychological support. Only the smallest of inferential leaps is needed to think of the extra contributions from cadres as OCB. Moreover, to the extent that the immediate supervisor acts as the 'face' of the organization, mediating the resources to which the cadre might attain access, one can easily imagine that subordinate sentiments about the organization derive in large measure from exchange with the leader.

Wayne, Shore, and Liden (1997) provide strong empirical support for the utility of connecting OCB to LMX. Their survey of 289 managers and 570 subordinates in a large national corporation found that perceived organizational support (POS) and LMX independently predicted OCB. While POS and LMX themselves were predicted by different sets of antecedents, they appeared to be reciprocally related to each other. Interestingly, POS showed no effect on how subordinates were rated on task performance, while LMX actually exerted a much larger effect on performance ratings than on OCB. The findings suggest rather at least two quite different interpretations. Possibly, as suggested by Dansereau, Graen and Haga (1975), leaders pursue social exchange with the more talented subordinates; the result is that those with the most ability to do the task also are the ones who then provide OCB 'in exchange' for other forms of favored treatment. Yet those who view the organization itself as offering support beyond what is contracted also reciprocate with OCB, even when they cannot do so with higher-than-the-norm performance on the task itself. An alternative interpretation, of course, is that some subordinates render OCB to ingratiate themselves with their leader, resulting in a more personal relationship of social exchange, and ultimately the benefit of higher performance ratings.

Studies by Settoon, Bennett, and Liden (1996) and Tierney and Bauer (1996) also support the case for a linkage between LMX and OCB. Moreover, the findings suggest that the linkage is one containing unique explained variance in OCB net of the effects of job satisfaction, personal affectivity as a trait, and perceived organizational support.

CONCLUSION

The overriding impression one gets from this survey of recent research and interpretive commentary is a diminished concern for attitudinal and dispositional correlates of individual OCB. The evidence is quite consistent that any affectively-toned measure of member perceptions will covary to a modest degree with others' ratings of that member's OCB, and it now appears fruitless to expect that any single such measure will emerge as 'definitive' in accounting for this finding. If there is any important work to be done along these lines, it probably would take the form of articulating the diffuse, underlying affective state ('morale'?) on which such affective or attitudinal measures tend to load.

Two exceptions may be noted to the above statement. Borman and Motowidlo (1997) continue to find support for 'contextual performance,' which we have noted is much akin to OCB, as the performance criterion that justifies the study of dispositional predictors. Of note is the fact that the predictors in question have at best faint suggestions of affective states; their measures have to do rather with the traits of perseverance, self-discipline, and achievement-striving. Also, the increasing attention to OCB as manifested in other cultures seeks to ascertain the cross-cultural robustness of the association between individual attitudes or affect and OCB.

In the main, however, the recent development of OCB reflects concern for 'going to the next level,' that is the group or organizational level of analysis; for exploring cultural variations on the meaning, nature, and texture of OCB; and for assessing the heuristic value of conceptual linkages between OCB and other workplace phenomena. As these three directions of inquiry proceed, we can expect to find, and have already seen, frequent occasions for revisiting construct definition of OCB. No doubt a recurring dilemma will present itself in the question of whether to conceptualize OCB more narrowly, in the interests of measurement reliability and denotative clarity, or more broadly, in the interest of greater organizational relevance. But the cumulative record of contributions in this area indicates that industrial and organizational psychology cannot make do without some construct akin to what is now called OCB or contextual performance.

REFERENCES

Bales, R.F. & Slater, P. (1955). Role differentiation in small decision-making groups. In T. Parsons & R.F. Bales (Eds), *Family, Socialization and Interaction Processes* (pp. 259–306). Glencoe, IL: Free Press.

Barnard, C.I. (1938). *The Functions of the Executive*. Cambridge, MA: Harvard University Press edition, 1964.

Bateman, T.S. & Organ, D.W. (1983). Job satisfaction and the good soldier: The relationship between affect and employee citizenship. *Academy of Management Journal*, **26**(4), 587–595.

Blau, P. (1964). *Exchange and Power in Social Life*. New York: Wiley.

Borman, W.C. & Motowidlo, S.J. (1993). Expanding the criterion domain to include elements of contextual performance. In N. Schmitt & W.C. Borman (Eds), *Personnel Selection* (pp. 71–98). San Francisco, CA: Jossey-Bass.

Borman, W.C. & Motowidlo, S.J. (1997). Task performance and contextual performance: The meaning for personnel selection research. *Human Performance*, **10**, 99–110.

Campbell, J.P. (1990). An overview of the Army Selection Classification Project (Project A). *Personnel Psychology*, **43**, 231–239.

Cook, T.D. & Campbell, D.T. (1979). *Quasi-experimental Design & Analysis Issues for Field Settings*. Boston: Houghton Mifflin.

Dansereau, F.D., Jr, Graen, G. & Haga, W.J. (1975). A vertical dyad linkage approach to leadership within formal organizations: A longitudinal investigation of the role making process. *Organizational Behavior and Human Performance*, **13**, 46–78.

Eastman, K.K. (1994). In the Eyes of the Beholder: An attributional approach to ingratiation and Organizational Citizenship Behavior. *Academy of Management Journal*, **37**(5), 1379–1391.

Farh, J.L., Earley, P.C. & Lin, S.C. (1997). Impetus for extraordinary action: A cultural analysis of justice and organizational citizenship behavior in Chinese society. *Administrative Science Quarterly*, **42**, 421–444.

Farh, J., Podsakoff, P.M. & Organ, D.W. (1990). Accounting for organizational citizenship behavior: Leader fairness and task scope versus satisfaction. *Journal of Management*, **16**, 705–722.

Feldman, J.M. (1981). Beyond attribution theory: Cognitive processes in performance appraisal. *Journal of Applied Psychology*, **66**(2), 127–148.

Ferris, G.R., Judge, T.A., Rowland, K.M. & Fitzgibbons, D.E. (1994). Subordinate influence and the performance evaluation process: Test of a model. *Organizational Behavior and Human Decision Processes*, **58**, 101–135.

Fleishman, E.A., Harris, E.H. & Burtt, H.E. (1955). Leadership and supervision in industry. *Ohio State Business Educational Research Monograph* (No. 33). Columbus: Ohio State University.

Graen, G.B. & Uhl-Bien, M. (1995). Relationship-based approach to leadership: Development of leader–member exchange (LMX) theory of leadership over 25 years: Applying a multi-level multi-domain perspective. *Leadership Quarterly*, **6**, 219–247.

Graham, J.W. (1986). Organizational citizenship informed by political theory. Paper presented at the meeting of the Academy of Management, Chicago.

Graham, J.W. (1986). Principled organizational dissent: A theoretical essay. In B.M. Staw & L.L. Cummings (Eds), *Research in Organizational Behavior* (Vol. 8, pp. 1–52). Greenwich, CT: JAI Press.

Hofstede, G. (1980). *Culture's Consequences: International Differences in Work-related Values*. Beverly Hills, CA: Sage Publications.

Hui, C., Organ, D.W. & Crooker, K. (1994). Time pressure, Type A behavior, and organizational citizenship behavior: A field study and an experiment. *Psychological Reports*, **75**, 199–208.

Karambaya, R. (1991). Contexts for organizational citizenship: Do high performing and satisfying units have better citizens? Unpublished manuscript, York University.

Katz, D. & Kahn, R.L. (1966). *The Social Psychology of Organizations*. New York: Wiley.

Kidwell, R.E., Jr & Bennett, N. (1993). Employee propensity to withhold effort: A conceptual model to intersect three avenues of research. *Academy of Management Review*, **18**, 429–456.

Konovsky, M.A., Elliot, J. & Pugh, S.D. (1997). The dispositional and contextual predictors of citizenship behavior in Mexico. Unpublished manuscript. New Orleans, LA: Tulane University.

Konovsky, M.A. & Folger, R. (1991). The effects of procedural and distributive justice on organizational citizenship behavior. Paper presented at the annual meetings of the Academy of Management, Miami Beach, FL.

Lawler, E.E. III & Porter, L.W. (1967). The effect of performance on job satisfaction. *Industrial Relations*, **7**, 20–28.

MacKenzie, S.B., Podsakoff, P.M. and Fetter, R. (1993). The impact of organizational citizenship behavior on evaluations of salesperson performance. *Journal of Marketing*, **57**, 70–80.

MacKenzie, S.B., Podsakoff, P.M. and Paine, J.E. (1997). The effects of organizational citizenship behaviors and productivity on evaluations of performance at different hierarchical levels in sales organizations. In press.

Moorman, R.H. (1991). Relationship between organizational justice and organizational citizenship behaviors: Do fairness perceptions influence employee citizenship? *Journal of Applied Psychology*, **76**(6), 845–855.

Moorman, R.H. & Blakeley, G.L. (1995). Individualism-Collectivism as an individual difference predictor of organizational citizenship behavior. *Journal of Organizational Behavior*, **16**, 127–142.

Morrison, E.W. (1994). Role definitions and organizational citizenship behavior: The importance of the employee's perspective. *The Academy of Management Journal*, **37**, 1543–1567.

Motowidlo, S.J., Borman, W.C. & Schmit, M.J. (1997). A theory of individual differences in task and contextual performance. *Human Performance*, **10**, 71–84.

Motowidlo, S.J. & Van Scotter, J.R. (1994). Evidence that task performance should be distinguished from contextual performance. *Journal of Applied Psychology*, **79**, 475–480.

Munene, J.C. (1995). Not on seat: An investigation of correlates of organizational citizenship in Nigeria. *Applied Psychology. An International Review*, **44**(2), 111–122.

Near, J.P. & Miceli, M.P. (1987). Whistle-blowers in organizations: Dissidents or reformers? In L.L. Cummings & B.M. Staw (Eds), *Research in Organizational Behavior* (Vol. 9, pp. 321–368). Greenwich, CT: JAI Press.

Niehoff, B.P. & Moorman, R.H. (1993). Justice as a mediator of the relationship between methods of monitoring and organizational citizenship behavior. *Academy of Management Journal*, **36**, 527–556.

Organ, D.W. (1977). A reappraisal and reinterpretation of the satisfaction–causes–performance hypothesis. *Academy of Management Review*, **2**, 46–53.

Organ, D.W. (1988). *Organizational Citizenship Behavior: The Good Soldier Syndrome*. Lexington, MA: Lexington Books.

Organ, D.W. (1990). The motivational basis of organizational citizenship behavior. In B.M. Staw & L.L. Cummings (Eds), *Research in Organizational Behavior* (Vol. 12, pp. 43–72). Greenwich, CT: JAI Press.

Organ, D.W. (1997). Organizational citizenship behavior: It's construct clean-up time. *Human Performance*, **10**, 85–98.

Organ, D.W. & Konovsky, M.A. (1989). Cognitive versus affective determinants of organizational citizenship behavior. *Journal of Applied Psychology*, **74**, 157–164.

Organ, D.W. & Lingl, A. (1995). Personality, satisfaction, and organizational citizenship behaviors. *Journal of Social Psychology*, **135**(3), 339–350.

Organ, D.W. & Ryan, K. (1995). A meta-analytic review of attitudinal and dispositional predictors of organizational citizenship behavior. *Personnel Psychology*, **48**, 775–802.

Paine, J.E. & Organ, D.W. (1997). Assessing the cultural robustness of organizational citizenship behavior. Working Paper. Bloomington, IN: Kelley School of Business, Indiana University.

Park, O. & Sims, H.P. Jr (1989). Beyond cognition in leadership: Prosocial behavior and affect in managerial judgment. Working Paper, Seoul National University and Pennsylvania State University.

Podsakoff, P.M., Ahearne, M. & MacKenzie, S.B. (1997). Organizational citizenship and the quantity and quality of work group performance. *Journal of Applied Psychology*, **82**(2), 262–270.

Podsakoff, P.M. & MacKenzie, S.B. (1992). Organizational citizenship behavior and sales unit performance. *Journal of Marketing Research*, **31**, 351–363.

Podsakoff, P.M., MacKenzie, S.B. & Hui, C. (1993). Organizational citizenship behaviors as determinants of managerial evaluations of employee performance: A review and suggestions for future research. In G.R. Ferris & K.M. Rowland (Eds), *Research in Personnel and Human Resources Management* (Vol. 11, pp. 1–40). Greenwich, CT: JAI Press.

Podsakoff, P.M., MacKenzie, S.B., Moorman, R.H. & Fetter, R. (1990). Transformational leader behaviors and their effects on followers' trust in leader, satisfaction, and organizational citizenship behavior. *The Leadership Quarterly*, **1**(2), 107–142.

Puffer, S.M. (1987). Prosocial behavior, noncompliant behavior, and work performance among commission salespeople. *Journal of Applied Psychology*, **72**, 615–621.

Robinson, S.L. & Wolfe-Morrison, E. (1995). Organizational citizenship behavior: A psychological contract perspective. *Journal of Organizational Behavior*, **16**, 289–298.

Roethlisberger, F.J. & Dickson, W.J. (1967), *Management and the Worker*. Cambridge, MA: Harvard University Press (original work published 1939).

Schneider, B. & Dachler, P. (1978). A note on the stability of the Job Descriptive Index. *Journal of Applied Psychology*, **63**, 650–653.

Scholl, R.W., Cooper, E.A. & McKenna, J.F. (1987). Referent selection in determining equity perceptions: Differential effects on behavioral and attitudinal outcomes. *Personnel Psychology*, **40**(1), 113–124.

Settoon, R.P., Bennett, & Liden, R.C. (1996). Social exchange in organizations: Perceived organizational support, leader–member exchange, and employee reciprocity. *Journal of Applied Psychology*, **81**, 219–227.

Skarlicki, D.P. & Folger, R. (1997). Retaliation in the workplace: The roles of distributive, procedural, and interactional justice. *Journal of Applied Psychology*, **82**, 434–443.

Skarlicki, D. & Latham, G. (1996). Increasing citizenship behavior within a labor union: A test of organization justice theory. *Journal of Applied Psychology*, **81**, 161–169.

Skarlicki, D. & Latham, G. (1997). Leadership training in organizational justice to increase citizenship behavior with a labor union: A replication. In press, *Personnel Psychology*.

Smith, C.A., Organ, D.W. & Near, J.P. (1983). Organizational citizenship behavior: Its nature and antecedents. *Journal of Applied Psychology*, **68**, 653–663.

Staw, B.M., Bell, N.E. & Clausen, J.A. (1986). The dispositional approach to job attitudes: A lifetime longitudinal test. *Administrative Science Quarterly*, **31**, 56–77.

Staw, B.M. & Ross, J. (1985). Stability in the midst of change: A dispositional approach to job attitudes. *Journal of Applied Psychology*, **70**, 469–480.

Tierney, P. & Bauer, T.N. (1996). A longitudinal assessment of LMX on extra-role behavior. Paper presented at Annual Conference of the Academy of Management, Cincinnati, OH.

Van Dyne, L., Cummings, L.L. & Parks, J.M. (1995). Extra role behaviors: In pursuit of construct and definitional clarity (a bridge over muddied waters). In L.L. Cummings & B.M. Staw (Eds), *Research in Organizational Behavior* (Vol. 17, pp. 215–285). Greenwich, CT: JAI Press.

Van Scotter, J.R. & Motowidlo, S.J. (1996). Evidence for two factors of contextual performance: Job dedication and interpersonal facilitation. *Journal of Applied Psychology*, **81**, 525–531.

Walz, S.M. (1995). Organizational citizenship behaviors: Their effect on organizational effectiveness in limited-menu restaurants. A dissertation submitted in partial fulfillment of the requirements for the degree of doctor of philosophy. Manhattan, KA: Kansas State University.

Walz, S.M. & Niehoff, B.P. (1996). Organizational citizenship behaviors and their effect on organizational effectiveness in limited menu restaurants. In J.B. Keys & L.N. Dosier (Eds), *Academy of Management Best Papers Proceedings*, pp. 307–311.

Wayne, S.J., Shore, L.M. & Liden, R.C. (1997). Perceived organizational support and leader-member exchange: A social exchange perspective. *Academy of Management Journal*, **40**, 82–111.

Werner, J.M. (1994). Dimensions that make a difference: Examining the impact of in-role and extra-role behaviors on supervisory ratings. *Journal of Applied Psychology*, **79**(1), 98–107.

Williams, L.J. & Anderson, S.E. (1991). Job satisfaction and organizational commitment as predictors of organizational citizenship and in-role behaviors. *Journal of Management*, **17**(3), 601–617.

Wolfe-Morrison, E. & Robinson, S.L. (1997). When employees feel betrayed: A model of how psychological contract violation develops. *Academy of Management Review*, **22**(1), 226–256.

Wright, P.M., George, J.M., Farnsworth, S.R. & McMahan, G.C. (1993). Productivity and extra-role behavior: The effects of goals and incentives on spontaneous helping. *Journal of Applied Psychology*, **78**, 374–381.

Part II

GROUPS AND TEAMS

Chapter 5

TEAM EFFECTIVENESS IN ORGANIZATIONS

Michael A. West, Carol S. Borrill and Kerrie L. Unsworth
University of Sheffield, UK

He makes tools (and does so within more than one technical tradition), builds shelters, takes over natural refuges by exploiting fire, and sallies out of them to hunt and gather his food. He does this in groups with a discipline that can sustain complicated operations; he therefore has some ability to exchange ideas by speech. The basic biological units of his hunting groups probably prefigure the nuclear family of man, being founded on the institutions of the home base and a sexual differentiation of activity. There may even be some complexity of social organization in so far as fire-bearers and gatherers or old creatures whose memories made them the data banks of their 'societies' could be supported by the labour of others. There has to be some social organization to permit the sharing of co-operatively obtained food, too. There is nothing to be usefully added to an account such as this by pretending to say where exactly can be found a pre-historical point or dividing line at which such things had come to be, but subsequent human history is unimaginable without them.

(J.M. Roberts, *The History of the World*, 1995, p. 18)

The activity of a group of people working cooperatively to achieve shared goals via differentiation of roles and using elaborate systems of communication is basic to our species. The current enthusiasm for teamworking in organizations reflects a deeper, perhaps unconscious, recognition that this way of working offers the promise of greater progress than can be achieved through individual endeavour or through mechanistic approaches to work. In this chapter, we examine many of the themes Roberts identifies, including types of groups, group composition, group processes and outcomes. We also critically examine the role of groups and teams in modern organizations. As far as is sensible, we avoid reviewing areas well covered in a previous volume in this series (Argote & McGrath, 1993), and particularly temporal changes in work group processes. The overall challenge is to answer the question—what factors determine the effectiveness of work teams? This chapter presents a critical overview

Team Effectiveness in Organizations by Michael A. West, Carol S. Borrill and Kerrie L. Unsworth taken from IRIOP 1998 v13, Edited by Cary L. Cooper and Ivan T. Robertson: © 1998 John Wiley & Sons, Ltd

of the research evidence of relevance to this question and highlights new and emerging theoretical developments which can contribute to clarifying current issues and shaping future research. First we consider what is meant by a group or team at work, then we outline the rationale for implementing teams as a way of working in organizations, and finally we show how researchers have approached their studies in this field.

WHAT ARE TEAMS?

Following Alderfer (1977) and Hackman (1987), Guzzo (1996) defines teams as social entities embedded in organizations, performing tasks which contribute to achieving the organization's goals; their work affects others within or outside the organization; members are dependent on each other in the performance of their work to a significant extent; and the group is identified as a group by those within and outside the group. What does this mean in practice? First, members of the group have shared objectives in relation to their work. Necessarily they must interact with each other in order to achieve those shared objectives. Team members have more or less well-defined and interdependent roles, some of which are differentiated from one another (e.g. in a primary health care team: doctors, nurses, receptionists) and they have an organizational identity as a work group with a defined organizational function (e.g. the public relations team for the pharmaceutical division of a major divisionalized company). Finally, they are not so large that they would be defined more appropriately as an organization, which has an internal structure of vertical and horizontal relationships characterized by subgroupings. In practice, this is likely to mean that a work group will be smaller than about 20 members and larger than two or perhaps three people (for a discussion of whether a dyad, triad or quad constitutes a team, see Weick, 1969).

THE RATIONALE FOR WORKING IN TEAMS

Why do people work in groups in modern organizations, and what evidence is there for their value? As organizations have grown in size and become structurally more complex, the need for groups of people to work together in co-ordinated ways to achieve objectives which contribute to the overall aims of the organization has become increasingly urgent. Trying to coordinate the activities of individuals in large organizations is like building a sandcastle using single grains of sand.

Mohrman, Cohen and Mohrman (1995) offer ten reasons for implementing team-based working in organizations:

- Teams are the best way to enact the strategy of (some) organizations, because of the need for consistency between organizational environment, strategy and design (Galbraith, Lawler & Associates, 1993).

- Teams enable organizations to speedily develop and deliver products and services cost-effectively, while retaining high quality.
- Teams enable organizations to learn (and retain learning) more effectively (Senge, 1990).
- Cross-functional teams promote improved quality management (Deming, 1986; Juran, 1989).
- Cross-functional design teams can undertake effective process re-engineering (Davenport, 1993).
- Time in production is saved if activities, formerly performed sequentially by individuals, can be performed concurrently by people working in teams (Myer, 1993).
- Innovation is promoted within team-based organizations because of cross-fertilisation of ideas (Senge, 1990; West & Pillinger, 1995).
- Flat organizations can be monitored, coordinated and directed more effectively if the functional unit is the team rather than the individual (Galbraith, 1993, 1994).
- As organizations have grown more complex, so too have their information processing requirements; teams can integrate and link in ways individuals cannot (Galbraith, 1993, 1994; Lawrence & Lorsch, 1967).

Clearly, work groups are not appropriate for every task or function within an organization, but there is evidence that the introduction of group goals leads to better performance and productivity in a variety of settings. Examples cited in a review of 30 studies (Weldon & Weingart, 1994) include loading trucks; performing work safely; harvesting and hauling timber; opening mail; operating spinning machines; running a restaurant; processing insurance appraisals; and raising money for voluntary organizations.

Macy and Izumi (1993) conducted a meta-analysis of 131 field studies of organizational change and found that interventions with the largest effects upon financial measures of organizational performance were team development interventions or the creation of autonomous work groups. Significantly, change was most effective when multiple elements of change were made simultaneously in technology, human resource management systems and organizational structure, and where teamworking was already present or a component of the change. It may be that teamworking represents a vehicle by which organizational change can most effectively be delivered for the reasons offered by Mohrman, Cohen and Mohrman (1995) though this is still to be determined empirically. Applebaum and Batt (1994) comment on recent developments in the American workplace by reviewing 12 large-scale surveys and 185 case studies of managerial practices. They conclude that team-based working leads to improvements in organizational performance on measures of both efficiency and quality. Similarly, Levine and D'Andrea-Tyson (1990) conclude that substantive participation leads to sustained increases in productivity and that teams effectively enable such participation. This finding is confirmed by Cotton (1993), in a study of a variety of forms of employee involvement.

This evidence, though stronger than that for the effectiveness of other elements of work design, must be viewed with caution since under the banner of 'teamwork' march a wide variety of practices and processes. There is also considerable research evidence which illustrates the difficulties associated with this way of organizing work.

PROBLEMS OF WORKING IN TEAMS

Steiner (1972), in an influential book, argued that, actual group productivity is usually less than potential productivity because of 'process losses'. These include poor group member coordination, competing objectives and poor communication. Another such process loss is called 'social loafing'. Individuals, in some circumstances, work less hard when their efforts are combined with and masked by those of others, than when they are individually accountable (Latané, Williams & Harkins, 1979). So are problems of group working confined simply to this relative lack of effort amongst group members? Studies of group decision-making suggest that other process losses hinder effective group functioning in a wide variety of ways.

A principal assumption behind the structuring of organizational activities into teams is that teams make better decisions than individuals. However, experimental research clearly indicates that while groups make decisions better than the average quality of decisions made by individual members (rated by experts external to the group), groups consistently fall short of the quality of decisions made by their most capable individual members (Rogelberg, Barnes-Farrell & Lower, 1992). Too little similar research has been conducted in work settings with *in vivo* groups to allow the applicability of these findings to work organizations to be assessed. Nevertheless, organizational and social psychologists have identified some processes which impede effective group decision-making. These include:

- *Personality* factors such as introversion can cause some group members to hesitate in offering their opinions and knowledge assertively (Eysenck & Eysenck, 1975; Wilson, 1977), thereby failing to contribute fully to the group's store of knowledge.
- Group members are also subject to *social conformity* effects, causing them to withhold opinions and information contrary to the majority view (Brown, 1988; Moscovici & Doise, 1994).
- Members of work groups may lack *communication* skills (West, Garrod & Carletta, 1997).
- There may be *domination* by particular individuals who take up disproportionate 'air time'. It is noteworthy that 'air time' and expertise are

correlated in high-performing groups and uncorrelated in groups that perform poorly (Rogelberg, Barnes-Farrell & Lowe, 1992).

- *Status, gender* and *hierarchy* effects also can cause some members' contributions to be valued and attended to disproportionately (Brown, 1988).
- 'Risky shift', or *group polarization*, is the tendency of work groups to make more extreme decisions than the average of members' decisions. When individuals discover the position of others, they tend to move along the scale of opinion partly because of a 'majority rule' influence— the largest subgroup tends to determine the group decision. Moreover, a process of social comparison may take place, whereby information about a socially preferred way of behaving leads to polarization. When we compare ourselves and identify with those immediately around us in the team, we tend to locate our position closer to the perceived ingroup mean, rather than retaining the integrity of our initial position (Hogg, Turner & Davidson, 1990; Myers & Lamm, 1976).
- *Diffusion of responsibility* can also inhibit individuals from taking responsibility for action when working with others. People often assume that responsibility will be shouldered by others who are present in a situation requiring action (Darley & Latané, 1968).
- The experimental study of 'brainstorming' groups has established that quantity and often quality of ideas produced by individuals working separately, consistently exceed those produced by a group working together (Diehl & Stroebe, 1987). This counter-intuitive finding is explained by '*production-blocking*' (Diehl & Stroebe, 1987). When people are speaking in groups, others (temporarily) cannot put ideas forward. Moreover, because they may be holding ideas in their memories, their ability to produce more is impaired by these competing verbalizations (but see also Sutton & Hargadon, 1996).
- Another process loss is '*satisficing*' or making decisions immediately acceptable to the group rather than the best decisions (Cyert & March, 1963).
- Janis (1982, 1989) identified a group syndrome—'*groupthink*'—whereby groups may err in decision-making, as a result of being more concerned with achieving agreement than with quality of decisions. Research on 'groupthink' suggests both that the phenomenon is most likely to occur in groups where a leader is particularly dominant, and that cohesiveness *per se* is not a crucial factor (McCaulay, 1989).

THEORIES OF GROUP EFFECTIVENESS

The source of the stream of research on group effectiveness can be traced to the Hawthorne studies (Roethlisberger & Dickson, 1939), which established the importance of intergroup relations in organizations (Brown, 1988; Hogg & Abrams, 1988), the influences of groups on their members (Hackman, 1992), and the importance of informal groups in influencing work-related behaviour (Hartley, 1996).

This stream culminated in a statement about group performance effectiveness by Hackman and Morris (1975) which argued that an implicit input–process–output model of group performance had dominated research and theorizing. Despite the coyness of researchers about this, the basic form of the model (inputs influencing processes and both determining outputs) has remained the most used template in subsequent years for theory development and research (Campion, Papper & Medsker, 1996; Goodman, Ravlin & Argote, 1986; Guzzo, 1996; Guzzo & Shea, 1992). However, we can offer less than confident assertions about the relative contributions of inputs and processes, as well as the relative strength of factors within each of these broad categories (Campion, Papper & Medsker, 1996; Guzzo & Dickson, 1996).

Two other springs of thought about groups and teams emerged in the 1960s and 1970s. The first focused on the whole group and examined unconscious phenomena in work groups (Bion, 1961). Bion argued that groups developed 'basic assumptions' (cf. Schein, 1992) in discussions of organizational culture, which could impede their effective functioning. These include basic assumptions of *dependence* (one of the group's members will look after the needs of the group and ensure its effectiveness); *pairing* (two group members will join together to produce a leader in some way—leading to a sense of Messianic anticipation in the group); and *fight-flight* (the group meets to fight an enemy or run away, and is consequently unable to do any effective work)—see Stein (1996) for a more elaborated discussion of unconscious phenomena in work groups. However, little research has been stimulated by this approach.

The second spring has led to considerably more theorizing and research internationally. The sociotechnical tradition (e.g. Bucklow, 1966; Cooper & Foster, 1971; Herbst, 1962; Miller, 1959; Rice, 1958; Trist, 1981; Trist & Bamforth, 1951; Trist, Higgin, Murray & Pollock, 1963) is dominated by a belief that social and task-related outcomes can be optimized through appropriate task and work design—the well-being of group members can be achieved in conjunction with group performance, through the joint optimization of the application of technology, organization and the use of human resources.

In the last 20 years, there has been an altogether new emphasis amongst writers concerned with understanding work group effectiveness—the organizational context within which teams perform. Hackman (1990), for example, has drawn attention to the influence of organizational reward, training, and information systems in influencing team effectiveness. Indeed, Campion, Medsker and Higgs (1993), in a cross-sectional study of 80 work groups, found a significant correlation between organizational factors such as training and managerial support with work group effectiveness.

Hackman's (1983) model of work group effectiveness has, until recently, been the most influential. It describes five categories of factors, which directly or indirectly influence team effectiveness:

1. *Group design*, including task structure, group composition, and group norms for performance processes.
2. *Organizational context*, including the reward system, education system (training, etc.), and information system.
3. *Group synergy* which results from process assistance from the organization.
4. *Process criteria of effectiveness*, including level of effort on the task, amount of relevant knowledge and skill applied to task work, and the appropriateness of task performance strategies.
5. *Material resources* refers to the sufficiency of material resources for efficient task performance.

Group effectiveness includes task output, viability of team (members' ability to work together is strengthened and maintained), and the extent to which members' needs are met.

This model has been tested in qualitative case studies of work group functioning with good support, and has influenced subsequent model development (Hackman, 1990). Campion and colleagues' empirical, quantitative work (1993, 1996) suggests many of these factors influence productivity, though weakly (and particularly weakly in longitudinal analyses).

Shea and Guzzo (1987) developed a reciprocal model of team effectiveness. They argue that outcome interdependence among group members leads to higher group effectiveness. Outcome interdependence refers to the extent to which group members are dependent on each other to achieve organizational rewards such as recognition, career advancement and financial rewards. *Task interdependence* moderates the relationship between outcome interdependence and effectiveness, because outcome interdependence can only lead to greater effectiveness if team members are required to work interdependently to get the job done. But the most significant element of the model (theoretically) is the concept of *potency*, similar to self-efficacy (Bandura, 1982), at the group level it is characterized by a group sense of likely success and ability to meet challenges. This is a direct predictor of team effectiveness in the model. Guzzo and Campbell (1990) have extended this approach by proposing that potency best predicts team effectiveness in conjunction with three other factors—the alignment of team goals with organizational goals, organizational rewards for team accomplishments, and the availability of resources for teams.

Another model of team effectiveness has been developed from a focus on group reflexivity (West, 1996). It is argued that most models of group performance tend to present static rather than dynamic processes; group variables, such as participation in decision-making, are assumed to have a consistent relationship with productivity (Beyerlein, Johnson & Beyerlein, 1995; West, 1996). Such models, are inappropriate for knowledge-based teams of professionals from diverse backgrounds (an increasingly common form) working in challenging and changing environments. The groups themselves often change rapidly as a result of experience and member turnover (e.g. Anderson & Thomas, 1996; Gersick, 1988, 1989; McGrath & O'Connor, 1996), requiring repeated adaptation of communication and decision-making processes. Groups even change their environments as a result of their own work via processes of innovation (e.g. Bunce & West, 1995; West & Anderson, 1992), political pressure or simply their own effectiveness.

West (1996) proposes that what may best predict group effectiveness is an overarching factor influencing all aspects of group performance—group task reflexivity. He argues that teams are effective to the extent that they reflect upon their task objectives, strategies, processes and environments and adapt these aspects of their task functional worlds accordingly. Reflexive groups plan strategies ahead and actively structure the situation, including potential feed-back (cf. Hacker, 1986); they have a more comprehensive and penetrating intellectual representation of their work; a longer time-frame; a larger invent-ory of environmental cues to which they respond; a better knowledge and anticipation of errors; and a more active orientation towards their work.

This brief account of some of the major theoretical approaches illustrates the move towards less descriptive models, which are more context specific and which are edging slowly toward the status of theory with clearly testable prop-ositions. It reveals too that researchers are coming to terms with the inherent complexity and cloudiness of real teams in organizations. But what is also revealed is the multiplicity of factors researchers have identified as important influences on team effectiveness. The thinking of most researchers has been dominated by the input–process–output structure, mainly because of its cat-egorical simplicity and utility. In the remainder of this chapter we therefore examine research evidence in relation to inputs and processes which link these various factors to effectiveness (see Figure 5.1).

INPUT FACTORS AND EFFECTS ON PROCESSES AND OUTPUTS

A team works towards specific outcomes defined by *the task*, which impacts upon team processes and effectiveness. Secondly, the team consists of a collec-tion of individuals—who represent the *group's composition*. The team works for and within an organization; thus it will be affected by the interaction with the surrounding *organizational context*. Finally, the team exists within a wider society which will effect the teams' fundamental beliefs and value systems, that is, *the cultural context*. We consider each of these four categories of factors in turn.

The Group's Task

In an experimental study conducted in 1969, Kent and McGrath found that group characteristics accounted for a meagre 3.4% of variance in group

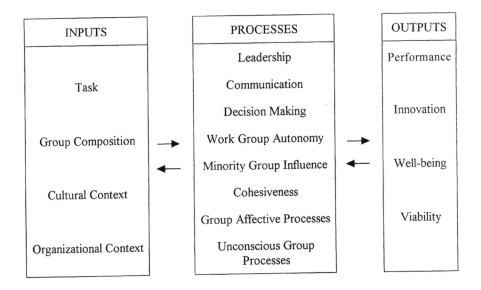

Figure 5.1   The input–process–output structure: influences on team effectiveness

performance; compared with 87.9% accounted for by task characteristics. Findings such as these have prompted a number of schemes for classifying task characteristics with dimensions such as difficulty, solution multiplicity, intrinsic interest, cooperative requirements (Shaw, 1976); unitary versus divisible, conjunctive, disjunctive and additive (Steiner, 1972); conflict versus cooperation, and conceptual versus behavioural (McGrath, 1984). However, such classification systems have proved easier to apply in laboratory settings than with work groups.

In the American tradition of research on team tasks, the classification of tasks and teams has been global, such that each team's task is assigned to one category (e.g. Hackman & Lawler, 1971; McGrath, 1984; Steiner, 1972). However, European researchers in this field have been influenced by Action Theory (Frese & Zapf, 1994; Hacker, 1986; Volpert, 1984) which has powerfully shaped their understanding of group behaviour (Tschan & von Cranach, 1996). The European approach to conceptualizing group tasks analyses them in relation to their *hierarchical* (goals and subgoals) and *sequential* (the order in which different parts of a task are carried out) requirements, as well as *cyclical process requirements* (generating goals, planning, decision-making, executing behaviour and reviewing performance for each element of the task). Such an orientation offers a level of sophistication and theoretical robustness to an area of study guided by rather shaky descriptive categories with limited theoretical underpinnings.

One of the most influential models of task classification, proposed by Hackman and colleagues (Hackman, 1990; Hackman & Lawler, 1971; Hackman & Oldham, 1975) identifies five characteristics of motivating tasks: autonomy, task variety, task significance, task identity and relevant task feedback. Variations in these characteristics are related to both job satisfaction (Drory & Shamir, 1988; Hackman & Lawler, 1971) and to work group effectiveness. Campion and colleagues (Campion, Medsker & Higgs, 1993; Campion, Papper & Medsker, 1996) studied employee and managerial work groups in a financial sector organization. Their first study analysed administrative groups' effectiveness and found that task design characteristics were relatively strong predictors of effectiveness. In particular, self-management and participation (i.e. group autonomy characteristics) were significantly correlated with the three measures of effectiveness. This finding was replicated by Campion, Papper and Medsker (1996) in a study of professional workers performing complex, knowledge-based tasks.

Hackman's task design characteristics have also predicted facets of team effectiveness for both self-managing and traditional teams. Cohen, Ledford and Spreitzer (1994) examined the differential patterns of predictors of effectiveness for each team type. The task design characteristics, however, only predicted self-rated productivity for self-managing teams, and absenteeism and self-rated quality of worklife for traditional teams. Cohen, Ledford and Spreitzer (1994) concentrated on the results for self-managing teams and therefore did not offer an explanation for this finding. However, it may be that when teams are self-managed and control their workloads, they are able to put more effort into those tasks that are highly motivating (i.e. high on Hackman's job characteristics), thereby increasing performance on those tasks. Traditional team structures, on the other hand, may not provide a choice of where team members place their efforts; thus task characteristics may only influence affective states.

Given the defining importance of group task to group processes and effectiveness, the need for research in this domain is a priority.

Group Composition

Group composition has been examined in two distinct lines of research. One examines the question of whether heterogeneity is advantageous to groups. The theoretical perspectives that have guided much of the research in this area include the attraction–selection–attrition model (Schneider, 1987), similarity–attraction theory (Byrne, 1971), and self-categorization theory (Turner, 1987). A basic premise of all three is that we are attracted to those who are similar to us and thus organize, and evaluate, our social worlds accordingly.

In the second line of research, it is assumed that heterogeneity is valuable but groups need to have the right mix of members. This approach questions which combination of roles, styles, or skills fit together particularly well and which types of people are needed within groups. Research in this area has focused on heterogeneity in skills, ability and demographic variables.

Although team composition has been widely recognized as potentially important in predicting team effectiveness, research evidence about its effects is limited (Guzzo & Dickson, 1996; Guzzo & Shea, 1992). The impact of diversity within a group clearly depends upon the type of diversity being studied, the task being performed and the way in which effectiveness is defined (Haythorn, 1968; Jackson, 1992, 1996). In addition, the self-categorization of each team member will impact upon the diversity–effectiveness relationship (Hogg & Abrams, 1988; Tajfel, 1978; Tajfel & Turner, 1979). If the individual identifies with the group as a whole then diversity on relations-oriented attributes may not be relevant as each team member views the others as part of their 'ingroup'. However, if other characteristics are more salient, that is, gender or ethnicity, there will be an ingroup/outgroup differentiation within the team, and thus a more pronounced effect of diversity on outputs.

Of the different classification systems for diversity, most differentiate between attributes that are role-related and task-relevant (e.g. organizational position and specialized knowledge), and those that are simply inherent in the person and relations-oriented (e.g. age, gender, ethnicity, social status and personality) (Maznevski, 1994). Jackson (1992, 1996), however, identifies another orthogonal dimension along which diversity could be classified: readily detected or underlying. For example, organizational position is a readily detected task attribute, while specialized knowledge is an underlying task-related attribute. Readily detected relations-oriented attributes include age, gender and ethnicity, but social status and personality would be classified as underlying relations-oriented attributes. Here we consider diversity classified along the task-related/relations-oriented dimension.

Task-related diversity

Although some debate has surrounded the question of whether it is advantageous to have groups that are homogeneous or heterogeneous with respect to cognitive ability, most research results support the view that level of ability, not heterogeneity of ability, is the critical factor. At least for tasks that are truly interdependent, high-ability homogeneous groups outperform, for example, low-ability homogeneous groups. This was demonstrated in Tziner and Eden's (1985) study of military groups in which they found that the contribution of one team member of high ability to the performance of the team was greatest when all other crew members were high in ability.

There is remarkable agreement that heterogeneity of skills in teams performing complex tasks is good for effectiveness (e.g. Campion, Medsker & Higgs, 1993; Guzzo & Dickson, 1996; Jackson, 1996; Maznevski, 1994; Milliken & Martins, 1996). Heterogeneity of skills and knowledge automatically implies that each team member will bring a different knowledge perspective to the problem, a necessary ingredient for creative solutions (Sternberg & Lubart, 1990; West, 1997). For example, Wiersema and Bantel (1992) reported that strategic management initiatives were more likely in groups that were heterogeneous with respect to educational specialization, while Bantel (1993) reported that the management teams of banks which were heterogeneous with respect to education and functional background developed clearer corporate strategies. Several experimental studies, particularly those involving complex tasks or requiring innovation, have shown similar effects (McGrath, 1984).

Relations-oriented diversity

However, teams which are diverse in task-related attributes are often diverse in relation to attributes inherent in the individual. These relations-oriented characteristics can trigger stereotypes and prejudice (Jackson, 1996) which, via intergroup conflict (Hogg & Abrams, 1988; Tajfel, 1978; Tajfel & Turner, 1979), can affect group processes and outcomes.

Experience of working in teams suggests that personalities play an important part in the effectiveness of teams working together. The questions often raised are: What personality types work best together? What mix of personalities is needed for a team to be effective? In what ways must group members be compatible in order to work together effectively?

A number of models of personality in teams have been proposed in the psychological literature. For example, some organizations have sought compatibility in teams by exploring the cognitive styles of team members using the Myers–Briggs assessment instrument (a questionnaire measure of cognitive style) (Guzzo & Shea, 1992). However, little research has examined relationships between personality, compatibility and team performance. An exception is the work of Schutz (1955, 1958, 1967) which seeks to explain how personal attributes of members affect group performance. Although some research has shown that compatibility on dimensions of control predicted time to task completion in groups of managers working in a laboratory setting, there is a good deal of evidence showing no relationships between compatibility and group performance (for example, Hill, 1982; Moos & Spiesman, 1962; Shaw & Nickols, 1964). Indeed, Hill (1982) found that incompatibility predicted productivity of teams of systems analysts.

Another popular approach to team personality issues is Belbin's Team Roles Model (Belbin, 1981, 1993). Belbin suggests that there are nine team personality types and that a balance of these team personality types is required within teams. However, there is no convincing evidence that the questionnaire has satisfactory psychometric validity (Broucek & Randell, 1996; Furnham, Steele & Pendleton, 1993), or that team effectiveness is demonstrated in teams characterized by the diversity of the team role types which Belbin identifies.

Stevens and Campion (1994) prefer to utilize knowledge, skills and abilities (KSAs) in team selection rather than personality, as these are more readily influenced by the organization and are not stable traits of the individual. They propose two main domains each with various KSAs and subKSAs. Interpersonal KSAs include conflict resolution, collaborative problem-solving, and communication; while self-management KSAs encompass goal-setting and performance management, and planning and task-coordination. However, as West and Allen (1997) note, these predictors have only been validated at the individual level and are still awaiting validation at team level.

Another form of relations-oriented diversity includes organizational cohorts who differ in age and tenure. Research evidence has shown cohort-related diversity is related to team effectiveness. For example, turnover rates are higher in groups that are heterogeneous with respect to age (Jackson, Brett, Sessa, Cooper, Julin & Peyronnin, 1991; Wagner, Pfeffer & O'Reilly, 1984), and team (or department) tenure (McCain, O'Reilly & Pfeffer, 1983).

What of ethnic and gender diversity? Two studies that have examined ethnicity diversity in groups have suggested that the effects of diversity may change over time. Milliken and Martins (1996) suggested that ethnic diversity in groups can have negative effects on individual and group outcomes, but only early in a group's life. Similarly, in one of the very few longitudinal studies in this area, Watson, Kumar and Michaelsen (1993) reported that groups that were heterogeneous with respect to culture initially performed, on a series of business case exercises, more poorly than culturally homogeneous groups. As group members gained experience with each other over time, however, performance differences between culturally homogeneous and heterogeneous groups largely disappeared.

Research examining gender and ethnic heterogeneity in teams has concentrated on effects on communication. Communication requires a certain degree of communality of meanings, linguistic conventions and appropriateness of behaviour, therefore it is easy for misunderstandings and misperceptions to occur (Brick, 1991). Consequences for errors in judgement range from interpersonal effects such as hostility and conflict, to organizational repercussions such as wasted expenditure of time, effort and money (Brick, 1991; Triandis & Albert, 1987). Campion, Medsker and Higgs (1993) reported that group communication was related to team productivity, and that ethnic and gender diverse groups communicate more formally and less frequently than homogeneous groups (Milliken & Martins, 1996).

The gender of speakers is an important influence on communication within the group. Not only are men consistently more assertive in public situations and confrontations (Kimble, Marsh & Kiska, 1984; Mathison & Tucker, 1982), but communication expectations differ for men and women. Sex-role stereotypes prescribe passive, submissive and expressive communication for women while men are expected to be active, controlling and less expressive communicators (LaFrance & Mayo, 1978); deviation from these sex roles has detrimental effects on the perceptions of the speaker (Unsworth, 1994). This punishment for violation of expectations may influence both the perceptions of women in groups and their willingness to participate in team communication (Jackson, Sullivan & Hodge, 1993; Jussim, 1986; Jussim, Coleman & Lerch, 1987).

For many immigrants, their work group is one of the few places in which they participate and interact with the host society (Yum & Wang, 1983), so in considering ethnic diversity, thought must be given both to the communality of the language spoken and to the contextual aspects of communication. For, although many immigrants are bilingual, wider values must still be mastered (Min-Hsi, 1989) and they must gain an understanding of the norms that facilitate daily interaction (Gallois & Callan, 1991).

In addition, the contributions made by ethnic minorities may be downgraded simply because of their accent. In general, non-English accents are perceived more unfavourably on status attributes than accents from the dominant population (Callan, Gallois, & Forbes, 1983; Gallois & Callan, 1981; Giles & Street, 1985). People upgrade dominant or prestigious group accents and dialects on dimensions of perceived competence, status, intelligence and success (Giles & Street, 1985) and therefore group members' accents act as cues that trigger ethnic schema (Singer & Eder, 1989).

Organizational Context

Perhaps the major change in emphasis in research on teams in the last 15 years has been the shift from discussion of intragroup processes to the impact of organizational context on the team. However, despite the significance attached to the context of team work, there is little empirical, field-based research. This is partly because research with real teams poses greater difficulties in general than work with individuals (e.g. 50 people are needed to cooperate in research with 50 people, but perhaps 300 people are required for work with 50 teams). But it also reflects the difficulty of conducting team research where context is an important variable. Comparing the organizational context of 50 teams requires 50 organizations which have teams carrying out similar tasks. Nevertheless, the size of the challenge should not deter researchers from undertaking the task, given the reviews of the potential beneficial outcomes of team-based working described earlier.

Various organizational contextual factors have been proposed as important in predicting team effectiveness. Hackman (1990) highlights three factors—reward systems, information and feedback, and training—which, in combination, have significant relationships with rated quality of worklife and managers' judgements of performance (Cohen, Ledford & Spreitzer, 1994).

Reward systems, such as public recognition, preferred work assignments and money (Sundstrom, DeMeuse & Futrell, 1990) have long been known to provide motivation (Vroom, 1964) and affect performance, particularly when the rewards are contingent upon task achievement (Hackman, 1990). Gladstein (1984), in a study of 100 sales teams, found that pay and recognition had an effect, especially upon the leader's behaviour and the way the group structured itself. Hackman (1990) identified two contingencies; whether the rewards are administered to the group as a whole or to individuals, and whether the rewards provide incentives for collaboration or delegation of tasks to individuals (group rewards and incentives for collaboration are associated with positive relationships between rewards and group effectiveness).

The second of Hackman's factors is ready access to data and feedback. Feedback is important for setting realistic goals and fostering high group commitment (Latham, Erez & Locke, 1988). In addition, high job satisfaction requires accurate feedback both from the task and from other group members (Drory & Shamir, 1988). However, group feedback can be difficult to provide to teams with either long cycles of work or one-off projects (Sundstrom, DeMeuse & Futrell, 1990).

Last, Hackman (1990) argues that training and technical assistance should be readily available for teams to function successfully. Limited empirical evidence suggests training is correlated both with team self-reported effectiveness (Gladstein, 1984) and with managers' judgements of effectiveness (Campion, Medsker & Higgs, 1993).

A more elaborated consideration of organizational context has been offered by Tannenbaum, Beard and Salas (1992) who consider eight aspects of the organizational context: rewards systems (individual or team-based); resource scarcity: management control; level of stress in the organization; organizational climate; competition; intergroup relations within the organization; and environmental uncertainty. These factors have high face validity in models of work group functioning and effectiveness, but there is still little evidence about their influence on work group effectiveness.

Physical conditions are another situational constraint which can affect the relationship between performance dimensions and effectiveness. For example, a team whose members are dispersed across the countries of the European Union will find decision-making more difficult and ineffective than a team whose members share the same physical location. Goodman (1986) reports significant differences between the effectiveness of mining crews dependent upon their performance, but only in situations where physical conditions were poor.

Allen (1996) argues that employees draw a meaningful affective distinction between their work groups and their organizations, and that these affective reactions have important consequences in both domains. Strong and positive affective reactions to both domains are elicited, she argues, only when attention is paid to the congruence between group and organizational-level variables (e.g. goals and leadership).

West (1996, 1997) suggests that views of team-organizational linkages have been dominated by a unitarist bias that sees team and organizational goals as aligned and coterminous. He suggests that teams, from a minority influence perspective (Nemeth & Owens, 1996), can create cognitive and organizational conflict, which can be important sources of innovation. Such a theoretical perspective offers an explanation for the link between the extent of teamworking and organizational effectiveness and innovation.

Thus, although little research has been carried out in this area, the context in which the team works may have a far-reaching effect on many areas of team effectiveness. However, there is also the cultural context which surrounds that of the organization. It is that broader context that we examine next.

Cultural Context

Another shift in emphasis in research has been to consider the cultural context of teams. In probably the most widely cited study in this field, Hofstede (1980, 1991) identified four dimensions along which cultures differ: *individualism/ collectivism* (whether people define themselves as individuals or as members of a group); *power distance* (the degree of formality of relationships with superiors); *uncertainty avoidance* (the degree of ambiguity about the future that can be tolerated); and *masculinity/femininity*(whether achievement or interpersonal relationships are valued in the workplace). A fifth dimension has since been acknowledged: *Confucian work dynamism* (immediate versus longer-term perspective) (Chinese Culture Connection, 1987). It is clear, therefore, that fundamental values and belief systems will differ depending upon their relative placements along these five dimensions.

Indeed the very definition of a team may change across cultures. As Smith and Noakes (1996) argue, an individualistic culture may view a team as a set of individuals each having a unique contribution to a specific part of the task, while a collectivist culture may define a team as having shared responsibility for all aspects of the task.

Group processes will also change depending upon the cultural context. Western leadership theorists have discounted trait theories in favour of situational theories (see Stogdill, 1974). However, consistently effective leadership styles have been identified in other cultures (Ayman & Chemers, 1983; Bond & Hwang, 1986; Misumi, 1985; Sinha, 1981). The social loafing effect identified in Western societies (e.g. Latané, Williams & Harkins, 1979), is apparently non-existent and sometimes reversed in China and Israel (Earley, 1987, 1993; Ereg & Somech, 1996). Similarly, conformity can be predicted by the value system espoused by the societal culture (Bond & Smith, 1996).

The effects of participation, in particular, are noteworthy. Current Western thinking is that group participation is useful in enhancing performance (e.g. Cummings & Worley, 1993). However, this is based upon studies performed in individualistic, low power distance cultures. Cultures with a high power distance, on the other hand, have reported negative effects of participation (Marrow, 1964). Participation in a collectivist culture may enhance performance (similar to an individualistic culture), but via a different process—by increasing social motivation (Erez & Earley, 1987; Smith & Noakes, 1996).

Finally, the implications of value systems stretch far wider than that immediately implied by Hofstede's dimensions. For example, attitudes towards time can have a substantial impact upon team working. Smith and Noakes (1996) argue that different cultures will have different attitudes and preferences regarding time. Indeed, Levine, West and Reis (1980) found that latecomers were perceived negatively in the USA, but positively in Brazil. This can have a significant effect on the simple logistics of meetings and team gatherings. It is apparent, therefore, that the cultural context within which the team operates has an effect: both at the individual level and at the team level.

In summary, it can be seen that the neglect of group task characteristics as a variable to consider in research and theorizing is hampering our progress in understanding factors determining work team effectiveness. The interest in diversity and composition in work teams has so far produced good research evidence, but there is a need for intelligent research designs in this area which use systematic variations in composition to test theoretical predictions. The study of newly created teams offers many possibilities for avenues towards richer understanding. There can be no doubt that organizational context powerfully influences team functioning in organizations and the dearth of research in this area makes theoretical progress highly unlikely. From the perspective of practitioners, industrial/organizational psychologists are not addressing an issue of contemporary relevance with sufficient energy.

GROUP PROCESS AND EFFECTS ON OUTPUTS

This section examines the processes within teams which enable them to achieve their goals, and examines the main factors which influence these processes and ultimately how effectively teams perform their task. A fundamental requirement for effectiveness is that team members' work is coordinated and integrated (Worchel, Wood & Simpson, 1992), so first we consider the contribution of leadership and communication to team effectiveness. For knowledge and skills to be converted into action involves processes of decision-making. These are discussed with respect to factors which inhibit and enhance effective decision-making. Other processes considered are cohesiveness; the development of group affective tone; and unconscious group phenomena.

Leadership

Early research on leadership focused on the personality characteristics of leaders (see Stogdill, 1974 for a review), but revealed little conclusive evidence. A contrasting approach provided explanations in terms of the functional demands of the situation (Bales, 1950), arguing that the most effective leader in a given context is the person best equipped to assist the group to fulfil its objectives in that context. More recently, research on leadership has focused on the leadership role and leadership processes.

The Ohio state leadership studies (e.g. Fleishman, 1973; Stogdill, 1974) consisted of a large number of investigations which examined the behaviour and effectiveness of teams. Two main themes relating to leadership behaviour emerged from these studies: concern for initiating structure and consideration for others. More recently, the leadership literature has identified two superordinate dimensions of leadership (see Hackman & Walton, 1986): monitoring (obtaining and interpreting data); and taking action to create or maintain favourable performance conditions.

Yammarino (1996) identifies three styles of leadership: instrumental, inspirational and informal. Instrumental leaders (e.g. see Schriesheim & Kerr, 1977; Yukl, 1994) focus on transactions, exchanges and contingent rewards and punishments to change team members' behaviour. In this approach there is an emphasis on the relationship between person- and task-oriented leader behaviour and effective group member performance. Examples of such leader behaviours which Yammarino outlines are 'goal-setting, coaching and the use of incentives, showing consideration, being participative, empowering and delegating'.

Inspirational leaders (see, e.g. Burns, 1978; House & Shamir, 1993) influence group members through transformation, charisma and visioning. These leaders use emotional or ideological appeals to change the behaviour of the group, moving them from self-interest in work values to a consideration of the whole group and organization. Informal group leaders (see Bass, 1990; Hollander, 1958; Yukl, 1994) are elected and non-appointed leaders. Such leaders always emerge as a result of team social interaction and consensus because a particular member is judged able to lead the team to its goals. These emergent leaders facilitate the work of others, and offer support, direction and collaboration. Emergent leaders adapt their style of performance to the needs of the team and are responsive to team members' needs.

There is considerable research evidence that leaders affect team performance (e.g. Beyerlein, Johnson & Beyerlein, 1996; Brewer, Wilson & Beck, 1994; Komaki, Desselles and Bowman, 1989) and evidence of the relationship between leadership style and team effectiveness. Eden (1990) examined the effects of platoon leaders' expectations on group performance. His work with the Israeli Defence Forces showed that those platoons which trained under leaders with high expectations performed better on physical and cognitive tests. Podsakoff and Todor (1985) investigated the relationship between team members' perceptions of leader reward and punishment behaviours and group cohesiveness, drive and productivity. Results showed that both leader contingent reward and punishment were positively related to group drive and productivity. Leader contingent reward was also related to cohesiveness, while leader non-contingent punishment behaviour was negatively related to group drive. Jacobs and Singell (1993) examined the effects of managers on the won-lost record of professional baseball teams over two decades and found that leaders were effectively influencing team performance, by exercising tactical skills and improving the performance of team members. George and Bettenhausen (1990) studied groups of sales associates reporting to a store manager and found that the favourability of leaders' moods was negatively related to employee turnover.

Work by Yammarino and colleagues (see Yammarino, 1996) suggests the need to take account of both leadership style (instrumental, inspirational, informal) and the level at which leadership is operating (*whole* level or *parts* level). When leadership is operating at a *whole* group level the leader displays a similar style towards each subordinate within a group. When the leader style differs in each relationship with subordinates in the group, this is the *parts* level. A similar approach is the *vertical dyad linkage/leader member exchange* model (Graen, Novak & Sommerkamp, 1982; Graen & Scandura, 1987) where the focus is on dyads within groups; relationships are seen as controlled, managed or influenced by the leader, who is linked more closely with some subordinates than others.

Some researchers have focused on leadership at the dyad level, examining the relationship between leader and subordinate. In the *whole* dyad approach the focus is on independent dyads which function as homogeneous entities. In some of the leader–subordinate dyads relationships are stronger than others, but the individual perceptions or behaviours within each dyad are balanced (see Yammarino & Dubinsky, 1992, 1994). In contrast, in the dyad *parts* view, in all the leader–subordinate dyads, the perceptions and behaviour are unbalanced (Adams, 1965; Berscheid, 1985). These differences in perceptions and behaviours arise because the dyads are composed of dissimilar individuals (Berscheid, 1985; Byrne, 1971; Hall & Lord, 1995; Pulakos & Wexley, 1983), or reflect status differences and disproportionate credit build-up between the individuals involved (Hollander, 1958).

Another approach to leadership is suggested by West (1994) who distinguishes between managing a team (e.g. clarifying objectives and roles, and monitoring performance), coaching individuals (e.g. by managing day-to-day interactions and processes), and leading a team (e.g. developing a long-term strategic view and facilitating team-organizational linkages). Hackman (1990) also offers practical prescriptions for leading a team in terms of creating favourable performance conditions, building and maintaining the team as a performing unit, and coaching and helping the team.

Leadership is an area of research on team effectiveness where conceptual clarity and clear research questions are required for progress to be made. The tensions between concepts such as self-managing teamwork and team leadership are apparent in both the research and practitioner literatures. Moreover, as concepts of leadership embodied in individuals are challenged (e.g. Mohrman, Cohen & Mohrman, 1995) and replaced by concepts of distributed leadership, demand for researchers to develop new theoretical models and research paradigms is increased.

Communication

The study of communication in social groups has a long history in social psychology (see Brown, 1988, for a review), but recent reviews by Guzzo and Dickson (1996) and Guzzo and Shea (1992) reveal the paucity of thorough industrial and organizational research in this area. Blakar (1985) proposes five preconditions for effective communication in teams. Team members must have shared social reality—they must have a common 'here and now' within which the exchange of messages can take place, including a shared language base and perception. Team members must be able to 'decentre', to take the perspective of others into account in relation both to their affective and to their cognitive position (Redmond, 1989, 1992). Team members must be motivated to communicate. There must be 'negotiated and endorsed contracts of behaviour' (i.e. agreement among team members about how interactions take place). Finally, the team must attribute communication difficulties appropriately, so if one of the other preconditions is not being met, the team is able to identify the problem correctly and develop a solution.

Research evidence provides no clear understanding of the relationships between team communication dimensions, such as frequency of interaction, communication style, communication patterns, and performance. Smith, Smith, Olian, Sims, O'Bannon & Scully (1994) investigated the relative effects on team performance of demographic factors and team processes, including informal communication and communication frequency. They found that, unusually, communication frequency was negatively related to performance. Smith et al. suggest that conflict and disagreement in groups may have resulted in increased communication which was concerned with conflict resolution, rather than with task performance.

More recent experimental research on group communication effectiveness (e.g. Krauss & Fussell, 1990) has been augmented by burgeoning work on computer-mediated technology which can aid or hinder work group communication (Finholt, Sproull & Kiesler, 1990; Hollingshead & McGrath, 1995; Sproull & Keisler, 1986). This technology included voice messaging (e.g. Rice & Shook, 1990), teleconferencing (e.g. Egido, 1990), and group project and decision support systems (Guzzo & Dickson, 1996; Kraemer & Pinsonneault, 1990; Olson & Atkins, 1990; Vogel & Nunamaker, 1990). The results reveal very mixed effects which are, not surprisingly, dependent upon the nature of the task, the group, the context and the technology. Before developing a good understanding of technology mediating communication in work groups, however, further theoretical and research progress is needed to understand traditional work group communication processes and outcomes.

Micro analysis of communication in team meetings may provide a better understanding of these issues (West, Garrod & Carletta, 1997). The work on communication can usefully focus on how interactions are controlled and understood in group discussions (see for example, Carletta, Fraser-Krauss & Garrod, 1997). Carletta and colleagues argue that people learn to communicate in dyads. Thus group discussion tends to be 'incoherent, difficult to understand, and irrelevant in parts to all members of the group, leading to deinvestment on the part of the members' (Carletta, Fraser-Krauss & Garrod, p. 3).

Overall, industrial/organizational psychologists are faced with the challenge of synthesizing the knowledge gleaned from social psychology with their appreciation of workplace realities. Distinguishing between group communication in general and communication in meetings may be one sensible starting point.

Decision-making

Effective decision-making and problem-solving processes are central to team performance. A thorough review of the literature on team effectiveness and decision-making in organizations has been edited by Guzzo and Salas (1995). This and other evidence from both social psychological and organizational research provide support for the general proposition that high-quality decision-making will be made by groups which are reflexive.

A coherent and major body of research developed by Maier and colleagues on decision-making in groups suggested that cognitive stimulation in groups may produce novel ideas, a unique combination of subideas, or a complex solution whose total value is 'greater than the sum of its parts'. Group effectiveness might be improved, Maier found, if groups were encouraged to be 'problem minded' rather than 'solution minded' (Maier & Solem, 1962); that is, to question and communicate about its current approach or to consider other aspects of the problem (see also Maier, 1970). Maier also found that group effectiveness was improved when the group analysed problem facets as subtasks, and if members separated and recombined problem-solving strategies. Similar effects on productivity were found when groups were encouraged to produce two different solutions to a problem, so that the better of the two might be adopted (Maier, 1970). Particularly for complex decision-making groups, more planning enhances group performance (Hackman, Brousseau & Weiss, 1976; Smith, Locke & Barry, 1990).

Another line of findings comes from research on problem identification by groups (Moreland & Levine, 1992). Group problem-solving, especially early on, is significantly improved when members examine the way in which they have defined the situation and considered whether or not they are solving the 'right' problem (see, e.g. Bottger & Yetton, 1987; Hirokawa, 1990; Landsberger, 1955; Maier, 1970; Schwenk, 1988).

A major factor determining group task effectiveness is group norms regarding problem-solving. In some groups problems are regarded as threats to morale and identification of problems by their members is discouraged (Janis, 1982; Miceli & Near, 1985; Smircich, 1983). Those who become aware of problems in such groups are reluctant to talk about them because they expect to be censored. When problems are brought into the awareness of such groups, the tension produced can prevent appropriate planning and action (cf. Lyles, 1981; Schwenk & Thomas, 1983). Groups that engage in more extensive scanning and discussion of their environments are also better than those which do not in identifying problems (Ancona & Caldwell, 1988; Main, 1989; Billings, Milburn & Schaalman, 1980).

Tjosvold (1990) describes constructive controversy within groups operating in a cooperative context as the open exploration of opposing opinions. He argues for a direct causal relationship with effectiveness and offers empirical support for this proposition (Tjosvold, 1985). Similar notions, though not well developed, have been proposed by Shiflett (1979) in relation to groups. At the organizational level, Argyris (1993) proposed the idea of 'double-loop learning' in organizations as an indication of members' ability to recognize and modify underlying assumptions about organizational functioning. Dean and Sharfman (1996) studied 52 decisions in 24 companies and demonstrated clearly that the decision process has a sizeable impact on strategic decision-making effectiveness.

Van Offenbeek and Koopman (1996) offer a sophisticated contingency model of decision-making in project teams, arguing that psychological knowledge about cognitive and political group processes can be usefully applied by considering the nature of group tasks in their organizational context. This approach offers a valuable framework for integrating work from social, industrial/organizational and cognitive psychology. Other useful reviews include those by Baron, Kerr and Miller (1992), Guzzo and Salas (1995) and Moscovici and Doise (1994).

Work Group Autonomy

Autonomous work groups are permanent groups of employees, frequently at shopfloor level, who collectively exercise a substantial degree of operational responsibility in relation to the performance of some natural unit of work (Cohen & Ledford, 1994).

There are sound reasons for assuming that autonomous work groups might contribute to organizational effectiveness (see Beyerlein & Johnson, 1994; Cordery, Sevastos & Parker, 1992; Wall & Davids, 1992). However, reviews indicate only modest improvements in productivity and quality (Cohen & Ledford, 1994; Cordery, 1996). One explanation proposed is the operation of contingency factors (Wall & Jackson, 1995), including individual differences such as employee motivation, satisfaction, knowledge, skills and ability

(Hackman & Oldham, 1975) and employee perceptions of autonomy (Pearce & Ravlin, 1987). Other contingency factors include the degree of uncertainty in the work context (Wall & Jackson, 1995), task or technical interdependence (Kiggundu, 1983), the interaction between the autonomous working arrangements and process control systems (Klein, 1991) and whether the product/market is characterized by turbulence or rapid change (Cohen, 1991). Cordery (1996) comments that little is known about the social processes which occur within autonomous work groups, which might impact on performance. He argues that these groups are as likely as any to suffer from 'group think' and process loss.

Minority Group Influence

Minority influence theory (Moscovici, 1976; Moscovici, Mugny & Avermaet, 1985; Nemeth, 1986; Nemeth & Owens, 1996) is a stimulating and important contribution from social psychology to the understanding of work groups. This seeks to explain how minorities in groups can have a sustained and powerful impact upon the attitudes and behaviour of others within the group. Minority group influence is the process whereby a numerical or power minority within a group or society brings about enduring change in the attitudes and behaviour of others.

Exposure to minority influence can cause private changes in attitudes in the direction of the deviant view, as a result of the cognitive or social conflict generated by the minority's disagreement with the dominant view. Repeated exposure to a consistent minority view can lead to marked and internalized changes in attitudes and behaviours. When people conform to a majority view they generally comply publicly without necessarily changing their private beliefs. Minorities, in contrast, appear to produce a shift in private views rather than mere public compliance (for a review of studies of this phenomenon see Wood, Lundgren, Oullette, Busceme & Blackstone, 1994).

More recent research by Nemeth (1986) and Nemeth and Owens (1996) is based on the premise that dissent stimulates cognitive effort, but the form that effort takes is very different, depending on whether the dissent emanates from a minority or a majority. Both forms of dissent result in increased cognitive effort within the group. However, when majorities offer a different viewpoint from the individual this induces stress, resulting in convergent thinking. Minorities on the other hand are initially derided by group members and assumed to be incorrect. However, Nemeth and Owens (1996) argue that, when group members come to reappraise the situation, they make a thorough, more broad-ranging analysis in the form of divergent thinking. Thus minority dissent can contribute significantly to improving group decision-making.

Minority dissent makes additional contributions to effective group decision-making. Other studies have shown that minorities can stimulate the search for and the recall of information (Nemeth, Mayseless, Sherman & Brown, 1990) and, perhaps more importantly, can increase the desire for additional information which is relatively unbiased (Nemeth & Rogers, 1996). This latter finding is important because evidence suggests that people favour information which is consistent with their own view and may actively avoid information which opposes their position (Frey, 1982). If minority dissent can stimulate unbiased information search, this can contribute to the quality of decision-making in a group. Nemeth and Owens conclude:

> we have found that dissenting minority views stimulate information search and thought processes that are divergent in form. People search for information in an unbiased way; they consider multiple perspectives; they utilize multiple strategies in the service of performance. Importantly, the effects of exposure to minority dissent do not depend on the correctness of the position. It is not because they might hold the truth or even the partial truth. It is because they maintain a dissenting view and, by casting doubt on the position held by the majority, they stimulate those individuals to engage in precisely the kinds of thought processes that, on balance, serve decision-making and creativity. (p. 137)

Cohesiveness

Cohesiveness refers to the degree of interpersonal attraction and liking among team members and their liking for the team as a whole. There are sound reasons for arguing that cohesiveness will affect team performance, by influencing team members' helping behaviour and generosity, cooperation and problem-solving orientation during negotiations, and their membership of the team (see Isen & Baron, 1991). This may translate into greater motivation to contribute fully and perform well as a means of gaining approval and recognition (Festinger, Schachter & Back, 1950).

There is some evidence suggesting that members of socially integrated groups experience higher morale and satisfaction, and exhibit greater efficiency in the coordination of tasks (Shaw, 1981; McGrath, 1984; O'Reilly, Caldwell & Barnett, 1989). Shaw and Shaw (1962) found that highly cohesive groups devoted more time to planning and problem-solving and that group members followed the established plan. Members in low-cohesion groups were hostile and aggressive; they tested each other immediately and did not engage in preliminary planning. Smith et al. (1994) found a substantial positive association between cohesion and the performance of top management teams. One explanation for this link between cohesion and effectiveness is suggested by the work of Ouchi (1980), who showed that highly socialized and cohesive groups have lower communication and coordination costs, are thus more efficient and flexible, and can apply greater attention to problems which require quick action. This explanation is supported by Zaccaro, Gualtieri and Minionis (1995) who found that highly task-cohesive military teams under high time pressure performed as well on decision-making tasks as did either high task-cohesive or low task-cohesive teams under low time urgency. This suggests that task cohesion can improve team decision-making under time pressure.

The most recent review (Mullen & Copper, 1994) involved a meta-analytical cross-lagged panel correlation, using 66 tests of the cohesiveness—performance effect. It revealed a consistent and highly significant relationship and that the direction of effect was stronger from performance to cohesion than from cohesion to performance. This is an important finding since it suggests that it is effective performance which influences cohesiveness more than the reverse association.

Group Affective Processes

Another important, but more controversial, approach to understanding work group processes and effectiveness is offered by the research on group affective tone. George (1990) suggests that if members of a group experience similar kinds of affective states at work (either negative or positive), then affect is meaningful not only in terms of their individual experiences, but also at a group level. A number of studies have demonstrated a significant relationship between group affective tone and behaviour such as absenteeism (George, 1989, 1990, 1995). George proposes that groups which are interested, strong, excited, enthusiastic, proud, alert, inspired, determined, attentive and active enable cognitive flexibility, creativity and effectiveness (George, 1996). However, she argues that group affective tone may not exist for all groups, so it cannot be assumed a priori that it is a relevant construct for every team.

George (1996) sees group affective tone and team mental models as having a reciprocal influence. So in a group with a negative affective tone, members would have different cognitive processes from those in a group with a positive affective tone, which then may influence group effectiveness. There is some evidence that team mental models play an important role in group decision-making (Klimoski & Mohammed, 1994), influencing aspects of group decision-making such as problem definition, speed and flexibility, alternative evaluation, and implementation (Walsh & Fahey, 1986; Walsh, Henderson & Deighton, 1988). A group which has a negative affective tone may tend to be more rigid when making decisions (Staw, Sandelands & Dutton, 1981). The nature and outcomes of group decision-making are therefore likely to be affected by the interaction between group affective tone and team mental models.

Unconscious Group Processes

George's work on affective tone reflects the resurgence of interest in the role of emotions in the workplace (e.g. Fineman, 1993). The psychodynamic tradition provides a valuable framework for understanding emotions. A central proposition in this tradition is that unconscious phenomena can influence group behaviour and therefore team effectiveness (Bion, 1961; Stein, 1996). Bion suggested that unconscious phenomena in a group may run counter to and therefore undermine the rational task. The group functions as if it is working on its task, but factors which the group is largely unaware of prevent it from doing so.

Stein (1996) proposes that a major constituent part of the group unconscious is the anxiety that group members are unable to bear, and so block from entering their consciousness. These anxieties relate to the nature of the work (i.e. 'the group will fail at the task') and to the organization (i.e. 'the management are against us'). Therefore, observable group processes may be unconsciously shaped by the need to avoid the experience of these anxieties (Menzies Lyth, 1989).

A work group may also have unconscious thoughts and feelings about an individual with whom it works, such as a manager. When these thoughts and feelings are transferred from other past or present relationships experienced by group members, this is termed 'transference'. Stein (1996) observes that envy is another relatively unexplored phenomenon in work groups. While members may be conscious of some envy, it is the unconscious feelings which are critical, resulting in, for example, group members inhibiting the development of skills of certain of its members. Such an approach to team processes offers an alternative perspective and draws our attention to neglected issues of power in teams at work.

The relative richness of research on group processes in comparison with that on team inputs is a consequence of the much longer history of research in this area, stretching back to the Hawthorne studies in the 1930s. Nevertheless, the reader will still struggle to clearly articulate general links between team processes and effectiveness, based on this review. This is partly because research on this relationship has proceeded piecemeal with an ironic failure amongst researchers to achieve a shared understanding of what is meant by group effectiveness. It is this nettle we grasp next!

OUTPUTS

In the three team domains of inputs, processes and outputs, the least progress in conceptual development has been made in the last. Not unusually in industrial/organizational psychology, researchers have focused on independent variables to the theoretical and empirical neglect of dependent measures (West, Patterson, & Lawthom, 1997). Recently, an excellent analysis of the group effectiveness construct has been made by Brodbeck (1996). After Campbell and Campbell (1988), he distinguishes between 'performance' as an aggregate of those behaviours which are relevant for achieving group goals (i.e. motivation to work; knowledge and skill brought to bear on the task; and collective performance strategies used by the group for internal and external, e.g. boundary-spanning), activities; 'effectiveness' as the degree to which performance outcomes approach goals; and 'productivity' as the efficiency with which a given level of effectiveness is achieved. These distinctions enable researchers to avoid the 'unmodified linear assumption', that more performance means more effectiveness, which is characteristic of the group-effectiveness literature.

Brodbeck argues that the relationship between work group performance and effectiveness will be moderated or 'contaminated' by situational constraints. These are either internal to the group (social loafing, production blocking, other process losses) or external. External constraints include material resources (Hackman, 1987), task complexity (Tschan & von Cranach, 1996), environmental uncertainty (e.g. Sundstrom, De Meuse & Futrell, 1990), market growth (Gladstein, 1984), and technology (Ulich & Weber, 1996).

Work group functioning also depends upon the stage in the group's life. McGrath and O'Connor (1996) have presented a cogent analysis of the temporal issues which impact on the effective functioning of work groups, based on the extensive work conducted by McGrath over the last 25 years. They suggest there are four important temporal domains which must be considered:

- The formation and subsequent development of groups as sociotechnical systems
- Temporal changes associated with the processes by which the group performs its task
- Changes that come about in the group as a function of its own development and task performance experience
- Dynamic changes that occur in groups as a function of changes in their constituent parts (e.g. their members) and in their environments

Argote and McGrath (1993) suggest that these four issues are reflected in four central processes in groups: group construction, group operations, group reconstructions, and external relations processes. All of these factors will affect group performance and effectiveness, so dynamic, temporally based models which emphasize reciprocal interdependence between variables are needed if we are to theorize better about group effectiveness in the workplace.

A number of conclusions can be drawn. Work group performance and effectiveness should be explicitly distinguished and separately measured (self-report measures of work group performance and effectiveness, common in the research literature, abuse this ideal). The various dimensions of performance and effectiveness should be conceptualized and operationalized as precisely as possible, rather than relying on convenience measures of, for example, productivity. Temporal factors should be considered; there is a need for research on newly created work teams, following their progress and measuring performance and effectiveness over time. Because effectiveness is a political concept, as much as an empirical concept in organizations, account should be taken of the criteria of effectiveness used by constituents of teams (managers, customers, group members, other groups), and built into operationalizations of work group effectiveness (Poulton & West, 1993, 1994). Researchers must carefully specify levels of analysis (Kozlowski & Hattrup, 1992; James, Demareé & Wolf, 1993; George & James, 1993, 1994) and justification needs to be offered for aggregating individual level phenomena (mental health, job satisfaction) to the group level as surrogate measures of aspects of group effectiveness.

The Productivity Measurement and Enhancement System (ProMES) (Pritchard, Jones, Roth et al., 1988, 1989; Pritchard, 1990) provides an approach to conceptualizing and operationalizing performance and effectiveness, while taking account of constituents' criteria. ProMES involves developing formal methods for measuring productivity which clearly specify the outputs, indicators of goal achievement and contribution of each indicator to overall effectiveness. Feedback on performance is used to develop strategies for improving performance.

Four effectiveness dimensions are specified in Brodbeck's work, largely reflecting the thinking of previous scholars in the area. These are productive output (e.g. sales revenues, patients treated, reduction in customer complaints); social criteria (willingness of group members to continue working together—'team viability'); individual outcomes (member mental health, member growth and well-being, and member satisfaction); and innovation. Productivity has been discussed in the previous sections, so therefore we focus here on the three outputs not yet considered: individual well-being, team viability, and innovation.

Individual Well-being

Does working in teams lead to better outcomes for members in terms of mental health, job satisfaction, growth and development, and career opportunities? Most research on group effectiveness has focused on issues of productivity (Gladstein, 1984; Goodman, 1986; Guzzo & Shea, 1992; Hackman & Morris, 1975; Worchel, Wood & Simpson, 1992; Brodbeck, 1996). There is comparatively little research or theorizing which addresses issues of well-being of group members, despite extensive work on individual work factors and well-being. Perhaps one of the reasons for this relative neglect is the problem of confounding levels of analysis, referred to earlier, when the effects of work group factors are examined in relation to individual well-being. This can lead to confusion about outcomes. For example, high group cohesion and support in a group does not mean that every individual in the group will experience a high level of support and warmth. Psychodynamic analyses of group processes (Stein, 1996) can reveal scapegoating of individuals in groups in order to achieve high support and cohesion for all other group members.

Early studies (Roethlisberger & Dickson, 1939; Trist & Bamforth, 1951) clearly revealed that group work has an impact upon attitudes and affect. Disbanding small stable work groups in Trist and Bamforth's (1951) study of coal mining was shown to lead to higher levels of neurotic and psychosomatic disorder amongst those forced to work in relative isolation. Hackman (1992) argues strongly for the impact of group membership on satisfaction, since membership can offer opportunities for social contact, boosts to self-esteem and other social rewards.

Moch (1980) found that amongst 522 employees of an assembly and packaging plant, those who worked in networks of work relationships had higher motivation, even controlling for job characteristics. Similar results for psychosomatic complaints (more team work associated with lower complaints) were reported for a study of police working in groups (Greller, Parsons & Mitchell, 1992). Rudolph, Schönfleder and Hacker (1987) found that clerical workers in cooperative settings were more satisfied than those who worked in settings which did not require cooperation.

Which aspects of group work affect member well-being? Sonnentag (1996) addresses these questions in relation to group size, composition and task, but results reveal no clear pattern in relation to group size and well-being. Homogeneity of the group similarly reveals no consistent relationships with well-being or satisfaction.

Does the group's task affect well-being of group members? Research at the individual level of analysis suggests it would (Frese, 1985; Karasek, Baker, Marxer et al., 1981; Leitner, 1993). The most relevant area of research is that on autonomous work groups (e.g. Cordery, Mueller & Smith, 1991; Wall & Clegg, 1981; Wall, Kemp, Jackson & Clegg, 1986). This suggests that the implementation of autonomous work groups is associated with increased satisfaction, though the temporal pattern of changes in satisfaction is inconsistent. In some studies early changes occur in mental health, with later ones occurring in job satisfaction (e.g. Wall & Clegg, 1981). In others, no changes in satisfaction over time were found (Cordery, Mueller & Smith, 1991). Sonnentag suggests these effects may be related to other factors, such as the company's overall performance (e.g. Antoni, 1994).

Sonnentag (1996) also examines the relationship between group process variables and well-being, showing consistently positive relationships, though she points out that the common method variance problems of eliciting self reports about processes and well-being are acute. Individual response bias may lead to those with good mental health reporting on their group process also in favourable terms, so that causality is from mental health to group process rather than vice versa. Where group level data (on group process) are used, the relationships still tend to reveal that group process is related to individual mental health and satisfaction, though the relationship is much weaker (around $r = -0.025$), than those at the individual level ($r = -0.04$ to -0.05).

Sonnentag reflects on the need for longitudinal studies which examine the causal effects of work group characteristics on individual well-being. These would be particularly powerful if they were studies of newly created work groups, since the effects of prior experience and success could effectively be ruled out. She also urges researchers to develop group level measures of work group characteristics whenever dealing with constructs conceptualized at the group level.

Team Viability

An outcome variable consistently referred to in the literature and which has an important place in influential models and theories (e.g. Hackman, 1987; Hackman, 1990; Sundstrom, De Meuse & Futrell, 1990) is team viability. This is the extent to which a group's processes lead the group to cohesion, shared purpose and continued commitment versus destructive conflict, intention to leave the group and dissatisfaction with group membership. Such a concept is theoretically important, though there are hard questions about the extent to which the imperatives of organizational functioning allow interpersonal difficulties to determine the composition and direction of group work, except perhaps at senior levels. Whatever, there is virtually no evidence about work group characteristics, group processes, and organizational context effects upon group viability. Some studies of turnover in groups exist but this is an inadequate surrogate measure of the construct under consideration. People leave groups for a variety of reasons, which may be task-determined (different membership is required at different stages of a project's life cycle); in some circumstances turnover is necessary to avoid the apparently unhelpful effects of sustained homogeneity. Researchers need to consider carefully the utility of the construct, rather than accepting its importance unquestioningly.

Another area where more understanding is required is in terms of the effects of team outcomes upon group context, organizational context and group processes. Because there have been so few longitudinal studies of teams at work and almost none of newly created teams, there are few data illustrating the reciprocal interdependence implied by some more recent theoretical approaches in the field (Guzzo, Yosst, Campbell & Shea, 1994; Sundstrom, De Meuse & Futrell, 1990).

Innovation

Since one of the main reasons for introducing team-based working is to promote organizational innovation, policy-makers and practitioners are increasingly asking what factors determine innovation in teams?

In relation to inputs, there is some evidence that heterogeneity of group composition is related to group innovation (Hoffman & Maier, 1961; McGrath, 1984; Jackson, 1996). There may be innovation differences too, consequent upon team tenure. Katz (1982) has argued that project new-comers represent a novelty-enhancing condition, challenging and improving the scope of existing methods and accumulated knowledge. He suggests that the longer group has been together, the less members communicate with key information sources, scan the environment, or communicate within the group and externally. There is certainly evidence that team tenure moderates the relationship between task complexity and performance (Kozlowski & Hults, 1986). Research on diversity in teams (Bantel & Jackson, 1989; Jackson, 1996) also suggests that longer tenure might be associated with increasing homogeneity, and consequent deleterious effects on team innovation.

Another element of group composition is the personality or dispositional characteristics of group members. West and Anderson (1996) suggest that team innovation will be determined by the proportion of innovative individuals who constitute the team (see also Burningham & West, 1995). This proposition derives from the assumption that the generation of a new idea is a cognitive process which is located within individuals, albeit fostered sometimes by interaction processes in teams (Mumford & Gustafson, 1988).

West and Anderson (1996) draw on existing reviews (Agrell & Gustafson, 1996; Anderson & King, 1993; Guzzo & Shea, 1992; King, 1990; Wolf, 1994) to identify four group process characteristics which theoretically might predict group innovation—commitment to and clarity of team objectives, team participation, task orientation, and support for innovation.

The most consistently important factor in determining group effectiveness is the existence of group goals or objectives (Guzzo & Shea, 1992; Latham & Yukl, 1975; Locke, 1968; Maier, 1963; Pritchard et al. 1988; Vroom & Yetton, 1973; Weldon & Weingart, 1993). In the context of group innovation, Pinto and Prescott (1987), in a study of 418 project teams, found that a clearly stated mission was the only factor that predicted success at all stages of the innovation process. Clarity of team objectives is likely to facilitate innovation by enabling focused development of new ideas, which can be assessed with greater precision than if team objectives are unclear. However, there is little direct evidence relating clarity of team goals and member goal commitment to the innovativeness of teams.

Research on participation in decision-making has a long history in both social and industrial/organizational psychology, revealing that participation tends to foster greater effectiveness and commitment (Bowers & Seashore, 1966; Coch & French, 1948; Lawler & Hackman, 1969; Wall & Lischeron, 1977). There are good reasons for supposing that this factor will also be of importance in team innovation. To the extent that information and influence over decision-making are shared within teams and there is a high level of interaction amongst team members, the cross-fertilization of perspectives which can spawn creativity and innovation (Cowan, 1986; Mumford & Gustafson, 1988; Pearce & Ravlin, 1987; Porac & Howard, 1990) is more likely to occur. More generally, high levels of participation in decision-making are associated with less resistance to change and therefore greater likelihood of innovations being implemented.

A central theme in the innovation and creativity literatures is that divergent thinking and the management of competing perspectives are important processes in the generation of creativity (Mumford & Gustafson, 1988). Such processes are characteristic of task-related team conflict and controversy. They can arise from a shared concern with excellence of quality of task performance in relation to shared objectives—what has been termed 'task orientation' (West, 1990). Task orientation may be evidenced by appraisal of, and constructive challenges to, the group's objectives, strategies, processes and performance; and by concern with high standards of performance. Tjosvold and colleagues (Tjosvold, 1982; Tjosvold & Field, 1983; Tjosvold & Johnson, 1977; Tjosvold, Wedley & Field, 1986) have argued similarly that constructive controversy in cooperative group contexts improves the quality of decision-making and, therefore, of innovation (Tjosvold, 1991).

A second theme in the innovation literature suggests that innovation is more likely to occur in contexts (be they organizational or group) where there is support for innovation, or where innovative attempts are rewarded rather than punished (Amabile, 1983; Kanter, 1983).

West and Anderson (1996) have carried out a longitudinal study of the functioning of top management teams in 27 hospitals and examined relationships between group and organizational factors and team innovation. The results suggested that group processes best predict the overall level of team innovation, while the proportion of innovative team members predicts the rated radicalness of innovations introduced. Resources available to teams do not predict overall team innovation.

DEVELOPING TEAMS IN ORGANIZATIONS

To what extent is it possible to develop team working to ensure higher levels of effectiveness? Tannenbaum, Salas and Cannon-Bowers (1996) have reviewed research in this area and related results to a comprehensive model of team effectiveness which integrates interventions (Tannenbaum, Beard & Salas, 1992). They describe a number of intervention types:

- *Team member selection.* Although organizations tend to use quite sophisticated methods for selecting employees for individual jobs, they rarely use systematic methods for selecting for teams. Selection interventions could improve team effectiveness by increasing the professional or skill diversity of team members, thereby increasing the range of competencies in the group. No systematic studies of such interventions have been undertaken.
- *Team-building.* Some team-building interventions focus on role clarification, some on interpersonal relationships or conflict resolution issues while

others take more of a general problem-solving approach (Tannenbaum, Salas & Cannon-Bowers, 1996). Many team processes, including communication, decision-making and mutual role understanding, are often direct targets of team-building interventions. Several reviews have examined the efficacy of team-building interventions (DeMeuse & Liebowitz, 1981; Guzzo & Shea, 1992; Sundstrom, De Meuse & Futrell, 1990; Tannenbaum et al., 1992, 1996). They suggest that no one team-building method consistently works better than others. The cumulative evidence suggests that while team-building interventions can have a positive impact on individual perceptions and attitudes, there is less support for any impact upon team performance.

Other strategies considered by Tannenbaum and colleagues include team training, leadership training, and teamwork redesign. However, no empirical evaluations of such interventions have been undertaken. Little thought appears to have been given by researchers to interventions designed to change organizational context, rather than group composition and processes, as ways of enhancing team effectiveness.

One of the most exciting developments in the field is the new emphasis upon the development of team-based working in organizations (Mohrman, Cohen & Mohrman, 1995; Markiewicz & West, 1996). This reflects a concern amongst practitioners with how team-based working can be effectively introduced. Mohrman, Cohen and Mohrman studied 25 teams in four companies using a grounded research methodology, involving managers and internal customers. In the second phase of their research they surveyed 178 teams across seven corporations, involving team members, managers and customers. In this way, they developed a five-stage design sequence for the transition to a team-based organization:

- *Identifying work teams and the nature of the task.* This involves process analysis to determine essential work activities that have to be conducted and integrated to produce products or services; deliberations analysis which identifies dialogues about issues that have to be repeatedly resolved in order to provide shared direction and enable people to complete their tasks; and task interdependence analysis which determines where and to what extent individuals and teams have to rely on each other to complete their tasks.
- *Specifying integration needs.* In order to integrate the work of teams which have to work together, Mohrman, Cohen and Mohrman recommend using liaison roles, overlapping memberships of teams, cross-integrating teams which include representatives from the teams required to coordinate their work. In order to integrate across multiple teams and components of business units, Mohrman, Cohen and Mohrman recommend management teams, representative integrating teams (where an overall coordinating team has representatives from each of those teams collectively involved

in producing a product or service), individual integrating roles, and improvement teams.

- *Clarifying management structure and roles.* This stage involves putting as much self-management responsibility into the teams as possible; involving team members in determining how leadership tasks will be performed and by whom; using lateral mechanisms for cross-team and organization-wide integration so that teams participate in that integration; and creating management roles which link teams to the organizational strategy and ensure they are responsive to the organizational and wider environmental context.
- *Designing integration processes.* The research evidence suggested that team-based organizations should set clear directions in the organization (e.g. by defining, communicating and operationalizing a strategy at all levels, aligning goals, assigning rewards in accordance with organizational goals, and planning collectively); managing information distribution and communication; and developing an appropriate decision-making strategy (by clarifying decision-making authority, and appropriately involving organizational contributors).
- *Developing performance management processes.* Finally, the model suggests the need to manage performance—defining, rewarding and reviewing performance and involving internal and external customers, and team members. Mohrman, Cohen and Mohrman report that the more people were rewarded for individual performance, the worse team performance was. The more people were rewarded for team performance, the better was the team and the business unit's performance, and the more process improvements the team and the business unit instituted.

CONCLUSIONS

This review has revealed the diversity of perspectives which industrial and organizational scientists have brought to the study of work teams. Their work takes place in a context of high demand for knowledge, yet their task is complex, uncertain and changing as teams evolve in organizational settings. The level of effort made by researchers is prodigious, though there has been too little truly interdisciplinary research in the field (for example linking the work of economists and industrial/organizational psychologists). The effectiveness of this effort has been limited, partly by the difficulty of the task of researching with real work groups within and across organizations.

We believe there is a need to develop more integrated, holistic views of organizational contexts, to enable better theory development (as opposed to testing atomistic influencing factors). We also look for theory and research examining linkages and effects from team effectiveness to organizational effectiveness—what are the processes, and what contingencies operate? How can we find out more about communication, power and leadership in teams?

What effects do processes and outputs have upon team inputs and organizational contexts, and by what means? We hope researchers will attack the big questions by better operationalizing effectiveness and intervening in groups at work to promote effectiveness. Examining contextual and environmental contingencies is also vital if the discipline is to offer valuable contributions to practitioners.

Above all, we must be reflexive as researchers, continually questioning what it is we are trying to achieve in this domain of research, challenging and modifying our strategies, and developing innovative research methods. Humans live and work in groups. How successfully they do so, is in part dependent upon their ability to turn the light of consciousness onto their own functioning, to reflect and to learn about how to live and work most effectively in these groups. With our unique skills and knowledge, industrial and organizational psychologists can aid considerably in this process.

REFERENCES

Adams, J. S. (1965). Inequity in social exchange. In L. Berkowitz (Ed.), *Advances in Experimental Social Psychology* (Vol. 2). New York: Academic Press.

Agrell, A. & Gustafson, R. (1996). Innovation and creativity in work groups. In M. A. West (Ed.), *Handbook of Work Group Psychology* (pp. 317–344). Chichester: Wiley.

Alderfer, C. P. (1977). Group and intergroup relations. In J. R. Hackman & J. L. Suttle (Eds), *Improving the Quality of Work Life* (pp. 227–296). Pallisades, CA: Goodyear.

Allen, N. J. (1996). Affective reactions to the group and organisation. In M. A. West (Ed.), *Handbook of Work Group Psychology* (pp. 371–396). Chichester: Wiley.

Amabile, T. M. (1983). The social psychology of creativity: A componential conceptualization. *Journal of Personality and Social Psychology*, **45**, 357–376.

Ancona, D. F. & Caldwell, D. F. (1988). Bridging the boundary: External activity and performance in organisational teams. *Administrative Science Quarterly*, **37**, 634–665.

Anderson, N. R. & King, N. (1993). Innovation in organisations. In C. L. Cooper & I. T. Robertson (Eds), *International Review of Industrial and Organizational Psychology* (Vol. 8). Chichester: Wiley.

Anderson, N. & Thomas, H. D. C. (1996). Work group socialization. In M. A. West (Ed.), *The Handbook of Work Group Psychology* (pp. 423–450). Chichester: Wiley.

Antoni, C. (1994). Auswirkungen von teilautonomen Arbeitsgruppen auf Kriterien humaner Arbeit und ökonomischer Effizienz. In K. Pawlik (Ed.), *Bericht über den 39. Kongreß der Deutschen Gessellschaft für Psychologie, Hamburg, 25–29 September 1994* (Vol. 1, p. 32). Hamburg: Psychologisches Institut I der Universität Hamburg.

Applebaum, E. & Batt, R. (1994). *The New American Workplace*. Ithaca, NY: ILR Press.

Argote, L. & McGrath, J. E. (1993). Group processes in organisations: Continuity and change. In C. L. Cooper & I. T. Robertson (Eds), *International Review of Industrial and Organizational Psychology* (Vol. 8). Chichester: Wiley.

Argyris, C. (1993). On the nature of actionable knowledge. *The Psychologist*, **6**, 29–32.

Ayman, R. & Chemers, M. M. (1983). Relationship of supervisory behavior ratings to work group effectiveness and subordinate satisfaction among Iranian managers. *Journal of Applied Psychology*, **68**, 338–341.

Bales, R. F. (1950). *Interaction Process Analysis: A Method for the Study of Small Groups*. Cambridge, MA: Addison-Wesley.

Bandura, A. (1982). Self-efficacy mechanism in human agency. *American Psychologist*, **37**, 122–147.

Bantel, K. A. (1993). Strategic clarity in banking: Role of top management team demography. *Psychological Reports*, **73**, 1187–1201.

Bantel, K. A. & Jackson, S. E. (1989). Top management and innovations in banking: Does the demography of the top team make a difference? *Strategic Management Journal*, **10**, 107–124.

Baron, R. S., Kerr, N. L. & Miller, N. (1992). *Group Process, Group Decision, Group Action*. Milton Keynes, Bucks: Open University Press.

Bass, B. M. (1990). *Bass and Stogdill's Handbook of Leadership*. New York: Free Press.

Belbin, R. M. (1981). *Management Teams: Why They Succeed or Fail*. London: Heinemann.

Belbin, R. M. (1993). *Team Roles at Work: A Strategy for Human Resource Management*. Oxford: Butterworth, Heinemann.

Berscheid, E. (1985). Interpersonal attraction. In G. Lindzey & E. Aronson (Eds), *Handbook of Social Psychology* (pp. 413–484). New York: Random House.

Beyerlein, M. M. & Johnson, D. A. (Eds) (1994). *Advances in the Interdisciplinary Study of Work Teams*. London: JAI Press.

Beyerlein, M. M., Johnson, D. A. & Beyerlein, S. T. (Eds) (1995). *Advances in the Interdisciplinary Study of Work Teams* (Vol. 2): *Knowledge Work in Teams*. London: JAI Press.

Beyerlein, M. M., Johnson, D. A. & Beyerlein, S. T. (Eds) (1996). *Advances in the Interdisciplinary Study of Work Teams* (Vol. 3): *Team Leadership*. London: JAI Press.

Billings, R. S., Milburn, T. W. & Schaalman, M. L. (1980). A model of crisis perception: A theoretical and empirical analysis. *Administrative Science Quarterly*, **25**, 300–316.

Bion, W. R. (1961). *Experiences in Groups and other Papers*. New York: Basic Books.

Blakar, R. M. (1985). Towards a theory of communication in terms of preconditions: A conceptual framework and some empirical explorations. In H. Giles & R. N. St Clair (Eds), *Recent Advances in Language, Communication and Social Psychology*. London: Lawrence Erlbaum.

Bond, M. H. & Hwang, K. K. (1986). The social psychology of Chinese people. In M. H. Bond (Ed.), *The Psychology of the Chinese People* (pp. 213–266). Hong Kong: Oxford University Press.

Bond, M. H. & Smith, P. B. (1996). Culture and conformity: A meta-analysis of studies using the Asch line judgement task. *Psychological Bulletin*, **119**, 111–137.

Bottger, P. C. & Yetton, P. W. (1987). Improving group performance by training in individual problem solving. *Journal of Applied Psychology*, **72**, 651–657.

Bowers, D. G. & Seashore, S. E. (1966). Predicting organisational effectiveness with a four-factor theory of leadership. *Administrative Science Quarterly*, **11**, 238–263.

Brewer, N., Wilson, C. & Beck, K. (1994). Supervisory behavior and team performance amongst police patrol sergeants. *Journal of Occupational and Organizational Psychology*, **67**, 69–78.

Brick, J. (1991). *China: A Handbook in Intercultural Communication*. Sydney: Macquarie University.

Brodbeck, F. (1996). Work group performance and effectiveness: Conceptual and measurement issues. In M. A. West (Ed.), *The Handbook of Work Group Psychology* (pp. 285–316). Chichester: Wiley.

Broucek, W. G. & Randell, G. (1996). An assessment of the construct validity of the belbin self-perception inventory and observer's assessment from the perspective of the five-factor model. *Journal of Occupational and Organizational Psychology*, **69**(4), 389–406.

Brown, R. J. (1988). *Group Processes: Dynamics Within and Between Groups*. London: Blackwell.

Bucklow, M. (1966). A new role for the work group. *Administrative Science Quarterly*, 11(1), 72–74.

Bunce, D. & West, M. A. (1995). Self perceptions and perceptions of group climate as predictors of individual innovation at work. *Applied Psychology: An International Review*, 44, 199–215.

Burningham, C. & West, M. A. (1995). Individual, climate and group interaction processes as predictors of work team innovation. *Small Group Research*, 26, 106–117.

Burns, J. M. (1978). *Leadership*. New York: Harper & Row.

Byrne, D. (1971). *The Attraction Paradigm*. New York: Academic Press.

Callan, V. J., Gallois, C. & Forbes, P. A. (1983). Evaluative reactions to accented English: Ethnicity, sex role and context. *Journal of Cross-Cultural Psychology*, 14(4), 407–426.

Campbell, J. P. & Campbell, R. J. (1988). Industrial-organizational psychology and productivity: The goodness of fit. In J.P. Campbell & R.J. Campbell (Eds), *Productivity in Organizations* (pp. 82–93). San Francisco: Jossey-Bass.

Campion, M. A., Medsker, G. J. & Higgs, A. C. (1993). Relations between work group characteristics and effectiveness: Implications for designing effective work groups. *Personnel Psychology*, 46, 823–850.

Campion, M. A., Papper, E. M. & Medsker, G. J. (1996). Relations between work team characteristics and effectiveness: A replication and extension. *Personnel Psychology*, 49, 429–689.

Carletta, J., Fraser-Krauss, H. & Garrod, S. (1997). Speaking turns in face-to-face workplace groups: The role of the communication mediator. Unpublished manuscript. Human Communication Research Centre, Universities of Edinburgh and Glasgow.

Chinese Culture Connection (1987). Chinese values and the search for culture-free dimensions of culture. *Journal of Cross-Cultural Psychology*, 18, 143–164.

Coch, L. & French, J. R. (1948). Overcoming resistance to change. *Human Relations*, 1, 512–532.

Cohen, S. G. (1991). *Teams and Teamwork: Future Directions* (CEO Publication No. G91-9(194)). University of Southern California.

Cohen, S. G. & Ledford, G. E. (1994). The effectiveness of self-managing teams: A field experiment. *Human Relations*, 47, 13–43.

Cohen, S. G., Ledford, G. E. & Spreitzer, G. M. (1994). *A Predictive Model of Self-managing Work Team Effectiveness* (CEO Publication No. T94-28(271)). University of Southern California.

Cooper, R. & Foster, M. (1971). Sociotechnical systems. *American Psychologist*, 26, 467–474.

Cordery, J. L. (1996). Autonomous work groups. In M.A. West (Ed.), *The Handbook of Work Group Psychology* (pp. 225–246). Chichester: Wiley.

Cordery, J. L., Mueller, W. S. & Smith, L. M. (1991). Attitudinal and behavioural outcomes of autonomous group working: A longitudinal field study. *Academy of Management Journal*, 34, 464–476.

Cordery, J. L., Sevastos, P. P. & Parker, S. (1992). *Job design, skill utilization and psychological well-being at work: Preliminary test of a model*. Paper presented at XXV International Congress of Psychology, Brussels, July.

Cotton, J. L. (1993). *Employee Involvement*. Newbury Park, CA: Sage.

Cowan, D. A. (1986). Developing a process model of problem recognition. *Academy of Management Review*, 11, 763–776.

Cummings, T. G. & Worley, C. G. (1993). *Organization Development and Change*. St Paul, MN: West.

Cyert, R. & March, J. (1963). *The Behavioral Theory of the Firm*. Englewood Cliffs, NJ: Prentice-Hall.

Darley, J. M. & Latané, B. (1968). Bystander intervention in emergencies: Diffusion of responsibility. *Journal of Personality and Social Psychology*, **8**, 377–383.

Davenport, T. H. (1993). *Process Innovation: Re-engineering Work Through Information Technology*. Cambridge, MA: Harvard Business School Press.

Dean, J. W. Jr & Sharfman, M. P. (1996). Does decision process matter? A study of strategic decision making effectiveness. *Academy of Management Journal*, **39**(2), 368–396.

DeMeuse, K. P. & Liebowitz, S. J. (1981). An empirical analysis of team-building research. *Group and Organization Studies*, **6**, 357–378.

Deming, W. E. (1986). *Out of the Crisis*. Cambridge, MA: Center for Advanced Engineering Study, Massachusetts Institute of Technology.

Diehl, M. & Stroebe, W. (1987). Productivity loss in brainstorming groups: Towards the solution of a riddle. *Journal of Personality and Social Psychology*, **53**, 447–509.

Drory, A. & Shamir, B. (1988). Effects of organizational and life variables on job satisfaction and burnout. *Group and Organization Studies*, **13**(4), 441–455.

Earley, P. C. (1987). Intercultural training for managers: A comparison of documentary and interpersonal methods. *Academy of Management Journal*, **30**, 685–698.

Earley, P. C. (1993). East meets West meets Mid-East: Further explorations of collectivistic and individualistic work groups. *Academy of Management Journal*, **36**, 319–348.

Eden, D. (1990). Pygmalion without interpersonal contrast effects: Whole groups gain from raising manager expectations. *Journal of Applied Psychology*, **75**, 394–398.

Egido, C. (1990). Teleconferencing as a technology to support cooperative work: Its possibilities and limitations. In J. Galegher, R. E. Kraut & C. Egido (Eds), *Intellectual Teamwork: Social and Technological Foundations of Cooperative Work*. Hillsdale, NJ: Lawrence Erlbaum.

Ereg, M. & Somech, A. (1996). Is group productivity loss the rule or the exception? Effects of culture and group-based motivation. *Academy of Management Journal*, **39**, 1513–1537.

Erez, M. & Earley, P. C. (1987). Comparative analysis of goal-setting strategies across cultures. *Journal of Applied Psychology*, **72**, 658–665.

Eysenck, H. J. & Eysenck, S. B. G. (1975). *Manual for the EPI*. London: Hodder & Stoughton.

Festinger, L., Schachter, S. & Back, K. (1950). *Social Pressures in Informal Groups: A Study of Human Factors in Housing*. New York: Harper.

Fineman, S. (Ed.) (1993). *Emotion in Organisations*. London: Sage.

Finholt, T., Sproull, L. & Kiesler, S. (1990). Communication and performance in ad hoc task groups. In J. Galegher, R. E. Kraut & C. Egido (Eds), *Intellectual Teamwork: Social and Technological Foundations of Cooperative Work*. Hillsdale, NJ: Lawrence Erlbaum.

Fleishman, E. A. (1973). Twenty years of consideration and structure. In E.A. Fleishman and J. F. Hunt (Eds), *Current Developments in the Study of Leadership*. Carbondale, IL: South Illinois University Press.

Frese, M. (1985). Stress at work and psychosomatic complaints: A causal interpretation. *Journal of Applied Psychology*, **70**, 314–328.

Frese, M. (1989). Theoretical models of control and health. In S. L. Sauter, J. J. Hurrell Jr & C. L. Cooper (Eds), *Job Control and Worker Health*. Chichester: Wiley.

Frese, M. & Zapf, D. (1994). Action as the core of work psychology: A German approach. In H. C. Triandis, M. D. Dunnette & J. M. Hough (Eds), *Handbook of Industrial and Organizational Psychology* (Vol. 4, pp. 271–340). Palo Alto, CA: Consulting Psychologists Press.

Frey, D. (1982). Different levels of cognitive dissonance, information seeking, and information avoidance. *Journal of Personality and Social Psychology*, **43**, 1175–1183.

Furnham, A., Steele, H. & Pendleton, D. (1993). A psychometric assessment of the Belbin Team-Role Self-perception Inventory. *Journal of Occupational and Organizational Psychology*, **66**, 245–257.

Galbraith, J. R. (1993). The business unit of the future. In J. R. Galbraith, E. E. Lawler III & Associates (Eds), *Organizing for the Future: The New Logic for Managing Complex Organizations*. San Francisco: Jossey-Bass.

Galbraith, J. R. (1994). *Competing with Flexible Lateral Organisations* (2nd edn). Reading, MA: Addison-Wesley.

Galbraith, J. R., Lawler, E. E. III & Associates (1993). *Organizing for the Future: The New Logic for Managing Complex Organizations*. San Francisco: Jossey-Bass.

Gallois, C. & Callan, V. J. (1981). Personality impressions elicited by accented English speech. *Journal of Cross-Cultural Psychology*, **12**(3), 347–359.

Gallois, C. & Callan, V. J. (1991). Interethnic accommodation: The role of norms. In H. Giles, J. Coupland & N. Coupland (Eds) *Contexts of Accommodation: Developments in Applied Sociolinguistics*. Cambridge: Cambridge University Press.

George, J. M. (1989). Mood and absence. *Journal of Applied Psychology*, **74**, 317–324.

George, J. M. (1990). Personality, affect, and behavior in groups. *Journal of Applied Psychology*, **75**, 107–166.

George, J. M. (1995). Leader positive mood and group performance: The case of customer service. *Journal of Applied Social Psychology*, **25**, 778–794.

George, J. M. (1996). Group affective tone. In M. A. West (Ed.), *Handbook of Work Group Psychology* (pp. 77–94). Chichester: Wiley.

George, J. M. & Bettenhausen, K. (1990). Understanding prosocial behaviour, sales performance and turnover: A group-level analysis in a service context. *Journal of Applied Psychology*, **75**, 698–709.

George, J. M. & James, L. R. (1993). Personality, affect and behavior in groups revisited: Comment on aggregation, levels of analysis and a recent application of within and between analysis. *Journal of Applied Psychology*, **78**, 798–804.

George, J. M. & James, L. R. (1994). Levels issues in theory development. *Academy of Management Review*, **19**, 636–640.

Gersick, C. J. G. (1988). Time and transition in work teams: toward a new model of group development. *Academy of Management Journal*, **31**, 9–41.

Gersick, C. J. G. (1989). Marking time: predictable transitions in task groups. *Academy of Management Journal*, **32**, 274–309.

Giles, H. & Street Jr, R. L. (1985). Communicator characteristics and behavior. In M. L. Knapp & G. R. Miller (Eds), *Handbook of Interpersonal Communication*. Newbury Park, CA: Sage Publications.

Gladstein, D. (1984). Groups in context: A model of task group effectiveness. *Administrative Science Quarterly*, **29**, 499–517.

Goodman, P. S. (1986). *Designing Effective Work Groups*. San Francisco: Jossey-Bass.

Goodman, P. S., Ravlin, E. C. & Argote, L. (1986). Current thinking about groups: Setting the stage for new ideas. In P. S. Goodman (Ed.), *Designing Effective Work Groups* (pp. 1–33). San Francisco: Jossey-Bass.

Graen, G., Novak, M. & Sommerkamp, P. (1982). The effects of leader–member exchange and job design on productivity and satisfaction: Testing a dual attachment model. *Organizational Behavior and Human Performance*, **30**, 109–131.

Graen, G. & Scandura, T. A. (1987). Toward a psychology of dyadic organizing. *Research in Organizational Behavior*, **9**, 175–209.

Greller, M. M., Parsons, C. K. & Mitchell, D. R. D. (1992). Additive effects and beyond: Occupational stressors and social buffers in a police organisation. In J. C. Quick, L. R. Murphy & J. J. Hurrell Jr (Eds), *Stress and Well-being at Work: Assessments and Interventions for Occupational Mental Health*. Washington, DC: American Psychological Association.

Guzzo, R. A. (1996). Fundamental considerations about work groups. In M.A. West (Ed.), *Handbook of Work Group Psychology* (pp. 3–24). Chichester: Wiley.

Guzzo, R. A. & Campbell, R. J. (1990). *Conditions for team effectiveness in management.* Paper presented at the annual meeting of the Academy of Management, San Francisco, August.

Guzzo, R. A. & Dickson, M. W. (1996). Teams in organisations: Recent research on performance and effectiveness. *Annual Review of Psychology*, **46**, 307–338.

Guzzo, R. A. & Salas, E. (Eds) (1995). *Team Effectiveness and Decision Making in Organisations.* San Francisco: Jossey-Bass.

Guzzo, R. A. & Shea, G. P. (1992). Group performance and intergroup relations in organisations. In M. D. Dunnette and L. M. Hough (Eds), *Handbook of Industrial and Organizational Psychology*, (Vol 3, pp. 269–313). Palo Alto, CA: Consulting Psychologists Press.

Guzzo, R. A., Yosst, P. R., Campbell, R. J. & Shea, G. P. (1993). Potency in groups: Articulating a construct. *British Journal of Social Psychology*, **32**, 87–106.

Hacker, W. (1986). Arbeitspsychologie, Psychische Regualtion von Arbeitstaetigkeiten. Berlin (DDR): Deutscher Verlag der Wissenschaften.

Hackman, J. R. (1983). *A normative model of work team effectiveness.* (Technical Report No. 2). Research Program on Group Effectiveness. Yale School of Organization and Management.

Hackman, J. R. (1987). The design of work teams. In J. W. Lorsch (Ed.), *Handbook of Organizational Behavior* (pp. 315–342). Englewood Cliffs, NJ: Prentice-Hall.

Hackman, J. R. (1990). (Ed), *Groups That Work (and Those That Don't): Creating Conditions for Effective Teamwork.* San Francisco: Jossey-Bass.

Hackman, J. R. (1992). Group influences on individuals in organizations. In M.D. Dunnette and L. M. Hough (Eds), *Handbook of Industrial and Organizational Psychology* (Vol. 3) (pp. 199–267). Palo Alto, CA: Consulting Psychologists Press.

Hackman, J. R., Brousseau, K. R. & Weiss, J. A. (1976). The interaction of task design and group performance strategies in determining group effectiveness. *Organizational Behavior and Human Performance*, **16**, 350–365.

Hackman, J. R. & Lawler, E. E. (1971). Employee reactions to job characteristics. *Journal of Applied Psychology*, **55**,(3), 259–286.

Hackman, J. R. & Morris, C. G. (1975). Group task, group interaction process, and group performance effectiveness: A review and proposed integration. In L. Berkowitz (Ed.), *Advances in Experimental Social Psychology*, (Vol. 8). New York: Academic Press.

Hackman, J. R. & Oldham, G. R. (1975). Development of the job diagnostic survey. *Journal of Applied Psychology*, **60**, 159–170.

Hackman, J. R. & Walton, R. E. (1986). Leading groups in organisations. In R. S. Goodman & Associates (Eds), *Designing Effective Work Groups* (pp. 72–119). San Francisco: Jossey-Bass.

Hall, R. J. & Lord, R. G. (1995). Multi-level information processing explanations of followers' leadership perception. *Leadership Quarterly*, **6**, 265–287.

Hartley, J. F. (1996). Intergroup relations in organisations. In M.A. West (Ed.), *Handbook of Work Group Psychology* (pp. 397–422). Chichester: Wiley.

Haythorn, W. W. (1968). The composition of groups: A review of the literature. *Acta Psychologica*, **28**, 97–128.

Herbst, P. G. (1962). *Alternatives to Hierarchies.* Leiden: Martinus Nijhoff.

Hill, G. W. (1982). Group versus individual performance: Are n + 1 heads better than one? *Psychological Bulletin*, **91**, 517–539.

Hirokawa, R. Y. (1990). The role of communication in group decision-making efficacy: A task-contingency perspective. *Small Group Research*, **21**, 190–204.

Hoffman, L. R. & Maier, N. R. F. (1961). Sex differences, sex composition, and group problem-solving. *Journal of Abnormal and Social Psychology*, **63**, 453–456.

Hofstede, G. (1980). *Culture's Consequences: International Differences in Work-related Values*. Beverly Hills, CA: Sage.

Hofstede, G. (1991). *Cultures and Organisations: Software of the Mind*. London: McGraw-Hill.

Hogg, M. & Abrams, D. (1988). *Social Identifications: A Social Psychology of Intergroup Relations and Group Processes*. London: Routledge.

Hogg, M., Turner, J. C. & Davidson, B. (1990). Polarized norms and social frames of reference: A test of the self-categorization theory of group polarization. *Basic and Applied Social Psychology*, **11**, 77–100.

Hollander, E. P. (1958). Conformity, status and idiosyncrasy credit. *Psychological Review*, **65**, 117–127.

Hollingshead, A. B. & McGrath, J. E. (1995). Computer-assisted groups: A Critical review of the empirical research. In R. A. Guzzo & E. Salas (Eds), *Team Effectiveness and Decision Making in Organizations*. San Francisco: Jossey-Bass.

House, R. J. & Shamir, B. (1993). Toward the integration of transformation, charismatic, and visionary theories. In M. M. Chemers & R. Ayman (Eds), *Leadership Theory and Research: Perspectives and Directions*. San Diego, CA: Academic Press.

Isen, A. M. & Baron, R. A. (1991). Positive affect as a factor in organizational behavior. In L. L. Cummings & B. M. Staw (Eds), *Research in Organizational Behavior* (Vol. 13). Greenwich, CT: JAI Press.

Jackson, L. A., Sullivan, L. A. & Hodge, L. N. (1993). Stereotype effects on attributions, predictions and evaluations: No two social judgements are quite alike. *Journal of Personality and Social Psychology*, **65**(1), 69–84.

Jackson, S. E. (1992). Consequences of group composition for the interpersonal dynamics of strategic issue processing. *Advances in Strategic Management*, **8**, 345–382.

Jackson, S. E. (1996). The consequences of diversity in multidisciplinary work teams. In M. A. West (Ed.), *Handbook of Work Group Psychology* (pp. 53–76). Chichester: Wiley.

Jackson, S. E., Brett, J. F., Sessa, V. I., Cooper, D. M., Julin, J. A. & Peyronnin, K. (1991). Some differences make a difference: Individual dissimilarity and group heterogeneity as correlates of recruitment, promotions and turnover. *Journal of Applied Psychology*, **76**, 675–689.

Jacobs, D. & Singell, L. (1993). Leadership and organizational performance: Isolating links between managers and collective success. *Social Science Research*, **22**, 165–189.

James, L. R., Demareé, R. G. & Wolf, G. (1993). r_{wg}: An assessment of within-group interrater agreement. *Journal of Applied Psychology*, **78**, 306–309.

Janis, I. L. (1982). *Groupthink: A Study of Foreign Policy Decisions and Fiascos*, 2nd edn. Boston: Houghton Mifflin.

Janis, I. L. (1989). *Crucial Decisions*. New York: Free Press.

Jervis, I. L. (1976). *Perception and Misperception in International Politics*. Princeton, NJ: Princeton University Press.

Juran, J. M. (1989). *Juran on Leadership for Quality*. New York: Free Press.

Jussim, L. (1986). Self-fulfilling prophecies: A theoretical and integrative review. *Psychological Review*, **93**(1), 429–445.

Jussim, L., Coleman, L. M. & Lerch (1987). The nature of stereotypes: A comparison and integration of 3 theories. *Journal of Personality and Social Psychology*, **52**(3), 536–546.

Kanter, R. M. (1983). *The Change Masters: Corporate Entrepreneurs at Work*. New York: Simon & Schuster.

Karasek, R., Baker, D., Marxer, F., Ahlbom, A. & Theorell, T. (1981). Job decision latitude, job demands, and cardiovascular disease: A prospective study of Swedish men. *American Journal of Public Health*, **71**, 694–705.

Katz, R. (1982). The effects of group longevity on project communication and performance. *Administrative Science Quarterly*, **27**, 81–104.

Kent, R. N. & McGrath, J. E. (1969). Task and group characteristics as factors influencing group performance. *Journal of Experimental Social Psychology*, 5, 429–440.

Kiggundu, M. V. (1983). Task interdependence and job design: Test of a theory. *Organizational Behavior and Human Performance*, 31, 145–172.

Kimble, C. E., Marsh, N. B. & Kiska, A. C. (1984). Sex, age and cultural differences in self-reported assertiveness. *Psychological Reports*, 55, 419–422.

King, N. (1990). Innovation at work: The research literature. In M. A. West & J. L. Farr (Eds), *Innovation and Creativity at Work: Psychological and Organisational Strategies* (pp. 15–59). Chichester: Wiley.

Klein, J. A. (1991). A re-examination of autonomy in light of new manufacturing practices. *Human Relations*, 44, 21–38.

Klimoski, R. & Mohammed, S. (1994). Team mental model: Construct or metaphor? *Journal of Management*, 20, 403–437.

Komaki, J. L., Desselles, M. L. & Bowman, E. D. (1989). Definitely not a breeze: Extending an operant model of effective supervision to teams. *Journal of Applied Psychology*, 74, 522–529.

Kozlowski, S. W. J. & Hattrup, K. (1992). A disagreement about within-group agreement: Disentangling issues of consistency versus consensus. *Journal of Applied Psychology*, 77, 161–177.

Kozlowski, S. W. J. & Hults, B. M. (1986). Joint moderation of the relation between task complexity and job performance for engineers. *Journal of Applied Psychology*, 71, 196–202.

Kraemer, K. L. & Pinsonneault, A. (1990). Technology and groups: Assessments of the empirical research. In J. Galegher, R. E. Kraut & C. Egido (Eds), *Intellectual Teamwork: Social and Technological Foundations of Cooperative Work*. Hillsdale, NJ: Lawrence Erlbaum.

Krauss, R. M. & Fussell, S. R. (1990). Mutual knowledge and communicable effectiveness. In J. Galegher, R. E. Kraut & C. Egido (Eds), *Intellectual Teamwork: Social and Technological Foundations of Cooperative Work*. Hillsdale, NJ: Lawrence Erlbaum.

LaFrance, M. & Mayo, C. (1978). *Moving Bodies: Nonverbal Communication in Social Relationships*. Monterey, C.A.: Brooks/Cole.

Landsberger, H. A. (1955). Interaction process analysis of the mediation of labor–management disputes. *Journal of Abnormal and Social Psychology*, 51, 522–528.

Latané, B., Williams, K. & Harkins, S. (1979). Many hands make light work: The causes and consequences of social loafing. *Journal of Personality and Social Psychology*, 37, 822–832.

Latham, G. P., Erez, M. & Locke, E. A. (1988). Resolving scientific disputes by the joint design of crucial experiments by the antagonists: Application to the Erez–Latham dispute regarding participation in goal setting. *Journal of Applied Psychology*, 73(4), 753–772.

Latham, G. P. & Yukl, G. A. (1975). A review of research on the application of goal setting in organisations. *Academy of Management Journal*, 18, 824–845.

Lawler, E. E. & Hackman, J. R. (1969). Impact of employee participation in development of pay incentive plans: A field experiment. *Journal of Applied Psychology*, 53, 467–471.

Lawrence, P. R. & Lorsch, J. (1967). *Organization and Environment*. Cambridge, MA: Harvard University Press.

Leitner, K. (1993). Auswirkungen von Arbeitsbedingungen auf die psychosoziale Gesundheit. *Zeitschrift für Arbeitswissenschaft*, 47, 98–107.

Levine, D. I. & D'Andrea-Tyson, L. (1990). Participation, productivity, and the firm's environment. In A. S. Blinder (Ed.), *Paying for Productivity* (pp. 183–237). Washington, DC: Brookings Institution.

Levine, R. V., West, L. J. & Reis, H. T. (1980). Perceptions of time and punctuality in the US and Brazil. *Journal of Personality and Social Psychology*, **38**, 541–550.

Locke, E. A. (1968). Toward a theory of task motivation and incentives. *Organizational Behavior and Human Performance*, **3**, 157–189.

Lyles, M. A. (1981). Formulating strategic problems: Empirical analysis and problem development. *Strategic Management Journal*, **2**, 61–75.

Macy, B. A. & Izumi, H. (1993). Organizational change, design and work innovation: A meta-analysis of 131 North American field studies—1961–1991. *Research in Organizational Change and Design* (Vol. 7). Greenwich, CT: JAI Press.

Maier, N. R. F. (1963). *Problem-solving Discussions and Conferences: Leadership Methods and Skills*. New York: McGraw-Hill.

Maier, N. R. F. (1970). *Problem Solving and Creativity in Individuals and Groups*. Monterey, CA: Brooks/Cole.

Maier, N. R. F. & Solem, A. R. (1962). Improving solutions by turning choice situations into problems. *Personnel Psychology*, **15**, 151–157.

Main, J. (1989). At last, software CEOs can use. *Fortune*, 13 March, 77–83.

Markiewicz, L. & West, M. A. (1996). *Team-based Organisation*. Aberdeen: Grampian/ECITB.

Marrow, A. J. (1964). Risks and uncertainties in action research. *Journal of Social Issues*, **20**, 5–20.

Mathison, D. L. & Tucker, R. K. (1982). Sex differences in assertive behaviour: A research extension. *Psychological Reports*, **51**(3), 943–948.

Maznevski, M. L. (1994). Understanding our differences: Performance in decision-making groups with diverse members. *Human Relations*, **47**(5), 531–552.

McCain, B. R., O'Reilly, C. C. III & Pfeffer, J. (1983). The effects of departmental demography on turnover. *Academy of Management Journal*, **26**, 626–641.

McCauley, C. (1989). The nature of social influence in groupthink: Compliance and internalization. *Journal of Personality and Social Psychology*, **57**, 250–260.

McGrath, J. E. (1984). *Groups: Interaction and Performance*. Englewood Cliffs, NJ: Prentice-Hall.

McGrath, J. E. & O'Connor, K. M. (1996). Temporal issues in work groups. In M.A. West (Ed.), *Handbook of Work Group Psychology* (pp. 25–52). Chichester: Wiley.

Menzies Lyth, I. (1989). *The Dynamics of the Social*. London: Free Association Books.

Miceli, M. P. & Near, J. P. (1985). Characteristics of organisational climate and perceived wrong-doing associated with whistle-blowing decisions. *Personnel Psychology*, **38**, 525–544.

Miller, E. J. (1959). Technology, territory and tie: The internal differentiation of complex production systems. *Human Relations*, **12**, 243–272.

Milliken, F. J. & Martins, L. L. (1996). Searching for common threads: Understanding the multiple effects of diversity in organizational groups. *Academy of Management Review*, **21**(2), 402–433.

Min-Hsi, H. C. (1989). The Chinese communities in Australia: The way ahead in a neglected field of research. *Journal of Intercultural Studies*, **10**(1), 33–48.

Misumi, J. (1985). *The Behavioral Science of leadership: An Interdisciplinary Japanese Research Program*. Ann Arbor, MI: University of Michigan Press.

Moch, M. K. (1980). Job involvement, internal motivation, and employees' integration into networks of work relationships. *Organizational Behavior and Human Performance*, **25**, 15–31.

Mohrman, S. A., Cohen, S. G. & Mohrman, A. M., Jr (1995). *Designing Team-Based Organizations*. San Francisco: Jossey-Bass.

Moos, R. H. & Spiesman, J. C. (1962). Group compatibility and productivity. *Journal of Abnormal and Social Psychology*, **65**, 190–196.

Moreland, R. L. & Levine, J. M. (1992). Problem identification by groups. In S. Worchel, W. Wood & J. A. Simpson (Eds), *Group Process and Productivity*. Newbury Park, CA: Sage.

Moscovici, S. (1976). *Social Influence and Social Change*. London: Academic Press.

Moscovici, S. & Doise, W. (1994). *Conflict and Consensus: A General Theory of Collective Decisions*. London: Sage.

Moscovici, S., Mugny, G. & van Avermaet, E. (Eds) (1985). *Perspectives on Minority Influence*. Cambridge: Cambridge University Press.

Mullen, B. & Copper, C. (1994). The relation between group cohesiveness and performance: An integration. *Psychological Bulletin*, **115**, 210–227.

Mumford, M. D. & Gustafson, S. B. (1988). Creativity syndrome: Integration, application and innovation. *Psychological Bulletin*, **103**, 27–43.

Myer, C. (1993). *How to Align Purpose, Strategy and Structure for Speed*. New York: Free Press.

Myers, D. G. & Lamm, H. (1976). The group polarization phenomenon. *Psychological Bulletin*, **83**, 602–627.

Nemeth, C. (1986). Differential contributions of majority and minority influence. *Psychological Review*, **93**, 23–32.

Nemeth, C., Mayseless, O., Sherman, J. & Brown, Y. (1990). Exposure to dissent and recall of information. *Journal of Personality and Social Psychology*, **58**, 429–437.

Nemeth, C. & Owens, J. (1996). Value of minority dissent. In M. A. West (Ed.), *Handbook of Work Group Psychology* (pp. 125–142). Chichester: Wiley.

Nemeth, C. & Rogers, J. (1996). Dissent and the search for information. *British Journal of Social Psychology*, **35**, 67–76.

O'Reilly, C. A., Caldwell, D. F. & Barnett, W. P. (1989). Work group demography, social integration and turnover. *Administrative Science Quarterly*, **34**, 21–37.

Olson, G. M. & Atkins, D. E. (1990). Supporting collaboration with advanced multimedia electronic mail: The NSF EXPRES project. In J. Galegher, R.E. Kraut & C. Egido (Eds), *Intellectual Teamwork: Social and Technological Foundations of Cooperative Work*. Hillsdale, NJ: Lawrence Erlbaum.

Ouchi, W. G. (1980). Markets, bureaucracies and clans. *Administrative Science Quarterly*, **34**, 21–37.

Pearce, J. A. & Ravlin, E. C. (1987). The design and activation of self-regulating work groups. *Human Relations*, **40**, 751–782.

Pinto, J. K. & Prescott, J. E. (1987). Changes in critical success factor importance over the life of a project. In F. Hoy (Ed.), *Academy of Management Proceedings* (pp. 328–332). New Orleans: Academy of Management.

Podsakoff, P. M. & Todor, W. D. (1985). Relationships between leader reward and punishment behavior and group processes and productivity. *Journal of Management*, **11**, 55–73.

Porac, J. F. & Howard, H. (1990). Taxonomic mental models in competitor definition. *Academy of Management Review*, **2**, 224–240.

Poulton, B. C. & West, M. A. (1993). Effective multidisciplinary teamwork in primary health care. *Journal of Advanced Nursing*, **18**, 918–925.

Poulton, B. C. & West, M. A. (1994). Primary health care team effectiveness: Developing a constituency approach. *Health and Social Care*, **2**, 77–84.

Pritchard, R. D. (1990). *Measuring and Improving Organizational Productivity*. New York: Praeger.

Pritchard, R. D., Jones, S. D., Roth, P. L., Stuebing, K. K. & Ekeberg, S. E. (1988). Effects of group feedback, goal setting, and incentives on organizational productivity. *Journal of Applied Psychology*, **73**, 337–358.

Pritchard, R. D., Jones, S. D., Roth, P. L., Stuebing, K. K. & Ekeberg, S. E. (1989). The evaluation of an integrated approach to measuring organizational productivity. *Personnel Psychology*, **42**, 69–115.

Pulakos, E. G. & Wexley, K. N. (1983). The relationship between perceptual similarity, sex and performance ratings in manager–subordinate dyads. *Academy of Management Journal*, **26**, 129–139.

Redmond, M. V. (1989). The functions of empathy (decentering) in human relations. *Human Relations*, **42**, 593–605.

Redmond, M. V. (1992). A multi-dimensional theory and measure of decentering. Unpublished manuscript.

Rice, A. K. (1958). *Productivity and Social Organisation: The Ahmedabad Experiment.* London: Tavistock.

Rice, R. E. & Shook, D. E. (1990). Voice messaging, coordination and communication. In J. Galegher, R. E. Kraut & C. Egido (Eds), *Intellectual Teamwork: Social and Technological Foundations of Cooperative Work*. Hillsdale, NJ: Lawrence Erlbaum.

Roberts, J. M. (1988). *The Penguin History of the World*. Harmondsworth, UK: Penguin Books.

Roethlisberger, F. J. & Dickson, W. J. (1939). *Management and the Worker*. Cambridge, MA: Harvard University Press.

Rogelberg, S. G., Barnes-Farrell, J. L. & Lowe, C. A. (1992). The stepladder technique: An alternative group structure facilitating effective group decision-making. *Journal of Applied Psychology*, **77**, 730–737.

Rudolph, E., Schönfleder, E. & Hacker, W. (1987). *Tätigkeitsbewertungssystem Geistige Arbeit. TBS-GA*. Berlin: Psychodiagnostisches Zentrum der Humboldt-Universität.

Schein, E. H. (1992). *Organizational culture and leadership*. San Francisco: Jossey-Bass.

Schneider, B. (1987). The people make the place. *Personnel Psychology*, **40**, 437–453.

Schriesheim, C. A. & Kerr, S. (1977). Theories and measures of leadership: A critical appraisal of current and future directions. In J. G. Hunt & L. L. Larson (Eds), *Leadership: The Cutting Edge* (pp. 9–45). Carbondale, IL: Southern Illinois University Press.

Schutz, W. C. (1995). What makes groups productive? *Human Relations*, **8**, 429–465.

Schutz, W. C. (1958). *FIRO: A Three-dimensional Theory of Interpersonal Behaviour*. New York: Holt Rinehart.

Schutz, W. C. (1967). *JOY: Expanding Human Awareness*. New York: Grove Press.

Schwenk, C. R. (1988). *The Essence of Strategic Decision-making*. Cambridge, MA: Heath.

Schwenk, C. R. & Thomas, H. (1983). Formulating the mess: The role of decision aids in problem formulation. *Omega*, **11**, 239–252.

Senge, P. (1990). *The Fifth Discipline: The Art and Practice of the Learning Organization*. New York: Doubleday Currency.

Shaw, M. E. (1976). *Group Dynamics: The Psychology of Small Group Behavior*. New York: McGraw-Hill.

Shaw, M. E. (1981). *Group Dynamics: The Psychology of Small Group Behavior*. New York: McGraw-Hill.

Shaw, M. E. & Nickols, S. A. (1964). *Group effectiveness as a function of group member compatibility and cooperation requirements of the task* (Technical report No. 4, ONR contract NR 170–266, Nonr-580[11]). Gainesville: University of Florida.

Shaw, M. E. & Shaw, L. M. (1962). Some effects of sociometric grouping upon learning in a second grade classroom. *Journal of Social Psychology*, **57**, 453–458.

Shea, G. P. & Guzzo, R. A. (1987). Groups as human resources. In K. M. Rowland & G. R. Ferris (Eds), *Research in Personnel and Human Resources Management* (Vol. 5). Greenwich, CT: JAI Press.

Shiflett, S. (1979). Towards a general model of small group productivity. *Psychological Bulletin*, **86**, 67–79.

Singer, M. & Eder, G. S. (1989). Effects of ethnicity, accent and job status on selection decisions. *International Journal of Psychology*, **24**, 13–34.

Sinha, J. B. P. (1981). *The Nurturant Task Manager: A Model of the Effective Executive*. Atlantic Highlands, NJ: Humanities Press.

Smircich, L. (1983). Organization as shared meaning. In L. R. Pondy, P. Frost, G. Morgan & T. Dandridge (Eds), *Organizational Symbolism* (pp. 55–65). Greenwich, CT: JAI Press.

Smith, K. G., Locke, E. A. & Barry, D. (1990). Goal setting, planning and organizational performance: An experimental simulation. *Organizational Behavior and Human Decision Processes*, **46**, 118–134.

Smith, K. G., Smith, K. A., Olian, J. D., Sims, H. P. Jr, O'Bannon, D. P. & Scully, J. A. (1994). Top management team demography and process: The role of social integration and communication. *Administrative Science Quarterly*, **39**, 412–438.

Smith, P. B. & Noakes, J. (1996). Cultural differences in group processes. In M.A. West (Ed.), *Handbook of Work Group Psychology* (pp. 477–502). Chichester: Wiley.

Sonnentag, S. (1996). Individual well-being. In M.A. West (Ed.), *Handbook of Work Group Psychology* (pp. 345–367). Chichester: Wiley.

Sproull, L. S. & Keisler, S. (1986). Reducing social context cues: Electronic mail in organizational communication. *Management Science*, **32**, 1492–1512.

Staw, B. M., Sandelands, L. E. & Dutton, J. E. (1981). Threat-rigidity effects on organizational behavior: A multilevel analysis. *Administrative Science Quarterly*, **26**, 501–524.

Stein, M. (1996). Unconscious phenomena in work groups. In M.A. West (Ed.), *Handbook of Work Group Psychology* (pp. 143–157). Chichester: Wiley.

Steiner, I. D. (1972). *Group Process and Productivity*. New York: Academic Press.

Sternberg, R. J. & Lubart, T. I. (1990). *Defying the Crowd: Cultivating Creativity in a Culture of Conformity*. New York: Free Press.

Stevens, M. J. & Campion, M. A. (1994). The knowledge, skill and ability requirements for teamwork: Implications for human resource management. *Journal of Management*, **20**(2), 503–530.

Stogdill, R. M. (1974). *Handbook of Leadership*. New York: Free Press.

Sundstrom, E., De Meuse, K. P. & Futrell, D. (1990). Work teams: Applications and effectiveness. *American Psychologist*, **45**, 120–133.

Sutton, R. I. & Hargadon, A. (1996). Brainstorming groups in context: Effectiveness in a product design firm. *Administrative Science Quarterly*, **41**, 685–718.

Tajfel, H. (1978). *Differentiation Between Social Groups: Studies in the Social Psychology of Intergroup Relations* (European Monographs in Social Psychology, No. 14). London: Academic Press.

Tajfel, H. & Turner, J. C. (1979). An integrative theory of intergroup conflict. In W. G. Austin and S. Worchel (Eds), *The Social Psychology of Intergroup Relations*. Monterey, CA: Brooks/Cole.

Tannenbaum, S. I., Beard, R. L. & Salas, E. (1992). Team building and its influence on team effectiveness: An examination of conceptual and empirical developments. In K. Kelley (Ed.), *Issues, Theory and Research in Industrial/Organizational Psychology* (pp. 117–153), London: North Holland.

Tannenbaum, S. I., Salas, E. & Cannon-Bowers, J. A. (1996). Promoting team effectiveness. In M. A. West (Ed.), *Handbook of Work Group Psychology*, (pp. 503–529). Chichester: Wiley.

Tjosvold, D. (1982). Effects of approach to controversy on superiors' incorporation of subordinates' information in decision making. *Journal of Applied Psychology*, **67**, 189–193.

Tjosvold, D. (1985). Implications of controversy research for management. *Journal of Management*, **11**, 21–37.

Tjosvold, D. (1991). *Team Organisation: An Enduring Competitive Advantage*. Chichester: Wiley.

Tjosvold, D. & Field, R. H. G. (1983). Effects of social context on consensus and majority vote decision making. *Academy of Management Journal*, **26**, 500–506.

Tjosvold, D. & Johnson, D. W. (1977). The effects of controversy on cognitive perspective-taking. *Journal of Educational Psychology*, **69**, 679–685.

Tjosvold, D., Wedley, W. C. & Field, R. H. G. (1986). Constructive controversy, the Vroom–Yetton model, and managerial decision making. *Journal of Occupational Behavior*, **7**, 125–138.

Triandis, H. C. & Albert, P. D. (1987). Cross cultural perspectives. In F. M. Jabin, L. L. Putnam, K. H. Roberts, L. W. Porter (Eds), Handbook of organizational communication: An Interdisciplinary Perspective (pp. 264–295). Newbury Park, CA: Sage.

Trist, E. (1981). *The Evolution of SocioTechnical Systems* (Paper No. 2). Toronto: Quality of Working Life Center.

Trist, E. & Bamforth, D. (1951). Some social and psychological consequences of the longwall method of coal gettting. *Human Relations*, 4, 3–38.

Trist, E. L., Higgin, G. W., Murray, H. & Pollock, A. B. (1963). *Organisational Choice: Capabilities of Groups at the Coal Face under Changing Technologies*. London: Tavistock.

Tschan, F. & von Cranach, M. (1996). Group task structure, processes and outcome. In M. A. West (Ed.), *Handbook of Work Group Psychology* (pp. 95–121). Chichester: Wiley.

Turner, J. C. (1987). *Rediscovering the Social Group: A Self-categorization Theory*. Oxford: Blackwell.

Tziner, A. E. & Eden, D. (1985). Effects of crew composition on crew performance: Does the whole equal the sum of its parts? *Journal of Applied Psychology*, 70, 85–93.

Ulich, E. & Weber, W. G. (1996). Dimensions, criteria and evaluatiion of work group autonomy. In M. A. West (Ed.), *Handbook of Work Group Psychology* (pp. 247–282). Chichester: Wiley.

Unsworth, K. L. (1995). Perceptions of assertion in the workplace: The impact of ethnicity, sex and organisational status. Unpublished manuscript, University of Queensland, Australia.

Van Offenbeek, M. & Koopman, P. (1996). Interaction and decision-making in project teams. In M. A. West (Ed.), *Handbook of Work Group Psychology* (pp. 159–188). Chichester: Wiley.

Vogel, D. R. & Nunamaker, J. F. (1990). Design and assessment of a group decision support system. In J. Galegher, R. E. Kraut & C. Egido (Eds), *Intellectual Teamwork: Social and Technological Foundations of Cooperative Work*. Hillsdale, NJ: Lawrence Erlbaum.

Volpert, W. (1984). *Handlungsstrukturanalyse als Beitrag zur Qualifikationsforschung*. Cologne: Pahl Rugenstein.

Vroom, V. H. (1964). *Work and Motivation*. New York: Wiley.

Vroom, V. H. & Yetton, P. W. (1973). *Leadership and Decision Making*. Pittsburgh, PA: University of Pittsburgh Press.

Wagner, W. G., Pfeffer, J. & O'Reilly, C. A. (1984). Organizational demography and turnover in top management groups. *Administrative Science Quarterly*, 29, 74–92.

Wall, T. D. & Clegg, C. W. (1981). A longitudinal field study of group work redesign. *Journal of Occupational Behaviour*, 2, 31–49.

Wall, T. D. & Davids, K. (1992). Shop floor work organisation and advanced manufacturing technology. In C. L. Cooper and L. T. Robertson (Eds), *International Review of Industrial and Organizational Psychology* (Vol. 7). Chichester: Wiley.

Wall, T. D. & Jackson, P. R. (1995). New manufacturing initiatives and shopfloor job design. In A. Howard (Ed.), *The Changing Nature of Work*. San Francisco: Jossey-Bass.

Wall, T. D., Kemp, N. J., Jackson, P. R. & Clegg, C. W. (1986). Outcomes of autonomous workgroups: A long-term field experiment. *Academy of Management Journal*, 29, 280–304.

Wall, T. D. & Lischeron, J. H. (1977). *Worker Participation: A Critique of the Literature and some Fresh Evidence*. Maidenhead, UK: McGraw-Hill.

Walsh, J. P. & Fahey, L. (1986). The role of negotiated belief structures in strategy making. *Journal of Management*, 12, 325–338.

Walsh, J. P., Henderson, C. M. & Deighton, J. (1988). Negotiated belief structures and decision performance: An empirical investigation. *Organizational Behavior and Human Decision Processes*, 42, 194–216.

Watson, W. E., Kumar, K. & Michaelsen, L. K. (1993). Cultural diversity's impact on interaction process and performance: Comparing homogeneous and diverse task groups. *Academy of Management Journal*, **36**, 590–602.

Weick, K. E. (1969). *The Social Psychology of Organizing*. Reading, MA: Addison Wesley.

Weldon, E. & Weingart, L. R. (1993). Group goals and group performance. *British Journal of Social Psychology*, **32**, 307–334.

West, M. A. (1990). The social psychology of innovation in groups. In M.A. West & J. L. Farr (Eds), *Innovation and Creativity at Work* (pp. 309–333). Chichester: Wiley.

West, M. A. (1994). *Effective Teamwork*. Leicester: British Psychological Society.

West, M. A. (1996). *The Handbook of Work Group Psychology*. Chichester: Wiley.

West, M. A. (1997). *Developing Creativity in Organisations*. Chichester: Wiley.

West, M. A. & Allen, N. J. (1977). Selecting for team work. In N. Anderson & P. Herriot (Eds), *Handbook of Selection and Appraisal* (2nd edn) (pp. 493–506). London: Wiley.

West, M. A. & Anderson, N. R. (1992). Innovation, cultural values and the management of change in British hospitals. *Work and Stress*, **6**, 293–310.

West, M. A. & Anderson, N. R. (1996). Innovation in top management teams. *Journal of Applied Psychology*, **81**(6), 680–693.

West, M. A., Garrod, S. & Carletta, J. (1997). Group decision making: Unexplored boundaries. In C. L. Cooper & S. E. Jackson (Eds), *New Developments in Organisational Behaviour* (pp. 293–317). Chichester: Wiley.

West, M. A., Patterson, M. G. & Lawthom, R. (1997). Psychological perspectives on company performance. Manuscript submitted for publication.

West, M. A. & Pillinger, T. (1995). *Innovation in UK manufacturing* (Research report). Institute of Work Psychology, University of Sheffield.

Wiersema, M. F. & Bantel, K. A. (1992). Top management team demography and corporate strategic change. *Academy of Management Journal*, **35**, 91–121.

Wilson, G. (1977). Introversion/extraversion. In T. Blass (Ed.), *Personality Variables in Social Behaviour*. New York: Wiley.

Wolf, R. A. (1994). Organizational innovation: Review, critique and suggested research directions. *Journal of Management Studies*, **31**, 405–431.

Wood, R. E., Hull, F. & Azumi, K. (1983). Evaluating quality circles: The American application. *California Management Review*, **26**, 37–49.

Wood, W., Lundgren, S., Oullette, J. A., Busceme, S. & Blackstone, T. (1994). Minority influence: A meta-analytic review of social influence processes. *Psychological Bulletin*, **115**(3), 323–345.

Worchel, S., Wood, W. & Simpson, J. A. (Eds) (1992). *Group Process and Productivity*. Newbury Park, CA: Sage.

Yammarino, F. J. (1996). Group leadership. In M.A. West (Ed.), *Handbook of Work Group Psychology* (pp. 189–224). Chichester: Wiley.

Yammarino, F. J. & Dubinsky, A. J. (1992). Superior–subordinate relationships: A multiple level of analysis approach. *Human Relations*, **45**, 575–600.

Yammarino, F. J. & Dubinsky, A. J. (1994). Transformational leadership theory: Using levels of analysis to determine boundary conditions. *Personnel Psychology*, **47**, 787–811.

Yukl, G. A. (1994). *Leadership in Organizations*. Englewood Cliffs, NJ: Prentice-Hall.

Yum, J. O. & Wang, G. (1983). Interethnic perception and the communication behavior among 5 ethnic groups in Hawaii. *International Journal of Intercultural Relations*, **7**, 285–308.

Zaccaro, S. J., Gualtieri, J. & Minionis, D. (1995). Task cohesion as a facilitator of team decision making under temporal urgency. *Military Psychology*, **7**(2), 77–93.

Chapter 6

CONFLICT AND PERFORMANCE IN GROUPS AND ORGANIZATIONS

Carsten K.W. De Dreu, Fieke Harinck and Annelies E.M. Van Vianen

University of Amsterdam

In a Dutch hospital, non-emergency surgery for 50 patients was delayed for one week because nurses refused to work any longer with their head of planning and collectively took sick-leave. Immediate cost was well over US$1m. An international trucking company shut down its Canadian business unit because it found no way out of an eight-month strike—over 1200 employees were fired. Ruud Gullit, player-manager of the Chelsea soccer team that won the 1997 FA Cup against Middlesbrough, increased his team's focus by stirring up conflict and disagreement. After the Bay of Pigs disaster in 1961, the then US President John F. Kennedy increased the influence of dissent in his decision-making team and avoided a nuclear war with the Soviet Union over Cuban missiles in 1963 (Forsyth, 1983).

Conflict in groups and organizations occurs, as these examples show, at different levels and it has diverse effects. Organizational conflict involves two or three colleagues fighting over office space, work teams hassling about the optimal way to perform a task, decision-making teams debating roles and procedures, and union and management disputing pension systems. Conflict increases absenteeism, disrupts the social climate in groups and organizations and interferes with efficient processes. Contrary to what is often assumed, however, conflict may have positive effects as well. Conflict increases individual creativity, it promotes communication and mutual understanding, it enhances the quality of group decision-making, and it sometimes increases team performance (Coser, 1956; De Dreu & Van de Vliert, 1997; Robbins, 1974; Tjosvold, 1991). Unfortunately, however, little systematic knowledge about the relationship between conflict and performance is available. In part this is because in organizational psychology conflict is often treated as a distinct rather than an integrated topic. For example, the last five *Annual*

Conflict and Performance in Groups and Organizations by Carsten K. W. De Dreu, Fieke Harinck and Annelies E. M. Van Vianen taken from IRIOP 1999 v14, Edited by Cary L. Cooper and Ivan T. Robertson: © 1999 John Wiley & Sons, Ltd

Review of Psychology chapters on I/O Psychology by Rousseau (1997), Wilpert (1995), O'Reilly (1991), Ilgen and Klein (1988), and Staw (1984) do not treat conflict management and dispute resolution at all. At the same time, update reviews on negotiation and mediation by Carnevale and Pruitt (1992), Greenhalgh (1987), Lewicki, Weiss and Lewin (1992), Levine and Thompson (1996) and Pruitt (in press) discuss conflict management and negotiation in isolation from the broader context of organizational structure, work-related attitudes, and performance.

This chapter concerns the relationship between conflict and performance. We discuss experimental research on bargaining and negotiation, and experimental and field research on conflict in production and decision-making teams. Our aim is to provide an overview of the existing evidence regarding the effects of conflict on performance, to highlight gaps in our knowledge, to identify important moderating and mediating variables, and to provide tools for effective intervention. Contrary to other reviews of the conflict literature, mainly dealing with the conflict process (e.g., Greenhalgh, 1987; Thomas, 1992), we also focus on the consequences of having versus not having conflict. The latter, often neglected, focus is especially useful in assessing the link between conflict and performance.

The chapter is organized in five sections. The first section defines conflict, and deals with conflict issues and prominent strategies for dealing with conflict. In addition, we define what we mean by performance in relation to conflict. The second section reviews research on bargaining and negotiation to highlight factors that increase or lower performance in *conflict over resources*. The third section reviews field research on conflict in groups and organizational teams to highlight factors that increase or lower performance in *conflict over information*. The fourth section of this chapter discusses strategies and objectives for conflict intervention that may be useful to managers and group leaders. We conclude with a summary of the main findings and offer some suggestions for future research.

CONFLICT AND PERFORMANCE: CONCEPTS AND DEFINITIONS

In this section we provide a definition of conflict and discuss key components of this definition in some detail. We distinguish between conflict as a process and conflict as a condition, and discuss these two perspectives in relation to performance.

The Conflict Process

In everyday speech conflict is seen as a fight, a struggle, or the clashing of opposed principles (e.g., *Concise Oxford Dictionary*, 1983). The problem with this definition is that it confounds conflict issues (what is the conflict about), feelings and cognitions (intraparty experiences), and conflict management (interparty experiences). In organizations people often avoid conflict, and those who instigate conflict are often unaware of doing so (Kolb & Bartunek, 1992; O'Connor, Gruenfeld & McGrath, 1993). These situations are not recognized as such as long as we define conflict as struggle and fight. For analytical purposes, we need a definition that is broader and separates conflict issues, intraparty and interparty experiences (cf. Pondy, 1967; Schmidt & Kogan, 1972).

Conflict can be considered as the tension an individual or group experiences because of perceived differences with another individual or group. Thus, scientists see conflict as the process that begins when one individual or group perceives differences between him or herself and another individual or group. Perceived differences produce psychological states, including feelings, cognitions and motivations that in turn produce behaviors intended to intensify, reduce or solve the tension (De Dreu & Van de Vliert, 1997; Pruitt, in press; Thomas, 1992; Wall & Callister, 1995). In a sense, an academic definition of conflict does not exist. Instead, *conflict issue* is defined as the substantive issue in which the tension is rooted, *conflict experience* is defined as the feelings, cognitions and intentions associated with the conflict issues and the interdependent other, *conflict management* is defined as the behavior oriented towards the intensification, reduction, and resolution of the tension, and *conflict outcome* is defined as the extent to which settlement is reached, as well as the quality of the settlement.

Conflict issues

Many different taxonomies of conflict issues have been proposed. Some argue that conflict involves resources or information (Kelley & Thibaut, 1969; Levine & Thompson, 1996). Conflict over *resources* involves access to and the distribution of scarce resources. Conflict over *information* involves debates over factual and evaluative issues. This distinction parallels Coombs' (1987) distinction between conflict of interest versus conflict of understanding and Rapoport's (1960) distinction between 'games' and 'debates.' Some go one step further and separate information issues into *intellective* issues and *evaluative* issues. Intellective issues have correct solutions according to commonly accepted standards. Examples are what is the shortest way from A to B, and which procedure is most efficient. Evaluative issues, however, have no correct solution and are a matter of taste. Examples are the question how to get from A to B, and whether efficiency should be the prevailing criterion in selecting a procedure (cf. Baron, Kerr & Miller, 1993; Kaplan & Miller, 1987). Intellective issues are associated with influence to accept information from another person about reality (informational influence), while evaluative issues are associated with the influence to conform with the positive expectations of another person (normative influence: Deutsch & Gerard, 1955).

Several authors have argued that since group members contribute to the group through task inputs and socio-emotional inputs (e.g., Forsyth, 1983), conflict issues are task- or identity-related (e.g., De Dreu, 1997; Amason & Schweiger, 1997; Jehn, 1997; Turner & Pratkanis, 1997). Examples of task issues are outcomes, procedures, judgments, and facts. Examples of identity issues are personal taste, political preference, and interpersonal style. Task and identity conflict may involve resource, intellective, and evaluative issues. However, identity conflict often involves a specific set of evaluative issues, namely those involving normative considerations of behavior (cf., Thomas, 1992).

There is both an advantage and a problem with classifying conflict as a function of conflict issue. The advantage is analytical—it helps one to focus on specific processes and to analyze specific features. This is particularly helpful in experimental research, but also useful in designing effective interventions. The problem is that conflict issues rarely come alone, and if they do, they are quickly joined by others (Rubin, Pruitt & Kim, 1994).[1] For example, preferences for particular procedures may be partially due to taste and interpersonal style, and political preferences may produce a preference for the distribution of outcomes. Moreover, in research on task versus identity conflicts, these two are usually correlated around 0.40 (e.g., Jehn, 1995). Thus, when we classify research according to conflict issue, this primarily suits analytical purposes.

Conflict experience: cognition and motivation

Conflict issues produce feelings, cognitions, and motivations. Prominent feelings in conflict are pride, resentment, anger and fear, but sometimes disputants experience elation, guilt and regret. Cognitions may relate to the other side in the conflict and involve stereotypes. Cognitions may also relate to the conflict itself and involve scripts about the evolution of conflict interaction. For example, Mikolic, Parker and Pruitt (1997) found that disputants have fairly strong scripts about how to deal with persistent annoyance.

Related to feelings and cognitions are frames. Research has identified outcome frames and conflict frames. Outcome frames refer to the way conflict outcomes are coded, as gains or as losses (Bottom & Studt, 1993; De Dreu & McCusker, 1997; Kahneman & Tversky, 1979; Neale & Bazerman, 1985). In the case of a gain frame, the conflict is about an undesirably low level of gains one anticipates, while in the case of a loss frame, the conflict is about an undesirably high level of losses one anticipates. Conflict frames define how conflict issues are perceived. Pinkley (1990) identified intellective frames that define whether the conflict is about intellective issues or about emotional issues, cooperative frames that define whether the conflict is about collaboration or competition, and relationship frames that define whether the conflict is about relationships or rational issues. Many other frames may exist (e.g., Putnam & Holmer, 1992). Interestingly, there is growing evidence that whenever disputants start with different conflict frames, they converge over time towards one and the same perspective (De Dreu, Carnevale, Emans & Van de Vliert, 1994; Pinkley & Northcraft, 1994).

Prominent motivations in conflict involve the desired distribution of outcomes between oneself and the other disputant (McClintock, 1977). In the case of a competitive motivation, disputants desire a relative advantage over the other party. In the case of an individualistic motivation, disputants desire to do well for themselves and ignore the other party's outcomes. And in the case of a prosocial motivation, disputants desire equality and good outcomes for themselves as well as for their opponent.[2] Social motives are partly rooted in individual differences. That is, some people are more inclined to approach their opposing negotiator in a cooperative manner than others (e.g., De Dreu & Van Lange, 1995; McClintock, 1977; Rubin & Brown, 1975). Motives may also be triggered by features of the situation: Future interaction, instructions from constituents and incentive structures may induce a (temporary) tendency to adopt a cooperative or more individualistic orientation (Deutsch, 1982; De Dreu & McCusker, 1997; Druckman, 1994; Sattler & Kerr, 1991). Adopting a cooperative rather than an individualistic or competitive motive may be for genuine reasons (one really likes the other party and wishes him well) or for instrumental reasons (one believes cooperation serves some egoistic goal; Pruitt & Carnevale, 1993).

Conflict management

Research and theory have identified many strategies for dealing with conflict and most subscribe to one of five global strategies (Blake & Mouton, 1964; Thomas, 1992; Pruitt & Rubin, 1986; Rahim, 1983; Van de Vliert & Kabanoff, 1990). *Dominating* behavior focuses on imposing one's will on the other side. It involves threats, bluffs and persuasive arguments, positional commitments, and strategic withdrawal. At the cognitive level, dominating involves a search for reasons why one is right and the other side is wrong, a cognitive justification of one's mean behaviors, and a derogation of the other's goodness. The flip side of dominating is *yielding*, which is oriented towards accepting and incorporating the other's will. It involves unilateral concessions, unconditional promises, and offering help. At the cognitive level, yielding involves a search for reasons why the other party is right and oneself is wrong, a cognitive justification of one's altruistic behavior, and an enhancement of the other's case. In between dominating and yielding is *compromising*, which is oriented towards splitting the difference. It involves the matching of each other's concessions, making conditional promises and threats, and an active search for a middle-ground.

Dominating, compromising, and yielding are located on a distributive dimension because they seek a particular allocation of outcomes. Other conflict behaviors diminish or expand the amount of outcomes to be allocated (Putnam & Jones, 1982). *Inaction* involves active withdrawal and passive avoidance. At the cognitive level, it involves reducing the importance of the issues, and attempts to suppress thinking about the issues. *Integration* is oriented towards an agreement that satisfies both one's own and the other's aspirations as much as possible. It involves an exchange of information about priorities and preferences, showing insights, and making trade-offs between important and unimportant issues. At the cognitive level, integration involves a reframing of interests and viewpoints, and a search for underlying organizing principles. Inaction and integration are the end-points on an integrative dimension because they both influence the total amount of outcomes to be distributed (Thomas, 1992; Van de Vliert & Kabanoff, 1990).

The conflict management strategies discussed above are used in conflict over *resources*; researchers have developed a similar taxonomy for dealing with *conflict over information*. Mann, Burnett, Radford, and Ford (1997) distinguished between unconflicted adherence, unconflicted change, defensive avoidance, hypervigilance, and vigilance. In unconflicted adherence, the decision-maker ignores information about the risk of losses and decides to continue the present course of action. This strategy resembles dominating. In unconflicted change, the decision-maker uncritically adopts whichever new course of action is most salient or most strongly recommended. This strategy resembles yielding. In defensive avoidance, the decision-maker escapes conflict by procrastinating, shifting responsibility to someone else, or constructing wishful rationalizations to bolster the least objectionable alternative. This strategy has much in common with inaction. In hypervigilance, the decision-maker searches frantically for a way out of the dilemma, and quickly seizes upon hastily contrived solutions that seem to promise immediate relief. Hypervigilance is similar to seeking 50:50 compromises. In vigilance, finally, the decision-maker clarifies objectives to be achieved by the decision, canvasses an array of alternatives, searches for relevant information, and evaluates carefully before making a decision. Vigilance has much in common with an integrating, problem-solving strategy.

An important issue is how sequences of conflict behavior unfold. In general, people have a strong tendency to reciprocate each other (e.g., Gouldner, 1960; Putnam & Jones, 1982). In conflict, many behaviors tend to be reciprocated, including procedural statements, integrative behaviors, distributive behaviors, conflict avoidance, and affect statements (Putnam, 1983; Donohue, 1981). However, in conflict we also witness a tendency to react in complementary fashion. This is the case, for example, when one party attacks, leading the other to defend (Putnam & Jones, 1982). In a study of both reciprocation and complementary conflict behavior, Weingart, Thompson, Bazerman and Carroll (1990) observed that negotiators mostly engage in reciprocation, regardless of whether their opponent's behavior was distributive or integrative. Although it was not mentioned in the Weingart study, we suspect that in many disputes conflicting parties may be tempted to take advantage of each other's cooperative behavior and to respond with dominating behavior. In addition, conflicting parties may suspect ulterior motives behind each other's yielding or problem-solving behavior and attempt to defend themselves through dominating responses. Thus, there is a general tendency in conflict to reciprocate, but with constructive behavior sometimes being 'undermatched' (cf., Pruitt & Carnevale, 1993).

Several authors noted that conflict management goes through different phases (Lewicki, Litterer, Minton, & Saunders, 1994). Walton (1969) distinguishes between a differentiation phase in which parties develop and defend their own interests and aspirations, and an integration phase in which parties seek possibilities to combine and integrate interests. Pruitt and Carnevale (1993) argue that early in negotiation parties respond with moderate demands when the other side is initially firm, and demand a lot if the other is initially conciliatory. They see this as 'tracking,' that is an effort to place one's goals and demands at a reasonable distance from the best offer that can be expected from the other. In the middle of the negotiation, when more information about each other's preferences and aspirations is available, negotiators closely match the frequency of each other's demands and concessions (but undermatch the magnitude of the other's concessions, see also above). At the end of the negotiation, when a deadline is looming, negotiators mismatch each other's demands—they are more conciliatory when the other remains firm, and remain firm when the other seems ready to give in. A general explanation for these stages in conflict management is that over time parties realize the cost of stalemate and impasse and shift from pure self-interest towards joint-interest.

Conflict outcomes

Conflict management may result in a victory to one and defeat to the other party, in an impasse, in a compromise in which both parties give and take a little, and in an integrative agreement. Integrative agreements are possible when the situation is variable-sum, and allows trade-offs among issues to reach higher joint outcomes than would have been realized in a 50:50 compromise (Pruitt, 1981; Walton & McKersie, 1965). Consider, for example, two managers who negotiate the number of temporary assistants they can appoint in the next year. Each manager wants as many assistants as possible, and they decide to divide their budget equally. The first manager decides to hire new assistants in the summer, and to fire them in the winter when business is slow. In contrast, the second manager decides to hire in the winter when backlogs are usually highest and to fire them in the summer. Obviously, albeit not to these managers, using the differences in time preferences would have allowed both managers to hire more assistants on a more permanent basis—both would have been better off had they exploited the integrative potential to a greater extent.

How conflict management influences conflict outcomes is discussed in the sections on managing resource conflict, and on managing information conflict. Here, it is important to note that integrative agreements are often assumed to be better solutions than victory or 50:50 compromises because they are more stable and enduring, and make parties happier (Thomas, 1992; Rubin, Pruitt & Kim, 1994; Van de Vliert, 1997). This assumption may be true in resource conflict but is untenable in many information conflicts. Brehmer and Hammond (1976) note that if people in a resource conflict agree any solution will do. In an intellective conflict, in contrast, the course of action or decision agreed upon has to be a *good* solution to the problem posed by the task. In intellective conflicts a victory for one may be superior to any other solution when it is the most accurate judgment.

Researchers often assume that the quality of conflict outcomes increases the more *equitable* the distribution of outcomes is. Equitable distributions produce greater satisfaction among conflict parties than disadvantageous and, interestingly, advantageous distributions (De Dreu, Lualhati & McCusker, 1994; Messick & Sentis, 1985; Loewenstein, Thompson, & Bazerman, 1989). Two issues are noteworthy, however. First, research on resource conflict usually confounds equitable distributions with integrative outcomes, in that parties realizing integrative potential automatically reach an equitable distribution of resources. An interesting and important question is whether and when parties are willing to sacrifice equity to realize integrative potential and, vice versa, sacrifice integrative potential to reach an equitable distribution. Second, (in)equity seems more important in resource conflict than in intellective and evaluative conflict where the goodness of a solution dominates. However, social justice research indicates that subjective experiences of fairness are more important than the actual, objective distribution of outcomes (Brockner & Wiesenfeld, 1996). Moreover, fair procedures appear equally or more important than fair distributions of outcomes (e.g., Van den Bos, Vermunt & Wilke, 1997). While distributive fairness may be more important in resource conflict than in information conflicts, procedural justice may be equally important in resource, intellective, and evaluative conflict.

Figure 6.1 summarizes the conflict process. Conflict issues produce conflict experiences including feelings and frames, and competitive, individualistic and prosocial motivations. Conflict experiences produce conflict behavior, including dominating, compromising, yielding, inaction, and integrating. As Thomas (1992) eloquently noted, conflict management produces or mitigates conflict issues in the other side, which subsequently intensifies or moderates conflict experiences. Thus, conflict is a complex interplay between conflict issues, parties' conflict experiences, and conflict behaviors. This complex

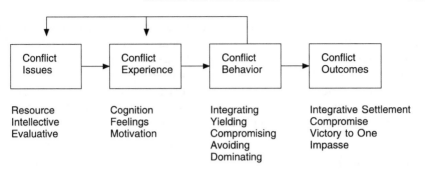

Figure 6.1   Schematic representation of the conflict process

interplay results in impasse, victory for one, compromise, or integrative agreements.

Conflict as a Condition

Theory and research traditionally focus on conflict processes, and conflict management in particular. A complementary perspective is to look at conflict as a condition. Some situations may have intense conflict, some are characterized by moderate conflict, and some lack conflict. Robinson (1995) discusses several trends in modern organizations that enhance the likelihood of conflict. For example, he argues that the increasing diversity of the workplace and the concomitant need to manage diversity is likely to bring new and more conflicts into today's organization (see also, Donnellon & Kolb, 1997). Similarly, he shows that the growing role of information technology with its fast and relatively anonymous way of communicating is likely to stimulate irritation and misunderstanding among its users. And the move away from traditional hierarchy and towards team-based work is yet another factor than enhances the likelihood of conflict in the workplace.

It would be simplistic to conceive of resource, intellective, and evaluative conflict as a state that is either absent or present. Rather, it should be operationalized in terms of its *intensity*, the relevant question being whether conflict is absent, moderate, or intense. The importance of conflict intensity is illustrated in research showing that moderate (information) conflict is better for task performance than either low or intense conflict (Jehn, 1995; Walton, 1969). Conflict as a condition should also be operationalized in terms of its *frequency*, the relevant question being whether conflict occurs never, sometimes, or very often.

The focus on conflict as a condition rather than a process requires a different level of analysis. The analysis of conflict process and outcomes orients towards the conflict parties and the analysis stops when the conflict is resolved. The analysis of conflict as a condition orients towards a comparison of individuals, groups, or entire organizations in which there is conflict with individuals, groups and organizations in which no conflict exists. Relevant questions then are (1) 'How is this individual, group or organization with conflict doing compared to other individuals, groups, or organizations without conflict?' and (2) 'How was this individual, group, or organization doing before conflict emerged, compared to how it is doing now?' Thus, in analyzing conflict as a condition we need a longer time-horizon that incorporates a substantial period after the conflict has been resolved.

Task and contextual performance

In studying the effects of conflict on performance, we need two complementary perspectives. First, we need to assess disputants' performance within the conflict process: How did conflicting parties resolve their conflict, what resources are used, and which goals are achieved? Second, we need to assess disputants' and their fellow group members' performance as a function of the conflict itself: How do conflict frequency and conflict intensity influence performance?

Performance may be operationalized in many different ways, such as the productivity relative to one's most salient competitor, as the supervisor's evaluation of her employees' commitment, as the quality of group decisions, and as the creativity in product development and individual thought processes (e.g., Pritchard, 1992). Several authors argue that group and organizational performance also involves less tangible issues. Organ (1988) coined the concept of organizational citizenship behavior, which involves behaviors such as compliance with collective goals, taking initiatives, and coordinating activities. It involves behaviors of a discretionary nature that are not part of the employee's formal role requirements, but nevertheless promote the effective functioning of the organization (Organ, 1988:4). Research shows that organizational citizenship behavior influences both the quantity and quality of work group performance (e.g. Podsakoff, Ahearne & MacKenzie, 1997).

Related to organizational citizenship behavior is contextual performance, defined as a set of interpersonal and volitional behaviors that support the social and motivational context in which organizational work is accomplished (Borman & Motowidlow, 1993). Van Scotter and Motowidlow (1996) proposed conceiving task performance as including task proficiency and motivation to perform one's own tasks effectively, and conceiving contextual performance as including interpersonal skills, the motivation to maintain good working relationships and help others perform their tasks.

Distinguishing between task and contextual performance is useful as it helps us to understand better the relationship between conflict management and outcomes on the one hand, and group and organizational performance on the other. Specifically, conflict may influence effectiveness at three distinct levels. First, conflict may influence personal effectiveness—personal development of skills, abilities, and knowledge. Second, conflict may influence interpersonal, or group effectiveness—learning to work together, developing relationships, or reaching high-quality group decisions. Third, conflict may influence organizational effectiveness—implementation of strategy, diagnosing and alleviating mismatches between components of organizational systems, product innovation, and learning to manage external threats and challenges. At any level, conflict may improve or reduce effectiveness, and improvements at one level (e.g., increase in individual creativity) may be offset by reductions at another level (e.g., disrupted coordination among group members). Thus, it is hypothesized that conflict enhances contextual performance because through conflict people become better equipped to deal with others and learn to communicate, or it reduces contextual performance because conflict interferes with interpersonal relations and increases distrust. In addition, conflict increases task performance because through conflict people learn skills and abilities and gain insights that foster task proficiency, or conflict hinders task performance because it distracts and lowers motivation to perform.

Thomas (1992) argued that the *time-horizon* of short- versus longer-term goal achievement is key to understanding the effects of conflict. Conflict as a condition may increase or decrease the likelihood of short-term achievement of a shared goal such as making profits. In the longer run, the positive or negative effects may persist, become stronger, or disappear. For example, the conflict between the head of operations and the nursing staff in the Dutch hospital may, in the long run, result in better working conditions, participative decision-making, and improved health care. The strike at the Canadian trucking company may have bolstered short-term efficiency to cope with the slowed-down production process, and perhaps reinforced union commitment among the employees; in the long run, however, the conflict led to exceedingly negative outcomes for all—the shutdown of the entire factory. The point is that conflict processes may have positive or negative effects on task performance in the short run, in the long run, or both.

Taken together, we explicitly distinguish between conflict process and outcomes on the one hand, and effects of conflict process and outcomes on contextual and task performance on the other. Our perspective includes trade-offs among individual, group and organizational performance, and incorporates both short-term and long-term effects of conflict on performance. Figure 6.2 summarizes this framework for thinking about conflict and performance. It shows that conflict issues influence contextual and task performance through conflict processes. For example, integrative conflict management may generate resources, interpersonal liking, and insights that help group members in their performance. On the other hand, dominating behavior and impasse reduce performance because conflicting parties are tired, angry and lack focus. Figure 6.2 also reveals that conflict issues may have a direct effect on performance, that is, regardless of the conflict management and outcomes. For example, conflict between two group members may distract or energize the

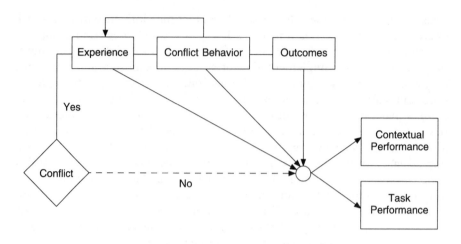

Figure 6.2   Relationship between conflict and performance

other members of the group. In the sections which follow we examine these relationships in resource conflicts and in information (i.e., intellective and evaluative) conflict.

RESOURCE CONFLICT

And if you calculate cost, then even in case of victory, one's losses greatly exceed the gains

Desiderius Erasmus (*Letters to Antonius van Bergen*, Oxford, 1906)

This section deals with conflict process and performance in resource conflict. Resource conflict can as suggested in the observation by the Dutch humanist Erasmus in 1514, have quite negative effects on contextual and task performance. To counter this, constructive, integrative conflict management is key. First we discuss conflict management, and subsequently we explicate how resource conflict impacts upon performance.

Managing Resource Conflict

Most of what we know about conflict processes derives from research on bargaining and negotiation. In negotiation, parties communicate about what each shall give and take, leave and perform in order to settle their divergent interests (Morley & Stephenson, 1977; Pruitt & Carnevale, 1993; Rubin & Brown, 1975). Key to managing resource conflict is whether disputants *reach agreement* and whether the agreement realizes *integrative potential*. Whether negotiators reach agreement is a positive function of the parties' willingness to make concessions. Druckman (1994) provides a meta-analytic review of variables that influence concession making. He concludes that negotiators are less willing to make concessions when: (1) they are representatives accountable to constituents who are responsible for deciding on the division of a significant tangible reward; (2) they prepare strategies in cohesive groups for a negotiation in which few issues are being contested; (3) relatively competitive orientations are induced by bureaucratic superiors; (4) they perform before an audience that creates strong face-saving pressures; (5) there are no time limits to reach agreements and no strike costs during bargaining; and (6) the opponent is tough and exploitative and his or her intentions are easy to discern (for narrative reviews yielding similar conclusions, see Carnevale & Pruitt, 1992; Pruitt, in press).

In research, integrative agreement is usually operationalized as the negotiators' joint outcome—the higher the more integrative negotiators have been (e.g., Pruitt, 1981; Neale & Bazerman, 1991). Other studies use Pareto Optimality, or the extent to which a solution is reached at which no party can do better without another party doing worse (Clyman, 1995; De Dreu, Giebels, & Van de Vliert, 1998; Tripp & Sondak, 1992; Weingart et al., 1990; Weingart, Hyder, & Prietula, 1996). Often, but not necessarily, measures of Pareto Optimality and joint outcomes are positively correlated.

Joint outcomes and Pareto Optimality are a function of the parties' use of integrative tactics. Rubin, Pruitt and Kim (1994) discuss five integrative tactics. First, negotiators may attempt to *expand the pie* by introducing new issues or by splitting existing issues into smaller ones. With multiple issues chances are slim that preferences are diametrically opposed on all issues and that all issues are equally important. Second, negotiators may engage in *logrolling* by giving in on less important issues and remaining firm on the more valuable ones. Third, parties may provide *non-specific compensation*, that is, consider what the party could do for the other side that would make the other side happy and have them allow the party to get their way on the key issue. Fourth, parties may engage in *cost cutting*; they may ask themselves what they can do to minimize the risks and costs associated with concessions demanded from the other side. Finally, negotiators may *bridge* and invent a solution that meets both sides' relative priorities and their underlying interests and needs (for other discussions, see Fisher, & Ury, 1981; Lax & Sebenius, 1986; Lewicki et al., 1994; Walton & McKersie, 1965).

Much is known about the antecedents of integrative behavior (for reviews, see Carnevale & Pruitt, 1992; Lewicki et al., 1994; Pruitt, in press; Thompson, 1990). Many studies take a motivational approach and suppose that negotiators often fail to realize the integrative potential because they lack a prosocial motivation. Other studies take a cognitive approach and show that negotiators often fail to realize the integrative potential because they lack the cognitive ability to see trade-offs, or fail to use their cognitive resources to integrate one's own and another's interests.

Motivational roots of integrative negotiation

The motivational approach is represented by the Dual Concern Theory (Pruitt & Rubin, 1986), and the Conflict Management Grid (Blake & Mouton, 1964). It argues that disputants turn to integrative tactics when they have a high concern for their own outcomes as well as a high concern for the other side's outcomes. Concern for the other's outcomes may be instrumental (one needs the other party again), or genuine (one really likes the other party and wishes him well). Consistent with Dual Concern Theory, research shows that when the concern for one's own outcomes is high, for example because of accountability to constituents, loss-framing, or high aspirations, higher joint outcomes are obtained when disputants have a high rather than low concern for each other's outcomes. Concern for others' outcomes is higher when negotiators expect future interaction, have a positive mood, have sympathetic feelings for the other party, or are instructed to value others' interests (e.g., Ben Yoav & Pruitt, 1984a,b; Butler, 1994; Carnevale & Isen, 1986; Fry, Firestone & Williams, 1983; Pruitt & Lewis, 1975). A similar conclusion derives from research on motivational orientations, which shows that negotiators with a prosocial motivation achieve higher joint outcomes than negotiators with an individualistic or competitive motivation (e.g., Carnevale & Lawler, 1986; De Dreu, Giebels & Van de Vliert, 1998; Giebels, De Dreu & Van de Vliert, 1998; Olekalns, Smith & Kibby, 1996; Schulz & Pruitt, 1978; Weingart, Bennett & Brett, 1993).

A problem with research on dual concern and motivational orientation is that most studies examined dyads in which both members shared the same motivational orientation. Obviously, in real life, negotiators with a prosocial motivation meet competitive negotiators, and research is needed to examine what happens in these mixed-orientation dyads. As mentioned, research on conflict frames indicates that when conflicting parties start with different frames they shift over time and converge to one and the same perspective (De Dreu et al., 1994; Pinkley & Northcraft, 1994). Similar processes may be at work in the case of motivational orientation and dual concerns. Another problem is that all studies involved student samples and research is needed to examine the generalizibility to samples involving more experienced disputants and to samples involving disputants who share a past and a future. However, despite these limitations, it seems safe to conclude that integrative negotiation is a positive function of the weight negotiators accord to their opposing party's outcomes. Provided this is the case, it would help if disputants have a high concern for their own interests as well.

Cognitive roots of integrative negotiation

The cognitive approach to integrative behavior is represented by Behavioral Decision Theory (Bazerman, 1983; Neale & Bazerman, 1991), which argues that negotiators are limited in their cognitive capacities and use short-cuts to deal with the complexities and uncertainties of the situation. As such, the cognitive approach subscribes to a tradition in psychology that views humans as cognitive misers who adopt strategies that simplify complex problems, strategies that may not be normatively correct but which emphasize efficiency (Fiske & Taylor, 1991). Research indeed shows that negotiators often use cognitive heuristics—simplifying strategies of inference (Neale & Bazerman, 1991). For example, negotiators simplify the situation by assuming that their own and the other's interests are diametrically opposed (i.e., fixed-pie heuristic) and this reduces integrative behavior and outcomes (Pinkley, Griffith & Northcraft, 1995; Thompson & Hastie, 1990; Thompson & Hrebec, 1996). Second, it appears that conflicting parties are prone to self-serving judgments and perceptions that interfere with constructive, integrative negotiation. Kramer, Newton, and Pommerenke (1994) showed that negotiators see themselves as fairer and more moral than the average negotiator. Thompson and Loewenstein (1992) showed that negotiators have self-serving ideas about what a fair distribution of outcomes would be and also found that self-serving bias was positively related to length of impasse. De Dreu, Nauta and Van de Vliert (1995) showed that disputants see themselves as more cooperative and less competitive than their opponent, and this self-serving perception of conflict management was positively associated with conflict escalation. Thus, it appears that self-serving judgments and perceptions hinder integrative conflict behavior and outcomes.

Combined influence of motivation and cognition

De Dreu and Koole (1997) showed that negotiators do not always act as cognitive misers and instead sometimes process information systematically (cf., Hoskin & Morley, 1992). Specifically, when the cost of inaccuracy was low and efficiency was valued, negotiators used heuristics to make decisions, and reached rather low joint outcomes. But when the cost of inaccuracy was high and efficiency less of an issue, negotiators acted as deep thinkers, did not rely on heuristics, and reached higher joint outcomes (see also De Dreu, Koole, & Oldersma, in press. Other research found that cooperative negotiators process information in rather different ways than individualistic and competitive negotiators (De Dreu & Boles, in press). All in all, the motivational and cognitive perspectives on integrative negotiation together suggest that managing resource conflict towards integrative outcomes is served best by a cooperative, prosocial motivation. In addition, a strong tendency to engage in deep processing of information appears to be useful as it counters the tendency to use suboptimal decision heuristics.

Resource Conflict and Performance

Two lines of research inform us about the influence of resource conflict on contextual and task performance. The first deals with effects of intergroup competition. The second concerns the role of distributive and procedural justice, including grievance filing, in work motivation and employee commitment.

Intergroup competition

Many consider the presence of intergroup competition as a liability to organizations (e.g., Schein, 1988). However, several pieces of evidence suggest that intergroup competition may improve performance. In a field experiment, Erev, Bornstein and Galili (1993) compared three conditions. In an individual incentive condition workers had to pick oranges and were paid on the basis of their individual performance. In a team incentive condition workers had to pick oranges and were paid on the basis of their team's task performance. In an intergroup competition condition workers were paid on the basis of their team outperforming the competitor. Results showed that the intergroup competition condition led to a higher task performance than the team condition, with the individual incentive condition being intermediate. Thus, intergroup competition increases task performance. A related finding was reported by Carnevale and Probst (1997) who found that individuals with a competitive motivation became more creative when they were in a group competing with another group, compared to a situation where they worked individually. Thus, intergroup competition fosters creativity, especially in competitive people.

Positive effects of intergroup conflict and competition on performance are not confined to the laboratory. Putnam (1997) analyzed teacher–board negotiations and concluded that active confrontation through negotiation promotes intergroup communication, increases mutual understanding and results in greater acceptance of agreements and decisions than more tacit coordination. Walton, Cutcher-Gershenfeld and McKersie (1994:72–73) reported both the negative and the positive consequences of union–management negotiations in the auto-supply, the pulp and paper, and the railroad industries. Inspection of their data reveals that within the pulp and paper industry 20% of the negotiations resulted in negative consequences only, such as costly strikes, while 20% of the negotiations improved contextual and/or task performance. For the auto-supply and the railroad industries, these percentages were 30 and 60, and 25 and 50, respectively. Apparently, active confrontation between union and management influences distal task performance in a fairly positive way.

Justice issues and grievance filing

Conflict management and outcomes, and its perceived fairness in particular, has important consequences for contextual and task performance. As mentioned above, research shows that people are less satisfied with outcomes they perceive to be unfair than with those they perceive to be fair. Such feelings and perceptions have been shown to result in poor performance (e.g., Cowherd & Levine, 1992; Pfeffer & Langton, 1993), including turnover and absenteeism (e.g., Hulin, 1991; Schwarzwald, Koslowsky, & Shalit, 1992). Thus, poor conflict management resulting in unfair outcomes is likely to reduce (contextual) performance. Related to this is the advice that one should avoid bragging about one's individual conflict outcomes and one's smart moves during conflict management (Pruitt, in press). Public disclosure may reveal to the other parties the unsettling news that they performed worse than they thought, and that they have been treated far less nobly than they thought. These feelings may well lead to new conflicts, but also reduce commitment, individual creativity, and group cohesion.

Research on layoffs suggests that group members not involved in resource conflict may actually be influenced by it as well. Survivors usually respond negatively to watching their co-workers lose their jobs (Cropanzano & Greenberg, 1997) and this results in reduced organizational commitment and task performance. In addition, conflict and issues of unfairness and injustice are likely to be surveyed in communication among coworkers. We speculate that witnessing poor conflict management and unfair conflict outcomes influences the observer's performance because of reduced work motivation and because it distracts.

Related to organizational justice is the grievance procedure for addressing organizational conflict. Grievance procedures have been created to provide labor and management with a means for resolving differences between them in the interpretation of labor contracts. Several studies examined the relationship between grievance filing as an indication of the level of conflict within a work unit or organization and contextual performance (i.e., absenteeism). Katz, Kochan and Weber (1985) found that absenteeism was positively correlated with grievance rate, a finding replicated by Lewin and Peterson (1988). Lewin and Peterson also found absenteeism to be higher among those whose grievance was denied, compared to those whose grievance was granted. Using a longitudinal design, Klaas, Heneman and Olson (1991) found that absenteeism was positively correlated with grievances about information conflict (i.e., policy differences, see below), and that absenteeism *decreased* the month after filing grievances about resource conflicts (i.e., disciplinary sanctions). Other research shows that managers punish grievance filers by giving them lower performance ratings and terminating their employment (e.g., Klaas & DeNisi, 1989; Lewin, 1987; Lewin & Peterson, 1988). Olson-Buchanan (1996) examined whether these 'punishment' effects reflected an actual change in the grievant's behavior. Her results showed that employees who had a basis for dispute had lower task performance and were less willing to continue working for the organization.

Taken together, there is some evidence from the justice and grievance literature to suggest that resource conflict influences contextual and task performance for those who are involved in the dispute as well as for those who are witnessing it. Performance includes lower organizational commitment in the case of perceived injustice, and lower productivity and continuance commitment in the case of grievance filing.

Conclusions and Unanswered Questions about Resource Conflict

The literature on resource conflict suggests that constructive, integrative conflict management benefits from disputants having a prosocial rather than competitive motivation, together with a strong tendency to engage in thorough information processing. The literature further suggests that contextual and task performance benefits from intergroup competition for scarce resources, in that it increases mutual cooperation, individual creativity, and work motivation. However, resource conflict also reduces performance, as injustice leads to lower organizational commitment and work motivation, and grievance filing is associated with reduced productivity. Overall, resource conflict appears to reduce contextual and task performance, the exception being the effects of some forms of intergroup competition. Figure 6.3 summarizes these conclusions. It shows that the conflict process becomes more constructive under high tendency to engage in deep information processing and a cooperative motivation. It also shows that the conflict process is likely to affect contextual and task performance, perhaps in a negative way (the dashed line indicates we have little direct evidence for this relationship, see also below).

Four issues that are important for groups and organizations are scarcely considered in research on resource conflicts. As mentioned above, most research on managing resource conflict is conducted in the laboratory with undergraduate or MBA students as participants. As a result, we know almost nothing about negotiations in which parties share a past and a future (Greenhalgh, 1987). Some research involving intimate partners has been conducted (e.g., Fry, Firestone & Williams, 1983), but more systematic research involving colleagues or co-workers is needed. Some evidence suggests that sharing a past or a future increases prosocial motivation (cf., Ben-Yoav & Pruitt, 1984a; Komorita & Carnevale, 1992), but sharing a future also increases the importance of building the tough and powerful image of someone not to be trifled with.

Second, little attention has been given to satisfaction with settlements, and to changes in interparty attitudes (Cross, 1995). These are important consequences of conflict management as they relate to the occurrence of new conflicts, and thus may impact more distal task performance. Thus, we

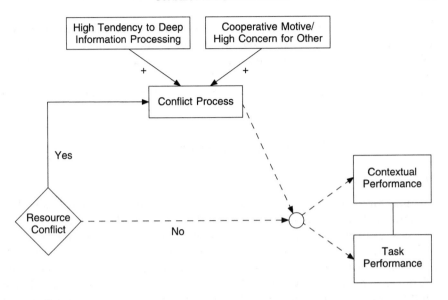

Figure 6.3 Management resource conflict and performance

would encourage research to assess conflict outcomes in terms of objective as well as subjective parameters.

Third, research has failed to address the aftermath of resource conflict, that is, the implementation of negotiated contracts (Pruitt, 1981; Saunders, 1985). This is particularly important to organizations where badly implemented contracts become a liability to co-workers, or to the organization as a whole. Finally, and relatedly, research is needed to better assess the more distal effects of resource conflict on contextual and task performance. We know quite well how participants manage and resolve resource conflict, but we know little about how conflict management and outcomes influence individual work motivation, group innovation, and organizational productivity. Research needs to confirm our tentative conclusion that resource conflict in groups and organizations generally lowers contextual and task performance.

INFORMATION CONFLICT

Conflict is the gadfly of thought. It stirs us to observation and memory. It instigates to invention. It shocks us out of sheep-like passivity, and sets us at noting and contriving. . . . Conflict is the sine qua non of reflection and ingenuity

John Dewey (*Human Nature and Conduct*, Holt & Company, 1922)

This section deals with conflict process and performance in information conflict, which we further divide into conflict over factual, intellective issues, and conflict over evaluative issues. Information conflict can have, as suggested by Dewey, quite positive effects on contextual and task performance. First we discuss conflict management, and subsequently we explicate how information conflicts impact upon performance.

Managing Information Conflict

Intellective conflict: social judgment theory

An important stream of research on conflict over factual, intellective issues has its roots in Social Judgment Theory and the Brunswikian 'lens model' in which a to-be-judged entity takes on some true value in the environment. Although the true value may not be known to the judge, relevant information is available in the form of multiple, redundant cues, each with some true relationship to the true value of the to-be-judged entity. Because the judge cannot observe the criterion directly, the judge must make a judgment based on the information provided by the cues. Whether a judge arrives at an accurate judgment depends on whether he or she uses valid cues and ignores invalid ones (Brehmer & Joyce, 1988).

Although initially developed for individual judgments, social judgment theory can be applied to understand intellective conflicts (Brehmer & Hammond, 1976; Gigone & Hastie, 1996). The situation is extended to two or more parties with different cues and different preferences for cue utilization (i.e., policies). Their task is to agree upon what cues to use. For example, disputants have to predict teachers' salaries based on demographic and economic data (Reagan-Ciricione, 1994), or disputants have to predict which horse will win a race, based on cues such as the horses' median speed, their positions at the start, their jockeys, and their winning records of last year (Harmon & Rohrbauch, 1990). By varying the cues disputants have at their disposal (e.g., the horses' median speed and starting position, versus their jockeys and last year's records) and/or by manipulating preferences for cue utilization (e.g., preference for median speed data rather than for last year's records) disputants arrive (1) at contradictory predictions that are (2) less than optimal as long as not all cues are entered in the judgment.

In a review of the earlier intellective conflict research, Brehmer (1976) reaches several conclusions that are relevant to managing intellective conflict. First, it appears that in cognitive conflict parties have a hard time reaching agreement. Specifically, research suggests that over a series of trials disputants rapidly reduce the systematic differences between their policies (i.e., what cues to use), but at the same time decrease the consistency with which they apply their policies. As Brehmer notes (1976:990): 'there was little change in the *amount* of disagreement, but its *structure* changed. In the beginning of the conflict stage, most of the subjects' disagreement was caused by the systematic differences between their policies . . . At the end, however, most of their disagreement was caused by a lack of consistency' (emphasis in the original).

The second major conclusion reached by Brehmer (1976) is that in intellective conflict judgment accuracy is more important to disputants than agreement or conflict reduction—in particular disputants with inadequate judgment policies change, while disputants with adequate policies remain committed. Other results suggest, however, that this conclusion is limited to situations in which feedback about actual accuracy is provided. When compromise will not lead to any obvious loss in judgmental accuracy, disputants change their policies to reduce conflict. Clearly, the absence of feedback about judgmental accuracy is likely to be a common characteristic in real-life groups and organizations. Related to this are task characteristics. Three formal characteristics of the task have been found to influence the level of conflict. A higher number of cues, nonlinearity of the relationship between the cues and the to-be-predicted criterion, and a higher level of task uncertainty lead to more conflict. Alone or in combination these characteristics lead to a lower task predictability, which causes more disagreement (Brehmer, 1976).

As an antidote to groupthink (Janis, 1972), decision-making groups often employ the procedure of *devil's advocacy*. Devil's advocacy refers to the decision aid strategy in which an individual or group formulates a plan, which is subsequently criticized by someone who attempts to find all that is wrong with the plan and to expound the reasons why the plan should not be adopted. Research suggests that devil's advocates promote decision quality in teams (Janis, 1972; Priem & Price, 1991; Schweiger, Sandberg & Ragan, 1986), most likely because devil's advocates stimulate the development of alternative, perhaps better plans and strategies. Indeed, a meta-analytic review of 16 experiments with students and professional decision-makers shows that the controversy introduced by devil's advocacy improves managerial decision-making, compared to expert-based approaches (Schwenk, 1990). However, the meta-analysis also suggests that devil's advocacy may reduce the quality of performance in situations that are stable and well understood, that is, in tasks that can be executed in a routine manner. The reason for this reversal is that when the task is well understood assumptions are usually valid. When the devil's advocate questions these otherwise valid assumptions, it may be that these assumptions are then rejected, thus reducing overall performance (see also, Rose, Menasco & Curry, 1982).

Several studies examined the role of motivational orientation on managing intellective conflicts. McCarthy (1977) found no differences between disputants instructed to grasp their other side's policies (cf. cooperative motivation) and disputants instructed to clarify and repeat their own viewpoints (cf. individualistic motivation). However, Summers (1968) showed that in an intellective conflict task using naturally occurring differences in beliefs, participants compromised more often when they were given a cooperative rather than competitive orientation. Similarly, Cosier and Rose (1977) showed that disputants given a competitive goal were less accurate in their predictions than disputants given no goal. Alexander (1979) showed that supportive communication, including messages intended to seek another's opinion and messages intended to obtain or give restatements, reduced intellective conflict. Supportive communication is more likely in the case of a cooperative rather than competitive or individualistic motivation. Thus, it appears that in intellective conflict cooperative motivation reduces conflict because it increases supportive communication. Note that this conclusion closely parallels the one we reached in reviewing the literature on conflict over resources.

Taken together, research on intellective conflict suggests: (1) that although the initial amount of disagreement may be reduced quickly, the conflict persists because disputants are inconsistent in the application of their policies; (2) that the goal of judgment accuracy prevails over the goal of conflict reduction when feedback about accuracy is provided, but not when feedback is absent; (3) that conflict management is more difficult when task predictability is lower and complexity is higher; and (4) that conflict management benefits from a cooperative as compared to a more competitive motivational orientation.

Evaluative conflicts

While social judgment theory deals with intellective conflicts, Druckman and colleagues conducted a series of studies concerned with evaluative conflicts— information conflicts in which no correct solution is available and disagreements involve taste, norms, and values (e.g., Druckman & Zechmeister, 1973). One of the main conclusions that derives from their research is that evaluative conflicts are difficult to resolve and often lead disputants into destructive, escalatory spirals (Druckman, Rozelle, & Zechmeister, 1976). An explanation may be that, contrary to resource and intellective conflict, disputants have more difficulty making concessions, or understand that the other does not possess the 'correct' solution. Matters of evaluation are likely to evoke intransigence. Research indeed revealed that in conflicts over interpersonal style and proper modes of conduct, disputants are most likely to engage in dominating behavior and least likely to engage in yielding, with problem-solving and avoiding taking intermediate positions (De Dreu, 1997; Janssen, Van de Vliert & Veenstra, in press). Thus, evaluative conflict in itself leads to poor conflict management.

In one series of studies, Druckman and colleagues compared three conditions of evaluative conflicts: where values were separated from interests (delinked condition); where they were not separated from interests (embedded condition), and where they were not separated in a situation in which parties explored their differences during prenegotiation sessions (facilitation condition). Specifically, parties in the facilitation condition were led to identify and explore values, to develop insight into the other side's values, and to develop an understanding of the difference between interests and values. Parties in the delinked and embedded conditions were not given this opportunity. Results typically show that facilitation reduces conflict intensity as indicated by more cooperative statements made during negotiation, greater satisfaction with the solution, and more positive perceptions of the negotiation climate. However, the number of issues resolved did not differ between the facilitation and delinked conditions: Both conditions produced more resolved issues than the embedded condition (Druckman, Korper & Broome, 1988; Korper, Druckman, & Broome, 1986). One could argue that the facilitation treatment reduces the disputants' competitive motivation and increases their perspective-taking ability, which is related to prosocial motivation (cf. Tjosvold, 1991). Support for this idea comes from Judd (1978) who found that two parties in an evaluative conflict focused on similarities when they were given a cooperative motive, and focused on differences when they were given a competitive motive. As such, these studies are consistent with other findings that a cooperative, prosocial motivation ameliorates conflict management.

Taken together, research shows that evaluative conflict in itself is likely to produce destructive conflict management. Consistent with findings from studies on resource and intellective conflict, research also suggests that a prosocial rather than competitive motivation reduces intransigence and improves conflict management.

Information Conflict and Performance

Two distinct lines of research concern performance in information conflict. The first line of investigation is captured in Tjosvold's (1991) constructive controversy, and in research concerned with task-related disagreements (e.g., Amason, 1996; Jehn, 1997). The second line of investigation concerns social influence processes and covers devil's advocacy and minority dissent (Nemeth & Staw, 1989; Schwenk, 1990).

Constructive controversy and task-related disagreements

Tjosvold's constructive controversy (Tjosvold, 1991, 1997) argues that (information) conflict occurs in cooperation, in independence, or in competition. Under cooperation, disputants perceive their goals to be positively linked—both swim or sink together. Under independence, parties perceive their goals to be independent—whether one swims has no influence on the other's fate. Under competition, parties perceive their goals to be negatively linked—one swims as the other sinks and vice versa. Cooperation, independence, and competition are closely related to the prosocial,

Table 6.1   Antecedents for cooperation and competition in information conflict

	Cases (nos)
Cooperation	
Shared Goals	33
Common Tasks	14
Complementary Roles	27
Need for Coordination	6
Shared Rewards	3
Competition	
Win–Lose Rewards	33
Desire to Get One's Way	13
Win–Lose Attitudes	27
Scarce Resources	58

Note. Entries indicate the number of cases in which the antecedent was mentioned ($n = 104$). Respondents were Dutch staff members and managers in a hospital and a manufacturing firm.

Source. Based on Kluwer et al. (1993).

individualistic, and competitive motivation discussed under resource conflict (Deutsch, 1949, 1973, 1982). Table 6.1 lists a series of antecedent conditions to perceived cooperation and competition, derived from a critical incident study in Dutch organizations by Kluwer, De Dreu, Dijkstra, Van der Glas, Kuiper and Tjosvold (1993). Cooperation is triggered by shared goals and complementary roles, while competition is due to win–lose rewards, scarcity, and competitive attitudes.

Whether information conflict occurs in cooperation, independence or competition is crucial for conflict management. Under cooperation, parties exchange information, discuss priorities and preferences in an open-minded fashion, they listen and develop trust, and they seek to incorporate each other's perspective. This is called *constructive controversy*. Under competition, in contrast, parties do not trust each other, they fail to disclose important information, they do not listen and they seek to overwhelm the other rather than to work together for mutual benefit. This is called *destructive controversy*. Under independence, parties tend to behave as if they were under competition, albeit less extreme.

In the past 20 years, Tjosvold and colleagues have conducted an impressive series of studies to assess the relationship between constructive and destructive controversy on the one hand, and performance on the other (for reviews, see Tjosvold, 1991, 1997). His research shows that, compared to destructive controversy, constructive controversy improves organizational decision-making (Tjosvold & Deemer, 1980), customer service (Tjosvold, Dann & Wong, 1992), and production and health care (Tjosvold & Tsao, 1989), to name but a few effects.

Related to Tjosvold's work are recent studies on so-called task-related conflict. West and Anderson (1996) obtained evidence to suggest that constructive task-oriented conflict influences the quality of innovation in top management teams. Amason (1996) and Amason and Sapienza (1996) examined top management teams and observed that teams reporting high levels of task-related conflict reported better decisions and greater commitment to these decisions. Similar findings were obtained by Jehn (1994, 1995) who studied production teams. Jehn (1995) also demonstrated that positive effects of task-related conflicts were especially strong in teams performing non-routine tasks. For teams involved in routine jobs, task-related conflict reduced performance. Consistent with Tjosvold's constructive controversy, Amason (1996) and Jehn (1995) finally showed that task-related conflict increases performance especially when the group values openness (see also, Janssen, Van de Vliert & Veenstra, in press).

A third line of research on information conflict and performance examines effects of minority dissent. Minority dissent can be defined as publicly advocating and pursuing beliefs, attitudes, ideas, procedures and policies that go against and challenge the status quo—the position or perspective assumed by the majority of the group or organization's members (De Dreu & De Vries, 1997). Examples are the decision-maker who challenges commonly shared assumptions, the colleague pleading for affirmative action, and the newly hired medical assistant who consistently advocates implementation of a novel treatment she was taught about at school. Minority dissent stimulates innovation and adaptiveness (De Dreu & De Vries, 1997; Levine & Russo, 1987; Nemeth & Staw, 1989). Nemeth (1986) suggests that being confronted with minority dissent elicits 'divergent' thinking. Her research shows that when recipients focus on the dissenter's message they attempt to understand why the minority thinks this way and at the same time attempt to falsify and counter-argue its position. As such, minority dissent facilitates the discovery of alternative, sometimes better, solutions, it induces more elaborate clustering strategies in memory, it enhances recall of previously learned information, it promotes creativity in individual thinking, it leads to more novel associations, and it produces more original proposals (e.g., Nemeth & Kwan, 1985, 1987; Peterson & Nemeth,1995; Volpato, Maass, Muchi-Faina & Vicci, 1990).

A field study by Cosier and Dalton (1990) examined the relationship between dissent in information conflict and distal variables such as job commitment and job satisfaction. Dissent was operationalized as whether discussion between organization members reflects disagreement and conflict, as whether the organization involves someone acting as a devil's advocate when input for risky decisions is needed, and whether decisions in the organization reflect the consideration of 'opposites.' Job commitment and job satisfaction were measured six weeks later. Results showed positive correlations between the amount of information conflict and job commitment, but not job satisfaction. The authors suppose that commitment increases information conflict because one does not get into conflict unless one really cares about the issue and the organization. Alternatively, it may be that the occurrence of information conflict produces better understanding of the issue and the organization, which results in greater commitment.

In recent years, several studies demonstrated that information conflict has a robust negative influence on contextual and task performance when the focus of the conflict is socio-emotional rather than task-related (Amason, 1996; Janssen, Van de Vliert & Veenstra, in press; Jehn, 1994, 1995; for reviews, see Amason & Schweiger, 1997; De Dreu, 1997; Jehn, 1997; Turner & Pratkanis, 1997). Thus, the finding that information conflict sometimes benefits performance seems limited to situations in which few socio-emotional issues are involved.

Taken together, information conflict can enhance personal and group effectiveness. That is, dissent increases individual creativity, it is associated with greater organizational commitment, and it leads to greater quality of group decision-making. This positive contribution of minority dissent and devil's advocacy seems restricted to complex, non-routine tasks for which no clearcut solutions are available. When tasks are simple and routine, dissent distracts and may lead to the rejection of otherwise valid assumptions and procedures, thus reducing individual and group performance. In addition, beneficial effects of information conflict come about especially when individuals and groups have cooperative goals and engage in constructive controversy. Finally, information conflict becomes detrimental as socio-emotional issues dominate the dispute.

Conclusions and Unanswered Questions about Information Conflict

Intellective and evaluative conflicts are difficult to resolve, because people apply policies in an inconsistent manner and because people have a hard time compromising their preferences and values. Nevertheless, when given a cooperative motivation conflict management improves and both intellective and evaluative conflict are reduced substantially. Intellective and evaluative conflicts benefit contextual and task performance when the group values openness and engages in constructive controversy, the task is complex and non-routine, and task-related rather than socio-emotional issues dominate the dispute (see Figure 6.4). Benefits include innovation, greater creativity, better decisions and increased organizational commitment.

Several issues have received little attention and require research. First, research on intellective and evaluative conflict has ignored almost entirely the effects of the motivation to engage in information processing on conflict

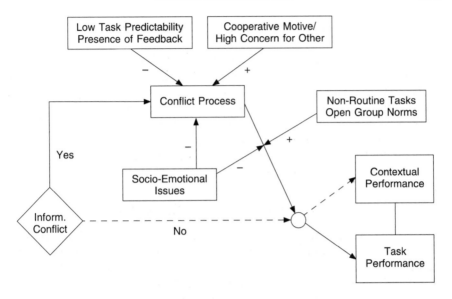

Figure 6.4 Managing information conflict and performance

management. In keeping with the effects found in resource conflict, we speculate that in intellective conflict increased ability and motivation to process information systematically improves conflict management as well as judgment accuracy and acceptance. This speculation is consistent with the finding that, in intellective conflict, having to justify one's judgments, which has been shown to increase systematic information processing (Tetlock, 1992), increases consistency in the judgment policy when task predictability is low and feedback about the actual judgment accuracy is absent (Hagafors & Brehmer, 1983). It would be interesting to explore these issues in evaluative conflict as well.

Another issue that requires attention is that most of the evidence linking information conflict to performance is cross-sectional. With some exceptions, most of the evidence for Tjosvold's constructive controversy is based on cross-sectional designs and most performance indicators are self-report measures. Fortunately, a large number of experiments on academic performance (Johnson & Johnson, 1989) yield similar conclusions to those reached by Tjosvold. More problematic is the stream of research on task-related versus socio-emotional conflict, which is entirely cross-sectional. It cannot be excluded that (perceived) performance influences (perceptions of) the amount of task-related and socio-emotional conflict. Controlled experiments and longitudinal field studies are needed to corroborate the idea that task-related conflict enhances group decision-making and productivity when groups perform non-routine tasks and have a cooperative motivation.

THIRD PARTY INTERVENTION

Up to this point we have reviewed and discussed research findings concerning resource conflict and information conflict. Several general conclusions emerged from this literature that are relevant to third parties seeking to help disputants resolve their differences in such a way that is beneficial to the conflict process, to contextual performance, and to task performance. Below, we first analyze the different roles third parties may adopt, and we review strategic choices third parties have at their disposal. Subsequently, we analyze third party intervention in resource conflicts, and in information conflicts.

Third Party Roles and Strategies

Research identified various roles third parties can adopt when intervening in conflict between subordinates or fellow group members. Building on the pioneering work by Thibaut and Walker (1975), Sheppard (1983, 1984) distinguished between a third party's control over the presentation and interpretation of dispute-relevant evidence (*process control*) and his or her control over the outcome of the dispute (*decision control*). These two dimensions jointly produce four distinct roles a third party may assume. When third parties exercise both process and decision control they assume an inquisitorial role, while they assume a mediational role when they exercise process control only. When third parties lack process and decision control they assume a role in which they provide impetus, and when they only exert decision control they assume an adjudicative role. Subsequent research corroborated the inquisitorial role (also called 'autocratic'), the mediational role, and the adjudicative role. In addition, managers as third parties sometimes assume a motivational role when using threats and rewards to motivate disputants to settle (Karambaya & Brett, 1989; Karambaya, Brett, & Lytle, 1992). An inductive analysis using multidimensional scaling by Pinkley, Brittain, Neale, and Northcraft (1995) provided further support for the distinction between process and decision control, and also revealed that managers sometimes choose to handle the dispute publicly.

In organizations managers and group leaders are the most likely third parties in a dispute. However, more and more organizations employ a corporate ombudsman intended to serve as a voice-giving mechanism. An ombudsman may be called a Director of Personnel Communications, a Work Problem Counsellor, or an Employee Relations Manager. The responsibilities usually include communications, policy interpretations and counselling, and providing feedback to senior management. Ombudsmen handle a variety of complaints regarding salaries, terminations, performance reviews, and harassment (Kolb, 1986:213–214). Ombudsmen have less formal authority than managers, and are likely to use different strategies. Kolb discusses several cases in which ombudsmen saw themselves as an arranger and advisor, or as an investigator. Their strategies reflect low decision control and moderate process control.

Elangovan (1995a) developed several criteria for effective intervention. He argued that an intervention is effective when: (1) the issues are fully addressed to produce a settlement consistent with the organizational objectives; (2) the resolution is timely; and (3) the disputants are committed to implement the agreed-upon settlement. He derived five intervention strategies that closely resemble the third party roles discussed above. In a means-control strategy, the manager intervenes by influencing the process of resolution. He or she facilitates the interaction, assists in communication and clarifies issues (cf., mediation). In an ends-control strategy, the manager intervenes by influencing the outcomes of the dispute, by deciding what the final decision will be (cf., arbitration). In a low-control strategy, the manager remains rather passive and stimulates the parties to resolve the conflict themselves, for instance through negotiation. In a full-control strategy, the manager intervenes by influencing both process and outcome (cf., inquisitorial intervention). In a part-control strategy, finally, the manager intervenes by sharing control over the process and outcome with the disputants. He or she attempts to persuade the parties to accept a particular solution and pushes for a settlement (cf., group problem-solving). Elangovan's prescriptive analysis suggests that part-control and means-control strategies are optimal in roughly 65% of the cases, while ends-control and full-control strategies are optimal in those 30% of the cases where there is a high probability that disputants will be committed to an imposed settlement.

Descriptive support for the advice offered by Elangovan (1995a) comes from research by Karambaya and Brett (1989), Karambaya, Brett and Lytle (1992), and Lewicki and Sheppard (1985). In experimental studies with experienced MBA students, these researchers found that mediation was most preferred, produced more settlements than more autocratic intervention strategies, and that settlements based on mediation produced greater satisfaction among disputants, and higher ratings of procedural fairness.

A descriptive model of mediation has been proposed by Carnevale (1986a,b). This Strategic Choice Model argues that mediation is guided by (1) the mediator's concern for the disputants' aspirations, and (2) the mediator's perception of common ground, that is the likelihood that parties will reach agreement. When concern for aspirations is high and perceived common ground is high, mediators are likely to choose an integrating, problem-solving strategy. When concern for aspirations is high and perceived common ground is low, mediators are predicted to use compensation to entice parties to make concessions. When concern for aspirations is low and perceived common ground is high, mediators tend towards forcing parties into a solution. And when concern for aspirations is low and perceived common ground is low mediators are predicted to remain inactive and to let the parties handle the dispute themselves.

Research has supported the strategic choice model (e.g., Carnevale & Conlon, 1988; Carnevale & Henry, 1989; Harris & Carnevale, 1990; for reviews, see Carnevale, Conlon, Hanisch, & Harris, 1989; Carnevale & Pruitt, 1992). Ross and Wieland (1996), for example, varied time pressure as an operationalization of the mediator's perceived common ground and between-disputants' trust as an operationalization of the mediator's concern for parties' aspirations. Results showed that high time pressure increased the mediators' use of forcing messages and decreased the use of inaction messages. Other research corroborated that professional mediators use tactics in a contingent manner (Rubin, 1986). In a study involving professional mediators, Lim and Carnevale (1990) showed that interparty hostility was associated with forcing and face-saving tactics, that male mediators were more likely to use forcing tactics than female mediators, and that labor disputes were more likely to be associated with forcing tactics than non-labor disputes. All in all, the Strategic Model of Mediation has firm support both from experimental research involving unexperienced mediators and from field research involving professional, experienced third parties.

Intervention in Resource and Information Conflict

Research and theory on third party intervention primarily considers the ways third parties assist disputants in managing their conflict, and does not take into account the fact that (managing) conflict may have both positive and negative effects on performance. In addition, third party research and theory does not consider the fact that disputes may be concerned with resources, with intellective issues, or with evaluative issues. For example, Carnevale's Strategic Choice Model of mediation appears to consider the mediation of resource conflicts. Our review of resource and information conflict suggests (1) that conflict sometimes increases task performance, suggesting that third parties may desire to stimulate rather than mitigate conflict, and (2) that resource and information conflict run very different courses, suggesting that third parties may desire to pay closer attention to the issues under debate.

The discussion of resource conflict showed that integrative behavior is least disruptive and prevents resource conflict having negative effects on performance. Our review revealed few positive effects of resource conflict on task performance, the sole exception being some forms of intergroup competition. In resource conflicts, third parties may try to help parties manage their conflict in a constructive, integrative way. In addition, we speculated that merely witnessing one's peers to be involved in a resource conflict lowers work motivation and distracts. This indicates that especially in resource conflict, third parties should stimulate private rather than public conflict management, and should try to isolate the conflict from the broader context of the group or organization within which it occurs.

The discussion of information conflict showed that intellective and evaluative conflicts need to be managed in a constructive, open way. Constructive controversy sometimes increases task performance, especially when tasks are complex and non-routine. Thus, while third parties should assist disputants to engage in constructive controversy, they also should seek ways to expand and stimulate the conflict whenever the group's task is complex and non-routine. When tasks are simple and routine, third parties should attempt to mitigate conflict. In addition, research revealed that conflict has negative effects on task performance whenever the focus is socio-emotional rather than task-related. Under all circumstances, third parties should attempt to avoid personal, identity-related issues entering the dispute. Finally, our discussion revealed that in intellective conflict where a correct solution exists, integrative agreements may be less desirable than a victory for one when this victory includes the correct solution. Third parties involved in intellective conflict may assist parties to cope with a victory-to-one solution, for example by compensating the losing disputant.

To intervene, third parties have several 'entry points' at their disposal (Van de Vliert, 1997). Staying close to the conflict-as-a-process-model outlined at the outset, these entry points are: (1) antecedent conditions and conflict issues; (2) conflict experience including cognition, feelings and motivations; (3) conflict behaviors; and (4) anticipated consequences. Van de Vliert argues that escalative intervention at the level of conflict management and (perceived) consequences is preferable to manipulating antecedent conditions and conflict issues because the former strategies require less manipulation and have a less permanent nature than manipulating antecedent conditions and the number or generality of conflict issues. Thus, (de)escalative intervention is more controllable and less permanent as one moves from antecedent conditions and conflict issues via conflict experience to conflict management and (perceived) conflict consequences. Since de-escalation is the primary objective in resource conflict, it seems advisable that third parties seek de-escalative intervention by manipulating antecedent conditions and the number and generality of issues. In the case of information conflict where controlled escalation is sometimes the goal, it seems advisable that third parties seek (de)-escalation by manipulating conflict management and (perceived) conflict consequences. Good overviews of ways to manipulate aspects of the conflict process are given by Fisher (1997), Robbins (1974), Van de Vliert (1997), and Walton (1969).

SUMMARY AND CONCLUSIONS

This chapter discussed resource and information conflict in relation to contextual and task performance. The review led to some new insights and revealed several questions for further research. Some pertain to conflict as a process and have relevance for the conflict literature in particular. Others pertain to conflict as a condition, and have relevance for organizational psychologists in general, and in particular for those interested in performance.

We defined conflict as the tension an individual or group experiences due to perceived differences with another individual or group. Perceived differences relate to interests, access to and distribution of scarce resources (resource conflicts), or to the accuracy, validity, and value of judgments and opinions (intellective and evaluative conflicts). The study of conflict in groups and organizations takes two approaches. The first, traditional approach is to study conflict processes and outcomes. Research in this tradition is predominantly experimental, using well-defined laboratory tasks such as experimental games, distributive and integrative negotiation simulations, and group problem-solving tasks. The second approach is to examine conflict as a condition, as a state in which individuals, groups, or organizations may, or may not be. The second approach is in its infancy and requires development, both theoretically and in terms of research methodology. The current chapter: (1) reviewed evidence on conflict processes in resource, intellective and evaluative conflict; (2) examined evidence on the relationship between conflict conditions and performance; and (3) connected conflict processes and conflict conditions to better understand the relationship between conflict and individual, group, and organizational performance. Below, we summarize the main conclusions and discuss avenues for future research.

Managing Resource and Information Conflict

Several good reviews cover the conflict process (Carnevale & Pruitt, 1992; Levine & Thompson, 1996; Pruitt, in press; Thomas, 1992). The current chapter adds to these reviews three new insights. First, we discover that the five strategies identified in resource conflict (i.e., dominating, yielding, compromising, avoiding, and integrating) have a close parallel in information conflict (i.e., unconflicted adherence, unconflicted change, hypervigilance, defensive avoidance, and vigilance). Thus, we are able to analyze and describe conflict management regardless of whether the conflict concerns resource, intellective, or evaluative issues. This opens up the possibility of examining whether conflict issue influences preferences for conflict management strategies. In addition, it allows us to connect research on bargaining and negotiation (e.g., Carnevale & Pruitt, 1992) with the literature on group decision-making, for which the strategies for dealing with information conflict have been developed (cf., Mann et al., 1997). The negotiation literature suggests variables that stimulate integrative, problem-solving behavior (e.g., Dual Concern Theory, Rubin, Pruitt & Kim, 1994), and it would be interesting to see whether similar factors promote vigilance in information conflict. Vice versa, group decision-making research has generated many variables that stimulate vigilant decision-making, and future research could examine these variables in the context of resource conflict.

Both within resource and within information disputes conflict management appeared highly contingent upon the disputants' competitive, individualistic, or prosocial motivation. In resource conflict, prosocial motivation usually leads to more constructive conflict management (integrating and yielding) than individualistic or competitive motivation. Often this produces higher joint outcomes, and more integrative agreements. In information conflicts we discovered a similar effect. In evaluative conflicts where parties learned other's values and understood their opponent's interests, impasse rate was lower and social perceptions more positive, compared to evaluative conflicts where parties did not learn each other's values or understand their opponent's interests. In intellective conflicts a cooperative motivation reduced conflict much more than an individualistic or competitive motivation, probably because the former leads to more supportive communication. Future research is needed, however, to determine whether a cooperative motivation emphasizes harmony and conflict reduction at the cost of decision quality.

Finally, we uncovered promising evidence to suggest that conflict management in both resource and intellective disputes is more effective when dispositional or situational factors stimulate disputants to engage in thorough, systematic information processing. In resource conflict, systematic information processing promotes conflict reduction and increases the discovery of integrative outcomes (De Dreu & Koole, 1997). In intellective conflict, systematic information processing reduces the inconsistency with which parties apply policies, and thus alleviates an important barrier to conflict reduction (Hagafors & Brehmer, 1983). We have not been able to find studies on the influence of the degree of information processing on behavior and outcomes in evaluative conflicts, and research is needed to uncover whether an increase in systematic information processing is as beneficial in evaluative conflicts as it appears to be in resource and intellective disputes.

That conflict management in resource, intellective and evaluative disputes depends on the disputants' cooperative or egoistic motivation as well as on their tendency to engage in systematic or heuristic information processing begs the question whether motivation and information processing are independent, or interact to influence conflict management and outcomes. Research is only beginning to explore this issue, and suggests that in resource conflict cooperative versus egoistic motivation biases information processing (De Dreu & Boles, in press). An interesting issue for future research is whether heightened tendency to engage in systematic information processing strengthens or dilutes this bias. In addition, future research could examine whether (interactive) effects of motivational orientation and tendency to engage in systematic information processing are equally strong in resource, intellective, and evaluative conflict.

Future research on the management of conflict needs to take a closer look at the various conflict outcomes parties attain. As already mentioned, research tends to confound integrative solutions with equitable, fair distributions of outcomes, and we do not know whether and when conflict parties are willing to sacrifice equity to realize integrative potential, or vice versa. In addition, we need to pay closer attention to attitudinal and affective aspects of conflict outcomes, such as changes in interpersonal attitudes and perceived procedural fairness. Both issues have serious consequences for more distal group processes, and for contextual and task performance.

Contextual and Task Performance

A central goal of the current review was to integrate findings on the relationship between conflict processes on the one hand, and contextual and task performance on the other. Concerning resource conflict, few studies addressed the relationship between conflict and performance, and more systematic research is much needed. The tentative conclusion based on the current review was that resource conflict has a predominantly negative effect on contextual and task performance, except when resource conflict is managed constructively to reach integrative outcomes. Concerning information conflict, more research is available. The conclusion was that information conflict may have both positive and negative effects on contextual and task performance. Negative consequences included absenteeism and reduced continuance commitment, distraction and lower performance ratings by superiors. Positive consequences include greater individual creativity and enhanced team productivity. Negative effects dominate when the information conflict contains many socio-emotional issues, when the group task is simple and routine, or when group members have competitive instead of cooperative goals. Positive effects dominate when there are few socio-emotional issues, the task is complex and non-routine, and group members value openness and cooperation.

Research has examined effects of conflict on conflicting parties, and their contextual and task performance. Research is needed to assess the effects of conflict on group members not involved but witnessing the conflict. Conflict is a vivid and salient event and likely to attract attention and be to surveyed in communication. As such, conflict may energize as well as distract group members who have no stake in the dispute, and do not wish to intervene. Put otherwise, conflict may have effects on contextual and task performance that surpass those involved in the dispute.

Implicit in our discussion was that conflict influences performance, and we did not consider the possibility that performance influences conflict. Space limitations require us to be brief about this extremely important issue. Poor performance, and how to improve, may become a conflict issue and outstanding performance may shape interpersonal attitudes such that conflict escalates less easily. It may well be that conflict and performance influence each other in a spiral yielding exceedingly positive or exceedingly negative outcomes for all.

A particularly important question for future research relates to the fact that almost all research covered in the current chapter examined conflict at one moment in time and ignored temporal processes from a longitudinal perspective (O'Connor, Gruenfeld & McGrath, 1993). Several models of group development exist (Levine & Moreland, 1990) and it would be useful to connect them with conflict management and with the relationship between conflict management and task performance. Conflict may serve different functions at different stages of group development.

The current chapter did not include the role of culture in conflict and performance. There is little research about the effects of conflict on performance in different cultures. Researchers interested in this question will find useful starting points in recent research on cultural differences in conflict management (e.g., Leung, 1987; Ting-Toomey, Gao, Trubisky et al., 1991) and third party intervention (e.g., Elangovan, 1995b). It would be particularly interesting to examine the generality of some of the current conclusions from individualistic to more collectivistic cultures. For example, collectivistic cultures appear more conflict avoidant (Leung, 1987) and third party interventions aimed at stimulating conflict may be far less desirable and effective than they seem to be in individualistic culture.

Distinguishing between resource versus information conflicts yielded some interesting implications for third party intervention. It was argued that third parties may manipulate the origins of the conflict, such as the antecedent conditions and the number and magnitude of the conflict issues, or intervene at the level of conflict experiences and conflict behavior. Since resource conflicts generally reduce contextual and task performance, third parties may seek to reduce the (likelihood of) conflict by manipulating antecedents and issue in the case of resource conflict. Because information conflicts sometimes enhance contextual and task performance, third parties may seek to stimulate (the intensity of) conflict by manipulating conflict experiences and behavior. Since stimulating conflict is playing with fire, manipulating conflict experiences and behavior is more desirable than manipulating antecedents and issue because the former conflict components are more controllable than the latter (Van de Vliert, 1997).

CONCLUSION

This chapter reviewed the literature on conflict involving resources and information. We distinguished between conflict as a process and conflict as a condition, and studied effects on contextual and task performance. Conflict management in both resource and information conflicts improves when parties have a cooperative instead of individualistic or competitive motivation, and when parties have the ability and motivation to engage in systematic information processing. Resource conflict basically hinders performance and only intergroup competition over scarce resources may yield beneficial effects in terms of enhanced individual creativity and intragroup cooperation. Information conflict hinders task performance when it centres on socio-emotional issues, and promotes performance when the group values openness, the conflict focuses on task-related, cognitive issues and the task is complex and non-routine.

ACKNOWLEDGMENTS

Preparation of this chapter was financially supported by a Royal Netherlands Academy of Sciences fellowship and grant NWO 575-31-006 from the Netherlands Organization for Scientific Research, both awarded to Carsten K.W. De Dreu. For the many stimulating discussions and their comments on previous drafts we thank Bianca Beersma, Peter Carnevale, Nel De Dreu-Davidse, Daniel Druckman, Michael Frese, Esther Kluwer, Chris McCusker, Dean Tjosvold, and Evert Van de Vliert.

NOTES

1. Increase in the number of conflict issues is indicative of conflict escalation (Rubin, Pruitt & Kim, 1994). As we will see in the section on conflict over information, conflict escalates to a greater degree when new conflict issues are related to socio-emotional inputs rather than task inputs.
2. Other motivational orientations exist, such as altruism. However, research has shown that approximately 90% of the disputants adopt a competitive, individualistic, or prosocial motivation (e.g., Deutsch, 1973; Kuhlman & Marshello, 1975; McClintock & Liebrand, 1988).

REFERENCES

Alexander, E.R. III (1979). The reduction of cognitive conflict. *Journal of Conflict Resolution*, **23**, 120–138.
Amason, A.C. (1996). Distinguishing the effects of functional and dysfunctional conflict on strategic decision making: Resolving a paradox for top management teams. *Academy of Management Journal*, **39**, 123–148.
Amason, A.C. & Sapienza, H.J. (1996). The effects of top management team size and interaction norms on cognitive and affective conflict. *Journal of Management*, in press.
Amason, A.C. & Schweiger, D. (1997). The effect of conflict on strategic decision making effectiveness and organizational performance. In C.K.W. De Dreu & E. Van de Vliert (Eds), *Using Conflict in Organizations* (pp. 101–115). London: Sage.

Axelrod, R. (1984). *The Evolution of Cooperation*. New York: Basic Books.

Baron, R.S., Kerr, N. & Miller, N. (1993). *Group Process, Group Decision, Group Action*. London: Open University Press.

Bazerman, M.H. (1983). Negotiator judgment. *American Behavioral Scientist*, 27, 211–228.

Ben-Yoav, O. & Pruitt, D.G. (1984a). Accountability to constituents: A two-edged sword. *Organizational Behavior and Human Decision Processes*, 34, 283–295.

Ben-Yoav, O. & Pruitt, D. (1984b). Resistance to yielding and the expectation of cooperative future interaction in negotiation. *Journal of Experimental Social Psychology*, 34, 323–335.

Blake, R.R. & Mouton, J.S. (1964). *The Managerial Grid*. Houston, TX: Gulf.

Borman, W.C. & Motowidlow, S.J. (1993). Expanding the criterion domain to include elements of contextual performance. In N. Schmitt & W. Borman (Eds), *Personnel Selection in Organizations* (pp. 71–98). New York: Jossey-Bass.

Bottom, W.P. & Studt, A. (1993). Framing and distributive aspects of integrative negotiation. *Organizational Behavior and Human Decision Processes*, 56, 459–474.

Brehmer, B. (1976). Social judgement theory and the analysis of interpersonal conflict. *Psychology Bulletin*, 83, 985–1003.

Brehmer, B. & Hammond, K.R. (1976). Cognitive factors in interpersonal conflict. In D. Druckman (Ed.), *Negotiations* (pp. 79–103). Thousand Oaks, CA: Sage.

Brehmer, B. & Joyce, C.R.B. (Eds) (1988). *Advances in Psychology*: Vol. 54. *Human Judgment: The SJT View*. North Holland: Elsevier.

Brockner, J. & Wiesenfeld, B. (1996). An integrative framework for explaining reactions to decisions: Interactive effects of outcomes and procedures. *Psychological Bulletin*, 120, 189–208.

Butler, J.K., Jr (1994). Conflict styles and outcomes in a negotiation with fully-integrative potential. *International Journal of Conflict Management*, 5, 309–325.

Carnevale, P.J. (1986a). Strategic choice in mediation. *Negotiation Journal*, 2, 41–56.

Carnevale, P.J. (1986b). Mediating disputes and decisions in organizations. In R.J. Lewicki, B.H. Sheppard & M.H. Bazerman (Eds), *Research on Negotiation in Organizations* (Vol. 1, pp. 251–270). Greenwich, CT: JAI Press.

Carnevale, P.J. & Conlon, D.E. (1988). Time pressure and strategic choice in mediation. *Organizational Behavior and Human Decision Processes*, 42, 111–133.

Carnevale, P.J., Conlon, D.E., Hanisch, K.A. & Harris, K.L. (1989). Experimental research on the strategic choice model of mediation. In K. Kressel & D.G. Pruitt (Eds), *Mediation Research* (pp. 344–367). San Francisco, CA: Jossey-Bass.

Carnevale, P.J. & Henry, R.A. (1989). Determinants of mediator behavior: A test of the strategic choice model. *Journal of Applied Social Psychology*, 19, 469–488.

Carnevale, P.J. & Isen, A. (1986). The influence of positive affect and visual access on the discovery of integrative solutions in bilateral negotiation. *Organizational Behavior and Human Decision Processes*, 37, 1–13.

Carnevale, P.J. & Lawler, E.J. (1986). Time pressure and the development of integrative agreements in bilateral negotiation. *Journal of Conflict Resolution*, 30, 636–659.

Carnevale, P.J. & Probst, T. (1997). Good news about competitive people. In C.K.W. De Dreu & E. Van de Vliert (Eds), *Using Conflict in Organizations* (pp. 129–146). London: Sage.

Carnevale, P.J. & Pruitt, D.G. (1992). Negotiation and mediation. *Annual Review of Psychology*, 43, 531–82.

Clyman, D.R. (1995). Measures of joint performance in dyadic mixed-motive negotiations. *Organizational Behavior and Human Decision Processes*, 64, 38–48.

Coombs, C.H. (1987). The structure of conflict. *American Psychologist*, 42, 355–363.

Coser, L.A. (1956). *The Functions of Social Conflict*. New York: Free Press.

Cosier, R. & Dalton, D.R. (1990). Positive effects of conflict: A field assessment. *International Journal of Conflict Management*, **1**, 81–92.

Cosier, R. & Rose, G. (1977). Cognitive conflict and goal conflict effects on task performance. *Organizational Behavior and Human Performance*, **19**, 378–391.

Cowherd, D.M. & Levine, D.I. (1992). Product quality and pay equity between lower level employees and top management: An investigation of distributive justice theory. *Administrative Science Quarterly*, **37**, 302–320.

Cropanzano, R. & Greenberg, J. (1997). Progress in organizational justice: Tunneling through the maze. In C.L. Cooper & I.T. Robertson (Eds), *International Review of Industrial and Organizational Psychology* (Vol. 12, pp. 317–372). Chichester: Wiley.

Cross, S. (1995). *Three types of negotiation: Effects on attitudes.* Paper presented at the 8th annual meeting of the International Association for Conflict Management, Elsinore (Denmark), 11–14 June.

De Dreu, C.K.W. (1997). Productive conflict: The importance of conflict management and conflict issue. In C.K.W. De Dreu & E. Van de Vliert (Eds), *Using Conflict in Organizations* (pp. 9–22). London: Sage.

De Dreu, C.K.W. & Boles, T. (in press). Motivated cognition in negotiation: Effects of social value orientation on choice and recall of decision heuristics. Organizational Behavior and Human Decision Processes.

De Dreu, C.K.W., Carnevale, P.J., Emans, B.J.M. & Van de Vliert, E. (1994). Effects of gain–loss frames in negotiation: Loss aversion, mismatching, and frame adoption. *Organizational Behavior and Human Decision Processes*, **60**, 90–107.

De Dreu, C.K.W. & De Vries, N.K. (1997). Minority dissent in organizations. In C.K.W. De Dreu & E. Van de Vliert (Eds), *Using Conflict in Organizations* (pp. 72–86). London: Sage.

De Dreu, C.K.W., Giebels, E. & Van de Vliert, E. (1998). Social motive and trust in integrative negotiation: disruptive effects of punitive capability. *Journal of Applied Psychology*, **83**, 408–422.

De Dreu, C.K.W., Koole, S., & Oldersma, F. (in press). On the seizing and freezing of negotiator inferences: Need for closure moderates the use of cognitive heuristics. *Personality and Social Psychology Bulletin.*

De Dreu, C.K.W. & Koole, S. (1997). Motivated use of heuristics in negotiation. Unpublished MS. University of Amsterdam.

De Dreu, C.K.W., Lualhati, J. & McCusker, C. (1994). Effects of gain–loss frames on satisfaction with self–other outcome-differences. *European Journal of Social Psychology*, **24**, 497–510.

De Dreu, C.K.W. & McCusker, C. (1997). Gain–loss frames and cooperation in two-person social dilemmas. *Journal of Personality and Social Psychology*, **72**, 1093–1106.

De Dreu, C.K.W., Nauta, A. & Van de Vliert, E. (1995). Self-serving evaluations of conflict behavior and escalation of the dispute. *Journal of Applied Social Psychology*, **25**, 2049–2066.

De Dreu, C.K.W. & Van de Vliert, E. (Eds) (1997). *Using Conflict in Organizations*. London: Sage.

De Dreu, C.K.W. & Van Lange, P.A.M. (1995). Impact of social value orientation on negotiator cognition and behavior. *Personality and Social Psychology Bulletin*, **21**, 778–789.

Deutsch, M. (1949). A theory of cooperation and competition. *Human Relations*, **2**, 129–151.

Deutsch, M. (1969). Conflicts: Productive and destructive. *Journal of Social Issues*, **25**, 7–41.

Deutsch, M. (1973). *The Resolution of Conflict: Constructive and Destructive Processes*. New Haven, CT: Yale University Press.

Deutsch, M. (1982). Interdependence and psychological orientation. In V. Derlega & J. Gezelak (Eds), *Cooperation and Helping Behavior* (pp. 15–42). Cambridge: Cambridge University Press.

Deutsch, M. & Gerard, H. (1955). A study of normative and informal social influences upon individual judgment. *Journal of Abnormal and Social Psychology*, 51, 629–636.

Donnellon, A. & Kolb, D. (1997). Constructive for whom? The fate of diversity disputes in organizations. In C.K.W. De Dreu & E. Van de Vliert (Eds), *Using Conflict in Organizations* (pp. 161–176). London: Sage.

Donohue, W.A. (1981). Analyzing negotiation tactics: Development of a negotiation interact system. *Human Communication Research*, 7, 273–287.

Druckman, D. (1994). Determinants of compromising behavior in negotiation. *Journal of Conflict Resolution*, 38, 507–556.

Druckman, D., Korper, S.H. & Broome, B.J. (1988). Value differences and conflict resolution: Facilitation or delinking? *Journal of Conflict Resolution*, 32, 489–510.

Druckman, D., Rozelle, R. & Zechmeister, K. (1976). Conflict of interest and value dissensus: Two perspectives. In D. Druckman (Ed.), *Negotiations* (pp. 105–131). Thousand Oaks, CA: Sage.

Druckman, D. & Zechmeister, K. (1973). Conflict of interest and value dissensus: Propositions in the sociology of conflict. *Human Relations*, 26, 449–466.

Elangovan, A.R. (1995a). Managerial third-party dispute intervention: A prescriptive model of strategy selection. *Academy of Management Journal*, 20, 800–830.

Elangovan, A.R. (1995b). Managerial conflict intervention in organizations: Traversing the cultural mosaic. *International Journal of Conflict Management*, 6, 124–146.

Erev, I., Bornstein, G. & Galili, R. (1993). Constructive intergroup competition as a solution to the free rider problem: A field experiment. *Journal of Experimental Social Psychology*, 29, 463–478.

Fisher, R.J. (1997). Third party consultation as the controlled stimulation of conflict. In C.K.W. De Dreu & E.Van de Vliert (Eds), *Using Conflict in Organizations* (pp. 192–207). London: Sage.

Fisher, R. & Ury, W. (1981). *Getting to Yes: Negotiating Agreement without Giving In*. London: Hutchinson.

Fiske, S.T. & Taylor, S.E. (1991). *Social Cognition*. New York: McGraw-Hill.

Forsyth, D. (1983). *An Introduction to Group Dynamics*. Belmont, CA: Brooks/Cole.

Fry, W.R., Firestone, I.J. & Williams, D.L. (1983). Negotiation process and outcome of stranger dyads and dating couples: Do lovers lose? *Basic and Applied Social Psychology*, 4, 1–16.

Giebels, E., De Dreu, C.K.W. & Van de Vliert, E. (1998). The alternative negotiator as the invisible third. *International Journal of Conflict Management*, 9, 5–21.

Gigone, D. & Hastie, R. (1996). The impact of information on group judgment: A model and computer simulation. In E. Witte & J.H. Davis (Eds), *Understanding Group Behavior* (Vol. 1, pp. 221–252). Hillsdale, NJ: Erlbaum.

Gouldner, A.W. (1960). The norm of reciprocity: A preliminary statement. *American Sociological Review*, 25, 161–178.

Greenhalgh, L. (1987). Interpersonal conflicts in organizations. In C.L. Cooper & I.T. Robertson (Eds), *International Review of Industrial and Organizational Psychology* (Vol. 2, pp. 229–272). Chichester: Wiley.

Hagafors, R. & Brehmer, B. (1983). Does having to justify one's judgments change the nature of the judgment process? *Organizational Behavior and Human Performance*, 31, 223–232.

Harmon, J. & Rohrbauch, J. (1990). Social judgment analysis and small group decision making: Cognitive feedback effects on individual and collective performance. *Organizational Behavior and Human Decision Processes*, 46, 34–54.

Harris, K.L. & Carnevale, P.J. (1990). Chilling and hastening: The influence of third-party power and interests on negotiation. *Organizational Behavior and Human Decision Processes*, 47, 138–160.

Hocker, J.L. & Wilmot, W.W. (1991). *Interpersonal Conflict*. Dubuque, IA: William Brown.

Hoskin, D.-M. & Morley, I.E. (1992). *A Social Psychology of Organizing*. London: Harvester Wheatsheaf.

Hulin, C.L. (1991). Adaptation, persistence, and commitment in organizations. In M.D. Dunnette & L.M. Hough (Eds), *Handbook of Industrial and Organizational Psychology* (2nd edn, pp. 445–506). Palo Alto, CA: Consulting Psychologists Press.

Ilgen, D.R. & Klein, H.J. (1988). Organizational behavior. *Annual Review of Psychology*, **40**, 327–351.

Janis, I.L. (1972). *Victims of Groupthink: A Psychological Study of Foreign-policy Decision and Fiascos*. Boston: Houghton Mifflin.

Janssen, P., Van de Vliert, E. & Veenstra, C. (in press). How task and person conflict shape the role of positive interdependence in management teams. *Journal of Management*.

Jehn, K. (1994). Enhancing effectiveness: An investigation of advantages and disadvantages of value-based intragroup conflict. *International Journal of Conflict Management*, **5**, 223–238.

Jehn, K. (1995). A multimethod examination of the benefits and detriments of intragroup conflict. *Administrative Science Quarterly*, **40**, 256–282.

Jehn, K. (1997). Affective and cognitive conflict in work groups: Increasing performance through value-based intragroup conflict. In C.K.W. De Dreu & E. Van de Vliert (Eds), *Using Conflict in Organizations* (pp. 87–100). London: Sage.

Johnson, D.W. & Johnson, R.T. (1989). *Cooperation and Competition: Theory and Research*. Edina, MN: Interaction Books.

Judd, C.M. (1978). cognitive effects of attitude conflict resolution. *Journal of Conflict Resolution*, **22**, 483–498.

Kahneman, D. & Tversky, A. (1979). Prospect Theory: An analysis of decision under risk. *Econometrica*, **47**, 263–291.

Kaplan, M.F. & Miller, C.E. (1987). Group decision making and normative versus informational influence: Effects of type of issue and assigned decision rule. *Journal of Personality and Social Psychology*, **53**, 306–313.

Karambaya, R. & Brett, J.M. (1989). Managers handling disputes: Third-party roles and perceptions of fairness. *Academy of Management Journal*, **32**, 687–704.

Karambaya, R., Brett, J.M. & Lytle, A. (1992). Effects of formal authority and experience on third-party roles, outcomes, and perceptions of fairness. *Academy of Management Journal*, **35**, 426–438.

Katz, H.C., Kochan, T.A. & Weber, M. (1985). Assessing the effects of industrial relations systems and efforts to improve the quality of working life on organizational effectiveness. *Academy of Management Journal*, **28**, 509–526.

Kelley, H.H. & Thibaut, J. (1969). Group problem solving. In G. Lindzey & E. Aronson (Eds), *The Handbook of Social Psychology* (2nd edn, Vol. 4). Reading, MA: Addison-Wesley.

Klaas, B.S. & DeNisi, A.S. (1989). Managerial reactions to employee dissent: The impact of grievance activity on performance ratings. *Academy of Management Journal*, **32**, 705–717.

Klaas, B.S., Heneman, H.G., III, & Olson, C.A. (1991). Effects of grievance activity on absenteeism. *Journal of Applied Psychology*, **76**, 818–824.

Kluwer, E., De Dreu, C.K.W., Dijkstra, S., Van der Glas, F., Kuiper, A. & Tjosvold, D. (1993). Doelinterdependentie en conflicthantering in profit- en non-profit-organisaties. (Goal interdependence and conflict management in profit and non-profit organizations) *Toegepaste Sociale Psychologie (Applied Social Psychology)*, Eburon: Delft, The Netherlands, 208–218.

Kolb, D. (1986). Who are organizational third parties and what do they do? In R.J. Lewicki, B.H. Sheppard & M.H. Bazerman (Eds), *Research on Negotiation in Organizations* (Vol. 1, pp. 207–228). Greenwich, CT: JAI Press.

Kolb, D. & Bartunek, J. (Eds) (1992). *Hidden Conflict in Organizations: Uncovering Behind the Scenes Disputes.* Newbury Park, CA: Sage.

Komorita, S.S. & Carnevale, P.J. (1992). Motivational arousal versus decision framing in social dilemmas. In W.B.G. Liebrand, D. Messick, & H.A.M. Wilke (Eds), *A Social Psychological Approach to Social Dilemmas* (pp. 209–223). London; Pergamon Press.

Korper, S.H., Druckman, D. & Broome, B.J. (1986). Value differences and conflict resolution. *Journal of Social Psychology,* **126,** 415–417.

Kramer, R.M., Newton, E. & Pommerenke, P.L. (1994). Self-enhancement biases and negotiator judgment: Effects of self-esteem and mood. *Organizational Behavior and Human Decision Processes,* **56,** 110–133.

Kuhlman, D.M. & Marshello, A. (1975). Individual differences in game motivation as moderators of preprogrammed strategic effects in prisoner's dilemma. *Journal of Personality and Social Psychology,* **32,** 922–931.

Lax, D.A. & Sebenius, J.K. (1986). *The Manager as Negotiator: Bargaining for Cooperation and Competitive Gain.* New York: Free Press.

Leung, K. (1987). Some determinants of reactions to procedural models for conflict resolution: A cross-national study. *Journal of Personality and Social Psychology,* **53,** 898–908.

Levine, J.M. & Moreland, R.L. (1990). Progress in small group research. *Annual Review of Psychology,* **41,** 585–634.

Levine, J.M. & Russo, E. (1987). Majority and minority influence. In C. Hendrick (Ed.), *Review of Personality and Social Psychology* (Vol. 8). London: Sage.

Levine, J.M. & Thompson, L.L. (1996). Conflict in groups. In E.T. Higgins & A.W. Kruglanski (Eds), *Social Psychology: Handbook of Basic Principles* (pp. 745–776). New York: Guilford.

Lewicki, R.J. & Sheppard, B.H. (1985). Choosing how to intervene: Factors affecting the use of process and outcome control in third party dispute resolution. *Journal of Occupational Behavior,* **6,** 49–64.

Lewicki, R.J., Litterer, J.A., Minton, J.W. & Saunders, D.M. (1994). *Negotiation.* Boston, MA: Irwin.

Lewicki, R.J., Weiss, S.E. & Lewin, D. (1992). Models of conflict, negotiation, and third party intervention: A review and synthesis. *Journal of Organizational Behavior,* **13,** 209–252.

Lewin, D. (1987). Dispute resolution in the non-union firm: A theoretical and empirical analysis. *Journal of Conflict Resolution,* **31,** 465–502.

Lewin, D. & Peterson, R.B. (1988). *The Modern Grievance Procedure in the United States.* Westport, CT: Quoram.

Lim, R. & Carnevale, P.J. (1990). Contingencies in the mediation of disputes. *Journal of Personality and Social Psychology,* **58,** 259–272.

Loewenstein, G.F., Thompson, L.L. & Bazerman, M.H. (1989). Social utility and decision making in interpersonal contexts. *Journal of Personality and Social Psychology,* **57,** 426–441.

Maier, N.R.F. (1963). *Problem-solving Discussions and Conferences: Leadership Methods and Skills.* New York: McGraw-Hill.

Mann, L., Burnett, P., Radford, M. & Ford, S. (1997). The Melbourne Decision Making Questionnaire: An instrument for measuring patterns for coping with decisional conflict. *Journal of Behavioral Decision Making,* **10,** 1–19.

McCarthy, H. (1977). Some situational factors improving cognitive conflict reduction and interpersonal understanding. *Journal of Conflict Resolution,* **21,** 217–234.

McClintock, C. (1977). Social motives in settings of outcome interdependence. In D. Druckman (Ed.), *Negotiations: Social Psychological Perspective* (pp. 49–77). Beverly Hills, CA: Sage.

McClintock, C.G. & Liebrand, W.B.G. (1988). Role of interdependence, individual orientation, and another's strategy in social decision making: A transformational analysis. *Journal of Personality and Social Psychology*, **55**, 396–409.

Messick, D.M. & Sentis, K.P. (1985). Estimating social and non-social utility functions from ordinal data. *European Journal of Social Psychology*, **15**, 389–399.

Mikolic, J.M., Parker, J.C. & Pruitt, D.G. (1997). Escalation in response to persistent annoyance: Groups versus individuals and gender effects. *Journal of Personality and Social Psychology*, **72**, 151–163.

Morley, I.E. & Stephenson, G.M. (1977). *The Social Psychology of Bargaining*. London: Allen & Unwin.

Neale, M.A. & Bazerman, M.H. (1985). The effects of framing and negotiator overconfidence on bargaining behaviors and outcomes. *Academy of Management Journal*, **28**, 34–49.

Neale, M.A. & Bazerman, M.H. (1991). *Rationality and Cognition in Negotiation*. New York: Free Press.

Nemeth, C. (1986). Differential contributions of majority and minority influence processes. *Psychological Review*, **93**, 10–20.

Nemeth, C. & Kwan, J. (1985). Originality of word associations as a function of majority versus minority influence. *Social Psychology Quarterly*, **48**, 277–282.

Nemeth, C. & Kwan, J. (1987). Minority influence, divergent thinking and detection of correct solutions. *Journal of Applied Social Psychology*, **17**, 786–797.

Nemeth, C.J. & Staw, B.M. (1989). The trade-offs of social control and innovation in groups and organizations. In L. Berkowitz (Ed.), *Advances in Experimental Social Psychology*, **22**, 175–210.

O'Connor, K.M., Gruenfeld, D.H. & McGrath, J.E. (1993). The experience and effects of conflict in continuing work groups. *Small Group Research*, **24**, 362–382.

Olekalns, M., Smith, P.L. & Kibby, R. (1996). Social value orientations and negotiator outcomes. *European Journal of Social Psychology*, **26**, 299–314.

Olson-Buchanan, J.B. (1996). Voicing discontent: What happens to the grievance filer after the grievance? *Journal of Applied Psychology*, **18**, 52–63.

O'Reilly, C. (1991). Organizational behavior: Where we've been; where we're going. *Annual Review of Psychology*, **42**, 427–458.

Organ, D.W. (1988). *Organizational Citizenship Behavior: The Good Soldier Syndrome*. Lexington, MA: Lexington Books.

Peterson, R.S. & Nemeth, C.J. (1995). Focus versus flexibility: Majority and minority influence can both improve performance. *Personality and Social Psychology Bulletin*, **22**, 14–23.

Pfeffer, J. & Langton, N. (1993). The effects of wage dispersion on satisfaction, productivity, and working collaboratively: Evidence from college and university faculty. *Administrative Science Quarterly*, **38**, 382–407.

Pinkley, R. (1990). Dimensions of conflict frame: Disputant interpretations of conflict. *Journal of Applied Psychology*, **75**, 117–126.

Pinkley, R.L. & Northcraft, G.B. (1994). Conflict frames of reference: Implications for dispute processes and outcomes. *Academy of Management Journal*, **37**, 193–205.

Pinkley, R.L., Brittain, J., Neale, M.A. & Northcraft, G.B. (1995). Managerial third-party dispute intervention: An inductive analysis of intervener strategy selection. *Journal of Applied Psychology*, **80**, 386–402.

Pinkley, R.L., Griffith, T.L. & Northcraft, G.B. (1995). 'Fixed Pie' à la Mode: Information availability, information processing, and the negotiation of suboptimal agreements. *Organizational Behavior and Human Decision Processes*, **62**, 101–112.

Podsakoff, P.M., Ahearne, M. & MacKenzie, S.B. (1997). Organizational citizenship behavior and the quantity and quality of work group performance. *Journal of Applied Psychology*, **82**, 262–270.

Pondy, L.R. (1967). Organizational conflict: Concepts and models. *Administrative Science Quarterly*, **12**, 296–320.

Priem, R.L. & Price, K.H. (1991). Process and outcome expectations for the dialectical inquiry, devil's advocacy, and consensus techniques of strategic decision making. *Group and Organization Studies*, **16**, 206–225.

Pritchard, R.D. (1992). Organizational productivity. In M.D. Dunnette & L.M. Hough (Eds), *Handbook of Industrial and Organizational Psychology* (2nd edn, Vol. 3, pp. 443–471). Palo Alto, CA: Consulting Psychologists Press.

Pruitt, D.G. (1981). *Negotiation Behavior*. New York: Academic Press.

Pruitt, D.G. (in press). Social conflict. In D. Gilbert, S.T. Fiske & G. Lindzey (Eds), *Handbook of Social Psychology* (4th edn). New York: McGraw Hill.

Pruitt, D.G. & Carnevale, P.J. (1993). *Negotiation in Social Conflict*. Pacific Grove, CA: Brooks/Cole.

Pruitt, D.G. & Lewis, S.A. (1975). Development of integrative solutions in bilateral negotiations. *Journal of Personality and Social Psychology*, **31**, 621–633.

Pruitt, D.G. & Rubin, J.Z. (1986). *Social Conflict: Escalation, Stalemate, and Settlement*. New York: Random House.

Putnam, L.L. (1983). Small group work climates: A lag sequential analysis of group interaction. *Small Group Behavior*, **14**, 465–494.

Putnam, L.L. (1997). Productive conflict: Negotiation as implicit coordination. In C.K.W. De Dreu & E Van de Vliert (Eds), *Using Conflict in Organizations* (pp. 147–160). London: Sage.

Putnam, L.L. & Holmer, M. (1992). Framing, reframing and issue development. In L.L. Putnam & M.E. Roloff (Eds), *Communication Perspectives on Negotiation*. Thousand Oaks, CA: Sage.

Putnam, L.L. & Jones, T.S. (1982). Reciprocity in negotiations: An analysis of bargaining interaction. *Communication Monographs*, **49**, 171–191.

Rahim, M.A. (1983). Measurement of organizational conflict. *Journal of General Psychology*, **109**, 189–199.

Rahim, M.A. (1992). *Managing Conflict in Organizations*. Westport, CT: Praeger.

Raiffa, H. (1982). *The Art and Science of Negotiation*. Cambridge, MA: Belknap.

Rapoport, A. (1960). *Fights, Games, and Debates*. Ann Arbor: University of Michigan Press.

Reagan-Ciricione, P. (1994). Improving the accuracy of group judgment: A process intervention combining group facilitation, social judgment analysis and information technology. *Organizational Behavior and Human Decision Processes*, **58**, 246–270.

Robbins, S.P. (1974). *Managing Organizational Conflict: A Nontraditional Approach*. Englewood Cliffs, NJ: Prentice-Hall.

Robinson, R.J. (1995). The conflict-competent organization: A research agenda for emerging organizational challenges. In R.M. Kramer & D.M. Messick (Eds), *Negotiation as a Social Process* (pp. 186–204). Thousand Oaks, CA: Sage.

Rose, G.L., Menasco, M.B. & Curry, D.J. (1982). When disagreement facilitates performance in judgment tasks: Effects of different forms of cognitive conflict, information environments, and human information processing characteristics. *Organizational Behavior and Human Performance*, **29**, 287–306.

Ross, W.H. & Wieland, C. (1996). Effects of interpersonal trust and time pressure on managerial mediation strategy in a simulated organizational dispute. *Journal of Applied Psychology*, **81**, 228–248.

Rousseau, D.M. (1997). Organizational behavior in the new organizational era. *Annual Review of Psychology*, **48**, 515–546.

Rubin, J.Z. (1986). Third parties within organizations: A responsive commentary. In R.J. Lewicki, B.H. Sheppard, & M.H. Bazerman (Eds), *Research on Negotiation in Organizations* (Vol. 1, pp. 271–286). Greenwich, CT: JAI Press.

Rubin, J.Z. & Brown, B.R. (1975). *The Social Psychology of Bargaining and Negotiation.* New York: Academic Press.

Rubin, J.Z., Pruitt, D.G. & Kim, S.H. (1994). *Social Conflict: Escalation, Stalemate, and Settlement.* New York: McGraw-Hill.

Sattler, N. & Kerr, N. (1991). Might versus morality: Motivational and cognitive bases for social motives. *Journal of Personality and Social Psychology,* **60,** 756–765.

Saunders, H. (1985). We need a larger theory of negotiation. *Negotiation Journal,* **3,** 249–262.

Schein, E. (1988). *Organizational Psychology.* Englewood Cliffs, NJ: Prentice-Hall.

Schmidt, S.M. & Kogan, T.A. (1972). Conflict: Toward conceptual clarity. *Administrative Science Quarterly,* **17,** 359–370.

Schwarzwald, J., Koslowski, M. & Shalit, B. (1992). A field study of employees' attitudes and behaviors after promotion decisions. *Journal of Applied Psychology,* **77,** 511–514.

Schweiger, D.M., Sandberg, W.R. & Ragan, J.W. (1986). Group approaches for improving strategic decision making: A comparative analysis of dialectical inquiry, devil's advocacy, and consensus. *Academy of Management Journal,* **29,** 51–71.

Schwenk, C.R. (1990). Effects of devil's advocacy and dialectical inquiry on decision making: A meta-analysis. *Organizational Behavior and Human Decision Processes,* **47,** 161–176.

Schwenk, C.R. & Cosier, R.A. (1980). Effects of the expert, devil's advocate, and dialectical inquiry methods on prediction performance. *Organizational Behavior and Human Performance,* **26,** 409–424.

Schulz, J.W. & Pruitt, D.G. (1978). The effects of mutual concern on joint welfare. *Journal of Experimental Social Psychology,* **14,** 480–491.

Sheppard, B.H. (1983). Managers as inquisitors: Some lessons from the law. In M. Bazerman & R.J. Lewicki (Eds), *Negotiation in Organizations.* Beverly Hills, CA: Sage.

Sheppard, B.H. (1984). Third party conflict intervention: A procedural framework. In B. Staw and L. Cummings (Eds), *Research in Organizational Behavior* (Vol. 6, pp. 141–190). Greenwich, CT: JAI Press.

Staw, B.M. (1984). Organizational behavior: A review and reformulation of the field's outcome variables. *Annual Review of Psychology,* **35,** 627–666.

Steiner, I.D. (1972). *Group Processes and Productivity.* New York: Academic Press.

Summers, D.A. (1968). Conflict, compromise, and belief change in a decision-making task. *Journal of Conflict Resolution,* **12,** 215–221.

Tetlock, P.E. (1992). The impact of accountability on judgment and choice: Toward a social contingency model. L. Berkowitz (Ed.), *Advances in Experimental Social Psychology.* (Vol. 25, pp. 331–376). New York: Academic Press.

Thibaut, J. & Walker, L. (1975). *Procedural Justice: A Psychological Analysis.* Hillsdale, NJ: Erlbaum.

Thomas, K.W. (1992). Conflict and negotiation processes in organizations. In M.D. Dunnette & L.M. Hough (Eds), *Handbook of Industrial and Organizational Psychology* (2nd edn, pp. 651–717). Palo Alto, CA: Consulting Psychologists Press.

Thompson, L. (1990). Negotiation behavior and outcomes: Empirical evidence and theoretical issues. *Psychological Bulletin,* **108,** 515–532.

Thompson, L. & Hastie, R. (1990). Social perception in negotiation. *Organizational Behavior and Human Decision Processes,* **47,** 98–123.

Thompson, L. & Hrebec, D. (1996). Lose–lose agreements in interdependent decision making. *Psychological Bulletin,* **120,** 396–409.

Thompson, L. & Loewenstein, G. (1992). Egocentric interpretations of fairness and interpersonal conflict. *Organizational Behavior and Human Decision Processes,* **51,** 176–197.

Ting-Toomey, S., Gao, G., Trubisky, P., Yang, Z., Kim, H.S., Lin, S.-L. & Nishida, T. (1991). Culture, face maintenance, and styles of handling interpersonal conflict: A study in five cultures. *International Journal of Conflict Management*, 2, 253–330.

Tjosvold, D. (1991). *The Conflict-positive Organization*. Reading, MA: Addison-Wesley.

Tjosvold, D. (1997). Conflict within interdependence: Its value for productivity and individuality. In C.K.W. De Dreu & E. Van de Vliert (Eds), *Using Conflict in Organizations* (pp. 23–37). London: Sage.

Tjosvold, D., Dann, V. & Wong, C. (1992). Managing conflict between departments to serve customers. *Human Relations*, 45, 1035–1054.

Tjosvold, D. & Deemer, D.K. (1980). Effects of controversy within a cooperative or competitive context on organizational decision-making. *Journal of Applied Psychology*, 65, 590–595.

Tjosvold, D. & Tsao, Y. (1989). Productive organizational collaboration: The role of values and cooperative goals. *Journal of Organizational Behavior*, 10, 189–195.

Tripp, T. & Sondak, H. (1992). An evaluation of dependent variables in experimental negotiation: Effects of decision rule, agenda, and aspiration. *Organizational Behavior and Human Decision Processes*, 51, 273–295.

Turner, M.E. & Pratkanis, A. (1997). Mitigating groupthink by stimulating constructive conflict. In C.K.W. De Dreu & E. Van de Vliert (Eds), *Using Conflict in Organizations* (pp. 53–71). London: Sage.

Valley, K.L., Neale, M.A. & Mannix, E.A. (1995). Friends, lovers, colleagues, strangers: The effects of relationships on the process and outcomes of negotiations. In R.J. Bies, R.J. Lewicki & B.H. Sheppard (Eds), *Research on Negotiation in Organizations* (Vol. 5, pp. 65–94). Greenwich, CT: JAI Press.

Van den Bos, K., Vermunt, R. & Wilke, H.A.M. (1997). Procedural and distributive justice: What is fair depends more on what comes first than what comes next. *Journal of Personality and Social Psychology*, 72, 95–104.

Van de Vliert, E. (1997). Enhancing performance by conflict-stimulating intervention. In C.K.W. De Dreu & E. Van de Vliert (Eds), *Using Conflict in Organizations* (pp. 208–222). London: Sage.

Van de Vliert, E. & De Dreu, C.K.W. (1994). Optimizing performance by stimulating conflict. *International Journal of Conflict Management*, 5, 211–222.

Van de Vliert, E., Euwema, M.C. & Huismans, S.E. (1995). Managing conflict with a subordinate or a superior: Effectiveness of conglomerated behavior. *Journal of Applied Psychology*, 80, 271–281.

Van de Vliert, E. & Kabanoff, B. (1990). Toward theory-based measures of conflict management. *Academy of Management Journal*, 33, 199–209.

Van de Vliert, E., Nauta, A., Euwema, M. & Janssen, O. (1997). The effectiveness of mixing problem solving and forcing. In C.K.W. De Dreu & E. Van de Vliert (Eds), *Using Conflict in Organizations* (pp. 38–52). London: Sage.

Van Scotter, J.R. & Motowidlow, S.J. (1996). Interpersonal facilitation and job dedication as separate facets of contextual performance. *Journal of Applied Psychology*, 81, 525–531.

Volpato, C., Maass, A., Mucchi-Faina, A. & Vitti, E. (1990). Minority influence and social categorization. *European Journal of Social Psychology*, 20, 119–132.

Wall, J. & Callister, R. (1995). Conflict and its management. *Journal of Management*, 21, 515–558.

Walton, R.E. (1969). *Interpersonal Peacemaking: Confrontations and Third Party Consultation*. Reading, MA: Addison-Wesley.

Walton, R.E. & McKersie, R.B. (1965). *A Behavioral Theory of Labor Negotiations: An Analysis of a Social Interaction System*. New York: McGraw-Hill.

Walton, R.E., Cutcher-Gershenfeld, J.E. & McKersie, R.B. (1994). *Strategic Negotiations: A Theory of Change in Labor–Management Relations*. Boston, MA: Harvard Business School Press.

Weingart, L.R., Bennet, R.J. & Brett, J.M. (1993). The impact of consideration of issues and motivational orientation on group negotiation process and outcome. *Journal of Applied Psychology*, **78**, 504–517.

Weingart, L.R., Hyder, E. & Prietula, M.J. (1996). Knowledge matters: The effect of tactical descriptions on negotiation behavior and outcome. *Journal of Personality and Social Psychology*, **70**, 1205–1217.

Weingart, L.R., Thompson, L.L., Bazerman, M.H. & Carroll, J.S. (1990). Tactical behavior and negotiation outcomes. *International Journal of Conflict Management*, **1**, 7–31.

West, M.A. & Anderson, N.R. (1996). Innovation in top management teams. *Journal of Applied Psychology*, **81**, 680–693.

Wilpert, B. (1995). Organizational behavior. *Annual Review of Psychology*, **46**, 59–90.

Part III

ORGANIZATIONAL ISSUES

Chapter 7

PROGRESS IN ORGANIZATIONAL JUSTICE: TUNNELING THROUGH THE MAZE

Russell Cropanzano
Colorado State University
and
Jerald Greenberg
Ohio State University

One of the topics of greatest interest to scientists in the fields of industrial-organizational psychology, human resources management, and organizational behavior in recent years has been *organizational justice*—people's perceptions of fairness in organizations. Whether we're talking about the fairness of large-scale organizational policies, such as pay systems, or individual practices at the local level, such as determining priorities for vacation scheduling in an office, questions of fairness on the job are ubiquitous. As both scentists and practitioners have become sensitive to the importance of such matters, the literature on organizational justice has proliferated. Witness, for example, the large number of books (e.g. Cropanzano, 1993; Folger & Cropanzano, in press; Greenberg, 1996a; Sheppard, Lewicki, & Minton, 1993; Steensma & Vermunt, 1991; Tyler, 1990; Vermunt & Steensma, 1991), and conceptual articles (e.g. Brockner & Weisenfeld, 1996; Folger, 1994; Greenberg, 1990a, 1993c; Lind, 1995; Lind & Earley, 1992; Tyler & Dawes, 1993; Tyler & Lind, 1992; Tyler & Smith, in press) that have appeared in recent years. Further evidence of the topic's current appeal is reflected by the fact that organizational justice consistently has been among the most popular topics of papers submitted for consideration on the program of the Organizational Behavior Division of the Academy of Management during the years 1993–1995. From our perspective, attention to matters of organizational justice appears to show no sign of abating in the foreseeable future.

With the recent growth in contributions to the organizational justice literature, the need has arisen to gain perspective on the field—to assess where it

---

Progress in Organizational Justice: Tunneling Through the Maze by Russell Cropanzano and Jerald Greenberg taken from IRIOP 1997 v12, Edited by Cary L. Cooper and Ivan T. Robertson: © 1997 John Wiley & Sons, Ltd

has been and where it is going. Insofar as previous reviews of the literature have covered earlier periods, in the present review we will concentrate on work appearing between 1990 and 1995—a span during which considerable growth may have left observers of the organizational justice literature feeling somewhat uncertain as to its major issues and directions. We attempt to remedy this situation in the present chapter. Specifically, we intend to shed light on recent progress in the field of organizational justice by 'tunneling through the maze' of ideas it has generated—highlighting major conceptual and applied advances, and putting them in perspective. In doing so, we hope to help readers see light at the end of the tunnel that may encourage them to enter, and that will guide them in their journey toward understanding organizational justice.

JUSTICE: ITS FUNDAMENTAL NATURE IN ORGANIZATIONS

Before starting this journey, it is important to specify our orientation. In keeping with social science tradition, our treatment of justice is completely *descriptive* in orientation—focusing on people's perceptions of what constitutes fairness, and their reactions to unfair situations. This is in contrast to the large body of work in moral philosophy (e.g. for a review, see Cohen & Greenberg, 1982) which is inherently *prescriptive*, specifying what should be done to achieve justice (for more on this distinction, see Greenberg & Bies, 1992). As such, when organizational scientists talk about justice, they generally are referring to individual perceptions, one's evaluations as to the appropriateness of a given outcome or process. Thus, as the term is used here, justice is subjective —as perceived by a person.

Questions about justice arise whenever decisions are made about the allocation of resources. For example, in organizations the manner in which profits are disbursed among investors or pay is distributed to employees may animate justice concerns. Indeed, the very fact that people work in order to receive economic gains (e.g. pay) and social benefits (e.g. status) suggests that organizations are settings in which matters of justice are likely to be salient (Greenberg & Tyler, 1987). Given the centrality of these outcomes for work life, it should come as no surprise that fairness is something that individuals use to define their relationships to their employers. It is with this idea in mind, that Greenberg (1987a) coined the term 'organizational justice' to refer to theories of social and interpersonal fairness that may be applied to understanding behavior in organizations. In this connection it is important to note that concerns about fairness are not unique to organizations and that much of our understanding of justice is based on other settings and disciplines (for reviews, see Bierhoff, Cohen & Greenberg, 1986; Cohen, 1986; Greenberg & Cohen, 1982a; Tyler & Smith, in press). However, as we will illustrate in this chapter, organizations have proven to be a rich venue for studying matters of fairness. Indeed, we have learned a great deal about organizations by studying justice and a great deal about justice by examining it within organizations.

In general, the study of organizational justice has focused on two major issues: employees' responses to the things they receive—that is, *outcomes*—and the means by which they obtain these outcomes—that is, *procedures*. It is almost tautological to claim that all allocation decisions are about outcomes. In fact, work settings may be characterized by the outcomes stemming from them. For example, performance appraisal results in some rating or ranking, a promotion decision culminates in a new job, a pay review results in a raise, a selection interview results in a hiring decision, and so on. Of course, outcomes also can be negative as well as positive. For example, decisions are also made about how to punish a poor performer, and whom to terminate during cutbacks. Allocations result in a certain configuration or pattern whereby some individuals get more and others get less. Individuals' evaluations of these outcomes are referred to as judgments of *distributive justice* (Leventhal, 1976a).

Although concerns about distributive justice are critical in organizations, and were the first form of justice to capture the attention of organizational scientists (see Greenberg, 1987a), they comprise only part of the story where organizational justice is concerned. Outcomes do not simply appear; they result from a specific set of processes or procedures. For example, people may raise questions about *how* their performance ratings, promotion decisions, pay raises, or selection decisions were determined. Were these based on procedures that are themselves fair? As we will detail in this chapter, people's perceptions of the fairness of the procedures used to determine allocations— referred to as *procedural justice*—are of considerable importance in organizations. Indeed, there are many benefits that result from perceived fair procedures, and problems that result from perceived unfair procedures.

Insofar as the concept of procedural justice was introduced into the study of organizations during a period in which interest in distributive justice was waning (Folger & Greenberg, 1985; Greenberg & Folger, 1983) it quickly became the center of attention among justice researchers (Greenberg & Tyler, 1987). Not surprisingly, contemporary empirical work has emphasized procedural justice. The balance of material in the present chapter reflects this trend: Although we review recent investigations of both types of fairness, procedural justice receives somewhat more attention. This skew reflects only the prevailing balance of attention in the literature, and not our judgment about their relative importance. Indeed, we have advocated the importance of both distributive and procedural justice in our own work (e.g. Folger & Cropanzano, in press; Greenberg, 1996a).

In the first half of this chapter we will review the latest advances in both distributive justice and procedural justice. We will discuss the basic concepts and review recent evidence examining these concepts within work organizations. Following a historical perspective, we will first examine distributive justice and then move to procedural justice. In the third section we will discuss recent evidence concerning the manner in which these two types of justice operate jointly to predict work outcomes. Then, in the second half of the chapter we will review organizational justice research focusing on applications. Specifically, we will describe evidence demonstrating the role of justice in various organizational practices and phenomena, such as strategic planning, staffing, drug testing, conflict-resolution, layoffs, organizational citizenship behavior, and employee theft. Throughout this chapter we will not only critically analyze the present state of knowledge, but also make recommendations for new directions that deserve to be taken in the future.

DISTRIBUTIVE JUSTICE

The concept of distributive justice can be traced back to Aristotle's *Nichomachean Ethics*: 'that which is manifested in distributions of honour or money or the things that fall to be divided among those who have a share in the constitution' (Ross, 1925, Book V, p. 1130). However, it was Homans (1961) whose conceptualization provided the modern roots of attention to distributive justice. According to Homans' 'rule of distributive justice', it is expected among parties to a social exchange relationship: (i) that the reward of each will be proportional to the costs of each, and (ii) that net rewards, or profits, will be proportional to their investments. Extending this concept to the context of organizations, Adams (1965) proposed his theory of inequity, according to which people are motivated to avoid the tension that results from states in which the ratio of one's own outcomes (i.e. rewards) compared to one's inputs (i.e. contributions) is unequal to the corresponding ratio of a comparison other. Complete historical overviews of these concepts are beyond the scope of the present work; for more information the reader is invited to consult Cohen and Greenberg (1982), Greenberg (1982), Törnblom (1990) and Tyler and Smith (in press). Following the lead of these earlier works, a distinction may be made between studies of how people judge and respond to unfair distributions (i.e. research focusing on recipients' behavior) and people's decisions about the allocation norms that should be followed (i.e. research focusing on allocators' behavior). Several studies within each category have been conducted in recent years.

Reactions to Allocation Outcomes

The study of distributive justice in organizations today focuses primarily on people's perceptions of the fairness of the outcomes (benefits or punishments) they receive—that is, their evaluations of the end state of the allocation process. In keeping with traditional equity theory research (for a review, see Greenberg, 1982), contemporary studies have found that people tend to be less satisfied with outcomes they perceive to be unfair than those they perceive to be fair. Such perceptions have been shown to result in poor performance (e.g. Cowherd & Levine, 1992; Pfeffer & Langton, 1993) and high rates of withdrawal behavior, such as turnover and absenteeism (e.g. Hulin, 1991;

Schwarzald, Koslowsky, & Shalit, 1992). In view of these costly consequences of perceived distributive injustice, and following from earlier conceptualizations (e.g. Leventhal, Karuza, & Fry, 1980), recent work has focused on understanding the processes by which individuals form judgments of distributive fairness.

This process is more complex than one may expect on an intuitive basis. It is not simply the case that people's perceptions of fairness are determined exclusively by self-fulfiling motives—that is, the more one gets, the more satisfied one is (although this motive is potent, to be sure; Greenberg, 1983, 1987b). One's absolute level of resources, in and of itself, is only one determinant of fairness (Summers & Hendrix, 1991; Sweeney, McFarlin, & Inderrieden, 1990). Rather, individuals base their evaluations of distributive justice not only one what they receive, but as suggested by Homans (1961) and Adams (1965), what they receive *relative* to some standard or referent. Although the comparative nature of distributive standards is rooted in theory, confusion has long existed in the literature as to the choice of comparison standards (Austin, 1977).

This is especially true in organizations, where comparison standards are often social in nature. For example, people may evaluate the fairness of their own pay by comparing it to the pay believed to be received by someone else. There are also other referent standards that may be used. For example, people may compare the adequacy of the rewards they receive to their expectations, needs, or general societal norms. This practice is quite plausible insofar as the value of many organizational outcomes cannot be classified objectively. Consequently, these evaluations can be based solely on social comparisons. Consider, for example, an outcome such as pay. The fairness of a specific level of pay may be difficult to evaluate in the absence of information about job title, the pay of similar others, one's pay history, and the like. Only by reference to such standards can pay outcomes be judged as 'adequate' or 'inadequate'. These issues are discussed in greater detail by Kulik and Ambrose (1992), and also have been the subject of recent research.

Illustrating the dynamics of referent standards, Sweeney, McFarlin, and Inderrieden (1990) measured pay satisfaction, actual salary, and various sorts of referents (including both social comparisons and personal expectations) in three large-scale survey studies. They found that although salary level was related to satisfaction, the various referents contributed substantial variance beyond objective information about the amount of one's income. Apparently, satisfaction with outcomes is determined not only by the magnitude of the outcomes received, but also by how these outcomes compare to referent standards.

The results of such comparisons have been found to affect important organizational outcomes. Consider, for example, Schwarzwald, Koslowsky, and Shalit's (1992) field study of work attitudes and absenteeism among individuals being considered for promotion. After failing to earn new positions, individuals had increases in absenteeism, and experienced lower feelings of commitment and higher feelings of inequity. The researchers reasoned that the promoted coworkers acted as referents. That is, individuals who were not initially disadvantaged now felt inequitably underpaid relative to those who had earned a promotion. Such inequities can have adverse effects on job performance. For example, Cowherd and Levine (1992) found that workers produced higher quality products when there was only a small pay differential between themselves and managers compared to when this differential was large. To the extent that large differences may have been perceived to be undeserved in view of relative work contributions, it follows from equity theory that people would withold their inputs, thereby accounting for the results. This finding is consistent with several classic tests of equity theory reporting that inequitably underpaid individuals produce low quality goods (for a review, see Greenberg, 1982).

A limitation of these studies—indeed, of most distributive justice research—is that the investigators measured people's referents and fairness perceptions at only a single point in time. This is problematic insofar as people's choices of referents may be dynamic and adjust to changing conditions. This possibility was demonstrated in a longitudinal study by Stepina and Perrewe (1991). These researchers first measured employees' comparative referents with regard to four job facets: compensation, security, job complexity, and supervision. Then, two years later these measures were readministered to the same participants. With regard to the security, job complexity, and supervision facets, referent choice was stable among those who perceived themselves to be advantaged relative to their referents. In contrast, those who believed themselves to be relatively disadvantaged were more likely to select a new (and lower) referent, thereby producing greater felt equity. However, for the compensation facet, consistent standards were used throughout the two-year period. People were less likely to alter their compensation referents and maintained the same points of comparison for the duration of the study. This stability existed even among employees who felt they were disadvantaged. Insofar as these findings illustrate the dynamic nature of referent comparisons—at least with respect to some dimensions—care needs to be exercised in interpreting people's reactions to inequity.

We close this section by pointing to some unfinished business: drawing a distinction between outcomes that are *unfavorable*, and those that are *unfair* from a distributive justice perspective. An unfavorable outcome is one that is not as advantageous as it could be, whereas an unfair outcome is one that is lower than it should be compared to some referent. Indeed, receiving a low allocation of a desired resource may be considered quite fair to the extent that one's limited contributions so merit. Although this distinction is conceptually explicit, some researchers have been more careful about separating these two constructs than others (for discussions of this problem, see Flinder & Hauenstein, 1994; Lind & Tyler, 1988; Lowe & Vodanovich, 1995). To take but two examples, both Cropanzano and Folger (1991) and Brockner and Wiesenfeld (in press) use the two terms interchangeably. This practice creates considerable conceptual confusion insofar as it can become unclear whether certain predictions or findings apply to outcomes that are inequitable, or simply unfavorable. Accordingly, we encourage future researchers to be more careful about distinguishing between these two terms.

Reward Allocation Behavior

Thus far, we have discussed distributive justice only from the perspective of the person who receives the allocation. If that allocation is believed to be inappropriate relative to some standard, then the recipient is likely to experience distributive injustice. However, following the work of Leventhal (1976a), we also can consider distributive justice from the perspective of the individual making the allocation. Indeed, several recent studies (e.g. Kabanoff, 1991; Skitka & Tetlock, 1992) have examined the rules by which decision makers distribute resources.

Perhaps the easiest way to describe decision rules is to start with the case that is presumed to be philosophically 'pure'—that is, a situation in which self-interest is eliminated, a condition of impartiality. To achieve this hypothetical state, the philosopher John Rawls (1971) proposed a thought experiment referred to as the 'original position'. Imagine that a group of people have assembled to plan a future society. They possess a rudimentary understanding of human nature, interpersonal relationships, and so on. However, they know absolutely nothing about the future economy, technology, or challenges that their new civilization will face. The planners even lack knowledge about themselves and the other people with whom they will be sharing their new society. No one knows what their own social position, abilities, and even preferences will be. In other words, everyone in the planning group is working from behind a 'veil of ignorance'. It is impossible to be self-serving when one does not even know one's own interests! Under these conditions, Rawls (1971) believed that individuals would decide to divide benefits in a way that made the worst-off person as well-off as possible. In other words, things would probably be allocated based on a rule of equality, or perhaps even need (cf. Deutsch, 1975).

The conditions necessary to test Rawls' (1971) supposition can never exist in the real world. No one can actually set-up a new society behind a veil of ignorance. However, the 'original position' can be approximated in the laboratory. In two imaginative experiments, Lissowski, Tyszka, and Okrasa (1991) had Polish undergraduates perform an experimental task. Before beginning, the students had to agree on a payment rule; some individuals could be paid more generously than others. After (or if) the group had reached a decision, individuals were assigned to their payment condition by lot. The bulk of these groups were able to reach consensus regarding a payment rule. However, they did not behave as suggested by Rawls (1971). Instead, subjects selected a distribution principle that maximized the average income (not the minimum income, as Rawls suggested), while simultaneously maintaining a so-called 'floor constraint'. That is, individuals also retained a minimum income for the worst-off member of their 'society'. Similar results were obtained by Frohlich, Oppenheimer, and Eavy (1987a,b) using samples of American and Canadian subjects. Although this situation is artificial in the extreme, the findings underscore a key point: When allocators do not know what outcomes will benefit themselves, they take steps to ensure their own well-being, and that of all concerned.

The implications of this fact come into focus when we consider that people generally make allocation decisions with some specific purpose in mind—typically either normative (e.g. being fair) or instrumental (e.g. stimulating performance or maintaining harmony) in nature (Greenberg & Cohen, 1982b; Skitka & Tetlock, 1992). For example, Kabanoff (1991), James (1993), and Martin and Harder (1994) all maintain that people in North American organizations are likely to distribute economic resources based upon a rule of equity. That is, rewards are assigned on the basis of merit: Those who contribute the most, earn the most. Kabanoff (1991) argues that equity distributions are used to spur productivity (for additional evidence see also James, 1993). The basic idea is simple (and consistent with expectancy theory; Vroom, 1964): To the extent that better performers receive higher rewards, people desiring these rewards will strive to attain high levels of performance (cf. Deutsch, 1975, 1985).

However, the matter appears to be more complicated than decision makers may realize. Although research does suggest that equitable rewards can boost positive work behaviors, such as work performance (Greenberg, 1990a; Sheppard, Lewicki, & Minton, 1993), this is by no means a foregone conclusion. The problem managers face is in ensuring that individuals on the low end of the pay scale will perceive their pay as equitable. Those who receive the allocations may not have the same perceptions as those who make them. If they do not, then it seems possible that an attempt to create equity from the organization's perspective could create unfair resource dispersion from the perspective of disadvantaged employees. To the extent that this occurs, the performance-boosting benefits of 'equity' (as defined by the persons assigning the outcomes) will simply not result. In fact, performance may even decline (cf. Greenberg & Cohen, 1982).

Evidence bearing on this point is provided in a noteworthy study by Pfeffer and Davis-Blake (1992) examining 'wage dispersion' (i.e. variability in salary) among university and college administrators. When wage dispersion was high, turnover was lower among individuals with high salaries and higher among individuals with low salaries. In a follow-up study among university and college faculty, Pfeffer and Langton (1993) found that as salary dispersion increased, research productivity dropped and faculty became less collaborative.

Harder (1992) reached similar conclusions in a study of professional athletes. To the extent that the colleges and universities were attempting to achieve pay equity (and it seems unlikely that they would be doing otherwise), their efforts would appear to have failed. Not only did performance fail to improve, but in some cases it declined. This is not to say that equity is unimportant. In fact, Greenberg (1990a), Kulik and Ambrose (1992), Sheppard, Lewicki, & Minton (1993), and Cropanzano and Randall (1993) all review evidence demonstrating that equity can indeed lead to positive work behaviors. However, the equitable feelings that produce these benefits are based on the perceptions of the recipient, and these may *not* coincide with those of the decision maker.

Our discussion thus far has focused on only one organizational reward—pay. Although money is a critically important reward in organizations (Miceli, 1993; Miceli & Lane, 1991), it is not the only reward that is distributed. Indeed, in their classic resource exchange theory, Foa and Foa (1974) have described a variety of valued resources that may be allocated following different normative standards than those which may be used for distributing money. In keeping with this tradition, the allocation of neo-economic outcomes has been studied in two in-basket experiments conducted by Martin and Harder (1994). Participants in these studies were managers who were asked to divide hypothetical rewards between recipients. Some of the rewards were financial (e.g. profits) and others were socioemotional (e.g. friendliness). The researchers found that different types of rewards were allocated following different standards. Specifically, whereas socioemotional rewards were most frequently divided equally, financial rewards were most frequently divided in accordance with people's relative contributions (i.e. equitably). These findings suggest that although it may be considered distributively fair to distinguish between recipients with respect to financial rewards, considered to be deserved by virtue of meritorious contributions, socioemotional rewards are not considered suitable for distinction in this manner. Rather, socioemotional rewards deserve to be provided equally to all, regardless of their performance-relevant contributions. This is in keeping with research showing that allocators are reluctant to distinguish between recipients with whom they have friendly relations (for a review and conceptual model, see Greenberg & Cohen, 1982b).

Another variable shown to influence the making of reward-allocation decisions is national culture (for a review, see Gergen, Morse, & Gergen, 1980). As Greenberg (1982) concluded a decade-and-a-half ago after reviewing cross-cultural differences in the use of justice norms, 'cultural norms of various nations appear to make the equity norm more or less prevalent' (p.424). Among the most reliable cultural differences found has been the tendency for people from collectivistic societies, such as the Chinese, to prefer equal allocations insofar as these promote group harmony, and for people from individualistic societies, such as Americans, to prefer equitable allocations insofar as allocations proportional to contributions promote productivity (Miles & Greenberg, 1993). Although such findings are consistent with Hofstede's (1980) conceptualization of culture, an emphasis on cultural differences diverts attention from the more immediate situational demands of a social setting. Recognizing this possibility, James (1993) and Triandis (1994) have raised the possibility that different cultures may value different transactional goals, and that these may be met by following different allocation practices.

Testing this notion, Bond, Leung, and Schwartz (1992, Study 1) had undergraduates from Israel and Hong Kong allocate rewards among members of a work group and indicate why they had made their allocation decisions. Interestingly, they found that the preferred distributions were largely based on subjects' expectancies that their decisions would produce positive consequences. In other words, the decision was not based on what was valued by their culture, but instead, on the outcomes one could expect to obtain: Subjects followed either equity or equality, depending on their beliefs about the consequences of doing so. Cultural differences by themselves did a limited job of predicting allocation behavior.

Chen (1995) has suggested that this may be the case because cultural differences are subject to change over time, and that multiple cultural forces may make preferences for allocation norms uncertain. Moreover, cultural differences in sensitivity to various goals are dynamic in nature. For example, there have been recent shifts in goal priorities within both American and Chinese companies: American organizations have become more humanistic, and less likely to be driven purely by profit, whereas Chinese organizations (following reforms initiated in 1978) have become more profit-driven, and less driven by interest in achieving harmony. As a result of these changes, Chen (1995) predicted that employees of contemporary American organizations would prefer equal allocations of material rewards whereas their Chinese counterparts would prefer equitable allocations. Chen had large numbers of American and Chinese employees of various companies, and at various levels, complete an in-basket exercise that allowed them to express preferences for various reward-allocation practices. It was found that allocation preferences were in keeping with the cultural shifts Chen described: Americans were more likely to make equal allocations of rewards, whereas the Chinese were more likely to make equitable allocations of rewards. Although these findings are completely opposite to those long noted, they illustrate the same dynamic in operation: People make reward allocation decisions that are consistent with the goals that are salient at the time, and these may well be reliably differentiated by culture. In fact, it is precisely because of this reversal that our confidence in the validity of this phenomenon is enhanced.

PROCEDURAL JUSTICE

In the mid-1970s several theorists (e.g. Deutsch, 1975, Leventhal, 1976b; Thibaut & Walker, 1975) first called our attention to the idea that justice demands paying attention not only to the 'ends' of social exchange, but also to the 'means' whereby those ends are attained. As noted earlier, this idea has been referred to as *procedural justice*—the perceived fairness of the procedures used to determine outcomes. Thibaut and Walker's (1975) research comparing various legal systems led to the conclusion that procedures perceived to be fair are ones that give people a voice in the procedures affecting them. Around this same time, Leventhal (1976b, 1980; Leventhal, Karuza, & Fry, 1980) proposed that fair processes involve more than just voice. He argued that procedures may be considered fair to the extent that they adhere to six criteria—they are: applied consistently, free from bias, accurate, correctable, representative of all concerns, and based on prevailing ethical standards. A few years later, Greenberg and his associates (e.g. Folger & Greenberg, 1985; Greenberg, 1987a; Greenberg & Folger, 1983; Greenberg & Tyler, 1987) articulated how the concept of procedural justice may be applied to the study of organizations. The subsequent work in this area has been considerable (for reviews, see Greenberg, 1990a, 1996; Sheppard, Lewicki, & Minton, 1993; Tyler & Smith, in press), and has seen a great deal of conceptual and practical development during the period covered by this review.

Perhaps the major reason for the popularity of the study of procedural justice in organizations is that fair procedures have been associated with a wide variety of desirable outcomes. For example, substantial evidence has demonstrated that procedurally fair treatment makes individuals more accepting of smoking bans (Greenberg, 1994a), pay systems (Miceli, 1993; Miceli & Lane, 1991), parental leave policies (Grover, 1991), and disciplinary actions (Ball, Treviño, & Sims, 1994). In fact, justice concerns appear to feature prominently in virtually all human resource interventions (for reviews see Folger & Cropanzano, in press; Greenberg, 1996a; Tyler & Smith, in press). Generally, people are more accepting of decisions that result from fair procedures than those that result from unfair procedures.

Furthermore, people who accept organizational decisions tend to cooperate with authority figures (Lind, 1995; Tyler & Dawes, 1993; Tyler & Lind, 1992). This occurs even among people who are harmed or inconvenienced by their organizations in some way—the very individuals whose favor may be difficult to court. For example, Tyler and Degoey (1995) found that the more strongly individuals believed that officials went about making water-rationing decisions on a fair basis, the more likely they were to cooperate with those decisions. Similarly, Greenberg (1994a) found that smokers more strongly accepted a smoking ban when they believed it was imposed by their company following fair procedures than when following unfair procedures. In another context, Schaubroeck, May, and Brown (1994) found that salaried employees reacted less negatively to a pay freeze when that freeze was implemented in a procedurally fair fashion than when it was implemented in an unfair fashion. Similarly, Greenberg (1990b) found that people were less likely to steal in response to pay cuts when these appeared to be the result of fair procedures than when they stemmed from unfair procedures. Taken together, these findings illustrate that the effectiveness of organizational procedures may be enhanced by incorporating process attributes that are perceived to be fair.

However, the matter is more involved than this. Employees use their experience with fair or unfair allocation procedures as information that reflects on the organization as a whole. As such, procedural fairness may be used as the basis by which people establish larger relationships with their employers, enhancing their loyalty toward the organization and their willingness to exert effort on its behalf (Tyler & Lind, 1992). In this regard, research has shown that compared to those who believe that their organizations' decision-making processes are unfair, those who perceive them to be fair exhibit higher levels of organizational commitment (Tyler, 1991), greater trust in management (Konovsky & Pugh, 1994), lower turnover intentions (Dailey & Kirk, 1992), a lower likelihood of litigation (Bies & Tyler, 1993), more generous citizenship behaviors (Konovsky & Pugh, 1994; Organ & Moorman, 1993), and to some extent, higher job performance (although the evidence for this connection is tentative, see Gilliland, 1994; Konovsky & Cropanzano, 1991; Lee, 1995).

Clearly, procedural justice has wide-ranging beneficial effects on organizational functioning. In this light, we will examine the components of procedural justice in more detail. When people make fairness evaluations they appear to be sensitive to two distinct 'focal determinants' (Greenberg, 1993b): *structural determinants*—those dealing with the environmental context within which interaction occurs—and *social determinants*—those dealing with the treatment of individuals. We will now turn our attention to each of these. Following this discussion, we will address the issue of *why* procedural justice produces the beneficial effects described above.

Structural Aspects of Procedural Justice

From a structural perspective a procedure may be considered procedurally fair to the extent that it is based on explicit formal organizational policies that people expect to lead to fair distributions (Greenberg, 1993b). The central issue investigated in this regard has to do with identifying the specific determinants of procedural fairness. Both Thibaut and Walker's (1975) findings about the importance of voice and Leventhal's (1976b, 1980; Leventhal, Karuza, & Fry, 1980) list of six criteria have proven useful in this regard, although these guidelines are highly abstract and general in nature.

In the past few years, however, several theorists have built upon these conceptualizations by proposing various structural determinants of procedural justice that are expected to operate in specific organizational settings. For example:

● Building on the empirical work of Greenberg (1986a), Folger, Konovsky, and Cropanzano (1992) proposed that three factors contribute to the

perceived fairness of performance evaluations: adequate notice, fair hear-
ing, and judgment based on evidence—each of which has been supported in
empirical research (Taylor, Tracy, Renard, Harrison, & Carroll, 1995).

- In the context of strategic planning, Kim and Mauborgne (1991, 1993)
  identified such process attributes as bilateral communication, ability to re-
  fute, consistency, and the presence of a social account as determinants of
  fairness.

- In the domain of workplace drug screening, Konovsky and Cropanzano
  (1993), reviewed research suggesting that fair drug screening procedures
  are ones that are accurate, allow for corrections to be made, provide opportunities for voice, and that are administered with advance notice. With the
  exception of this last criterion, these other variables are all completely predictable from procedural justice theories.

- Gilliland (1993) identified nine procedural rules expected to enhance the
  fairness of personnel selection decisions: job relatedness, the opportunity to
  perform, reconsideration opportunity, consistency, feedback, selection information, honesty, two-way communication, and the propriety of questions. Although these are closely linked to procedural justice theories,
  Gilliland (1993) also identified two additional rules that may contribute to
  the perceived fairness of selection decisions, but which have not been previously identified by justice theorists: ease of faking answers, and the invasiveness of questions.

For the most part, these contributions have identified determinants of fairness
consistent with Leventhal's (1976b, 1980) rules and the use of voice identified
by Thibaut and Walker (1975). In keeping with earlier studies (Greenberg,
1986; Sheppard & Lewicki, 1987), it would appear that these general determinants of fairness *do* apply in organizations although they may take different
forms in different contexts. Moreover, it is also possible that some unique
determinants of fairness manifest themselves in different organizational settings.

The notion that procedural fairness may be context-sensitive is not meant to
imply that completely idiosyncratic criteria are used in different settings—that
is, justice is not totally context-specific. Rather, it appears that many of the
same general procedural guidelines are brought to all organizational environments although their relative weights and specific forms are shaped by the
demands of the context in which they operate. In other words, general determinants of fairness may come to life by being altered to fit their settings. It is
with this idea in mind that Greenberg (1996a) has recommended carefully
tailoring measures of procedural justice to the specific settings in which they
are being assessed: 'What makes a set of questions appropriate in one context
may not make them equally appropriate in another. Questions about justice
should be carefully matched to the context of interest . . .' (p.402). To the
extent that research measures tapping justice perceptions are context-
sensitive, our confidence in interpreting them may be enhanced.

Social Aspects of Procedural Justice

Following largely from the work of Bies and his associates (e.g. Folger & Bies, 1989; Greenberg, Bies, & Eskew, 1991; Tyler & Bies, 1990), interest in the structural aspects of procedural justice has been supplemented by the social aspects of procedural justice. The basic idea is that people are concerned with the quality of the interpersonal treatment they receive at the hands of decision-makers—what many researchers have referred to as *interactional justice* (Bies & Moag, 1986). In tracing the history of this concept, Greenberg (1993b) noted that interactional justice was originally treated as a separate construct, a third type of justice (e.g. Bies, 1987). Although subsequent research demonstrated the importance of interpersonal determinants of fairness, the concept became increasingly difficult to distinguish from structural procedural justice. For one thing, both the formal procedures and the interpersonal interactions jointly comprise the process that leads to an allocation decision. Additionally, inter-actional and structural procedural justice had similar consequences and correlates (e.g. Clemmer, 1993). Indeed, some studies found them to be highly related to one another (e.g. Konovsky & Cropanzano, 1991; Koper, Van Knippenberg, Bouhuijs, Vermunt, & Wilke, 1993). For these reasons, most current researchers now treat interactional justice as a social aspect of procedural fairness as opposed to separate forms of justice (e.g. Tyler & Bies, 1990; Tyler & Lind, 1992), and we will follow suit.

Following the lead of Greenberg (1993b) and Tyler and Bies (1990) we also will distinguish between two aspects of interpersonal treatment. The first is *social sensitivity*—the extent to which people believe that they have been treated with dignity and respect. The second is *informational justification*—the extent to which people believe they have adequate information about the procedures affecting them. Below we discuss each.

Social sensitivity: The role of dignity and respect

Although it is commonsensical to claim that people like being treated in an interpersonally sensitive manner, it represents a conceptual extension to claim that such treatment contributes to perceptions of fairness. Indeed, several researchers have found that treating people with dignity and respect enhances their perceptions of fairness and their acceptance of the outcomes associated with the discussion. For example, in their study of grievance resolution procedures used by coal miners, Shapiro and Brett (1993) found that fair decisions were believed to be made by adjudicating parties who demonstrated high degrees of knowledge, impartiality, and a willingness to consider the grievants' perspectives and feelings. Similarly, in a field experiment Greenberg (1994a) had company officials explain a pending company-wide smoking ban to workers in a manner that demonstrated either high or low levels of sensitivity to the nature of the disruption they were likely to face. As expected, he found that employees were more accepting of the ban, believing it to be fairer, when higher levels of sensitivity were shown.

Interestingly, it is not only perceptions of fairness that are enhanced by socially sensitive treatment, but a general reluctance to retaliate against harmdoers in response to unfair outcomes. For example, Greenberg (1994b) studied theft reactions following from underpayment. Although all underpaid people stole, those who were treated in a disrespectful manner stole objects that were of no value to themselves, but that were of value to their employers. In other words, disrespectful treatment, adding insult to the injury of unfair treatment, encouraged people to retaliate against their employers—seeking to harm them in exchange for harming themselves, even if so doing did nothing more than even the score between them symbolically.

It is important to note that the importance of social sensitivity as a determinant of justice is not limited to Americans. Leung, Chiu, and Au (1993) conducted a study in Hong Kong in which they examined observers' responses to hypothetical industrial actions such as strikes and sit-ins. Respondents were found to be more sympathetic to industrial actions when management had treated workers with a lack of consideration and respect. This research provides a useful cross-cultural addition to the burgeoning literature on the social determinants of fairness. More such cross-cultural work of this type is needed (cf. Lind & Earley, 1992), not only to determine the generalizability of existing phenomena, but also to determine the extent to which normative differences with respect to politeness and social sensitivity qualify existing conclusions.

Informational justification: The role of social accounts

In addition to fairness defined in terms of courteous treatment, research also supports the idea that fairness demands having access to information regarding the reasons underlying how outcomes are determined. For example, Daly and Geyer (1994) surveyed employees' reactions to a major facilities relocation. They found that individuals responded more positively when the move was adequately explained than when no such explanation was given. In a follow-up study, these same researchers found that adequate explanations were effective in maintaining workers' feelings of organizational commitment during periods of organizational decline (Daly & Geyer, 1995). The benefits of informational justifications for undesirable outcomes have been exhibited consistently in several additional empirical studies conducted in a wide variety of settings (e.g. Brockner, DeWitt, Grover, & Reed, 1990; Greenberg, 1993a, 1994a; Konovsky & Folger, 1991a; Schaubroeck, May & Brown, 1994). All of these studies demonstrate that providing people with information that justifies the need for negative outcomes enhances the extent to which they come to accept those outcomes as fair.

Recent studies have examined various characteristics of informtion that contribute to its perceived adequacy in mitigating reactions to undesirable outcomes. For example, in a laboratory study Shapiro (1991) assessed the perceived adequacy of three different types of causal accounts: an external attribution to an uncontrollable event, an internal attribution to an altruistic motive, and an internal attribution to a selfish motive. She found that the most effective excuses were external in nature, events over which actors had no control. By contrast, explanations that led to the belief that the actor was selfish were considered least adequate. In fact, explanations that are not particularly convincing might not only be inadequate when it comes to cultivating positive impressions, but may backfire, leading to negative impressions (Greenberg, 1996b).

It is not only the adequacy of information that contributes to its effectiveness in mitigating reactions to unfair situations, but also the medium by which that information is conveyed. In this connection, Shapiro, Butner, and Barry (1994, Study 2) compared the perceived adequacy of accounts presented in face-to-face verbal interaction and in written notes. They found that the added richness of face-to-face verbal interaction enhanced perceptions of the adequacy of messages compared to the same messages presented in written form. These findings are in keeping with earlier studies suggesting that commUnciations media differ with respect to the degree of information they convey, and that richer media are considered preferable for communicating socially sensitive information (Lengel & Daft, 1988). In an era in which working people frequently interact by using such impersonal means as computers, fax machines, and satellite transmissions, Shapiro, Batner, and Barry's (1994, Study 2) findings are worthy of further consideration.

Not only might information presented via one medium be more effective than the same information presented via another medium, but also, the same explanation may be more effective in some situations than in others. Brockner et al. (1990) examined this possibility using a sample of layoff survivors. Although survivors responded negatively when their coworkers lost their jobs, justifications attenuated these negative reactions. These mitigating accounts were most effective under two conditions: when the workers were uncertain about the way that their employer was allocating organizational resources, and when the layoff was especially important to the survivors. According to Brockner et al. (1990), uncertainty and importance created a high need for information, and social accounts are useful in this regard. On the other hand, when uncertainty was low and the layoffs were unimportant, survivors' need for information was lower, and the accounts given had less impact.

Why Do Procedures Matter?

As we have noted, research suggests that matters of justice involve more than just economic gain; they also involve the manner in which people are treated. The question of why this occurs has been the topic of considerable recent research. In general, two approaches have been suggested, both of which have received empirical support—the *instrumental model* and the *relational model*. We now will review the evidence for each.

The instrumental model

The instrumental, or self-interest, model of procedural justice accepts the traditional notion that economic incentives promote fairness. It simply claims that individuals may take a long-term focus when evaluating their economic gains. As a result, people may become tolerant of short-term economic losses so long as they expect that advantageous outcomes will be forthcoming in the future. Procedural justice is highly valued insofar as it suggests the existence of a system that will yield the greatest benefits in the long run. Thus, short-term failures can be overlooked when there is some promise of future gain (for reviews, see Greenberg, 1990a, Shapiro, 1993; Tyler, 1990).

There is a good deal of evidence suggesting that individuals value procedural justice, in part, for instrumental reasons. Perhaps the most compelling evidence for the instrumental model is that people evaluate processes more favorably when they lead to positive outcomes than when they lead to negative outcomes. This effect has been observed repeatedly (e.g. Ambrose, Harland, & Kulik, 1991; Conlon, 1993; Conlon & Fasolo, 1990; Conlon & Ross, 1993; Flinder & Hauenstein, 1994; Krzystofiak, Lillis, & Newman, 1995; Lind, Kanfer, & Earley, 1990; Lind, Kulik, Ambrose, & de Vera Park, 1993; Lowe & Vodanovich, 1995), although sometimes the effect sizes are small (e.g. Tyler, 1989, 1991) and exceptions occur (e.g. Giacobbe-Miller, 1995; Tyler, 1994).

If the instrumental model identified the only cause of procedural justice, then one would expect that process fairness would be entirely determined by short-term and long-term economic concerns. On the other hand, to the extent that noninstrumental considerations matter, then process characteristics should enhance perceptions of procedural justice even when no direct economic benefits are expected. To test this possibility, researchers have examined the impact of process characteristics (such as voice or advance notice) under conditions in which advantageous outcomes are precluded. For example, in a laboratory experiment conducted by Lind, Kanfer, and Earley, (1990) undergraduate subjects were assigned performance goals, the successful attainment of which would lead to a desired reward. Some subjects were given an effective voice in determining their goal. For others, their voice had no effect on the outcome. Finally, in a control group subjects had no voice whatsoever. The lowest levels of perceived fairness were reported by subjects in the control group, for whom no voice was allowed. The highest levels of perceived fairness were found when voice was permitted and capable of influencing the goal. In this condition, voice is presumed to have both an instrumental effect—increasing the opportunity to meet the goal—and a noninstrumental effect—enhancing the belief that one's input is welcomed.

Most relevant to our point is that even when individuals could not influence their outcomes, they still reported greater fairness when they had voice than when they didn't have voice.

Parallel findings were obtained by Cropanzano and Randall (1995). These researchers were interested in investigating the effects of advance notice on perceptions of procedural justice. Subjects were assigned to work on an anagram-solving task. High performance on this task would yield a bonus unit of experimental credit. Some individuals were disadvantaged due to a change in the scoring procedure. When the change was announced in advance, perceptions of procedural fairness were relatively high. However, when the change was announced after the task was conducted, perceptions of procedural fairness were much lower. Thus, although the outcomes were identical in both conditions, the manner in which the change was announced had an effect on the perceived fairness of those outcomes. The noninstrumental, purely procedural variable, advance notice, raised procedural justice perceptions despite the fact that procedures had no impact on outcomes—that is, they had no instrumental effects.

Evidence of this phenomenon is not limited exclusively to the lab. Conlon (1993) examined defendants' procedural justice judgments after appealing parking violations. He found that both instrumental considerations (the value of the fine) and noninstrumental considerations (voice in the legal procedure) affected perceptions of process fairness, although the effects of the instrumental factors were substantially larger. Slightly different results were obtained in a field study by Shapiro and Brett (1993). These researchers assessed the reactions of coal miners to various grievance procedures. Like Conlon (1993), Shapiro and Brett (1993) found evidence for both instrumental and noninstrumental determinants of procedural justice. However, in this study the noninstrumental concerns explained the preponderance of variance.

Taken together, these investigations suggest that although instrumental concerns are important, people also formulate procedural justice judgments based on other considerations. However, none of the work reviewed thus far directly measured these 'other concerns'. Although these concerns appear to be important, without such direct measurement they cannot be explicitly identified. Fortunately, research has begun to address this issue by suggesting a complementary model of procedural justice.

The relational model

The relational model (formally called the group-value model) has been proposed as a supplement to the instrumental model (for reviews see Lind, 1995; Lind & Tyler, 1988; Tyler, 1990; Tyler & Dawes, 1993; Tyler & Lind, 1992). Proponents of the relational model agree that people join groups as a means of obtaining valuable economic resources. In this sense, the relational and instrumental models are consistent. However, the relational model maintains that groups offer more than material rewards. Group affiliation is also a means of achieving social status and self-esteem, and these considerations are every bit as potent as the economic incentives emphasized by the instrumental approach. Even within the most individualistic cultures people need to be valued by some group or groups (Lind & Earley, 1992), in as much as this is an important means by which people acquire a sense of personal worth (Tyler & Lind, 1992). For this reason, people tend to be keenly aware of their positions within groups and the groups' potential for providing them with these valuable social rewards.

Tyler (1989, 1990) has argued that people have three *relational concerns*, and that these stem from people's desires for dignity and worth—neutrality, trust, and standing. *Neutrality* is something that a decision-maker expresses to an individual. If neutrality exists, then the decision-maker is free from tendentiousness and bias. He or she uses facts and not opinions and attempts to make choices that create a level playing field for all. Neutrality implies openness and honesty, and the absence of any hidden agendas. *Trust* refers to the degree to which people believe that the decision-maker intends to act in a fair manner. Employees generally wish to count on the trustworthiness of authority figures. *Standing* is something that an individual possesses, but that is conveyed by the decision-maker. When a person's standing is high, his or her status has been affirmed, such as by implementing procedures with politeness and care.

Evidence for the relational model generally has been supportive: Procedural fairness perceptions are enhanced when these three relational concerns have been fulfilled (for reviews, see Lind & Tyler, 1992; Tyler, 1990). For example, there is good support for the relational model in the context of citizens' interactions with civil authorities (Tyler, 1989, 1994). However, only now is the evidence beginning to accumulate in organizational settings. In two field studies, Lind et al. (1993) examined the manner in which individuals reacted to court-ordered arbitration in response to a lawsuit. They found that when relational concerns were met, the litigants had greater perceptions of procedural justice. These feelings, in turn, led them to accept the arbitrated settlement. Although these findings support the relational model, it is important to note that they do not contradict the instrumental approach. In fact, Lind et al. (1993) present evidence suggesting that outcome favorability may impact procedural justice judgments as well as the acceptance of outcomes themselves. Analogous results were obtained by Giacobbe-Miller (1995) in a study of labor–management disputes.

Brockner, Tyler, and Cooper-Schneider (1992) examined the relational model from a different perspective. They argued that if individuals are guided by relational concerns, then those who are most committed to their institutions will be the most upset by violations of procedural justice. This would suggest an interaction between commitment and procedural justice such that procedural justice is more strongly related to various outcomes when commitment is high. When commitment is low, however, the effects of procedural justice should be weaker. Supportive results were obtained in two field studies, one dealing with layoff survivors (Brockner, Tyler, & Cooper-Schneider, 1992, Study 1), and the other examining citizen interactions with legal authoroities (Brockner, Tyler, & Cooper-Schneider, 1992, Study 2).

In conclusion, evidence supports both the instrumental and relational models of procedural justice. Both perspectives provide important insight into the underlying reasons why procedural justice has been shown to be so important in organizations.

THE RELATIONSHIP BETWEEN PROCEDURAL AND DISTRIBUTIVE JUSTICE

Thus far, our discussion of organizational justice has focused on the unique impact of distributive justice and procedural justice. However, from the time that the concept of procedural justice was first introduced to the social sciences, theorists have acknowledged that it may be related to distributive justice (Leventhal, 1976a, 1980; Thibaut & Walker, 1975), although the nature of this relationship was not systematically studied. Recently, however, theorists have focused on two possibilities that we will review here—that distributive justice and procedural justice operate independently, as main effects, and that they operate jointly, as interacting effects.

The Two-Factor Model: Different Effects of Different Types of Justice

In a review article, Greenberg (1990a) distinguished between the different consequences that procedural and distributive justice appeared to have: Procedural justice was linked to system satisfaction whereas distributive justice was linked to outcome satisfaction. To a great extent, this distinction continues to hold today. Evidence suggests that distributive justice primarily influences one's satisfaction with the outcome in question or the results of some decision (Brockner & Wiesenfeld, in press). For example, the belief that one's pay is not suitable compensation for one's achievements results in perceptions of inequity that, in turn, produce low pay satisfaction (Harder, 1992; McFarlin & Sweeney, 1992; Sweeney & McFarlin, 1993; Sweeney, McFarlin, & Inderrieden, 1990; Summers & Hendrix, 1991). By contrast, procedural justice primarily influences attitudes and behaviors that are relevant to the larger organization. Procedures, in other words, are central determinants of one's trust in management and loyalty to the institution or system that rendered the decision in question (Krystofiak, Lillis, & Newman, 1995; Lind, 1995; Tyler & Degoey, 1995). Continuing with pay as an example, evidence suggests that when pay decisions are made using fair procedures, people are likely to remain committed to their organizations—even when the decisions are unfavorable (Cooper, Dyck, & Frohlich, 1992; McFarlin & Sweeney, 1992; Schaubroeck, May, & Brown, 1994; Sweeney & McFarlin, 1993). Sweeney and McFarlin (1993) have dubbed these different effects the *two-factor model*: Although procedures and outcomes are both important determinants of justice, they affect different factors.

Despite considerable evidence supporting the two-factor model (for reviews, see Lind & Earley, 1992; Tyler, 1990; Tyler & Lind, 1992), the evidence is not unequivocal. Lowe and Vodanovich (1995), for example, suggested that the relationship of distributive justice and procedural justice to organizationally relevant criteria may vary over time. They propose that perceptions of organizational outcomes are most strongly influenced by distributive injustices immediately after the injustices occur. As time elapses, however, this effect dissipates. Employees then adapt a longer-term perspective and alter their impressions of organizations so that these are more firmly based upon procedures. If this reasoning is correct, then support for the two-factor model should only appear as time has passed following defining-episodes of distributive injustice.

Lowe and Vodanovich (1995) tested these ideas using a sample of university employees who had undergone a restructuring of their job classifications, an event that triggered feelings of distributive injustice in many employees. Their survey, administered two months after the restructuring occurred (while respondents apparently were still feeling the sting), found that feelings of organizational commitment were more strongly linked to the unfavorability of the outcome than they were to the procedures whereby these outcomes were determined. Unfortunately, insofar as the investigators failed to administer a follow-up survey to assess the extent to which procedures became more important with the passage of time, their hypotheses were not completely tested. However, their idea warrants future research. Based on our earlier conclusions regarding the mitigating influences of explanations, these may be expected to be likely moderators of the time-sensitive effects Lowe and Vodanovich (1995) proposed. After all, as time passes it is likely that people will receive information that qualifies their interpretation of earlier events.

The Interaction Model:
Conjoint Effects of Distributive and Procedural Justice

According to the two-factor model, procedures and outcomes predict different types of reactions, and therefore it speaks only to main effects. Additional research, however, suggests that procedural justice and distributive justice interact (for reviews, see Brockner & Wiesenfeld, 1996; Cropanzano & Folger, 1991). Following Brockner and Wiesenfeld (1966), this interaction can be described from the perspective of either the procedures or the

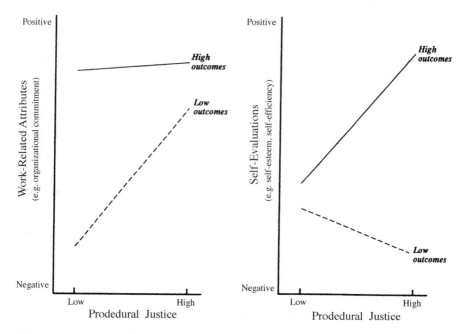

Figure 7.1   General form of procedure-by-outcome interactions for work-related attitudes (left panel) and self-evaluations (right panel)

outcomes (see left panel of Figure 7.1). One might say that procedural justice is more strongly related to work attitudes when outcomes are low than when they are high. Conversely, one also might say that outcomes are more strongly related to work attitudes when procedures are unfair than when they are fair. Brockner and Wiesenfeld (1996) examined the evidence documenting the existence of this interaction and offered several possible explanations for it.

Work-related attitudes

Notably, Brockner and Wiesenfeld (1996) suggested that the procedure-by-outcome interaction has been generally associated with organizationally relevant outcomes. For example, in research, conducted by Brockner et al. (1990) and by Daly and Geyer (1994) the procedure-by-outcome interaction significantly predicted organizational commitment. However, less research has linked the procedure-by-outcome interaction to criteria that could clearly be considered personal, such as pay satisfaction. The work of McFarlin and Sweeney (1992) is an exception. These researchers found that the procedure-by-outcome interaction was significant for commitment, but not for pay satisfaction. Clearly, more research is needed before definite conclusions can be drawn about the nature of the procedure-by-outcome interaction. At this point, however, the available evidence suggests that the procedure-by-outcome interaction behaves the same as the procedural main effect described in conjunction with the two-factor model—that is, the interaction is more clearly related to attitudes toward the system or institution than attitudes toward one's job.

It is important to note that the interaction effect has not been consistently obtained. Researchers either have not tested for it (cf. Brockner and Wiesenfeld, in press), or have found it to be nonsignificant in their research (Cropanzano & Konovsky, 1995; Lowe & Vodanovich, 1995). Nonsignificant interactions are particularly likely to occur in studies (e.g. Lowe & Vodanovich, 1995) in which sample sizes are too low to have adequate statistical power to detect interactions (cf. Stone, 1988). Interaction effects also might not be found in the case of certain dependent variables which may be sensitive only to the main effects of outcome. For example, in the context of workplace drug screening, Cropanzano and Konovsky (1995) found that some process characteristics (e.g. voice, advance notice) interacted with outcome negativity as expected whereas another (i.e. the presence or absence of a grievance system) did not. Such findings suggest that it may be misleading to ignore the possibility that all determinants of fair procedures do not have the same effects. As noted in our earlier discussion of context-sensitive variables, some determinants of procedural justice may have different effects than others.

Brockner and Siegel (1995) have offered a novel interpretation of the interaction effect. They claim that it is not procedures themselves that interact with outcomes, but that outcome favorability moderates the effect of trust: The relevant interaction is between trust and outcomes; procedures are not directly involved. Brockner and Siegel (1995) hypothesize that procedural justice is still important, but indirectly, insofar as it serves as the primary determinant of trust. Nevertheless, it is trust that takes part in the actual interaction. To date, the evidence for this idea is limited, but promising. For example, in a retrospective study Siegel, Brockner, and Tyler (1995) asked workers to recall problems they had with their supervisors. Consistent with Brockner and Siegel's (1995) reasoning, outcome favorability interacted with both procedures and trust to predict employees' acceptance of the supervisors' decisions. However, the trust-by-outcome interaction accounted for considerably more variance. Moreover, when both interactions were simultaneously used to predict decision acceptance, only the trust-by-outcome interaction remained significant; the procedure-by-outcome interaction was not. Although it is premature to draw firm conclusions about the role of trust in determining the acceptance of outcomes, it does appear to be an important factor.

Self-evaluations

Thus far, we have seen that procedures and outcomes may interact to foster different reactions to different aspects of the work environment. Insightful as this work has been, none of it has examined self-relevant cognitions. However, in light of literature demonstrating the importance of self-esteem (e.g. Brockner, 1988) and self-efficacy (e.g. Gist & Mitchell, 1992) in organizations, attention deserves to be paid to what fair or unfair treatment leads people to think about themselves.

Several recent studies have examined how procedures and outcomes work together to influence self-esteem and perceptions of self-efficacy. For the most part, these studies find a different interaction pattern than the one previously described (see right panel of Figure 7.1). For example, in two laboratory experiments Koper et al. (1993), gave university students bogus feedback about their performance on a test of basic abilities. When the students were given positive feedback and the test was believed to have been graded fairly (i.e. carefully and accurately), state self-esteem was relatively high. However, when the students were given negative feedback, the fairness of the test-grading procedure had little impact on their self-esteem. These studies suggest that procedures and outcomes interact to predict self-relevant cognitions such that outcome favorability exerts a stronger effect on state self-esteem when fair procedures are used compared to when unfair procedures are used. In a related field study, Gilliland (1994) examined the impact of procedures and outcomes on self-efficacy. He found that when people were not hired (an unfavorable outcome) using a test that was job-related (a fair procedure), their self-efficacy perceptions were low. However, unfair tests had less effect on self-efficacy than did fair tests. Gilliland's (1994) findings are generally consistent with the self-esteem research reviewed previously. As summarized in Figure 7.1, the interactions obtained by both Koper et al. (1993) and Gilliland (1994), measuring self-relevant perceptions, were different from those found in the earlier cited studies measuring organizational attitudes.

Why might this interaction occur? Tyler and Degoey (1995) consider the question from the perspective of the relational model: When a process is fair, individuals see themselves as valued; when a process is unfair, they see themselves as less valued. For this reason, people should evaluate themselves more positively when procedures are fair, and less positively when procedures are unfair. This explanation implies that it is the fairness of the presentation, and not the favorability of the feedback, that determines self-esteem. One might posit from Tyler and Degoey (1995), therefore, that people's self-esteem will be raised even when feedback is negative, so long as a fair process is maintained. This hypothesis, however, has not received support. In fact, procedural fairness does not exhibit a positive relationship to self-evaluations in the case of negative feedback. Rather, evidence suggests that people receiving negative feedback evaluate themselves less positively when that feedback is considered procedurally fair than when it is considered procedurally unfair (Gilliland, 1994; Koper et al., 1993). In other words, people receiving negative feedback may feel better about themselves when the process used to assess their performance is considered to be unfair than when it is considered to be fair. Tyler and Degoey's (1995) reasoning cannot account for these findings.

Thus, we need a model that explains why people react favorably to feedback that is procedurally fair and positive, while also reacting unfavorably to feedback that is procedurally fair and negative. We can resolve this issue by considering the dimension along which the feedback is diagnostic. For Tyler and Degoey (1995) the principal dimension in question is the individual's relationship with the group. They maintain that procedures, more than outcomes, provide information about this relationship. However, performance feedback supplies information about other things as well. In particular, feedback also can suggest things about a person's skills and abilities. In the studies by Koper et al. (1993) and Gilliland (1994), subjects received some type of evaluative feedback, such as their basic abilities or their abilities to do their jobs. A fair process might lead individuals to more fully accept their feedback as valid. Thus, when the procedures are believed to be fair, the negative feedback resulting from these procedures will have greater diagnostic value. However, when a procedure is unfair, the value of the feedback resulting from it is circumspect, and may be readily dismissed. To state the matter more succinctly, information has greater force when it is based on fair procedures compared to unfair procedures. For this reason, fairly given positive feedback leads people to evaluate themselves more favorably, whereas fairly given negative feedback leads people to evaluate themselves less favorably. This analysis suggests that allocation procedures may trigger more than just the concern for personal dignity. They also may provide information about how people should evaluate their own abilities and skills.

JUSTICE RESEARCH IN ORGANIZATIONAL SETTINGS: TOWARD PRACTICAL APPLICATIONS

Greenberg (1990a, 1993c, 1996a) has argued that the major value of studying organizational justice phenomena lies in the insight it provides with respect to understanding and managing various aspects of organizational behavior. Specifically, he claims that general, context-neutral studies of fairness are less informative than those examining fairness issues arising in specific organizational settings (Greenberg, 1996a). There are three reasons for this. First, studying the perceived fairness of organizational phenomena is a valuable way of learning about those phenomena themselves. Second, unique aspects of justice are likely to arise in specific organizational contexts. And finally, studying justice concepts in various organizational settings provides a good opportunity to assess their generalizability. Greenberg's point is that studying justice in organizations not only sheds light on matters of justice, but also on organizations themselves. For this reason, he advocates applying justice concepts to a broad set of organizational phenomena.

When the study of organizational justice first emerged, Greenberg identified several aspects of organizational settings that stood to benefit from being analyzed through the lens of organizational justice (e.g. Greenberg, 1987a). Indeed, he conducted justice-directed *post hoc* analyses of such phenomena as performance evaluations (Greenberg, 1986b,c), comparable worth (Greenberg & McCarty, 1990) and various human resources management practices (Greenberg & Folger, 1983; Folger & Greenberg, 1985). Today, researchers have not only accepted, but embraced the premise that 'justice matters' in organizations, and they have conducted many investigations focusing on the role of justice in organizations. Indeed, the past few years have seen many significant applications of justice concepts to organizational issues. In view of the voluminous nature of this literature, we will review only the highlights of this work (for a more complete presentation, see Folger & Cropanzano, in press).

Strategic Planning

Earlier, we noted that among the benefits derived from using fair procedures is that they enhance employees' acceptance of institutional authorities. This is likely to be especially important in the context of strategic planning, in which it is vital to organizational success that employees endorse their firms' strategic plans (Miller & Cardinal, 1994). Recent research suggests that one important determinant of the acceptance of strategic plans is the extent to which employees believe that the plans were formulated and implemented in a procedurally fair manner. In general, research has shown that organizational changes that are believed to be based on fair procedures are better accepted than those believed to be based on unfair procedures (Novelli, Kirkman, & Shapiro, 1995).

This phenomenon is demonstrated clearly in a survey of subsidiary managers from multinational coporations conducted by Kim and Mauborgne (1991). These researchers were interested in determining the extent to which managers believed that their companies' headquarters used procedurally fair decision techniques during the planning process. They found, as expected, that perceptions of procedural justice were positively associated with feelings of organizational commitment, trust in the head office, social harmony, and satisfaction with the outcomes of the planning process. Moreover, the procedural justice effects were greater than the impact of outcome fairness. The same researchers later replicated and extended these findings in a longitudinal study. Kim and Mauborgne (1993) found that procedural justice was associated positively with perceptions of commitment, trust, and outcome satisfaction. They also found that these feelings, in turn, led managers to be supportive of the strategic plan.

A complementary approach was taken by Korsgaard, Schweiger, and Sapienza (1995). These researchers were interested in the strategic planning process used by members of intact management teams. They presented a hypothetical business case to team members who were participating in an executive training program. Consistent with the field research of Kim and Mauborgne (1991, 1993), Korsgaard and her colleagues found that

perceptions of procedural fairness were affected significantly by two independent variables: allowing team members to influence the decision, and consideration of their viewpoints. These feelings of procedural justice, in turn, led to
higher levels of trust, decision commitment, and group attachment. In sum,
research has shown that fair procedures enhance employees' acceptance of
their organizations' strategic plans.

Organizational Staffing

Historically, when industrial/organizational psychologists have discussed 'selection fairness' they were referring to various psychometric properties of
assessment instruments, such as concerns of differential validity, adverse impact, and so forth. This literature continues to be important (Arvey & Sackett,
1993). However, more recent work has begun to examine the test-takers'
perceptions of fairness (Arvey, 1992), especially distributive and procedural
justice (for reviews, see Gilliland, 1993; Schuler, 1993a; Singer, 1993). Generally speaking, this work suggests that staffing procedures perceived as being
unfair have pernicious consequences.

Gilliland (1993) maintains that selection tests incite concerns about all
three aspects of procedural justice—structural characteristics (what Gilliland
calls 'formal characteristics'), explanations and interpersonal treatment. This
work is important insofar as some selection methodologies are less likely to
engender fairness perceptions than others (Gilliland, 1994; Singer, 1992).
Perceived injustice, in turn, gives rise to a host of negative outcomes, such as
poor work attitudes and lower job performance (Gilliland, 1994). For example, Gilliland (1994) found that workers who believed that they were selected by unfair means had poorer work attitudes and lower job performance
than those who believed they were selected by fair means. Similarly, several
studies by Singer (1992, 1993) found that individuals who believed that staffing procedures were unfair were less likely to accept a job than those who
believed them to be fair. (It should be noted, however, that this effect may be
stronger when job opportunities are considered sequentially than when they
are examined in pairs; Bazerman, Schroth, Shah, et al., 1994, Study 2.)

Fortunately, these consequences can be avoided by incorporating procedural justice into selection systems. In fact, research conducted over the
past few years can serve as explicit guides as to how this may be accomplished.
With this in mind, we will consider the fairness of several of the most widely
used staffing procedures (see also reviews by Folger and Cropanzano, in press;
Gilliland, 1993).

Interviews

Employment interviews, especially the unstructured variety, are used very
widely (Harris, Dworking, & Park, 1990). Studies have found that applicants

view them as fair (Harland & Biasotto, 1993; Kravitz, Stinson, & Chavez, in press; Smither, Reilly, Millsap, et al., 1993), although these results can vary depending on the content of the interview (Rynes & Connerley, 1993). Job applicants even expect to participate in unstructured interviews—in fact, they consider selection procedures unfair when interviews are not used (Singer, 1992, 1993). Although these findings paint an encouraging picture of the benefits of unstructured interviews, it remains problematic that unstructured interviews yield lower validity coefficients than their structured counterparts (Latham & Finnegan, 1993). At the same time, however, applicants perceive unstructured interviews to be more fair than structured interviews (Latham & Finnegan, 1993; Schuler, 1993b). This probably stems from the fact that unstructured interviews provide greater opportunities for candidates to express themselves, thereby providing voice—a well-established criterion of procedural justice (Thibaut & Walker, 1975). In so far as there are justice-enhancing benefits associated with unstructured interviews, and validity-enhancing benefits associated with structured interviews, it would appear wise to consider using both types of interviews in the selection process.

Assessment centers and work simulations

Both Gilliland (1993) and Singer (1993) suggest that perceptions of fairness are enhanced when a selection instrument is ostensibly job-related or 'transparent' (Schuler, 1993a)—that is, when it has 'face validity' (Mosier, 1947). Various work simulations and assessment centers have this quality (Finkle, 1976). Applicants can readily reocgnize the tests' relevance for the job and, therefore, should view these tools favorably. In fact, considerable research suggests that this is the case. For example, in surveys conducted by Rynes and Connerley (1993), and Kravitz, Stinson, and Chavez (in press), it was found that work simulations and job-sample tests consistently were among the most favored selection devices. Studies of assessment centers yield similar results (Davis, 1993; Macan, Avedon, Paese, & Smith, 1994). These findings are encouraging insofar as work simulations and assessment centers yield substantial validity coefficients (Thornton & Cleveland, 1990). Thus, work simulations appear to constitute a selection instrument that is both useful and fair.

Biographical inventories

If face-valid assessment tools are perceived to be fair it follows that those with questionable face validity, and inherent opportunities for violations of privacy, would be considered unfair. This appears to be the case in studies of biographical inventories. Indeed, Smither et al. (1993) found that biographical inventories were believed to be less fair than other selection techniques.

Similarly, Kluger and Rothstein (1993) found that applicants generally held negative opinions of organizations that used biographical inventories. Likewise, Stoffey, Millsap, Smither, and Reilly (1991) found that the use of biodata lowered applicants' job-pursuit intentions. These findings, considered along with the fact that the US government has long restricted the kinds of questions that can be asked on an application blank (Lowell & DeLoach, 1984), raise serious questions about the costs that may be incurred by the continued use of biographical inventories as selection tools.

Personality tests

The issue of perceived job-relevance of test procedures and invasions of privacy manifests itself as well in the context of personality tests. Research has shown that personality tests are sometimes valid predictors of job performance (Guion, 1991), although this depends greatly on the personality trait measured and on the characteristics of the particular job (Tett, Jackson, & Rothstein, 1991). Generally, however, applicants do not like personality inventories. In fact, many people react negatively to them (Ambrose & Rosse, 1993; Harland & Biasotto, 1993; Kavitz, Stinson, & Chavez, in press; Rosse, Miller, & Stecher, 1994; Rynes & Connerley, 1993) and form negative opinions of the organizations using them (Smither et al., 1993). For example, in a large-scale survey of employees, Westin (1978) found that 44% of the respondents wanted personality testing banned. Not surprisingly, applicants selected by use of personality inventories are less likely to accept job offers than individuals selected by other means (Rosse, Ringer, & Miller, in press). In view of this negative picture, it should come as no surprise to find that managers are reluctant to use personality tests (Harris, Dworkin, & Park, 1990).

Despite these concerns, there may be something that can be done to enhance the acceptance of personality tests. Many personality instruments were originally designed for diagnosing personality disorders in clinical populations (for a review, see Guion, 1965). As a result, some of the questions may come across as invasive and offensive when used in nonclinical settings. If so, then it may be possible to revise offending items or to select only those items that are relevant to occupational settings. Doing so may enhance the perceived fairness of personality screening. Some evidence suggests that this will indeed occur. For example, Jones (1991) discovered that test-takers responded far more favorably when only work-related personality items were used in selection tests than when these were supplemented by unrelated items. The suggestion to limit the focus of personality tests is in keeping with the trend toward using narrow, situationally explicit, personality variables in personnel testing (Guion, 1991). Of course, to the extent that items from established personality inventories are revised or omitted, it is essential to revalidate them to ensure that their predictive power has not been attenuated.

Reference checks

Reference checks are in widespread use (Harris, Dworkin, & Park, 1990) despite the fact that they do not have particularly high levels of statistical validity (except, perhaps in certain limited conditions; Knouse, 1989). Regardless, applicants do consider reference checks to be fair. A study by Rynes and Connerley (1993), for example, found that applicants preferred reference checks to other selection techniques. Additionally, in a study in which people were asked to assess their reactions to various selection devices Kravitz, Stinson, and Chavez (in press) found that reference letters were judged quite favorably.

Cognitive abilities tests

Cognitive abilities, or so-called 'intelligence', tests are useful tools for predicting job performance (Wigdor & Sackett, 1993). However, several studies suggest that job applicants often reject them. Kluger and Rothstein (1993, Study 1) gave subjects negative feedback regarding their performance on one of four selection tests. Responses were especially negative among people who scored low on a test of cognitive ability. In a follow-up study the researchers found that the actual and perceived difficulty of the intelligence tests may have lowered test-takers' perceptions of control and distracted them (Kluger & Rothstein, 1993, Study 2). Similar results also were obtained by Macan et al. (1994).

This is not to say that people's feelings about intelligence tests are completely negative. For example, Rosse, Miller, and Stecher (1994) found that the inclusion of a cognitive ability test in a battery with a personality test actually improved people's reactions to the personality test. In addition, of the 16 selection instruments evaluated by participants in the study by Kravitz and his associates (in press), cognitive abilities tests were ranked seventh— approximately in the middle of their list. Test-takers' reactions also may depend less on the type of test and more on the particular test items. In support of this contention, Rynes and Connerley (1993) found that intelligence tests were evaluated more favorably when they included job-related items than when they did not. Likewise, Smither et al. (1993) discovered that cognitive ability tests with concrete items were perceived more positively than those containing abstract items.

To conclude this section, many recent studies have demonstrated that certain characteristics can be incorporated into selection procedures to enhance their perceived fairness. Moreover, perceived fair procedures lead to a variety of beneficial personal and organizational outcomes. Clearly, research and theory on organizational justice holds a great deal of promise when it comes to identifying ways of enhancing people's reactions to selection instruments.

Workplace Drug Screening

Although drug testing can be a valid predictor of work behavior, surveys have shown that people's reactions to this practice are highly variable (for a review, see Konovsky & Cropanzano, 1993). Many individuals perceive drug screening favorably whereas others do not (Labig, 1992; Murphy, Thornton, & Prue, 1991; Murphy, Thornton, & Reynolds, 1990). Nonetheless, studies have documented at least some concerns regarding drug-testing fairness (e.g. Harris, Dworking, & Park, 1990), although some other staffing methods are considered even less fair (Kravitz, Stinson, & Chavez, in press; Rosse, Ringer, & Miller, in press; Rynes & Connerley, 1993).

These findings are of more than academic interest. Notably, Konovsky and Cropanzano (1991) found that those employees who believed that a workplace drug screening program was procedurally unfair also had lower organizational commitment, lower job satisfaction, higher turnover intentions, and lower assessments of their work performance by their supervisors. Generally consistent results also were obtained in a role-playing study conducted by Crant and Bateman (1990). To the extent that unfair drug screening procedures may interfere with an organization's effectiveness, it is important for managers to recognize the characteristics of fair and unfair practices, and to promote the use of fair practices.

There are several possible reasons why diverse evaluations of drug testing are found. One possibility is that there are individual differences in people's attitudes toward drug testing. Research by Crant and Bateman (1993) and by Rosse, Miller, and Ringer (in press) suggests that people who use illegal drugs tend to have more negative opinions of drug testing programs than those who do not. This is in keeping with the self-interest bias in procedural justice perceptions to which we alluded earlier (cf. Grover, 1991).

However, as we have already discussed, self-interest appears to be only one determinant of procedural fairness judgments. Evaluations of drug screening also may vary because drug screening programs themselves are highly diverse. Any particular drug test may or may not have associated with it a variety of procedural safeguards (Konovsky & Cropanzano, 1993). Furthermore, even if these safeguards do exist, they may not be evident to the test-taker (suggesting that it is important for people who are behaving fairly to publicize their efforts; Greenberg, 1990c). For example, Tepper and Braun (1995) found that employees felt favorable toward drug testing procedures to the extent that they believed these procedures yielded accurate results (i.e. Leventhal's, 1980, 'accuracy' rule was followed), and that leniency was shown to those who tested positively.

In another recent study, Cropanzano and Konovsky (1995) determined that drug screening was considered fair to the extent that the procedure used contained elements of voice, advance notice, justifications, a grievance system, and when testing was conducted 'for cause'. (As mentioned earlier, all five of these process attributes except presence/absence of a grievance system interacted with outcome negativity.) Taken together, research suggests that drug testing can indeed give rise to perceptions of injustice. However, to the extent that the system is designed in a manner that incorporates appropriate procedural safeguards, these concerns may be assuaged.

Organizational Image Management

Earlier, we discussed the use of social accounts as a means of legitimizing the behavior of individuals. Extending this line of thinking, we also can see that it is not only individuals who need to have their behavior justified as fair, but organizations as well (Gatewood, Gowan, & Lautenschlager, 1993). In fact, recent research suggests that organizations go through similar processes of image-maintenance—especially following actions that might be seen as unfair (cf. Greenberg, 1990c). Although attention to this topic is fairly recent, some interesting findings already have emerged.

In a qualitative study Dutton and Dukerich (1991) examined the manner in which the New York and New Jersey Port Authority responded to the large number of homeless people congregating in their transportation facilities. Port Authority officials were concerned that these individuals constituted an obstacle for effective service delivery. As such, they took a variety of measures, many of which were subsequently criticized by the media. Among other things, Dutton and Dukerich (1991) were interested in how the Port Authority responded to these critiques.

Initially, officials denied engaging in some of the more controversial behaviors. However, as public outcry grew, the Port Authority's image further eroded in the public eye. As a result, the organization shifted its reactions from denial to a series of 'legitimizing actions' such as making a capital investment in new facilities for the homeless, and forming a task force on the problem. One might say that the Port Authority partially acquiesced to its critics and began to address their concerns. Presumably, had denial been more effective as an impression-management technique, these other institutional changes would not have been initiated.

Another perspective on organizational accounts is provided by the work of Elsbach and Sutton (1992) in their study of two social-activist groups: The AIDS Coalition to Unleash Power (ACT-UP) and Earth First! ACT-UP and Earth First! members engage in many activities that are widely accepted as legitimate. Indeed, most people wish to assist AIDS sufferers and to protect the environment, or at least, believe that it is reasonable to do so. Nevertheless, in the course of pursuing these goals, members of these organizations sometimes engaged in actions that were perceived as illegitimate (e.g. the disruption of a religious service by ACT-UP members, and an injurious tree-spiking incident committed by members of Earth First!). The investigators were interested in how these two organizations could maintain a positive public image in the face of these questionable actions.

Elsbach and Sutton (1992) found evidence that these organizations actually anticipated the need to provide social accounts, and built provisions for doing so into their structures. This was done in two ways. First, ACT-UP and Earth First! engaged in 'institutional conformity'. That is, their visible structures and actions were consistent with the values and norms of the larger society. Few people, for example, would object to a group that provides assistance to AIDS victims or that educates people about ecology. (As such, these activities are much like the legitimizing actions observed by Dutton and Dukerich, 1991.) Second, the organizations adopted a highly de-centralized structure. The roles of different chapters or spokespersons were separated from the rest of the organization. For example, Earth First! members went so far as to create an *ad hoc* group that engaged in tree-spiking. These two structural adaptations came in handy after an illegitimate event occurred.

Following controversial events ACT-UP and Earth First! were able to rely on their structures for help. For one, they could point to many legitimate activities in which they participated. This had a chilling effect on criticism insofar as any broad attacks on the organization would also constitute attacks on these favorable activities. Second, they were able to dissociate the organization from those individuals who performed the illegitimate activity. For example, ACT-UP has local chapters that operate in a relatively autonomous fashion. The overall organization simply attributed the attack on the church to the over-zealous New York chapter, thereby protecting its image by distancing itself from those illegitimate actions. Indeed, Elsbach and Sutton (1992) provide evidence that these accounts were effective at putting an end to the public censure.

In a more recent investigation on this topic, Elsbach (1994) studied the manner in which the California cattle industry responded to various allegations of wrongdoing. Her focus here was less on structure and more on the nature of the social accounts themselves. In particular, Elsbach (1994, Study 1) found that the accounts used by the maligned cattle industry took two broad forms. There were *denials*, whereby industry spokespeople maintained that nothing bad had occurred. There also were *acknowledgements*—concessions that something bad had happened, accompanied by explanations as to why the problem was not really so severe or why it was not the fault of most ranchers. (The analogous behavior on the part of individuals has been referred to as *justifications* by Tedeschi & Reiss, 1981, and *techniques of neutralization* by Sykes & Matza, 1957.)

Each of these two forms of accounts could have one of two different types of contents. One content referred to *characteristics of the institution*, such as the legitimate goals pursued by ranchers. Another content referred to *characteristics of the technology*, such as the efficiency of modern ranching techniques. Combining form and context, Elsbach (1994, Study 2) identified four prototypical accounts:

- denial based on institutional reasons (e.g. there is no safety problem due to federal monitoring);

- denial based on technical reasons (e.g. cattle are handled compassionately because that's what is profitable);
- acknowledgement, but explained by institutional reasons (e.g. grazing in a state park reduces fire hazards); and
- acknowledgement, but explained by technical reasons (e.g. enforcing a ban on growth hormones would not be economically viable).

All four of these prototypical acounts received at least some use. However, Elsbach (1994, Studies 2 and 3) found that acknowledgements did a better job than denials at maintaining the industry's image. Additionally, accounts based on institutional characteristics were more effective than those based on technical characteristics. As one might expect, the form and the content of the account also worked together. The most effective explanation of all was an acknowledgement that something negative had occurred, but that explained the event in terms of an institutional characteristic of the industry.

Although research on social accounts at the level of the organization is still in its infancy, the work conducted thus far has considerable promise. Such research represents an innovative application of organizational justice, as it moves from the level of the individual to the level of the firm as a whole. This leads us to wonder whether justice findings in other domains would generalize as readily across levels of analysis. Clearly, this represents a promising avenue for future inquiry.

Informal Conflict Resolution

Managers frequently are required to intervene in disputes between subordinates (for reviews see Dworkin, 1994; Karambayya & Brett, 1994; Wall & Callister, 1995). When they do, they are said to be acting as 'informal' third-parties, as compared to the 'formal' interventions by judges and arbitrators (Kolb, 1986). Although there are many important considerations involved in making third-party interventions effective (Elangovan, 1995), maintaining justice is one of the most important. Indeed, research has shown that managers who behave fairly resolve conflict more effectively than those who do not (Cropanzano, Aguinis, Schminke, & Denham, 1996; Karambayya, Brett, & Lytle, 1992; Kozan & Ilter, 1994). The role of justice in informal conflict resolution has a long history (for an overview, see Folger & Cropanzano, in press), although our discussion will focus only on recent contributions to this literature.

How much participation do managers allow?

As we have already discussed, giving people voice in the procedures affecting them is likely to enhance their perceptions of the fairness of those procedures and the resulting outcomes. This generalization holds true in the domain of conflict resolution as well. For example, in a field study conducted in a school Rasinski (1992, Study 1) found that a large percentage of teachers preferred to resolve conflicts between students in a participative fashion rather than in a nonparticipative fashion. Likewise, in a role-playing study, Cropanzano et al. (1996) discovered that simulated disputants in the US, the Dominican Republic, and Argentina preferred that their supervisors intervened in a way that preserved their voice in the matter. Cropanzano et al.'s (1996) respondents also believed that participative procedures were more fair and more likely to alleviate future tensions than nonparticipative procedures. Finally, in a laboratory experiment Schoorman and Champagne (1994) gave simulated supervisors negative information about their subordinates. Although this information harmed the supervisor–subordinate relationship, they found that if the two individuals openly discussed the problem, their relationship improved. This finding suggests that participation could act to strengthen the interpersonal ties between workers and managers. In view of such evidence it should come as no surprise to find that practitioners widely recommend using participative interventions for most types of conflicts (e.g. Weeks, 1992).

Research has shown that the beneficial effects of participative conflict resolution practices are not limited to American samples. For example, in a study of Turkish workers Kozan and Ilter (1994) found that managers typically used a participative process in their conflict resolution efforts. Specifically, Turkish supervisors were most likely to mediate (i.e. let the two disputants speak freely, but reserve control over the decision to themselves) and facilitate (lower tension levels, but let the subordinates work through the problem). In addition, when the supervisors used these voice-oriented strategies, subordinates reported more favorable outcomes than when they did not use such tactics. Despite this, it is most common for American managers to intervene in an autocratic fashion (see Dworkin, 1994; Folger & Cropanzano, in press), although this can vary substantially depending upon the nature of the dispute (Shapiro & Rosen, 1994). In general, American managers tend to control both the discussion of the problem as well as the choice of a settlement.

Several studies shed light on the underlying reasons for this autocratic preference. For example, Sheppard, Blumenfeld-Jones, Minton, and Hyder (1994) interviewed managers concerning the manner in which they had settled recent disputes. In keeping with previous research, they found that autocratic approaches were preferred. Part of the reason for this had to do with managerial goals. When supervisors were concerned with the need for a fast, high-quality decision, they relied on an autocratic strategy. However, when quality and speed were of less concern, supervisors were more participative. In addition, Sheppard et al. (1994) also found that the major reason why American managers use autocratic tactics had to do with the way they frame conflicts. That is, they think of their conflict-resolution obligations as decisions that have to be made, much as their other managerial tasks. Consequently, they make these decisions in much the same autocratic fashion.

Another reason why American supervisors tend to make conflict-resolution decisions autocratically is that they may not know any better. In an interesting experiment, Karambayya, Brett, and Lytle (1992) had inexperienced MBA students and actual managers role-play a simulated organizational dispute. The subjects either were or were not granted formal power. It was found that if subjects lacked formal power, they did not intervene in an autocratic fashion, and were more participative. This was true of both MBA students and actual managers. However, among those individuals who were granted formal power, significant differences emerged. The inexperienced MBA students utilized autocratic tactics, whereas the more experienced managers used more participative strategies. Finally, regardless of the condition, the simulated disputants reported that the outcomes were fairer and more effective when they were given voice in the procedures than when voice was not allowed. These findings support the notion that supervisors learn from experience, initially using less effective, autocratic approaches and gradually learning to use more participative procedures. These findings lend cause for optimism about the potential effectivness of efforts at training managers to enhance their dispute-resolution skills (Kolb, 1985).

Timing of third-party interventions

Closely related to the issue of participation in dispute resolution is the matter of timing. People in conflict with each other often prefer to resolve their disagreements by themselves (cf. Bergmann & Volkema, 1994; Rasinski, 1992). This enables both parties to control both the process and the outcome, and avoids relinquishing control to intervening authority figures. However, when a supervisor intervenes prematurely, control is stripped from the disputants. To the extent that disputants believe they did not have sufficient time to resolve their differences on their own, they are likely to believe that they were treated unfairly and to feel dissatisfied with those managers who stepped-in too quickly. These ideas were directly tested by Conlon and Fasolo (1990), who examined disputants' reactions to a simulated conflict. As expected, a hasty intervention by informal third parties lowered the disputants' perceptions of procedural fairness.

Third-party partisanship

When managers intervene in conflicts they typically are not dispassionate observers. They often have vested interests—sometimes, legitimate ones—in the way conflicts are settled. From the perspective of the disputant, however, these interests may introduce unacceptable bias into the decision-making process. In other words, supervisors may be unable to provide the neutrality that Tyler and Lind (1992) maintain is important to procedural justice. As an obvious example, when the adjudicating third party is affiliated with one of the disputants, justice is compromised. For example, several studies have found that when third parties benefited from the outcomes of the settlements they made, disputants were prone to question the fairness of the process (Welton & Pruitt, 1987; Wittmer, Carnevale, & Walker, 1991).

As obvious as these findings may be, third-party affiliations also can have some unusual effects. In one experiment, subjects either did or did not observe a third party chatting in a friendly fashion with the opposing disputant (Lind & Lissak, 1985). This friendly discourse was perceived to be improper insofar as it might bias the outcome of the decision. The effects of this type of impropriety depended upon the outcome that the third party assigned. When the outcome was unfavorable, subjects responded very negatively, attributing the result to biased decision-making. However, when the outcome was favorable, subjects responded quite positively. The cordial relations between the third paty and their opponent served to lower the subjects' expectations of receiving beneficial outcomes. When these negative expectations were not met, disputants were very pleased. (This is akin to the augmentation effect in impression management demonstrated recently by Greenberg, 1996b.)

These ideas were further tested by Conlon and Ross (1993). In two laboratory experiments they found that when a third party was partisan, the non-affiliated disputant lowered his or her expectations. This made settlements easier to achieve. In addition, favorable outcomes were evaluated positively in as much as these were substantially greater than imagined coming from a partisan decision-maker. Conlon and Ross's findings (1993) suggest that partisanship is not necessarily harmful. To a large extent, it depends on the circumstances and the nature of the settlement. However, to the extent that it can be avoided and neutrality can be demonstrated, the tactic of manipulating expectations via displays of partisanship can be avoided in the first place.

Layoffs

As organizations have downsized and restructured their operations in recent years, layoffs have become a troubling fact of organizational life for millions of Americans (Richman, 1993), and experts predict that the hardships they endure will continue in the future (Cascio, 1995). Research in organizational justice appears to provide some valuable insights into ways of mitigating the negative impact of job loss on both victims of layoffs (those who lost their jobs) and survivors (those who remain on the job after others have been laid off) (for reviews, see Brockner, 1994; Brockner & Greenberg, 1990; Konovsky & Brockner, 1993).

Layoff victims

Several studies have examined the impact of various determinants of fairness on the reactions of layoff victims. For example, Konovsky and Folger (1991a) surveyed people who had been laid off from a variety of different industries. They found that formal procedures predicted victims' willingness to speak positively about their companies and to eschew government regulation of layoffs. Interestingly, however, neither social accounts nor benefits level (an index of outcome favorability) were associated with these outcomes.

However, in a more recent study, Greenberg, Lind, Scott, and Welchans (1995) found that the fairness of the social treatment people received as their layoffs were announced had a great effect not only on their perceptions of fairness, but also on their interest in seeking legal damages against their former employers. Their interviews of a large number of laid-off people indicated that 40% considered initiating a lawsuit or an EEOC complaint. Some 23% actually talked to a lawyer or EEOC official, and 7% actually filed a suit or a complaint. Logistic regression analyses found that the strongest predictor of the willingness to consider legal action, or to actually take action, was respondents' perceptions that they were treated without dignity or in a disrespectful fashion at the time of their dismissal. In fact, whereas only 16% of those treated well thought about suing, 66% of those treated poorly thought about suing. Additional evidence suggests that victims' reactions to layoffs depended on the degree of harm the layoff caused them: the perceived fairness of the layoff procedures predicted the reactions of victims who felt harmed by the layoffs better than it did the reactions of those who were less adversely affected. These findings replicate an identical reaction identified by Brockner et al. (1994, Study 1).

Layoff survivors

Considerable research also has examined the reactions of layoff survivors. As one might imagine, survivors do not respond positively to watching their coworkers lose their jobs, often arousing 'survivor guilt'. As we described earlier, Brockner et al. (1990) found that when a justification was provided for others' layoffs, survivors responded more positively than when an explanation was lacking. However, this occurred only under conditions in which survivors had a high need for information—that is, when individuals were uncertain about the process used to determine the layoffs and when these negative outcomes were important to them. Although social accounts are important, this is only the case when these accounts are believed to be true. Mellor (1992) examined survivors' commitment to their union following layoffs. The company blamed the job terminations on the union. Survivors who believed this account expressed low commitment to their union when the layoff was severe. However, when the account was not believed or when the layoffs were less severe, commitment to the union was higher.

Brockner et al. (1994, Studies 2 and 3) also examined survivors' reactions to layoffs as a function of procedural justice, operationalized as advance notice of a forthcoming layoff, and outcomes, the level of layoff benefits provided.

They found the expected interaction: Procedures were stronger determinants of employees' responses to layoffs when benefits were unfavorable compared to when they were favorable. These findings need to be considered in light of those obtained by Brockner et al. (1990). In each case, an aspect of procedural justice (be it a social account or advance notice) was an important predictor of reactions, but only when the outcome was severely negative (i.e. when the endangered job was important or the level of benefits was low). These findings provide strong support for the interaction model of justice described earlier. They also send a clear message to organizations who are forced to layoff employees: To minimize negative reactions among survivors, conduct layoffs fairly (such as by fully explaining its need and by giving advance notice), and clearly elucidate that these practices were followed. Reaping the benefits of carrying out fair procedures frequently requires calling others' attention to them (Greenberg, 1990c).

Organizational Citizenship Behaviors

To the extent that people are strongly committed to organizations they believe have treated them fairly, it follows that they would be willing to contribute to its well-being, even if this involves going above and beyond the call of duty. This is the idea behind organizational citizenship behaviors (OCBs)—those helpful and supportive actions by employees that are not part of their formal job description. Examples include showing courtesy to others, being conscientious about work, being a 'good sport' about doing extra work, and generally protecting the organization's property. Insofar as people may have only limited control over some of their work outcomes, and may be reluctant to lower them in response to underpayment, work output may not be the most sensitive indicant of feelings of injustice (Greenberg, 1982). However, given that OCBs are discretionary, and people are free to engage in them or to forgo them if they wish, these behaviors may be highly reactive to fair and unfair treatment (Greenberg, 1993d). Not surprisingly, considerable attention has been paid to understanding the relationship between justice and OCBs (for a review, see Organ & Moorman, 1993).

As Organ (1990) and Reed and Kelly (1993) discuss, OCBs are based on employees' notions of social exchange. When an organization treats individuals fairly, they are likely to reciprocate by exerting extra effort on the firm's behalf (cf. Organ & Konovsky, 1989). Empirical evidence suggests that justice, especially procedural justice, is related to OCB (e.g. Ball, Treviño, & Sims, 1994; Konovsky & Folger, 1991b). Some OCB studies have demonstrated this effect, although they have been nonspecific as to the type of justice involved. For example, Deluga (1994) found that a general measure of fairness was associated with several aspects of OCB. Likewise, Konovsky and Organ (in press) found that a composite variable that they called justice/satisfaction predicted various OCB dimensions.

One of the earliest studies to examine different types of justice was conducted in a Taiwanese government ministry. Farh, Podsakoff, and Organ (1990) found that procedural justice was related to the altruism dimension of OCB. However, for the compliance dimension, procedural justice did not account for a significant amount of the variance above and beyond the effect of job scope. Extending the work of Farh, Podsakoff, and Organ (1990) in an American sample, Moorman (1991) assessed five dimensions of OCB: altruism, courtesy, sportsmanship, conscientiousness, and civic virtue. Neither distributive justice nor formal procedural justice predicted any of these dimensions. However, interactional justice predicted all but civic virtue. Similarly, Lee (1995) also found that the social aspects of justice predicted all of these dimensions except civic virtue, but that formal procedures were related to OCB. Finally, Niehoff and Moorman (1993) obtained a mixed pattern. Formal procedures predicted courtesy, sportsmanship, and conscientiousness, although interactional justice was associated with only sportsmanship. Further muddying the waters, Konovsky, Elliott, and Pugh (1995) found that procedural justice was the better predictor of OCB in an American sample, whereas distributive justice was the better predictor of OCB in a Mexican sample.

The best summary that can be given at this time is that procedural justice is a better predictor of OCB than distributive justice (for Americans, at least). However, it remains unclear which particular components of procedural justice, structural or social, best predict which particular forms of OCB. The picture is further complicated by the possibility that procedural justice may be an indirect predictor of OCB. This possibility has been suggested by Konovsky, Elliott, and Pugh (1995), who found that procedural justice was correlated with trust in their survey of hospital workers. Trust, in turn, was associated with OCB. These findings call our attention to the possibility that procedural justice is only correlated with OCB by way of its influence on trust. This possibility is in keeping with the role of trust as a mediator of procedural justice identified by Brockner and Siegel (in press; Siegel, Brockner, & Tyler, 1995).

Employee Theft

Our discussion of the link between justice and prosocial acts of organizaitonal citizenship may be juxtaposed with an emerging literature on justice and the antisocial act of employee theft (Greenberg, 1997). From the perspective of distributive justice, stealing company property may be understood as an attempt to re-establish equity between the parties involved in a social exchange relationship (for a review, see Greenberg & Scott, 1996). Specifically, in terms of equity theory (Adams, 1965), employees who believe they are receiving insufficient outcomes (e.g. pay) in exchange for their work contributions may effectively raise these outcomes by stealing, thereby redressing their perceived inequities with their employers.

Greenberg has empirically demonstrated this phenomenon in a series of studies. In the first, a quasi-experiment conducted in an organization, Greenberg (1990b) compared the theft rates within three manufacturing plants belonging to the same company. In two of these factories (comprising the experimental groups), all employees encountered a pay-cut of 15% over a 10-week period as the company's response to a financial crisis. A third plant, with demographically similar employees, in which there were no pay cuts, served as the control group. Insofar as employees in the first two plants received lower pay than they had in the past, they were considered to have suffered underpayment inequity. To assess theft, standard measures of shrinkage were taken by agents unaware of the study. Consistent with equity theory, Greenberg (1990b) found that theft rates were significantly higher within the plants in which employees' pay was cut than in the control group. These differences are particularly dramatic when one considers that theft rates were consistently low in all three plants both before the pay cut, and also after regular rates of pay were reinstated.

Going beyond this straightforward test of equity theory, this investigation also considered the social determinants of justice by examining the manner in which the pay cut was explained to the workers in the two experimental groups. Employees at one plant, selected at random, were given an elaborate and caring explanation of the need for pay to be cut (the adequate explanation condition). By contrast, workers in the other experimental plant were given limited information about the need for the pay cut, accompanied by only superficial expressions of remorse (the inadequate explanation condition). The differences between these two plants was striking: Over twice as much theft occurred in the plant whose employees received the inadequate explanation compared to the plant whose employees received the adequate explanation.

These dramatic findings are limited by the confounding of two key variables—the amount of information presented about the reason for the pay cut, and the amount of sensitivity shown regarding the impact of the pay cut. To eliminate this confounding, Greenberg (1993a) independently manipulated these variables in a follow-up experiment conducted in a laboratory setting. Undergraduates were hired to perform a clerical task in exchange for $5 per hour, a rate shown in pretesting to be perceived as fair. After performing the task, a random half of the participants (the underpaid group) were told that they would be paid only $3. The other half of the participants (the equitably paid group) were told they would be paid the $5 promised.

As he announced the pay rate, Greenberg systematically manipulated the quality of the information used as the basis for establishing the pay rate, giving an explanation that was either extremely thorough and based on ostensibly verified facts (the high valid information condition) or one that was extremely incomplete and based on questionable facts (the low valid information condition). He also manipulated, via his remarks, the amount of remorse and concern shown for having caused the underpayment, demonstrating either great amounts (the high social sensitivity condition) or very limited amounts (the low social sensitivity condition). After treating the subjects in these manners, the experiment left subjects alone in a room with an ostensibly unknown sum of money and invited them to take the amount they were supposed to take (i.e. $3 in the underpayment group and $5 in the equitable payment group). However, because the experimenter knew the exact amount of money left on the desk, he was able to determine precisely how much was taken. Amounts of in excess of the stated wages were considered theft.

Consistent with equity theory, subjects who were equitably paid did not steal, whereas those who were underpaid did steal. In particular, the amount they stole was dependent upon the way they were treated. Subjects receiving high amounts of information stole less than those receiving low amounts. Likewise, those treated with high levels of social sensitivity stole less than those receiving low levels. Furthermore, these effects combined in an additive fashion: Those receiving high amounts of both variables stole the least, whereas those receiving low amounts of both stole the most.

These findings suggest not only that pay inequity induces theft, but also that the amount of theft in which the people engage depends on the nature of the interpersonal treatment they receive: Positive treatment (i.e., thorough information presented in a socially sensitive manner) at the hands of an authority figure lowers theft. People are interested in evening the score with those who have treated them inequitably, and use theft as a device for doing so— particularly when the source of the inequity shows little concern and remorse. When Greenberg's (1993a) subjects stole the money they may have been attempting to make up for the underpayment they received at the hands of the investigator, or they may have been attempting to retaliate against the investigator by taking too much money. Indeed, both restitution and retaliation are possible responses to theft-induced inequities. Because taking more money than one is supposed to simultaneously advantages oneself and disadvantages the authority figure, it is impossible to distinguish between the restitution and retaliation motives for theft. Acknowledging this limitation, Greenberg (1994b) replicated and extended this study in a manner that made it possible to deduce subjects' underlying motives for stealing.

The task subjects performed consisted of counting small round objects and packaging them into rolls so they could be easily counted. In one condition the objects were 25¢ coins (quarters). In another condition, they were similarly sized objects—lithium batteries said to be valuable experimental prototypes. Subjects performed the task alone in rooms in which buckets of either quarters or batteries were put in front of them. Some subjects encountered an underpayment inequity as they completed the task: they were told that they would only be paid $3 for the half-hour's work instead of the $6.00 they were initially promised. After this announcement was made, the experimenter left the room, but not before giving subjects three $1 bills. Subjects then completed a questionnaire while in the presence of the coins or batteries they were counting. As in the Greenberg (1993a) study, the explanation for this surprising negative turn of events was either thoroughly explained or not thoroughly explained, and in a manner that demonstrated either a high or low level of dignity and personal concern. Because the number of batteries or coins in the bucket was known in advance (although subjects were led to believe otherwise), it was possible to determine if they had stolen anything. It was reasoned that any theft of the batteries could be interpreted as an act of retaliation insofar as it only would harm the company but be of no value to the subjects themselves. However, theft of the quarters would mutually harm the company while benefiting themselves (making the motive at least retaliation, but also possibly restitution). Thus, in this study, the items stolen were taken as cues to the underlying motives for the theft.

When the subjects were working with quarters, the results replicated those of Greenberg (1993a). That is, both information and sensitivity independently affected theft: When both were high theft was lowest; when both were low, theft was highest; and when one factor was high and the other low, theft was intermediate. However, when subjects were working with allegedly valuable lithium batteries the only variable that affected theft was the amount of respect and dignity shown while explaining the inequity. When the level of dignity displayed was high, theft was low or nonexistent. However, when it was low, the level of theft rose considerably. By contrast, the amount of information presented about the reasons for the unexpectedly low pay had no effects on the stealing of batteries; the level of theft observed in this condition was quite low. These results suggest that the combined effects of treating people inequitably while failing to treat them with dignity and respect led them to retaliate against the source of their harm, the authority figure.

The sociologist Kemper (1996) has referred to this type of retaliative behavior as *reciprocal deviance*—the deviance that results when an authority figure defaults on his or her obligations to an individual. In fact the acts of 'striking back' observed here in response to an inequity, are conceptually consistent with the inequitable conditions Kemper (1966) identified as inviting reciprocal deviance. However, it is interesting to note that it was not just the inequity that triggered theft, but the inequity augmented by a lack of personal sensitivity. This combination appears to have added insult to injury, triggering an interest in retaliation. This is not to say that the retaliation response is purely without benefit for the harmdoer. Although acts of reciprocal deviance may fail to redress an inequity financially, they may do so symbolically. That is, if one cannot directly benefit oneself, then at least one can derive satisfaction from knowing that one has harmed another who has harmed oneself.

Taken together, the Greenberg studies (1990b, 1993a, 1994b) suggest that it is not only the magnitude of the inequity that determines theft, but also the *way* that inequity is presented—that is, the treatment of employees. Further illustrating this point, Greenberg (1994c) administered a questionnaire to workers assessing their perceptions of various aspects of unfairness in their workplace. The respondents were approached as they recorded their 'punch out' times on a piece of paper while the investigator surreptitiously noted the actual times they stopped in front of the clock. (A sign informed the workers that the time clock was being repaired, and directed them to record their names and 'punch out' times on a form provided for that purpose. A large digital clock was placed where the time clock was usually found.) By comparing the actual 'punch out' times with those recorded, a measure of time theft was created—the reporting of more time than actually worked. Although the actual amount of time theft was rather low, variance in this measure was significantly accounted for by responses to several questionnaire items. Two variables best predicted time theft: the amount of compassion shown by supervisors, and the degree of respect employers show for employees. By contrast, general measures of pay fairness were weaker predictors of theft. Again, these findings suggest that theft is associated with unfair treatment of an interpersonal nature. Uncaring, inconsiderate supervision is a key determinant of employee theft.

In summary, it appears that employee theft is more than simply an attempt to restore a mathematical balance between outcomes and inputs. Such inequities appear to be necessary for theft to occur, but may not always be sufficient. What needs to be added to the formula for predicting employee theft is improper social treatment—variously called social insensitivity, lack of dignity, rudeness, disrespect, or lack of compassion. Thus, whereas insufficient outcomes may stimulate awareness of inequitable states, it requires social insensitivity to this condition to trigger the theft response.

CONCLUSION

Our review of the recent literature on organizational justice has distinguished between various types of justice and has examined the relationships between them. We saw that fairness is an important determinant of a variety of important work outcomes, such as commitment, turnover intentions, and organizational citizenship behaviors. Especially consequential is the manner in which organizational justice theories have been applied to a host of managerial practices, including selection, theft-prevention, and conflict-resolution. When fairness is incorporated into these practices, beneficial outcomes accrue to both individuals and the organizations employing them.

If nothing else, our analysis demonstrates that justice is a common theme that cuts across all aspects of work life, providing coherence and unity to an array of organizational practices that otherwise might appear unconnected. This is not to say that fairness is the only, or even the most important consideration in organizational practice. Our point is more modest—but only slightly so: Justice can be a consideration in virtually everything that an organization does because it is through its policies and procedures that a company defines its relationship to each employee. In other words, fairness partially determines how an organization and its members treat one another. It provides a framework within which individuals and institutions interact. This relationship, when characterized by fairness and mutual respect, is a healthy source of morale and productive behavior (Rosen, 1991). We believe that it is implicit recognition of this important point that has stimulated so much attention to matters of organizational justice in recent years. In a field lacking any established research paradigm or unifying theory, and only limited conceptual agreement, the maze of research on organizational justice has grown increasingly complex. Hopefully, by tunneling through this maze, our guided tour of the literature has convinced readers that the journey is worthwhile.

AUTHOR NOTE

Preparation of this chapter was provided in part by National Science Foundation grant number SBR-9224169 awarded to Jerald Greenberg.

REFERENCES

Adams, J. S. (1965) Inequity in social exchange. In L. Berkowitz (ed.), *Advances in Experimental Social Psychology*, Vol. 2 (pp. 267–299). New York: Adcademic Press.

Ambrose, M. L., Harland, L. K., & Kulik, C. T. (1991) Influence of social comparisons on perceptions of organizational fairness. *Journal of Applied Psychology*, 76, 239–246.

Ambrose, M. L. & Rosse, J. G. (1993) Relational justice and personality testing: Sometimes nice guys do finish last. Unpublished manuscript. University of Colorado, Boulder, CO.

Arvey, R. D. (1992) Fairness and ethical considerations in employee selection. In D. M. Saunders (ed.), *New Approaches in Employee Selection*, Vol. 1 (pp. 1–19). Greenwich, CT: JAI Press.

Arvey, R. D. & Sackett, P. R. (1993) Fairness in selection: Current developments and perspectives. In N. Schmitt & W. Borman (eds), *Personnel Selection* (pp. 171–202). San Francisco: Jossey-Bass.

Austin, W. (1977) Equity theory and social comparison processes. In J. M. Suls & R. M. Miller (eds), *Social Comparison Processes* (pp. 279–306). Washington, DC: Hemisphere.

Ball, G. A., Treviño, L. K., & Sims, H. P., Jr (1994) Just and unjust punishment: Influences on subordinate performance and citizenship. *Academy of Management Journal*, 37, 299–322.

Bazerman, M. H., Schroth, H. A., Shah, P. P., Diekmann, K. A., & Tenbrunsel, A. E. (1994) The inconsistent role of comparison others and procedural justice in reactions to hypothetical job descriptions: Implications for job acceptance decisions. *Organizational Behavior and Human Decision Processes*, 60, 326–352.

Bergmann, T. J. & Volkema, R. J. (1994) Issues, behavioral responses and consequences in interpersonal conflicts. *Journal of Organizational Behavior*, 15, 467–471.

Bierhoff, H. W., Cohen, R. L., & Greenberg, J. (1986) *Justice in Social Relations*. New York: Plenum.

Bies, R. J. (1987) The predicament of injustice: The management of moral outrage. In L. L. Cummings & B. M. Staw (eds), *Research in Organizational Behavior*, Vol. 9 (pp. 289–319). Greenwich, CT: JAI Press.

Bies, R. J. & Moag, J. S. (1986) Interactional justice: Communication criteria of fairness. In R. J. Lewicki, B. H. Sheppard, & M. Bazerman (eds), *Research on Negotiation in Organizations*, Vol. 1 (pp. 43–55). Greenwich, CT: JAI Press.

Bies, R. J. & Tyler, T. R. (1993) The 'litigation mentality' in organizations: A test of alternative psychological explanations. *Organizational Science*, 4, 352–366.

Bond, M. H., Leung, K., & Schwartz, S. (1992) Explaining choices in procedural and distributive justice across cultures. *International Journal of Psychology*, 27, 211–225.

Brockner, J. (1988) *Self-esteem at Work: Reserach, Theory, and Practice*. Lexington, MA: Lexington Press.

Brockner, J. (1994) Perceived fairness and survivors' reactions to layoffs, or how downsizing organizations can do well by doing good. *Social Justice Research*, 7, 345–363.

Brockner, J., DeWitt, R. L., Grover, S., & Reed, T. (1990) When it is especially important to explain why: Factors affecting the relationship between managers' explanations of a layoff and survivors' reactions to the layoff. *Journal of Experimental Social Psychology*, 26, 389–407.

Brockner, J. & Greenberg, J. (1990) The impact of layoffs on survivors: An organizational justice perspective. In J. S. Carroll (eds), *Applied Social Psychology and Organizational Settings* (pp. 45–75). Hillsdale, NJ: Erlbaum.

Brockner, J., Konovsky, M., Cooper-Schneider, R., Folger, R., Martin, C., & Bies, R. J. (1994) Interactive effects of procedural justice and outcome negativity on victims and survivors of job loss. *Academy of Management Journal*, 37, 397–409.

Brockner, J. & Siegel, P. (1995) Understanding the interaction between procedural and distributive justice. In R. M. Kramer & T. R. Tyler (eds), *Trust in Organizations*. Newbury Park, CA: Sage.

Brockner, J., Tyler, T. R., & Cooper-Schneider, R. (1992) The influence of prior commitment to an institution on reactions to perceived unfairness: The higher they are, the harder they fall. *Administrative Science Quarterly*, 37, 241–261.

Brockner, J. & Wiesenfeld, B. M (1996) An integrative framework for explaining reactions to decisions: The interactive effects of outcomes and procedures. *Psychological Bulletin*, 120, 189–208.

Cascio, W. F. (1995) Whither industrial and organizational psychology in a changing world of work? *American Psychologist*, 50, 928–939.

Chen, C. C. (1995) New trends in rewards allocation preferences: A Sino-US comparison. *Academy of Management Journal*, 38, 408–428.

Clemmer, E. C. (1993) An investigation into the relationship of fairness and customer satisfaction with services. In R. Cropanzano (ed.), *Justice in the Workplace: Approaching Fairness in Human Resource Management* (pp. 193–207). Hillsdale, NJ: Erlbaum.

Cohen, R. L. (1986) *Justice: Views from the Social Sciences*. New York: Plenum.

Cohen, R. L. & Greenberg, J. (1982) The justice concept in social psychology. In J. Greenberg & R. L. Cohen (eds), *Equity and Justice in Social Behavior* (pp. 1–41). New York: Academic Press.

Conlon, D. E. (1993) Some tests of the self-interest and group-value models of procedural justice: Evidence from an organizational appeal procedure. *Academy of Management Journal*, 36, 1109–1124.

Conlon, D. E. & Fasolo, P. M. (1990) Influence of speed of third-party intervention and outcome on negotiator and constituent fairness judgments. *Academy of Management Journal*, 33, 833–846.

Conlon, D. E. & Ross, W. H. (1993) The effects of partisan third parties on negotiator behavior and outcome perception. *Journal of Applied Psychology*, 78, 280–290.

Cooper, C. L., Dyck, B., & Frohlich, N. (1992) Improving the effectiveness of gain-sharing: The role of fairness and participation. *Administrative Science Quarterly*, **37**, 471–490.

Cowherd, D. M. & Levine, D. I. (1992) Product quality and pay equity between lower-level employees and top management: An investigation of distributive justice theory. *Administrative Science Quarterly*, **37**, 302–320.

Crant, J. M. & Bateman, T. S. (1990) An experimental test of the impact of drug-testing programs on potential job applicants' attitudes and intentions. *Journal of Applied Psychology*, **75**, 127–131.

Crant, J. M. & Bateman, T. S. (1993) Potential job applicant reactions to employee drug testing: The effects of program characteristics and individual differences. *Journal of Business and Psychology*, **7**, 279–290.

Cropanzano, R. (ed.) (1993) *Justice in the Workplace: Approaching Fairness in Human Resource Management*. Hillsdale, NJ: Erlbaum.

Cropanzano, R., Aguinis, H., Schminke, M., & Denham, D. L. (August 1996) Disputant reactions to managerial conflict intervention strategies: A comparison among Argentina, the Dominican Republic, Mexico and the United States. In J. G. Rosse (chair), *Justice and Fairness in Organizations*. Symposium conducted at the 1996 meeting of the Academy of Management. Cincinnati, OH.

Cropanzano, R. & Folger, R. (1991) Procedural justice and worker motivation. In R. M. Steers & L. W. Porter (eds), *Motivation and Work Behavior*. Fifth edition (pp. 131–143). New York: McGraw-Hill.

Cropanzano, R. & Konovsky, M. A. (1995) Resolving the justice dilemma by improving the outcomes: The case of employee drug screening. *Journal of Business and Psychology*, **10**, 221–243.

Cropanzano, R. & Randall, M. L. (1993). Injustice and work behavior: A historical review. In R. Cropanzano (ed.), *Justice in the Workplace: Approaching Fairness in Human Resource Management* (pp. 1–20). Hillsdale, NJ: Erlbaum.

Cropanzano, R. & Randall, M. L. (1995) Advance notice as a means of reducing relative deprivation. *Social Justice Research*, **8**, 217–238.

Dailey, R. C. & Kirk, D. J. (1992) Distributive and procedural justice as antecedents of job dissatisfaction and intent to turnover. *Human Relations*, **45**, 305–317.

Daly, J. P. & Geyer, P. D. (1994) The role of fairness in implementing large-scale change: Employee evaluations of process and outcome in seven facility relocations. *Journal of Organizational Behavior*, **15**, 623–638.

Daly, J. P. & Geyer, P. D. (1995) Procedural fairness and organizational commitment under conditions of growth and decline. *Social Justice Research*, **8**, 137–151.

Davis, R. (1993) When applicants rate the examinations: Feedback from 2000 people. In B. Nevo & R. S. Jäger (eds), *Educational and Psychological Testing: The Test Taker's Outlook* (pp. 221–237). Toronto, Canada: Hogrefe & Huber.

Deluga, R. J. (1994) Supervisor trust building, leader-member exchange and organizational citizenship behaviour. *Journal of Occupational and Organizational Psychology*, **67**, 315–326.

Deutsch, M. (1975) Equity, equality, and need: What determines which value will be used as the basis for distributive justice? *Journal of Social Issues*, **31**(3), 137–149.

Deutsch, M. (1985) *Distributive Justice: A Social-Psychological Perspective*. New Haven, CT: Yale University Press.

Dutton, J. E. & Dukerich, J. M. (1991) Keeping an eye on the mirror: Image and identity in organizational adaptation. *Academy of Management Journal*, **34**, 517–554.

Dworkin, J. B. (1994) Managerial third party dispute resolution: An overview and introduction to the special issue. *Employee Responsibilities and Rights Journal*, **7**, 1–8.

Elangovan, A. R. (1995) Managerial third-party dispute intervention: A perspective model of strategy selection. *Academy of Management Review*, **20**, 800–830.

Elsbach, K. D. (1994) Managing organizational legitimacy in the California cattle industry: The construction and effectiveness of verbal accounts. *Administrative Science Quarterly*, **39**, 57–88.

Elsbach, K. D. & Sutton, R. I. (1992) Acquiring organizational legitimacy through illegitimate actions: A marriage of institutional and impression management theories. *Academy of Management Journal*, **35**, 699–738.

Farh, J., Podsakoff, P. M., & Organ, D. W. (1990) Accounting for organizational citizenship behavior: Leader fairness and task scope versus satisfaction. *Journal of Management*, **16**. 705–721.

Finkle, R. B. (1976) Managerial assessment centers. In M. D. Dunnette (ed.), *Handbook of Industrial and Organizational Psychology*. Second edition (pp. 861–888). Chicago: Rand McNally.

Flinder, S. W. & Hauenstein, M. A. N. (1994) Antecedents of distributive and procedural justice perceptions. Unpublished manuscript, Virginia Polytechnic Institution and State University, Blacksburg, VA.

Foa, U. G. & Foa, E. B. (1974) *Social Structures of the Mind*. Springfield, IL: Charles C. Thomas.

Folger, R. (1994) Workplace justice and employee worth. *Social Justice Research*, **7**, 225–241.

Folger, R. & Bies, R. J. (1989) Managerial responsibilities and procedural justice. *Employee Responsibilities and Rights Journal*, **2**, 79–90.

Folger, R. & Cropanzano, R. (in press) *Organizational Justice and Human Resource Management*. Thousand Oaks, CA: Sage.

Folger, R. & Greenberg, J. (1985) Procedural justice: An interpretative analysis of personnel systems. In K. Rowland & G. Ferris (eds), *Research in Personnel and Human Resources Management*, Vol. 3 (pp. 141–183). Greenwich, CT: JAI Press.

Folger, R., Konovsky, M. A., & Cropanzano, R. (1992) A due process metaphor for performance appraisal. In B. M. Staw & L. L. Cummings (eds), *Research in Organizational Behavior*, Vol. 14 (pp. 129–177). Greenwich, CT: JAI Press.

Frohlich, N., Oppenheimer, J. A., & Eavy, C. L. (1987a) Laboratory results on Rawls's distributive justice. *British Journal of Political Science*, **17**, 1–21.

Frohlich, N., Oppenheimer, J. A., & Eavy, C. L. (1987b) Choice of principles of distributive justice in experimental groups. *American Journal of Political Science*, **45**, 606–636.

Gatewood, R. D., Gowan, M., & Lautenschlager, G. J. (1993) Corporate image, recruitment image, and initial job choice decisions. *Academy of Management Journal*, **36**, 414–427.

Gergen, K. J., Morse, S. J., & Gergen, M. M. (1980) Behavior exchange in cross-cultural perspective. In H. C. Triandis & R. W. Brislin (eds), *Handbook of Cross-cultural Psychology: Social Psychology*, Vol. 5 (pp. 121–153). Boston: Allyn & Bacon.

Giacobbe-Miller, J. (1995) A test of the group-values and control models of procedural justice from competing perspectives of labor and management. *Personnel Psychology*, **48**, 115–142.

Gilliland, S. W. (1993) The perceived fairness of selection systems: An organizational justice perspective. *Academy of Management Review*, **18**, 694–734.

Gilliland, S. W. (1994) Effects of procedural and distributive justice on reactions to a selection system. *Journal of Applied Psychology*, **79**, 691–701.

Gist, M. E. & Mitchell, T. R. (1992) Self-efficacy: A theoretical analysis of its determinants and malleability. *Academy of Management Journal*, **17**, 183–211.

Greenberg, J. (1982) Approaching equity and avoiding inequity in groups and organizations. In J. Greenberg & R. L. Cohen (eds), *Equity and Justice in Social Behavior* (pp. 389–435). New York: Academic Press.

Greenberg, J. (1983) Overcoming egocentric bias in perceived fairness through self-awareness. *Social Psychology Quarterly*, **46**, 152–156.

Greenberg, J. (1986a) Determinants of perceived fairness of performance evaluations. *Journal of Applied Psychology*, 71, 340–342.

Greenberg, J. (1986b) The distributive justice of organizational performance evaluations. In H. W. Bierhoff, R. L. Cohen & J. Greenberg (eds), *Justice in Social Relations* (pp. 337–351). New York: Plenum.

Greenberg, J. (1986c) Organizational performance appraisal procedures: What makes them fair? In R. J. Lewicki, B. H. Sheppard, & M. H. Bazerman (eds), *Research on Negotiation in Organizations* Vol. 1 (pp. 25–41). Greenwich, CT: JAI Press.

Greenberg, J. (1987a) A taxonomy of organizational justice theories. *Academy of Management Review*, 12, 9–22.

Greenberg, J. (1987b) Reactions to procedural injustice in payment distributions: Do the means justify the ends? *Journal of Applied Psychology*, 72, 55–61.

Greenberg, J. (1990a) Organizational justice: Yesterday, today, and tomorow. *Journal of Management*, 16, 399–432.

Greenberg, J. (1990b) Employee theft as a reaction to underpayment inequity: The hidden cost of pay cuts. *Journal of Applied Psychology*, 75, 561–568.

Greenberg, J. (1990c) Looking fair vs being fair: Managing impressions of organizational justice. In B. M. Staw & L. L. Cummings (eds), *Research in Organizational Behavior*, Vol. 12 (pp. 111–157). Greenwich, CT: JAI Press.

Greenberg, J. (1993a) Stealing in the name of justice: Informational and interpersonal moderators of theft reactions to underpayment inequity. *Organizational Behavior and Human Decision Processes*, 54, 81–103.

Greenberg, J. (1993b) The social side of fairness: Interpersonal and informational classes of organizational justice. In R. Cropanzano (ed.), *Justice in the Workplace: Approaching Fairness in Human Resource Management* (pp. 79–103). Hillsdale, NJ: Erlbaum.

Greenberg, J. (1993c) The intellectual adolescence of organizational justice: You've come a long way, maybe. *Social Justice Research*, 6, 135–147.

Greenberg, J. (1993d) Justice and organizational citizenship: A commentary on the state of the science. *Employee Responsibilities and Rights Journal*, 6, 227–237.

Greenberg, J. (1994a) Using socially fair treatment to promote acceptance of a work site smoking ban. *Journal of Applied Psychology*, 79, 288–297.

Greenberg, J. (1994b) Restitution and retaliation as motives for inequity-induced pilferage. Unpublished manuscript, Ohio State University.

Greenberg, J. (1994c) Interpersonal determinants of time theft in the workplace. Unpublished manuscript, Ohio State University.

Greenberg, J. (1996a) *The Quest for Justice on the Job: Essays and Experiments*. Thousand Oaks, CA: Sage.

Greenberg, J. (1996b) 'Forgive me, I'm new': Three experimental demonstrations of the effects of attempts to excuse poor performance. *Organizational Behavior and Human Decision Processes*, 66, 165–178.

Greenberg, J. (1997) The STEAL Motive: Managing the social determinants of employee theft. In R. Giacalone & J. Greenberg (eds), *Antisocial Behavior in the Workplace* (pp. 85–108). Thousand Oaks, CA: Sage.

Greenberg, J. & Bies, R. J. (1992) Establishing the role of empirical studies of organizational justice in philosophical inquiries into business ethics. *Journal of Business Ethics*, 11, 433–444.

Greenberg, J., Bies, R. J., & Eskew, D. E. (1991) Establishing fairness in the eye of the beholder: Managing impressions of organizational justice. In R. Giacalone & P. Rosenfeld (eds), *Applied Impression Management: How Image Making Affects Managerial Decisions* (pp. 111–132). Newbury Park, CA: Sage.

Greenberg, J. & Cohen, R. L. (1982a) *Equity and Justice in Social Behavior*. New York: Academic Press.

Greenberg, J. & Cohen, R. L. (1982b) Why justice? Normative and instrumental interpretations. In J. Greenberg & R. L. Cohen (eds), *Equity and Justice in Social Behavior* (pp. 437–469). New York: Academic Press.

Greenberg, J. & Folger, R. (1983) Procedural justice, participation, and the fair process effect in groups and organizations. In P. B. Paulus (ed.), *Basic Group Processes* (pp. 235–256). New York: Springer-Verlag.

Greenberg, J., Lind, E. A., Scott, K. S., & Welchans, T. D. (1995) [Wrongful termination litigation in response to perceived injustice among layoff victims.] Unpublished raw data.

Greenberg, J. & McCarty, C. (1990) Comparable worth: A matter of justice. In G. R. Ferris & K. M. Rowland (eds), *Research in Personnel and Human Resources Management*, Vol. 8 (pp. 265–301). Greenwich, CT: JAI Press.

Greenberg, J. & Scott, K. S. (1996) Why do employees bite the hands that feed them? Employee theft as a social exchange process. In B. M. Staw & L. L. Cummings (eds), *Research in Organizational Behavior* (pp. 111–166). Greenwich, CT: JAI Press.

Greenberg, J. & Tyler, T. R. (1987) Why procedural justice in organizations? *Social Justice Research*, **1**, 127–142.

Grover, S. L. (1991) Predicting the perceived fairness of parental leave policies. *Journal of Applied Psychology*, **76**, 247–255.

Guion, R. M. (1965) *Personnel Testing.* New York: McGraw-Hill.

Guion, R. M. (1991) Personnel assessment, selection, and placement. In M. D. Dunnette & L. M. Hough (eds), *Handbook of Industrial and Organizational Psychology.* Second edition, Vol. 2 (pp. 327–398). Palo Alto, CA: Consulting Psychologists Press.

Harder, J. W. (1992) Play for pay: Effects of inequity in pay-for-performance context. *Administrative Science Quarterly*, **37**, 321–335.

Harland, L. K. & Biasotto, M. M. (1993, August) An evaluation of the procedural fairness of personality tests. Paper presented at the annual meeting of the Academy of Management, Atlanta, GA.

Harris, M. M., Dworkin, J. B., & Park, J. (1990) Preemployment screening procedures: How human resource managers perceive them. *Journal of Business and Psychology*, **4**, 279–292.

Hofstede, G. (1980) *Culture's Consequences.* London: Sage.

Homans, G. C. (1986) *Social Behavior: Its Elementary Forms.* New York: Harcourt, Brace, & World.

Hulin, C. L. (1991) Adaptation, persistence, and commitment in organizations. In M. D. Dunnette & L. M. Hough (eds), *Handbook of Industrial and Organizational Psychology.* Second edition, Vol. 2 (pp. 445–506). Palo Alto, CA: Consulting Psychologists Press.

James, K. (1993) The social context of organizational justice: Cultural, intergroup, and structural effects on justice behaviors and perceptions. In R. Cropanzano (ed.), *Justice in the Workplace: Approaching Fairness in Human Resource Management* (pp. 21–50). Hillsdale, NJ: Erlbaum.

Jones, J. W. (1991) Assessing privacy invasiveness of psychological test items: Job relevant versus clinical masures of integrity. *Journal of Business and Psychology*, **5**, 531–535.

Kabanoff, B. (1991) Equity, equality, power, and conflict. *Academy of Management Review*, **16**, 416–441.

Karambayya, R. & Brett, J. M. (1994) Managerial third parties: Intervention strategies, process, and consequences. In J. Folger & T. Jones (eds), *New Directions in Mediation: Communication Research and Perspectives* (pp. 175–192). Thousand Oaks, CA: Sage.

Karambayya, R., Brett, J. M., & Lytle, A. (1992) Effects of formal authority and experience on third-party roles, outcomes, and perceptions of fairness. *Academy of Management Journal*, **35**, 426–438.

Kemper, T. D. (1966) Representative roles and the legitimization of deviance. *Social Problems*, **13**, 288–298.

Kim, W. C. & Mauborgne, R. A. (1991) Implementing global strategies: The role of procedural justice. *Strategic Management Journal*, **12**, 125–143.

Kim, W. C. & Mauborgne, R. A. (1993) Procedural justice, attitudes, and subsidiary top management compliance with multinationals' corporate strategic decsions. *Academy of Management Journal*, **36**, 502–526.

Kluger, A. N. & Rothstein, H. R. (1993) The influence of selection test type on applicant reactions to employment testing. *Journal of Business and Psychology*, **8**, 3–25.

Knouse, S. P. (1989) Impression management and letters of recommendation. In R. A. Giacalone & R. Rosenfeld (eds), *Impression Management in the Organization* (pp. 283–296). Hillsdale, NJ: Erlbaum.

Kolb, D. M. (1985) To be a mediator: Expressive tactics in mediation. *Journal of Social Issues*, **41**, 1–25.

Kolb, D. M. (1986) Who are organizational third parties and what do they do? In R. J. Lewicki, B. H. Sheppard, & M. H. Bazerman (eds), *Research on Negotiation in Organizations* (pp. 207–228). Greenwich, CT: JAI Press.

Konovsky, M. A. & Brockner, J. (1993) Managing victim and survivor layoff reactions: A procedural justice perspective. In R. Cropanzano (ed.), *Justice in the Workplace: Approaching Fairness in Human Resource Management* (pp. 133–153). Hillsdale, NJ: Erlbaum.

Konovsky, M. A. & Cropanzano, R. (1991) The perceived fairness of employee drug testing as a predictor of employee attitudes and job performance. *Journal of Applied Psychology*, **76**, 698–707.

Konovsky, M. A. & Cropanzano, R. (1993) Justice considerations in employee drug testing. In R. Cropanzano (ed.), *Justice in the Workplace: Approaching Fairness in Human Resource Management* (pp. 171–192). Hillsdale, NJ: Erlbaum.

Konovsky, M. A., Elliott, J., & Pugh, S. D. (1995, August) The dispositional and contextual predictors of citizenship behavior in Mexico. Paper presented at the annual meeting of the Academy of Management, Vancouver, BC, Canada.

Konovsky, M. A. & Folger, R. (1991a) The effects of procedures, social accounts, and benefits level on victims' layoff reactions. *Journal of Applied Social Psychology*, **21**, 630–650.

Konovsky, M. A. & Folger, R. (1991b, August) The effects of procedural and distributive justice on organizational citizenship behavior. Paper presented at the annual meeting of the Academy of Management, Miami Beach, FL.

Konovsky, M. A. & Organ, D. W. (in press) Dispositional and contextual determinants of organizational citizenship behaviors. *Journal of Organizational Behavior*.

Konovsky, M. A. & Pugh, S. D. (1994) Citizenship behavior and social exchange. *Academy of Management Journal*, **37**, 656–669.

Koper, G., Van Knippenberg, D., Bouhuijs, F., Vermunt, R., & Wilke, H. (1993) Procedural fairness and self-esteem. *European Journal of Social Psychology*, **23**, 313–325.

Korsgaard, M. A., Schweiger, D. M., & Sapienza, H. J. (1995) Building commitment, attachment, and trust in strategic decision-making teams: The role of procedural justice. *Academy of Management Journal*, **38**, 60–84.

Kozan, M. K., & Ilter, S. S. (1994) Third party roles played by Turkish managers in subordinates' conflicts. *Journal of Organizational Behavior*, **15**, 453–466.

Kravitz, D. A., Stinson, V., & Chavez, T. L. (in press) Evaluations of tests used for making selection and promotion decisions. *International Journal of Selection and Assessment*.

Krzystofiak, F. J., Lillis, M., & Newman, J. M. (1995, August) Justice along the scarcity continuum. Paper presented at the annual meeting of the Academy of Management. Vancouver, BC, Canada.

Kulik, C. T. & Ambrose, M. L. (1992) Personal and situational determinants of referent choice. *Academy of Management Review*, **17**, 212–237.

Labig, C. E. Jr (1992) Supervisory and nonsupervisory employee attitude about drug testing. *Employee Responsibilities and Rights Journal*, **5**, 131–141.

Latham, G. P. & Finnegan, B. J. (1993) Perceived practicality of unstructured, patterned, and situational interviews. In H. Schuler, J. L. Farr, & M. Smith (eds), *Personnel Selection and Assessment: Individual and Organizational Perspectives* (pp. 41–55). Hillsdale, NJ: Erlbaum.

Lee, C. (1995) Prosocial organizational behaviors: The roles of workplace justice, achievement striving, and pay satisfaction. *Journal of Business and Psychology*, **10**, 197–206.

Lengel, R. H. & Daft, R. L. (1988) The selection of communication media as an executive skill. *Academy of Management Executive*, **2**, 225–232.

Leung, K., Chiu, W.-H., & Au, Y.-F. (1993) Sympathy and support for industrial actions: A justice analysis. *Journal of Applied Psychology*, **78**, 781–787.

Leventhal, G. S. (1976a) The distribution of rewards and resources in groups and organizations. In L. Berkowitz & E. Walster (eds), *Advances in Experimental Social Psychology*, Vol. 9 (pp. 91–131). New York: Academic Press.

Leventhal, G. S. (1976b) Fairness in social relationships. In J. W. Thibaut, J. T. Spence, & R. C. Carson (eds), *Contemporary Topics in Social Psychology* (pp. 211–240). Morristown, NJ: General Learning Press.

Leventhal, G. S. (1980) What should be done with equity theory? In K. J. Gergen, M. S. Greenberg, & R. H. Willis (eds), *Social Exchanges: Advances in Theory and Research* (pp. 27–55). New York: Plenum.

Leventhal, G. S., Karuza, J., & Fry, W. R. (1980) Beyond fairness: A theory of allocation preferences. In G. Milkula (ed.), *Justice and Social Interaction* (pp. 167–218). New York: Springer-Verlag.

Lind, E. A. (1995) Justice and authority relations in organizations. In R. Cropanzano & M. K. Kacmar (eds), *Organizational Politics, Justice, and Support: Managing the Social Climate of the Workplace* (pp. 83–96). Westport, CT: Quorum Books.

Lind, E. A. & Earley, P. C. (1992) Procedural justice and culture. *International Journal of Psychology*, **27**, 227–242.

Lind, E. A., Kanfer, R., & Earley, P. C. (1990) Voice, control, and procedural justice: Instrumental and noninstrumental concerns in fairness judgments. *Journal of Personality and Social Psychology*, **59**, 952–959.

Lind, E. A., Kulik, C. A., Ambrose, M., & de Vera Park, M. V. (1993) Individual and corporate dispute resolution: Using procedural fairness as a decision heuristic. *Administrative Science Quarterly*, **38**, 224–251.

Lind, E. A. & Lissak, R. I. (1985) Apparent impropriety and procedural fairness judgments. *Journal of Experimental Social Psychology*, **21**, 19–29.

Lind, E. A. & Tyler, T. R. (1988) *The Social Psychology of Procedural Justice*. New York: Plenum.

Lissowski, G., Tyszka, T., & Okrasa, W. (1991) Principles of distributive justice: Experiments in Poland and America. *Journal of Conflict Resolution*, **35**, 98–119.

Lowe, R. H. & Vodanovich, S. H. (1995) A field study of distributive and procedural justice as predictors of satisfaction and organizational commitment. *Journal of Business and Psychology*, **10**. 99–114.

Lowell, R. S. & DeLoach, J. A. (1984) Equal employment opportunity: Are you overlooking the application form? In R. S. Schuler & S. A. Youngblood (eds), *Reading in Personnel and Human Resource Management*. Second edition (pp. 115–120). St Paul, MN: West.

Macan, T. H., Avedon, M. J., Paese, M., & Smith, D. E. (1994) The effects of applicants' reactions to cognitive ability tests and an assessment center. *Personnel Psychology*, **47** 715–738.

Martin, J. & Harder, J. W. (1994) Bread and roses: Justice and the distribution of financial and socioemotional rewards in organizations. *Social Justice Research,* 7, 241–264.

McFarlin, D. B. & Sweeney, P. D. (1992) Distributive and procedural justice as predictors of satisfaction with personal and organizational outcomes. *Academy of Management Journal,* 35, 626–637.

Mellor, S. (1992) The influence of layoff severity on postlayoff union commitment among survivors: The moderating effect of the perceived legitimacy of a layoff account. *Personnel Psychology,* 45, 579–600.

Miceli, M. P. (1993) Justice and pay system satisfaction. In R. Cropanzano (ed.), *Justice in the Workplace: Approaching Fairness in Human Resource Management* (pp. 257–283). Hillsdale, NJ: Erlbaum.

Miceli, M. P. & Lane, M. C. (1991) Antecedents of pay satisfaction: A review and extension. In K. M. Rowland & G. R. Ferris (eds), *Research in Personnel and Human Resources Management,* Vol. 9 (pp. 235–309). Greenwich, CT: JAI Press.

Miles, J.A. & Greenberg, J. (1993) Cross-national differences in preferences for distributive justice norms: The challenge of establishing fair resource allocations in the European Community. In J. B. Shaw, P. S., Kirkbride, & K. M Rowlands (eds), *Research in Personnel and Human Resources Management* (Suppl. 3, pp. 133–156). Greenwich, CT: JAI Press.

Miller, C. C. & Cardinal, L. B. (1994) Strategic planning and firm performance: A synthesis of more than two decades of research. *Academy of Management Journal,* 37, 1649–1665.

Moorman, R. H. (1991) Relationship between organizational justice and organizational citizenship behaviors: Do fairness perceptions influence employee citizenship? *Journal of Applied Psychology,* 76, 845–855.

Mosier, C. I. (1947) A critical examination of the concept of face validity. *Educational and Psychological Measurement,* 7, 5–12.

Murphy, K. R., Thornton, G. C., III., & Prue, K. (1991) Influence of job characteristics on the acceptability of employee drug testing. *Journal of Applied Psychology,* 76, 447–453.

Murphy, K. R., Thornton, G. C., III., & Reynolds, D. H. (1990) College students' attitudes toward employee drug testing programs. *Personnel Psychology,* 43, 615–631.

Niehoff, B. P. & Moorman, R. H. (1993) Justice as a mediator of the relationship between methods of monitoring and organizational citizenship behavior. *Academy of Management Journal,* 36, 527–556.

Novelli, L., Jr, Kirkman, B. L., & Shapiro, D. L. (1995) Effective implementation of organizational change: An organizational justice perspective. In C. L. Cooper & D. M. Rousseau (eds), *Trends in Organizational Behavior,* Vol. 2 (pp. 15–36). Chichester, UK: Wiley.

Organ, D. W. (1990) The motivational basis of organizational citizenship behavior. In B. M. Staw & L. L. Cummings (eds), *Research in Organizational Behavior,* Vol. 12 (pp. 43–72). Greenwich, CT: JAI Press.

Organ, D. W. & Konovsky, M. A. (1989) Cognitive versus affective determinants of organizational citizenship behavior. *Journal of Applied Psychology,* 74, 157–164.

Organ, D. W. & Moorman, R. H. (1993) Fairness and organizational citizenship behavior: What are the connections? *Social Justice Research,* 6, 5–18.

Pfeffer, J. & Davis-Blake, A. (1992) Salary dispersion, location in the salary distribution, and turnover among college administrators. *Industrial and Labor Relations Review,* 45, 753–763.

Pfeffer, J. & Langton, N. (1993) The effects of wage dispersion on satisfaction, productivity, and working collaboratively: Evidence from college and university faculty. *Administrative Science Quarterly,* 38, 382–407.

Rasinski, K. A. (1992) Preference for decision control in organizational decision making. *Social Justice Research,* 5, 343–357.

Rawls, J. (1971) *A Theory of Justice.* Cambridge, MA: Harvard University Press.

Reed, T. F. & Kelly, D. (1993) An exchange theory of organizational citizenship. In G. R. Ferris (ed.), *Research in Personnel and Human Resources Management,* Vol. 11 (pp. 41–82). Greenwich, CT: JAI Press.

Richman, L. S. (1993, September 20) When will the layoffs end? *Fortune,* pp. 54–56.

Rosen, R. H. (1991) *The Healthy Company.* New York: Jeremy P. Archer/Perigree.

Ross, W. D. (ed.) (1925) *The Oxford Translation of Aristotle. Vol. IX: The Nicomachean Ethics.* London: Oxford University Press.

Rosse, J. G., Miller, J. L., & Ringer, R. C. (in press) The deterrent value of drug and integrity testing. *Journal of Business and Psychology.*

Rosse, J. G., Miller, J. L., & Stecher, M. D. (1994) A field study of job applicants' reactions to personality and cognitive ability testing. *Journal of Applied Psychology,* 79, 987–992.

Rosse, J. G., Ringer, R. C., & Miller, J. L. (in press) Personality and drug testing: An exploration of perceived fairness of alternatives to urinalysis. *Journal of Business and Psychology.*

Rynes, S. L. & Connerley, M. L. (1993) Applicant reactions to alternative selection procedures. *Journal of Business and Psychology,* 7, 261–277.

Schaubroeck, J., May, D. R., & Brown, F. W. (1994) Procedural justice explanations and employee reactions to economic hardship: A field experiment. *Journal of Applied Psychology,* 79, 455–460.

Schoorman, F. D. & Champagne, M. V. (1994) Managers as informal third parties: The impact of supervisor–subordinate relationships on interventions. *Employee Responsibilities and Rights Journal,* 7, 73–84.

Schuler, H. (1993a) Social validity of selection situations: A concept and some empirical results. In H. Schuler, J. L. Farr, & M. Smith (eds), *Personnel Selection and Assessment: Individual and Organizational Perspectives* (pp. 11–26). Hillsdale, NJ: Erlbaum.

Schuler, H. (1993b) Is there a dilemma between validity and acceptance in the employment interview? In B. Nevo & R. S. Jäger (eds), *Educational and Psychological Testing: The Test Taker's Outlook* (pp. 239–250). Toronto, Canada: Hogrefe & Huber.

Schwarzwald, J., Koslowsky, M. & Shalit, B. (1992) A field study of employees' attitudes and behaviors after promotion decisions. *Journal of Applied Psychology,* 77, 511–514.

Shapiro, D. L. (1991) The effects of explanations on negative reactions to deceit. *Administrative Science Quarterly,* 36, 614–630.

Shapiro, D. L. (1993) Reconciling theoretical differences among procedural justice researchers by re-evaluating what it means to have one's view 'considered': Implications for third-party managers. In R. Cropanzano (ed.), *Justice in the Workplace: Approaching Fairness in Human Resource Management* (pp. 51–78). Hillsdale, NJ: Erlbaum.

Shapiro, D. L. & Brett, J. M. (1993) Comparing three processes underlying judgments of procedural justice: A field study of mediation and arbitration. *Journal of Personality and Social Psychology,* 65, 1167–1177.

Shapiro, D. L., Buttner, E. H., & Barry, B. (1994) Explanations for rejection decisions: What factors enhance their perceived adequacy and moderate their enhancement of justice perceptions? *Organizational Behavior and Human Decision Processes,* 58, 346–368.

Shapiro, D. L. & Rosen, B. (1994) An investigation of managerial interventions in employee disputes. *Employee Responsibilities and Rights Journal,* 7, 37–51.

Sheppard, B. H., Blumenfeld-Jones, K., Minton, W. J., & Hyder, E. (1994) Informal conflict intervention: Advice and dissent. *Employee Responsibilities and Rights Journal,* **7**, 53–72.

Sheppard, B. H. & Lewicki, R. J. (1987) Toward general principles of managerial fairness. *Social Justice Research,* **1**, 161–176.

Sheppard, B. H., Lewicki, R. J., & Minton, J. W. (1993) *Organizational Justice: The Search for Fairness in the Workplace.* Lexington, MA: Lexington Press.

Siegel, P., Brockner, J., & Tyler, T. (August, 1995) Revisiting the relationship between procedural and distributive justice: The role of trust. Paper presented at the Annual Meeting of the Academy of Management. Vancouver, BC, Canada.

Singer, M. S. (1992) Procedural justice in managerial selection: Identification of fairness determinants and associations of fairness perceptions. *Social Justice Research,* **5**, 49–70.

Singer, M. S. (1993) *Fairness in Personnel Selection.* Aldershot, New Zealand: Avebury.

Skitka, L. J. & Tetlock, P. E. (1992) Allocating scarce resources: A contingency model of distributive justice. *Journal of Experimental Social Psychology,* **28**, 491–522.

Smither, J. W., Reilly, R. R., Millsap, R. E., Pearlman, K., & Stoffey, R. W. (1993) Applicants' reactions to selection procedures. *Personnel Psychology,* **46**, 49–75.

Steensma, H. & Vermunt, R. (1991) *Social Justice in Human Relations. Vol. 2: Societal and Psychological Consequences of Justice and Injustice.* New York: Plenum.

Stepina, L. P. & Perrewe, P. L. (1991) The stability of comparative referent choice and feelings of inequity: A longitudinal field study. *Journal of Organizational Behavior,* **12**, 185–200.

Stoffey, R. W., Millsap, R. E., Smither, J. W., & Reilly, R. R. (1991, April) The influence of selection procedures on attitudes about the organization and job pursuit intentions. In R. R. Reilly (Chair), *Perceived validity of selection procedures: Implications for organizations.* Symposium presented at the annual meeting of the Society for Industrial and Organizational Psychology, Saint Louis, MO.

Stone, E. F. (1988) Moderator variables in research: A review and analysis of conceptual and methodological issues. In K. R. Rowland & G. R. Ferris (eds), *Research in Personnel and Human Resources Management* Vol. 6 (pp. 191–230). Greenwich, CT: JAI.

Summers, T. P. & Hendrix, W. H. (1991) Modeling the role of pay equity perceptions: A field study. *Journal of Occupational Psychology,* **64**, 145–157.

Sweeney, P. D. & McFarlin, D. B. (1993) Workers' evaluations of the 'ends' and the 'means': An examination of four models of distributive and procedural justice. *Organizational Behavior and Human Decision Processes,* **55**, 23–40.

Sweeney, P. D., McFarlin, D. B., & Inderrieden, E. J. (1990) Using relative deprivation theory to explain satisfaction with income and pay level: A multistudy examination. *Academy of Management Journal,* **33**, 423–436.

Sykes, G. & Matza, D. (1957) Techniques of neutralization: A theory of delinquency. *American Journal of Sociology,* **22**, 664–670.

Taylor, M. S., Tracy, K. B., Renard, M. K., Harrison, J. K., & Carroll, S. J. (1995) Due process in performance appraisal: A quasi-experiment in procedural justice. *Administrative Science Quarterly,* **40**, 495–523.

Tedeschi, J. T. & Reiss, M. (1981) Verbal strategies in impression management. In C. Antaki (ed.), *The Psychology of Ordinary Explanations of Social Behaviour* (pp. 271–309). London: Academic Press.

Tepper, B. J. & Braun, C. K. (1995) Does the experience of organizational justice mitigate the invasion of privacy engendered by random drug testing? An empirical investigation. *Basic and Applied Social Psychology,* **16**, 211–225.

Tett, R. P., Jackson, D. N., & Rothstein, M. (1991) Personality measures as predictors of job performance: A meta-analysis. *Personnel Psychology,* **44**, 703–742.

Thibaut, J. & Walker, L. (1975) *Procedural Justice: A Psychological Analysis.* Hillsdale, NJ: Erlbaum.

Thornton, G. C., III & Cleveland, J. C. (1990) Developing managerial talent through simulation. *American Psychologist,* **45**, 190–199.

Törnblom, K. Y. (1990) The social psychology of distributive justice. In K. Scherer (ed.), *The Nature and Administration of Justice: Interdisciplinary Approaches* (pp. 45–70). Cambridge, UK: Cambridge University Press.

Treviño, L. K. & Ball, G. A. (1992) The social implications of punishing unethical behavior: Observers' cognitive and affective reactions. *Journal of Management,* **18**, 751–768.

Triandis, H. C. (1994) *Culture and Social Behavior.* New York: McGraw-Hill.

Tyler, T. R. (1989) The psychology of procedural justice: A test of the group-value model. *Journal of Personality and Social Psychology,* **57**, 830–838.

Tyler, T. R. (1990) *Why People Obey the Law: Procedural Justice, Legitimacy, and Compliance.* New Haven, CT: Yale University Press.

Tyler, T. R. (1991) Using procedures to justify outcomes: Testing the viability of a procedural justice strategy for managing conflict and allocating resources in work organizations. *Basic and Applied Social Psychology,* **12**, 259–279.

Tyler, T. R. (1994) Psychological models of the justice motive: Antecedents of distributive and procedural justice. *Journal of Personality and Social Psychology,* **67**, 850–863.

Tyler, T. R. & Bies, R. J. (1990) Beyond formal procedures: The interpersonal context of procedural justice. In J. S. Carroll (ed.), *Applied Social Psychology and Organizational Settings* (pp. 77–98). Hillsdale, NJ: Erlbaum.

Tyler, T. R. & Dawes, R. M. (1993) Fairness in groups: Comparing self-interest and social identity perspectives. In B. A. Mellers & J. Baron (eds), *Psychological Perspectives on Justice: Theory and Applications* (pp. 87–108). New York: Cambridge University Press.

Tyler, T. R. & Degoey, P. (1995) Collective restraint in social dilemmas: Procedural justice and social identification effects on support for authorities. *Journal of Personality and Social Psychology,* **69**, 482–497.

Tyler, T. R. & Lind, E. A. (1992) A relational model of authority in groups. In M. P. Zanna (ed.), *Advances in Experimental Social Psychology,* Vol. 25 (pp. 115–191). San Diego, CA: Academic Press.

Tyler, T. R. & Smith, H. J. (in press) Social justice and social movements. In D. Gilbert, S. T. Fiske, & G. Lindzey (eds), *Handbook of Social Psychology.* Fourth edition. New York: McGraw-Hill.

Vermunt, R. & Steensma, H. (1991) *Social Justice in Human Relations, Vol. 1: Societal and Psychological Origins of Justice.* New York: Plenum.

Vroom, V. (1964) *Work and Motivation.* New York: Wiley.

Wall, J. A. & Callister, R. R. (1995) Conflict and its management. *Journal of Management,* **21**, 515–558.

Weeks, D. (1992) *The Eight Essential Steps to Conflict Resolution: Preserving Relationships at Work, at Home, and in the Community.* New York: Putnam.

Welton, G. L. & Pruitt, D. G. (1987) The mediation process: The effect of mediator bias and disputant power. *Personality and Social Psychology Bulletin,* **13**, 123–133.

Westin, A. F. (1978) Privacy and personnel records: A look at employee attitudes. *Civil Liberties Review,* **4**(5), 28–34.

Wigdor, A. K. & Sackett, P. R. (1993) Employment testing and public policy: The case of the General Aptitude Test Battery. In H. Schuler, J. L. Farr, & M. Smith (eds), *Personnel Selection and Assessment: Individual and Organizational Perspectives* (pp. 183–204). Hillsdale, NJ: Erlbaum.

Wittmer, J. M., Carnevale, P. J., & Walker, M. E. (1991) General alignment and oversupport in biased mediation. *Journal of Conflict Resolution,* **35**, 594–610.

Chapter 8

CONSEQUENCES OF ALTERNATIVE WORK SCHEDULES

Catherine S. Daus, David N. Sanders
Southern Illinois University – Edwardsville, USA

and

David P. Campbell
Center For Creative Leadership – Colorado Springs, USA

INTRODUCTION

With our fast-paced society's current demand for immediacy, technology has responded by enabling businesses to provide products and services in record time. The trend for fast and immediate interactions has spurred the development of everything from the fax machine to telephone availability on airplanes. We truly can communicate with almost anyone, anywhere in the world, at any time. While increases in efficiency and productivity for organizations can in part be attributed to the current technological revolution, many people forget about the deleterious effects that such an age is having on a substantial and growing percentage of the population.

In order for companies to respond to demands for faster service and products, many have had to increase their hours of operation to 24 hours a day. Often, employees are required to work on a night or evening shift to accommodate the company's operating demands. Additionally, there are companies which, by the nature of their business, must remain open around-the-clock. Employees such as nuclear reactor operators, emergency room workers, and policemen are a few examples of occupations that are directly affected. These occupations have had to require some workers to work on a shift system.

This chapter will discuss consequences of shiftwork to the individual as well as to the employing organization. Such consequences include physiological, psychological, and performance-related phenomena. Suggestions for short- and long-term preventions, and interventions both for the individual

Consequences of Alternative Work Schedules by Catherine S. Daus, David N. Sanders and David P. Campbell
taken from IRIOP 1998 v13, Edited by Cary L. Cooper and Ivan T. Robertson: © 1998 John Wiley & Sons, Ltd

shiftworker as well as for the employing organization will be presented. Individual differences which predispose persons to tolerate the effects of shiftwork better than others will be identified. The specific design of the shift system has significant consequences for individual adjustment, and literature on this point will be given considerable attention. This review will also discuss in depth two other common alternative work schedules related to, but distinct from, shiftwork regarding the end goals of the system: compressed work weeks (also known as the '4/40') and flextime. Finally, the manuscript will consider future research directions which include the study of new and innovative scheduling policies as well as research methodologies.

SHIFTWORK

Shiftwork, broadly defined as working day, evening, or night shifts, has been shown to have adverse effects on individuals and organizations (Adams, Folkard & Young, 1986; Akerstedt, 1990; Bohle & Tilley, 1989; Gadbois, 1984; Harrington, 1978; Rutenfranz, Haider & Koller, 1985; Walker, 1985). However, shiftwork is necessary in industries which require 24-hour operation. Shiftwork can vary in its specific characteristics; for example, continuous shift systems require weekend working whereas discontinuous systems occur in organizations which operate Monday through Friday. Shiftwork varies according to: start and stop times of employees; length of shifts; length of time off between shifts; and order of shift rotation. Shiftwork can be permanent where each crew works only one shift, or it can be rotating where each crew rotates their hours to include each type of shift. Rotating shifts, in particular, are increasing in popularity: in 1992, approximately one-third of the US labor market worked a rotating schedule (Mitler, 1992).

Regardless of the specific characteristics of the shiftwork system, a common problem with shiftwork is that an individual engages in activity (working) at a time of the day when he or she is supposed to be inactive (sleeping). One major source of difficulty for shiftworkers is the inversion of the rest and activity cycles from a 'normal' day orientation. Normally, temperature, sleep, metabolism, and production of most hormones all cycle close to a 24-hour, or circadian, pattern for most people. The biological clock, an endogenous 'pacemaker', in combination with exogenous environmental cues, keeps people synchronized to a 24-hour cycle. Each day, certain exogenous cues (*zeitgebers*) such as the day–night light cycle, 'reset' our bodies to synchronize with the 24-hour cycling of our world. Without these environmental cues, many of these rhythms would fall into a 'free running' pattern lasting closer to a 25-hour cycle.

We therefore have two types of cues, endogenous and exogenous, which interact to influence the timing of the physiological processing of our bodies. These influences strongly encourage a basic pattern of sleep at night and activity during the day. When we continuously counter the natural tendencies of our bodies by, for example, working at night and sleeping during the day, the circadian system becomes disrupted or desynchronized, meaning that behavior and biological rhythms are out of phase. While this may appear inconsequential, circadian rhythms control many of the human body's activities. When the natural order of the body is disrupted, there can be adverse physical and psychological consequences to the individual as well as negative effects for the employing organization.

Physical Consequences to the Individual

As mentioned above, engaging in night shiftwork can result in the disruption of an individual's circadian rhythms. This disruption is mainly due to the body being active in the absence of light. The suprachasmatic nucleus (SCN) in the hypothalamus is a structure which has been shown to be sensitive to light. The SCN reacts to the presence or absence of light as a cue to what time of the day it is. Through the course of time, the availability of light has been associated with activity, and the absence of light associated with inactivity. Thus, when an individual works at night in the absence of light, the body is receiving conflicting signals. These conflicting signals result in the disruption of many bodily functions. Also, desyncrhonization of the body's circadian rhythms can lead to pervasive feelings of fatigue and malaise: 'occupational jet lag' (Mitler, 1992, p. 135). This section will discuss the major physical and physiological effects reported in the shiftwork literature.

Sleep

The problem of poor sleep quality is probably the most burdensome and pervasive consequence of shiftwork. Several studies and reviews (Akerstedt, 1990; Akerstedt & Gillberg, 1981; Costa, Lievore, Casaletti, Gaffuri & Folkard, 1989; Minor, Healey & Waterhouse, 1994; Moore-Ede, 1993; Regestein & Monk, 1991; Skipper, Jung & Coffey, 1990; Smith & Folkard, 1993b; Torsvall, Akerstedt & Gillberg, 1981) have indicated that night shiftwork is related to poor quality of sleep, decreased duration of sleep, and fatigue. This is due, in large part, to the sleep of the shiftworker being shifted to a time of day that is least appropriate for sleep (Akerstedt & Gillberg, 1981). Experiments have also shown that total sleep time is longer and of much better depth and quality for workers on a day shift and/or non-rotators compared to those on a night shift and/or rotators (Czeisler, Moore-Ede & Coleman, 1982; Monk, 1990; Monk & Folkard, 1985; Rosa, Colligan & Lewis, 1989). The erratic sleep cycle, once initiated, is difficult to terminate as switching on and off different shifts makes it nearly impossible to adjust. Even permanent shiftworkers will experience sleep disturbances as there is greater environmental noise during the day which reduces both the duration and quality of sleep for those on the night shift (Knauth & Rutenfranz, 1975; Rutenfranz, Colquhoun, Knauth & Ghata, 1977). This results in an accumulated sleep deficit toward the end of a shift series commonly referred to as 'sleep debt'.

Alertness/concentration

The second physical consequence is related to cognitive functioning and can result directly from poor sleep quality. Individuals engaged in night shiftwork and/or rotating shifts have reported lower levels of alertness, concentration, and vigor, and higher levels of fatigue and confusion (Akerstedt, 1988; Bohle & Tilley, 1993; Moore-Ede, 1993; Tasto, Colligan, Skiel & Polly, 1987). This consequence is particularly important to individuals whose work requires a high degree of monitoring, for example, a nuclear power plant employee or an intensive care nurse. While the importance is obvious for individuals who must continuously monitor, alertness/concentration problems are also in evident in situations where an individual is producing a product where concentration problems can negatively impact the quality of production. These problems will be further discussed in the section on organizational consequences–performance problems.

Gastrointestinal problems

The third physical consequence is related to hormone levels in the body. Much research has indicated that a pervasive problem with shiftworkers is gastrointestinal disruption (Cervinka, 1993; Costa, Apostoli, d'Andrea, F. & Gaffuri, 1981; Gordon, Cleary, Parlan & Czeisler, 1986; Moore-Ede, 1993; Moore-Ede & Richardson, 1985; Skipper, Jung & Coffey, 1990; Tasto et al., 1978). Mitler (1992) suggests that approximately 20% of shiftworkers experience gastrointestinal disorders. At night when the body is normally inactive, hormone levels associated with gastrointestinal functioning are at their lowest levels. When an individual is active, hormone levels may increase, causing problems such as indigestion, chronic diarrhoea, and peptic ulcers, to name a few. Vener, Szabo and Moore (1989) review the effects of shiftwork on gastrointestinal functioning and literature regarding (a) the central nervous system control and integration of circadian rhythms; and (b) shiftwork and gastrointestinal symptoms/disease.

Research has also found an association between shiftwork and cardiovascular disease, musculoskeletal functioning, and peptic ulcers. While physical problems are discussed independently, taken together, one can see the toll that night shiftwork, either acute or chronic, can take on an individual. However, the true extent of working shifts on an individual's physiological systems may still not be fully appreciated. Recent research (Spelten, Barton & Folkard, 1993) suggests that the shiftworkers themselves may not even realize the toll that shiftwork is taking on their body, and may be underestimating its effects. For more comprehensive reviews of the physical consequences of shiftwork, see Angersbach, Knauth, Loskant et al. (1980); Costa, Cesana, Kogi and Wedderburn (1990); Costa et al. (1981); Harrington (1978); Mott, Mann, McLoughlin, and Warwick (1965); Rutenfranz, Haider, and Koller (1985); Tasto et al. (1978(.

Psychological Consequences to the Individual

When an individual chooses or is required to engage in night shiftwork, psychological consequences often arise. The psychological effects may or may not be related to the physical consequences associated with night shiftwork. Whatever the case may be, shiftwork is correlated with two main psychological problems: increased stress and affect or mood disturbances.

Stress and strain

Stress, both job- and non-job-related, is usually higher for rotating shiftworkers and night shiftworkers compared to non-rotating, daytime employees (Barton & Folkard, 1991; Bohle & Tilley, 1989; Coffey, Skipper & Jung, 1988; Gordon et al., 1986; Jamal & Baba, 1992; Skipper, Jung & Coffey, 1990). Research has also demonstrated that stress increases incrementally as the number and length of night shifts (called night shift dose) increase (Cervinka, 1993). The increased level of stress may be a result of several things. Stress may result from the physical strain the body is under due to the night-shift and/or nature of the work which consequently results in a disturbance of circadian rhythms. Lack of sleep and/or gastrointestinal disturbances may result in increased levels of stress. Here, the physical consequence contributes to a psychological consequence.

Another source of stress may come from strained social relationships. Several studies (Charles & Brown, 1981; Costa, 1996; Koller, Kundi, & Cervinka, 1978; Mott et al., 1965; Smith & Folkard, 1993; Tasto et al., 1978; Walker, 1985) have documented a relationship between night shiftwork and social relationship strains. Shiftworkers have trouble maintaining friendships and relationships with others who do not share their schedule. Furthermore, constant fatigue affects shiftworker's social lives as they often do not have the energy or motivation to participate socially. Finally, on a pragmatic level, membership of social organizations and participation in social activities may be difficult because of the meeting times; a shiftworker may not be able to attend weekly or monthly evening meetings if he or she works the evening shift. 'Shiftworkers are less likely than dayworkers to be members of organizations or to be office holders once they have joined' (Walker, 1985, p. 218).

Social relationship strain may also manifest itself through work–family conflict. Alternative work schedules, such as flextime and 4/40 have been thought to reduce the degree of work–family conflict; however, night shiftwork may increase the degree of conflict. A shiftworking individual experiencing work–family conflict feels increased stress due to work and family life conflicting with one another. Shiftwork interferes with family time; many studies report that relationships with spouses and children who are on a different time schedule than the shiftworking family members are inevitably compromised (Charles & Brown, 1981; Koller et al., 1978; Moore-Ede, 1993; Mott et al., 1965; Pleck, Staines & Lang, 1980; Tasto et al., 1978; Walker, 1985(. Disruptions of social and family life magnify and compound the physical stress associated with shiftwork. Flexible schedules are thought to ease work–family conflict by allowing personal scheduling of work hours more congruent with family responsibilities. These schedules will be discussed later in the manuscript.

However, research has not been unequivocal in its findings regarding family life disruption due to shiftwork (Skipper, Jung & Coffey, 1990). In fact, some research has found that night shifts allow flexibility for families in that there is usually at least one parent home to care for the children, rather than the parents having to rely constantly on paid caregivers. This is supported by research which reports *fewer* domestic problems for night workers compared to day workers (Barton & Folkard, 1991). While these results may seem directly contradictory to previous literature, it actually illuminates one of the major problems with the shiftwork research: the sample characteristics from different studies may differ so substantially that the generalizability of the results from one study to another shiftworking population is questionable. Further, much early shiftwork research was conducted in industrial settings with males who had no choice regarding what shift they worked. A major question that arises is: do the results from this literature generalize to other very different groups of workers (e.g. predominantly female nurses who choose to work the night shift)? The issue of choice appears to have a great impact on whether employees experience adverse effects from shiftwork and will be discussed in depth.

Affect

The second psychological consequence is related to an individual's affect. Psychological problems such as irritability, apathy, restlessness, and depression may arise due to an individual engaging in night shiftwork. While an individual may experience mood disturbances from normal working hours, individuals engaging in night shiftwork experience greater degrees of such problems (Healy, Minors & Waterhouse, 1993; Jamal & Jamal, 1982; Moore-Ede, 1993; Tasto et al., 1978). Additionally, because work–family conflict is related to depression (Thomas & Ganster, 1995), shiftwork which contributes to work–family conflict may also indirectly contribute to depression. There is even some indication that shiftwork, especially night shiftwork, may have long-lasting severe consequences on some individuals. In a questionnaire/ interview study of 270 oil refinery workers, it was found in the 'drop-out' group that in certain individuals very long-lasting psychosomatic, pseudo-neurotic, or sensitization reactions may develop (Koller, Kundi & Cervinka, 1978). Further, in telephone interviews with more than 2500 workers, Gordon et al. (1986) found evidence of 'severe emotional problems' due to shift-work. These affect-related problems, while directly impacting the individual, may indirectly impact the organization via employee withdrawal behaviors (lateness, absenteeism, turnover), or a lack of extraorganizational behaviors, or 'organizational citizenship behaviors' (e.g. voluntarily helping a co-worker; staying late to finish a project; speaking highly of the organization to outsiders). These extrarole behaviors have been found to positively impact organizational productivity and profitability (Organ, 1988).

Drug use

The use of both legal and illegal drugs can be considered as a consequence of shiftwork as well as a treatment or prevention of the adverse consequences from shiftwork. Increased alcohol, caffeine and sleeping pill usage are potential consequences of shiftwork (Mitler, 1992; Moore-Ede, 1993). However, each of these drugs may also be used, and possibly even prescribed as a treatment (albeit questionable, and certainly short term) for different effects from shiftwork such as tension/irritability, sleepiness or fatigue at work, and sleeplessness/restlessness during off hours. To this end, there will be a brief discussion of the effects of drugs in both sections of the chapter.

While the literature on drug usage and shiftwork is particularly scant, there is some evidence for increased drug usage. Shiftworkers often will use caffeine as the 'boost' needed to get them through the seemingly everlasting night shift. Gordon et al. (1986) found much heavier use of caffeine by shift workers compared to non-shiftworkers. Additionally, these researchers found heavier alcohol consumption: 16% of men on variable shifts reported having more than four drinks daily (Gordon et al., 1986). The exploration of increased drug usage as a consequence of shiftwork appears to be ripe for inquiry.

As discussed, physical and psychological problems often reported by shift-workers are multitudinous and diverse in nature: poor quality and not enough sleep; persistent fatigue; digestive/gastrointestinal trouble and disturbances; frequent mood changes; irritability and depression; and increased use or dependence upon sleeping pills, alcohol, and/or caffeine. Several of these effects can compound by interaction. For example, a worker is exhausted and finds herself grumpy and moody all the time due to lack of sleep. She has trouble in the early morning hours of work so she drinks coffee around 3.30 a.m. to keep her awake until her shift ends at 5.00 a.m. Since the effects of the caffeine have not yet worn off and she is trying to sleep at a time when her body is naturally awakening itself, she has trouble sleeping. She decides to buy sleeping pills.

She sleeps longer but soon becomes resistant to the effects of one pill and needs more of the drug to sleep. Additionally, no longer grumpy, she finds herself depressed during the night due to the traces of a depressant drug (the sleep medication) in her system. Finally, her stomach begins to hurt quite often due to digestive problems caused by the increased use of caffeine and drugs.

This section has discussed some of the consequences an individual may incur from working a night shift. The next section will discuss what consequences night shiftwork may have on the organization.

Organizational Consequences

The previous two sections have focused on the consequences to the individual of engaging in an alternative work schedule. This section deals with organizational consequences. While the organization may attempt to enhance the employees' quality of life, the organization must also be concerned with its own well-being. Some alternative work schedules such as flextime and 4/40, may help the organization via the individual; other alternative work schedules may be dictated by the nature of the organization. As mentioned previously, hospitals, law enforcement agencies, and nuclear power plants by their very nature require around-the-clock shifts. The next two sections discuss several consequences resulting from shiftwork that directly impact the organization.

Performance

A company may find lower performance as well as more unsafe behaviors and accidents performed by the night shift crew or rotating shift personnel compared to the day shift and/or non-rotating personnel (Coffey, Skipper & Jung, 1988; Folkard, 1987, 1990; Moore-Ede, 1993; Skipper, Jung & Coffey, 1990; Tasto et al., 1978). It is known that the neural processes controlling alertness and sleep produce an increased sleep tendency and diminished capacity to function during certain early morning hours (approximately 2–7 a.m.) regardless of whether one has slept or not (Mitler, 1992). Studies have shown that individuals who engage in night shiftwork tend to have a greater number of performance failures and lower productivity and efficiency (Costa, 1996; Mitler, 1992; Rosekind, Gander, Miller & Gregory, 1994; Scott, 1994). Bonnet (1990) claims that a company should expect a 5–10% decline in the capacity for work during nocturnal work periods compared to daytime work periods, which will dissipate somewhat if workers maintain a consistent sleep–wake routine. However, Rosa, Colligan and Lewis (1989) also found performance decrements or increased errors (187%) for workers on a 12-hour compressed schedule compared to the same workers who had previously been on an 8-hour schedule, *even after seven months of adjustment time*.

The performance problems associated with night shiftwork may be the result of the previously mentioned physical and psychological consequences.

For example, fatigue, which may contribute to lower levels of alertness and concentration, may also contribute to performance failure and lower levels of productivity/efficiency. Rosa, Colligan, and Lewis (1989) as well as Tepas and Monk (1987) feel that performance problems are due to increased fatigue and decreased alertness due to an ever-accumulating sleep debt. This sleep debt contributes to a chronic state of exhaustion for some workers which often ends in the worker falling asleep on the job. In fact, in surveys of 1500 workers in a variety of industrial sites, over 55% of them admitted to falling asleep on the job during a given week (Mitler, 1992). In a study of locomotive engineers, regarding night trips, 11% admitted to 'dozing off on most trips', while 59% admitted to falling asleep at least once (Akerstedt, 1988). Thus, increased individual errors, lower levels of productivity/efficiency, as well as falling asleep at work will obviously impact the overall performance of the organization.

The consequences of performance problems vary according to the type of organization. For example, an individual's performance failure while working a night shift at an assembly facility may result in a defective product, while an individual's performance failure working at a nuclear power plant may result in contaminated water being released into the environment. While either of these occurrences may take place on any shift, it is the night shift where the likelihood is greatest.

Withdrawal behaviors

Attendance, tardiness, and turnover problems are potential negative consequences of shiftwork. While most alternative work schedules are designed with the intent of reducing withdrawal behaviors of employees, night shiftwork, particularly rotating schedules, may result in increased absenteeism, tardiness, and even turnover (Costa, Micciolo, Bertoldi & Tommasini, 1990; Moore-Ede, 1993). Jamal's research (1990; Jamal & Baba, 1992; Jamal & Jamal, 1982) reports that nurses on rotating shifts have higher absenteeism and tardiness, and report higher rates of turnover intention compared to nurses on non-rotating shifts. The increase in withdrawal behaviors of employees may be the result of physical problems and/or psychological problems. If an individual is apathetic about an upcoming night shift, he/she may choose to call in sick or be late in reporting to work. Furthermore, if an individual is experiencing fatigue due to night shiftwork, the individual may call in sick to an upcoming day shift. In fact, research (Nicholson, Jackson & Howes, 1978) has demonstrated a relationship between shiftworkers' absence and day of the week: absences are higher for shiftworkers on days of the week when rest days are several days in the future. So not only is the nightshift staffing impacted by night shiftwork, it is possible day and evening staffing are also impacted.

An interesting feature of the absence and withdrawal literature with regard to shiftwork, is that not all of the research has shown detrimental effects. In fact, Taylor, Pocock and Sergaen (1972) demonstrated the absence rate of shiftworkers to be *lower* than that of their counterparts who worked during the day. Some researchers have suggested that there is, in fact, a moderating influence of certain sample characteristics regarding whether or not they will show negative effects due to shiftwork. In particular, those workers who voluntarily choose to work the night shift or rotating shift may not experience the adverse effects. This topic will be explored further later in the manuscript.

COMPRESSED, 4/40 WORK WEEK

The compressed, or '4/40' work week, where employees work four fixed days per week, 10 hours per day, is an alternative work schedule related to shiftwork and length of shifts in that in some organizations, the length of the required shift can be 10 or 12 hours, or even longer. In fact, many organizations utilize 12-hour shifts to 'make up' for requiring employees to work at night: an increase of hours worked on each shift in exchange for fewer afternoons, evenings, and weekends worked. The term compressed refers to any schedule where employees are working a regular number of hours (usually 40) in less than the normal five days. Thus, employees working the night shift can just as easily work compressed schedules (and often do) as those in more 'traditional' organizations without evening and night shifts. In fact, some organizations offer their employees compressed schedules as a 'perk'. The advantage of such schedules is that employees get a three-day weekend every week, or every other week, depending on the particular characteristics of the schedule. As evidence substantiating that employees do, indeed, view compressed schedules as a perquisite, is research reporting that the primary reasons cited for favoring 4/40 schedules are associated with extra leisure and social participation/time and the long weekend (Knauth & Rutenfranz, 1982; Nollen, 1979; Steele & Poor, 1970).

Compressed schedules have been found to have other advantages for the employee. For example, Williamson, Gower, and Clarke (1994) found that when 75 computer operators changed from a predominantly 8-hour shift to a 12-hour shift, improvements in health, especially psychological, and reduced feelings of tiredness were reported, and these changes were not detrimental to job attitudes (job satisfaction, in particular). However, the shift change also included a change from an 8-hour *irregular* shift to a 12-hour *regular* or relatively permanent shift. Since some research has found that permanent shifts result in fewer adverse effects, it is unknown in this study whether the longer time interval (the compressed schedule) or the regularity of the shift was responsible for the reported positive effects.

Not all reports in the research regarding compressed schedules are positive. Workers on a compressed schedule may suffer from many of the same problems as shiftworkers. Individuals are more fatigued, especially toward the end of the shift (Goodale & Aagaard, 1975; Kenny, 1974) compared to those working shorter shifts, and are often working shifts longer than is appropriate in terms of their body's physical capacities and limitations. Older workers, particularly, who are more susceptible to fatigue may suffer the most from compressed schedules and thus be 'less than enthusiastic' about its implementation (Nollen, 1979; Northrup, Wilson & Rose, 1979).

Perhaps an obvious expected consequence of compressed work schedules is an increase in employee job attitudes, particularly job satisfaction. Indeed, some literature supports this: Hartman and Weaver (1977) and Steele and Poor (1970) claimed positive effects on job satisfaction due to the 4/40 schedules. Further, Ivancevich and Lyon (1977) found that over a 12-month period, employee job satisfaction showed a significant improvement. Northrup, Wilson and Rose (1979) report in field surveys of managers in 50 plants in the United States and Canada, that one of the most important effects of the 12-hour shift was a significant improvement in employee morale which did not impair job efficiency, job safety, or workers' health. Also, much research (Breaugh, 1983; Dunham, Pierce & Castaneda, 1987; Foster, Latack & Reindl, 1979; Harrick, Vanek & Michlitsch, 1986; Northrup, Wilson & Rose, 1979) reports that worker satisfaction with schedules is improved with compressed schedules.

The impact of compressed work schedules in performance is not clear. Many organizations fear that productivity will be negatively impacted due to a rise in accidents from increased fatigue. Yet the research has not borne this out. In fact, in a survey of US and Canadian managers, Northrup, Wilson, and Rose (1979) reported that *none of the 50 locations surveyed* reported increased accidents as a result of 12-hour shifts; indeed, four locations were experiencing the longest periods in their history without time lost because of injuries. Some research has even reported productivity increases (Hartman & Weaver, 1977; Wheeler, 1970). Dunham, Pierce, and Castaneda (1987) reported improvement in six of seven organizational effectiveness measures, (although improved client service was the only change which was statistically significant) when employees switched from a 5/40 schedule to a 4/40 schedule. These researchers also guarded against the Hawthorne effect as the measures showed a subsequent decrease when employees switched back to a 5/40 schedule. Foster, Latack, and Reindl (1979) also found higher productivity in both quantity and quality of computer operations personnel working a 3/38 schedule compared to those working a 5/40 schedule. Ivancevich and Lyon (1977) found improved quality of performance over a 12-month period, as indexed by supervisor ratings of quality, quantity, and overall performance. The compressed work week may further impact productivity indirectly through reduced absenteeism and turnover. Northrup, Wilson and Rose (1979) report that both absenteeism and turnover, if impacted at all by the introduction of a 12-hour shift, showed reductions. Harrick and colleagues (1986) as well as Latack and Foster (1985) also report a reduction in sick leave, personal leave, and annual leave due, in part, to compressed schedules.

However, there is research which reports productivity decreases or increased error rates. Rosa and Colligan (1988) examined a group of data entry personnel working on a compressed work week schedule (a 12-hour, four-day week). Job performance was measured with a data entry task operated throughout the day. Performance deficits were indicated by progressively higher error rates over the four-day work week. However, an interesting thing happened on the final workday. There was an increase in performance which the researchers called the 'end-spurt'. It was suggested that the anticipation of the extended weekend motivated the employees to perform better. Rosa and Bonnett (1991) also examined the effects of a compressed work week schedule at another facility (a natural gas utility) and found consistent results: after ten months of transition from a traditional 8-hour, 5–7-day schedule to a 12-hour, 2–4-day schedule, employees continued to experience decrements in performance and alertness. In a review of fitness factors regarding shiftwork, Bonnett (1990) summarizes data which suggest that decreases in physical capacity to perform night work will be magnified on longer, 12-hour shifts.

Some research reported no significant productivity changes (Calvasina & Boxx, 1975; Goodale & Aagaard, 1975) or offsetting positive and negative effects (Harrick, Vanek & Michlitsch, 1986). Finally, there is research which has reported mixed results: Ivancevich (1974) found a one-year performance increase following the introduction of a 4/40 schedule, but a 24-month follow-up (Ivancevich & Lyon, 1977) showed no long-term impact on performance. This highlights one of the problems with the compressed work week literature: How long will results last?/Are they only short term? Ivancevich (1974; Ivancevich & Lyon, 1977) suggests that conversions to the 4/40 work week may not be as beneficial as originally hoped. Certainly more research comparing short- and long-term effects is warranted.

Regarding the employing organization, there do not appear to be any major administrative or overhead costs (except possibly providing supervision across the longer shift) associated with longer shifts. In fact, if management cooperates with employees when employees when implementing longer shifts, longer shift schedules are seen as a bar to unionism (Northrup, Wilson & Rose, 1979). Latack and Foster (1985) found that a critical variable in successful implementation of compressed schedules was employee participation in the decision to implement. Therefore, it is often the situation where both management and workers alike must support the implementation of compressed schedules, in order for it to be successful, Northrup, Wilson and Rose (1979) report that generally employers have supported 12-hour shifts given the following four contingencies:

- continued employee support
- no increased difficulty in administration (e.g. covering overtime)
- no decrease in productivity and efficiency, and
- no increase in accidents and no violations of OSHA regulations

Most reports of the compressed work weeks appear positive. Of the negative consequences and effects reported, the majority appear to be related to the longer nature of the shifts and how it disrupts sleep and physiological processes, much as with shiftwork. The next section of this chapter discusses prevention of deleterious effects and intervention strategies to combat negative consequences of shiftwork and/or compressed schedules.

INTERVENTION AND PREVENTION OF ADVERSE EFFECTS TO THE INDIVIDUAL

The primary purpose of physical interventions/preventions is to readjust an individual's circadian rhythms. As noted before, this problem mainly stems from night shiftwork. However, there is a caveat: much research has suggested that full adjustment can never really take place (Daniel, 1990; Folkard, 1988, 1990; Knauth & Rutenfranz, 1992). No matter how much time a worker has to adjust, the circadian systems will never *completely* adapt to the night schedule; indeed, complete adaptation is 'practically impossible' (Daniel, 1990). This is due, partly, to the probability that on their days off, most workers try to maintain a normal societal 24-hour schedule such that they sleep at night and are active in the morning. Thus, each week, the worker becomes entrained, or readjusted, to the night schedule again. Daniel (1990) found that it takes 10 to 20 days of continuous night work to come close to a complete reversal of circadian rhythms.

Currently, the two most popular means of circadian adjustment are light therapy and melatonin therapy. Each approach uses the circadian characteristics of individuals to counteract potential problems.

Light Therapy

Light therapy as a physical intervention/prevention seeks to simulate the overall availability of light in a normal day. The goal of light therapy is to trick the body into believing it is day time when it is actually night time. The premise behind this therapy is that simulated light will entrain an individual's circadian rhythm via the SCN. This therapy can be given in two ways. The first type of light therapy is increasing the intensity of light in the work area. This type of therapy may be appropriate in organizational settings where individuals are not required to move around a great deal, for example an assembly line. The second type of light therapy involves wearing what looks like a sun visor. Immediately above an individual's eyes on the visor are two lights which focus light on the individual's eyes. This type of therapy may be more appropriate for organizational settings where individuals are required to move about, for example a hospital.

Numerous studies have shown that availability of light can entrain circadian rhythms. Furthermore, several studies (Czeisler, Johnson & Duffy, 1990;

Dawson & Campbell, 1991; Dawson, Encel & Lushington, 1995; Elmore Betrus, & Burr, 1994; Wever, 1989) have been conducted to examine the relationship between light therapy and night shiftwork. The summary results of these studies are: light is an important cue for entraining an individual's circadian rhythm; light therapy can lessen the problems associated with sleep and alertness; and light therapy can suppress melatonin secretion (this implication will be discussed in the next section). While light therapy by itself seems to counteract some of the problems associated with night shiftwork, it can be used in conjunction with other interventions. The next section will examine melatonin as a means of counteracting problems associated with night shiftwork.

Melatonin

Currently, melatonin is being billed as a wonder drug that does everything from improving quality of sleep to reversing the aging process. Much of melatonin's popularity is rooted in its use to counteract problems associated with circadian disruption. As society suddenly became more global, mainly via airline travel, melatonin was utilized to counteract jet lag. Travellers using melatonin reported decreases in jet lag, and thus a phenomenon was born.

Melatonin is a hormone responsible for seasonal rhythms in animals. The chief production of it usually occurs at night (or in the absence of light): there is an increase in the production rate of a factor anywhere from 10 to 50 after dusk (Lewy, Ahmed, Jackson & Sack, 1992). Studies have shown that melatonin has a circadian periodicity and thus is controlled by the overall circadian rhythm. Additionally, light therapy has been shown to suppress melatonin secretion (Eastman, 1990; Lewy et al., 1992).

Melatonin therapy would involve the administration of low doses of melatonin taken after the shift to simulate the onset of night, or lack of light, and thus sleep. Oral melatonin actually shifts forward (phase advance) or shifts backwards (phase delay) the body's production of natural melatonin (Lewy et al., 1992). These phase shifts run counter to, and to some extent, override the *zeitgeber* from the competing light–dark cycle. If examined in conjunction with light therapy, there is a possibility for shiftwork disorders to be treated with appropriately timed bright light exposure in combination with an appropriately timed administration of melatonin. One can begin to see how you can trick your body into thinking it is another time. Cassone (1990) found that sleep can even be induced via the administration of melatonin in the late afternoon and early evening. While melatonin is riding a popularity wave, it does seem to help counteract some problems associated with night shiftwork and is a promising possible therapy for circadian clock dysfunction. It should be noted that melatonin tends to counteract many of the secondary effects (poor sleep quality and duration) of night shiftwork.

Drug Therapy

One very prevalent, common drug that might counteract some of the primary effects (decreased alertness, cognitive functioning, concentration, and increased fatigue) of night shiftwork is caffeine. Decreased cognitive functioning includes decreased computational speed, and slower reaction times. In an organizational context, decreased cognitive functioning may be the most important side-effect of circadian rhythm desynchronization because of the inherent safety and performance implications. Caffeine has been shown to increase subjectively reported levels of alertness during shiftwork (Schweitzer, Muehlbach & Walsh, 1992). One thing to note is that, as with any drug, one may become tolerant or unresponsive to its effects. While caffeine may provide a short-term fix by addressing levels of alertness, it fails to do anything as regards synchronizing circadian rhythms.

In a similar vein of research, other investigators have examined the effects of administering drugs which alter circadian rhythms. In particular, the benzodiazepine drug triazolam is a commonly prescribed hypnotic drug which is used to treat depression. The benzodiazepines are the drugs of choice for anxiety and stress-related conditions as well as sleep disorders; basically any disorder where there is some disruption of the normal circadian rhythms (Turek & Reeth, 1988). Triazolam can shorten the time it takes for the activity rhythm to be resynchronized to new lighting schedules following a shift change. Therefore, it is possible to restore normal rhythmic patterns of people whose endogenous and exogenous cycles have become desynchronized with the appropriately timed administration of certain drugs.

However, the use of drugs, including caffeine and alcohol, to combat the problems may, in the long run, be worse for the shiftworker as dependence may develop. Additionally, drugs affect many other functions such as mood and performance and do not seem to be a very viable solution.

Stress Interventions

While problems with alertness and concentration are important on the job, problems associated with stress influence individuals both on and off the job. Preventions for problems associated with stress from alternative work schedules can be either short- or long-term solutions. Short-term solutions to stress include flexibility in work schedules, work break activities, and sensory stimulation. Flexible work schedules prevent stress and lessen work–family conflict by allowing individuals to determine working times (within a set range identified according to the company's needs) which minimize strain (Cervinka, 1993; Knauth, 1993; Knauth & Rutenfranz, 1982). For example, delaying the starting time of a shift by even two hours allows a parent either to be at home for breakfast and to send the children to school (day shift); to be at home when children return from school and to have dinner together (evening shift); or to be at home when children go to sleep (night shift). The design of the shift system has the potential to exacerbate or alleviate stress and will be discussed in extensive detail later in the chapter.

Regarding the individual, coping strategies associated with any stress are critical. These strategies include physical exercise, cognitive restructuring, meditation, and relaxation, to name a few. However, research has not consistently demonstrated that organizationally sponsored stress management programs work. Ganster, Mayes, Sime and Tharp (1982) used an experimental design to assess the effects of the stress reduction interventions of cognitive restructuring and progressive relaxation. In a field experiment with public agency employees, results were promising: depression and epinephrine levels (which increase in response to stressful situations) were lower for the experimental group compared to the control group, even at 4-month follow-up times. However, the treatment effects were not replicated in a subsequent intervention with the control group. The researchers suggest that adoption of stress management programs such as these is questionable for the following reasons: the effect sizes are small; the efficacy of such programs when implemented by less specialized management consultants is questionable (they employed a clinical psychologist who specialized in cognitive therapy techniques who was assisted by an exercise and stress physiologist); and training employees to 'better tolerate poorly designed organizations' is a less desirable strategy than one that attempts to make the organization less stressful (Ganster et al., 1982). Thus, we agree with Ganster and colleagues in that stress management programs may be most advantageous as supplements to organizational change programs.

One potential reason for lack of strong empirical support for stress management programs may be the inherent individual differences associated with stress reduction techniques. If organizations do offer stress reduction techniques to their employees, at best they will probably offer one or two different types. Many employees may not see the one or two chosen types as viable or desirable options for them. A stress reduction program should be very individualized according to the particular person's needs, problems, and preferences. However, an interesting caveat is that an individual needs to match the coping strategy according to whether cognitive or somatic functioning is most disrupted (Schwartz, Davidson & Coleman, 1978). In a study designed to separate the cognitive from somatic components of anxiety and consequent coping mechanisms, Schwartz and colleagues (1978) found that physical exercise was most necessary for anxiety which manifested itself somatically; and meditation was most helpful for cognitively manifested anxiety. We therefore advocate that in terms of coping with stress, the individual should employ stress reduction techniques best suited to his/her lifestyle needs and desires. For reviews of stress management techniques, see Kahn and Byosiere (1992); Newman and

Beehr (1979); Sarason and Spielberger (1975); and Spielberger and Sarason (1975).

While the individual can do a considerable amount to reduce consequences associated with alternative work schedules, the organization can also contribute to the reduction of consequences. Yet an organization must also realize that certain individuals are less likely to be able to adjust well to shiftwork, either physically and/or psychologically, and that this needs to be considered before implementation of solutions is undertaken.

INDIVIDUAL DIFFERENCES IN SHIFTWORK TOLERANCE

Several studies have identified individuals who are 'shift intolerant' (Costa et al., 1989; Daniel, 1990; Knauth & Harma, 1992; Motohashi, 1992) and exhibit higher levels of adverse reactions such as gastrointestinal problems and sleep disturbances than do 'shift tolerant' persons. Healy and Waterhouse (1991) suggest that there is a certain type of predisposition to shiftwork intolerance which is very similar to the profile of a person with an affective disorder. These researchers propose a mismatch between exogenous and endogenous influences on circadian rhythmicity, which causes dysphoria, lethargy, and listlessness found both in clinical depression and in poor adjustment to shiftwork. The implication is that persons with an affective disorder may be particularly intolerant to shiftwork. These observations by Healy and Waterhouse (1991) coincide with results found by Costa et al. (1989) that persons with lower manifest anxiety had better tolerance to shiftwork.

Personality Variables: Morningness, Introversion

One individual difference variable, 'morningness', has been studied extensively and has been shown to be a reliable predictor of desynchronization; that is, the more of a 'morning' type a person is, the more trouble the worker will have adjusting to a night work schedule and will then show more physiological disruption (Akerstedt & Froberg, 1976; Folkard, Monk & Lobban, 1979; Monk & Folkard, 1985; Motahashi, 1992; Ostberg, 1973). In a study of computer operators, Ostberg (1973) found that the night shift was associated with the worst sleep–wake patterns of the morning types ('larks'), who slept best when they were on the morning shift; and night shift was associated with the best sleep–wake patterns of the evening types ('owls').

An additional personality trait which may predict adjustment is that of introversion vs extraversion in the Eysenck-type classification scheme. Introverts are generally more emotionally unstable and this variable has been implicated in predicting people with poorer adjustment (Costa et al., 1989; Folkard, Monk & Lobban, 1979; Monk & Folkard, 1985; Nachreiner, 1975).

Physical Characteristics: Age, Physical Fitness

Physical characteristics of individuals have also been implicated in the study of circadian disruption. Since sleep patterns of older persons differ significantly from those of younger persons with decreased delta-wave amplitude, increased number and length of arousals from sleep, and increased daytime napping (Monk & Folkard, 1985), it is natural to think that older workers may adjust differently to shiftwork than younger workers. Indeed, older workers (over 50 years of age) have been found to be more inflexible in their circadian system functioning and thus to experience more problems due to shiftwork (Harma, Knauth, Ilmarinen & Ollila, 1990; Matsumoto & Morita, 1987; Torsvall, Akerstedt & Gillberg, 1981). According to Monk and Folkard, 'as the shiftworker enters his 50s, things start to get dramatically worse' (1985, p. 228). Age effects corroborate research regarding morningness, since age and morningness scores are positively correlated (Monk & Folkard, 1985). When studied individually, these two variables have similar effects on circadian rhythm desynchronization.

The decreased flexibility of the circadian system might possibly be attributed to older workers generally being less physically fit and therefore less able to withstand strong physical pressure and disruption (Monk & Folkard, 1985). Intuitively, a physically fit person should be more resistant to deleterious effects, but this has not been directly supported by research. However, indirect positive effects have been found. For example, in a study by Atkinson, Coldwells, Reilly, and Waterhouse (1993), participants who were physically fit had higher rhythm amplitudes than the non-physically fit. The amplitude of circadian rhythms is associated with the ability to adjust circadian rhythms. The implication is that the more active an individual is, the higher their circadian rhythm amplitudes, the better the individual will be able to adjust to changes in circadian rhythms. Harma, Ilmarinen, and Yletyinen (1982) also found larger circadian rhythm amplitudes as well as lower heart rates and less perceived exertion for physically fit workers compared to workers of average fitness. Fitness may also influence adjustment through increased positive mood states. People who are more physically fit overall, have a better mood which counters some of the negative forces (Bonnet, 1990).

Sleeping Patterns

Research has found that flexible sleeping patterns and vigor, or ability to overcome drowsiness, are individual difference variables which are extremely important not only in short-term circadian adjustment, but are critical in long-term adjustment as well (Bohle & Tilley, 1993; Costa et al., 1989; Folkard, Monk & Lobban, 1979; Vidacek, Kaliterna, Rodosevic-Vidacek & Prizmic, 1990). The next two sections will consider both short- and long-term organizational intervention and prevention strategies.

INTERVENTION AND PREVENTION OF ADVERSE EFFECTS TO THE ORGANIZATION

Short-term Solutions

Short-term solutions attempt to address consequences associated with performance. Decreases in productivity and efficiency as well as increased performance failures can be counteracted by the organization. As mentioned previously, increasing light intensity in the work area or providing light visors may increase alertness and concentration enough to minimize detrimental performance consequences. Additionally, some research (Bonnet, 1990; Schweitzer, Muehlback & Walsh, 1992; Motohashi & Takano, 1993) has suggested that night-time napping contributes to increased alertness and performance. 'Prophylactic naps' have been shown to ameliorate negative effects and assist the adjustment process (Bonnet, 1990). This type of nap is one which is taken prior to a period of sleep loss and helps to maintain alertness as opposed to a nap taken subsequent to a sleep loss which is intended to make up for lost sleep. We have suggested several measures organizations can employ to reduce short-term consequences associated with alternative work schedules. The organization also has several options which are more critical to long-term adjustment.

Long-term Solutions

Selection

Selection in organizations requiring night and evening shiftwork would entail organizations selecting employees for their ability to stay awake (Mitler, 1992) or who would be predicted to be shift tolerant (Czeisler, Moore-Ede & Coleman, 1982; Folkard, Monk & Lobban, 1979) or stress resistant (Cervinka, 1993). The Standard Shiftwork Index (SSI; Folkard, Barton, Costa et al., 1993) is a set of questionnaires specifically designed to assess the severity of health, sleep, and social disruption experienced as a result of shiftwork, as well as the individual differences which may predict the disruption. The questionnaire is composed of the following variables: chronic fatigue; psychological well-being; physical health; cognitive and somatic anxiety; neuroticism; sleep quality and disturbances; social and domestic disruption; general job satisfaction; flexibility and languidity (measures of circadian type); morningness; reasons for working shifts; and biographical information (Barton, 1994). However, a company might find itself defending its employment practices in a court of law due to the questionable moral and ethical ramifications of selecting individuals on a basis of sleep factors and social disruption. Further, laws (in the United States) such as the Age Discrimination in Employment Act and the Americans With Disabilities legally prohibit discrimination in selection procedures based on age factors (which would be relevant since sleep patterns of older persons are related to shiftwork intolerance) and disabilities, which include mental disabilities as well as physical disabilities. Thus, selection for shift tolerance is not likely to be a feasible solution for most organizations due to the legal restrictions.

Moore-Ede (1993) discusses how many of the laws and regulations in existence now aggravate and intensify problems from shiftwork. For example, airline pilots are not supposed to take naps in the cockpit according to FAA regulations. This regulation makes sense: Who wants his/her pilot sleeping? However, a multitude of airline accidents have been caused by fatigued pilots who either unavoidably end up falling asleep at the controls, or who enter a type of stupor due to the erratic schedules and lack of sleep. Anecdotal evidence as well as controlled experiments establish that naps, even 15-minute ones if appropriately timed, can alleviate fatigue and keep a pilot alert and safe. It is quite easy to conceive of a schedule where the pilots take turns allowing each other to take short naps. In cockpits where the captain allows this (against regulations), the instances of accidents are much less frequent (Moore-Ede, 1993).

Self-selection/choice

An alternative possibility, rather than the organization selecting individuals for shiftwork, or requiring employees to work certain shifts, is to allow the employees to self-select for shiftwork. Employees vary in their shift preference. For example, many nurses who work the night shift do so to enable them to spend time with their young children during the day (Gadbois, 1981; Robson & Wedderburn, 1990; Skipper, Jung & Coffey, 1990). Barton's research (1994; Barton & Folkard, 1991; Barton, Smith, Totterdell, Spelten & Folkard, 1993) has consistently demonstrated that when nurses specifically choose to work the night shift, rather than being mandated to, the health, sleep, social and domestic disruptions usually associated with night shiftwork are minimized. When people choose to work permanent night shifts, they are able to structure their work and non-work lives to reduce disruption, and subsequently may experience fewer problems associated with shiftwork (Barton & Folkard, 1991; Knauth & Rutenfranz, 1982; Skipper, Jung & Coffey, 1990; Verhaegen, Cober, De Smedt et al., 1987). Regarding nurses in particular, systematic reduction in participation (reduced work schedules) is an important source of nursing resource loss in some hospitals (Wise, 1993). Perhaps if nurses were allowed to choose their own schedules, these hospitals would not experience such losses.

While the research results regarding choice seem to be promising, freedom of choice may be denied in certain instances. For example, many companies have night shifts that have to be filled; if there are not enough 'volunteers' to fill them, some workers will be forced to work night shifts or will be out of a job. Furthermore, some industries, such as hospitals, are moving away from permanent day and night work toward an internal rotation system which requires *both* day and night work (Sadler, 1990). Choice, therefore, may not always be a viable option for organizations.

If we examine the type of work performed, we find many more predictors of desynchronization. Certain types of tasks are more fit for night-time performance than others, and certain types are particularly inappropriate for late night hours. Vigilance or monitoring type tasks, such as an air traffic controller might perform, are especially dangerous when performed at night. Unless the worker has some intermittent type of attention-demanding activity, he or she will inadvertently and unavoidably become fatigued and lapses in attention may occur as a result (Mitler, 1992). However, memory tasks, because they tax the cognitive load of a person and force functioning, are resistant to lapses in attention which produce poor performance and can thus be performed relatively safely at later night hours. According to Monk (1990) vigilance tasks follow a cyclical type of rhythm with troughs in performance occurring in the early hours of the morning and peaks in mid-to-late evening. However, memory-type tasks follow the opposite pattern with the worst performance occurring at night and the best performance in the early morning.

Therefore, a simple recommendation is to avoid performing vigilance tasks during the late night/early morning hours. It would be nice if it were as simple as this; yet it is impossible for the types of activities which must be performed around-the-clock like most monitoring tasks. You simply cannot tell a nuclear reactor operator to 'do something else' during those hours.

Moore-Ede (1993) in his book *The Twenty-four Hour Society* reviews many problems caused by the technological revolution. He discusses how most of the catastrophic events not caused by natural forces, such as Chernobyl and the *Exxon Valdez* have been caused at some level by fatigued operators and workers, which inevitably produced lapses in attention. Mitler (1992) also discusses dangers of accumulated sleep loss. Coping mechanisms such as physical activity and dietary stimulants may temporarily mask the sleep debt. However, when 'defenses are "let down," such as a period requiring immobility, overwhelming sleepiness ensues' (Mitler, 1992, p. 132). These instances may account for the seemingly incomprehensible times when individuals have fallen asleep in situations that caused great danger for themselves and others. To compound the problem, companies and engineers design workspaces in an effort to increase the comfort and decrease the workload demand. Unfortunately, this approach may actually exacerbate situations and now, by design, workers are required to do less in a more comfortable environment at a time when their bodies are craving sleep. This problem is not difficult to discern.

The Design of the Shift System

Alternative work schedules are often designed to accommodate individual needs. Organizations requiring around-the-clock operation can reduce problems from shiftwork by designing schedules that take advantage of established circadian rhythm principles. There are two primary factors regarding the design of the shift schedule which need to be considered: rotation of the shifts and number of recovery days. The direction of rotation will predict circadian adjustment: a forward rotation which involves phase delays (days, evenings, nights), rather than backward rotation involving phase advances (nights, evenings, days), predicts much better adjustment due to circadian rhythm synchronization (Barton & Folkard, 1993; Czeisler, Moore-Ede & Coleman, 1982; Knauth, 1993; Knauth & Kiesswetter, 1987; Knauth & Rutenfranz, 1982; Monk, 1990; Mitler, 1992; Monk & Folkard, 1985). Individual adjustment may lead to organizational productivity. In fact, Czeisler, Moore-Ede and Coleman (1982) reported *productivity increases for the plant* when a work schedule was redesigned to rotate forward rather than backward, every 21 days instead of every week. In this particular study, it is difficult to discern whether the direction or speed of rotation (or a combination of the two) was responsible for the productivity increase. However, one principle is clear from this body of literature: if a company must have rotating night shifts, it should make sure that the shift is scheduled in a forward rotating manner to induce phase delays rather than phase advances.

The speed of a shift rotation is a matter of debate. Europeans regard the problems with the circadian disharmony due to partial temporal adjustment as being most harmful and thus they rotate workers very rapidly during a week since the problem does not occur until later in the week (Knauth, 1993; Knauth & Kiesswetter, 1987; Knauth & Rutenfranz, 1982; Monk, 1990). The intention is that by rapidly rotating the workers, the disharmony problems will not have a chance to develop. By working only a few consecutive night shifts (one or two), the circadian disruption is minimized and the development of a chronic sleep debt is avoided (Barton, 1994; Knauth, 1993; Knauth & Kiesswetter, 1987; Knauth & Rutenfranz, 1982). Knauth (1993) advocated reducing the requirement to work the night shift as much as possible since it is the most disruptive of all shifts in terms of physiological adjustment, sleep/ fatigue, and alertness.

Conversely, North Americans generally view the inappropriate phasing problem as most harmful and therefore have less rapid rotation, or a slower speed (three weeks days, three weeks evenings, and three weeks nights vs three days days, three days evenings, and three days nights) thus allowing the phasing problem to occur less frequently. As discussed above, Czeisler, Moore-Ede and Coleman (1982) found that a slower rotation may have positively impacted the overall productivity of the plant. Barton (1994; Barton & Folkard, 1991; Barton et al., 1993) has found that nurses on permanent night shifts report fewer health, sleep, social and domestic complaints compared to nurses working on rotating-shift schedules. Czeisler, Moore-Ed and Coleman (1982) also found that a significantly greater percentage (65%) of continually rotating shiftworkers reported poor quality of sleep compared to reports of non-rotating workers (20%). Additionally, Jamal and Baba (1992) found that nurses on fixed schedules reported less job stress, higher job satisfaction and organizational commitment, and less of an intent to leave the organization. Wilkinson (1992) also strongly argues in favor of a permanent night shift which will maximize adaptation and minimize disruption. Neither schedule is free from problems, however. As previously mentioned, even when allowed to adapt for quite long periods of time, workers still never fully recover because of the weekend 'rebounding' of other opposing patterns of activity. For more comprehensive recent reviews of the rotation debate see Monk (1986); Folkard (1992); Wedderburn (1992) and Wilkinson (1992).

Mitler (1992) discusses how management's primary concern in designing a rotating schedule should be to alleviate the biological problems. Mitler (1992) reports a study conducted by the Center for the Design of Industrial Schedules (CDIS), a non-profit organization affiliated with Harvard University, where a new schedule was designed for Philadelphia police officers to combat circadian adjustment problems. The CDIS recommended a schedule which had the following characteristics: (a) the direction of rotation was changed from backward to forward; (b) the rate of rotation was reduced from one week to three weeks; and (c) the six-day work week was reduced to four or five work days in a row. Results after 11 months were that the officers reported a four-fold decrease in the frequency of poor sleep; officers reported a 25% decline in number of sleep episodes on the night shift; officers reported using less alcohol and fewer sleeping pills; officers' families reported nearly five-fold increase in satisfaction with their work schedule; and twice as many officers preferred the improved schedule over the old schedule (Mitler, 1992). Mitler's 1992 research corroborated Knauth and Kiesswetter's 1987 research which found that a forward rotating system reduced sleep difficulties (compared to a backward rotating system), and a majority of workers (83.9%) favored the new system, *despite a loss of money* from less overtime.

Czeisler, Moore-Ede and Coleman's (1982) research also demonstrated how workers' satisfaction, health, attendance, and productivity were all improved by designing systems which incorporated known circadian principles. In their study, the researchers designed a schedule which incorporated phase delays, rather than advances, and also gave workers a longer interval between shift schedules than they had had previously. Thus organizations can also help adjustment by giving employees plenty of time for their bodies to adapt. Because physiological adaptation to shiftwork takes place very slowly (Daniel, 1990), research has consistently shown that the longer a worker has to adjust to the night schedule, the fewer problems occur as a result. Also, research has demonstrated that the interval between phase shifts should be as great as possible and practical to the organization to allow workers maximum time for adjustment (Barton & Folkard, 1993; Czeisler, Moore-Ede & Coleman, 1982; Knauth & Rutenfranz, 1982).

One simple thing an organization can do is to adjust the start times of shifts to be most advantageous to the worker. Knauth (1993; Knauth & Rutenfranz,

1982) reviews literature regarding shift start times and concludes that early-starting morning shifts (especially before 7.00 a.m.) appear to be linked with higher accident and error rates. Increasing the number of work breaks during the evening and night shifts has also been shown to reduce adverse effects of shiftwork. A final measure organizations can take to minimize consequences of shiftwork is to allow a recovery day. This entails giving the individual the day off after a night shift in order to synchronize his/her life and thus his/her circadian rhythms.

Common sense seems to be a theme: encouraging comfort and lower work-load will increase the tendency toward drowsiness; prohibiting naps will increase fatigue; monotonous tasks are performed worse when the body needs excitement to keep awake. The best advice for the shiftworker is to keep as regular a schedule as possible and to arrange the environment to facilitate sleep by reducing noise distractions. Companies need to examine their policies and practices as well as their work demands, keeping the known circadian principles in mind. If the company chooses not to, it may find itself in the undesirable position of being forced to by law: some countries are beginning to recognize the consequences of shiftwork and are enacting legislation to combat the adverse effects. Cervinka (1993) reports that Austria enacted legislation in 1981 entitled 'Night Shift Hard Labour Law' which contains a variety of preventive regulations such as additional work breaks, additional days off, funding for earlier retirement for employees who work more than 60 night shifts per year. Monk (1988) provides an excellent review of various countries' legislation efforts to make shiftwork safe and less negative for the shiftworker.

One consistent theme that has surface is for the company to allow flexibility in scheduling (Burke & Greenglass, 1987; Cervinka, 1993; Knauth, 1993; Knauth & Rutenfranz, 1982; Staines & Pleck, 1986). Staines and Pleck (1986) found that there was a buffering effect of flexibility against the negative effects, particularly on family life, of alternative, or non-standard, work schedules. Flexible scheduling ideas have contributed to a very popular trend in many organizations, including both those with shifts *as well as* those companies which do not require shiftwork: Flextime.

FLEXTIME

Flextime was first introduced in West Germany in the late 1960s. The original intentions were to ease commuting and energy problems as well as to attract skilled mothers back into the labor force during a time of labor shortage. Today, flextime and flexible scheduling have grown in popularity as employees, particularly single mothers/fathers, and dual-career couples with children, express the need for more flexibility in their jobs. With increases in work–family conflict (described above) due in part to both parents in most households working, employees are finding that a rigid workday schedule is not acceptable.

Flextime (a.k.a. *flexitime or flexitour*) refers to any schedule which allows employees to vary work arrival and departure times (e.g. employees may arrive any time between the band hours of 7–9 a.m., with the earliest arrivers eligible to depart at 3.30 p.m.). Usually, there is a company-prescribed 'core time' (e.g. 10 a.m.–3 p.m.) which coincides with the busiest part of the workday, when all employees must be on the job. For comprehensive reviews of the different types or models of flextime, see Baum and McEvan Young (1974); Ronen (1984); Rubin (1979); and Swart (1978).

Individual Effects from Flextime

Many reports have indicated overwhelming positive effects from implementing flextime. The freedom to set their own schedules often enables employees to spend less money on childcare services, as well as to spend more time with the family in the evening. Flextime may also broaden work opportunities for individuals who are unable to work in fixed schedule jobs (Coltrin & Barendse, 1981). Data indicate that flextime may enhance the quality of family relationships (Bohen & Viveros-Long, 1981; Nollen, 1979) and reduce work–family conflict (Nollen, 1979; Shinn, Wong, Simko & Ortiz-Torres, 1989; Walker, Fletcher & McLeod, 1975) which is why flextime is usually included in reference to 'family-friendly', 'family-supportive', work environments and policies.

Employee work attitudes such as job satisfaction may also be improved (Bohen & Viveros-Long, 1981; Dunham, Pierce & Castaneda, 1987; Narayanan & Nath, 1982b; Nollen, 1979; Nollen & Martin, 1978; Orpen, 1981) as employees' higher order needs for control and growth are more fulfilled than with schedules where the employee has no choice in when he or she works (Allenspach, 1972; Elbing, Gadon & Gordon, 1973; Krausz & Hermann, 1991; Ronen, 1984; Thomas & Ganster, 1985). Some authors have suggested flextime is a type of job enrichment policy because it allows employees more autonomy (Huse & Cummings, 1985; Narayanan & Nath, 1982b; Pierce & Newstrom, 1980; Ronen, 1981a). Due to reduced supervisory control over employees' time, flextime may also improve supervisor–employee relations (Buckley, Kicza & Crane, 1987; Narayanan & Nath, 1982b).

Organizational Effects from Flextime

Research has not consistently demonstrated that 'bottom line' organizational productivity is improved as a result of flextime implementation (Harrick, Vanek & Michlitsch, 1986; McGuire & Liro, 1986; Schein, Mauner & Novak, 1977). Some studies do report performance increases (although negligible) from flexible work schedules (Kim & Campagna, 1981; Orpen, 1981). In a study on claims processed in an insurance company, Walch and Gordon (1980) reported a significant increase in annual productivity following implementation of flextime. Similar increases in productivity are reported in the literature by Craddock, Lewis, and Rose (1981), Golembiewski and Hilles (1977), Gomze-Mejia, Hopp, and Sommerstad (1978), and Morgan (1977). Nollen (1979) reports that, based on approximately 40 case studies and surveys, a conservative estimate is that flextime yields productivity increases for a third to a half of organizations that implement it. A major problem with many of the reported productivity increases is that they are anecdotal in nature and do not contain an experimental design to rule out alternative explanations.

However, research *has* consistently reported that organizational performance is improved indirectly as indexed by less absenteeism, tardiness, and turnover as well as less use of sick leave and overtime (Baum & McEvan Young, 1974; Coltrin & Barendse, 1981; Dalton & Mesch, 1990; Golembiewski, Hilles & Kagno, 1974; Harrick, Vanek & Michlitsch, 1986; Kim & Campagna, 1981; Narayanan & Nath, 1982a; Nollen, 1979; Ralston, Anthony & Gustafson, 1985; Ralston & Flanagan, 1985; Ronen, 1984; Swart, 1978). In fact, a recent meta-analysis of 92 organizations concluded that absenteeism, tardiness, and turnover were reduced as a result of alternative work schedules which included flextime (Pierce, Newstrom, Dunham & Barber, 1989).

Yet still other research has concluded that the magnitude of the problems encountered with dual-career or single-parent households cannot be alleviated much by 'minor changes in daily work schedules' (Bohen & Viveros-Long, 1981). Some authors (Buckley, Kicza & Crane, 1987; Krausz & Hermann, 1991; Ronen, 1981a, b) have noted that flextime is not the 'universal panacea' it has been touted: 'Reports of flextime success can be matched invariably with examples of flextime failure' (Buckley, Kicza & Crane, 1987, p. 260). Not all workers are even in favor of the practice. In fact, workers (particularly young, single, childless) who do not have a need for the flexibility, may react negatively to the schedule. Flextime often reduces overtime which may be particularly essential for unionized workers and workers who have increased their standard wages through overtime (Coltrin & Barendse, 1981; Nollen, 1979; Rubin, 1979). In addition, administration and/or management may regard flextime as problematic because it requires more time and effort on their part to coordinate work schedules and, while employees gain some control and autonomy, supervisors inevitably lose some control over employees (Buckley, Kicza & Crane, 1987; Krausz & Hermann, 1991; Nollen, 1979). Finally, the costs of implementing flextime (e.g. administrative, overhead, maintenance and security) can also be a major deterrent and create obvious negative consequences, even though costs may not inevitably rise (Buckley, Kicza & Crane, 1987; Ronen, 1984). In fact, fear of increased costs is a major reason cited why flextime is not used more frequently (Bohlander, Werther & Wolfe,

1980). Therefore, organizations need to anticipate both positive and negative flextime outcomes before choosing implementation (Buckley, Kicza & Crane, 1987). Swart (1978) recommends that instead of implementing a flextime system in all departments of an organization, one or more representative work units should be used as a pilot study.

Other Effects from Flextime

One of the original intentions was that flextime would reduce traffic congestion and commuting times which translates into time and gas saved for employees. In support of this, the Environmental Protection Agency found that flexible working schedules resulted in a reduction of energy consumption by commuters because of increased travel speed from improved traffic flow (Swart, 1978). Additionally, Petersen (1980) found that flextime cut employee commuting time by more than 75%. Thus, rush hour traffic is reduced which leads to less road abuse and more tax savings (Swart, 1978). Working at off-peak hours can also reduce congestion in the work environment itself (Swart, 1978). Less congestion leads to less noise pollution. The list could go on indefinitely; the point is that there are potentially many positive benefits beyond those to the employees and the employing organization.

Clients and customers external to the employing organization, as well as other organizations with whom the company conducts business, may also be positively impacted. Customer service may increase as a result of flextime due to there being more hours in the day in which to contact an organization (Coltrin & Barendse, 1981). Communication over time zones may be improved in organizations with flexible bandwidths of time. An employee who stays late into the evening, or who comes in very early, may be more able to talk to companies across continents during their regular business hours.

FUTURE RESEARCH DIRECTIONS

Other Alternative Work Schedules

While this review was intended to be fairly comprehensive regarding alternative work schedules, there are still many other alternative or 'non-standard' schedules which we did not discuss. The reason is that the research and literature of these other schedules is so scant, most likely because they are either relatively new in concept, or they have increased in importance and emphasis in the last decade.

Part-time workers have been studied more recently as researchers have begun to realize that they are a distinct type of employee who do not necessarily have the same work attitudes, needs, and goals as full-time employees. Also, as organizations are looking for ways to cut costs and overheads, they are utilizing part-time workers more (who don't usually receive benefits). Part-time workers thus represent an understudied group and the literature is beginning to reflect this.

Job sharing is related to part-time work and is a concept that is gaining popularity as it offers an alternative for many employees who may not be able to commit to an organization full time. Job sharing involves two or more people splitting up a 40-hour-per-week job. Many organizations are letting people who wish to share a job to do so if the employees agree to be responsible for coordinating the administration and logistics of the schedule. The literature, particularly experimentally designed studies, is particularly sparse regarding job sharing. Related to job sharing is a notion called 'flexible working years' which involves the coordination of two or more employees working alternative years at a particular job. We only found one reference in the literature to such a schedule.

Finally, there is a relatively new concept called 'telecommuting' (also home-based work, flexible place, flexiplace) which involves the employee working out of his or her home. Telecommuting appears to be particularly amenable to jobs that entail mainly computer work (e.g. data entry), or phone work (e.g. phone sales/solicitation). The most obvious major concern with telecommuting is the monitoring of the system.

Family-friendly Policies

Actually, what all of the alternative schedules have in common is that at some time they have all been referred to or categorized as 'family-friendly' policies an organization can implement. As discussed, shiftwork can enable parents to work when their children are sleeping and thus to be at home for mealtimes; compressed schedules often have extended weekends as an advantage; and flextime enables a parent to adjust work hours to coincide with when they need to be home in the mornings and/or afternoons. Part-time work and job sharing are considered family-friendly in that they enable people (often a parent who does not want to work full time because of family commitments) to work who cannot or will not commit full time to a job. Telecommuting offers obvious advantages for families as it allows a parent to be home continuously. Other family-friendly policies which are gaining in popularity, yet have relatively little research support, are company-sponsored wellness/fitness programs and on-site or company-sponsored childcare centers.

Methodological Considerations

As mentioned in the text of this review, one of the main concerns regarding the literature on alternative work schedules is the generalizability of the results from different samples. This is especially a concern for the shiftwork literature as much of the research has been conducted with either nurses or mostly male-dominated industrial workers. Replications of some of the major research findings in more diverse settings thus appears to be warranted.

Another concern involves the criterion measures: much of the data is from questionnaires and surveys and revolves around a handful of dependent variables (i.e. job satisfaction and satisfaction with work, withdrawal behaviors, health and sleep symptoms). There is a gap in the literature linking alternative work schedules to much of the recent work in the last decade in organizational attitudes and behaviors. We feel that a notable addition to the literature would be studies involving more behaviorally based criterion measures. A particularly fruitful avenue for further exploration is the impact of alternative work schedules on organizational citizenship behaviors (OCBs). Other suggestions include a consideration of the impact of alternative work schedules on the organizational attitudes of perceived organizational support and organizational commitment.

Finally, we feel that longitudinal studies are particularly necessary in this field. A few studies made mention that some of the adverse effects of shiftwork appeared to be very long-lived; however, a majority studied a snapshot in time. While the consequences discussed are important regardless of whether they are acute or chronic, long-term effects, particularly physical and mental health-related ones, are much more onerous. Established long-term consequences would also help with legislation efforts to make shiftwork, in particular, more safe.

In a related vein, some researchers mentioned that jet lag was similar to shiftwork in its physiological disruptions to the individual, yet distinct because jet lag benefits from time cues that encourage adjustment, and it is usually acute rather than chronic (Regestein & Monk, 1991). It would be very interesting to utilize the jet lag literature and test some preventions for jet lag with shiftworkers. A melding of the two literatures may further shed light on the distinction between acute and chronic problems resulting from shiftwork.

Related to the nature of longitudinal studies is the notion of studying persons who drop out of shiftwork. At first blush this may seem akin to asking researchers to do more studies on turnover and who left the organization and why; the difficulties of such research are readily apparent. Yet, with alternative work schedules, persons who drop out of the particular schedule may actually stay with the organization. Thus, it would be possible to study those who have 'quit shiftwork' but continued working for the employing organization. The variables of perceived organizational support, organizational citizenship behaviors, and organizational commitment would all seem to be logically related to reasons why persons drop out.

Finally, it is possible that the people who drop out of shiftwork could have been either counseled on strategies to prevent adverse consequences, or deterred from entering into shiftwork in the first place. In fact, the question of clinical management of individual problems from shiftwork has recently arisen in the literature (e.g. is the poor sleep that shiftworkers experience to be considered a sleep disorder? Regestein & Monk, 1991). Clinical and counseling strategies for shiftworkers thus seems to be another potential avenue for future research.

CONCLUDING REMARKS

Before an organization implements any alternative work schedule, it should carefully evaluate its own scheduling needs, the needs of its employees, and the work environment. While this may sound like elementary advice, many organizations implement such policies based on anecdotal evidence from other organizations and reports from non-research-based journals. According to Dunham and Pierce (1983; Dunham, Pierce & Castaneda, 1987), most users of alternative work schedules have chosen one based on intuition or have copied the practices of other organizations. If those in administration have strong expectations about what the implementation of the schedule will accomplish, they may be setting themselves up for disappointment and possibly failure. As Buckley, Kicza and Crane (1987) point out, it is erroneous to assume that 'what worked in one organization will work in another'.

The organizational culture, then, will be a major determining factor in whether a particular work schedule is needed and/or accepted in a particular organization (Buckley, Kicza and Crane, 1987). For example, telecommuting may not be a viable option for organizations which have established excellent reputations based on quality, personal, face-to-face service (e.g. banks, accounting firms). Thus, if an organization makes a commitment to family-friendly policies and decides to implement an alternative work schedule, they may have the task of actually changing their organization's culture. Organizations need to consider if this is an additional challenge they are willing to tackle. In summary, we offer five critical concerns management must evaluate before implementing any alternative schedule.

- Policy Adoption Issues: What is the impetus behind adopting this particular schedule? Is it due to hunch, intuition, or because another organization reported 'amazing' effects? Implementation should be based on a sound assessment of one's own operating needs, the needs and desires of one's employees; and the feasibility of the proposed schedule: not all jobs and/or positions are amenable to alternative schedules.
- Administrative and Financial Issues: How will the administration of the system be monitored? Will the organization incur extra overhead cost for utilities, support services such as cafeteria and security, or personnel administration? Often organizations choose to implement schedules without realizing the extra administrative time and overhead expenses.
- Union and Legal Issues: Is there likely to be union opposition? Does the chosen schedule have potential to adversely impact any protected classes

of employees? Organizations may find legal consultation extremely advantageous in preventing future legal battles.

● Design of the System: Is the design of the chosen system threatening to employees' physical and/or mental health? Will measures be taken to reduce adverse consequences? Keeping known circadian rhythm principles in mind when designing the system will prevent and alleviate deleterious effects.

● Long-term Monitoring: What procedures are in place to ensure that the system continues to meet organizational and employee needs? Long-term monitoring and adjustments to the system are critical in enabling organizations to capitalize on potential value added.

REFERENCES

Adams, J., Folkard, S. & Young, M. (1986). Coping strategies used by nurses on night duty. *Ergonomics*, **29**(2), 185–196.

Akerstedt, T. (1988). Sleepiness as a consequence of shift work. *Sleep*, **11**, 17–34.

Akerstedt, T. (1990). Psychological and physiological effects of shiftwork. *Scandinavian Journal of Work and Environmental Health*, **16**, 67–73.

Akerstedt, T. & Froberg, J. (1976). Shift work and health—interdisciplinary aspects. In P. Rentos & R. Shepard (Eds), *Shift Work and Health* (pp. 179–197). Washington, DC: US Department of Health, Education and Welfare.

Akerstedt, T. & Gillberg, M. (1981). The circadian variation of experimental displaced sleep. *Sleep*, **4**, 159–169.

Allenspach, H. (1972). Flexible working time—its development application in Switzerland. *Occupational Psychology*, **46**, 209–215.

Angersbach, D., Knauth, P., Loskant, H., Karvonen, M. J., Undeutsch, K. & Rutenfranz, J. (1980). A retrospective cohort study comparing complaints and diseases in day and shift workers. *International Archives of Occupational and Environmental Health*, **45**, 127–140.

Arendt, J. (1994). Clinical perspectives for melatonin and its agonists. *Biological Psychiatry*, **35**(1), 1–2.

Atkinson, G., Coldwells, A., Reilly, T. & Waterhouse, J. (1993). A comparison of circadian rhythms in work performance between physically active and inactive subjects. *Ergonomics*, **36**(1–3), 273–281.

Barton, J. (1994). Choosing to work at night: A moderating influence on individual tolerance to shift work. *Journal of Applied Psychology*, **79**(3), 449–454.

Barton, J. & Folkard, S. (1991). The response of day and night nurses to their work schedules. *Journal of Occupational Psychology*, **64**, 207–218.

Barton, J. & Folkard, S. (1993). Advancing versus delaying shift systems. *Ergonomics*, **36**(1–3), 59–64.

Barton, J., Smith, L., Totterdell, P., Spelten, E. & Folkard, S. (1993). Does individual choice determine shift system acceptability? *Ergonomics*, **36**(1–3), 93–99.

Baum, S. & McEvan Young, W. (1974). *A Practical Guide to Flexible Working Hours*. Park Ridge, NJ: Noyes Data Corporation.

Bohen, H.H. & Viveros-Long, A. (1981). *Balancing Jobs and Family Life*. Philadelphia: Temple University Press.

Bohlander, G. W., Werther, W. B. & Wolfe, M. N. (1980). An update of nonstandard work schedules. *Arizona Business*, **2**, 16–24.

Bohle, P. & Tilley, A. J. (1989). The impact of night work on psychological well-being. *Ergonomics*, **32**(9), 1089–1099.

Bonnet, M.H. (1990). Dealing with shift work: Physical fitness, temperature, and napping. *Work and Stress*, **4**(3), 261–274.

Breaugh, J. A. (1983). The 12-hour work day: Differing employee reactions. *Personnel Psychology*, **36**, 277–288.

Buckley, M. R., Kicza, D. C. & Crane, N. (1987). A note of the effectiveness of flextime as an organizational intervention. *Public Personnel Management*, **16**(3), 259–267.

Burke, R. J. & Greenglass, E. R. (1987). Work and family. In C. L. Cooper & I. T. Robertson (Eds), *International Review of Industrial and Organizational Psychology* (Ch. 9, pp. 273–321). Chichester: Wiley.

Calvasina, E. & Boxx, R. (1975). Efficiency of workers on the four day work week. *Academy of Management Journal*, **18**, 604–610.

Campbell, S. S. (1992). Effects of sleep and circadian rhythms on performance. *Handbook of Human Performance*, **3**, 195–215.

Cassone, V. M. (1990). Effects of melatonin on vertebrate circadian systems. *TINS*, **13**(11), 457–461.

Cervinka, R. (1993). Night shift dose and stress at work. *Ergonomics*, **361**(1–3), 155–160.

Charles, N. & Brown, D. (1981). Women, shiftwork and the sexual division of labour. *Sociological Review*, **29**(4), 685–704.

Coffey, L., Skipper, J. & Jung, F. (1988). Nurses and shift work: Effects on job performance and job-related stress. *Journal of Advanced Nursing*, **13**(2), 245–254.

Cohen, A. R. & Gadon, H. (1978). *Alternative Work Schedules: Integrating Individual and Organizational Needs*. Reading, MA: Addison-Wesley.

Coltrin, S. A. & Barendse, B.D. (1981). Is your organization a good candidate for flextime? *Personnel Journal*, **60**(9), 712–715.

Costa, G. (1996). The impact of shift and night work on health. International Congress on Occupational Health. *Applied Ergonomics*, **27**(1), 9–16.

Costa, G., Apostoli, P., d'Andrea, F. & Gaffuri, E. (1981). Gastrointestinal and neurotic disorders in textile shift workers. In A. Reinberg, N. Vieux & P. Andlauer (Eds), *Night and Shift Work: Biological and Social Aspects* (pp. 215–221). Oxford: Pergamon Press.

Costa, G., Cesana, G., Kogi, K. & Wedderburn, A. (Eds) (1990). *Shiftwork: Health, Sleep, and Performance*. Frankfurt: Peter Lang.

Costa, G., Lievore, F., Casaletti, G., Gaffuri, E. & Folkard, S. (1989). Circadian characteristics influencing interindividual differences in tolerance and adjustment to shiftwork. *Ergonomics*, **32**(4), 373–385.

Costa, G., Micciolo, R., Bertoldi, L. & Tommasini, M. (1990). Absenteeism among female and male nurses on day and shiftwork. In G. Costa, G. Cesana, K. Kogi & A. Wedderburn (Eds), *Shiftwork: Health, Sleep, and Performance*. Frankfurt: Peter Lang.

Craddock, S., Lewis, T. & Rose, J. (1981). Flexitime: The Kentucky experiments. *Public Personnel Management*, **10**, 244–252.

Czeisler, C. A., Moore-Ede, M. C. & Coleman, R. M. (1982). Rotating shift work schedules that disrupt sleep are improved by applying circadian principles. *Science*, **217**(30), 460–462.

Czeisler, C. A., Johnson, M. P. & Duffy, J. F. (1990). Exposure to bright light and darkness to treat physiologic maladaptation to night work. *New England Journal of Medicine*, **322**(18), 1253–1259.

Dalton, D. R. & Mesch, D. J. (1990). The impact of flexible scheduling on employee attendance and turnover. *Administrative Science Quarterly*, **35**(2), 370–387.

Daniel, J. (1990). Circadian patterns of changes in psychophysiological indicators of adaptation to shift work. *Studia Psychologica*, **32**, 173–177.

Dawson, D. & Campbell, S. S. (1991). Time exposure to bright light improves sleep and alertness during simulated night shifts. *Sleep*, **14**(6), 511–516.

Dawson, D., Encel, N. & Lushington, K. (1995). Improving adaptation to simulated night shift: Time exposure to bright light versus daytime melatonin administration. *Sleep*, **18**(1), 11–21.

De Vries, G. M. & De Vries-Griever, A. H. G. (1990). The process of developing health complaints: A longitudinal study of the effects of abnormal, irregular and condensed working hours. In G. Costa, G. Cesana, K. Kogi & A. Wedderburn (Eds), *Shiftwork: Health, Sleep, and Performance*. Frankfurt: Peter Lang.

Dunham, R. B. & Pierce, J. L. (1983). The design and evaluation of alternative work schedules: A study of employee and organizational consequences. *Personnel Administrator*, **28**, 67–75.

Dunham, R. B., Pierce, J. L. & Castaneda, M. B. (1987). Alternative work schedules: Two field quasi-experiments. *Personnel Psychology*, **40**, 215–242.

Eastman, C. I. (1990). Circadian rhythms and bright light recommendations for shift work. *Work & Stress*, **4**, 245–260.

Elbing, A. O., Gadon, H. & Gordon, J. R. M. (1973). Time for a human timetable. *European Business*, **39**, 46–54.

Elmore, S. K., Betrus, P. A. & Burr, R. (1994). Light, social *zeitgebers*, and the sleep–wake cycle in the entrainment of human circadian rhythms. *Research in Nursing and Health*, **17**(6), 471–478.

Feldman, D. C. (1990). Reconceptualizing the nature and consequences of part-time work. *Academy of Management Review*, **15**(1), 103–112.

Folkard, S. (1987). Circadian rhythms and hours of work. In P. Warr (Ed.), *Psychology at Work* (3rd edn.). Harmondsworth: Penguin.

Folkard, S. (1988). Circadian rhythms and shiftwork: Adjustment or masking. *Advances in the Biosciences*, **73**, 173–182.

Folkard, S. (1990). Circadian performance rhythms: Some practical and theoretical implications. *Philosophical Transactions of the Royal Society of London, Series B*, **327**, 543–553.

Folkard, S. (1992). Is there a 'best compromise' shift system? *Ergonomics*, **35**(12), 1453–1463.

Folkard, S., Barton, J., Costa, G., Smith, L., Spelten, E. & Totterdell, P. (1993). The Standard Shiftwork Index. *Ergonomics*, **36**, 313–314.

Folkard, S., Monk, T. H. & Lobban, M. C. (1979). Towards a predictive test of adjustment to shift work. *Ergonomics*, **22**(1), 79–91.

Foster, L. W., Latack, J. C. & Reindl, L. J. (1979). Effects and promises of the shortened work week. *Academy of Management Proceedings*, 226–230.

Gadbois, C. (1981). Women on night shifts: Interdependence of sleep and off the job activities. In A. Reinberg, N. Vieux & P. Andlauer (Eds), *Night and Shift Work: Biological and Social Aspects* (pp. 13.1–13.14). Elmsford, NY: Pergamon Press.

Gadbois, C. (1984). Time budget strategies regulating off the job activities of night nurses. In A. Wedderburn & P. Smith (Eds), *Psychological Aspects of Shiftwork*. Edinburgh: Herriot Watt University.

Ganster, D. C., Mayes, B. T., Sime, W. E. & Tharp, G. D. (1982). Managing organizational stress: A field experiment. *Journal of Applied Psychology*, **67**(5), 533–542.

Gold, D. R., Rogacz, S., Bock, N. & Tosteson, T. D. (1992). Rotating shiftwork, sleep, and accidents related to sleepiness in hospital nurses. *American Journal of Public Health*, **82**(7), 1011–1014.

Golembiewski, R. & Hilles, R. J. (1977). Drug company workers like new schedules. *Monthly Labor Review*, **100**, 65–69.

Golembiewski, R., Hilles, R. & Kagno, M. (1974). A longitudinal study of flextime effects: Some consequences of an OD structural intervention. *Journal of Behavioral Science*, **4**, 503–532.

Gomez-Meija, L. R., Hopp, M. S. & Sommerstad, C. R. (1978). Implementation and evaluation of flexible work hours: A case study. *Personnel Administrator*, **23**, 39–41.

Goodale, J. G. & Aagaard, A. K. (1975). Factors relating to varying reactions of the four-day work week. *Journal of Applied Psychology*, **69**, 33–38.

Gordon, N., Cleary, P., Parlan, C. & Czeisler, C. (1986). The prevalence and health impact of shiftwork. *American Journal of Public Health*, **76**(10), 1225–1228.

Gupta, S. & Pati, A. (1994). Desynchronization of circadian rhythms in a group of shift working nurses: Effects of pattern of shift rotation. *Journal of Human Ergology*, **23**(2), 121–131.

Harma, M. I., Ilmarinen, J. & Yletyinen, I. (1982). Circadian variation of physiological functions in physically average and very fit dayworkers. *Journal of Human Ergology*, **11**, Supplement, 33–46.

Harma, M., Knauth, P., Ilmarinen, J. & Ollila, H. (1990). The relation of age to the adjustment of the circadian rythms of oral temperature and sleepiness to shift work. *Chronology International*, **7**(3), 227–233.

Harrick, E. J., Vanek, G. R. & Michlitsch, J. F. (1986). Alternate work schedules, productivity, leave usage, and employee attitudes: A field study. *Public Personnel Management*, **15**(2), 159–169.

Harrington, J. M. (1978). *Shift Work and Health. A Critical Review of the Literature*. London: HMSO.

Hartman, R. I. & Weaver, K. M. (1977). Four factors influencing conversion to a four-day work week. *Human Resource Management*, **16**, 24–27.

Healy, D., Minors, D. S. & Waterhouse, J. M. (1993). Shiftwork, helplessness, and depression. *Journal of Affective Disorders*, **29**(1), 17–25.

Healy, D. & Waterhouse, J. M. (1991). Reactive rhythms and endogenous clocks. *Psychological Medicine*, **21**, 557–564.

Huse, E. F. & Cummings, T. G. (1985). *Organizational Development and Change* (3rd edn.). St Paul, MN: West Publishing.

Ivancevich, J. M. (1974). Effects of the shorter workweek on selected satisfaction and performance measures. *Journal of Applied Psychology*, **59**, 717–721.

Ivancevich, J. M. & Lyon, H. L. (1977). The shortened workweek: A field experiment. *Journal of Applied Psychology*, **62**(1), 34–37.

Jamal, M. (1990). Relationships of job stress and Type A behaviour to employees' job satisfaction, organizational commitment, psychosomatic health problems and turnover motivation. *Human Relations*, **43**, 727–738.

Jamal, M. & Baba, V. V. (1992). Shiftwork and department-type related to job stress, work attitudes and behavioral intentions: A study of nurses. *Journal of Organizational Behavior*, **13**, 449–464.

Jamal, M. & Jamal, S. (1982). Work and nonwork experiences of employees on fixed and rotating shifts: An empirical assessment. *Journal of Vocational Behavior*, **20**(3), 282–293.

Kahn, R. L. & Byosiere, P. (1992). Stress in organizations. In M. D. Dunnette & L. M. Hough (Eds), *Handbook of Industrial and Organizaitonal Psychology* (Vol. 3, pp. 571–650). Palo Alto, CA: Consulting Psychologists Press.

Kenny, M. T. (1974). Public employee attitudes toward the four-day week. *Public Personnel Management,*3, 159–161.

Kim, J. & Campagna, A. (1981). Effects of flextime on employee attendance and performance: A field experiment. *Academy of Management Journal,* 24, 729–741.

Knaugh, P. (1993). The design of shift systems. *Ergonomics,* 36, 15–28.

Knauth, P. & Harma, M. (1992). The relation of shift work tolerance to the circadian adjustment. *Chronobiology International,* 9(1), 46–54.

Knauth, P. & Kiesswetter, E. (1987). A change from weekly to quicker shift rotations: A field study of discontinuous three-shift workers. *Ergonomics,* 30(9), 1311–1321.

Knauth, P. & Rutenfranz, J. (1975). The effects of noise on the sleep of nightworkers. In W. Colquhoun, S. Folkard, P. Knauth & J. Rutenfranz (Eds), *Experimental Studies of Shift Work.* Opladen: Westdeutscher Verlag.

Knauth, P. & Rutenfranz, J. (1982). Development of criteria for the design of shiftwork systems. In K. Kogi, T. Miura & H. Saito (Eds), *Shiftwork: Its practice and improvement. Journal of Human Ergology,* 2 (Supplement), 337–367.

Kogi, K. (1996). Improving shift workers' health and tolerance to shiftwork: Recent advances. *Applied Ergonomics,* 27(1), 5–8.

Koller, M., Kundi, M. & Cervinka, R. (1978). Field studies of shift work at an Austrian oil refinery: I. Health and psychosocial wellbeing of workers who drop out of shiftwork. *Ergonomics,* 21(10), 835–847.

Kossek, E. E. (1989). The acceptance of human resource innovation by multiple constituencies. *Personnel Psychology,* 42, 263–281.

Krausz, M. & Hermann, E. (1991). Who is afraid of flextime: Correlates of personal choice of a flexitime schedule. *Applied Psychology: An International Review,* 40(3), 315–326.

Latack, J. C. & Foster, L. W. (1985). Implementation of compressed work schedules: Participation and job redesign as critical factors for employee acceptance. *Personnel Psychology,* 38, 75–92.

Lee, T. W. & Johnson, D. R. (1991). The effects of work schedules and employment status on the organizational commitment and job satisfaction of full versus part time employees. *Journal of Vocational Behavior,* 38, 208–224.

Lewy, A. J., Ahmed, S., Jackson, J. M. L. & Sack, R. L. (1992). Melatonin shifts human circadian rhythms according to a phase-response curve. *Chronobiology International,* 9(5), 380–392.

Mason, J. C. (1992). Flexing more than muscle: Employees want time on their side. *Management Review,* 81(4), 6–12.

Matsumoto, K. & Morita, Y. (1987). Effect of nighttime nap and age on sleep patterns of shift workers. *Sleep,* 10, 580–589.

McGuire, J. B. & Liro, J. R. (1986). Flexible work schedules, work attitudes, and perceptions of productivity. *Public Personnel Management,* 15, 65–73.

Meijman, T. F., Thunnissen, M. J. & de Vries-Griever, A. G. H. (1990). The aftereffects of a prolonged period of day-sleep on subjective sleep quality. *Work and Stress,* 4(1), 65–70.

Minor, D. S., Healy, D. & Waterhouse, J. M. (1994). The attitudes and general health of student nurses before and immediately after their first eight weeks of nightwork. *Ergonomics,* 37(8), 1355–1362.

Mitler, M. M. (1992). The realpolitik of narcolepsy and other disorders with impaired alertness. *Psychosocial Aspects of Narcolepsy.* Binghampton, NY: Haworth Press.

Monk, T. H. (1986). Advantages and disadvantages of rapidly rotating shift schedules: A circadian viewpoint. *Human Factors,* 38, 553–557.

Monk, T. H. (1988). *How to Make Shift Work Safe and Productive.* DesPlaines, IL: American Society of Safety Engineers.

Monk, T. H. (1990). The relationship of chronobiology to sleep schedules and performance demands. *Work and Stress*, **4**(3), 227–236.

Monk, T. H. & Folkard, S. (1985). Individual differences in shiftwork adjustment. In S. Folkard & T. H. Monk (Eds), *Hours of Work: Temporal Factors in Work Scheduling* (pp. 227–237). New York: Wiley.

Moore-Ede, M. (1993). *The Twenty-four Hour Society*: Reading, MA: Addison-Wesley.

Moore-Ede, M. & Richardson, G. (1985). Medical implications of shiftwork. *Annual Review of Medicine*, **36**, 607–617.

Morgan, F. T. (1977). Your (flex) time may come. *Personnel Journal*, **56**, 82–85, 96.

Motohashi, Y. (1992). Alteration of circadian rhythm in shift-working ambulance personnel. Monitoring of salivary cortisol rhythm. *Ergonomics*, **35**(11), 1331–1340.

Motohashi, Y. & Takano, T. (1993). Effects of 23-hour shiftwork with nighttime napping on circadian rhythm characteristics in ambulance personnel. *Chronobiology International*, **10**(6), 461–470.

Mott, P. E., Mann, F. C., McLoughlin, Q. & Warwick, D. P. (1965). *Shiftwork: The Social, Psychological, and Physical Consequences*. Ann Arbor, MI: University of Michigan Press.

Nachreiner, F. (1975). Role perceptions, job satisfaction and attitudes towards shift work of workers in different shift systems are related to situational and personal factors. In W. Colquhoun, S. Folkard, P. Knauth & J. Rutenfranz (Eds), *Experimental Studies of Shift Work*. Opladen: Westdeutscher Verlag.

Narayanan, V. K. & Nath, R. (1982a). A field test of some attitudinal and behavioral consequences of flexitime. *Journal of Applied Psychology*, **67**, 214–218.

Narayanan, V. K. & Nath, R. (1982b). Hierarchical level and the impact of flextime. *Industrial Relations*, **21**, 216–229.

Newman, J. E. & Beehr, T. A. (1979). Personal and organizational strategies for handling job stress: A review of research and opinon. *Personnel Psychology*, **32**, 1–43.

Nicholson, N., Jackson, P. & Howes, G. (1978). Shiftwork and absence: An analysis of temporal trends. *Journal of Occupational Psychology*, **51**, 127–137.

Nollen, S. D. (1979). *Highlights of the Literature, 7: New Patterns of Work*. Scarsdale, NY: Work in America Institute.

Nollen, S. D. & Martin, V. H. (1978). *Alternative Work Schedules, Part I: Flextime*, New York: AMACOM, a division of American Management Associations.

Northrup, H. R., Wilson, J. T. & Rose, K. M. (1979). The twelve-hour shift in the petroleum and chemical industries. *Industrial and Labor Relations Review*, **32**(3), 312–321.

Organ, D. W. (1988). *Organizational Citizenship Behavior: The Good Soldier Syndrome*. Lexington, MA: D.C. Heath.

Orpen, C. (1981). Effects of flexible working hours on employee satisfaction and performance: A field experiment. *Journal of Applied Psychology*, **66**(1), 113–115.

Ostberg, O. (1973). Interindividual differences in circadian fatigue patterns of shift workers. *British Journal of Industrial Medicine*, **30**, 341–351.

Ottmann, W., Karvonen, M. J., Schmidt, K. H., Knauth, P. & Rutenfranz, J. (1989). Subjective health status of day and shift-working policemen. *Ergonomics*, **32**(7), 847–854.

Petersen, D. J. (1980). Flextime in the United States: The lessons of experience. *Personnel*, **57**, 21–31.

Pierce, J. L. & Newstrom, J. W. (1980). Toward a conceptual clarification of employee responses to flexible working hours: A work adjustment approach. *Journal of Management*, **6**, 117–134.

Pierce, J. L., Newstrom, J. W., Dunham, R. B. & Barber, A. E. (1989). *Alternative Work Schedules*. Boston: Allyn & Bacon.

Pleck, J. H., Staines, G. L. & Lang, L. (1980). Conflict between work and family life. *Monthly Labor Review*, **103**(3), 29–32.

Ralston, D. A., Anthony, W. P. & Gustafson, D. J. (1985). Employees may love flextime, but what does it do to the organization's productivity? *Journal of Applied Psychology*, **70**, 272–279.

Ralston, D. & Flanagan, M. (1985). The effect of flex-time on absenteeism and turnover for male and female employees. *Journal of Vocational Behavior*, **26**, 206–217.

Regestein, Q. R. & Monk, T. H. (1991). Is the poor sleep of shift workers a disorder? *American Journal of Psychiatry*, **148**(11), 1487–1493.

Robson, M. & Wedderburn, A. (1990). Women's shiftwork and their domestic commitments. In G. Costa, G. Cesana, K. Kogi & A. Wedderburn (Eds), *Shiftwork: Health, Sleep and Performance* (pp. 137–142). Frankfurt: Peter Lang.

Ronen, S. (1981a). *Flexible Working Hours*. New York: McGraw-Hill.

Ronen, S. (1981b). Arrival and departure patterns of public sector employees before and after implementation of flexitime. *Personnel Psychology*, **34**, 817–822.

Ronen, S. (1984). *Alternative Work Schedules*. Homewood, IL: Dow Jones–Irwin Publishers.

Rosa, R. R. & Bonnett, M. H. (1991). Performance and alertness on 8 h and 12 h rotating shifts at a natural gas utility. Report, NIOSH, Cincinnati, OH.

Rosa, R. R. & Colligan, M. J. (1988). Long workdays versus restdays: Assessing fatigue and alertness with a portable performance battery. *Human Factors*, **30**(3), 305–317.

Rosa, R. R., Colligan, M. J. & Lewis, P. (1989). Extended workdays: Effects of 8-hour and 12-hour rotating shift schedules on performance, subjective alertness, sleep patterns, and psycho-social variables. *Work & Stress*, **3**(1), 21–32.

Rosekind, M. R., Gander, P. H., Miller, D. L. & Gregory, K. B. (1994). Fatigue in operational settings: Examples from the aviation environment. Special Issue: Fatigue. *Human Factors*, **36**(2), 327–338.

Rubin, R. S. (1979). Flextime: Its implementation in the public sector. *Public Administration Review*, **39**, 277–281.

Rutenfranz, J., Colquhoun, W. P., Knaugh, P. & Ghata, J. N. (1977). Biomedical and psychosocial aspects of shift work. *Scandinavian Journal of Work and Environmental Health*, **3**, 165–182.

Rutenfranz, J., Haider, M. & Koller, M. (1985). Occupational health measures for night workers and shiftworkers. In S. Folkard & T. Monk (Eds), *Hours of Work: Temporal Factors in Work Scheduling*. New York: Wiley.

Sadler, C. (1990). Shift work: Beat the clock. *Nursing Times*, **86**(38), 28–31.

Sarason, I. G. & Spielberger, C. D. (Eds) (1975). *Stress and Anxiety* (Vol. 2). New York: Halsted Press.

Schein, V. E., Maurer, E. H. & Novak, J. F. (1977). Impact of flexible working hours on productivity. *Journal of Applied Psychology*, **62**(4), 463–465.

Schwartz, G. E., Davidson, R. J. & Goleman, D. J. (1978). Patterning of cognitive and somatic processes in the self-regulation of anxiety: Effects of meditation versus exercise. *Psychosomatic Medicine*, **40**(4), 321–328.

Schweitzer, P. K., Muehlbach, M. J. & Walsh, J. K. (1992). Countermeasure for night work performance deficits: The effect of napping or caffeine on continuous performance at night. *Work and Stress*, **6**(4), 355–365.

Scott, A. J. (1994). Chronobiological considerations in shiftworker sleep and performance and shiftwork scheduling. Special Issue: State-dependent cognitive functioning: II. *Human Performance*, **7**(3), 207–233.

Shinn, M., Wong, N. W., Simko, P. A. & Ortiz-Torres, B. (1989). Promoting the well-being of working parents: Coping, social support, and flexible job schedules. *American Journal of Community Psychology*, **17**, 31–55.

Siegel, G. B. (1989). Learning from personnel research: 1963–1988. Compensation, benefits and work schedules. *Public Personnel Management*, **18**(2), 176–192.

Skipper, J. K., Jung, F. D. & Coffey, L. C. (1990). Nurses and shiftwork: Effects on physical health and mental depression. *Journal of Advanced Nursing*, **15**, 835–842.

Smith, A. P. (1992). Time of day and performance. *Handbook of Human Performance*, **3**, 217–235.

Smith, L. & Folkard, S. (1993a). The perceptions and feelings of shiftworkers' partners. Special Issue: Night and Shiftwork. *Ergonomics*, **36**(1–3), 299–305.

Smith, L. & Folkard, S. (1993b). The impact of shiftwork on personnel at a nuclear power plant: An exploratory survey study. *Work and Stress*, **7**(4), 341–350.

Spelten, E., Barton, J. & Folkard, S. (1993). Have we underestimated shiftworkers' problems? Evidence from a 'reminiscence' study. *Ergonomics*, **36**, 307–312.

Spielberger, C. D. & Sarason, I. G. (Eds) (1975). *Stress and Anxiety* (Vol. 1). New York: Halsted Press.

Staines, G. L. & Pleck, J. H. (1986). Work schedule flexibility and family life. *Journal of Occuaptional Behavior*, **7**, 147–223.

Steele, J. L. & Poor, R. (1970). Work and leisure: The reactions of people at 4-day firms. In R. Poor (Ed.), *4 Days, 40 Hours* (pp. 105–122). Cambridge, MA: Bursk & Poor.

Swart, J. C. (1978). *A Flexible Approach to Working Hours*. New York: AMACOM, a division of American Management Associations.

Tasto, D. L., Colligan, M. J., Skiel, E. W. & Polly, S. J. (1978). Health consequences of shift work. DHEW (NIOSH) Publication No. 78–154, Washington, DC.

Taylor, P. J., Pocock, S. J. & Sergaen, R. (1972). Shift and day workers' absence: A relationship with some terms and conditions of service. *British Journal of Industrial Medicine*, **29**, 338–340.

Tepas, D. I. & Monk, T. H. (1987). Work schedules. In G. Salvendy (Ed.), *Handbook of Human Factors* (pp. 819–843). New York: Wiley.

Tepas, D. I., Walsh, J. K., Moss, P. D. & Armstrong, D. R. (1981). Polysomnographic correlates of shift worker performance in the laboratory. In A. Reinberg, N. Vieux & P. Andlauer (Eds), *Night and Shift Work: Biological and Social Aspects*. (pp. 179–186). Oxford: Pergamon Press.

Thomas, L. T. & Ganster, D. C. (1995). Impact of family-supportive work variables on work–family conflict and strain: A control perspective. *Journal of Applied Psychology*, **80**(1), 6–15.

Tilley, A. & Brown, S. (1992). Sleep Deprivation. *Handbook of Human Performance*, **3**, 237–259.

Torsvall, L., Akerstedt, T. & Gillberg, M. (1981). Age, sleep and irregular work hours. *Scandinavian Journal of Work and Environmental Health*, **7**, 196–203.

Turek, F. W. & Reeth, O. V. (1988). Altering the mammalian circadian clock with the short-benzodiazepine, triazolam. *TINS*, **11**(12), 535–541.

Vener, K. J., Szabo, S. & Moore, J. G. (1989). The effect of shiftwork on gastrointestinal (GI) function: A review. *Chronobiologia*, **16**(4), 421–439.

Verhaegen, P., Cober, R., De Smedt, M., Dirkx, J., Kerstens, J., Ryvers, D. & Van Daele, P. (1987). The adaptation of night nurses to different work schedules. *Ergonomics*, **30**, 1301–1309.

Vidacek, S., Kaliterna, L., Radosevic-Vidacek, B. & Prizmic, Z. (1990). Tolerance to shiftwork assessed by means of the way of life questionnaire. In G. Costa, G. Cesana, K. Kogi & A. Wedderburn (Eds), *Shiftwork: Health, Sleep, and Performance* (pp. 214–219). Frankfurt: Peter Lang.

Walch, J. L. & Gordon, D. (1980). Assessing the impact of flexitime on productivity. *Business Horizons*, **23**, 61–65.

Walker, J. (1985). Social problems of shiftwork. In S. Folkard & T. Monk (Eds) *Hours of Work: Temporal Factors in Work Scheduling*. New York: Wiley.

Walker, J., Fletcher, C. & McLeod, D. (1975). Flexible working hours in two British government offices. *Public Personnel Management*, 4, 216–222.

Wedderburn, A. A. I. (1992). How fast should the night shift rotate? A rejoinder. *Ergonomics*, 35(12), 1447–1451.

Wever, R. A. (1989). Light effects of human circadian rhythms: A review of recent Andechs experiments. *Journal of Biological Rhythms*, 4(2), 161–185.

Wheeler, M. E. (1970). Four days, forty hours: A case study. *California Management Review*, 17, 74–81.

Wilkinson, R. T. (1992). How fast should the night shift rotate? *Ergonomics*, 35, 1425–1446.

Williamson, A. M., Gower, C. G. I. & Clarke, B. C. (1994). Changing the hours of shiftwork: A comparison of 8- and 12-hour shift rosters in a group of computer operators. *Ergonomics*, 37(2), 287–298.

Wise, L. C. (1993). The erosion of nursing resources: Employee withdrawal behaviors. *Research in Nursing and Health*, 16(1), 67–75.

Chapter 9

IMPACTS OF TELEWORK ON INDIVIDUALS, ORGANIZATIONS AND FAMILIES—A CRITICAL REVIEW

Udo Konradt, Renate Schmook and Mike Mälecke
University of Kiel

INTRODUCTION

Telework is defined as a form of work organization where the work is done partially or completely outside the conventional company workplace with the aid of information and telecommunication services. Although originally designed to overcome long distances (Olson, 1983; Pratt, 1984; Nilles, 1985), telework today offers more flexibility and agility for organizations beside telemanagement (coordination and management of distributed work) and teleservices (service as a product of geographically distributed work) (Hiltz & Turoff, 1987).

In the context of telework different forms have evolved. Besides home-based telework, where work is done exclusively at home, various forms of alternating or mobile telework can be differentiated. Home-based telework is most similar to classical home-based work where teleworkers work only at home either with a regular contract of employment (according to statutes of domestic work) or as self-employed. Alternating telework is nowadays the most common type of telework. Apart from their workplace at home, teleworkers usually still have a workplace at their organization. Location and timing of their work are determined by changing job requirements. In most cases the transition to this form of work is happening stepwise so that social ties with the organization remain.

Employees who do centre-based telework usually work in offices close to their home. These workplaces are used as so-called satellite offices by the main organization or, less often, are jointly used as neighbourhood offices by different organizations. However, coordination in this work setting can be difficult. Centre-based telework is well suited to foster employment in structurally

Impacts of Telework on Individuals, Organizations and Families—A Critical Review by Udo Konradt, Renate Schmook and Mike Mälecke taken from IRIOP 2000 v15, Edited by Cary L. Cooper and Ivan T. Robertson: © 2000 John Wiley & Sons, Ltd

weak regions (PATRA, 1992–1994; Crellin, Graham & Powell, 1996). The demand for centre-based telework consequently varies strongly between different countries.

Finally, mobile telework can be considered as a further form of telework. Executives and employees who work outside the office, and also craftsmen and building companies, already make wide use of this type of telework. People who work directly with customers can link up via computer with the database of their organizations from a hotel, a construction site, a car or public transport to professionally prepare for a next meeting or respond to short notice requests from customers.

The transition to other forms of on-site telework is fluid. This term describes telework that is situated at the site of the customer or contractor. In a lot of professional areas, for example management consulting and software development, this kind of on-site telework has already been established. Teleworkers can work face to face with the client and at the same time have constant access to their organization via telecommunication. We will return to this issue in the context of the distribution of telework.

Besides providing the potential for more flexibility within organizations, structures underlying telework can support the evolution of virtual enterprises and cooperative joint ventures. Virtual enterprises are legally independent and geographically separated organizations, mainly self-employed entrepreneurs, that in general only connect to conduct a defined project. The communication within the enterprise is exclusively carried out through telecommunication technologies (Davidow & Malone, 1992). Thus a project manager can assemble the best and financially most advantageous organizations within a virtual enterprise or workgroup even when those organizations are located in a different region or country.

Because of its grand potential, telework has gained importance in industry, administration and science. It is estimated that at present 1.25–17.5 million positions in telework have been implemented throughout the EC (European Community) (EITO, 1997; Kordey & Korte, 1997). In the US, 3–20 million people are estimated to engage in telework (summarized in Büssing, 1997). Studies that incorporate the interest of employees and employers in telework as well as the feasibility of telework calculate a potential of 10 million positions in telework throughout the whole of Europe, including 2.5 million in Germany (DG XIII-B, 1996; summarized in Pollmann, 1997; Table 9.1). Giving an outlook on the year 2000, the EC expects a total of 2 million people to be employed in telework in the states of the EC. For Germany, national estimates assume several hundred thousand positions in telework around the year 2000 (ZVEI/VDMA, 1995). In a Delphi-based study on the use of the inter- and intranet, experts conclude that within the time-frame from 2005 to 2012, 30% of all employees working in offices will work at home on two to five days a week (State Department for Research and Technology, 1998).

Table 9.1 Potential of telework in Europe (Empirica, 1995)

	Germany (%)	France (%)	UK (%)	Italy (%)	Spain (%)
Interest among gainfully employed	42.4	52.6	48.4	48.1	61.4
Interest among executives within the organization	40.4	39.3	34.4	41.8	29.6
Potential interest in telework	17.1	20.6	16.6	20.1	18.2
Realistic potential of telework	6.8	8.2	6.6	8.0	7.3
Realistic number of potential teleworkers (millions)	2.48	1.81	1.69	1.68	0.91

Reasons for the strongly deviating estimates can be found in the broad and rather unclear definition of telework. In a review on the definitions of telework Di Martino and Wirth (1990) isolate three basic concepts that give rise to most definitions: organization, location and technology. Assuming a relatively broad definition, telework can be done either online or offline, it can be organized either individually or collectively, it can cover either all working hours or a part of the working hours of a person, and it can be done either by an employee or a self-employed person. Within the European study, all decentralized or domestic workplaces that at least had an offline PC and a telephone are denoted as telework places (Empirica, 1994). A second reason lies in the fact that hidden forms of telework such as working outside the office or freelance work are also included. It is presently unresolved how narrow a definition would be useful. A too narrow definition could be counterproductive, as new forms of telecooperative work could then possibly not be integrated formally and in terms of research.

In an attempt to differentiate various forms of telework, Watson Fritz, Higa and Narasimhan (1994) chose a two-dimensional scheme of classification with the dimensions 'level of coordination' and 'traditional vs non-traditional organization'. According to this scheme traditional forms of organization employing methods of telecooperation exist, when features such as physical proximity to customers and contractors as well as availability of coworkers are given. This differentiation reveals that the extent of applied telecommunication technology does not suffice to discriminate selectively between telework and office-based computer work. Rather, the technical prerequisites have to be complemented by new forms of organization.

Figure 9.1 shows a taxonomy of telecooperative forms of work and organizations expanding the above mentioned reflections. Depending on the level of cooperation, isolated workers, non-interactive, interactive intra- and inter-working groups are taken into account. The second dimension represents to what degree telework is integrated (level of integration) within an organization (intra-organizational) or between a network of different organizations (inter-organizational). Virtual enterprises, as a form of telecooperative work, are based on inter-group relations between different organizations. Telework, in the sense of alternating telework, is in general understood as isolated work within an organization. The empty fields in this taxonomy illustrate further possible forms of telecooperative work.

The impacts of telework on people and organizations have been discussed (see Olson, 1989; Mehlmann, 1988; Kraut, 1988). Table 9.2 lists some of the impacts usually considered in early reviews. It is undeniable that telecooperation can lead to direct economic opportunities and a competitive chance (see the section below on profitability of telework). Moreover, closer commuting distances represent an important element of environmental planning. Finally, telecooperation also entails desirable aspects of social politics, as groups of the population suffering from reduced mobility such as disabled people or imprisoned persons can be, at least partially, integrated into working structures (Godehardt, 1994a; Cullen & Robinson, 1997).

A survey of 60 organizations that had already implemented telework showed that the major motivations to do so were cost reduction, keeping or recruiting qualified personnel, planned organizational restructuring,

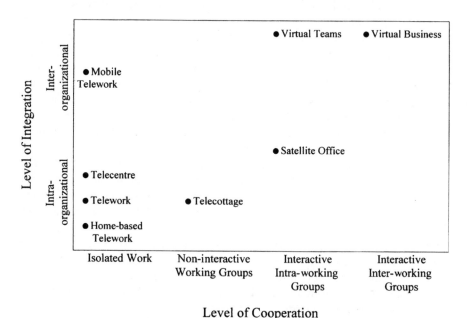

Figure 9.1 Taxonomy of telecooperative forms of work

Table 9.2 Chances and risks of telework regarding the interests of different groups (according to Kern & Wawrzinek, 1985)

Effects	Employees	Organization	Society
Positive	• work comfort • work opportunities • commuting time • individual organization • residence • being more independent from the organization • flexible working hours	• productivity • additional wage costs (e.g. social contributions) • securing of location • rationalization • room costs • compensation of work overload • flexibility • workforce potential	• global competitiveness • energy conservation • protection of the environment • problematic issues • conurbation • structural measures • traffic situation
Ambiguously	• family situation • social security contributions • wage • qualifications • work contents	• wage costs • fluctuation	• self-employed/ employed • women's situation • demand behaviour
Negative	• contacts (social isolation) • work safety • career opportunities • control	• overheads • control • opportunities to obtain information • organizational effort • selection of personnel • identification with the organization	• occupational situation • data protection • parties involved in wage settlements

increasing the motivation and productivity of the employees and more efficient coping with increased workloads (TELDET-Projekt, see also Wheeler & Zackin, 1994). Employees valued the easier coordination of professional and private life, particularly the quieter work situation and the decrease of commuting time. Employees' reasons for engaging in telework can be separated into three major fields:

1. Financial-economic reasons: e.g. in the context of an increased financial burden (acquisition of real estate, birth, divorce, maintenance) or aiming for a higher standard of living (weekend house, leisure goods, travelling).
2. Status and professional reasons such as maintenance and enrichment of professional qualifications, social contacts, financial independence, approved social status.

3. Reasons related to specific life situations or life plans such as health problems or disability, minimizing commuting distance, lack of child-care options, reintegration after maternity leave.

The growing interest in telework is reflected in the increasing number of books as much in the German (e.g. Reichwald, Möslein & Oldenburg, 1998; Wedde, 1994; Weissbach, Lampe & Späker, 1997; Büssing & Aumann, 1999) as in the Anglo-American literature (e.g. Jackson & van der Wielen, 1998; Bertin & Denbigh, 1996; Hodson, 1992). At the same time a great number of guides on how to install telework have been developed (Gordon & Kelly, 1986; Kugelmass, 1995; Nilles, 1994; Reid, 1994; Kordey & Korte, 1996; Godehardt, 1994a; Godehardt, Kork, Michelsen & Quadt, 1997; Johanning, 1997). In light of this background the present review intends to pursue two lines of reasoning. First, the results of research on the effects of telework will be systematically reviewed. The effects of telework will be scrutinized using a broad set of criteria, including the influence on work, family and profitability. Second, special attention will be directed towards the underlying methodical standards of the studies. It will be shown that in the majority of investigations the opportunities and risks of telework were only summed up by those in management positions without any direct assessment of the effects with personnel. Furthermore, it has seldom been tried to explain theoretically the results of the respective investigations. This review is therefore meant to concentrate the discussion of the development and evaluation of telework once more on scientifically sound findings and to take a new look at the often quoted opportunities and risks of telework in light of these findings. In doing this, deficits in current research will be delineated and guidelines for prospect investigations will be developed.

The review is structured as follows: in the next section a model for the investigation of the effects of telework will be introduced. Opportunities and risks of telework that have been frequently mentioned in the literature will be discussed in the third section. In the fourth section the procedure of the literature research is described, followed by the results on the effects of telework in the fifth section. Finally, an outlook on further research needs and goals is given.

A MODEL FOR THE INVESTIGATION OF THE EFFECTS OF TELEWORK

In the discussion of the opportunities and risks of telework a model for the explanation and prediction of the effects of telework has been repeatedly called for (Van Sell & Jacobs, 1994; Watson Fritz, Higa & Narashiman, 1994). In our view, this model should satisfy the following criteria:

1. A broad number of physical, spatio-temporal, personal and organizational aspects of the work situation should be taken into account.
2. Effects of telework on individual experience and behaviour should also be investigated beside performance.
3. Positive as well as negative consequences need to be considered.
4. Individual features of a person such as coping strategies, motivational and emotional resources, should be integrated.
5. Beside factors that cause work-related stress, stress and strain experienced during housework and leisure time should also be included.

Despite considerable efforts, neither research in industrial and organizational psychology nor stress research in the social sciences has succeeded in providing a model covering all the above issues. We therefore propose a two-step procedure to develop an adequate model. In the first step factors will be determined that are designed to modulate the generation of stress responses. In this context objective stimulus-oriented factors and subjective response-oriented features are discriminated. In the second step, objectively and subjectively stressing aspects of telework can be consequently used within a model of structural equations to predict actual stress during telework.

An expanded strain-stress model is proposed as the base for this model (Schönpflug, 1987; Wieland-Eckelmann, 1992; Richter & Hacker, 1998). In the field of professional work all factors externally affecting the individual and requiring his or her effort will be termed strains. Strain is defined as the sum of all influences that affect the individual within the work system. Stress is caused by strains and is expressed in respective changes in physiological and psychological functioning and subjective well-being during work performance. The consequences of stress, following the strain-stress process, are evident in work output or work performance as well as in short-, middle- and long-term changes in physical and mental power and energetic, emotional and motivational well-being.

As the type and magnitude of work-related strain are not independent of the working individual, strain needs to be understood as a relational term. This means that strains and demands (e.g. work tasks, equipment, organizational and procedural regulations, spatio-temporal and physical conditions) should be put in relation to the individual resources (e.g. physical, performance, motivational and emotional). Figure 9.2 shows a relevant model.

Strains that can arise in free time are, for example, the extent and temporal distribution of different kinds of housework. Studies investigating the participation of employees in telework projects have repeatedly shown that in particular the compatibility of housework and childcare with professional work is an important motivating factor. But equally other activities during leisure time such as cultural, social or sporting events can be pursued in a more flexible way by teleworkers (Burke, 1986). If this is not possible, then participation in telework projects can be seriously endangered. Burke shows that strains

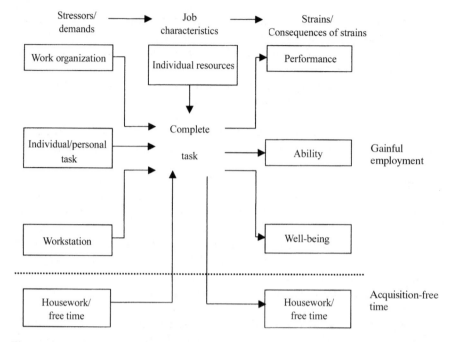

Figure 9.2   Model for the investigation of the effects of telework

experienced during leisure time can also contribute to the overall sum of strains in the context of telework.

HYPOTHESES REGARDING THE EFFECTS OF TELEWORK

In the discussion of the effects and the future shaping of telework, far-reaching personal and organizational changes have been repeatedly stressed beside technical opportunities within this field. Benefits of telework such as the improvement of women's situation due to an improved compatibility of occupational and family duties, autonomy in the choice of working hours, increase of spare time because no commuting is needed, have been contrasted with costs such as perpetuating the discrimination of disadvantaged groups of employees, disruption of family life, lack of career opportunities, social isolation, increase of work demands and personal exploitation. Because theoretical models are lacking, benefits and costs are in general not linked.

In recent years, several reviews have been published on the consequences of telework on communication (Andriessen, 1991), organization (Watson Fritz, Higa & Narashimhan, 1994; Chapman, Sheehy, Heywood et al., 1995) and quality of life and work (Büssing, 1997; Van Sell & Jacobs, 1994; Mundorf, Meyer, Schulze & Zoche, 1994; Shamir & Salomon, 1985).

Although the planned and systematic introduction of telework in the context of measures of organizational and personnel development is of fundamental importance, only very few empirical studies, and these suffering from severe methodical flaws, have focused on this particular aspect. Current representative surveys throughout the EC emphasize this point: major obstacles to the dissemination of telework can be found in the lack of information about ways of organizing telework, potentials and risks on the one hand and anticipated problems in leading and instructing the 'invisible employees' (Reichwald & Möslein, 1996) on the other hand. These results have been confirmed in other international studies (see also Wheeler & Zackin, 1994).

The following possible effects of telework will be dealt with more thoroughly:

1. What effects does telework have on social contacts? To answer this question , social contacts, personality traits and consequences for training and career are investigated.
2. What effects does telework have on family and leisure time? This question will be discussed in the light of time autonomy, attitudes towards the mixing of work and leisure time, the structure of the social surroundings and the perceived use.
3. How do communication within the organization, concepts of management and management behaviour change? Furthermore, effects on the whole organization are looked at.
4. Which economic benefits does telework provide? Costs and benefits will be discussed.

IDENTIFICATION AND SELECTION OF EMPIRICAL STUDIES

A literature search was conducted to identify all relevant empirical studies. The search included articles published between 1982 and mid-1997 using various databases[1] relevant to the field. The aim of the literature search was to identify only empirical, independent research investigating the effects of telework. The studies should focus on the effects of actually implemented telework places on teleworkers. Studies dealing with speculations, claims or projections concerning future telework projects were not included. The empirical character of a study was deduced from specific information about the size and composition of the sample and about the type of telework investigated as well as from the description of the applied measures.

Out of the 665 references gained in the second step, 215 empirical papers were selected based on the content of the abstract. After eliminating articles which dealt with the prognoses or projections of managers concerning the opportunities and risks of telework, 27 original empirical papers remained. After careful evaluation, studies investigating the potential of telework were also excluded, so that the present literature review on the effects of telework is based on 20 empirical studies.

The studies were categorized according to the following aspects: (a) type of study (personal report, case study, quasi-experimental field study); (b) sample size; (c) type of telework investigated; (d) trade; (e) type of work; and (f) applied methods. According to Nullmeier (1988) four basic types of telework were distinguished (see Table 9.3): executive tasks, high-profile professional tasks, low-profile professional tasks, supporting tasks. These tasks can be discriminated according to the central dimension of the task, to what extent work can be planned and structured ahead, the need for information, the cooperating partners and how problems are solved.

The papers that were selected are predominantly case or field studies with sample sizes of less than 50 people (approx. 80%). In 40% of the studies even

Table 9.3   Basic types of office work (modified according to Nullmeier, 1988)

Tasks	Task characteristics	Examples
Executive tasks	Leading and motivation of employees, representative duties, development of communicational structures, gathering and dissemination of information, problem-solving and decision-making in the case of uncertainty/risk, finding consensus	Members of the board, managers on different hierarchical levels of the organization
High-profile professional task	Mastering of tasks that involve a great deal of expertise, independent organization of low-structured work, development of initiative, task-oriented	Qualified buyers and sellers, scientists and engineers in R&D as well as in production and DV, attorneys, judges, organizers, tax consultants, advertising specialists, publicists, accountants
Low-profile professional tasks	Mastering of tasks that involve only little expertise and are rather structured and repetitive, process- and result-oriented	Officials in charge of purchase and sale, officials working for insurance companies, banks, shipping agencies; book-keepers, administrative employees, counter clerks
Supporting tasks	Support of the other professional groups, processing, transcription and storage of information	Typists and secretaries, distributor of mail, operators

fewer than 15 individuals are investigated. In some cases information about the sample size is based on whole organizational units (e.g. department, firms, neighbourhood offices) so that the actual sample size is actually higher. The number of organizational units within a study usually lies below 20. In the majority of studies interviews or questionnaires are the predominant measures. The content and procedure are, however, often not specified. The studies cover all four types of telework that are mentioned above, although most studies focus on alternating telework, home-based telework and telecentres. Only very few studies looked at the effects of mobile telework. Virtual enterprises were not considered in any study.

The samples cover all trades, although electronic data processing, service, banks and insurance companies are represented more strongly. The tasks mainly belong to the low-profile professional domain, followed by supporting and high-profile professional functions; executive functions can be found less often. This result corresponds with the finding that typical tasks and functions pursued by teleworkers can be generally assigned to office and administrative functions (Gray, Hodson & Gordon, 1993). Telework is especially suited for tasks that do not require a great deal of personal communication or the continual presence of the employee within the organization.

Finally, the effects of telework on social contracts, family and leisure time, management and communication and profitability were determined. Table 9.4 gives an overview of the empirical studies on the effects of telework that were taken into account.

EFFECTS OF TELEWORK

In the following the results concerning the effects of telework on social contacts, family and leisure time, management and communication and profitability will be described in detail.

Effects of Telework on Social Contacts

Negative effects of telework have been suspected to exist to a large extent in the area of social contacts. The relevant hypothesis is that telework leads to social isolation and in consequence to social alienation as it is generally pursued without direct contact with colleagues or superiors. This is supposed to be even more true for telehomeworkers exclusively working at home. Important variables in this context are not only the quantity but also the quality of social contacts, as well as the subjective importance teleworkers ascribe to social bonds. This importance depends not only on personal needs but also on a person's degree of extraversion and their job demands. Furthermore, a certain number of contacts is seen as an important prerequisite for a career within the organization. Of the 20 studies 11 analysed the effects of telework on social contacts.

Table 9.4   Studies on the effects of telework

No.	Author(s), year	Type of study	Sample	Methods	Form of telework	Trades
1	Aichholzer & Kirschner, 1995 (AUS, GB, G)	Personal report	N^1=7 $N^2{}_1$=6, n_2=15, n_3=4, n_4=3	Not mentioned	Neighbourhood offices ATW[3]	Electronic data processing, Training, Public administration, Agrar
2	Baylin, 1989 (GB)	Case study	N_1=49, n_2=40 CG[4]	Questionnaire	THW[5]	Electronic data processing
3	Büssing & Aumann, 1997 (G)	Field study	N=5	Questionnaire	Centre-based telework, ATW	Electronic data processing Service
4	Büssing, Kunst & Michel, 1996 (G)	Field study	N_1=11 n_2=9 CG n_3=10 CG	Questionnaire, Interview	THW	Insurance
5	Euler, Froschle & Klein, 1987 (G)	Case studies	N=14 N=17	Interview, Group discussion	THW, Neighbourhood-, Satellite offices	Public administration, not mentioned
6	Fisher, Späker & Weissbach, 1987 (G)	Case studies	N=6 N_1=180, n_2=15, n_3= ca. 30, n_4= ca. 300	Not mentioned	ATW, Satellite offices	Electronic data processing, Service, Advertising
7	Glaser & Glaser, 1995 (G)	Field study	N_1=38, n_2=33 M[6]	Interview, Questionnaire	ATW	Electronic data processing
8	Godehardt, 1994b (G)	Case studies	N=22	Interview, Expert dialogue, Group questioning	ATW, THW, Satellite offices	Service
9	Goldmann & Richter, 1991 (G)	Case studies	N1=5 n_1=4, n_2=3, n_3=4, n_4=12, n_5=3 (not mentioned for printing trade) N2=15 n_1=11, n_2=90 Experts N3=3, n_3=16 (electronic data processing, service)	Questionnaire, Interview	ATW, mobile TW, THW	Printing trade, Electronic data processing, Service
10	Grantham & Paul, 1995 (USA)	Case studies	N=3 n_1=35+25 M, n_2=34 n_3=88 M	Questionnaire	ATW	Public administration, Electronic data processing, not mentioned
11	Hartman, Stoner & Arora, 1991 (USA)	Field study	N=11 n=97	Questionnaire	ATW	Telecommunication, Banks, Insurance, Printing trade, Public administration
12	Kreibich, Drüke, Dunkelmainn & Feverstein, 1990 (G)	Field study, Case studies	N1=105, N2=208, N3=20	Questionnaire, Interview	THW, mobile TW, ATW, Satellite offices and others	Industry Banks, Insurance, Public administration, Service, others
13	Morgan, 1985 (GB)	Field study	n=78	Questionnaire	THW	Electronic data processing
14	Müller & Reuschenbach, 1992 (G)	Field study	n=25 M	Questionnaire, Interview	THW, ATW, mobile TW	Electronic data processing, Insurance
15	Olson, 1983 (USA)	Field study	n=32	Interview	THW, ATW	Electronic data processing, not mentioned

			Effect on				
No.	Author(s), year	Type of work at telework	Social contact	Family & leisure time	Management & communication	Profitability	Comments
1	Aichholzer & Kirschner, 1995 (AUS, GB, G)	High-profile functions, Low-profile functions, Supporting functions	Yes	Yes	Yes	Yes	Pilot projects
2	Baylin, 1989 (GB)	High-profile functions, Low-profile functions	–	Yes	–	–	
3	Büssing & Aumann, 1997 (G)	Low-profile functions, Supporting functions	–	–	Yes	Yes	
4	Büssing, Kunst & Michel, 1996 (G)	Low-profile functions, Supporting functions	Yes	Yes	Yes	–	Pilot projects
5	Euler, Froschle & Klein, 1987 (G)	Supporting functions	–	Yes	Yes	Yes	Model study
6	Fisher, Späker & Weissbach, 1997 (G)	High-profile functions, Low-profile functions	Yes	Yes	Yes	Yes	Model studies
7	Glaser & Glaser, 1995 (G)	High-profile functions, Low-profile functions	Yes	Yes	Yes	Yes	
8	Godehardt, 1994b (G)	Executive functions, High-profile functions, Low-profile functions, Supporting functions	Yes	Yes	Yes	Yes	
9	Goldmann & Richter, 1991 (G)	High-profile functions, Low-profile functions, Supporting functions	Yes	Yes	Yes	Yes	
10	Grantham & Paul, 1995 (USA)	Executive functions, Low-profile functions	Yes	Yes	Yes	Yes	Pilot project
11	Hartman, Stoner & Arora, 1991 (USA)	Executive functions, Low-profile functions	–	Yes	–	Yes	
12	Kreibich, Drüke, Dunkelmainn & Feverstein, 1999 (G)	Executive functions, High-profile functions, Low-profile functions, Supporting functions	–	Yes	–	Yes	
13	Morgan, 1985 (GB)	High-profile functions, Low-profile functions, Supporting funcions	Yes	Yes	Yes	Yes	
14	Müller & Reuschenbach, 1992 (G)	Executive functions, High-profile functions, Low-profile functions	–	–	Yes	Yes	
15	Olson, 1983 (USA)	Executive functions, Low-profile functions, Supporting functions	Yes	Yes	Yes	Yes	Pilot project

(Continued over)

Table 9.4 (*Continued*)

No.	Author(s), year	Type of study	Sample	Methods	Form of telework	Trades
16	Pupke, 1994 (Japan)	Field study	n=21	Interview	THW	Construction, Commerce, Transport, Manufacturing industry, Service
17	Rüttinger, Grünebaum & Jost, 1995 (G)	Field study	N=29 n=87 M	Interview	ATW, THW, mobile TW	Industry, Commerce, Banks, Insurance, Service
18	Soares & Vargas, 1992 (Brazil)	Case study	n_1=12, n_2= 3 M	Interview	Centre based telework	Electronic data processing
19	Strauf & Nagele, 1996 (G)	Case studies	N=11 n=69	Interview, Questionnaire	THW, ATW, Centre based telework, Satellite offices	Service, Construction, Manufacturing industry
20	Ulich, 1988 (Japan)	Case study	N=10	Interview, Questionnaire	Satellite offices	Electronic data processing

[1]Number of organizational units.
[2]Number of persons (teleworkers if not mentioned otherwise).
[3]Alternating telework.
[4]Control group.
[5]Telehomework.
[6]Managers.

Social contacts

In most studies social contacts include contacts with colleagues at the workplace as well as contacts with family members, friends, and acquaintances. The latter occur in private activities, whereas social contacts with colleagues refer to goal-oriented meetings.

Exclusively looking at the quantity of social contacts, eight studies (Büssing, Kunst, & Michel, 1996; Godehardt, 1994b; Goldmann & Richter, 1991; Hartman, Stoner & Arora, 1991; Morgan, 1985; Olson, 1983; Rüttinger, Grünebaum & Jost, 1995; Soares & Vargas, 1992) found a decrease in contacts, characteristic social isolation due to telework. However, employees regard this phenomenon according to their professional and private situation. Telework, especially home-based telework, can lead to social isolation. However, this need not be the case. An important modulating variable in this context is the perceived quality of the actual social contacts, which is experienced very differently among teleworkers.

Three studies (Goehardt, 1994b; Grantham & Paul, 1995; Rüttinger, Grünebaum & Jost, 1995) merely mention that social isolation is a problem that can occur temporarily especially during extended periods of home-based telework. A more detailed analysis of the development of social contacts can be found in Büssing, Kunst and Michel (1996). This study shows that changes

			Effect on				
No.	Author(s), year	Type of work at telework	Social contact	Family & leisure time	Management & communi-cation	Profitability	Comments
16	Pupke, 1994 (Japan)	High-profile functions Low-profile functions Supporting functions	–	Yes	–	Yes	
17	Rüttinger, Grünebaum & Jost, 1995 (G)	Executive functions, High-profile functions, Low-profile functions, Supporting functions	Yes	Yes	Yes	–	
18	Soares & Vargas, 1992 (Brazil)	Supporting functions	Yes	–	Yes	Yes	
19	Strauf & Nagele, 1996 (G)	Executive functions, Low-profile functions, High-profile functions, Supporting functions	–	Yes	–	Yes	
20	Ulich, 1988 (Japan)	Low-profile functions, Supporting functions	–	–	Yes	Yes	Pilot project

take place in various forms. Of the teleworkers questioned, 80% reported they had less contact with colleagues whereas 20% experienced no difference. While 46% said that they had less contact with friends, 36% actually reported an increase in contacts and 18% of the teleworkers noticed no change in the number of contacts with friends. The evaluation of social contacts depends to a large degree on the type of work teleworkers engage in. In different case studies (Goldmann & Richter, 1991) generally half of the participants view social isolation as the major problem whereas the remainder do not experience it as a problem. If routine jobs are to be carried out, contact between teleworkers is considered unnecessary. Tasks that require regular team communication as, for example, in the software business can be most efficiently pursued by alternating telework, as this mode of telework offers the opportunity to work on problems in the privacy of one's own home (Goldmann & Richter, 1991). Working at home is experienced and judged as very effective in this context, because one's attention is not distracted by colleagues (Glaser & Glaser, 1995; Goldmann & Richter, 1991). These people evaluate their social contacts with family members, friends and acquaintances as positive and do not feel 'caged in' at home. At the same time, however, the lack of contact with colleagues is viewed as a potential danger fostering the development of social isolation (Goldmann & Richter, 1991; Morgan, 1985; Olson, 1983; Soares & Vargas, 1992). This situation is particularly problematic when participants miss informal exchanges with their colleagues and the opportunity of aiming for mutual goals. Occasional gatherings to meet these demands can be initiated by teleworkers themselves or by the management (Büssing, Kunst, & Michel, 1996; Goldman & Richter, 1991). Consequently social isolation is not perceived as a problem when institutionalized meetings are held and when their frequency can be adjusted according to the needs of the employees.

Personality traits

In the discussion of social contacts in the context of telework, attention is also drawn to the suitability of certain personality types to carry out telework. This personality type is described as rather introverted with little need for social contact and exchange. Extraverted employees, having a stronger need for social relations, are in contrast expected to suffer more strongly from the feeling of alienation that is anticipated as a consequence of telework. However, this hypothesis could not be confirmed empirically (Glaser & Glaser, 1995). Interviews provided evidence that extraverted employees were actually more likely to cope with the social consequences of home-based work. They have in general enough self-confidence to adjust the intensity of their social relations according to their personal needs. They can therefore compensate their limited occupational contacts with private social activities.

Training and career

Changing organization-bound workplaces into telework places can result in a loss of integration and might therefore cause isolation. However, for a freelance, telework can actually lead to a gain of integration. The integration of freelances through telework has not been explicitly examined in any of the studies, therefore no empirically based findings exist on this topic. The investigations of employees holding permanent positions in telework have mainly focused on social contact or social isolation respectively. Apart from a few exceptions, statements are made on the training and career opportunities of teleworkers (Glaser & Glaser, 1995).

The few studies on this topic emphasize that teleworkers can participate as much in training measures as organization-bound employees do and that they have the same career opportunities. Concerning career progress, teleworkers are actually thought to have a greater chance as their motivation and performance were positively valued by the management (Fischer, Späker & Weissbach, 1994).

Conclusion

When teleworkers are looked at as a general group, no clear trends regarding changes in social contacts can be identified. Whereas one section of the teleworkers perceived a decline of contacts, the other section either judged the number of contacts with colleagues as still sufficient or they compensated for limited occuaptional contacts with an increase of private contacts. When teleworkers are differentiated according to the main task they carry out, it becomes clear that especially routine tasks which are typically done by tele-homeworkers lead to feelings of social isolation. This finding is also confirmed in international comparison (Goldmann & Richter, 1991; Morgan, 1985; Olson, 1983; Soares & Vargas, 1992). The situation, however, differs for teleworkers who have at least the status of officials in different fields of exper-tise. They are especially more likely to perceive their social contacts as suffi-cient or to make up for fewer occupational contacts with more private contacts. Furthermore, this group of employees, according to personal estima-tion, works more efficiently at home, as they are not disturbed by colleagues.

Alternating telework seems to offer the benefits of undisturbed, efficient work at home without the risk of social isolation, Kraut (1988) concludes that alter-nating teleworkers use their workplace within the organization for social and interactive tasks whereas the workplace at home is preferred for mental tasks.

Empirical studies could provide no evidence that a specific personality type is better suited for telework. Watson, Fritz, Higa and Narasimhan (1994), review-ing the literature, come to the conclusion that certain key qualifications are necessary for the successful pursuit of telework such as the ability for time management, self-monitoring and self-motivation, a lower need for social con-tacts as well as a higher need for autonomy (see also Büssing & Aumann, 1996).

The present review suggests that teleworkers in comparison to organization-bound employees are not disadvantaged in terms of career opportunities if they make use of the training opportunities within the organization. Although it has frequently been stated in the literature that the lack of daily contact within the organization might endanger the chances of being promoted, the current studies could not confirm this fear (see also Di Martino & Wirth, 1990; Olson & Primps, 1984).

Effects of Telework on Leisure Time and Family

The importance of telework lies not only in the possibility of organizing work hours more flexibly, but also in the resulting opportunity to combine pre-viously separated spheres of life more easily: gainful employment, housework and leisure time. If and to what degree these goals can be accomplished is dealt with in 13 of the 20 studies. The studies show that the compatibility of these spheres depends on a variety of occupational, personal and family condi-tions. Important factors are sovereignty over work hours, type and extent of household duties, attitudes towards the separation of work and private mat-ters, social support from the family, and the perceived use of opportunities to re-enter or continue work.

Flexible use of time during work and within the family

Flexible use of time is only possible in telework if the employer agrees to this flexibility. It does not suffice to restrict flexibility to the rims of the daily working hours, that is translating the already widespread flextime with stable core hours to telework jobs or demanding—taking the extreme case—fixed work hours for teleworkers that cover the complete regular working hours. However, the flexible use of working hours can be restricted when specific task and work demands arise through job demands. This can, for example, be the case when clients can only be reached at certain times or when the workload varies depending on the season. Working hours of qualified employees with fairly algorithmic or plannable tasks should not be linked to specific times of the day. In a current study, however, only one fifth of alternating teleworkers engaging in high- and low-profile professional tasks could make flexible use of their working hours (Glaser & Glaser, 1995).

Even when flexible working hours have been officially agreed upon, family demands can lead to a determination and condensation of the working hours, similar to or even stricter than at conventional workplaces. Furthermore, household and family tasks that follow a fixed circadian rhythm inevitably create a working rhythm adjusted to family and personal conditions (Glaser & Glaser, 1995). Working hours are therefore typically in the early morning and/or the late evening (Büssing, Kunst & Michel, 1996; Euler, Fröschle & Klein, 1987; Pupke, 1994). In many cases this leads to a reciprocal adjustment between occupational demands and the needs of the family, which implies that working hours are generally placed respective to the working hours of the spouse and to the times spent on childcare (Büssing, Kunst & Michel, 1996; Glaser & Glaser, 1995). A so-called 'fictitious flexibility' most often occurs when children or other relatives need to be taken care of. However, it cannot be assumed that paid work and housework cause a permanent overburdening. Just one study reported that this problem occurred sporadically, but that it was not experienced as particularly burdensome (Glaser & Glaser, 1995). Teleworkers generally appreciate that they have more time for family members or their partner (Glaser & Glaser, 1995; Grantham & Paul, 1995), and that they are available in the event of unpredictable events (Büssing, Kunst & Michel, 1996), and emergencies (Euler, Fröschle & Klein, B., 1987), as well as for occasional errands and administrative tasks (Glaser & Glaser, 1995).

Attitude towards the separation of work and private sphere

Telework requires the acceptance of a workplace within the domestic environment and consequently giving up, at least partly, the separation of private and work spheres. In individual cases, the separation of work and family spheres was not successful even under advantageous spatial conditions, such as the existence of a separate room (Euler, Fröschle & Klein, 1987). Results from a pilot project (Fischer, Späker & Weissbach, 1994) could show that around every tenth employee perceived the superposition of work and private spheres as unpleasant and therefore cancelled telework. This finding gives an idea of the importance of this problem.

A further survey found a close connection between satisfaction with telework and disturbances by the family, with an increase in satisfaction with telework corresponding to a decrease of disturbances and interruptions by members of the family (Hartman, Stoner & Arora, 1991). Environmental factors have consequently proven to be important determinants for the satisfaction of teleworkers with this specific way of work. When it is not possible to create an appropriate social environment and to adjust individual role definitions, job satisfaction declines and can lead to the termination of telework. Quite often changes in the distribution of family roles and consequently 'periods of intensified family adjustment' become necessary (Euler, Fröschle & Klein, 1987; Glaser & Glaser, 1995; Grantham & Paul, 1995).

Social surroundings

Aspects of the social surroundings are closely connected with the distribution of roles within the family. In households with pre-schoolers undisturbed home-based work can be assured by other caretakers. Relatives, friends and acquaintances, neighbours, but also paid helpers (e.g. day mother, daycare centre, au pairs) can take charge of the children and/or the household (Goldmann & Richter, 1991). So far, however, there have been only very few relevant findings on this topic in the context of telework.

Perceived benefit

According to the re-entry hypothesis telework is supposed to offer employees a convenient opportunity to re-enter the work process. The current results do not support this hypothesis. The resumption of professional activity is more likely to be motivated by local changes, new and extended social relations and the opportunity to be mobile (Fischer, Späker & Weissbach, 1994). It is additionally reported that telehomeworkers would not have chosen this way of working if they did not have children to take care of (Euler, Fröschle & Klein, 1987; Morgan, 1985). Specifically telehomeworkers see a major importance in the 'intrinsic character' of family duties that temporarily arise (Bailyn, 1989). However, this is only valid for those employees who do not live in areas with poor infrastructures and who have a sufficient amount of professional alternatives in acceptable commuting distance (Euler, Fröschle & Klein, 1987; Strauf & Nägele, 1996). For long-term employees telework can provide an increase in motivation and self-esteem: there are indications that this group of employees views working outside the organization as a privilege reflecting the confidence of the management (Glaser & Glaser, 1995). An increased sense of responsibility and a better identification with the organization were mentioned as a consequence.

The decision to take up telework is predominantly judged as a decision for the family. The possibility of taking care of the children is therefore specified as the major benefit of home-based telework (Morgan, 1985; Olson, 1983), limited, at least during the planning phase, to the time of the children's education (Euler, Fröschle & Klein, 1987) to facilitate re-entry into the organization after maternity leave (Goldmann & Richter, 1991; Rüttinger, Grünebaum & Jost, 1995). When the motivations and reasons of employees and employers to start telework are put into focus, the major motive is to maintain employment during changes within the family. Women taking their maternity leave often use home-based telework as a transient solution in order to be able to continue employment in the legally defined way. When these situations do not exist, home-based telework is often found to be less attractive, indicating that the evaluation of telework can be primarily influenced by the current life situation (see also Gutscher, 1988).

Overall, it is evident that the compatibility model of paid work and housework can only be applied to women (Goldmann & Richter, 1991). The feasibility is evaluated differently depending on the organization, the qualification of the employee and other circumstances. It has been found to be limited to bad for employees with highly qualified jobs in an organization with a strong team orientation (Goldmann & Richter, 1991). In addition executive functions or jobs involving high mobility are viewed as less compatible with home-based telework.

Conclusion

To actually make use of one of the major benefits of telework—the opportunity to have more sovereignty of time—the distribution of work hours should be prescribed as little as possible by the organization. Home-based telework is most often undertaken by women taking their educational leave. The flexible use of time and the success of an individually structured timetable are nevertheless determined by professional demands as well as by family demands. Problems can be expected to arise when full-time employment in combination with specific constellations within the family (children, taking care of relatives) leads to an ongoing double stressor (see also Shamir & Salomon, 1985). However, this was a theoretical assumption that could not be supported empirically. Instead it could be shown that telework is often viewed as a transitional solution, for example during periods of childcare. This implies that changes within the life situation (when the children grow more independent) also lead to a reconsideration of the current work situation causing a new decision for or against telework.

The consequences of the superposition of work and private spheres are also important. Teleworkers need to be aware to what degree they wish for or reject a mingling of both spheres. In the latter case, measures should be taken that allow a separation of work and private space, for example by setting up a separate study or arranging external childcare.

Effects of Telework on Management and Communication within the Organization

One of the major obstacles in the implementation of telework can be found in the attitudes of executive personnel (Korte & Wynne, 1996; Wheeler & Zackin, 1994). Executives often reject telework because they anticipate losing control over their subordinates. They do not feel capable of supervising 'invisible' coworkers. It should be therefore investigated whether superiors supervise teleworkers significantly differently than employees working within the organization.

As communication is a fundamental supervising task, the question arises whether the executive's style of communication is particularly affected. As telework inevitably requires computer-based forms of communication instead of personal contact, changes in formal aspects and content of communication are expected. Work in computer-based cooperative groups appears to be related (Andriessen, 1991).

The issue of management, especially leadership, is mentioned in 10 of the 20 studies; work-related communication is covered in 15 studies. Four studies do not deal with either topic. Altogether managerial and communicational issues are an important topic, they are treated very generally in all investigations. Differentiating the results according to type of study, method, type of telework or type of job is hardly possible.

Management

Management in telework cannot be accomplished with conventional measures such as detailed control. Furthermore, executives must get rid of the idea that employees only work when they are closely supervised. Management should instead focus on result-orientation or goal-orientation respectively (see e.g. Guzzo, Jette & Katzell, 1985). Out of the 10 studies that covered management, 9 stress the necessity of this principle (Büssing & Aumann, 1997; Euler, Fröschle & Klein, 1987; Fischer, Späker & Weissbach, 1994; Glaser & Glaser, 1995; Godehardt, 1994b; Grantham & Paul, 1995; Müller & Reuschenbach, 1992; Olson, 1983; Rüttinger, Grünebaum & Jost, 1995). At the same time it is emphasized that this form of management requires a certain amount of trust (Rüttinger, Grünebaum & Jost, 1995). The basis for truse lies in the assumption that someone who strives for space and autonomy in his or her work, knows that he or she needs to work reliably (Fischer, Späker & Weissbach, 1994). Prerequisites on the side of the employee are maturity, organizational abilities, good time management and responsibility. Adequate management, however, cannot be considered to be a sufficient condition for the success of telework (Olson, 1983). A further important component is the appropriate selection of jobs and employees in telework. Moreover, executives should possess particular management qualities (Fischer, Späker & Weissbach, 1994) or should be trained in the handling of teleworkers (Grantham & Paul, 1995).

The concept of management by objectives (MbO) is evaluated positive both for telework places and for conventional workplaces (Fischer, Späker & Weissbach, 1994; Glaser & Glaser, 1995; Godehardt, 1994b; Grantham & Paul, 1995). Thus MbO does not constitute a specific way of leading in the context of telework, even though it is often regarded as a necessary prerequisite for the successful establishment of telecooperative work. Problems of MbO are not brought up. Just one study points out that when goal-oriented management, especially control, is applied, an objective comparison of the work results of different teleworkers is sometimes not possible because of specific influences during the work progress (Euler, Fröschle & Klein, 1987). Further analyses regarding positive and negative effects of goal-oriented management are not reported.

The attitudes of executives towards telework were assessed in only one study (Glaser & Glaser, 1995), that found the attitudes were in general positive. In the study by Fischer, Späker and Weissbach (1994) it is implicitly assumed that a positive attitude on the part of the executives is essential for the success of telework. It is stressed that an agreement between executive and subordinate is necessary for the implementation of a telework place. A further important task of executives is to function as a link between teleworkers and the organization (Fischer, Späker & Weissbach, 1994).

In summary, none of the reviewed studies focused on the possible effects of telework on management. Rather it is assumed without scrutinizing it that an adequate style of management is a prerequisite for the success of telework.

Communication within the organization

Because of the increasing delinkage of location and time of communication between sender and receiver, communication has changed. Compared to other forms of communication, messages within electronic mail systems clearly contain less personal and social information. Furthermore, norms of communication are more often transitioned as during direct communication. It can therefore be expected that the social competence of group members will decline as electronic communication substitutes for conventional forms of communication (see also Kiesler & Sproull, 1986; Kiesler, Siegel & McGuire, 1984). As the exchange of information with the teleworkers increasingly needs to take place over longer distances and as the greater flexibility of working hours leads to a more intensive use of the respective media, the communication of and with teleworkers becomes particularly significant.

The analyses of teleworkers' communicative behaviour are most often restricted to a description of the media used for communication (Büssing & Aumann, 1997; Fischer, Späker & Weissbach, 1994; Godehardt, 1994b; Goldmann & Richter, 1991; Morgan, 1985; Olson, 1983; Rüttinger, Grünebaum & Jost, 1995; Ulich, 1988). In this connection the improved possibilities in computer-aided communication arising from continuing technical development should also be considered. Thus e-mail is mentioned in only one of the studies conducted in the eighties, whereas newer studies all report the use of electronic mail. As the studies cover a time range from 1982 to 1997 in which significant technological innovations have taken place, a detailed analysis of the communication media described in the studies is not useful as the studies are not compatible in this regard.

Beside a mere description of the media used the importance of functioning structures of communication (Aichholzer & Kirschner, 1995; Grantham & Paul, 1995), according to the communicative skills of the involved personnel, is stressed in several studies, as well as the training of these skills (Goldmann & Richter, 1991; Grantham & Paul, 1995). The need for communication, however, is at the same time viewed as a limiting factor of telework. When the need for communication and/or cooperation increases, the expenses (for the organization) are perceived as unacceptable and telework, accordingly, does not seem to be justified as a way of organizing work (Fischer, Späker & Weissbach, 1994; Goldmann & Richter, 1991; Pupke, 1994).

If and how communicative and/or informative behaviour concerning work-related information is changed because of the implementation of telework or is different from other forms of work organization, has been investigated sporadically (Büssing & Aumann, 1997; Büssing, Kunst & Michel, 1996). In these studies a restriction in the supply of information as well as in the active search for information has been reported for teleworkers.

The importance of informal communication is emphasized in studies by Glaser and Glaser (1995), Goldmann and Richter (1991), Grantham and Paul (1995) and Soares and Vargas (1992). The study by Glaser and Glaser (1995) assesses the importance of informal communication. Employees judge the opportunity to ask colleagues for help as important. Getting to know the latest rumour, however, was considered unimportant. The studies by Goldmann and Richter (1991), Grantham and Paul (1995) and Soares and Vargas (1992) simply state the lack of informal communication in telework that in return leads to social isolation. These studies stress the negative consequences of telework.

One of the case studies (Fischer, Späker & Weissbach, 1994), however, observes a change in communication due to the introduction of technical aids. This leads to the conclusion that altered communicative behaviour is not the result of the new way of organizing work, but can be caused by the general changes in communication inherent to computer workplaces. Negative consequences such as social isolation that might arise from altered communicative behaviour might therefore be better explained by the introduction of new techniques of information and communication.

The organization

It is repeatedly emphasized that the implementation of telework requires extensive measures of reorganization within the organization. The studies by

Fischer, Späker and Weissbach (1994) and Soares and Vargas (1992) take a closer look at some far-reaching effects of telework on the total organization. In the study by Fischer, Späker and Weissbach (1994), a case study, it is not expected that telework can stimulate a reduction of hierarchies or can democratize decisional structures. Soares and Vargas (1992), however, fear that the introduction of telework will lead to clearly negative consequences such as a more rigid or static organizational structure.

Conclusion

Concerning management in telework, there is consensus that a delegative, goal-oriented concept of management is the most adequate for the successful implementation of telework (see also Di Martino & Wirth, 1990; Van Sell & Jacobs, 1994). Beside these rather general and unvalidated statements no specific study investigated topics such as the effect of telework on management behaviour, the influence of management style on different areas of telework or the interaction of management behaviour and teleworkers.

It can be further stated that telework alters the communicative behaviour of the people involved in it, although it cannot be clearly decided against the background of the current studies whether this effect can be directly attributed to telework or to the overall use of new techniques. Communicative behaviour may also be different in employees who work within the organization. However, studies employing control group designs that are able to reliably answer this question are lacking. The application of new media requires certain communicative skills on the part of teleworkers as well as of their counterparts within the organization (e.g. executives and colleagues) that possibly need to be conveyed in training.

Profitability of telework

Although Reichwald and Möslein (1996) portray the anticipation of problems in management as the main obstacle to the installation of telework, Kordey and Gareis (1997) state that profitability, at least from the perspective of the organization, is the essential argument for introducing and maintaining telework. IBM Germany, for example, only installs telework places when the potential increase of productivity justifies the costs of investment. They deviate from this principle only in specific cases, for example when urgent family problems force an employee to take up telework.

Costs and benefits of telework depend on the type of the workplace as well as on the technical equipment and the general economic conditions (Kordey & Gareis, 1997). Consequently, on the one hand, high costs were named as a negative consequence of telework (12% of the questioned organizations), but on the other hand, a decrease of costs was mentioned as a benefit (19%) (Strauf & Nägele, 1996). A cost-benefit calculation is further complicated by the large number of factors that need to be considered, for example also qualitative factors that are not clearly quantifiable (Kordey & Gareis, 1997). Of the 20 studies, 16 concentrated on the profitability of telework.

Costs

Kordey and Gareis (1997) divide potential costs into four categories: decentralized infrastructure, central infrastructure, communication, as well as organization and coordination. Investments into the decentralized infrastructure represent the largest portion in this context. Beside single costs arising from the investment into hard- and software, telecommunication and further auxiliary devices, the running costs for maintenance and insurance need to be included as well. Energy consumption and rent are usually proportionally covered by a monthly flat rate by the employer. The furniture at the workplace most often consists of the employee's property; ergonomic aspects in the arrangement of the telework place, however, are only considered in individual cases. Adequate technical conditions for communication with teleworkers also need to be created within the organization. Moreover, premises for regular meetings should be available. The costs of telecommunication strongly depend on the distance between the central organization and the workplace, the time of day and the duration of the on-line connection (Kordey & Gareis, 1997).

The costs for the technical infrastructure and telecommunication depend on the type of job and the required amount of communication with the central organization. It is therefore difficult to generalize the respective costs (Kordey & Gareis, 1997). Furthermore they are quickly outdated as prices fall consequent to technical development and the demand situation (Fischer, Späker & Weissbach, 1994; Goldmann & Richter, 1991). Although the installation of a telework place is in general regarded as more cost-effective than that of a conventional office place (Godehardt, 1994b) it needs to be considered to what extent the already implemented decentralized infrastructure is used. Thus home-based telework places that are only used half-time are less profitable for the organization (Euler, Fröschle & Klein, 1987).

Costs for organization and coordination entail, for example, planning and conducting the preparation, development of a security concept and selection of project participants. The expenses per teleworker are the higher the fewer telework places are planned. After the implementation further costs needed for training, supervision and coordination should be taken into account (Kordey & Gareis, 1997). The necessary extra expenditure for the organization and the coordination involved in the introduction of telework are not considered in any of the studies on the profitability of telework. Only studies that have scientifically monitored the implementation of neighbourhood offices and telecentres point out that problems with the acquisition of clients and the like are often underestimated in the beginning (Aichholzer & Kirschner, 1995; Euler, Fröschle & Klein, 1987; Fischer, Späker & Weissbach, 1994).

Benefits

The economic benefits of telework can be summed up in two points: increased work performance and work quality as well as saving of work and running costs (Kordey & Gareis, 1997).

The literature reports on differently sized increases in productivity. However, it is rarely evident which aspects were actually included in the calculations. The discussion on the conditions of eventual increases in productivity often appears speculative due to the lack of empirical data. The decisive factor is seen in the undisturbed atmosphere of the own home (Glaser & Glaser, 1995; Strauf & Nägele, 1996). However, teleworkers who were often contacted by their colleagues at home report a smaller improvement in efficiency (Glaser & Glaser, 1995). Jobs involving contact with customers use the benefits of closer proximity (Aichholzer & Kirschner, 1995) and temporal flexibility, working outside regular business hours (Strauf & Nägele, 1996), to contribute to the profitability of telework. In one study, teleworkers reported that customers were more content (Grantham & Paul, 1995). Quantifications or statements by the customers themselves or independent observers, however, are not available.

In some cases, the increase in productivity cannot be attributed to the specifics of telework but to factors closely connected to the innovative character of its implementation. Thus the improvement in efficiency and productivity in a satellite office was due not to the undisturbed atmosphere but to the ergonomic design of the workplace and the excellent technical equipment (Ulich, 1988).

Several studies look at the potential for increases in performance in the context of qualification. The latter is closely linked to personnel costs which vary considerably depending on the region and country. In Germany, the outsourcing of low-level, monotonous jobs does not appear to be profitable despite low wages (Fischer, Späker & Weissbach, 1994). Thus in the mid-eighties a project in Baden-Württemberg in which paperwork was transferred to a satellite office failed (Euler, Fröschle & Klein, 1987). The lack of the anticipated performance improvement is ascribed to the scattering of office work inherent to decentralization. This leads to an increase in coordinating effort while at the same time the motivation and satisfaction of the employees decreases.

The productivity shown in creative, high-level jobs, however, is more likely to improve as these jobs are more vulnerable to interference and disturbances (Fischer, Späker & Weissbach, 1994). This is supported by results gained by the telework initiative of IBM Germany, as only highly qualified employees profited from telework. Teleworkers as well as superiors judged working at home as being more productive and efficient, although the latter were more reserved in their evaluation (Glaser & Glaser, 1995).

Investigations outside Europe obtained different results regarding the importance of qualification. A North American study stresses that the observed increase in productivity of 16% can be found for jobs with different demands. The actual level of qualification of the persons investigated, however, was not specified (Grantham & Paul, 1995). The outsourcing of low-level data entry jobs leads to more productivity in Brazil, although the 'decentralization' is carried out from the suburbs to the town centre, causing higher costs for rent (Soares & Vargas, 1992). Examples showing that the outsourcing of low-level jobs is profitable for the organization due to low wages also exist in Japan (Pupke, 1994).

In introducing telework it is possible to establish a lower wage level. On the one hand additional wage costs such as pension scheme payments do not arise when people work freelance or are self-employed, on the other hand organizations can recruit cost-effective employees from structurally weak regions. Transferring regular employees to a freelance basis is said to yield potential savings of 30–40% (Christensen, 1987). Although decentralization of work places is cost-effective for the organization, it sometimes entails a deterioration of the employees' financial situation. German and British mothers who try to combine childcare and professional re-entry with the aid of telework, receive wages below average in respect to their qualification (Bailyn, 1989; Büssing, Kunst & Michel, 1996). In Great Britain women are the dominant group in the electronic telework which spread rapidly at the beginning of the eighties. They work in pseudo self-employment and have to face an unsteady order situation (Morgan, 1985). Their wages are way below average in comparison to those that are obtained in comparable areas of business, social security is insufficient, and they are sometimes even burdened with the costs for the technical equipment (Morgan, 1985).

Kordey and Gareis (1997) see further benefits in the opportunity to retain an employment in the event of moving and to stay with family members who are in need of constant care. Organizations are apparently interested in keeping their personnel, especially in the case of highly qualified employees, to reduce costs due to fluctuation. This aspect, however, is not emphasized in any of the studies.

Costs are further reduced by the discontinuation of voluntary social benefits (subsidies for fares and meals) and financial compensation of overtime (Morgan, 1985). In this context it should be pointed out that widespread informal homework is promoted by large number of enterprises (Fischer, Späker & Weissbach, 1994; Müller & Reuschenbach, 1992). While working at home, outside office hours, employees probably do more overtime without causing additional costs for the organization. Moreover, because of insufficient legal background problems concerning data protection as well as obligations to provide welfare for employees and liability of the organization occur.

Conclusion

It seems to be very difficult to make general statements concerning the profitability of telework. Costs and benefits need to be evaluated in the context of the respective situation and condition. When examining the profitability of telework the organization-based workplaces should be included in the analysis as an increase in performance at telework places could be due to a disadvantageous distribution of work, leaving the organization-based employee with less efficient jobs. The technical costs and the organizational expenditure depend on the demands of the workplace and the original structures within the organization. The personal costs vary with the qualification, the form of contract and the local region. Cost reduction results from the cancellation of additional financial benefits and overall from the free resources within the central infrastructure. Concerning productivity, telework influences quantity and quality of products and services not only directly, but also indirectly by reducing absenteeism, improved customer service and maybe a more efficient work organization. The level of qualification, flexible use of time, being undisturbed and technical equipment are also of importance. The significance of factors that are hard to quantify is judged by the persons involved. For example, work within a telecentre is cited because of good results and a higher job satisfaction despite lacking cost reduction (Fischer, Späker & Weissbach, 1994). Overall, it seems to be highly possible that telework can be realized as either cost-neutral or even bearing financial profit, especially as technical, organizational and economic impediments tend to be on the decline.

CONCLUSIONS AND PERSPECTIVES

The review has shown that the research on the effects of telework is still fragmentary. Central topics such as management and self-leadership, models of flexible working time and ergonomics of the work setting are not or just barely covered. Classical elements of organizational development such as individual training, special team training and quality circles are rarely applied. The need to consider a wide range of various factors that could explain success and failure of telework is met by only very few methodically sound empirical studies. The attempt to develop a model explaining the effects of telework has not yet been made (see also Van Sell & Jacobs, 1994).

In content there are hardly any homogeneous findings within the reviewed research on family, social contacts, communication and management as well as profitability. Looking at profitability, for example, it could be shown that a general statement on the efficiency of telework cannot be made but that a multitude of organizational, personal and task-related factors influence its profitability. But the review shows a lot of prevailing conditions leading to positive consequences.

Due to the spatial and organizational proximity of telecooperative forms of paid work and housework the rigid separation of paid work and 'non-work' in the sense of housework, family duties and leisure time becomes more and more obsolete. There are good reasons to deliver the assumption of neutrality assuming no interaction, for telework. Because of the demands on the future working society such as increasing flexibility, autonomy and responsibility as well as fusion of gainful employment, family and leisure time it will become inevitable that we abolish our traditional understanding of work focusing too narrowly on gainful employment.

Problems in the Evaluation of the Effects of Telework

All studies investigating the effects of telework are subject to three basic problems denoted as the technology problem, the phase problem, and the intercultural problem. These problems make it difficult to draw a general evaluation of the impacts of telework. The technology problem is evident in the fact that due to increasingly powerful technology forms of cooperation and communication can now be realized that, years ago, were unthinkable. Evaluation studies from the mid-eighties, for example, do not mention the use of e-mail. Work-related problems, however, can also be solved with the aid of the technical infrastructure. Reactivity, being the basic problem of evaluation studies, weighs more heavily in the highly dynamic area of technical development than in other areas, as qualitatively new forms of computer-aided communication become available and comparisons between current and older studies can only be drawn to a very limited extent.

The second problem, the phase problem, can be found on the organizational as well as on the individual level. On the organizational level it must be taken into account that enterprises that implemented telework are within different project phases. Basing the implementation of telework on a simple phase model covering the initial taking up of the concept, the pilot or model phase and the optimization and consolidation (Chapman et al., 1995, see Qvortrup, 1992), each phase leads to inherent problems. In the first phase, the fragmentation, single, divisable jobs are subject to outsourcing. The focus is on the adequate selection and limiting of organizational options. In the second phase, the dispersion, expansion and dispersion of the respective jobs take place, questioning the importance of the central organization as a whole/as a unit. During this phase it is important to spot the specific opportunities and risks of the newly installed workplaces to obtain, beside a general evaluation, information for the optimization. The third phase, finally, is characterized by diffusion, creating specialized service centres and highly specialized individuals. In the phase of optimization and consolidation even informational and organizational adaptations that concern the whole organization are decisive. So far there are no investigations integrating the life-cycle of telework into the evaluation of telework.

On the individual level the phase problem can be described as follow: in the context of looking at the effects of home-based telework on the family it was obvious that duties within the family that depend on the current life phase play an important role in the decision to take up telework and in its evaluation.

When duties are discontinued, the valence of telework can change. The dynamic in individual valence and instrumentality consequently needs to be considered.

The inter-cultural problem is caused by differences in the understanding of paid work and leisure time that can be also seen in the differing national labour and social laws. In international comparison, Germany, Italy and Austria are 'highly regulating' countries whereas the US and Great Britain have far fewer respective regulations (see Späker & Weissbach, 1997). From the perspective of 'high regulators' a special danger could lie in the lack of adherence to work time control, regulations concerning breaks, work environment and the representation of employees. Therefore it ought to be positively stressed that special precautions are indeed guaranteed during the introduction of telework. Excluding freelances and employees working outside the office, taking up telework is in general done voluntarily. The preliminary character of telework is evident in the fact that, at least in Europe, telework is implemented within limited model projects. By modifying the existing work contract teleworkers can return to their previous work situation without having to fear negative consequences. However, if the perceptions of social effects of telework in Germany and North America are compared, it can be shown that the conflict of paid work and leisure time does not exist in North American samples, giving further evidence for inter-cultural differences (Garhammer, 1997).

Critical Reflection of Evaluation Methods

The majority of the reviewed studies were carried out using relatively unsophisticated methods (see Van Sell & Jacobs, 1994). They were mostly case or field studies that often employed free, non-structured interviews or questionnaires. On the one hand precise pre-post measurements are also lacking that would allow us to state whether telework is actually the cause of observed changes in behaviour and experience. On the other hand control data from employees still working in conventional work settings rarely exist. Due to this lack it cannot be clarified whether problems named in the context of telework can be attributed to this new form of work organization or to a general increase of the workload. Finally, little is known about the long-term effects of telework because of the lack of longitudinal studies.

Beside these general methodical flaws, a large number of studies just give a recollection of diverse subjective impressions. Precise definitions and translations into experimental variables, however, as well as clear quantifications, are necessary to reliably measure constructs of individual behaviour and experience and to facilitate the compatibility of results. It was also not possible to integrate in our analysis how much of the complete working time was actually spent at the workplace at home, as only very few studies differentiated between home-based telework, home-based alternating telework, and office-based alternating telework. In some studies it was unclear whether a differentiation had been made. The review, however, shows that considerable differences exist between the motives to take up different types of telework and between the effects they exert. Andriessen (1991) for example, emphasizes the discrimination between clerical homeworkers who work freelance and are less well supported by legal regulations and professional homeworkers who are full-time employees. The importance of this discrimination is evident in differing effects on the individual, the family and the organization (see also Mehlmann, 1988). Our own studies illustrate that perceived stress and strain are dependent on the type of telework (Konradt & Schmook, 1999). Home-based telework and home-based alternating telework with a telework proportion over 50% is predominantly used by mothers during maternity leave in order to continue their current employment. Alternating teleworkers on the other hand, who spend less than 50% of their time engaging in telework, usually take up telework to work overtime. In future it will therefore be of major importance to differentiate more strongly between the various forms of telework. In this context the small sample size of most studies should be pointed out, which is not suited to adequately represent characteristics of the population.

Furthermore, the reviewed studies most often do not clearly separate between results stemming from empirical investigation and information or speculations obtained from other sources. Methodological problems of empirical studies on telecommuting are also discussed by McCloskey and Igbaria (1998). They mention small sample sizes, lack of control groups, heavy reliance on self-reports, failure to control extraneous factors and the entanglement of gender and employment status as factors which make it difficult to interpret the results.

Consequences for the Modification of Telework—What Should be Done?

It still must be assumed that there is hardly any empirically based knowledge on the effects of telework so that recommendations on the modification of telework inevitably remain speculative. Therefore scientific research accompanying projects especially in multinational enterprises (e.g. IBM, BMW, SNI, HP) is much to be desired. However, the transfer of possible findings to the situation of small and middle-sized enterprises would still be difficult. A further problem could lie in the enormous diversity among different types of telework, as recommendations would need to be either very general or very specific, naturally limiting their applicability. Despite the lack of empirical research, the number of telework places is growing slowly but steadily. Because of the lack of appropriate research, however, one must fear that preventive and prospective forms of organizing work will be applied less often.

In the current review the theoretical, methodological and methodical problems and weaknesses of the studies that investigated the effects of telework were repeatedly stressed and numerous demands for future research were deduced. In the following, suggestions that could be directly translated into empirical research designs will be finally suggested.

1. Further prognoses, projections and statements concerning the development of telework as well as the opportunities and risks involved are not necessary. The review of the literature has shown that only very few empirical studies could serve as a basis for a fruitful discussion of the impacts of telework.

2. Investigations should be conducted with more sophisticated methodology. This means that standardized, reliable and valid measures should be employed, allowing a quantitative assessment of the effects of telework. Furthermore, studies are urgently needed that directly compare teleworkers with strictly organization-based employees, engaging in similar jobs.

3. Longitudinal studies should be launched that investigate stress, strains and successful coping strategies in the course of ongoing telework. Evaluation studies could then not only offer summative evaluation but also formative evaluation which would provide a direct contribution to the preventive and prospective organization of work. In this connection the use of classical elements of organizational development such as health circles (for an example see Konradt, Schmook & Hertel, in press), participating in structuring of work and individually tailored training should be stressed as they could lead to a successive improvement of situational and organizational work conditions of teleworkers.

4. The management views leading and supervising teleworkers as the major obstacle in the context of introducing telecooperative forms of work. Although this concern has been identified, the literature does not provide usable empirical information. Therefore research is clearly needed in this area.

These demands could be directly integrated into the planning and conducting of studies investigating the effects of telework, thereby providing definite progress in the discussion on the evaluation and development of telework.

NOTE

1. PsycLIT, PSYNDEX, WISO III, Bildung, ADG (Archiv der Gegenwart—politics and economy), APS (ABC Political Science—politics, sociology and economy), CAB ABSTRACTS and CAB International (agricultural sciences), DISS (dissertations and habilitations), DNB (Deutsche Nationalbibliogrpahic—all areas), IBZ (Internationale Bibliographie der Zeitschriftenliteratur—all areas), ISTP (Index to Scientific & Technical Proceedings), ISSHP (Index to Social Sciences & Humanities Proceedings), MEDLINE and SERLINE. Most hits were found within data

banks on psychology, pedagogy, business administration and social sciences. Technical and medical databases as well as databases for political science contributed only few references.

ACKNOWLEDGEMENTS

The preparation of this chapter was supported by a grant from the Technology Foundation Schleswig-Holstein. We are grateful to Silke Sorgenfrey and Kerstin Krauel for their assistance on the preparation and comments on an earlier version of the manuscript.

Correspondence should be addressed to Udo Konradt, University of Kiel, Institute for Psychology, Olshausenstr. 40, 24 098 Kiel, Germany. E-mail: *konradt@PSychologie.uni-kiel.de*

REFERENCES

(Studies included in the empirical review are marked with *)

*Aichholzer, G. & Kirschner, A. (1995). *An Evaluation of the Neighbourhood Office Model of Teleworking*. Projektbericht am Institut für Technikfolgenabschätzung der Österreichischen Akademie der Wissenschaften, Vienna.

Andriessen, J. H. E. (1991). Mediated communication and new organizational forms. In C. L. Cooper & I. T. Robertson (Eds), *International Review of Industrial and Organizational Psychology*, Vol. 6 (pp. 17–70) Chichester: Wiley.

*Bailyn, L. (1989). Toward the perfect workplace. *Communications of the ACM*, **32**(4), 460–471.

Bertin, I. & Denbigh, A. (1996). *The Teleworking Handbook. New Ways to Work in the Information Society*. Warwickshire: TCA.

Burke, R. J. (1986). Occupational and life stress and the family: Conceptual frameworks and research findings. *International Review of Applied Psychology*, **35**, 347–369.

Büssing, A. (1997). Telearbeit und Telekooperation—Interdisziplinäre Perspektiven. *Zeitschrift für Arbeitswissenschaft*, **51**, 194–196.

Büssing, A. (1998). Teleworking and quality of life. In P.J. Jackson & J.H. van der Wielen (Eds), *Teleworking: International Perspectives: From Telecommuting to the Virtual Organization* (pp. 144–165). London: Routledge.

Büssing, A. & Aumann, S. (1996). Telearbeit im Spannungsfeld der Interessen betrieblicher Aketure: Implikationen für das Personalmanagement. *Zeitschrift für Personalforschung*, **10**, 223–239.

*Büssing, A. & Aumann, S. (1997). Telezentren im bayerischen Raum. Organizationsanalyse von kollektiver Telearbeit in Telezentren. In A. Büssing (Ed.), *Berichte aus dem Lehrstuhl für Psychologie der TU München* (Nr. 38). München: Technische Universität München.

Büssing, A. & Aumann, S. (1999). *Telearbeit. Analyse, Bewertung und Gestaltung ortsungebundener Arbeit*. Göttingen: Verlag für Angewandt Psychologie.

*Büssing, A., Kunst, R. & Michel, S. (1996). Qualifikationsanforderungen, berufliche qualifizierung und Mehrfachbelastung unter Telearbeig. In A. Büssing (Ed.), *Berichte aus dem Lehrstuhl für Psychologie der TU München* (Nr. 31). München: Technische Universität München.

Chapman, A. J., Sheehy, N. P., Heywood, S., Dooley, B. & Collins, S. C. (1995). The organizational implications of teleworking. In C. L. Cooper & I. T. Robertson (Eds). *International Review of Industrial and Organizaitonal Psychology*, Vol. 10 (pp. 229–248). Chichester: Wiley.

Christensen, K. E. (1987). Impacts of computer-mediated home-based work on women and their families. *Office: Technology and People*, **3**, 211–230.

Crellin, J., Graham, J. & Powell, A.-P. (1996). The Australian telecentres program: Providing public access to information networks for people in rural and remote regions. *Quarterly Bulletin of IAALD*, **41**, 173–177.

Cullen, K. & Robinson, S. (Eds) (1997). *Telecoms for Older People and People with Disabilities in Euorope*. Amsterdam: IOS Press.

Davidow, W. H. & Malone, M. S. (1992). *The Virtual Corporation*. New York: Harper Collins.

DG XIII-B (1996). *Action for stimulation of transborder telework and research cooperation in Europe. Telework 1996. Final Report on Telework Stimulate Actions (1994–1995)*. European Commission, Brussels.

Di Martino, V. & Wirth, L. (1990). Telework: An overview. *Conditions of Work Digest*, **9**, 3–42.

Empirica (1994). *Pan-europiaische Befragung zur Telearbeit* (Vols. 1–6). Bonn.

Empirica (Ed.) (1995). *Telematik- und Teleservices. Entwicklungen in deutschen Städten in 1995 und 2005* (Internes Arbeitspapier). Bonn.

*Euler, H., Fröschle, H.-P. & Klein, B. (1987). Dezentrale Arbeitsplätze unter Einsatz von Teletex. In F. Gehrmann (Ed.), *Neue Informations- und Kommunikationstechnologien* (pp. 55–71). Frankfurt: Campus.

European Information Technology Observatory (EITO) (1997). *EITO Yearbook 1997*, Frankfurt/M. [see *http://www.fvit-eurobit.de/eito*].

*Fischer, U. L., Späker, G. & Weissbach, H. J. (1994). *Neue Entwicklungen bei der sozialen Gestaltung von Telearbeit* (Materialien und Berichte des IuK-Instituts. Dortmund: IUK-GmbH.

Garhammer, M. (1997). Teleheimarbeit und Telecommuting: ein deutschamerikanischer Vergleich über kulturelle Bedingungen und soziale Auswirkungen einer neuen Arbeitsform. *Zeitschrift für Arbeitswissenschaft*, **23**, 232–239.

*Glaser, W. R. & Glaser, M. O. (1995). *Telearbeit in der Praxis. Psychologische Erfahrungen mit außerbetrieblichen Arbeitsstätten bei der IBM Deutschland GmbH*. Berlin: Luchterhand.

Godehardt, B. (1994a). *Telearbeit. Rahmenbedingungen und Potentiale*. Opladen: Westdeutscher Verlag.

*Godehardt, B. (1994b). *Telearbeit: Rahmenbedingungen und Potentiale* (ISDN-Forschungskommission des Landes ordrhein-Westfalen, Materialien und Berichte Nr. 15). Düsseldorf: Ministerium für Wirtschaft, Mittelstand und Technologie des Landes Nordrhein-Westfalen.

Godehardt, B., Kork, W. B., Michelsen, U. & Quadt, H. P. (Eds) (1997). *Management Handbuch Telearbeit*. Heidelberg: Hüthig/HVS.

*Goldmann, M. & Richter, G. (1991). *Beruf und Familie: Endlich vereinbar? Teleheimarbeit von Frauen*. Dortmund: Montania Druck- und Verlagsgesellschaft mbH.

Gordon, G. E. & Kelly, M. M. (1986). *Telecommuting: How to Make it Work for You and your Company*. Englewood Cliffs, NJ: Prentice-Hall.

*Grantham, C. E. & Paul, E. D. (1995). The 'Greening' of organizational change: A case study. *Innovation*, **8**, 221–233.

Gray, M., Hodson, N. & Gordon, G. (1993). *Teleworking Explained*. Chichester: Wiley.

Gutscher, H. (1988). Telearbeit: Neue Arbeitsformen, neue Risiken, neue Chancen. *Report Psychologie*, **13**, 10–17.

Guzzo, R. A., Jette, R. D. & Katzell, R. A. (1985). The effects of psychologically based intervention programs on worker productivity. *Personnel Psychology*, **38**, 275–291.

*Hartman, R. I., Stoner, C. R. & Arora, R. (1991). An investigation of selected variables affecting telecommuting productivity and satisfaction. *Journal of Business and Psychology*, **6**, 207–225.

Hiltz, S. R. & Turoff, M. (1987). *The Network Nation: Human Communication via Computer*. Cambridge, MA: MIT Press.

Hodson, N. (1992). *The Economies of Teleworking*. London: British Telecom.

Jackson, P. J. & van der Wielen, J. H. (Eds) (1998). *Teleworking: International Perspectives: From Telecommuting to the Virtual Organization*. London: Routledge.

Johanning, D. (1997). *Telearbeit.Einführung und Leitfaden für Unternehmer und Mitarbeiter*. München: Hanser.

Kern, P. & Wawrzinek, S. (1985). Homework—dezentraler produktiver arbeiten? *Arbeitspapier des Fraunhofer Instituts für Arbeitswissenschaft und Organization*.

Kiesler, S., Siegel, J. & McGuire, T. (1984). Social psychological aspects of computer-mediated communication. *Ameircan Psychologist*, **39**, 1123–1134.

Kiesler, S. & Sproull, L. S. (1986). Response effects in the electronic survey, *Public Opinion Quarterly*, **50**, 402–413.

Konradt, U. & Schmook, R. (1999). Telearbeit—Belastungen und Beanspruchungen im Längsschnitt. *Zeitschrift für Arbeits-und Organizationspsychologie*, **43**, 142–150.

Konradt, U., Schmook, R. & Hertel, G. (in press). Health circles for teleworkers: Selective results on stress, strain, and coping strategies. *Health Education Research*.

Kordey, N. & Gareis, K. (1997). Wirtschaftlichkeitsbetrachtungen bei der Einführung von Telearbeit. In Ministerium für Wirtschaft und Mittelstand, Technologie und Verkehr (Ed.), *Telearbeit und Telekooperation* (Schriftenreihe des Landes NRW—media NRW), Vol. 4 (pp. 94–109). Dusseldorf: Ministerium für Wirtschaft und Mittelstand, Technologie und Verkehr.

Kordey, N. & Korte, W. B. (1996). *Telearbeit Erfolgreich Realisieren*. Wiesbaden: Vieweg.

Kordey, N. & Korte, W. B. (1997). Verbreitung und Potential der Telearbeit in Europea. In Ministerium für Wirtschaft und Mittelstand, Technologie und Verkehr (Ed.), *Telearbeit und Telekooperation* (Schriftenreihe des Landes NRW—media NRW). Vol. 4 (pp. 18–40). Düsseldorf: Ministerium für Wirtschaft und Mittelstand, Technologie und Verkehr.

Korte, W. B. & Wynne, R. (1996). *Telework, Penetration, Potential and Practice in Europe*. Amsterdam: IOS Press.

Kraut, R. E. (1988). Telework as a work-style innovation. In B. D. Ruben (Ed.), *Information and Behavior*, Vol. 2 (pp. 116–146). New Brunswick: Transaction Books.

*Kreibich, R., Drüke, H., Dunkelmann, H. & Feuerstein, G. (1990). *Zakunft der Telearbeit. Empirische Untersuchung zur Dezentralisierung und Flexibilisierung von Angestelltentätigkeiten mit Hilfe neuer Informations- und Kommunikations-technologien*. Eschborn: RKW-Verlag.

Kugelmass, J. (1995). *Telecommuting: A Manager Guide to Flexible Work Arrangements*. New York: Lexington Books.

McCloskey, D. W. & Igbaria, M. (1998). A review of the empirical resarch on telecommuting and directions for future research. In M. Igbaria & M. Tan (Eds), *The Virtual Workplace* (pp. 338–358). Hershey, PA: Idea Group Publishing.

Mehlmann, M. (1988). Social aspects of telework: Facts, hopes, fears, ideas. In W. B. Korte, S. Robinson & W. J. Steinle (Eds), *Telework: Present situation and Future Development of a New Form of Work Organization* (pp. 101–110). Amsterdam: Elsevier Science.

*Morgan, V. M. (1985). Die neue Heimarbeiterin. *Frauen und Arbeit*, **3**, 17–20.

*Müller, T. & Reuschenbach, T. (1992). *Dezentrale Organisiationsformen von rechnergestützter Arbeit* (Unveröff. Projektbericht), Technische Universität Berlin, Berlin.

Mundorf, N., Meyer, S., Schulze, E. & Zoche, P. (1994). Families, information technologies, and the quality of life: German research findings. *Informatics and Telematics*, 11, 137–146.

Nilles, J. (1985). Teleworking from home. In T. Forester (Ed.), *The Information Technology Revolution*. Oxford: Blackwell.

Nilles, J. (1994). *Making Telecommuting Happen. A Guide for Telemanagers and Telecommuters*. New York: International Thomson Publ./van Nostrand Reinhold.

Nullmeier, E. (1988). Gestaltung rechnergestützter Arbeitsplätze in Büro und Verwaltung. In E. Nullmeier & K. H. Rödiger (Eds), *Dialogsysteme in der Arbeitswelt* (pp. 109–121). Mannheim: Wissenschaftsverlag.

*Olson, M. H. (1983). Remote office work: Changing work patterns in space and time. *Communications of the ACM*, 26, 182–187.

Olson, M. H. (1989). Work at home for computer professionals: Current attitudes and future prospects. *ACM Transactions on Office Information Systems*, 7, 317–338.

Olson, M. H. & Primps, S. B. (1984). Working at home with computers: Work and nonwork issues. *Journal of Social Issues*, 40(3), 97–112.

Psychological and Social Aspects of Teleworking in Rural Areas [PATRA] (1992–1994). CEC/DGXIII Contract Number 02004, Opportunities for Rural Areas (ORA Programme).

Pollmann, R. (1997). Entwicklung der Telearbeit in Europa—Eine Standortbestimmung. In B. Godehardt, W. B. Kork, U. Michelsen & H. P. Quadt (Eds), *Management Handbuch Telearbeit* (ch. 120.2), Heidelberg: Hüthig/HVS.

Pratt, J. (1984). Home Teleworking: A study of its pioneers. *Technological Forecasting and Social Change*, 25, 1–14.

*Pupke, H. (1994). *Tele-Heimarbeit in Japan. Berliner Beiträge zur sozial- und wirtschaftswissenschaftlichen Japan-Forschung* (Vol. 25). Bochum: Brockmeyer.

Qvortrup, L. (1992). Visions, definitions, realities, barriers. In OECD (Ed.), *Cities and New Technologies* (pp. 77–108). Paris: OECD.

Reichwald, R. & Möslein, K. (1996). Telearbeit und Telekooperation. In H.-J. Bullinger & H. J. Warnecke (Eds), *Neue Organizationsformen im Unternehmen.* (pp. 671–708). Berlin: Springer.

Reichwald, P., Möslein, K. & Oldenburg, S. (1998). *Telearbeit, Telekooperation und virtuelle Unternehmen*. Berlin: Springer.

Reid, A. (1994). *Teleworking: A Guide to Good Practice*. New York: Blackwell.

Richter, P. & Hacker, W. (1998). *Belastung und Beanspruchung*. Heidelberg: Asanger.

*Rüttinger, B., Grünebaum, B. & Jost, D. (1995). *Der Status der Telearbeit in der Bundesrepublik Deutschland 1994* (Institutsbericht). Darmstadt: Technische Hochschule Darmstadt.

Schönpflug, W. (1987). Beanspruchung und Belastung bei der Arbeit—Konzepte und Theorien. *Enzyklopädie der Psychologie* (1). Göttingen: Hogrefe.

Shamir, B. & Salomon, I. (1985). Work-at-home and the quality of work life. *Academy of Management Review*, 10, 455–464.

*Soares, A. S. & Vargas, F. G. (1992). Telework and communication in data processing centres in Brazil. In U. E. Gattiker (Ed.), *Studies in Technological Innovation and Human Resources*, Vol. 3 (pp. 117–149). Berlin: De Gruyter.

Späker, G. & Weissbach, H.-J. (1997). Regulationsmodelle für Telearbeit—ein europäischer Vergleich. *Zeitschrift für Arbveitswissenschaft*, 51, 214–223.

State Department for Research and Technology (BMBF) (1995). *Telearbeit—Definition, Potential und Probleme*. Bonn.

State Department for Research and Technology (BMBF) (1998). *Delphi '98. Studie zur globalen Entwicklung von Wissenschaft und Technik*. FhG-ISI, Karlsruhe.

*Stauf, S. & Nägele, B. (1996). *Möglichkeiten und Grenzen der Telearbeit*. Freiburg: Institut für Regionale Studeien in Europa.

*Ulich, E. (1988). Überlegungen zur Aufhebung der Ortsgebundenheit von Arbeit. *Psychosozial*, 11, 83–91.

Van Sell, M. & Jacobs, S.M. (1994). Telecommuting and quality of life: A review of the literature and a model for research. *Telematics and Informatics*, 11, 81–95.

Watson Fritz, M. E., Higa, K. & Narasimhan, S. (1994). Telework: Exploring the borderless office. *Proceedings of the Twenty-Seventh Annual Hawaii International Conference on System Sciences* (pp. 149–158).

Wedde, P. (1994). *Telearbeit. Handbuch für Arbeitnehmer, Betriebswirte und Anwender* (2nd edn). Köln: Bund-Verlag.

Weissbach, H.-J., Lampe, N. & Späker, G. (1997). *Telearbeit*. Marburg: Schüren.

Wheeler, M. & Zackin, D. (1994). Work–family roundtable: Telecommuting. *The Conference Board*, 4(1).

Wieland-Eckelmann, R. (1992). *Kognition, Emotion und Psychische Beanspruchung*. Göttingen: Hogrefe.

Zentralverband Elektrotechnik und Elkektronikindustrie e. V. (ZVEI)/Verband Deutscher Maschinen- und Anlagenbau e. V. (VDMA) (1995). *Informationsgesellschaft—Herauforderungen für Politik, Wirtschaft und Gesellschaft*. Frankfurt.

Chapter 10

THE PSYCHOLOGY OF STRATEGIC MANAGEMENT: DIVERSITY AND COGNITION REVISITED

Gerard P. Hodgkinson
Leeds University Business School, The University of Leeds, UK

INTRODUCTION

The purpose of this chapter is to review a number of developments in the psychology of strategic management that have taken place during the period that has elapsed since the publication of the previous review on this topic in the *International Review of Industrial and Organizational Psychology*, conducted by Sparrow (1994). During the current review period the literature has proliferated on a massive scale. Consequently, coverage must be selective and attention will be confined to an analysis of key developments in the study of cognitive processes in strategic management. Specifically, the present review will centre on the principal advances that have occurred in relation to four overlapping areas of inquiry, namely: (a) theoretical and empirical developments in the analysis of mental representations of competition; (b) theoretical and empirical developments in the analysis of cognitive processes in top management teams; (c) methodological issues and advances in the assessment of managerial and organizational cognition; and (d) the design and evaluation of psychologically based techniques for intervening in the strategy process.

Two of the core themes identified for coverage in the present review (cognitive processes in top management teams and mental representations of competition) were also addressed by Sparrow (1994). Although this means that there is an inevitable degree of overlap in the territories covered by the present chapter and the previous review in this series, there have been a sufficient number of significant theoretical, methodological and empirical developments during the intervening period to warrant this degree of additional attention.

As noted by Sparrow (1994), arguably the most exciting advances in strategic management are presently occurring at the interface between several key base disciplines. Recent advances in the analysis of actors' mental representations of competition, for example, have drawn on a variety of perspectives

Psychology of Strategic Management by Gerard Hodgkinson taken from IRIOP 2001 v16, Edited by Cary L. Cooper and Ivan T. Robertson: © 2001 John Wiley & Sons, Ltd

from a range of disciplines, including psychology, but also industrial organization economics (e.g. Porter, 1980), and evolutionary theories stemming from an ecological analysis of populations and subpopulations of organizations (Aldrich, 1999) in combination with the insights of institutional theory (Scott & Christensen, 1995) from the field of organizational sociology. Inevitably, therefore, the subject matter addressed by this chapter, although predominantly psychological in emphasis, by necessity cannot be isolated from these wider developments.

The earlier Sparrow chapter sought primarily to establish the legitimacy of the psychology of strategic management as an emerging topic within the field of I/O psychology, to map some of its principal boundaries and to outline the major challenges that lay ahead. Building on these foundations, the present chapter provides a critical assessment of the extent to which significant progress has been achieved during the intervening period in seeking to meet these challenges. The orientation of the present review is predominantly methodological in emphasis, arguing that there is a fundamental requirement for greater rigour if we are to develop robust empirical findings in this topic area.

The vast majority of developments that have taken place within the psychology of strategic management have been published in special issues of journals, monographs, edited books, and conference symposia and workshops devoted to the topic of *managerial and organizational cognition*. Since the publication of Sparrow's (1994) review two major management journals, *Organization Science* and the *Journal of Management Studies*, have published special issues (Hodgkinson & Thomas, 1997; Meindl, Stubbart & Porac, 1994) and there have been several edited books and monographs (e.g. Eden & Spender, 1998; Finkelstein & Hambrick, 1996; Flood, Dromgoole, Carroll and Gorman, 2000; Weick, 1995), in addition to numerous articles in regular journal issues in which the topic of strategic cognition has featured prominently. The papers contained in the 1994 special issue of *Organization Science* were subsequently reprinted in an edited book of readings (Meindl, Stubbart & Porac, 1996) which usefully incorporates a number of additional papers published in regular issues of this and several other major scholarly journals on the theme of managerial and organizational cognition, together with an expanded introductory editorial that places these 'classic papers' in a broader context. The Hodgkinson and Thomas special issue of the *Journal of Management Studies* contains a collection of peer reviewed articles based on papers presented at an earlier professional meeting of the European Group for Organization Studies (EGOS). In addition to an introductory editorial, which similarly places this particular collection of papers in the broader context of management and organization studies as a whole, an invited commentary by Huff (1997) critically evaluates the extent to which the managerial and organizational cognition field has advanced over the preceding decade or so, using the contents of this volume to review progress and highlight some of the further challenges that have yet to be confronted. This is the third guest-edited special issue of the *Journal of Management Studies* in little over a decade that has addressed the topic of managerial and organizational cognition, thus signalling its growing importance as an emerging subdiscipline, the previous special issues having been guest edited by Porac and Thomas (1989) and Eden (1992). The Eden and Spender (1998) volume comprises a further collection of papers based on an earlier conference workshop, placed in context by an accompanying editorial and afterword, while the books by Weick and Finkelstein and Hambrick are monographs that provide comprehensive overviews of the literature on 'Sensemaking in Organizations' and 'Strategic Leadership' respectively. The volume by Flood and his colleagues comprises yet another useful edited collection of readings (again stemming from the proceedings of a conference) devoted to implementation issues.

The present chapter is organized in four main sections, each section being devoted to one of the main subthemes selected for coverage, as listed above. An additional, concluding section draws together the main issues and trends common to each of these interrelated lines of inquiry and offers an assessment of the future prospects for the development of the psychology of strategic management from its continuing status as an emergent topic in I/O psychology to a fully established area of study within this field.

MENTAL REPRESENTATIONS OF COMPETITION

The identification of competitors and the bases on which they compete is one of the most fundamental issues of concern to strategy academics and practitioners alike (see, for example, Abell, 1980; Oster, 1990). Not surprisingly, therefore, the analysis of actors' mental representations of competitive business environments has continued to command considerable research attention during the current review period.

Background: The Theory of Strategic Groups

Conventional approaches to the analysis of business competition in industries and markets have been dominated by the structure → conduct → performance paradigm of industrial organization economics (Bain, 1956; Mason, 1957), and have centred on the notion of strategic groups. The writings of Michael Porter, a Harvard Professor of Strategic Management, have contributed greatly to the literature on competitive analysis and the commonly accepted definition of the strategic groups concept is that provided by Porter (1980, p.129):

> A strategic group is the group of firms in an industry following the same or a similar strategy along the strategic dimensions. An industry could have only one strategic group if all the firms followed essentially the same strategy. At the other extreme, each firm could be a different strategic group. Usually, however, there are a small number of strategic groups which capture the essential strategic differences among firms in the industry.

The main purpose of the economic theory underpinning the notion of strategic groups is to explain variations in the strategic behaviour (conduct) and performance of firms within industries. According to this theory, once strategic groups have formed, the various players develop isolating mechanisms (barriers to entry and mobility) that serve to deter new entrants from stepping into the competitive arena and to deter existing players from attempting to switch membership from one group to another (Caves & Porter, 1977). The theory predicts significant between-groups performance differences will accrue, over and above differences within groups, due to the fact that mobility barriers afford stable advantages to particular groups at the expense of other groups within the same industry. Hence the concept of mobility barriers provides both an explanation for intergroup performance differences and a conceptual basis for competitively positioning rival firms (Porter, 1981, p. 615).

A number of studies have failed to yield significant between-groups performance differences (for reviews see McGee & Thomas, 1986; Thomas & Venkatraman, 1988) and in recent years the notion of strategic groups has come under increasingly critical scrutiny. Several researchers (e.g. Hodgkinson & Johnson, 1994; Reger, 1990; Reger & Huff, 1993) have questioned the extent to which secondary financial and accounting information derived from company records or commercially available generic databases, as typically employed by strategic groups researchers, can adequately capture bases of competition. A major limitation of this predominantly economic approach is its inability to explain how or why competitive structures in industries and markets come to develop in the first place, and on what basis particular strategies are chosen. Arguably, the most extreme criticisms have come from Hatten and Hatten (1987) and Barney and Hoskisson (1990). These researchers contend that the theoretical base underpinning strategic groups is insufficiently developed to justify the notion, and that in reality strategic groups are merely analytical artefacts of the multivariate data analysis techniques employed to detect such groups.

Socio-cognitive Explanations for the Emergence of Competitive Industry Structures

Over the past ten to fifteen years, a number of researchers have responded to these criticisms by advancing 'socio-cognitive' (Lant & Phelps, 1999) or 'social constructionist' (Hodgkinson, 1997a) explanations for the emergence of competitive structures in industries and markets (e.g. Abrahamson & Fombrun, 1994; Bogner & Thomas, 1993; Levenhagen, Porac & Thomas, 1993; Peteraf & Shanley, 1997; Porac, Thomas & Baden-Fuller, 1989; Reger & Huff, 1993). According to this rapidly evolving body of theory, discernible competitive structures emerge because over time strategists from rival firms develop highly similar (or 'shared') mental models of the competitive arena, due to the fact that they share similar technical and material problems and frequently exchange information in the conduct of their business transactions.

This process of social exchange, in turn, leads to the development of a shared understanding—throughout the community of firms within the marketplace—of how to compete.

Drawing on the work of Berger and Luckmann (1967) and Weick's (1979) observation that organizations often create their environments through collective sense-making processes, then act as if their cognitive constructions were true, Porac, Thomas and Baden-Fuller (1989) have termed this process of social construction 'competitive enactment' (see also Porac & Rosa, 1996; Porac & Thomas, 1990; Weick, 1995). The basic features of this notion were demonstrated empirically in a study of the Scottish knitwear industry by Porac, Thomas and Baden-Fuller (1989), which revealed an overwhelming tendency for managers from a number of rival firms to disregard as competitors firms located outside the immediate vicinity of Scotland. Despite the fact that Scottish knitwear producers account for a mere 3% of the total amount of knitted outerwear manufactured on a worldwide basis, only firms within the immediate locality, and who produced a similar range of goods to one another, using similar technological processes of production and common channels of distribution, were regarded as serious competition. More recently, in a follow-up investigation, Porac, Thomas, Wilson, Patton and Kanfer (1995) have identified a six-category model of organizational forms which seems to capture actors' common perceptions of competition within this industry, with several attributes (principally size, technology, product style, and geographic location) forming the underlying basis for this commonly perceived structure.

Researchers advancing socio-cognitive explanations for the emergence of competitive structures contend that this tendency for individuals to attend to a limited subset of potential competitors and only consider a restricted range of strategic options—borne out by a number of other studies that have investigated actors' mental representations of competitors (e.g. Clark & Montgomery, 1999; Gripsrud & Gronhaug, 1985; Hodgkinson & Johnson, 1994; Johnson, Daniels & Asch, 1998; Porac & Thomas, 1994; Porac, Thomas & Emme, 1987; Reger & Huff, 1993)—arises due to fundamental information processing limitations. Extrapolating from cognitive categorization theory and research conducted by experimental psychologists and cognitive anthropologists (e.g. Lakeoff, 1987; Rosch, 1978) a number of strategy researchers (e.g. Porac, Thomas & Emme, 1987; Porac, Thomas & Baden-Fuller, 1989; Porac & Thomas, 1990; Reger & Huff, 1993) have argued that managers' mental representations of competitors take the form of a hierarchical taxonomy, in which intermediate, 'basic level' categories provide a cognitive analogue to the conventional notion of strategic groups. According to these researchers, the categorization of competitors in this way enables actors to simplify reality and hence take action within the constraints imposed by bounded rationality (March & Simon, 1958). It is as these basic-level cognitive categories come to be shared amongst groups of rivals, through mutual enactment processes, that discernible competitive structures are hypothesized to emerge.

This body of work, stressing the importance of categorization processes in competitor definition and advancing the notion of competitive enactment, has laid the foundations for subsequent theorizing. Building on these earlier developments, considerable research effort has been expended over recent years, in an attempt to flesh out the details of how competitive structures are socially constructed and reconstructed over time.

The cognitive lifecycle of market domains

Taking the earlier Scottish knitwear study (Porac, Thomas and Baden-Fuller, 1989) as their point of departure, Levenhagen, Porac and Thomas (1993) have introduced the notion of the 'cognitive lifecycle of market domains', in an effort to further explain the formation and development of competitive structures in industries and markets. Levenhagen, Porac and Thomas posit a four-stage lifecycle (concept formation → concept championing → concept appropriation → the institutionalization of market domains), preceded by a preliminary phase of 'pre-competitive knowledge development', in which multiple knowledge streams are disconnected from one another, separated temporally and spatially, with differential rates of development.[1]

Drawing on concepts from a variety of theoretical perspectives on competition including population ecology (Wholey & Brittain, 1986) and industrial organization economics (e.g. Penrose, 1959), together with marketing strategy (Day, Shocker & Shrivistava, 1979), resource dependency (Pfeffer & Salancik, 1978) and institutional theory (Zucker, 1986), Levenhagen and his colleagues contend that the social construction processes underpinning the development of 'market domains' are initiated by 'frame-making' and 'frame-breaking entrepreneurs'. According to this view, the role of leadership in this process is paramount. The prime contribution of the leader is to destroy the legitimacy of producers' and consumers' extant mental models, while selling new visions:

> There is more to leadership than the internal leadership of firms. There are important opportunities residing in and between all industrial domains for *industry leadership* as well. These opportunities exist at all times in almost all markets because market domains are not 'real' in any objective sense. They are 'constructed' through implicit agreement by their participants. In that markets have important cognitive and perceptual elements that influence what and how material transactions occur among stakeholders, almost any market can be maintained or destroyed through persuasive industrial leadership efforts—but *not* without good economic reasons. Since uncertainty and ambiguity reside in all market domains, good economic reasons are always in abundance. (Levenhagen, Porac & Thomas, 1993, p. 85).

Although the cognitive lifecycle conception has considerable intuitive appeal, the main assertions arising from this notion have yet to be tested empirically, on a rigorous and systematic basis (Hodgkinson, 1997a).

Managerial cognition and the institutionalization of competitive behaviour

In a separate development, Lant and Baum (1995) have explored the mechanisms through which firms might determine their *competitive sets* (the term employed by Lant and Baum, to denote the cognitive analogue to conventional strategic groups). In similar vein to Porac and his colleagues, Lant and Baum contend that managers *enact* a structure of strategic groups, responding to, and creating, their competitive worlds in a manner consistent with their own cognitions.

A central concept to have emerged from writings on institutional theory (e.g. DiMaggio & Powell, 1983; Meyer & Rowan, 1977) is the notion of 'isomorphism', that is the observed tendency for firms to develop shared beliefs, structures, practices, strategies and networks of relations. Drawing on this notion, Lant and Baum predicted that they would find evidence within a sample of $N = 43$ hotel managers in the Manhattan district of New York for the existence of mutually enacted competitive sets, in which rivals with similar characteristics and strategies would tend to identify one another as relevant competitors. They also predicted that the perceptions and attributions of managers within such competitive groups would be more similar than the perceptions and attributions of managers drawn from different groups.

Lant and Baum suggested that the isomorphism they expected to observe might arise from managers' conceptualizations of their strategic identities. According to Lant and Baum, two principal sources provide actors with clues about their organization's strategic identity and hence its appropriate strategy: cues arising from the monitoring of firms within the relevant competitive set *(mimetic isomorphism)* and cues arising from a variety of normative sources such as the parent company (if the hotel is part of a conglomerate), and agents in the institutional environment who act as transmitters of information, including travel agents, higher education institutions, and industry consultants *(normative isomorphism)*.

Using a form of network analysis (Borgatti, Everett & Freeman, 1992) in conjunction with hierarchical cluster analysis, some 14 competitive groupings were identified from a total of 167 hotels. As predicted, managers within each discernible group of hotels tended to regard one another as relevant competitors. Also as predicted, a number of significant differences emerged between the competitive groups in relation to the mean size, price and location (street and avenue) of the hotels, indicating that the aggregation the competitive sets elicited from the individual managers reveals relatively homogeneous groups of hotels.

Like the Scottish knitwear study discussed earlier, the findings of this study offer broad support for the general proposition that competitive structures may evolve through processes of social construction, involving competitive enactment. However, as the authors themselves readily acknowledge, due to limitations in the research design, this study contributes very little to understanding of the precise mechanisms through which such managerial perceptions converge over time, thereby giving rise to institutional isomorphism. Given that this study utilized a cross-sectional design, it was not possible to discern which of the various hypothesized forms of mimetic and normative isomorphism ultimately accounts for the observed pattern of findings. As with the Scottish knitwear study, the findings of this research should be regarded as tentative rather than conclusive, opening the field to further lines of inquiry, with larger samples and greater controls.

Greve's (1998) recent investigation of mimetic adoption processes in a population ecology study of the spread of new radio formats in the US provides a useful illustration of one way in which this preliminary work might inform future research in this area (see also Greve, 1996). Employing a range of documentary data sources, Greve (1998) modelled processes of innovation diffusion, using the technique of event history analysis (Tauma & Hannan, 1984), the study population being commercial radio stations. On the basis of his findings Greve concluded that the major driver of the mimetic adoption of new market positions is managers' mental models, which in turn are informed by information access (the degree to which they are able to observe competitors by virtue of geographical proximity) and relevancy judgements (as measured by market size). According to Greve, differential access to information, coupled with variations in perceived relevance, has given rise to the emergence of new strategic groups within this industry, through selective mimetic adoption. These results, suggesting that managers distinguish markets using market size as a relevancy criterion for deciding which competitors' practices are worthy of imitation, represent the beginnings of a journey to discover how managers categorize and distinguish markets.

Peteraf and Shanley's identity theory of strategic groups

Peteraf and Shanley (1997) have attempted to further enrich this emerging body of socio-cognitive theory by borrowing concepts from social learning theory (Bandura, 1986; Wood & Bandura, 1989) and social identification theory (Ashforth & Mael, 1989; Tajfel & Turner, 1985). Building on the earlier social constructionist accounts reviewed above, which emphasize the importance of direct and indirect interaction in the marketplace as a basis for the emergence of cognitive strategic groups, Peteraf and Shanley (1997) have introduced the notion of relational modelling and vicarious learning from social learning theory.

According to Peteraf and Shanley, managers reflect on their accumulated experiences of interorganizational interactions, both direct and vicarious, in order to discern which firms are important for them to observe and emulate or otherwise, and which are of significance in competitive terms or for reasons of mutual concern. Over time these observations and inferences about fellow firms are encoded into a series of organizational routines that guide the future search behaviours of organizations, whether they be looking to solve difficult problems, gather intelligence about competitors, or seek additional resources from cooperative partners. Irrespective of why the information is sought, Peteraf and Shanley argue that these routines steer organizations in such a way that they will tend to look to the same group of firms on repeated occasions, which in the long run leads to the development of a relatively stable cognitive entity. The accumulated experience gained through social learning enables organizations to reduce their transaction costs, by promoting continued exchange only with those firms found to be reliable interaction partners, predictable in their behaviours and providing tolerable levels of risk.

According to Peteraf and Shanley (1997) these processes of social learning are a necessary but insufficient condition for the emergence of strategic groups that have real and measurable effects, that is groups that will ultimately influence the conduct and performance of their individual members. In addition, social identification must occur; group members must not only perceive the fact that a group exists ('identification of the group'), but also *identify with* the group. For Peteraf and Shanley it is the identity strength of a strategic group that ultimately determines the extent to which group membership impacts on the conduct and performance of firms within a given industry. Potentially, this notion might explain why previous attempts to identify significant differences in organizational performance on the basis of strategic group membership *per se* have yielded inconsistent findings from study to study. Peteraf and Shanley contend that the previously hypothesized performance differences will only consistently emerge in situations where strategic groups are characterized by strong identities. As with the cognitive lifecycle notion, however, the various testable propositions arising from this theory have yet to be subjected to the rigours of empirical scrutiny.

Lant and Phelps's situated learning perspective

In yet another theoretical development, drawing on the work of Wenger (1998), Lant (1999) and Lant and Phelps (1999) have advanced a 'situated learning perspective' on strategic groups and the emergence of knowledge and identity within cognitive communities. Lant and Phelps contend that the existing body of socio-cognitive theory relating to the formation of competitive groups and cognitive communities has underemphasized the extent to which learning within and between cognitive groups is embedded in a social milieu, treating learning primarily as a vicarious process, whereas in reality the emergence and evolution of such groups is underpinned by a relatively complex, dynamic process, in which ongoing interactions among the various players both central and peripheral to the group yields not only common and predictable patterns of behaviour within strategic groups, but also helps preserve variations in the structures, strategies and beliefs within these groups. According to this view, such variations are vital to the accomplishment of learning and change, thereby enhancing the longer-term survival capabilities of the wider population of organizations.

Recognizing that the various major developments in the emerging socio-cognitive theory of strategic groups outlined above (categorization, competitive enactment and social identification) have undoubtedly enhanced understanding of the dynamics of competition in industries, Lant and Phelps (1999) nevertheless challenge several of the assumptions implicit within this body of theory and research. Firstly, citing the work of Tsoukas (1992), Araujo (1998) and Palinscar (1998), they question the adequacy of the 'topographic' view of organizations portrayed within this body of work and indeed much of the field of organization studies more generally. Two assumptions implicit within this perspective are challenged by Lant and Phelps, namely, the assumption that knowledge is localized in individual minds or other anthropomorphized entities such as organizations, and the assumption that organizations are relatively self-contained, bounded entities that learn through key individuals, such as top managers. Secondly, they question the adequacy of the way in which learning is portrayed within much of this work, as a predominantly vicarious process, in which referent others are modelled or imitated, as exemplified in the paper by Peteraf and Shanley (1997).

Lant (1999) and Lant and Phelps (1999) contend that the theory of learning and identification portrayed in extant social constructionist accounts of the emergence of strategic groups and identity in cognitive communities represents an *undersituated* perspective:

> In contrast, we assume that learning, cognition, and knowledge are inherently situated in a broader social context consisting of actors, artefacts, language, time and space. According to a situated learning perspective, knowledge and its meaning are negotiated and constructed by actors who interact within a community with which they identify and who share the practices of the community . . .
>
> Situated learning encompasses meaning (learning as experience), practice (learning as doing), community (learning as becoming), and identity (learning as belonging). Such a view affords a much richer sense of the learning processes that occur within and among organizations than a focus on vicarious learning by top managers. (Lant & Phelps, 1999, pp. 230–231).

As in the case of Levenhagen, Porac and Thomas's (1993) cognitive lifecycle notion and the work of Lant and Baum (1995) and Greve (1996, 1998), discussed earlier, this perspective has the potential to enrich considerably not only understanding of the strategic groups phenomenon, but also the dynamics of population-level competitive strategy, and learning and change more generally. Through its dynamic emphasis on the importance of *both* variation *and* consistency in cognition and action over varying time periods, the situated learning perspective draws attention to the importance of multi-level system interaction effects within and between firms and groups of firms.

This new perspective not only calls into question a number of fundamental assumptions concerning the nature of cognition and learning in organizational fields, but also challenges fundamental aspects of conventional strategic groups theory, particularly the nature and role of mobility barriers as protective devices which preserve the competitive positions of established industry players (cf. Caves & Porter, 1977). Contrary to conventional wisdom, according to Lant and Phelps (1999), strategic groups with high mobility barriers will have lower long-term survival chances than groups with lower barriers, due to the fact that these barriers inhibit learning by preventing players with new beliefs and practices from entering the group. Over time, this will result in reduced variation in structures, strategies and beliefs, thus rendering the wider population of firms vulnerable to competency-destroying technological changes of the sort discussed by Tushman and Anderson (1990)[2]

The conceptual and empirical status of socio-cognitive explanations for the emergence of competitive structures: a critical evaluation

Supported by appropriately designed, rigorous empirical studies, this emerging body of theory stands to greatly enrich the theory and practice of strategic management. To the extent that we can better understand the processes by which actors create, legitimize, destroy and recreate industries and markets this might not only have considerable implications for the regulation of competition, but could also inform the design of interventions to facilitate organizational learning and strategic renewal at the level of the individual firm. Presently, however, theory building is running well ahead of supporting empirical research, with a rapid succession of concepts, theoretical frameworks and testable propositions having evolved over a relatively short timespan.

Matters are not helped by the fact that differing authors have generated alternative concepts to describe essentially the same phenomena. Thus, for example, Porac, Thomas and Baden-Fuller (1989) employ the term 'primary competitive group' as a cognitive analogue to the conventional notion of the strategic group, while Lant and Baum (1995) speak of 'competitive sets'. Peteraf and Shanley (1997), by contrast, adopt the label 'cognitive strategic groups' in the development of their theory of strategic group identity, a term which Lant and Phelps (1999) also favour. Clearly there is a need for scholars to reflect at some length before further terms are introduced into what is very rapidly becoming an overcrowded field.

Theory development in this area has amassed largely on the basis of reviews of the extant literature in adjacent subfields, in conjunction with studies based on limited research designs and/or inadequate samples. Ultimately what is required, if social constructionist notions such as competitive enactment and the related cognitive lifecycle conception, outlined above, are to be tested with an acceptable degree of rigour, are large-scale longitudinal field studies, in which the mental representations of multiple informants, situated at differing vantage points within and between organizations in the same industrial sector are assessed repeatedly in conjunction with measurable aspects of strategic behaviour and organizational performance, over extended time periods (Hodgkinson, 1997a). Such studies would enable researchers to explore the extent to which, under what circumstances, and over what time-scale and with what effect, actors' mental representations of competition converge, diverge, stabilize and change. Only then would we be able to disentangle the myriad of cause–effect relationships and potentially competing explanations for the evolution of competitive structures implied by this emerging body of socio-cognitive theory.

Unfortunately, such high-quality studies have not been forthcoming. To date, just three studies (Gronhaugh & Falkenberg, 1989; Hodgkinson, 1997b; Reger & Palmer, 1996) have employed any form of longitudinal design, with only one of these (Hodgkinson's study of competitor cognition in the UK residential estate agency industry) being prospective in nature. The Gronhaugh and Falkenberg study, an investigation of the Norwegian forest products industry, utilized a retrospective design, in which participants were required to report perceptions of their own firm's competitive strategy, and those of its competitors, during periods of growth and recession ('boom' and 'bust') on the basis of subjective recall and was limited to just seven participants from four organizations. The reliability and validity of such retrospective recall techniques in strategy research in general, let alone on such a limited sample, has been seriously questioned in recent years and clearly should only be used in circumstances when no feasible alternative is possible (Golden, 1992, 1997; Miller, Cardinal & Glick, 1997).

The Reger and Palmer study comprised a comparison of executives' cognitive maps of competitive positioning in the US financial services industry, over a nine-year period. As with the Gronhaug and Falkenberg study, however, there are several methodological weaknesses associated with the design of this research that render the findings inconclusive, not least the fact that the data were actually drawn from three *separate* studies and compared retrospectively by means of a qualitative content analysis. While the data were gathered over differing time periods (1981, 1986 and 1989), as Reger and Palmer themselves acknowledge, there are several locational and industry segment disparities across the three studies. These potentially confound a number of outcomes which Reger and Palmer would otherwise have been able to attribute with much greater certainty to increasing environmental turbulence. Furthermore, there are several differences in the data analysis methods employed within each study that might also account for some of the outcomes.

Thus far, the overwhelming majority of studies used to support the development of theory in this area have been relatively small-scale, exploratory studies, characterized by poor or non-existent controls, thereby rendering problematic the extent to which alternative explanations for the findings can be ruled out. Typically, the mental representations of a single informant from each participating company (usually the owner-manager, managing director or CEO) are elicited, on a cross-sectional basis, by means of one or more cognitive mapping procedures, as exemplified by the Scottish knitwear (Porac, Thomas & Baden-Fuller, 1989; Porac et al., 1995) and Manhattan hotel industry (Lant & Baum, 1995) studies outlined above (see also Dess & Davis, 1984; Fombrun & Zajac, 1987; Porac, Thomas & Emme,1987; Porac & Thomas, 1994). These and a number of other researchers investigating strategic groups from a cognitive perspective have implicitly or explicitly assumed away the significance of potential intra- and interorganizational variations in cognition, treating the responses of the individual informant as representative of the organization and/or industry as a whole. When viewed from the situated learning perspective advanced by Lant (1999) and Lant and Phelps (1999), however, this core assumption of intra- and interfirm cognitive homogeneity becomes highly questionable. In the meantime, the findings of a number of recent studies that have deliberately utilized multiple informant research designs (e.g. Bowman & Ambrosini, 1997a,b; Bowman & Johnson, 1992; Calori, Johnson & Sarnin, 1992, 1994; Daniels, Johnson & de Chernatony, 1994; Hodgkinson & Johnson, 1994; Johnson, Daniels & Asch, 1998) suggest that these doubts may well be justified. Unfortunately, however, the wide range of cognitive mapping methods employed in these studies, coupled with the fact that they have been carried out in a diverse range of industries, means that the varying levels of homogeneity observed from one study to another are confounded, thereby severely limiting the interpretation which can be placed on the findings.

Summary and Conclusions

In summary, a number of major theoretical developments have occurred within the current review period, all highly cumulative on the surface, but giving rise to potentially competing explanations for the emergence and evolution of competitive structures in industries and markets. Each of the main conceptual building blocks within the emerging socio-cognitive theory of strategic groups has been greatly under-researched empirically, with a tendency to appeal to extant supporting secondary literatures within the base disciplines of psychology, sociology and economics, at the expense of conducting high-quality, primary field studies, designed to test key hypotheses in a hypothetico-deductive fashion. Recently, a number of empirical findings have begun to accumulate which cast doubt on the validity of some of the core assumptions underpinning the limited primary work that has hitherto been cited in support of this emerging body of theory. Unfortunately, however, a number of methodological limitations restrict the inferences that can be drawn from this work. Nevertheless, the fact that such intraorganizational variations in actors' mental representations of competition have been uncovered, utilizing a wide range of methods of data collection and analysis, points overwhelmingly to the need for a fine-grained analysis of socio-cognitive strategy-making processes within the firm, particularly at the level of the top management team, and it is to recent developments in the analysis of the antecedents and consequences of strategic cognition within executive teams that we now turn.

COGNITIVE PROCESSES IN TOP MANAGEMENT TEAMS

In the previous *IRIOP* review covering this topic, Sparrow (1994) summarized the findings of a number of studies that have investigated the inter-relationships between top management team (TMT) diversity and organizational outcomes (e.g. Bantel & Jackson, 1989; Murray, 1989; Norburn & Birley, 1988; Wiersema & Bantel, 1992) within the confines of the 'upper echelons perspective' (Hambrick & Mason, 1984). According to Hambrick and Mason (1984, p. 193) organizational outcomes such as strategy and effectiveness are ultimately a reflection of the values and 'cognitive bases' of 'the dominant coalition' within the firm. Since, by definition, the dominant coalition constitutes the organization's power elite, it is the cognitions and values of this group of actors that ultimately determine its strategic choices. Drawing on a range of psychological and sociological studies, Hambrick and Mason argued that a variety of observable managerial characteristics such as age, socio-economic roots, functional background, executive tenure and education shape the values and beliefs of the individual manager. In view of the obvious practical difficulties associated with attempting to study directly the psychological characteristics of senior executives, Hambrick and Mason (1984, p. 196) advocated the use of these external, observable characteristics as indicators of the givens that members of the TMT bring to bear on their administrative situation. Subsequently, a voluminous literature has developed in which researchers have explored the theoretical and empirical relationships between the demographic composition (homogeneity vs heterogeneity) of TMTs on the one hand, and a variety of organizational outcomes, outcomes as varied as innovation (e.g. Bantel & Jackson, 1989), firm performance (Norburn & Birley, 1988), the nature and extent of strategic change (Wiersema & Bantel, 1992), bankruptcy (D'Avini, 1990) and, more recently, corporate illegal activity (Daboub Rasheed, Priem & Gray, 1995), firms' competitive moves (Hambrick, Cho & Chen, 1996) and levels of international involvement in diversification strategies (Sambharya, 1996) on the other. Recently, however, a number of highly significant developments have occurred that challenge the central tenets of this approach.

Conceptual and Empirical Limitations of the Demographic Approach

Whereas initial findings generally supported Hambrick and Mason's (1984) theoretical predictions concerning the linkages between TMT composition and outcomes, the picture is now exceedingly complex, a large number of studies (reviewed in Finkelstein & Hambrick, 1996; Lau & Murnighan, 1998; Milliken & Martins, 1996; Pelled, 1996; Pettigrew, 1992; and Williams & O'Reilly, 1998) having yielded inconsistent and contradictory findings, particularly in the case of studies exploring the linkage between group demography and organizational performance and the question as to whether homogeneous or heterogeneous teams best contribute to team and organizational success. Recent studies investigating the linkage between the degree of TMT functional background diversity and financial performance, for example, have revealed mixed findings. Thus, Roure and Keeley (1990) found TMT diversity to be predictive of financial performance in respect of this particular characteristic, while West and Schwenk (1996) did not.

With remarkable foresight, Jackson (1992, p. 348) warned:

> Unless we develop a better theoretical understanding of the mediating processes through which team composition shapes organizational outcomes, the accumulation of evidence may not translate into an improved ability to formulate accurate predictions. In the longer term, this could be detrimental to the upper echelons paradigm for it may lead some to suspect the validity of the paradigm's basic underlying premise.

Naturally, the variability of results arising from this stream of research has led to the adoption of increasingly sophisticated research designs, incorporating a variety of control variables, in an effort to disentangle cause–effect relationships and clarify the reasons for such anomalous findings. Thus, for example, several of the more recent studies into the effects of TMT characteristics on performance have incorporated contingency factors such as environmental turbulence (Haleblain & Finkelstein, 1993; Keck, 1997) and strategy process variables such as communication and social integration (e.g. Smith et al., 1994) and decision comprehensiveness and debate (Simons, Pelled & Smith, 1999) in an effort to strengthen results. Whilst readily conceding that, like the basic input-output research that preceded it, this more sophisticated line of work has also yielded a number of empirical inconsistencies, Finkelstein and Hambrick (1996) contend that it nevertheless offers the potential for redirecting future research into the performance consequences of TMTs. Other researches, however, have called into question the fundamental assumptions underpinning this whole approach.

Pettigrew and Lawrence's theoretical contributions

Whilst the use of control variables and other recent methodological enhancements, such as the adoption of longitudinal designs incorporating the use of time-series data (e.g. Keck & Tushman, 1993), are to be welcomed, Pettigrew (1992, p. 174) has called for the development of new questions and methods that take us beyond the use of demographic data as proxy variables for cognition, in order that research within this tradition does not degenerate into 'another triumph of method over substance'. Ultimately, the validity of the upper-echelon tradition rests on a key, but highly dubious, assumption dating back to a paper by Pfeffer, which appeared in the year prior to Hambrick and Mason's (1984) seminal article. In this paper, Pfeffer (1983) outlined the case for demography as a potentially important factor that might indirectly influence a range of organizational outcomes, via a variety of intervening variables, but also added an important caveat, namely, that the fulfilment of the promise of the demographic approach to organizational analysis would be dependent on the resolution of several key empirical and philosophy of social science issues.

In the present context, the primary empirical question that needs to be addressed concerns the extent to which demography (the independent variable) predicts and explains not only variation in the dependent variables (strategy process and organizational performance outcomes) characteristic of the TMT research which has been conducted within the Hambrick and Mason tradition, but also the extent to which it predicts or explains managerial cognition (the intervening construct). Pettigrew quotes Pfeffer (1983, p. 351) directly, in order to summarize the bigger philosophical question that needs to be resolved:

> To what extent is it incumbent on the research to trace through a demographic effect on the various intervening constructs; or, to what extent can the postulating effect of demographic effect and a plausible mechanism be examined simply by investigating the empirical relationship between demography and what demography affects?

According to Pfeffer (1983) an understanding of intervening constructs or processes is not necessary or desirable, on the grounds that to embark on the search for such understanding will invariably lead to an infinite regress from which the researcher cannot logically escape. In a carefully constructed theoretical critique of the original Pfeffer paper, however, Lawrence (1997) has demonstrated how multiple and potentially conflicting processes might intervene between demography on the one hand and organizational outcomes on the other, thus revealing the fundamental limitations of Pfeffer's original line of reasoning and hence the adequacy of the demographic approach as a basis for studying cognitive processes and outcomes in TMTs.

Building on the Pettigrew–Lawrence critique, a number of scholars have begun to develop new theoretical constructs in an effort to refine understanding of the linkages between team composition on the one hand, and team processes and outcomes on the other. Pelled (1996), for example, has introduced the notions of 'visibility' (the extent to which the demographic variables in question are observable by group members) and 'job relatedness' (the extent to which the variables in question shape perspectives and skills directly related to tasks) in an attempt to account for the mixed effects of diversity on performance observed in previous studies. High-visibility variables (e.g. age, gender and race) are hypothesized to influence affective conflict within the team, while high-job-relatedness variables (e.g. organizational tenure, educational and functional background) are hypothesized to influence substantive (task) conflict. According to Pelled, both of these relationships are mediated by group longevity, and turnover in the team is determined by affective conflict, whereas cognitive task performance is jointly influenced by substantive and affective conflict.

In another recent development, Lau and Murnighan (1998) have introduced the notion of 'demographic faultlines' as an explanation for subgroup processes of conflict and a basis for opening up the black box of demography. Here, the focus is on processes of group formation and development, including the formation and development of subgroups. Demographic faultlines are hypothetical dividing lines the effect of which is to split groups into subgroups on the basis of one or more key attributes, such as age or educational experience. According to Lau and Murnighan, the formation of conflicting subgroups becomes much more likely when the demographic characteristics within a group form a faultline and are related to the group's task.

Markoczy's empirical contribution

Whilst these more recent conceptual innovations address some of the issues raised by Petttigrew (1992) and Lawrence (1997), suggesting new hypotheses that may account for several of the discrepancies observed in traditional upper-echelon research, the fundamental question still remains: to what extent are the external, background characteristics of the executive, adequate proxy variables for the assessment of perceptions and beliefs? Unaware of the Pettigrew–Lawrence critique, Markoczy (1997) has recently addressed this question empirically and her findings serve to reinforce the theoretical concerns and objections raised by these scholars.

Relatively few studies have directly tested the assumed relationship between individual external characteristics and cognition and those that have, have yielded mixed results. An early study by Dearborn and Simon (1958) (upon which Hambrick and Mason (1984) partially derived their original theoretical formulation) indicated that managers' views are biased by their functional positions. Subsequent research, however, has yielded contradictory and inconsistent findings. A study by Bowman and Daniels (1995), for example, which revisited Dearborn and Simon's research on methodological grounds, has confirmed their original claim, whereas other studies by Walsh (1988), and Beyer et al. (1997) have not. Another recent study running contrary to Hambrick and Mason's theory, by Waller, Huber and Glick (1995) found no evidence linking the functional backgrounds of CEOs and chief administrators to perceptions of changes in the perceived environment, but did find a link between functional background and perceptions of changes in organizational effectiveness. Several recent studies investigating managerial representations of competitive structures (reviewed earlier in this chapter) have also yielded inconsistent and contradictory findings in respect of the claim that functional position influences cognition (Daniels, Johnson & de Chernatony, 1994; Hodgkinson & Johnson, 1994; Johnson, Daniels & Asch, 1998).

According to Markoczy (1997) equivocal findings can similarly be listed in respect of the relationships between cognition and a number of other background characteristics, such as age and national culture. Consequently, additional studies are required in order to further investigate the validity of using external characteristics as substitutes for the direct measurement of perceptions and beliefs.

As part of a wider multicultural study of managers employed by Hungarian companies which have recently come under foreign ownership, Markoczy (1997) investigated the relationships between functional background, age, hierarchical position, and national culture and actors' causal belief systems with respect to organizational success—assessed by means of a causal mapping technique devised by Markoczy and Goldberg (1995)—arguing that these particular characteristics have received the strongest support on the basis of previous theory and research within the Hambrick and Mason tradition. Partial relationships were observed between three of the four background characteristics investigated (output functional background, age and non-Hungarian nationality) and the measured causal beliefs. In total, these characteristics accounted for 17.2% of the variance (change in adjusted R^2) of the similarity to one of two empirically derived clusters formed on the basis of the participants' causal maps. On the basis of these findings, Markoczy concluded that the case for substitutability was not supported:

> There is a substantial loss in the measurement, and the gain of convenience is not as great as it first appears to be. Researchers should determine what it is that they want to measure and continue to develop and refine tools for doing so instead of relying on convenient substitutes that may turn out to be neither particularly good substitutes nor extremely convenient ones. (Markoczy, 1997, p. 1240)

This is not to say that future research into TMT strategic cognition should cease to consider the external individual characteristics of TMT members, on the grounds that these characteristics are inconsequential. On the contrary, the fact that inconsistent and contradictory findings have emerged from this general stream of research points overwhelmingly to a need for further studies in which the search for correlates of executive perceptions and beliefs is widened, in an attempt to better understand the antecedents of managerial cognition (Walsh, 1995). Such understanding may have important implications not only for future theory and research, but also for the design of interventions for facilitating processes of strategy formulation and implementation. To the extent that executive beliefs impact on organizational processes and outcomes, knowledge of the various factors that shape these beliefs might also have important implications for the selection and development of TMTs.

Determinants of Executive Beliefs and Perceptions: Beyond Demographic Composition

Drawing on various competing theoretical arguments, researchers are now beginning to investigate the relative influence of a range of factors (including the external characteristics of the individual incorporated in traditional TMT studies, but also a variety of contextualizing (organizational and environmental) factors) as potential determinants of executive cognition, with a view to refining theoretical models of strategic decision processes (see, e.g., Chattopadhyay Glick, Miller & Huber, 1999; Knight, Pearce, Smith et al., 1999; Miller, Burke & Glick, 1998; Sutcliffe, 1994; Sutcliffe & Huber, 1998; Tyler & Steensma, 1998). In the remainder of this section, two of these recent studies are examined in detail, in order to illustrate the considerable potential of this approach.

Firm versus industry

Two broad, opposing, theoretical arguments prevail concerning the relative importance of firm and industry as determinants of executive perceptions of the environment: the first (e.g. Abrahamson & Fombrun, 1994; DiMaggio & Powell, 1983; Huff, 1982; Porac, Thomas, Baden-Fuller, 1989; Spender, 1989) suggests that a variety of social processes give rise to common perceptions within and among organizational subpopulations inhabiting the same environment; the second, that executive perceptions differ significantly between organizations inhabiting the same environment, due to variations in organizational structures and processes (e.g. Daniels, Johnson & de Chernatony, 1994; Hodgkinson & Johnson, 1994; Huber, 1991; Jablin, 1997; Nelson & Winter, 1982). From a practitioner perspective, this is a non-trivial issue since, as observed earlier, commonality of perceptions within industries may or may not be beneficial to the longer-term survival of entire populations and subpopulations of firms, depending on the extent to which such commonalities facilitate interorganizational coordination and processes of coalition and/or give rise to 'industry blindspots' (Zajac & Bazerman, 1991) thereby rendering the industry impervious to the threat of new entrants and innovative competitive practices.

In light of this unresolved controversy, a recent study by Sutcliffe and Huber (1998) has further explored the role of firm and industry as determinants of perceptual commonality among executives. In contrast to the studies of mental representations of competition reviewed earlier, which have utilized a variety of cognitive mapping techniques in an effort to capture actors' perceptions of the structure and dynamics of the business environment, Sutcliffe and Huber employed a series of multi-item Likert scales in order to assess executive perceptions of five particular environmental attributes, namely, instability, munificence, complexity, hostility and controllability. The sample for this study comprised a total of $N = 307$ TMT members of $N = 58$ organizations drawn from $N = 19$ industries. The relative contribution of industry and organizational membership as determinants of the participants' environmental perceptions along the five dimensions was investigated by means of a nested random-effects MANOVA, accompanied by a series of univariate ANOVAs. The MANOVA, estimating the significance of the overall relationship between the five dependent variables and the hypothesized explanatory factors (industry and TMT/organizational membership) was significant at the $p < 0.01$ level, indicating that the univariate analyses were justified. The results of the five individual ANOVAS, reproduced in Table 10.1, revealed that TMT membership was a significant predictor of the individual informants' perceptions in relation to all five environmental characteristics.

Table 10.1   Analysis of variance (nested model): The effects of organization and industry on TMT members' perceptions of environmental attributes

Source	Instability	Munificence	Complexity	Hostility	Controllability
Industry[b]	2.69**[a]	2.99**	1.59+	0.83	1.14
	(0.22)	(0.31)	(0.16)	(–)	(–)
Organization	1.52*	2.42***	2.11**	2.90***	2.98***
within industry[c]	(0.15)	(0.19)	(0.21)	(0.29)	(0.28)
Model R^2	0.37**	0.50***	0.37**	0.38***	0.42***

Source: Reproduced with permission of the publisher from K. M. Sutcliffe and G. P. Huber (1998). Firm and industry as determinants of executive perceptions of the environment. *Strategic Management Journal*, **19**, 793–807. © John Wiley and Sons, Ltd.

[a]F-statistics are reported. Values in parentheses are the proportion of variance explained when the F-statistic is statistically significant.
[b]$(n = 19)$
[c]$(n = 58)$
+p < 0.10; *p < 0.05; **p < 0.01; ***p < 0.001. $N = 307$

As can be seen in Table 10.1, industry membership was found to be a significant predictor of perceptions of instability and munificence and a marginally significant predictor of complexity ($p < 0.10$). On the basis of these findings, Sutcliffe and Huber concluded that there was evidence of significant commonality in environmental perceptions amongst top managers both within organizations and within industries, but that commonalities of perception exist within TMTs over and above those within industries.

Functional conditioning versus social influence

In another recent study seeking to identify the determinants of executive beliefs, Chattopadhyay et al. (1999) developed and tested two opposing theoretical models. The *functional conditioning model* reproduced in Figure 10.1 is predicated on a stream of psychological theory and research evidence

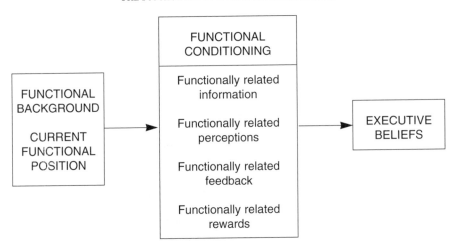

Figure 10.1 Effects of functional conditioning on beliefs of upper-echelon executives
Source: Reproduced with permission of the publisher from P. Chattopadhyay, W. H. Glick, C. C. Miller and G. P. Huber. (1999). Determinants of executive beliefs: comparing functional conditioning and social influence. *Strategic Management Journal*, **20**, 763–789. © John Wiley and Sons, Ltd.

emphasizing the fact that beliefs develop through experiences (Fiske & Taylor, 1984; Lord & Foti, 1986) by virtue of feedback and rewards associated with those experiences, which in turn serve to amplify the salience of particular goals and processes (Locke & Latham, 1990). According to this view, a combination of functionally related factors associated with organizational rewards and recognition processes jointly serve to condition managerial perceptions and beliefs.

Chattopadhyay et al. contend that a possible explanation for the empirical inconsistencies observed across previous studies of functional conditioning is model misspecification. In particular, researchers may have failed to consider the impact of one or more key factors that have a bearing on executive belief formation. None of the studies reviewed above (e.g. Dearborn & Simon, 1958; Walsh, 1988; Beyer et al., 1997) have considered additional explanatory variables other than the external characteristics of the individual manager.

In an attempt to address this limitation, Chattopadhyay et al. have developed an alternative, social influence model, which is reproduced in Figure 10.2. This model takes into account the overlapping social processes of communication, socialization and social information processing in an attempt to better explain the formation of executive beliefs. As shown in Figure 10.2, within this model, the functional background similarity and other relational demographic characteristics of the upper-echelon team are hypothesized to moderate the impact of the beliefs of the wider team on the beliefs of the focal executive. This model is predicated on a body of theory and research within social and organizational psychology (e.g. Gioia, 1986; Salancik & Pfeffer, 1978; Weick, 1995) that suggests the beliefs of individual TMT members are

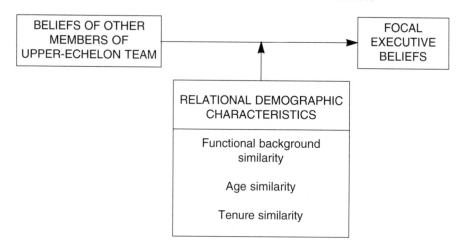

Figure 10.2   Social influence effects on focal upper-echelon executive beliefs
Source: Reproduced with permission of the publisher from P. Chattopadhyay, W. H. Glick, C. C. Miller and G. P. Huber. (1999). Determinants of executive beliefs: comparing functional conditioning and social influence. *Strategic Management Journal*, 20, 763–789. © John Wiley & Sons, Ltd.

likely to both shape, and be shaped by, a variety of social influence processes including shared sensemaking and verbal and non-verbal communication. The impact of the beliefs of the other members of the upper-echelon team on the formation of focal executives' beliefs is unlikely to be uniform, however, with some individuals exerting differentially greater levels of influence than others. One factor in particular singled out by Chattopadhyay et al. in this respect is the degree of demographic similarity between the focal executive and the wider team. Drawing on referent choice theory (Kulik & Ambrose, 1992) and similarity-attraction theory (Byrne, 1971), Chattopadhyay et al. contend that functional background similarity (and similarity on the other demographic dimensions shown in Figure 10.2) might moderate the relationship between the beliefs of other members of the team and the beliefs of the focal executive by influencing the degree to which the various wider team members communicate with the focal executive and one another. These relational demographic characteristics might also affect the extent to which team members attend to one another's behaviour and/or are receptive to one another's views regarding organizational matters.

In order to empirically test the relative explanatory power of these alternative theoretical models, Chattopadhyay et al. (1999) measured executives' beliefs concerning the efficacy of a broad set of business strategies and goals in achieving long-term profitability. As in the Sutcliffe and Huber (1998) study, the sampling strategy entailed collecting data from across a diverse range of industries, so as to increase the generalizability of the findings. The sample comprised $N = 371$ executives from $N = 58$ strategic business units, spanning

$N = 26$ industries. In addition to measuring executive beliefs and gathering the necessary demographic data, Chattopadhyay et al. controlled for various contextual features of the research setting that might independently influence the beliefs of individual participants, thereby giving rise to shared beliefs through processes unrelated to those incorporated in the hypothesized social influence model. Specifically, Chattopadhyay et al. controlled for environmental turbulence and environmental munificence, degree of SBU autonomy from the parent organization, the extent to which the participating organizations were functionally or divisionally structured, organization size and organizational effectiveness. The results of a series of multiple regression analyses did not support the functional conditioning model outlined in Figure 10.2, with just three out of the possible 25 effects tested for functional background and 5 of the possible 25 effects tested for current functional position yielding statistically significant standardized beta coefficients (p <0.05). The hypotheses associated with the social influence model outlined in Figure 10.2, by contrast, were substantially supported.

Strong support was obtained for the hypothesis that the beliefs held by a focal executive are related to the beliefs of the other members of the same upper echelon team, with significant betas ($p < 0.01$) in relation to all six of the belief dimensions investigated. Tests of the interactions between the various relational demographic variables constructed from the database and focal executive beliefs, however, yielded a mixed pattern of findings. Thus, for example, the interaction between the beliefs of other team members and functional background was found to be significant for three of the six belief dimensions at $p < 0.05$ and in the predicted direction. Although three of the six interaction terms associated with the tests conducted to investigate the hypothesized link between tenure similarity and focal executive beliefs were also significant, contrary to the predictions of the model, these results suggested that a team member's beliefs were most similar to the focal executive's beliefs when the member was more dissimilar in tenure to the focal executive.

Commendably, Chattopadhyay et al. conducted a statistical power analysis in order to assess the extent to which the null results reported in respect of several of their hypotheses might be due to Type II errors (i.e. falsely accepting the null hypothesis). On the basis of this analysis (indicating statistical power of 0.97) they concluded that any true effects that were not observed were probably negligible.

The overall conclusion derived from this study was that the effects of functional conditioning on executive beliefs, whether in the form of past experiences or current rewards and responsibilities, are minimal, whereas the impact of social influence is moderate, but larger, by comparison. The moderating effect of demographics on executive beliefs, however, is considerably more complex than that hypothesized on the basis of previous theory and research, with neither of the two models tested in this study adequately accounting for the results obtained. A given variable influences beliefs about some issues, but not others.

Evaluation

Studies such as these, incorporating direct measures of executive perceptions and beliefs, together with a range of contextual and control variables, are clearly beginning to reshape the agenda of upper-echelons research, potentially opening up the black box of organizational demography. However, there is a considerable way to go in the quest to understand the causal antecedents and consequences of executive cognition.

It is highly likely that a great many factors ultimately condition executive perceptions and beliefs, in a complex, dynamic interplay. In an attempt to capture this complexity, several of the more recent studies have incorporated a variety of team process variables, previously identified as potential mediators and moderators of executive perceptions and beliefs in the traditional upper-echelons literature. Knight et al. (1999), for example, incorporated measures of agreement seeking and interpersonal conflict in a LISREL analysis (Joreskog & Sorbom, 1993) which competitively tested four rival theoretical models seeking to explicate the relationships between demographic diversity, team processes and strategic consensus, while Miller, Burke and Glick (1998) incorporated measures of decision comprehensiveness and extensiveness in three separate studies into the effects of cognitive diversity on profitability.

Whilst these and the other recent studies exploring the determinants of executive perceptions and beliefs represent a major advance over traditional upper-echelons research, there is still considerable room for further improvement. For example, the Knight et al. study, although commendable for illustrating the potential of LISREL in this particular context, was based on a limited sample of $N = 76$ cases, once the dataset (based on the responses of $N = 328$ individuals) had been aggregated to the team-level, the focal unit of analysis. The question as to what constitutes an appropriate sample size for the legitimate application of structural equation modelling techniques, such as LISREL, has been the subject of intense debate over recent years. However, there is general agreement that large sample sizes are required if high levels of confidence are to be placed in the findings and it is well-known that the chi-square statistic underpinning a number of the commonly employed estimation procedures and goodness of fit measures associated with LISREL and related techniques is insensitive for samples of $N<100$–150, with a consequent increased likelihood that incorrect models will be wrongly accepted (James & James, 1989; Kelloway, 1996). Clearly, larger-scale replication studies are required in order to ascertain the extent to which the findings reported by Knight and his colleagues are in fact robust or otherwise.

Despite Sutcliffe's (1994) call for studies that utilize richer perceptual measures, specifically, causal mapping techniques (Axelrod, 1976), in conjunction with longitudinal research designs, all of these recent studies have employed cross-sectional designs and the vast majority have employed relatively simple summated rating scales for the assessment of executive cognition (along the lines of the Sutcliffe and Huber and Chattopadhyay et al. studies, reviewed above). Although relatively convenient to administer, score, and interpret, these measures of 'cognitive content' are no match for formal mapping procedures, such as causal mapping, in terms, of the depth of insight attained (cf. Miller, Burke & Glick, 1998, p. 52).

Summary and Conclusions

As with the analysis of mental representations of competition, research into cognitive processes in TMTs has advanced considerably within the current review period. Researchers are increasingly moving away from studies of the input-output variety, characteristic of the 1980s and early 1990s, in order to study executive perceptions and beliefs directly, in a concerted attempt to open up the black box of organizational demography. Ultimately, however, there are several non-trivial methodological hurdles associated with the assessment of managerial and organizational cognition that have yet to be overcome if the empirical knowledge base in a number of key areas within the psychology of strategic management is to advance beyond present levels. The next section highlights some of the complexities involved and offers an assessment of the extent to which progress has been achieved in addressing these fundamental problems.

METHODOLOGICAL ISSUES AND ADVANCES IN THE ASSESSMENT OF MANAGERIAL AND ORGANIZATIONAL COGNITION

Within a remarkably short time period, the field of strategic management has witnessed a proliferation in the range of techniques being applied in an effort to 'map' the mental representations of decision-makers (see, for example, Eden & Spender, 1998; Fiol & Huff, 1992; Huff, 1990; Huff & Jenkins, 2001; Walsh, 1995). Techniques employed by researchers investigating actors' mental representations of competition, for example, have ranged from relatively simple procedures that merely require a listing of competitors by name (Gripsrud & Gronhaug, 1985; de Chernatony, Daniels & Johnson, 1993), through semi-structured interviews, using taxonomic mapping procedures (Calori, Johnson & Sarnin, 1994; Hodgkinson & Johnson, 1994; Porac, Thomas & Baden-Fuller, 1989; Porac et al., 1995; Porac & Thomas, 1994) and network analysis, using block modelling procedures (Lant & Baum, 1995; Porac et al., 1995), to repertory grid (Daniels, Johnson & de Chernatony, 1994; Reger, 1990; Reger & Huff, 1993) and related multidimensional scaling and clustering techniques (Hodgkinson, 1997b; Hodgkinson, Padmore &

Tomes, 1991, Hodgkinson, Tomes & Padmore, 1996; Walton, 1986), and fully structured questionnaires based on extant typologies of competitive strategy (Bowman & Ambrosini, 1997a,b; Bowman & Johnson, 1992; Dess & Davis, 1984). Whilst the development and application of such a wide and varied range of alternative mapping procedures is generally to be welcomed, in many cases a number of fundamental questions regarding their psychometric efficacy (particularly in respect of reliability and validity) have yet to be addressed. A second, related set of issues concerns the comparison of maps elicited from multiple informants and/or the same informants over differing time periods. Which features of the data should form the basis of such comparisons and how should the data be analysed? Within the current review period, limited inroads have been made into each of these problem areas.

Reliability and Validity of Cognitive Mapping Procedures

Background

In her preface to *Mapping Strategic Thought,* Huff (1990, p. xv) warned that the significant enthusiasm for cognitive studies in strategic management and the other organization sciences was in danger of outreaching its methodological foundation, relatively little having been written about the technical aspects of how to conduct such investigations. Indeed, one of the primary reasons that the Huff volume was published was in order to introduce various cognitive mapping techniques, with a view to expanding the range and complexity of future research within the emerging field of managerial and organizational cognition. Although the book as a whole undoubtedly met in full its methodological agenda, explaining in an accessible form the underlying rationale of each technique so introduced, including detailed guidelines regarding the key stages of data collection, analysis and interpretation, issues associated with the reliability and validity of these procedures received, and have subsequently continued to receive, scant attention.

The extent to which the nature and significance of these issues has generally been downplayed and/or misunderstood by many members of the cognitive mapping community is perhaps best exemplified by the following quotation, taken from Laukkanan (1998), the context being a discussion of problems associated with the direct elicitation of participants' beliefs in the conduct of comparative causal mapping studies:

> It is only common sense to observe that acquiring good data is not easy and, disturbingly, we can seldom know how far we have come in any specific case . . . It is possible that sometimes the problem factors work at random or cancel each other out, especially over several domains and persons. Again, we cannot usually know if this is so and to what extent. The pragmatic conclusion is to do one's best to enhance data quality by acting on areas that are obviously critical and controll-

able. This starts with the choice of optimal subjects and the time and place of data acquisition. We should plan and prepare for the probing, for example, by knowing as much as possible about the situation and by testing our instruments in benevolent, predictable circumstances. In the field, we should increase the likelihood that our subjects do know what we want to tap and, second, that they feel relatively committed to produce as valid data as possible. Also, the interviewing should observe commonsense rules, which have been tested and are explained in most qualitative research guides. (Laukkanen, 1998, p. 175).

This quotation clearly highlights the gulf that currently exists in terms of levels of understanding of methodological issues between a number of researchers operating in this vitally important, yet highly underdeveloped, topic area and scholars working within the more traditional areas of I/O psychology. Notwithstanding the considerable practical difficulties that inevitably arise when attempting to conduct research which is not only methodologically rigorous, but also of relevance to practitioners, there can be no justification for disregarding the basic principles of psychometrics that have formed the bedrock of our field. If research into the psychology of strategic management is to fulfil its ultimate potential, it is essential that the procedures employed for mapping strategic thought meet the same basic requirements of psychometric rigour applicable to any other method of psychological assessment (e.g. Kline, 1993; Nunnally, 1978).

Basic requirements for direct elicitation procedures

Drawing on the standards normally applied in the better established areas of I/O psychology, especially personnel selection and assessment (e.g. Cook, 1998) it seems reasonable to stipulate that in contexts where the intended application of cognitive mapping is to access the relatively enduring features of actors' strategic perceptions and beliefs, as a basic minimum requirement, the procedure(s) employed should exhibit acceptable test-retest reliability and construct validity. Where appropriate, as, for example, in the case of multi-item Likert scales, the procedures adopted should also exhibit acceptable levels of internal consistency, as measured by Cronbach's Alpha (Cronbach, 1951).

In cases where the intended application is largely practical in nature, for example in the context of interventions designed to facilitate strategy debates among the TMT with a view to challenging the assumptions of key decision makers (e.g. Eden & Ackermann, 1998a), arguably, it is still the case that the mapping procedures so employed should exhibit test-retest reliability, albeit over relatively shorter time periods. If the aim of such interventions is to act as a catalyst for cognitive change, ultimately we need to ensure that the changes resulting from such applications are in fact non-trivial, deeper-level changes concerning actors' enduring thoughts (cf. Daniels, de Chernatony & Johnson, 1995; Stubbart & Ramaprasad, 1990).

The recent studies of executive cognition by Sutcliffe and Huber (1998) and Chattopadhyay et al. (1999), discussed at length in the previous section, are exemplary in their attempts to meet the basic requirements of psycho-metric rigour stipulated above. In both cases, the researchers reported the results of factor analyses and the accompanying reliabilities (alphas) of the instruments employed to assess executive perceptions and beliefs. In the Chattopadhyay et al. study, interrater reliabilities (ICC(1,k), Shrout & Fleiss, 1979) were also reported for scales in those cases where the executives were treated as key informants, and for the coded measure of functional position, interrater reliability was assessed via Cohen's kappa (Cohen, 1960).

When assessed by these standards, basic requirements in virtually any other area of I/O psychology, many of the published studies in the psychology of strategic management fall a long way short of the mark. Virtually none of the numerous alternative procedures employed in the cognitive analysis of competitive structures, for example, have been subjected to any form of psychometric evaluation. A notable exception in this respect, however, is to be found in a recently reported study by Daniels, de Chernatony and Johnson (1995), in which participants' cognitions elicited by means of a visual card sort technique, devised by the authors, were compared to cognitions elicited by means of a repertory grid approach (Kelly, 1955; Fransella & Bannister, 1977). The aim of this study was to explore the extent to which the two methods were psychometrically comparable to one another, with a view to establishing the convergent validity of the techniques. The results indicated that the methods do in fact yield comparable findings, to the extent that Daniels and his associates suggested that when the degree of access to research participants, for example due to time constraints, poses a problem for researchers, the visual card sort technique, which is relatively quick to administer in comparison to the grid technique, may be used in isolation, with relatively little loss of information.

While such evidence of convergent validity represents a useful step forward, ultimately, studies are required which explore the extent to which actors' mental representations of competition, elicited through these and the many other cognitive mapping techniques employed in recent investigations, are correlated with exogenous variables of theoretical interest, such as the background characteristics of the participants, environmental scanning behaviours, and the strategic, structural and performance characteristics of the organization, in much the same way that scholars have, *inter alia*, begun exploring the correlates of executives' perceptions of the organization's strategic orientation (Knight et al., 1999), potential technological alliances (Tyler & Steensma, 1998) and the wider business environment (Sutcliffe, 1994; Sutcliffe & Huber, 1998) in an attempt to further understanding of cognitive processes in TMTs. In the absence of adequate empirical evidence that such meaningful relationships exist, the extent to which cognitive approaches for the assessment of competitive environments can significantly further understanding of intra- and interorganizational processes of strategy development is open to question (Ginsberg, 1994; Hodgkinson, 1997a).

However, virtually no studies, to date, have directly explored the correlates of actors' mental representations of competitive positioning strategies (though for notable exceptions see Bowman & Ambrosini, 1997a; Bowman & Johnson, 1992; Calori Johnson & Sarnin, 1994). As observed by Hodgkinson (1997a), this may be due partly to the fact that there is a dearth of techniques suitable for capturing key aspects of actors' mental representations in a form which will enable researchers to detect *systematically* individual and/or subgroup differences and explore the extent to which these differences are related to exogenous variables of theoretical interest, an issue to which we shall return shortly.

Basic requirements for the construction of maps from secondary sources

In cases where cognitive maps are inferred from secondary sources, such as interview transcripts or documentary evidence, it seems reasonable to propose that, as a basic minimum, the coding schemes employed should meet the dual requirements of acceptable test-retest and intercoder reliability and that, wherever possible, researchers should attempt to demonstrate the validity of maps derived in this way by correlating the various structural and content indices with key process and/or outcome variables. The degree of code-recode reliability ultimately has a bearing on the attainment or otherwise of acceptable levels of intercoder reliability. Hence, as noted by Huff and Fletcher (1990, p. 410) both of these forms of reliability are necessary prerequisites for a coding scheme to be deemed technically adequate. It is heartening, therefore, that the majority of researchers utilizing documentary and other secondary sources for the coding of causal cognitive maps routinely take steps to ensure that their coding schemes exhibit acceptable intercoder reliability. Typically, however, this merely takes the form of an analysis of the number of instances where two or more coders are in basic agreement with one another (i.e. percentage agreement) with regard to the assignment of the various elements of data to each of the predetermined categories within the coding scheme, and which parts of the various assertions coded contain the causal concept and the sign of the causal assertion (for representative examples, see Barr, 1998; Barr & Huff, 1997; Calori, Johnson & Sarnin, 1994; Jenkins & Johnson, 1997a,b). Unfortunately, code-recode reliability statistics for maps derived in this way are not routinely reported at the present time and, as with maps derived from direct elicitation techniques, it is rarely the case that researchers attempt any form of rigorous statistical validation. Future studies employing secondary data for mapping strategic thought should adopt more sophisticated procedures for the assessment of intercoder reliability, such as the procedures employed by Chattopadhyay et al. (1999) in order to establish intercoder reliabilities on scales for use with key informants, and should also seek to establish the code-recode reliabilities of the coding schemes so adopted.

A study conducted by Calori and his colleagues illustrates the potential to statistically validate maps derived from interview transcripts and other secondary sources. Calori, Johnson & Sarnin (1994) investigated the extent to which the degree of complexity associated with CEOs' cognitive maps of the structure and dynamics of their industries correlated with the scope of the organization in terms of the business portfolio of the firm (degree of focus vs diversity), its geographic scope, and the extent to which the firm had foreign links with parent organizations. Using analysis of covariance (ANCOVA), Calori and his colleagues were able to control for the effect of the variable length of their interviews on map complexity (operationalized in terms of comprehensiveness and connectedness). Partial support was obtained for the hypothesis that the complexity of CEOs' cognitive structures match the complexity of the environment. Unfortunately, however, only relatively modest amounts of variance were explained with relatively low levels of statistical significance. As the authors themselves acknowledge, this is probably due to the small size of the sample ($N = 26$ CEOs drawn from four industries, spanning two countries). Nevertheless, the findings of this study are sufficiently encouraging to warrant further testing on larger samples, incorporating additional control variables. Notwithstanding its sampling limitations, this study clearly demonstrates that research which is not only technically adequate, but also methodologically acceptable to top-level managers (in terms of securing their participation) is within our grasp.

The Comparison of Cognitive Maps

If the various theoretical developments outlined in the preceding sections of this chapter are to be tested with an acceptable degree of rigour, ultimately techniques are required that will enable quantitative, longitudinal comparisons of the cognitive maps of multiple informants from large numbers of organizations in a multilevel fashion. Within the current review period, several significant methodological advances have occurred which have increased our capabilities to conduct such investigations.

Techniques for the comparison of causal maps

Causal mapping techniques fall within a general class of procedures that Huff (1990, p. 16) has categorized as methods for revealing understanding of 'influence, causality and system dynamics'. In their most basic form, cause maps can be depicted graphically, using the medium of the influence diagram (Diffenbach, 1982). Using this approach, variables are depicted as nodes in a network, interconnected by a series of arrow-headed pathways, terminating in each case on the dependent variable(s). The simplest forms of the technique are restricted to a consideration of positive (increases in one variable cause corresponding increases in one or more other variables), negative (increases in one variable cause corresponding decreases in one or more other variables), and neutral (no causality implied) relationships. More sophisticated variants of the technique enable these relationships to be differentially weighted, on the basis of the participant's belief strength, for example, or on the degree of certainty/uncertainty surrounding each particular causal assertion.

Whilst relatively simple causal maps can be conveniently summarized in visual form, this medium is not so convenient in situations where the purpose is to investigate the properties of much larger maps or to compare maps across large numbers of participants and/or over several points in time. Under these circumstances, it is more appropriate to employ the various specialist coding procedures (e.g. Huff, Narapareddy & Fletcher, 1990; Wrightson, 1976) and numerical measures, based on the mathematics of graph theory (e.g. Axelrod, 1976; Langfield-Smith & Wirth, 1992), that have been derived for the qualitative and quantitative analysis of causal maps.

Unfortunately, the analysis of cause maps in general has been hampered by a lack of suitable computer software for assisting in this task. Within the past decade, however, several major software developments have occurred that, collectively, stand to enhance the comparative analysis of ideographic and nomothetic data within a causal mapping framework, in much the same way that Slater's *INGRID* package and related procedures (Shaw, 1981; Slater, 1976, 1977) represented a major step-change in the elicitation and analysis of repertory grids, some two to three decades earlier.

Firstly, Laukkanan (1994) has reported the development of *CMAP2*, a computer program designed for the comparative analysis of cause maps derived through interview transcripts and/or documentary sources. This program is described by its author as a non-commercial, database oriented PC program, designed specifically for use in settings where the input data take the form of natural communication and key parameters such as the number of concepts explored, the number of mapped relationships and indeed the number of participants must be flexible (Laukkanan, 1998, p. 189, note 2). In addition to modules for the inputting of raw data and the creation of a standard language vocabulary for coding the natural language expressions and achieving comparability over research participants, the program also contains a variety of tools for editing the input data and the generation of analysable databases. Key numerical outputs from the program include measures of the distances between the map systems of individual participants or clusters of participants. Two limitations of this system, however, as noted by Jenkins (1998), concern the fact that, thus far, there does not appear to have been any attempt to assess the reliability of the processes by which the input data are transformed into comparable units of analysis, and the focus of analysis is restricted to the level of concepts and their links across groups of informants, as opposed to a consideration of the individual and the context in which he or she uses particular concepts. A further limitation of Laukkanan's procedure, as acknowledged by the author himself, concerns the fact that the various outputs from the software, currently written in DOS mode, are not easily exported into better-developed user interface environments such as Windows, thus rendering problematic any supplementary analyses that the researcher may wish to perform, using standard software packages. Moreover, the absence of methods for direct raw data acquisition and input by the actors themselves, in conjunction with primary-level standardization facilities and opportunities for concurrent feedback, render the whole process extremely labour intensive on the part of the researcher.

The processing limitations of the Laukkanan software contrast sharply with Graphics *COPE*, the system developed several years earlier by Eden, and his colleagues for use in the context of group decision support (e.g. Ackermann, Eden & Cropper, 1990; Eden, Ackermann & Cropper, 1992). Recently re-launched as *Decision Explorer*, this program enables the graphical representation of maps as well as the calculation of a variety of quantitative indices of a structural nature, as discussed in Eden, Ackermann and Cropper (1992). Unlike CMAP2, Decision Explorer operates in a Windows environment, thus enabling material to be imported and exported to and from a number of other standard packages for the qualitative analysis of social science data, such as NUD.IST. As noted by Eden and Ackermann (1998b), these features of Decision Explorer render this software invaluable in the comparative analysis of ideographic causal maps.

In a third development, building on the earlier work of Langfield-Smith and Wirth (1992), Markoczy and Goldberg (1995, p. 30), have devised a systematic method for eliciting and comparing causal maps, involving five key stages, which obviates the need for subjective researcher judgement in making such comparisons (with all the attendant problems of test-retest and intercoder reliability, discussed above):

1. Develop a *pool of constructs* by conducting and analysing interviews with managers and a review of relevant literature. This is done prior to the study so that each subject selects constructs from the same pool.
2. Have each subject select a fixed number of constructs by identifying items from a constant pool of constructs.
3. Construct the *causal map* of each individual subject by having her/him assess the influence of each of her/his selected constructs on her/his other selected constructs.
4. Calculate *distance ratios* between causal maps using a generalized version of Langfield-Smith and Wirth's (1992) formula.
5. Perform a variety of statistical tests on the distance ratios to identify what *characteristics* account for similarities in thinking.

The distance ratios derived from this procedure can be meaningfully employed in order to investigate patterns of similarity and difference among subgroups of participants, in addition to conducting correlational analyses. In order to conduct such analyses, it is first necessary to empirically derive multiple clusters of participants using cluster analysis. Once the centre of each cluster so formed has been identified, distances between the centres and each individual map can be calculated. In turn, these distances form the basis for standard statistical analyses. Markoczy (1997) adopted this approach in her recent investigation of the validity of using external, individual characteristics as proxy variables for executive cognition, reviewed earlier (for additional applications see also Markoczy, 1995).

Goldberg (1996) has devised a set of computer programs, known collectively as *the distrat/askmap suite of programs,* which perform various of the tasks associated with the Markoczy–Goldberg approach. Although this collection of programs is available to researchers on a non-commercial basis, like the Laukkanan system, the various algorithms are not in a form that readily facilitates the transfer of input and output data to and from other systems, especially of the larger, fully integrated, interactive variety. Notwithstanding these software limitations, the Markoczy–Goldberg approach to comparative causal mapping represents a significant methodological breakthrough that stands to greatly enrich the quality of future investigations into the correlates of strategic cognition.

Finally, for the sake of completeness, it is also worth noting that Wang (1996) has proposed (and illustrated) the use of a neural network approach for the measurement of differences between causal cognitive maps.

Methods for comparing maps showing the relationships between concepts

Paralleling recent methodological developments in relation to causal mapping, there have also been several advances in the comparative analysis of 'maps that show dimensions of categories and cognitive taxonomies' (Huff, 1990, p. 15). Techniques for revealing this type of map, which include repertory grid techniques, multidimensional scaling procedures, hierarchical taxonomic mapping techniques and card-sort procedures, have formed the bedrock of research into managerial mental representations of competitive structures, as observed earlier. As noted above, there has been a dearth of procedures to enable the systematic comparison of maps generated by these largely ideographic approaches, thus rendering problematic any large-scale theory testing, using statistically robust methods of analysis. Within this review period, however, two developments have taken place in an attempt to help to rectify this state of affairs.

Rating techniques for the comparison of maps. Firstly, Daniels, Markoczy and de Chernatony (1994) have advocated a relatively simple approach for the comparison of maps in general that has applicability in this particular context. This entails knowledgeable judges, such as industry experts or the actual participants themselves, assessing the overall degree of similarity/dissimilarity between maps in a pairwise fashion using a numerical rating scale. Daniels, Johnson and de Chernatony (1994) employed a variant of this approach to the comparison of maps in their study of managerial mental representations of competition, reviewed earlier.

In this study the participants were required to compare the overall degree of similarity of a series of maps (including their own) to their personal 'mental model' that prevailed at the time of the rating exercise, using a single-item, five-point Likert scale devised for this purpose. A comparison of the ratings (averaged over the three types of mapping procedure employed: visual card-sort maps, cluster analysis-derived repertory grid maps and principal components-derived repertory grid maps) on the basis of who the maps belonged to, using a repeated measures analysis of variance (ANOVA), revealed a systematic pattern, the overall degree of similarity decreasing monotonically as a function of the social distance between the rater and the target individual. As expected, participants rated their own maps as most similar to their own mental models.

Although it is highly attractive in terms of the apparent ease with which such ratings can be obtained, there are several potential problems associated with this approach. Studies of the cognitive processes underpinning similarities judgements (reviewed in Farjoun & Lai, 1997) have revealed that when individuals are required to evaluate conceptual stimuli in this way, often the judgements are flawed. Similarity judgements have been found to be both context sensitive and asymmetric, for example, and when faced with numerous complex judgements, individuals tend to use heuristics in order to simplify the processing of information (e.g. Tversky, 1977; Tversky & Gati, 1978). Hence, individuals required to evaluate the overall (dis)similarity of cognitive maps using the rating procedure advocated by Daniels and his associates are likely to vary in terms of which particular features of the maps they attend to and the weighting they give to common features. Moreover, in cases where the same individual is required to perform multiple comparisons, it is highly likely that they will attend to different features and/or adjust the weightings they give to common features as they switch from one pair of maps to another. As acknowledged by Daniels, Markoczy and de Chernatony (1994, p. 155), the number of pairwise comparisons required increases dramatically as a function of the number of maps involved, thus giving rise to the possibility of rater fatigue or boredom. In summary, it is highly likely that map comparisons derived in this way are prone to cognitive bias, resulting in problems of low test-retest and interrater reliability, especially in cases where large numbers of comparisons are involved.

Three-way scaling procedures for the comparison of dimensional maps. Ultimately, if cognitive maps are to be compared systematically, as noted by Markoczy and Goldberg (1995), the maps to be subjected to the comparison process also need to be elicited on a systematic basis. In a development paralleling the Markoczy–Goldberg advance in the systematic elicitation and comparison of causal maps, Hodgkinson (1997b) devised a procedure for systematically eliciting and comparing dimensional representations of competitor categories in his longitudinal study of the UK residential estate agency industry. This procedure utilizes a 'three-way scaling' (Arabie, Carroll & DeSarbo, 1987) approach in order to compare maps elicited via a modified repertory grid technique. In this system, which entails a substantial departure from Kelly's (1955) personal construct theory, both the competition categories and the constructs are supplied by the researcher, on the basis of a careful preliminary investigation involving the use of industry insiders and the consultation of relevant documentary sources, in order to ensure comprehensiveness, in terms of the coverage of the domain to be mapped, and that the rating tasks are meaningful to the individual participants (cf. Markoczy & Goldberg, 1995). The elements comprise a personalized list of named competitors, elicited in response to the various category titles, each depicting a different type of competitor. Participants are required to evaluate in turn each of the competitors contained within their individual, personalized lists (including their own firm) using the various bipolar rating scales (constructs) supplied by the researcher on the basis of the preliminary industry study. Using a procedure for the analysis of 'profile proximities' as set out in Kruskal and Wish (1978, pp. 70–73), the data derived from this approach to the elicitation of competitor assessments can be formed into a series of Euclidean distance matrices, which in turn form the basis of a three-way scaling exercise.

Adopting this approach, Hodgkinson (1997b) found that a two-dimensional group space configuration ('quality' $\times$ 'market power') meaningfully represented the aggregated judgements of $N = 206$ participants from $N = 58$ organizations in relation to 20 competitor categories across 21 bipolar rating scales. A follow-up investigation of a subsample of $n = 114$ of the original participants from $n = 41$ of the organizations concerned, some 12–18 months later, revealed that neither the group space configuration, nor the 'source weight' (Arabie, Carroll & DeSarbo, 1987) vectors, reflecting individual differences in the relative salience of the underlying dimensions of the group space configuration, differed significantly, despite a highly significant downturn in the domestic housing market from T1 to T2. Hodgkinson interpreted these findings as offering strong support for the cognitive inertia hypothesis, that is the notion that once formed, actors' assessments of competitors become highly resistant to change, often to the detriment of the individuals and organizations concerned (see also Reger & Palmer, 1996).

With a little imagination on the part of future researchers, this procedure could easily be adapted in order to facilitate the rigorous investigation of actors' mental representations of a range of strategic issues and problems. As with the Markoczy–Goldberg procedure for eliciting and comparing causal maps, the fact that participants' judgements are elicited on a systematic basis, the stimuli to be rated and the bipolar rating scales forming the bases of the judgements both being presented in a common language format, greatly facilitates the analysis of the resulting maps, obviating the need for cumbersome, post hoc coding procedures.

However, it should also be noted that the use of MDS techniques in this fashion also has its limitations. Tversky (1977) has demonstrated that similarity evaluations of many conceptual stimuli are better represented using non-spatial modelling techniques, based on an alternative to the basic Euclidean distance model, known as the *contrast model*, in which similarity judgements are modelled as a linear combination of common and distinctive features (see also Tversky & Hutchinson, 1986). For this reason, Farjoun and Lai (1997) have called on strategy researchers to extend their repertoire of mapping procedures to include methods predicated on feature-based models of similarity judgement in an effort to further refine understanding of strategists' conceptual structures. Two such procedures that meet this requirement are ADDTREE (Sattath & Tversky, 1977) and EXTREE (Corter & Tversky, 1986) as recently employed in conjunction with MDS techniques by Hodgkinson and his colleagues in several studies of consumers' mental representations of competitive structures (Hodgkinson, Padmore & Tomes, 1991; Hodgkinson, Tomes & Padmore, 1996). Clearly, the use of ADDTREE and EXTREE could readily be extended to an analysis of managers' (and other organizational actors') mental representations in future work.

Summary and Conclusions

The rigorous testing of the many theoretical developments currently taking place within the psychology of strategic management is being hampered by a lack of procedures suitable for the mass assessment of managerial and organizational cognition. Few of the techniques presently available for mapping strategic thought yield data in a form amenable to large-scale, multilevel hypothesis testing of the sort required to enable research within this topic area to progress to levels of maturity that would be comparable to those of the better-established subfields of I/O psychology. All too often, researchers have employed cognitive mapping procedures that have yet to be screened in terms of their basic psychometric efficacy and/or which yield data in a form unsuitable for the comparison of large numbers of maps on a systematic basis. Fortunately, however, within the current review period, a number of developments have occurred which, over the longer term, should help to rectify this state of affairs.

PSYCHOLOGICAL INTERVENTIONS

From a prescriptive point of view, the ultimate goal of research into the psychology of strategic management is to enhance organizational effectiveness, through the development and evaluation of intervention techniques (based on sound psychological principles) in order to facilitate processes of strategy formulation and implementation. One way in which I/O psychologists might assist with this endeavour is through the design and evaluation of procedures to enable individuals and groups to overcome a variety of limitations of a cognitive nature that might otherwise impede organizational learning and strategic renewal. Two problems in particular, which potentially could be ameliorated through such interventions, are cognitive bias and cognitive inertia.

Behavioural decision researchers (e.g. Tversky & Kahneman, 1974) have amassed a considerable volume of evidence which suggests that, in order to render the world manageable, decision-makers employ a variety of heuristics (or 'rules-of-thumb'). Whilst these heuristics enable decision-makers to cope with a complex and uncertain world by making a number of simplifying assumptions that reduce the burden of information processing that would otherwise ensue, an unfortunate, latent consequence is that they can give rise to a variety of cognitive biases which in turn may result in inappropriate/suboptimal decisions (for details see Bazerman, 1998; Goodwin & Wright, 1998). A growing body of theory and research within the strategy field—reviewed in Schwenk (1995) and Das and Teng (1999)—indicates that a number of the cognitive biases identified by behavioural decision researchers, primarily in the context of laboratory investigations, are also evident within strategy-making processes in organizational field settings. To the extent that this is the case, intervention techniques are required that will enable strategists to question their underlying assumptions with a view to de-biasing their judgements. Moreover, in so far as current functional responsibility and functional background determine the structure and content of actors' mental models of strategic decision problems, it is essential that these models are challenged from time to time, through processes of debate and dialogue, involving individuals drawn from a diverse range of functional areas and organizational levels.

Cognitive inertia, the tendency for changes in actors' mental models to lag significantly behind important changes in the business environment, has been identified by a number of scholars as a major barrier to organizational learning and strategic renewal, which, left unchecked, in the final analysis may threaten the adaptive capabilities of a firm, or entire subpopulations of firms, to the point of extinction (see, for example, Abrahamson & Fombrun, 1994; Barr & Huff, 1997; Barr, Stimpert & Huff, 1992; Hodgkinson, 1997b; Huff, Huff & Thomas, 1992; Porac & Thomas, 1990; Reger & Palmer, 1996). The implications of this work, as with the work on heuristics and biases in strategic decision-making, are that intervention techniques are required that challenge strategists to question their fundamental operating assumptions, with a view to attaining the requisite variety in mental models necessary in order to anticipate the future and develop a strategically responsive organization.

Causal Mapping Techniques for Overcoming the Effects of Cognitive Bias and Cognitive Inertia

One way in which cognitive bias and cognitive inertia might be minimized in the context of strategic decision-making is through the use of cognitive mapping techniques. *A priori*, causal mapping techniques, which require the decision-maker to consider the current situation in relation to past events and future consequences, would appear to be particularly suitable for this purpose. Causal mapping techniques and related procedures are increasingly being used as a tool of intervention for facilitating strategy development in both private and public sector organizations (Eden, 1993; Eden & Ackermann, 1998a, 2000; Morecroft, 1994). However, to date, there have been virtually no studies to demonstrate their efficacy for use in this context. To the extent that cognitive biases of the sort identified by behavioural decision researchers, under laboratory conditions, can be attenuated by recourse to causal mapping, this would provide tangible evidence that potentially there are indeed positive benefits to be gained from the use of these techniques in such practical settings.

Following this line of reasoning, Hodgkinson et al. (1999) have recently investigated the efficacy of causal cognitive mapping as a basis for attenuating the framing bias, a factor known to reduce the quality of decision-making in a broad range of situations, and which previous studies have implicated as a contributor to the well-documented escalation of commitment phenomenon in the context of strategic reinvestment decisions (Bateman & Zeithaml, 1989). This bias arises when trivial changes to the way in which a decision problem is presented, emphasizing either the potential gains or potential losses, lead to reversals of preference, with decision-makers being risk averse when gains are highlighted and risk seeking when losses are highlighted (Kahneman & Tversky, 1984). To overcome this bias decision-makers are encouraged to adopt procedures 'that will transform equivalent versions of any problem into the same canonical representation' (Kahneman & Tversky, 1984, p. 344) in order to bring about the normatively desirable state of affairs whereby individuals' preferences conform to the basic axioms of rational choice. In other words, decision-makers need to develop more elaborate models of problems, taking into account both the potential gains and losses involved, to ensure that trivial features of the decision context do not unduly influence choice behaviour.

Hodgkinson et al. (1999) conducted two studies, using elaborated decision scenarios under relatively controlled, experimental conditions. In study 1, final year undergraduate students of management studies were allocated at random to one of four treatment groups: positively vs negatively framed decision scenarios, with pre-choice vs post-choice mapping task orders. As predicted, participants allocated to the post-choice mapping conditions succumbed to the framing bias, whereas those allocated to the pre-choice mapping conditions did not. Study 2 replicated and extended these findings in an organizational field setting, on a sample of senior managers, using a decision scenario that closely mirrored a strategic dilemma confronting the organization in question, at the time of the investigation.

As with any new line of inquiry, the findings of these studies raise more questions than they resolve. What is the underlying mechanism by which this particular intervention attenuates the framing bias? To what extent do causal mapping procedures, in this prescriptive context, represent an advance over other intervention techniques involving effortful thought, which are also known to attenuate the framing bias, such as the frame analysis worksheet (Russo & Schoemaker, 1989) or merely requiring individuals to account for their decision choices (Sieck & Yates, 1997)? Doubtless more sophisticated research designs are required, involving the use of control groups and the direct comparison of multiple interventions one with another, before the value-added contribution of cognitive mapping procedures *per se* can be truly ascertained. Additional studies are required, not only to address these fundamental concerns, but also to determine the extent to which causal mapping techniques will enable strategic decision-makers to overcome other cognitive biases identified by behavioural decision researchers (Tversky & Kahneman, 1974) and strategy scholars (e.g. Bateman & Zeithaml, 1989; Bukszar & Connolly, 1988; Das & Teng, 1999; Lant, Milliken & Batra, 1992; Schwenk, 1995; Wagner & Gooding, 1997). In sum, the studies reported by Hodgkinson and his colleagues represent but the vital first steps in attempting to demonstrate the practical benefits to be gained from the use of cognitive mapping as a basis for intervening in processes of strategic decision-making.

Scenario Techniques for Overcoming Cognitive Bias and Cognitive Inertia

Another technique that has been advocated as a means for overcoming the potentially deleterious consequences of cognitive bias and cognitive inertia is the method of scenario planning (e.g. Fahay & Randall, 1998; Goodwin & Wright, in press; Grinyer, 2000; van der Heijden, 1996; Schoemaker, 1995; Wright & Goodwin, 1999). While there are a variety of approaches in the literature that may be grouped under the umbrella of 'scenarios', nevertheless, there are several discernible key features common to each which render this technique in general potentially useful as a basis for facilitating organizational learning and strategic renewal:

- A systematic yet highly flexible approach.
- Highly participative, involving extensive data gathering and reflection, both at an individual and a collective level.
- Scenario planning techniques force strategists to explicitly confront the changing world and consider its implications for the current strategy.
- Not an attempt to predict the future. Rather, scenario-planning techniques involve the use of speculation and human judgement in an attempt to gain fresh insights and 'bound' future uncertainties.

In contrast to traditional strategic planning techniques, which seek to forecast the future in probabilistic terms in an attempt to plan for a predetermined future, scenario planning techniques seek to develop a series of stylized portraits of the future, which capture what may or may not happen, thereby providing a basis for developing a strategy for dealing with the various contingencies so identified, thus directly incorporating uncertainty within the analysis (van der Heijden, 1994). According to van der Heijden (1996, p. 41) the benefits stemming from the application of scenario methods are two-fold:

- In the shorter term, increased adaptability by more skilful observation of the business environment.
- In the longer term, development of a more robust organizational system, better able to withstand the unexpected shocks that will come its way.

Using *Decision Explorer*, the specialist group decision support software for cognitive mapping reviewed earlier, Eden and colleagues (e.g. Eden & Ackermann, 1998a; van der Heijden, 1996) have developed a variety of cognitive mapping approaches which can be readily incorporated within the scenario planning process, as a basis for eliciting in systematic and structured ways managers' views of the future. The object of such an exercise is to help individuals and teams to share and reconcile multiple ideas about the future environment (Eden & van der Heijden, 1995).

Scenario planning is not without its critics, however. Two problems in particular have been highlighted which the would-be user of scenarios would be well advised to consider. First, the technique is a practitioner-derived method with very little supporting evidence, other than basic anecdotal evidence, for its efficacy (though for a notable exception in this respect see Schoemaker, 1993). Secondly, as noted by Mintzberg (1994), accounts of the use of scenarios in the (limited) extant literature have been restricted to 'success stories', such as Pierre Wack's highly acclaimed account of scenario planning in the Royal Dutch Shell organization (Wack, 1985a,b), which enabled the company to anticipate the dramatic shift in the world market for petroleum that occurred in 1973. One of the dangers of this approach is that it may not always be possible to identify viable alternatives to the present course of action, even in circumstances where major strategic change is clearly warranted, thereby compounding the difficulties confronting the organization (Hodgkinson & Wright, 1997).

Summary and Conclusions

This section has briefly considered the nature and role of causal mapping and scenario techniques as methods of psychological intervention for use in strategy-making processes. The ultimate purpose of such interventions in this context is to challenge the otherwise taken for granted beliefs and assumptions of key decision-makers, with a view to overcoming a number of fundamental limitations of human information processing identified by behavioural decision researchers, cognitive psychologists and strategy scholars. Given the widespread popularity of scenario and causal mapping techniques as methods of intervention, it is a matter of great concern that virtually no attempts have been made to rigorously evaluate the efficacy of either of these closely related procedures for use in this prescriptive fashion.

CONCLUSIONS AND FUTURE DIRECTIONS

This chapter has comprehensively surveyed a number of key developments that have taken place in the psychology of strategic management over the past decade or so, concentrating primarily on advances that have occurred within the period following the publication of Sparrow's (1994) *IRIOP* chapter, which previously addressed this topic. The overwhelming conclusion to be drawn from the present review is that although considerable progress has been achieved over a relatively short time period, there is still a long way to go before research on this topic matures to levels comparable with the better-established subfields of I/O psychology. As with any newly emerging topic area, until relatively recently studies investigating psychological issues in strategic management have, for the most part, been relatively small in scale and scope, being conducted largely on an exploratory basis.

There are, however, encouraging signs that research in this topic area is entering a new phase in its development. A number of recent methodological advances in the quantitative assessment of managerial and organizational cognition have created the potential for larger-scale theory testing, using longitudinal research designs of a form that will permit researchers to systematically disentangle cause–effect relationships. Suitably adapted, there is no reason why techniques for systematically eliciting and comparing actors' mental representations should not be used in conjunction with LISREL or the other structural equation modelling procedures now commonplace within the better-established subfields of I/O psychology (James & James, 1989; Kelloway, 1996). These procedures, and related techniques for the modelling of multilevel datasets (e.g. Bryk & Raudenbush, 1992; Goldstein, 1995), are ideally suited for rigorously testing the various socio-cognitive explanations for the emergence of competitive industry structures reviewed at the outset of this chapter. As we have seen, researchers are now beginning to employ LISREL and associated multiple regression techniques in an effort to further understanding of the causal antecedents and consequences of executive cognition in TMTs. The recent advances that have occurred in multilevel modelling over recent years could be fruitfully exploited in this context also.

Previous studies investigating the correlates of executive cognition have focused almost exclusively on the external characteristics of the individuals concerned, such as age and educational and functional background. There are encouraging signs, however, that this work is approaching new levels of sophistication, with recent studies incorporating a range of measures to control for key characteristics of the organization and its environment. While these developments are to be welcomed, there is a compelling need to balance the incorporation of such contextual features in the modelling process with a consideration of a number of psychological variables that might also mediate and/or moderate executive cognition. One such variable that might be incorporated in future studies is 'propensity to innovate', a factor which has been demonstrated to correlate with team composition and a variety of process variables and outcome measures of innovation in a recent study of TMTs in UK healthcare settings by West and Anderson (1996). Two other variables that might be usefully incorporated in future work are locus of control (Hodgkinson, 1992, 1993; Rotter, 1966) and cognitive style (Allinson & Hayes, 1996; Streufert & Nogami, 1989). There is a substantial literature (reviewed in Finkelstein & Hambrick, 1996; and Hayes & Allinson, 1998) to suggest that both of these variables will predict significant differences in the complexity levels of individuals' mental representations of strategic issues and problems. Consequently, either or both of these variables might account for some of the discrepancies arising in recent studies seeking to identify the correlates of executive cognition.

From a prescriptive standpoint, the extent to which greater levels of complexity in the mental models of executives facilitates or inhibits the longer-term performance of the wider organization is an entirely different matter, which also warrants significant research attention. Arguably, greater levels of complexity, particularly when distributed amongst several members of the executive team, may foster creativity and innovation while minimizing the dangers of group level myopia and cognitive inertia. On the other hand, overly complex mental representations of the organization and its environment may inhibit successful adaptation. Calori, Johnson and Sarnin (1994) were careful not to suggest that cognitive maps characterized by greater levels of complexity would automatically lead CEOs to superior performance, arguing that CEOs' cognitive complexity levels should match the complexity levels of the environment. More recent work by Wells and Bantel (2000), which has considered this issue at the team level, suggests that the attainment of high levels of team-level cognitive complexity is a fundamental prerequisite for competitive success among companies operating in environments characterized by complexity, scarcity, and unpredictable change. The extent to which the tentative findings emerging from this research, based on a limited number of interviews with key individuals from just five organizations, and the earlier study by Calori and his colleagues, generalize to other organizations and industry settings needs to be rigorously evaluated through a series of larger-scale investigations. To the extent that the findings of these preliminary studies are confirmed, this would clearly have important implications for the selection and development of executive teams, not least the need to ensure that such teams are well-balanced in terms of their membership, so as to ensure optimum levels of cognitive complexity (both with respect to cognitive differentiation and cognitive integration) at the team level. The extent to which greater complexity in strategic thinking can be systematically developed at the individual and/or team level through the use of cognitive mapping procedures and related techniques such as scenarios is another issue that warrants urgent attention.

In the absence of rigorous research evidence in respect of these issues, it is difficult to specify at the present time the extent to which it is desirable for organizations to select for, and/or develop, this particular attribute in CEOs and senior managers more generally, or indeed how such selection and/or development might best be accomplished. Given the current state of knowledge in respect of these vitally important issues, perhaps it is little wonder that senior managers tend to view our profession as a purely operational-level, technical activity and that I/O psychologists are not routinely included in strategic level decision-making (Anderson, 1998).

Finally, as noted by Daniels (1998, 1999), the recent upsurge of interest in cognitive processes in strategic management has neglected to consider the potential impact of emotions on strategic cognition (see also Langley, Mintzberg, Pitcher et al., 1995; and Walsh, 1995). Since a number of studies in laboratory (e.g. Dalgleish & Watts, 1990; MacCleod, 1991; Matt, Vazquez & Campbell, 1992) and organizational field settings (e.g. Burke, Brief & George, 1993; Spector & O'Connell, 1994; Williams, Gavin & Williams, 1996) have demonstrated significant linkages between affect and cognition, it follows that, potentially, affective processes could account for much of the variance in actors' strategic perceptions and beliefs. On the basis of this reasoning, Daniels (1998) has conducted an exploratory investigation of the relationships between trait negative affectivity and perceptions of the strategic environment, as assessed by means of a series of Likert scale items designed to tap the perceived performance, growth, complexity and competitiveness of participants' organizations relative to industry norms. The results of this study, based on two samples, suggest that this is a fruitful line of investigation worthy of longer-term follow-up, with several of the relationships tested yielding highly significant correlations, even after controlling for other variables such as age, gender, number of organizational levels from the CEO, tenure in current position and organizational size. These findings are sufficiently strong to suggest that future studies of cognitive processes in executive teams, along the lines of those conducted by Sutcliffe and Huber (1998) and Chattopadhyay et al. (1999), would benefit from the incorporation of this variable, as would studies seeking to elucidate the antecedents of actors' mental representations of competition. Meanwhile, in a separate development, Elsbach and Barr (1999) have begun investigating the effects of mood on the use of structured decision protocols under laboratory conditions. Their findings suggest that in situations where the use of such protocols is the usual method adopted, individuals in moderately negative, as opposed to moderately positive mood states, are more likely to carefully execute all the steps of the protocol, in the correct sequence, and rely on the outcome of the protocol as the primary basis for their decision. As demonstrated by the more recent work of Finucane, Alhakami, Slovic and Johnson (2000), in the final analysis, judgements of the risks and benefits associated with particular hazards may ultim ately be determined by the operation of an 'affect heuristic'. Hence, the incorporation of affective variables in future studies of strategic decision processes may not only enhance understanding of strategic management, but also clarify our understanding of the role of affect in judgement and decision-making more generally.

These are highly exciting times to be working in the field of strategic management. In the world of business, a number of major problems are currently unfolding that defy simplistic analysis from the perspective of any one base discipline of the social sciences, but which provide a rich opportunity for I/O psychologists to make a major contribution, both at the level of theory-building and, more particularly, in terms of the development and application of rigorous research methods. Here, there is a rare opportunity indeed for I/O psychologists to contribute to the generation of new knowledge of a form that will have an impact on organizations at the very highest levels, while breaking the vicious cycle of non-involvement in strategic/organizational decision-making that for too long has undermined our professional standing in the eyes of top management.

NOTES

1. Although the analytical approach adopted by Levenhagen and his associates is that of a lifecycle, it should be noted that these authors are at pains to point out that their framework is intended merely as a 'pedagogical device', i.e. 'No linear, lock-step, sequential set of events is implied. Such an approach would be a contradiction of the basic theoretical stand taken by social constructionists that cognitive and transactional events interact continually with one another' (Levenhagen, Porac & Thomas, 1993, p. 76).
2. Meanwhile, Dandrove, Peteraf and Shanley (1998) have outlined an alternative framework based on the 'new economics of industrial organization', which accommodates behavioural and economic factors, in an effort to better model the relationship between structure, conduct and performance. Within this framework, although strategic interactions are viewed as critical for a group level effect on profits, mobility barriers are necessary for the preservation of groups and their effects over time. For the sake of completeness, it is also worth noting that Rindova and Fombrun (1999) have recently advanced a new theoretical framework, which combines this general stream of literature on socio-cognitive aspects of competition with the resource-based theory of the firm and a number of other perspectives, in an attempt to better account for the social construction of *competitive advantage*.

REFERENCES

Abell, D. F. (1980). *Defining the Business: A Starting Point for Strategic Planning.* Englewood Cliffs, NJ: Prentice-Hall.

Abrahamson, E. & Fombrun, C. J. (1994). Macrocultures: determinants and consequences. Academy of Management Review, 19, 728–755.

Ackermann, F., Eden, C. & Cropper, S. (1990). Cognitive Mapping: A User's Guide. Working Paper No. 12, Department of Management Science, University of Strathclyde, UK.

Aldrich, H. (1999). Organizations Evolving. London: Sage.

Allinson, C. W. & Hayes, J. (1996). The cognitive style index: a measure of intuition-analysis for organizational research. Journal of Management Studies, 33, 119–135.

Anderson, N. (1998). The practitioner–researcher divide in work and organizational psychology. The Occupational Psychologist, no. 34, 7–16.

Arabie, P., Carroll, J. D. & DeSarbo, W. S. (1987). Three-Way Scaling and Clustering. Sage University Paper Series on Quantitative Applications in the Social Sciences, 07–065. London: Sage.

Araujo, L. (1998). Knowing and learning as networking. Management Learning, 29, 317–336.

Ashforth, B. & Mael, F. (1989). Social identity theory and the organization. Academy of Management Review, 14, 20–39.

Axelrod, R. M. (1976). The mathematics of cognitive maps. In R. M. Axelrod (Ed.), Structure of Decision: The Cognitive Maps of Political Elites (pp. 343–348). Princeton, NJ: Princeton University Press.

Bain, J. S. (1956). Barriers to New Competition. Cambridge, MA: Harvard University Press.

Bandura, A. (1986). Social Foundations of Thought and Action. Englewood Cliffs, NJ: Prentice-Hall.

Bantel, K. & Jackson, S. E. (1989). Top management and innovation in banking. Does the composition of top teams make a difference? Strategic Management Journal, 10, 107–124.

Barney, J. B. & Hoskisson, R. E. (1990). Strategic groups: Untested assertions and research proposals. Managerial and Decision Economics, 11, 187–198.

Barr, P. S. (1998). Adapting to unfamiliar environmental events: A look at the evolution of interpretation and its role in strategic change. Organization Science, 9, 644–669.

Barr, P. S. & Huff, A. S. (1997). Seeing isn't believing: Understanding diversity in the timing of strategic response. Journal of Management Studies, 34, 337–370.

Barr, P. S., Stimpert, J. L. and Huff, A. S. (1992). Cognitive change, strategic action, and organizational renewal. Strategic Management Journal, 13, 15–36.

Bateman T. S. and Zeithaml, C. P. (1989). The psychological context of strategic decisions: A model and convergent experimental findings. Strategic Management Journal, 10, 59–74.

Bazerman, M. H. (1998). Judgment in Managerial Decision Making, 4th edn. New York: Wiley.

Berger, P. L. & Luckmann, T. (1967). The Social Construction of Reality.Harmondsworth: Penguin.

Beyer, J., Chattopadhyay, P., George, E., Glick, W. H., ogilvie, d. & Pugliese, D. (1997). The selective perception of managers revisited. Academy of Management Journal, 40, 716–737.

Bogner, W. C. & Thomas, H. (1993). The role of competitive groups in strategy formulation: A dynamic integration of two competing models. Journal of Management Studies, 30, 51–67.

Borgatti, S. P., Everett, M. G. & Freeman, L. C. (1992). UCINET IV Version 1.0. Columbia: Analytic Technologies.

Bowman, C. & Ambrosini, V. (1997a). Perceptions of strategic priorities, consensus and firm performance. Journal of Management Studies, 34, 241–258.

Bowman, C. and Ambrosini, V. (1997b). Using single respondents in strategy research. *British Journal of Management*, **8**, 119–131.

Bowman, C. & Daniels, K. (1995). The influence of functional experience on perception of strategic priorities. *British Journal of Management* , **6**, 157–167.

Bowman, C. and Johnson, G. (1992). Surfacing competitive strategies. *European Management Journal*, **10**, 210–219.

Bryk, A. S. & Raudenbush, S. W. (1992). *Hierarchical Linear Models: Applications and Data Analysis Methods*. Newbury Park, CA: Sage.

Bukszar, E. & Connolly, T. (1988). Hindsight bias and strategic choice: Some problems in learning from experience. *Academy of Management Journal*, **31**, 628–641.

Burke, M. J. A., Brief, A. P. & George, J. M. (1993). The role of negative affectivity in understanding relations between self-reports of stressors and strains: A comment on the applied psychology literature. *Journal of Applied Psychology*, **78**, 402–412.

Byrne, D. (1971). *The Attraction Paradigm*. New York: Academic Press.

Calori, R., Johnson, G. & Sarnin, P. (1992). French and British top managers' understanding of the structure and dynamics of their industries: A cognitive analysis and comparison. *British Journal of Management*, **3**, 61–78.

Calori, R., Johnson, G. & Sarnin, P. (1994). CEOs' cognitive maps and the scope of the organization. *Strategic Management Journal*, **15**, 437–457.

Caves, R. E. & Porter, M. E. (1977). From entry barriers to mobility barriers: Conjectural decisions and contrived deterrence to new competition. *Quarterly Journal of Economics*, **91**, 421–434.

Chattopadhyay, P., Glick, W. H., Miller, C. C. & Huber, G. P. (1999). Determinants of executive beliefs: Comparing functional conditioning and social influence. *Strategic Management Journal*, **20**, 763–789.

Clark, B. H. & Montgomery, D. B. (1999). Managerial identification of competitors. *Journal of Marketing*, **63**, 67–83.

Cohen, J. (1960). A coefficient of agreement for nominal scales. *Educational and Psychological Measurement*, **20**, 31–46.

Cook, M. (1998). *Personnel Selection: Adding Value Through People*, 3rd edn. Chichester: Wiley.

Corter, J. E. & Tversky, A. (1986). Extended similarity trees. *Psychometrika*. **51**, 429–451.

Cronbach, L. J. (1951). Coefficient Alpha and the internal structure of tests. *Psychometrika*. **16**, 297–334.

Daboub, A. L, Rasheed, A. M. A., Priem, R. L. & Gray, D. A. (1995). Top management team characteristics and corporate illegal activity. *Academy of Management Review*, **20**, 138–170.

Dalgleish, T. & Watts, F. N. (1990). Biases of attention and memory in disorders of anxiety and depression. *Clinical Psychology Review*, **10**, 589–604.

Dandrove, D., Peteraf, M. & Shanley, M. (1998). Do Strategic Groups exist? An economic framework for analysis. *Strategic Management Journal*, **19**, 1029–1044.

Daniels, K. (1998). Towards integrating emotions into strategic management research: Trait affect and perceptions of the strategic environment. *British Journal of Management*, **9**, 163–168.

Daniels, K. (1999). Affect and strategic decision making. *The Psychologist*, **12**, 24–28.

Daniels, K., de Chernatony, L. & Johnson, G. (1995). Validating a method for mapping managers' mental models of competitive industry structures. *Human Relations*, **48**, 975–991.

Daniels, K., Johnson, G. and de Chernatony, L. (1994). Differences in managerial cognitions of competition'. *British Journal of Management*. **5**, S21–S29.

Daniels, K., Markoczy, L., & de Chernatony, L. (1994). Techniques to compare cognitive maps. *Advances in Managerial Cognition and Human Information Processing*, **5**, 141–164.

Das, T. K. & Teng, B.-S. (1999). Cognitive biases and strategic decision processes. *Journal of Management Studies*, **36**, 757–778.

D'Avini, R. A. (1990). Top managerial prestige and organizational bankruptcy. *Organization Science*, **1**, 121–142.

Day, G. S., Shocker, A. D. & Shrivistava, R. K. (1979). Customer-oriented approaches to identifying product markets. *Journal of Marketing*, **43**, 8–19.

Dearborn, D. C. & Simon, H. A. (1958). Selective perception: A note on the departmental identification of executives. *Sociometry*, **21**, 140–144.

de Chernatony, L., Daniels, K. & Johnson, G. (1993). A cognitive perspective on managers' perceptions of competition. *Journal of Marketing Management*, **9**, 373–381.

Dess, G. G. & Davis, P. S. (1984). Porter's (1980) generic strategies as determinants of strategic group membership and organizational performance. *Academy of Management Journal*, **27**, 467–488.

Diffenbach, J. (1982). Influence diagrams for complex strategic issues, *Strategic Management* Journal, **3**, 133–146.

DiMaggio, P. J. & Powell, W. W. (1983). The iron cage revisited: Institutional isomorphism and collective rationality in organizational fields. *American Sociological Review*, **48**, 147–160.

Eden, C. (Ed.) (1992). On the nature of cognitive maps. *Journal of Management Studies*, **29** (Special Issue), 261–389.

Eden, C. (1993). Strategy development and implementation: Cognitive mapping for group support. In J. Hendry, & G. Johnson with J. Newton (Eds), *Strategic Thinking: Leadership and the Management of Change* (pp. 115–136). Chichester: Wiley.

Eden, C. & Ackermann, F. (1998a). *Making Strategy: The Journey of Strategic Management*. London: Sage.

Eden, C. & Ackermann, F. (1998b). Analysing and comparing ideographic causal maps. In C. Eden & J.-C. Spender (Eds), *Managerial and Organizational Cognition: Theory, Methods and Research* (pp. 192–209). London: Sage.

Eden, C. & Ackermann, F. (2000). Mapping distinctive competencies: A systematic approach. *Journal of the Operational Research Society*, **51**, 12–20.

Eden, C., Ackermann, F. & Cropper, S. (1992). The analysis of cause maps. *Journal of Management Studies*, **29**, 309–324.

Eden, C. & van der Heijden, K. (1995). Detecting emergent strategy. In H. Thomas & D. O'Neil (Eds), *Strategic Renaissance and Business Transformation* (pp. 331–347). Chichester: Wiley.

Eden, C. & J.-C. Spender (Eds) (1998). *Managerial and Organizational Cognition: Theory, Methods and Research*. London: Sage.

Elsbach, K. D. & Barr, P. S. (1999). The effects of mood on individuals' use of structured decision protocols. *Organization Science*, **10**, 181–198.

Fahay, L. & Randall, R. M. (Eds) (1998). *Learning from the Future: Competitive Foresight Scenarios*. New York: Wiley.

Farjoun, M. & Lai, L. (1997). Similarity judgments in strategy formulation: Role, process and implications. *Strategic Management Journal*, **18**, 255–273.

Finkelstein, S. & Hambrick, D. C. (1996). *Strategic Leadership: Top Executives and Their Effects on Organizations*. St Paul, MN: West.

Finucane, M. L., Alhakami, A., Slovic, P. & Johnson, S. (2000). The affect heuristic in judgments of risks and benefits. *Journal of Behavioral Decision Making*, **13**, 1–17.

Fiol, C. M. & Huff, A. S. (1992). Maps for managers. Where are we? Where do we go from here? *Journal of Management Studies*, **29**, 267–285.

Fiske, S. T. & Taylor, S. E. (1984). *Social Cognition*. Reading, MA: Addison-Wesley.

Flood, P. C, Dromgoole, T., Carroll, S. & Gorman, L. (Eds), (2000). *Managing Strategy Implementation*. Oxford: Blackwell.

Fombrun, C. J. & Zajac, E. J. (1987). Structural and perceptual influences on intra-industry stratification. *Academy of Management Journal*, **30**, 33–50.

Fransella, F. & Bannister, D. (1977). *A Manual for Repertory Grid Technique*. New York: Academic Press.

Ginsberg, A. (1994). Minding the competition: From mapping to mastery. *Strategic Management Journal*, **15** (Winter Special Issue), 153–174.

Gioia, D. A. (1986). 'Conclusion: the state of the art in organizational social cognition—a personal view. In H. P. Sims & D. A. Gioia (Eds), *The Thinking Organization: Dynamics of Organizational Social Cognition* (pp. 336–356). San Francisco: Jossey-Bass.

Goldberg, J. (1996). The Distrat/Askmap Suite of Programs for Cause Map Analysis: A User's Guide. Unpublished manuscript available from Cranfield University Computer Centre, Cranfield University, UK.

Golden, B. (1992). The past is past—or is it? The use of retrospective accounts as indicators of past strategy. *Academy of Management Journal*, **35**, 848–860.

Golden, B. R. (1997). Further remarks on retrospective accounts in organizational and strategic management research. *Academy of Management Journal*, **40**, 1243–1252.

Goldstein, H. (1995). *Multilevel Statistical Models*. London: Edward Arnold.

Goodwin, P. & Wright, G. (1998). *Decision Analysis for Management Judgment*, 2nd ed. Chichester: Wiley.

Goodwin, P. & Wright, G. (in press). Enhancing strategy evaluation in scenario planning: A role for decision analysis. *Journal of Management Studies*.

Greve, H. R. (1996). Patterns of competition: The diffusion of market position in radio broadcasting. *Administrative Science Quarterly*, **41**, 29–60.

Greve, H. R. (1998). Managerial cognition and the mimetic adoption of market positions: What you see is what you do. *Strategic Management Journal*, **19**, 967–988.

Grinyer, P. H. (2000). A cognitive approach to group decision taking: A discussion of evolved practice in the light of received research results. *Journal of the Operational Research Society*, **51**, 21–35.

Gripsrud, G. & Gronhaug, K. (1985). Structure and strategy in grocery retailing: A sociometric approach. *Journal of Industrial Economics*, **XXXIII**, 339–347.

Gronhaug, K. & Falkenberg, J. S. (1989). Exploring strategy perceptions in changing environments. *Journal of Management Studies*, **26**, 349–359.

Haleblain, J. & Finkelstein, S. (1993). Top management team size, CEO dominance and firm performance: The moderating roles of environmental turbulence and discretion. *Academy of Management Journal*, **36**, 844–863.

Hambrick, D. C. & Mason, P. A. (1984). Upper echelons: The organization as a reflection of its top managers. *Academy of Management Review*, **9**, 193–206.

Hambrick, D. C., Cho, T. S. & Chen, M-J. (1996). The influence of top management team heterogeneity on firms' competitive moves. *Administrative Science Quarterly*, **41**, 659–684.

Hatten, K. J. & Hatten, M. L. (1987). Strategic groups, asymmetrical mobility barriers and contestability. *Strategic Management Journal*, **8**, 329–342.

Hayes J. & Allinson, C. W. (1998). Cognitive style and the theory and practice of individual and collective learning in organizations. *Human Relations*, **51**, 847–871.

van der Heijden, K. (1994). Probabilistic planning and scenario planning. In G. Wright & P. Ayton (Eds). *Subjective Probability*. Chichester: Wiley.

van der Heijden, K. (1996). *Scenarios: The Art of Strategic Conversation*. Chichester: Wiley.

Hodgkinson, G. P. (1992). Development and validation of the strategic locus of control scale. *Strategic Management Journal*, **13**, 311–317.

Hodgkinson, G. P. (1993). Doubts about the conceptual and empirical status of context-free and firm-specific control expectancies: A reply to Boone and De Brabander. *Strategic Management Journal*, **14**, 627–631.

Hodgkinson, G. P. (1997a). The cognitive analysis of competitive structures: A review and critique. *Human Relations, 50*, 625–654.

Hodgkinson, G. P. (1997b). Cognitive inertia in a turbulent market: The case of UK residential estate agents. *Journal of Management Studies, 34*, 921–945.

Hodgkinson, G. P., Bown, N., Maule, A. J., Glaister, K. W. and Pearman, A. D. (1999). Breaking the frame: An analysis of strategic cognition and decision making under uncertainty. *Strategic Management Journal, 20*, 977–985.

Hodgkinson, G. P. & Johnson, G. (1994). Exploring the mental models of competitive strategists: The case for a processual approach. *Journal of Management Studies, 31*, 525–551.

Hodgkinson, G. P., Padmore, J. & Tomes, A. E. (1991). Mapping consumers' cognitive structures: A comparison of similarity trees with multidimensional scaling and cluster analysis. *European Journal of Marketing, 25*(7), 41–60.

Hodgkinson, G. P. & Thomas, A. B. (Eds) (1997). Thinking in organizations. *Journal of Management Studies, 34* (Special Issue), 845–952.

Hodgkinson, G. P., Tomes, A. E. & Padmore, J. (1996). Using consumers' perceptions for the cognitive analysis of corporate-level competitive structures. *Journal of Strategic Marketing, 4*, 1–22.

Hodgkinson, G. P. & Wright, G. (1997). Confronting strategic inertia in a top management team: Learning from failure. Paper presented at the Fifth EIASM International Workshop on Managerial and Organizational Cognition: Let Reality Question Our Cognitive Concepts, Namur, Belgium, September.

Huber, G. (1991). Organizational learning: The contributing processes and the literatures. *Organization Science, 2*, 88–115.

Huff, A. S. (1982). Industry influences on strategy formulation. *Strategic Management Journal. 3*, 119–130.

Huff, A. S. (Ed.), (1990). *Mapping Strategic Thought.* Chichester: Wiley.

Huff, A. S. (1997). A current and future agenda for cognitive research in organizations. *Journal of Management Studies, 34*, 947–952.

Huff, A. S. & Fletcher, K. E. (1990). Conclusion: Key mapping decisions. In A. S. Huff, (Ed.), *Mapping Strategic Thought* (pp. 403–412). Chichester: Wiley.

Huff, J. O., Huff, A. S. and Thomas, H. (1992). Strategic renewal and the interaction of cumulative stress and inertia. *Strategic Management Journal, 13*, 55–75.

Huff, A. S. & Jenkins, M. (Eds) (2001). *Mapping Strategic Knowledge.* London: Sage.

Huff, A. S., Narapareddy, V. & Fletcher, K. E. (1990). Coding the causal association of concepts. In A. S. Huff, (Ed.), *Mapping Strategic Thought* (pp. 311–325). Chichester: Wiley.

Jablin, F. M. (1997). Organizational entry, assimilation and exit. In F. Jablin & L. Putnam (Eds), *The New Handbook of Organizational Communication* (pp. 679–740). Thousand Oakes, CA: Sage.

Jackson, S. E. (1992). Consequences of group composition for the interpersonal dynamics of strategic issue processing. *Advances in Strategic Management, 8*, 345—382.

James, L. R. & James, L. A. (1989). Causal modelling in organizational research. In C. L. Cooper & I. T. Robertson (Eds), *International Review of Industrial and Organizational Psychology*, Vol. 4 (pp. 372–404). Chichester: Wiley.

Jenkins, M. (1998). The theory and practice of comparing causal maps. In C. Eden & J.-C. Spender (Eds), *Managerial and Organizational Cognition: Theory, Methods and Research* (pp. 231–249). London: Sage.

Jenkins, M. & Johnson, G. (1997a). Linking managerial cognition and organizational performance: A preliminary investigation using causal maps. *British Journal of Management, 8*, (Special Issue), S77–S90.

Jenkins, M. & Johnson, G. (1997b). Entrepreneurial intentions and outcomes: a comparative causal mapping study. *Journal of Management Studies, 34*, 895–920.

Johnson, P., Daniels, K. and Asch, R. (1998). Mental models of competition. In C. Eden and J.-C. Spender (Eds), *Managerial and Organizational Cognition: Theory, Methods and Research* (pp. 130–146). London: Sage.

Joreskog, K. G. & Sorbom, D. (1993). *LISREL 8: Structural Equation Modelling with the SIMPLIS Command Language*. Hillsdale, NJ: Erlbaum.

Kahneman, D. & Tversky, A. (1984). Choices, values and frames. *American Psychologist*, **39**, 341–350.

Keck, S. L. (1997). Top management team structure: differential effects by environmental context. *Organization Science*, **8**, 143–156.

Keck, S. L. & Tushman, M. L. (1993). Environmental and organizational context and executive team structure, *Academy of Management Journal*, **36**, 314–344.

Kelloway, E. K. (1996). Common practices in structural equation modeling. In C. L. Cooper and I. T. Robertson (Eds), *International Review of Industrial and Organizational Psychology*, Vol. 11 (pp. 141–180). Chichester: Wiley.

Kelly, G. A. (1955). *The Psychology of Personal Constructs* (in 2 vols). New York: Norton.

Kline, P. (1993). *The Handbook of Psychological Testing*. London: Routledge.

Knight, D., Pearce, C. L., Smith, K. G., Olian, J. D., Sims, H. P., Smith, K. A. & Flood, P. (1999). Top management team diversity, group process, and strategic consensus. *Strategic Management Journal*, **20**, 445–465.

Kruskal, J. B. and Wish, M. (1978). *Multidimensional Scaling*. Sage University Paper Series on Quantitative Applications in the Social Sciences, 07–011. London: Sage.

Kulik, C. T. & Ambrose, M. C. (1992). Personal and situational determinants of referent choice. Academy *of Management Review*, **17**, 212–238.

Lakeoff, G. (1987). *Women, Fire and Dangerous Things: What Categories Reveal About the Mind*. Chicago, IL: University of Chicago Press.

Langfield-Smith, K. M. & Wirth, A. (1992). Measuring differences between cognitive maps. *Journal of the Operational Research Society*, **43**, 1135–1150.

Langley, A., Mintzberg, H., Pitcher, P., Posada, E. & Saint-Macary, J. (1995). Opening up decision making: the view from the black stool. *Organization Science*, **6**, 260–279.

Lant, T. K. (1999). A situated learning perspective on the emergence of knowledge and identity in cognitive communities. *Advances in Management Cognition and Organizational Information Processing*, **6**, 171–194.

Lant, T. K. & Baum, J. C. (1995). Cognitive sources of socially constructed competitive groups: Examples from the Manhattan Hotel Industry. In W. R. Scott & S. Christensen (Eds), *The Institutional Construction of Organizations: International and Longitudinal Studies* (pp. 15–38). Thousand Oaks, CA: Sage.

Lant, T. K., Milliken, F. J. & Batra, B. (1992). The role of managerial learning and interpretation in strategic persistence and reorientation: An empirical exploration. *Strategic Management Journal*, **13**, 585–608.

Lant, T. K. & Phelps, C. (1999). Strategic groups: A situated learning perspective. *Advances in Strategic Management*, **16**, 221–247.

Lau, J. & Murnighan, J. K. (1998). Demographic diversity and faultlines: the compositional dynamics of organizational groups. *Academy of Management Review*, **23**, 325–340.

Laukkanan, M. (1994). Comparative cause mapping of organizational cognitions. *Organization Science*, **5**, 322–343.

Laukkanan, M. (1998). Conducting causal mapping research: Opportunities and challenges. In C. Eden & J.-C. Spender (Eds), *Managerial and Organizational Cognition: Theory, Methods and Research* (pp. 168–191). London: Sage.

Lawrence, B. S. (1997). The black box of organizational demography. *Organization Science*, **8**, 1–22.

Levenhagen, M., Porac, J. F. & Thomas, H. (1993). Emergent industry leadership and the selling of technological visions: A social constructionist view. In J. Hendry & G. Johnson, with J. Newton, (Eds.), *Strategic Thinking: Leadership and the Management of Change* (pp. 69–87). Chichester: Wiley.

Locke, E. and Latham, G. (1990). *A Theory of Goal Setting and Task Performance*. Englewood Cliffs NJ: Prentice-Hall.

Lord, R. & Foti, R. (1986). Schema theories, information processing and organizational behavior. In H. P. Sims & D. A. Gioia (Eds), *The Thinking Organization: Dynamics of Organizational Social Cognition* (pp. 20–48). San Francisco: Jossey-Bass.

MacCleod, C. (1991). Clinical anxiety and the selective coding of threatening information. *International Review of Psychology*, 3, 279–292.

March, J. G. & Simon, H. A. (1958). *Organizations*. New York: Wiley.

Markoczy, L. (1995). States and belief states. *International Journal of Human Resource Management*, 6, 249–270.

Markoczy, L. (1997). Measuring beliefs: Accept no substitutes. *Academy of Management Journal*, 40, 1228–1242.

Markoczy, L. & Goldberg, J. (1995). A method for eliciting and comparing causal maps. *Journal of Management*, 21, 305–333.

Mason, E. (1957). *Economic Concentration and the Monopoly Problem*. Cambridge, MA: Harvard University Press.

Matt, G. E., Vazquez, C. & Campbell, W. K. (1992). Mood congruent recall of affectively toned stimuli: A meta-analytic review. *Clinical Psychology Review*, 12, 227–255.

McGee, J. & Thomas, H. (1986). Strategic groups: Theory, research and taxonomy. *Strategic Management Journal*, 7, 141–160.

Meindl, J. R., Stubbart, C. & Porac, J. F. (Eds) (1994). Cognition. *Organization Science*, 5 (Special Issue), 288–477.

Meindl, J. R., Stubbart, C. & Porac, J. F. (Eds) (1996). *Cognition Within and Between Organizations*. Thousand Oaks, CA: Sage.

Meyer, J. W. & Rowan, B. (1977). Institutionalized organizations: Formal structure as myth and ceremony. *American Journal of Sociology*, 83, 340–363.

Miller, C. C., Burke, L. M. & Glick, W. H. (1998). Cognitive diversity among upper-echelon executives: Implications for strategic decision processes. *Strategic Management Journal*, 19, 39–58.

Miller, C. C., Cardinal, L. B. & Glick, W. H. (1997). Retrospective reports in organizational research: A reexamination of recent evidence. *Academy of Management Journal*, 40, 189–204.

Milliken, F. & Martins, L. (1996). Searching for common threads: understanding the multiple effects of diversity in organizational groups. *Academy of Management Review*, 21, 402–433.

Mintzberg, H. (1994). *The Rise and Fall of Strategic Planning*. London: Prentice-Hall.

Morecroft, J. D. W. (1994). Executive knowledge, models and learning. In J. D. W. Morecroft & J. D. Sterman (Eds). *Modelling for Learning Organizations*. Portland, OR: Productivity Press.

Murray, A. (1989). Top management group heterogeneity and firm performance. *Strategic Management Journal*, 10, 125–141.

Nelson, R. R. & Winter, S. G. (1982). *An Evolutionary Theory of Economic Change*. Cambridge, MA: Harvard University Press.

Norburn, D. & Birley, S. (1988). The top management team and corporate performance. *Strategic Management Journal*, 9, 225–237.

Nunnally, J. C. (1978). *Psychometric Theory*. New York: McGraw-Hill.

Oster, S. M. (1990). *Modern Competitive Analysis*. Oxford: Oxford University Press.

Palinscar, A. S. (1998). Social constructivist perspectives on teaching and learning. *Annual Review of Pgychology*, 49, 345–375.

Pelled, L. H. (1996). Demographic diversity, conflict, and work group outcomes: an intervening process theory. *Organization Science*, 7, 615–631.

Penrose, E. (1959). *The Theory of the Growth of the Firm*. New York: Wiley.

Peteraf, M. and Shanley, M. (1997). Getting to know you: A theory of strategic group identity. *Strategic Management Journal*, 18 (Summer Special Issue), 165–186.

Pettigrew, A. M. (1992). On studying managerial elites. *Strategic Management Journal*, 13, 163–182.

Pfeffer, J. (1983). Organizational demography. In B. Staw and L. Cummings (Eds), *Research in Organizational Behavior*, Vol. 5 (pp. 299–357). Greenwich, CT: JAI Press.

Pfeffer, J. and Salancik G. R. (1978). *The External Control of Organizations*. New York: Harper and Row.

Porac, J. & Rosa, A. (1996). Rivalry, industry models, and the cognitive embeddedness of the comparable firm. *Advances in Strategic Management*, 13, 363–388.

Porac, J. F. & Thomas, H. (Eds) (1989). Managerial thinking in business environments. *Journal of Management Studies*, 26 (Special Issue), 323–438.

Porac, J. F. & Thomas, H. (1990). Taxonomic mental models in competitor definition. *Academy of Management Review*. 15, 224–240.

Porac, J. F. & Thomas, H. (1994). Cognitive categorization and subjective rivalry among retailers in a small city. *Journal of Applied Psychology*, 79, 54–66.

Porac, J. F., Thomas, H. & Baden-Fuller, C. (1989). Competitive groups as cognitive communities: The case of Scottish knitwear manufacturers. *Journal of Management Studies*, 26, 397–416.

Porac, J. F., Thomas H. & Emme, B. (1987). Knowing the competition: The mental models of retailing strategists. In G. Johnson (Ed.), *Business Strategy and Retailing* (pp 59–79) Chichester: Wiley.

Porac, J. F., Thomas, H., Wilson, F., Paton, D. & Kanfer, A. (1995). Rivalry and the industry model of Scottish knitwear producers. *Administrative Science Quarterly*, 40, 203–227.

Porter, M. E. (1980). *Competitive Strategy: Techniques for Analyzing Industries and Competitors*. New York: Free Press.

Porter, M. E. (1981). The contributions of industrial organization to strategic management. *Academy of Management Review*, 6, 609–620.

Reger, R. K. (1990). Managerial thought structures and competitive positioning. In A. S. Huff (Ed.), *Mapping Strategic Thought* (pp. 71–88). Chichester: Wiley.

Reger, R. K. & Huff, A. S. (1993). Strategic groups: A cognitive perspective. *Strategic Management Journal*, 14, 103–124.

Reger, R. K. & Palmer, T. B. (1996). Managerial categorization of competitors: Using old maps to navigate new environments. *Organization Science*, 7, 22–39.

Rindova, V. P. and Fombrun, C. J. (1999). Constructing competitive advantage: The role of firm–constituent interactions. *Strategic Management Journal*, 20, 691–710.

Rosch, E. (1978). Principles of categorization. In E. Rosch and B. B. Lloyd (Eds), *Cognition and Categorization* (pp. 27–48). Hillsdale, NJ: Erlbaum.

Rotter, J. B. (1966). Generalized expectancies for internal versus external control of reinforcement. *Psychological Monographs: General and Applied*, 80: Whole No. 609.

Roure, J. B. & Keeley, R. H. (1990). Predictors of success in new technology-based ventures. *Journal of Business Venturing*, 5, 201–220.

Russo, J. E. & Schoemaker, P. J. H. (1989). *Decision Traps*. New York: Doubleday.

Salancik, G. R. & Pfeffer, J (1978). A social information processing approach to job attitudes and task design. *Administrative Science Quarterly*, 23, 224–252.

Sambharya, R. B. (1996). Foreign experience of top management teams and international diversification strategies of US multinational corporations. *Strategic Management Journal*, 17, 739–746.

Sattath, S. & Tversky, A. (1977). Additive similarity trees. *Psychometrika*, **42**, 319–345.

Schoemaker, P. J. H. (1993). Multiple scenario development: Its conceptual and behavioral foundation. *Strategic Management Journal*, **14**, 193–213.

Schoemaker, P. J. H. (1995). Scenario planning: A tool for strategic thinking. *Sloan Management Review*, **Winter**, 25–40.

Schwenk, C. R. (1995). Strategic decision making. *Journal of Management*, **21**, 471–493.

Scott, W. R. & Christensen, S. (Eds) (1995). *The Institutional Construction of Organizations: International and Longitudinal Studies*. Thousand Oaks, CA: Sage.

Shaw, M. L. G. (Ed.) (1981). *Recent Advances in Personal Construct Technology*. London: Academic Press.

Shrout, P. E. & Fleiss, J. L. (1979). Intraclass correlations: Uses in assessing rater reliability. *Psychological Bulletin*, **86**, 420–428.

Sieck, W. & Yates, J. F. (1997). Exposition effects on decision making: Choice and confidence in choice. *Organizational Behavior and Human Decision Processes*, **70**, 207–219.

Simons, T., Pelled, L. H. & Smith, K. A. (1999). Making use of difference: Diversity, debate and decision comprehensiveness in top management teams. *Academy of Management Journal*, **42**, 662–673.

Slater, P. (Ed.) (1976). *The Measurement of Intrapersonal Space by Grid Technique: Vol. I—Explorations of Intrapersonal Space*. Chichester: Wiley.

Slater, P. (Ed.) (1977). *The Measurement of Intrapersonal Space by Grid Technique: Vol. II—Dimensions of Intrapersonal Space*. Chichester: Wiley.

Smith, K. G., Smith, K. A., Olian, J. D., Sims, H. P., O'Bannon, D. P. and Scully, J. A. (1994). Top management team demography and process: The role of social integration and communication. *Administrative Science Quarterly*, **39**, 412–438.

Sparrow, P. R. (1994). The psychology of strategic management: Emerging themes of diversity and cognition. In C. L. Cooper & I. T. Robertson (Eds), *International Review of Industrial and Organizational Psychology*, Vol. 9 (pp. 147–181). Chichester: Wiley.

Spector, P. E. & O'Connell, B. J. (1994). The contribution of personality traits, negative affectivity, locus of control and type A to subsequent reports of job stressors and job strains. *Journal of Occupational and Organizational Psychology*, **67**, 1–12.

Spender, J. C. (1989). *Industry Recipes: The Nature and Sources of Managerial Judgement*. Oxford: Basil Blackwell.

Streufert, S. & Nogami, G. Y. (1989). Cognitive style and complexity: Implications for I/O psychology. In C. L. Cooper & I. T. Robertson (Eds), *International Review of Industrial and Organizational Psychology*, Vol. 4 (pp. 93–143). Chichester: Wiley.

Stubbart, C. I. & Ramaprasad, A. (1990). Comments on the empirical articles and recommendations for future research. In A. S. Huff (Ed.), *Mapping Strategic Thought* (pp. 251–288). Chichester: Wiley.

Sutcliffe, K. M. (1994). What executives notice: Accurate perceptions in top management teams. *Academy of Management Journal*, **37**, 1360–1378.

Sutcliffe, K. M. & Huber, G. P. (1998). Firm and industry as determinants of executive perceptions of the environment. *Strategic Management Journal*, **19**, 793–807.

Tajfel, H. & Turner, J. C. (1985). The social identity theory of intergroup behavior. In S. Worchel & W. G. Austin (Eds), *Psychology of Intergroup Relations*, 2nd edn (pp. 7–24). Chicago, IL: Nelson-Hall.

Thomas, H. & Venkatraman, N. (1988). Research on strategic groups: Progress and prognosis. *Journal of Management Studies*, **25**, 537–555.

Tsoukas, H. (1992). Ways of seeing: Topographic and network representations in organization theory. *Systems Practice*, **5**, 441–456.

Tuma, N. B. & Hannan, M. T. (1984). *Social Dynamics: Models and Methods*. Orlando, FL: Academic Press.

Tushman, M. L. & Anderson, P. (1990). Technological discontinuities and dominant designs: A cyclical model of technological change. *Administrative Science Quarterly*, **35**, 604–633.

Tversky, A.(1977). Features of similarity. *Psychological Review*, **84**, 327–352.

Tversky, A. & Gati, I.(1978). Studies of similarity. In E. Rosch and B. B. Lloyd (Eds), *Cognition and Categorization* (pp. 79–98). Hillsdale, NJ: Erlbaum.

Tversky, A. & Hutchinson, J. W. (1986). Nearest neighbor analysis of psychological spaces. *Psychological Review*, **93**, 3–22.

Tversky, A. & Kahneman, D. (1974). Judgment under uncertainty: Heuristics and biases. *Science*, **185**, 1124–1131.

Tyler, B. B. & Steensma, H. K. (1998). The effects of executives' experiences and perceptions on their assessment of potential technological alliances. *Strategic Management Journal*, **19**, 939–965.

Wack, P. (1985a). Scenarios: Uncharted waters ahead. *Harvard Business Review*, **Sept.–Oct**, 73–90.

Wack, P. (1985b). Scenarios: Shooting the rapids. *Harvard Business Review*, **Nov.–Dec**, 131–142.

Wagner, J. A. & Gooding, R. Z. (1997). Equivocal information and attribution: An investigation of patterns of managerial sensemaking. *Strategic Management Journal*, **18**, 275–286.

Waller, M. J., Huber, G. P. & Glick, W. H. (1995). Functional background as a determinant of executives' selective perception. *Academy of Management Journal*, **38**, 943–974.

Walsh, J. P. (1988). Selectivity and selective perception: An investigation of managers' belief structures and information processing. *Academy of Management Journal*, **31**, 873–896.

Walsh, J. P. (1995). Managerial and organizational cognition: Notes from a trip down memory lane. *Organization Science*, **6**, 280–321.

Walton, E. J. (1986). Managers' prototypes of financial firms. *Journal of Management Studies*, **23**, 679–698.

Wang, S. (1996) A dynamic perspective of differences between cognitive maps. *Journal of the Operational Research Society*, **47**, 538–549.

Weick K. E. (1979), *The Social Psychology of Organizing*, (2nd edn). Reading, MA: Addison-Wesley.

Weick, K. E. (1995). *Sensemaking in Organizations*. Thousand Oaks, CA: Sage.

Wells, R. S. & Bantel, K. A. (2000). Competitive external pressures: Building top management teams to sustain competitive advantage in a changing world. In R. E. Quinn, R. M. O'Neill & L. St. Clair (Eds), *Pressing Problems in Modern Organizations (That Keep Us Up at Night): Transforming Agendas for Research and Practice* (pp. 175–196) New York: AMACOM.

Wenger, E. (1998). *Communities of Practice: Learning, Meaning and Identity*. Cambridge: Cambridge University Press.

West, C. and Schwenk, C. (1996). Top management team strategic consensus, demographic homogeneity and firm performance: A report of resounding non-findings. *Strategic Management Journal*, **17**, 571–576.

West, M. A. & Anderson, N. R. (1996). Innovation in top management teams. *Journal of Applied Psychology*, **81**, 680–693.

Wholey, D. R. & Brittain, J. W. (1986). Organizational ecology: Findings and implications. *Academy of Management Journal*, **11**, 513–533.

Wiersema, M. F. & Bantel, K. A. (1992). Top team demography and corporate strategic change. *Academy of Management Journal*, **35**, 91–121.

Williams, K. Y. & O'Reilly, C. A. (1998). Demography and diversity in organizations: A review of 40 years of research. In L. L. Cummings & B. M. Staw (Eds), *Research in Organizational Behavior*, Vol. 20 (pp. 77–140). Greenwich, CT: JAI Press.

Williams, L. J., Gavin, M. B. and Williams, M. L. (1996). Measurement and non-measurement processes with negative affectivity and employee attitudes. *Journal of Applied Psychology*, **81**, 88–101.

Wood, R. & Bandura, A. (1989). Social cognitive theory of organizational management. *Academy of Management Review*, **14**, 361–384.

Wright, G. & Goodwin, P. (1999). Future focused thinking: combining scenario planning with decision analysis. *Journal of Multicriteria Decision Analysis*, **8**, 311–321.

Wrightson, M. T. (1976). The documentary coding method. In R. M. Axelrod (Ed.), *Structure of Decision: The Cognitive Maps of Political Elites* (pp. 291–332). Princeton, NJ: Princeton University Press.

Zajac, E. J. & Bazerman, M. H. (1991). Blindspots in industry and competitor analysis: Implications of interfirm (mis)perceptions for strategic decisions. *Academy of Management Review*, **16**, 37–56.

Zucker, L. G. (1986). Production of trust: Institutional sources of economic structure, 1840–1920. In B. M. Staw & L. L. Cummings (Eds), *Research in Organizational Behavior*, Vol. 8. Greenwich, CT: JAI Press.

INDEX